-00

SWIFT

GULLIVER'S TRAVELS
AND SELECTED WRITINGS
IN PROSE & VERSE

Edited by JOHN HAYWARD for

the NONESUCH PRESS, London, 1949

NEW YORK: RANDOM HOUSE

First edition November 1934

PRINTED AND MADE IN SCOTLAND
BY R. & R. CLARK, LTD., EDINBURGH

J. S.

TOTO ORBE DIVISAE

AMICITIAE MEMOR

QUAE FUIT

J. H.

CONTENTS

v

CHRONOLOGICAL TABLE

Jonathan Swift born in Dublin	Nov. 30, 1667
At Kilkenny Grammar School	[c.] 1673–1681
Esther [Stella] Johnson born	March 13, 1680/1
Enters Trinity College, Dublin	April 24, 1682
Takes his Degree *speciali gratiâ*	Feb. 15, 1685/6
Settles with his mother at Leicester	1688
Joins Sir William Temple's household at Sheen	June 1689
Returns to Ireland	May 1690
Returns to Temple at Moor Park; Early Poems	Aug. 1691
M.A., Hart Hall, Oxford	July 5, 1692
Leaves Moor Park for Ireland	May 1694
Ordained Deacon [Priest, Jan. 13, 1694/5]	Oct. 25, 1694
Settles at Kilroot	[c.] Jan. 1695
Returns to Moor Park	May 1696
A Tale of a Tub. Battle of the Books written [pub. 1704]	1696/7
Chaplain to Lord Berkeley at Dublin Castle	Summer 1699
Presented with livings of Laracor &c.	Feb. 1699/1700
Prebend of St. Patrick's Cathedral, Dublin	Oct. 22, 1700
D.D. of Dublin	Feb. 1700/01
Returns to London with Berkeley	April 1701
Returns to Ireland	Sept. 1701
Resident in England	April–Nov. 1702, Nov. 1703 – May 1704

Resident in Ireland	June 1704 – Nov. 1707
Petitions in London for Remission of First Fruits	Nov. 1707 – May 1709
Lands in Ireland. Goes to Laracor	June 30, 1709
Returns to London	Sept. 7, 1710
Journal to Stella. Main period of political activity	Sept. 1710 – June 1713
Deserts the Whigs for the Tories	1710
Writes for the Tory *Examiner*	Nov. 2, 1710–June 14, 1711
Miscellanies in Prose and Verse published	Feb. 27, 1710/11
Retires to Chelsea	Spring 1711
The Conduct of the Allies published	Nov. 27, 1711
Triumph of the Tory Party	Dec. 31, 1711
Leaves London	June 1, 1713
Dean of St. Patrick's Cathedral, Dublin	June 13, 1713
Returns to London	Sept. 9, 1713
Cadenus & Vanessa written [pub. 1726]	1712/3 [?]
The Public Spirit of the Whigs published	March 1713/4
Retires to Letcombe, Berkshire	June 1714
Fall of the Tory Party	July 1714
Returns to Ireland	Sept. 1714
Death of Esther [Vanessa] Vanhomrigh	June 2, 1723
The Drapier's Letters I–V written and published	Mar.–Dec. 1724
Arrives in London	March 19, 1725/6

Stays with Pope at Twickenham	Summer 1726
Leaves London for Dublin	Aug. 15, 1726
Gulliver's Travels [written *c.* 1720–5] published	Oct. 28, 1726
Leaves Ireland for last visit to England	April 9, 1727
Pope & Swift's *Miscellanies.* Volumes I & II published	June 24, 1727
Returns to Dublin	Oct. 1727
Death of Stella	Jan. 28, 1727/8
Miscellanies. The Last [Third] *Volume* published	March 7, 1727/8
Stays at Market Hill with Sir Arthur Acheson	June 1728 – Feb. 1728/9
Freedom of the City of Dublin	1729
Verses on the Death of Dr Swift written [pub. 1739]	1731
Miscellanies. The Third [Fourth] *Volume* published	Oct. 4, 1732
First Collected Edition of his Works. 4 Volumes	1735
Miscellanies. Volume the Fifth published	1735
Breakdown of his health	[*c.*] 1738
Guardians in Chancery appointed	March 1741/2
Crisis of his illness	Sept. 1742
Dies in the Deanery, Dublin	Oct. 19, 1745
Buried in St. Patrick's Cathedral	Oct. 22. 1745

NOTE TO THE
SECOND IMPRESSION

IT is satisfactory to be able to record that some part of the hope with which the Introduction to the first impression of this edition concluded has already been fulfilled. In the last four years considerable progress has been made towards the completion of " a definitive edition and bibliography " of Swift's works. The poems have been magisterially edited by Mr Harold Williams (*Clarendon Press.* 3 *vols.* 1937) ; the prose writings are to be re-edited in their entirety by Professor Herbert Davis (*Shakespeare Head Press.* 7 *vols.*). On a smaller scale, but no less authoritative, are the editions of " The Drapier's Letters " (*Ed. Herbert Davis. Clarendon Press.* 1935) and " Swift's Letters to Charles Ford " (*Ed. Nichol Smith. Clarendon Press.* 1934). Dr. H. Teerink's " Bibliography " (*The Hague.* 1937), though imperfect in several respects and often misleading or confusing, is far superior to Spencer Jackson's sketch, and, despite its limitations, represents a useful advance towards finality.

No material changes have been made in this, the second impression. Errors and misprints, discovered in the first impression, have, however, been corrected and a few omissions supplied. For assistance in this connection I wish once more to thank Mr Harold Williams ; and, further, to express my gratitude to Lord Rothschild for the help I have received from the study of certain volumes in his incomparable collection of Swift.

J. H.

INTRODUCTION

SWIFT shares with Bunyan and Defoe the distinction of having given pleasure to a greater number of people in the last two hundred years than any other English author. *Gulliver's Travels*, like *The Pilgrim's Progress* and *Robinson Crusoe*, is a book which everyone who enjoys reading has read without any *arrière pensée* of having performed a social duty. Yet it is doubtful if very many of these thousands of readers have read anything else by Swift or could even give titles to his other books. Like Defoe, Swift was first and foremost a pamphleteer. Most of his writings in prose and verse were written to serve an immediate purpose, and if they are neglected to-day, it is chiefly because the subjects they were originally supposed to attack or defend are no longer important except to the historian. It would therefore be foolish to pretend that any of them possess the same permanent interest and charm as *Gulliver's Travels*; but some of them certainly deserve to be remembered and are well worth the attention of those who value simplicity and precision in the use of words and can respond to the subtle suggestions and insinuations of irony and satire — qualities which are not exclusive to *Gulliver's Travels* but distinguish everything Swift wrote in prose, and much of his verse as well. It is perhaps Swift's greatest gift and a measure of his genius that even now his style can knit together the dry bones of forgotten controversies and make them seem to live again.

In making the present selection, the chief problem has been to decide, not what to include but what to reject; and in order to solve or rather to simplify it, certain examples of Swift's work have been deliberately left out, while others have been severely curtailed. Thus, rather than sacrifice space to an inadequate selection of Swift's letters I have preferred to omit his correspondence altogether. An exception to this, of course, are the extracts from *The Journal to Stella*, which can claim to be a complete work in itself, a fragment of autobiography rather than a series of unrelated letters. I have also excluded specimens of Swift's contributions to periodicals such as *The Tatler* and *The Examiner* in the belief that nothing they contain cannot be matched equally well in the pamphlets I have printed. A more regrettable omission, perhaps, but justified, I hope, by the impossibility of printing the whole thing except at the expense of more important material, is that humorous interlude in Swift's youth, a masterpiece of bantering ridicule — the Partridge-Bickerstaff papers. For the rest, I have printed only a small selection of Swift's purely political and religious writings, from which inevitably the significance has faded more than from any other of his works; nevertheless I regret having had to exclude *The Public Spirit of The Whigs* and *Mr Collins's Discourse of Free-thinking*.

Swift had his own methods of publishing what he wrote and they are characteristic of him. With very few exceptions—and these are mainly attributable to indiscreet or opportunist publishers and printers—all his books, pamphlets and poems were issued from the press anonymously. But it need hardly be said that Swift's reputation in England and Ireland, his place in the public affairs of both countries, and not least his inimitable style were too well known to be hidden successfully beneath such an artless disguise. It is true that there is still some doubt about the authenticity of a few pieces in prose and verse that have been ascribed to him, but the vast majority of his writings were recognized as his from the day of their publication. The whole world knew who had written *Gulliver's Travels*; no one failed to connect the unknown Draper with the great Dean; and Swift's identification with the author of *A Tale of a Tub* was the unlucky, if inevitable, cause of his exclusion from the highest preferment.

The volume of his work and the peculiar and often complicated circumstances in which it was composed and published; the variety and confusion of editions, some authorized but many pirated; the author's apparent indifference to the whole business—it is said that *Gulliver's Travels* was the only book he was paid for—which must be qualified by the fact that he revised some of his work for later editions, and by the survival of his own annotated copies of *Miscellanies in Prose and Verse* and Faulkner's collected *Works*; * these are some of the problems that have still to be investigated by the methods and with the resources of modern scholarship. With two notable and splendid exceptions — Mr Harold Williams's *Gulliver's Travels* [First Edition Club. 1926] and The Clarendon Press edition of *A Tale of A Tub &c.* [Ed. Guthkelch & Nichol Smith. 1920] — Swift's work has never been adequately edited. [But *v*. " Note to the Second Impression ", p. xii.]

A very modest attempt has been made in this volume of selections to establish a faithful and unexpurgated text. It may be doubted whether such an attempt was worth making, since the general reader, whose pleasure must be considered before anything else, will certainly not waste his time over variant readings and collations; while the student, whose pleasure largely depends upon such things, will probably ignore them because they are not sufficiently elaborate. Yet there would seem to be this justification: that if an author is to be read at all, he should be read in a text which resembles as closely as possible his original manuscript. With very few exceptions—and I have mentioned the two outstanding ones—Swift has been denied this right. The main purpose, therefore, of the collations in this volume is to justify the attempted restoration and rehabilitation of the text itself, and at the same time possibly to encourage a more scholarly treatment of Swift's text in the future. If, in addition to satisfying the general reader, the following pages arouse the curiosity of the student to the point of studying Swift's text with a view to preparing a definitive edition and bibliography of his works, these initial steps will not have been taken in vain.

JOHN HAYWARD

---

* In his later years Swift began to " modernize " the text of his early books to the extent of expanding such abbreviations as *'tis* and *tho'* which had been in general use at the beginning of the century. Faulkner, his Irish publisher, is commonly blamed for these innovations.

NOTE ON THE TEXT

THE text of this edition has been set up from rotographs, transcripts and actual copies of the early editions listed in the Textual Notes. Apart from the correction of obvious printer's errors—misprints, dropped, turned and inverted types —and the substitution of lower-case initial and medial *s* for the long ſ, the original spelling and punctuation of these editions has been exactly preserved. Where, however, the punctuation is positively misleading, it has been silently emended from later editions printed in Swift's lifetime. In a few places readings from these later editions have been introduced into the original text where it is corrupt or where there is reason to believe that Swift himself was responsible for the alteration. Every one of these emendations is recorded in the notes; differences in spelling and punctuation, however—a thorough collation of which would occupy a lifetime to little purpose—are not shown. With the notable exception of *Gulliver's Travels* and one or two other less important pieces, the texts chosen are, as far as may be ascertained, those of the first editions or printings. Since, however, many of Swift's writings in prose and verse were published simultaneously in London and Dublin, and sometimes by different publishers in the same city, it is often impossible to state categorically which of two or more editions of the same work is actually the first. For example, it is impossible to be sure which of the several editions of *Cadenus and Vanessa*, printed in 1726, has priority over the rest; or, again, to identify the first issue of the first of the *Drapier's Letters*. An examination of the separate volumes and sets of Faulkner's and Bathurst's collected editions, and an attempt to decide to which state, issue, impression or edition they belong, will show at once the difficult nature of the subject. The confusions and contradictions in Swift's bibliography—unparalleled except, possibly, in Defoe's —have still to be resolved. Spencer Jackson's bibliographical sketch [London. 1908], to which I owe much, introduces almost as many problems as it solves.

In addition to separate editions, I have had occasion to use or refer to the following collections, amongst which the four volumes printed by George Faulkner—" the Prince of Dublin printers "—in 1735 are of outstanding importance. The textual value of these volumes has received far too little recognition from Swift's editors, and reference to the variants from them recorded in the notes to this edition provides sufficient proof— even if no other existed—that Swift himself made many of the corrections they contain. [For Swift's relations with Faulkner, *v. Correspondence*. Ed. F. E. Ball. Vol. V. *passim* and *Letters of Swift to Ford*. Ed. Nichol Smith.]

[1]. *Miscellanies in Prose & Verse*. 1711. Reprinted 1713.

[2]. *Miscellanies in Prose & Verse*. 1727. Three volumes edited by Pope, incorporating the contents of [1]. These are the original volumes of what are generally called *Swift & Pope's Miscellanies*—" that jumble in three volumes ", as Swift's friend Ford calls them, " which put me in a rage whenever I meet them ". Additional volumes were published in 1732 and 1735 respectively. These five volumes, each of which was separately reprinted from time to time, were subsequently extended to thirteen volumes, of each of which, again, various reprints exist. No one has yet attempted to investigate the apparently inconsequent dating, numbering and collation of this series. [But *v.* Teerink's *Bibliography*. 1937.]

[3]. *The Works of J. S. D.D. D.S.P.D.* 1735. Four volumes published by George Faulkner in Dublin. Re-issued with two additional volumes in 1738, and with two more, making eight volumes in all, in 1746. Faulkner's edition was later extended to 20 volumes.

[4]. *The Works of Jonathan Swift*. Ed. Hawksworth, Deane Swift, & Nichols. 14 volumes in 4to. 1755–1779, published by C. Bathurst. This edition was also issued in 25 vols. large 8vo, 27 vols. small 8vo and 27 vols. 18mo, and became the foundation of many irregularly dated sets.

[5]. *Works*. Ed. Sir Walter Scott. 19 volumes. 1814. Second Edition, corrected, 1824. The second edition of this collection is still the best for general purposes. Scott's editions were based on Nichols' edition, 1808, and enlarged with new material.

[6]. *Works*. Ed. Temple Scott and others. 12 volumes [Vol. XII contains Spencer Jackson's bibliography]. 1897–1908. The only modern collected edition, a very unequal work and now partly out of print. The text is completely modernized.

[7]. *Poems*. Ed. W. E. Browning. Two volumes. 1910. An unsatisfactory, modernized text.

[8]. *The Correspondence of Jonathan Swift*. Ed. F. Elrington Ball. 6 volumes. 1910. A masterly and invaluable edition.

[9]. The Forster bequest of books and MSS. by Swift or relating to him, in the library of the Victoria and Albert Museum.

Besides these and other editions mentioned elsewhere, I would add M. E. Pons' *Les Années de Jeunesse et le Conte du Tonneau* [1925], the first part of an exhaustive critical biography; F. Elrington Ball's *Swift's Verse: An Essay* [1929], an important contribution to Swift's bibliography; and Mr Harold Williams's *Swift's Library* [1932], a model of elegant scholarship.

ACKNOWLEDGEMENTS

I WISH to express my very grateful thanks to all those who, by their advice or by their lending me rare and early editions of Swift's writings, have lightened my work and saved me from errors which otherwise I might not have avoided. And in particular: to Mr Harold Williams, whose knowledge of Swift's bibliography is unrivalled; to Mr Richard Jennings for trusting me with his immaculate quartos of Bathurst's edition and other volumes; to Mr Hugh Macdonald and the Lady Ottoline Morrell for long-term loans of indispensable books; to the Duke of Bedford for presenting me with transcripts of three poems from a manuscript in his library at Woburn Abbey; to Mr A. F. Scholfield, the Librarian, and the Syndics of the Cambridge University Library for permission to photograph two tracts; to Mr George Manwaring of the London Library; to the following friends, booksellers of London, for their unfailing generosity—Mr P. J. Dobell, Mr Dudley Massey, Mr Kenneth Maggs, Messrs Elkin Mathews, Messrs Birrell and Garnett; and finally to Mr Francis Meynell and the staff of the Nonesuch Press for their co-operation.

J. H.

GULLIVER'S TRAVELS

" THE chief end I propose to myself in all my labours is to vex the world rather than divert it." So Swift wrote from Dublin in the autumn of 1725 when he was finishing the most celebrated of all his works. *Gulliver's Travels*, as the book is commonly called, was published in two volumes a year later, on October 28, and as Dr Johnson remarks " was read by the high and the low, the learned and illiterate. Criticism was for a while lost in wonder." What was to have vexed the world diverted it then and has continued to do so ever since.

According to Swift's habit, the publication was arranged mysteriously, and it is believed that Pope or Ford delivered the manuscript to Motte, the publisher, by the odd expedient of dropping it at his door from the window of a hackney coach. It was, however, generally known that Swift was the author.

The text, particularly of the third and fourth parts, of Motte's early editions—there were six of them between 1726 and 1735 —is unsatisfactory in several respects. Owing to Motte's timidity, words and whole passages in the MS. were altered or omitted without the author's knowledge. Fortunately, Swift indicated these alterations and omissions to his friend Charles Ford of Woodpark, who corrected them in his own interleaved large-paper copy of the first edition. This volume, now in the Forster collection, is of the highest textual importance. Although Motte had received a list of verbal and typographical corrections from Ford in January 1726/7 and incorporated nearly all of them in his fourth octavo edition [1727], it was not until Swift's Irish publisher, George Faulkner, published *Gulliver's Travels* as the third volume of the first collected edition of Swift's works in 1735 that all the words and passages noted by Ford in his own copy were restored. It is now known that Swift, though originally antagonistic to Faulkner's proposal, eventually submitted to it and was persuaded to look over the sheets of the first four volumes [*v*. Swift to Ford, Oct. 9, 1733].

While it is true that the text of the first edition has a sentimental interest as the original version given to the world, it is obvious that Faulkner's revision follows more closely Swift's MS. The principle hitherto adopted by editors of *Gulliver's Travels* has been to reprint Motte's edition incorporating Ford's corrections. I have preferred to reprint Faulkner's text and to indicate in the notes the readings of the first edition. The result, I venture to believe, is a more exact and reliable text than any that has been published in the last two hundred years.

TRAVELS
into Several Remote Nations of the World

In Four Parts,

viz.

I. A Voyage to Lilliput.

II. A Voyage to Brobdingnag.

III. A Voyage to Laputa, Balnibarbi,
Luggnagg, Glubbdubdrib
and Japan.

IV. A Voyage to the Country of the
Houyhnhnms.

By Lemuel Gulliver, first
a Surgeon, and then a
Captain of several
Ships.

TRAVELS

Into Several Remote Nations of the World

In Four Parts,

viz.

I. A Voyage to Lilliput

II. A Voyage to Brobdingnag

III. A Voyage to Laputa, Balnibarbi, Luggnagg, Glubbdubdrib, and Japan.

IV. A Voyage to the Country of the Houyhnhnms.

By Lemuel Gulliver, first a Surgeon, and then a Captain of several Ships.

A LETTER
from Capt. Gulliver, to his Cousin Sympson

I HOPE *you will be ready to own publickly, whenever you shall be called to it, that by your great and frequent Urgency you prevailed on me to publish a very loose and uncorrect Account of my Travels; with Direction to hire some young Gentlemen of either University to put them in Order, and correct the Style, as my Cousin* Dampier *did by my Advice, in his Book called,* A Voyage round the World. *But I do not remember I gave you Power to consent, that any thing should be omitted, and much less that any thing should be inserted: Therefore, as to the latter, I do here renounce every thing of that Kind; particularly a Paragraph about her Majesty the late Queen* Anne, *of most pious and glorious Memory; although I did reverence and esteem her more than any of human Species. But you, or your Interpolator, ought to have considered, that as it was not my Inclination, so was it not decent to praise any Animal of our Composition before my Master* Houyhnhnm: *And besides, the Fact was altogether false; for to my Knowledge, being in* England *during some Part of her Majesty's Reign, she did govern by a chief Minister; nay, even by two successively; the first whereof was the Lord of* Godolphin, *and the second the Lord of* Oxford; *so that you have made me* say the thing that was not. *Likewise, in the Account of the Academy of Projectors, and several Passages of my Discourse to my Master* Houyhnhnm, *you have either omitted some material Circumstances, or minced or changed them in such a Manner, that I do hardly know mine own Work. When I formerly hinted to you something of this in a Letter, you were pleased to answer, that you were afraid of giving Offence; that People in Power were very watchful over the Press; and apt not only to interpret, but to punish every thing which looked like an* Inuendo *(as I think you called it.) But pray, how could that which I spoke so many Years ago, and at above five Thousand Leagues distance, in another Reign, be applyed to any of the* Yahoos, *who now are said to govern the Herd; especially, at a time when I little thought on or feared the Unhappiness of living under them. Have not I the most Reason to complain, when I see these very* Yahoos *carried by* Houyhnhnms *in a Vehicle, as if these were Brutes, and those the rational Creatures? And, indeed, to avoid so monstrous and detestable a Sight, was one principal Motive of my Retirement hither.*

THUS *much I thought proper to tell you in Relation to your self, and to the Trust I reposed in you.*

I DO *in the next Place complain of my own great Want of Judgment, in being prevailed upon by the Intreaties and false Reasonings of you and some others, very much against mine own Opinion, to suffer my Travels to be published. Pray bring to your Mind how often I desired you to consider, when you insisted on the Motive of* publick Good; *that the* Yahoos *were a Species of Animals utterly incapable of Amendment by Precepts or Examples: And so it hath proved; for instead of seeing a full Stop put to all Abuses and Corruptions, at least in this little Island, as I had Reason to expect: Behold, after above six Months Warning, I cannot learn that my Book hath produced one single Effect according to mine Intentions: I desired you would let me know by a Letter, when Party and Faction were extinguished; Judges learned and upright; Pleaders honest and modest, with some Tincture of common Sense; and* Smithfield *blazing with Pyramids of Law-Books; the young Nobility's Education entirely changed; the Physicians banished; the Female* Yahoos *abounding in Virtue, Honour, Truth and good Sense: Courts and Levees of great Ministers thoroughly weeded and swept; Wit, Merit and Learning rewarded; all Disgracers of the Press in Prose and Verse, condemned to eat nothing but their own Cotten, and quench their Thirst with their own Ink. These, and a Thousand other Reformations, I firmly counted upon by your Encouragement; as indeed they were plainly deducible from the Precepts delivered in my Book. And, it must be owned that seven Months were a sufficient Time to correct every Vice and Folly to which* Yahoos *are subject; if their Natures*

*had been capable of the least Disposition to Virtue or Wis-
dom: Yet so far have you been from answering mine Expectation in any of your Letters; that on the contrary, you
are loading our Carrier every Week with Libels, and Keys,
and Reflections, and Memoirs, and Second Parts; wherein I
see myself accused of reflecting upon great States-Folk; of
degrading human Nature, (for so they have still the Confidence to stile it) and of abusing the Female Sex. I find likewise, that the Writers of those Bundles are not agreed among
themselves; for some of them will not allow me to be Author
of mine own Travels; and others make me Author of Books
to which I am wholly a Stranger.*

*I FIND likewise, that your Printer hath been so careless
as to confound the Times, and mistake the Dates of my
several Voyages and Returns; neither assigning the true Year,
or the true Month, or Day of the Month: And I hear the
original Manuscript is all destroyed, since the Publication of
my Book. Neither have I any Copy left; however, I have sent
you some Corrections, which you may insert, if ever there
should be a second Edition: And yet I cannot stand to
them, but shall leave that Matter to my judicious and candid
Readers, to adjust it as they please.*

*I HEAR some of our Sea-Yahoos find Fault with my Sea-
Language, as not proper in many Parts, nor now in Use. I
cannot help it. In my first Voyages, while I was young, I was
instructed by the oldest Mariners, and learned to speak as
they did. But I have since found that the Sea-Yahoos are
apt, like the Land ones, to become new fangled in their
Words; which the latter change every Year; insomuch, as I
remember upon each Return to mine own Country, their old
Dialect was so altered, that I could hardly understand the
new. And I observe, when any Yahoo comes from London
out of Curiosity to visit me at mine own House, we neither
of us are able to deliver our Conceptions in a Manner intelligible to the other.*

*IF the Censure of Yahoos could any Way affect me, I
should have great Reason to complain, that some of them
are so bold as to think my Book of Travels a meer Fiction
out of mine own Brain; and have gone so far as to drop Hints,*

that the Houyhnhnms, *and* Yahoos *have no more Existence than the Inhabitants of* Utopia.

INDEED I must confess, that as to the People of Lilliput, Brobdingrag, (*for so the Word should have been spelt, and not erroneously* Brobdingnag) *and* Laputa; *I have never yet heard of any* Yahoo *so presumptuous as to dispute their Being, or the Facts I have related concerning them; because the Truth immediately strikes every Reader with Conviction. And, is there less Probability in my Account of the* Houyhnhnms *or* Yahoos, *when it is manifest as to the latter, there are so many Thousands even in this City, who only differ from their Brother Brutes in* Houyhnhnmland, *because they use a Sort of a* Jabber, *and do not go naked. I wrote for their Amendment, and not their Approbation. The* united *Praise of the whole Race would be of less Consequence to me, than the neighing of those two degenerate* Houyhnhnms *I keep in my Stable; because, from these, degenerate as they are, I still improve in some Virtues, without any Mixture of Vice.*

DO these miserable Animals presume to think that I am so far degenerated as to defend my Veracity; Yahoo as I am, it is well known through all Houyhnhnmland, *that by the Instructions and Example of my illustrious Master, I was able in the Compass of two Years (although I confess with the utmost Difficulty) to remove that infernal Habit of Lying, Shuffling, Deceiving, and Equivocating, so deeply rooted in the very Souls of all my Species; especially the* Europeans.

I HAVE other Complaints to make upon this vexatious Occasion; but I forbear troubling myself or you any further. I must freely confess, that since my last Return, some Corruptions of my Yahoo *Nature have revived in me by conversing with a few of your Species, and particularly those of mine own Family, by an unavoidable Necessity; else I should never have attempted so absurd a Project as that of reforming the* Yahoo *Race in this Kingdom; but, I have now done with all such visionary Schemes for ever.*

April 2, 1727.

THE PUBLISHER TO
THE READER

THE *AUTHOR of these Travels, Mr.* Lemuel Gulliver, *is my antient and intimate Friend; there is likewise some Relation between us by the Mother's Side. About three Years ago Mr.* Gulliver *growing weary of the Concourse of curious People coming to him at his House in* Redriff, *made a small Purchase of Land, with a convenient House, near* Newark, *in* Nottinghamshire, *his native Country; where he now lives retired, yet in good Esteem among his Neighbours.*

ALTHOUGH *Mr.* Gulliver *were born in* Nottinghamshire, *where his Father dwelt, yet I have heard him say, his Family came from* Oxfordshire; *to confirm which, I have observed in the Church-Yard at* Banbury, *in that County, several Tombs and Monuments of the* Gullivers.

BEFORE *he quitted* Redriff, *he left the Custody of the following Papers in my Hands, with the Liberty to dispose of them as I should think fit. I have carefully perused them three Times; The Style is very plain and simple; and the only Fault I find is, that the Author, after the Manner of Travellers, is a little too circumstantial. There is an Air of Truth apparent through the whole; and indeed the Author was so distinguished for his Veracity, that it became a Sort of Proverb among his Neighbours at* Redriff, *when any one affirmed a Thing, to say, it was as true as if Mr.* Gulliver *had spoke it.*

BY *the Advice of several worthy Persons, to whom, with the Author's Permission, I communicated these Papers, I now venture to send them into the World; hoping they may be, at least for some time, a better Entertainment to our young Noblemen, than the common Scribbles of Politicks and Party.*

THIS *Volume would have been at least twice as large, if I had not made bold to strike out innumerable Passages relating to the Winds and Tides, as well as to the Variations*

9

and Bearings in the several Voyages; together with the minute Descriptions of the Management of the Ship in Storms, in the Style of Sailors: Likewise the Account of the Longitudes and Latitudes; wherein I have Reason to apprehend that Mr. Gulliver may be a little dissatisfied: But I was resolved to fit the Work as much as possible to the general Capacity of Readers. However, if my own Ignorance in Sea-Affairs shall have led me to commit some Mistakes, I alone am answerable for them: And if any Traveller hath a Curiosity to see the whole Work at large, as it came from the Hand of the Author, I will be ready to gratify him.

As for any further Particulars relating to the Author, the Reader will receive Satisfaction from the first Pages of the Book.

Richard Sympson

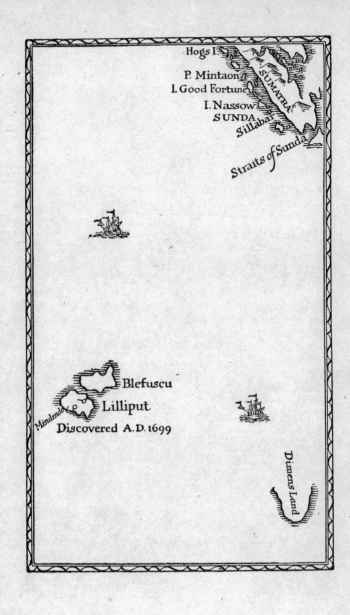

Hogs I.

P. Mintaon
I. Good Fortune
I. Nassow
SUNDA
Sillabar

SUMATRA

Straits of Sunda

Blefuscu
Lilliput
Mindendo
Discovered A.D. 1699

Dimens Land

PART I.

A VOYAGE TO LILLIPUT

CHAPTER I.

THE AUTHOR GIVETH SOME ACCOUNT OF HIMSELF AND
FAMILY; HIS FIRST INDUCEMENTS TO TRAVEL. HE IS
SHIPWRECKED, AND SWIMS FOR HIS LIFE; GETS SAFE ON
SHOAR IN THE COUNTRY OF LILLIPUT; IS MADE A
PRISONER, AND CARRIED UP THE COUNTRY.

M Y Father had a small Estate in *Nottinghamshire*;
I was the Third of five Sons. He sent me to
Emanuel-College in *Cambridge*, at Fourteen Years
old, where I resided three Years, and applied my self close
to my Studies: But the Charge of maintaining me (although
I had a very scanty Allowance) being too great for a narrow
Fortune; I was bound Apprentice to Mr. *James Bates*, an
eminent Surgeon in *London*, with whom I continued four
Years; and my Father now and then sending me small
Sums of Money, I laid them out in learning Navigation,
and other Parts of the Mathematicks, useful to those who
intend to travel, as I always believed it would be some time
or other my Fortune to do. When I left Mr. *Bates*, I went
down to my Father; where, by the Assistance of him and
my Uncle *John*, and some other Relations, I got Forty
Pounds, and a Promise of Thirty Pounds a Year to maintain me at *Leyden*: There I studied Physick two Years and
seven Months, knowing it would be useful in long Voyages.

SOON after my Return from *Leyden*, I was recommended
by my good Master Mr. *Bates*, to be Surgeon to the
Swallow, Captain *Abraham Pannell* Commander; with
whom I continued three Years and a half, making a Voyage
or two into the *Levant*, and some other Parts. When I came

back, I resolved to settle in *London*, to which Mr. *Bates*, my Master, encouraged me; and by him I was recommended to several Patients. I took Part of a small House in the *Old Jury*; and being advised to alter my Condition, I married Mrs. *Mary Burton*, second Daughter to Mr. *Edmond Burton*, Hosier, in *Newgate-street*, with whom I received four Hundred Pounds for a Portion.

But, my good Master *Bates* dying in two Years after, and I having few Friends, my Business began to fail; for my Conscience would not suffer me to imitate the bad Practice of too many among my Brethren. Having therefore consulted with my Wife, and some of my Acquaintance, I determined to go again to Sea. I was Surgeon successively in two Ships, and made several Voyages, for six Years, to the *East* and *West-Indies*; by which I got some Addition to my Fortune. My Hours of Leisure I spent in reading the best Authors, ancient and modern; being always provided with a good Number of Books; and when I was ashore, in observing the Manners and Dispositions of the People, as well as learning their Language; wherein I had a great Facility by the Strength of my Memory.

The last of these Voyages not proving very fortunate, I grew weary of the Sea, and intended to stay at home with my Wife and Family. I removed from the *Old Jury* to *Fetter Lane*, and from thence to *Wapping*, hoping to get Business among the Sailors; but it would not turn to account. After three Years Expectation that things would mend, I accepted an advantageous Offer from Captain *William Prichard*, Master of the *Antelope*, who was making a Voyage to the *South-Sea*. We set sail from *Bristol*, *May* 4th, 1699, and our Voyage at first was very prosperous.

It would not be proper for some Reasons, to trouble the Reader with the Particulars of our Adventures in those Seas: Let it suffice to inform him, that in our Passage from thence to the *East-Indies*, we were driven by a violent Storm to the North-west of *Van Diemen's* Land. By an Observation, we found ourselves in the Latitude of 30 Degrees 2 Minutes South. Twelve of our Crew were dead by immoderate Labour, and ill Food; the rest were in a very weak

Condition. On the fifth of *November*, which was the beginning of Summer in those Parts, the Weather being very hazy, the Seamen spyed a Rock, within half a Cable's length of the Ship; but the Wind was so strong, that we were driven directly upon it, and immediately split. Six of the Crew, of whom I was one, having let down the Boat into the Sea, made a Shift to get clear of the Ship, and the Rock. We rowed by my Computation, about three Leagues, till we were able to work no longer, being already spent with Labour while we were in the Ship. We therefore trusted ourselves to the Mercy of the Waves; and in about half an Hour the Boat was overset by a sudden Flurry from the North. What became of my Companions in the Boat, as well as of those who escaped on the Rock, or were left in the Vessel, I cannot tell; but conclude they were all lost. For my own Part, I swam as Fortune directed me, and was pushed forward by Wind and Tide. I often let my Legs drop, and could feel no Bottom: But when I was almost gone, and able to struggle no longer, I found myself within my Depth; and by this Time the Storm was much abated. The Declivity was so small, that I walked near a Mile before I got to the Shore, which I conjectured was about Eight o'Clock in the Evening. I then advanced forward near half a Mile, but could not discover any Sign of Houses or Inhabitants; at least I was in so weak a Condition, that I did not observe them. I was extremely tired, and with that, and the Heat of the Weather, and about half a Pint of Brandy that I drank as I left the Ship, I found my self much inclined to sleep. I lay down on the Grass, which was very short and soft; where I slept sounder than ever I remember to have done in my Life, and as I reckoned, above Nine Hours; for when I awaked, it was just Day-light. I attempted to rise, but was not able to stir: For as I happened to lie on my Back, I found my Arms and Legs were strongly fastened on each Side to the Ground; and my Hair, which was long and thick, tied down in the same Manner. I likewise felt several slender Ligatures across my Body, from my Armpits to my Thighs. I could only look upwards; the Sun began to grow hot, and the Light offended my

Eyes. I heard a confused Noise about me, but in the Posture I lay, could see nothing except the Sky. In a little time
I felt something alive moving on my left Leg, which advancing gently forward over my Breast, came almost up to my
Chin; when bending my Eyes downwards as much as I
could, I perceived it to be a human Creature not six Inches
high, with a Bow and Arrow in his Hands, and a Quiver at
his Back. In the mean time, I felt at least Forty more of
the same Kind (as I conjectured) following the first. I was
in the utmost Astonishment, and roared so loud, that they
all ran back in a Fright; and some of them, as I was afterwards told, were hurt with the Falls they got by leaping
from my Sides upon the Ground. However, they soon returned; and one of them, who ventured so far as to get a
full Sight of my Face, lifting up his Hands and Eyes by way
of Admiration, cryed out in a shrill, but distinct Voice,
Hekinah Degul: The others repeated the same Words several
times, but I then knew not what they meant. I lay all this
while, as the Reader may believe, in great Uneasiness: At
length, struggling to get loose, I had the Fortune to break
the Strings, and wrench out the Pegs that fastened my left
Arm to the Ground; for, by lifting it up to my Face, I discovered the Methods they had taken to bind me; and, at
the same time, with a violent Pull, which gave me excessive
Pain, I a little loosened the Strings that tied down my Hair
on the left Side; so that I was just able to turn my Head
about two Inches. But the Creatures ran off a second time,
before I could seize them; whereupon there was a great
Shout in a very shrill Accent; and after it ceased, I heard
one of them cry aloud, *Tolgo Phonac*; when in an Instant
I felt above an Hundred Arrows discharged on my left
Hand, which pricked me like so many Needles; and besides,
they shot another Flight into the Air, as we do Bombs in
Europe; whereof many, I suppose, fell on my Body, (though
I felt them not) and some on my Face, which I immediately
covered with my left Hand. When this Shower of Arrows
was over, I fell a groaning with Grief and Pain; and then
striving again to get loose, they discharged another Volly
larger than the first; and some of them attempted with

Spears to stick me in the Sides; but, by good Luck, I had on me a Buff Jerkin, which they could not pierce. I thought it the most prudent Method to lie still; and my Design was to continue so till Night, when my left Hand being already loose, I could easily free myself: And as for the Inhabitants, I had Reason to believe I might be a Match for the greatest Armies they could bring against me, if they were all of the same Size with him that I saw. But Fortune disposed otherwise of me. When the People observed I was quiet, they discharged no more Arrows: But by the Noise increasing, I knew their Numbers were greater; and about four Yards from me, over-against my right Ear, I heard a Knocking for above an Hour, like People at work; when turning my Head that Way, as well as the Pegs and Strings would permit me, I saw a Stage erected about a Foot and a half from the Ground, capable of holding four of the Inhabitants, with two or three Ladders to mount it: From whence one of them, who seemed to be a Person of Quality, made me a long Speech, whereof I understood not one Syllable. But I should have mentioned, that before the principal Person began his Oration, he cryed out three times *Langro Dehul san*: (these Words and the former were afterwards repeated and explained to me.) Whereupon immediately about fifty of the Inhabitants came, and cut the Strings that fastened the left side of my Head, which gave me the Liberty of turning it to the right, and of observing the Person and Gesture of him who was to speak. He appeared to be of a middle Age, and taller than any of the other three who attended him; whereof one was a Page, who held up his Train, and seemed to be somewhat longer than my middle Finger; the other two stood one on each side to support him. He acted every part of an Orator; and I could observe many Periods of Threatnings, and others of Promises, Pity, and Kindness. I answered in a few Words, but in the most submissive Manner, lifting up my left Hand and both my eyes to the Sun, as calling him for a Witness; and being almost famished with Hunger, having not eaten a Morsel for some Hours before I left the Ship, I found the Demands of Nature so strong upon me, that I could not forbear shew-

ing my Impatience (perhaps against the strict Rules of Decency) by putting my Finger frequently on my Mouth, to
signify that I wanted Food. The *Hurgo* (for so they call a
great Lord, as I afterwards learnt) understood me very well:
He descended from the Stage, and commanded that several
Ladders should be applied to my Sides, on which above
an hundred of the Inhabitants mounted, and walked towards my Mouth, laden with Baskets full of Meat, which
had been provided, and sent thither by the King's Orders
upon the first Intelligence he received of me. I observed
there was the Flesh of several Animals, but could not distinguish them by the Taste. There were Shoulders, Legs,
and Loins shaped like those of Mutton, and very well
dressed, but smaller than the Wings of a Lark. I eat them
by two or three at a Mouthful; and took three Loaves at a
time, about the bigness of Musket Bullets. They supplyed
me as fast as they could, shewing a thousand Marks of
Wonder and Astonishment at my Bulk and Appetite. I
then made another Sign that I wanted Drink. They found
by my eating that a small Quantity would not suffice me;
and being a most ingenious People, they slung up with great
Dexterity one of their largest Hogsheads; then rolled it towards my Hand, and beat out the Top; I drank it off at a
Draught, which I might well do, for it hardly held half a
Pint, and tasted like a small Wine of *Burgundy*, but much
more delicious. They brought me a second Hogshead,
which I drank in the same Manner, and made Signs for
more, but they had none to give me. When I had performed
these Wonders, they shouted for Joy, and danced upon my
Breast, repeating several times as they did at first, *Hekinah
Degul*. They made me a Sign that I should throw down the
two Hogsheads, but first warned the People below to stand
out of the Way, crying aloud, *Borach Mivola*; and when
they saw the Vessels in the Air, there was an universal Shout
of *Hekinah Degul*. I confess I was often tempted, while
they were passing backwards and forwards on my Body,
to seize Forty or Fifty of the first that came in my Reach,
and dash them against the Ground. But the Remembrance
of what I had felt, which probably might not be the worst

they could do; and the Promise of Honour I made them, for so I interpreted my submissive Behaviour, soon drove out those Imaginations. Besides, I now considered my self as bound by the Laws of Hospitality to a People who had treated me with so much Expence and Magnificence. However, in my Thoughts I could not sufficiently wonder at the Intrepidity of these diminutive Mortals, who durst venture to mount and walk on my Body, while one of my Hands was at Liberty, without trembling at the very Sight of so prodigious a Creature as I must appear to them. After some time, when they observed that I made no more Demands for Meat, there appeared before me a Person of high Rank from his Imperial Majesty. His Excellency having mounted on the Small of my Right Leg, advanced forwards up to my Face, with about a Dozen of his Retinue; And producing his Credentials under the Signet Royal, which he applied close to my Eyes, spoke about ten Minutes, without any Signs of Anger, but with a kind of determinate Resolution; often pointing forwards, which, as I afterwards found, was towards the Capital City, about half a Mile distant, whither it was agreed by his Majesty in Council that I must be conveyed. I answered in few Words, but to no Purpose, and made a Sign with my Hand that was loose, putting it to the other, (but over his Excellency's Head, for Fear of hurting him or his Train) and then to my own Head and Body, to signify that I desired my Liberty. It appeared that he understood me well enough; for he shook his Head by way of Disapprobation, and held his Hand in a Posture to shew that I must be carried as a Prisoner. However, he made other Signs to let me understand that I should have Meat and Drink enough, and very good Treatment. Whereupon I once more thought of attempting to break my Bonds; but again, when I felt the Smart of their Arrows upon my Face and Hands, which were all in Blisters, and many of the Darts still sticking in them; and observing likewise that the Number of my Enemies encreased; I gave Tokens to let them know that they might do with me what they pleased. Upon this, the *Hurgo* and his Train withdrew, with much Civility and chearful Countenances. Soon after

I heard a general Shout, with frequent Repetitions of the Words, *Peplom Selan,* and I felt great Numbers of the People on my Left Side relaxing the Cords to such a Degree, that I was able to turn upon my Right, and to ease my self with making Water; which I very plentifully did, to the great Astonishment of the People, who conjecturing by my Motions what I was going to do, immediately opened to the right and left on that Side, to avoid the Torrent which fell with such Noise and Violence from me. But before this, they had dawbed my Face and both my Hands with a sort of Ointment very pleasant to the Smell, which in a few Minutes removed all the Smart of their Arrows. These Circumstances, added to the Refreshment I had received by their Victuals and Drink, which were very nourishing, disposed me to sleep. I slept about eight Hours as I was afterwards assured; and it was no Wonder; for the Physicians, by the Emperor's Order, had mingled a sleeping Potion in the Hogsheads of Wine.

IT seems that upon the first Moment I was discovered sleeping on the Ground after my Landing, the Emperor had early Notice of it by an Express; and determined in Council that I should be tyed in the Manner I have related, (which was done in the Night while I slept) that Plenty of Meat and Drink should be sent me, and a Machine prepared to carry me to the Capital City.

THIS Resolution perhaps may appear very bold and dangerous, and I am confident would not be imitated by any Prince in *Europe* on the like Occasion; however, in my Opinion it was extremely Prudent as well as Generous. For supposing these People had endeavoured to kill me with their Spears and Arrows while I was asleep; I should certainly have awaked with the first Sense of Smart, which might so far have rouzed my Rage and Strength, as to enable me to break the Strings wherewith I was tyed; after which, as they were not able to make Resistance, so they could expect no Mercy.

THESE People are most excellent Mathematicians, and arrived to a great Perfection in Mechanicks by the Countenance and Encouragement of the Emperor, who is a re-

nowned Patron of Learning. This Prince hath several
Machines fixed on Wheels, for the Carriage of Trees and
other great Weights. He often buildeth his largest Men of
War, whereof some are Nine Foot long, in the Woods
where the Timber grows, and has them carried on these
Engines three or four Hundred Yards to the Sea. Five
Hundred Carpenters and Engineers were immediately set
at work to prepare the greatest Engine they had. It was a
Frame of Wood raised three Inches from the Ground, about
seven Foot long and four wide, moving upon twenty two
Wheels. The Shout I heard, was upon the Arrival of this
Engine, which, it seems, set out in four Hours after my
Landing. It was brought parallel to me as I lay. But the
principal Difficulty was to raise and place me in this Vehicle.
Eighty Poles, each of one Foot high, were erected for this
Purpose, and very strong Cords of the bigness of Packthread were fastened by Hooks to many Bandages, which
the Workmen had girt round my Neck, my Hands, my Body,
and my Legs. Nine Hundred of the strongest Men were
employed to draw up these Cords by many Pullies fastned
on the Poles; and thus in less than three Hours, I was raised
and slung into the Engine, and there tyed fast. All this I
was told; for while the whole Operation was performing,
I lay in a profound Sleep, by the Force of that soporiferous
Medicine infused into my Liquor. Fifteen hundred of the
Emperor's largest Horses, each about four Inches and a
half high, were employed to draw me towards the Metropolis, which, as I said, was half a Mile distant.

ABOUT four Hours after we began our Journey, I awaked
by a very ridiculous Accident; for the Carriage being stopt
a while to adjust something that was out of Order, two or
three of the young Natives had the Curiosity to see how I
looked when I was asleep; they climbed up into the Engine,
and advancing very softly to my Face, one of them, an
Officer in the Guards, put the sharp End of his Half-Pike
a good way up into my left Nostril, which tickled my Nose
like a Straw, and made me sneeze violently: Whereupon
they stole off unperceived; and it was three Weeks before I
knew the Cause of my awaking so suddenly. We made a

long March the remaining Part of the Day, and rested at
Night with Five Hundred Guards on each Side of me, half
with Torches, and half with Bows and Arrows, ready to
shoot me if I should offer to stir. The next Morning at Sun-
rise we continued our March, and arrived within two
Hundred Yards of the City-Gates about Noon. The Emperor, and all his Court, came out to meet us; but his great
Officers would by no Means suffer his Majesty to endanger
his Person by mounting on my Body.

At the Place where the Carriage stopt, there stood an
ancient Temple, esteemed to be the largest in the whole
Kingdom; which having been polluted some Years before
by an unnatural Murder, was, according to the Zeal of those
People, looked upon as Prophane, and therefore had been
applied to common Uses, and all the Ornaments and Furniture carried away. In this Edifice it was determined I should
lodge. The great Gate fronting to the North was about four
Foot high, and almost two Foot wide, through which I
could easily creep. On each Side of the Gate was a small
Window not above six Inches from the Ground: Into that
on the Left Side, the King's Smiths conveyed fourscore and
eleven Chains, like those that hang to a Lady's Watch in
Europe, and almost as large, which were locked to my Left
Leg with six and thirty Padlocks. Over against this Temple,
on the other Side of the great Highway, at twenty Foot
Distance, there was a Turret at least five Foot high. Here
the Emperor ascended with many principal Lords of his
Court, to have an Opportunity of viewing me, as I was told,
for I could not see them. It was reckoned that above an
hundred thousand Inhabitants came out of the Town upon
the same Errand; and in spight of my Guards, I believe
there could not be fewer than ten thousand, at several
Times, who mounted upon my Body by the Help of Ladders.
But a Proclamation was soon issued to forbid it, upon Pain
of Death. When the Workmen found it was impossible for
me to break loose, they cut all the Strings that bound me;
whereupon I rose up with as melancholy a Disposition as
ever I had in my Life. But the Noise and Astonishment of
the People at seeing me rise and walk, are not to be ex-

pressed. The Chains that held my left Leg were about two Yards long, and gave me not only the Liberty of walking backwards and forwards in a Semicircle; but being fixed within four Inches of the Gate, allowed me to creep in, and lie at my full Length in the Temple.

CHAPTER II.

THE EMPEROR OF LILLIPUT, ATTENDED BY SEVERAL OF THE NOBILITY, COMES TO SEE THE AUTHOR IN HIS CONFINEMENT. THE EMPEROR'S PERSON AND HABIT DESCRIBED. LEARNED MEN APPOINTED TO TEACH THE AUTHOR THEIR LANGUAGE. HE GAINS FAVOUR BY HIS MILD DISPOSITION. HIS POCKETS ARE SEARCHED, AND HIS SWORD AND PISTOLS TAKEN FROM HIM.

WHEN I found myself on my Feet, I looked about me, and must confess I never beheld a more entertaining Prospect. The Country round appeared like a continued Garden; and the inclosed Fields, which were generally Forty Foot square, resembled so many Beds of Flowers. These Fields were intermingled with Woods of half a Stang, and the tallest Trees, as I could judge, appeared to be seven Foot high. I viewed the Town on my left Hand, which looked like the painted Scene of a City in a Theatre.

I HAD been for some Hours extremely pressed by the Necessities of Nature; which was no Wonder, it being almost two Days since I had last disburthened myself. I was under great Difficulties between Urgency and Shame. The best Expedient I could think on, was to creep into my House, which I accordingly did; and shutting the Gate after me, I went as far as the Length of my Chain would suffer; and discharged my Body of that uneasy Load. But this was the only Time I was ever guilty of so uncleanly an Action;

for which I cannot but hope the candid Reader will give
some Allowance, after he hath maturely and impartially
considered my Case, and the Distress I was in. From this
Time my constant Practice was, as soon as I rose, to perform that Business in open Air, at the full Extent of my
Chain; and due Care was taken every Morning before Company came, that the offensive Matter should be carried off
in Wheel-barrows, by two Servants appointed for that Purpose. I would not have dwelt so long upon a Circumstance,
that perhaps at first Sight may appear not very momentous;
if I had not thought it necessary to justify my Character in
Point of Cleanliness to the World; which I am told, some
of my Maligners have been pleased, upon this and other
Occasions, to call in Question.

WHEN this Adventure was at an End, I came back out
of my House, having Occasion for fresh Air. The Emperor
was already descended from the Tower, and advancing on
Horseback towards me, which had like to have cost him
dear; for the Beast, although very well trained, yet wholly
unused to such a Sight, which appeared as if a Mountain
moved before him, reared up on his hinder Feet: But that
Prince, who is an excellent Horseman, kept his Seat, until
his Attendants ran in, and held the Bridle, while his Majesty
had Time to dismount. When he alighted, he surveyed me
round with great Admiration, but kept beyond the Length
of my Chains. He ordered his Cooks and Butlers, who
were already prepared, to give me Victuals and Drink,
which they pushed forward in a sort of Vehicles upon Wheels
until I could reach them. I took these Vehicles, and soon
emptied them all; twenty of them were filled with Meat,
and ten with Liquor; each of the former afforded me two
or three good Mouthfuls, and I emptied the Liquor of ten
Vessels, which was contained in earthen Vials, into one
Vehicle, drinking it off at a Draught; and so I did with the
rest. The Empress, and young Princes of the Blood, of both
Sexes, attended by many Ladies, sate at some Distance in
their Chairs; but upon the Accident that happened to the
Emperor's Horse, they alighted, and came near his Person;
which I am now going to describe. He is taller by almost

the Breadth of my Nail, than any of his Court; which alone is enough to strike an Awe into the Beholders. His Features are strong and masculine, with an *Austrian* Lip, and arched Nose, his Complexion olive, his Countenance erect, his Body and Limbs well proportioned, all his Motions graceful, and his Deportment majestick. He was then past his Prime, being twenty-eight Years and three Quarters old, of which he had reigned about seven, in great Felicity, and generally victorious. For the better Convenience of beholding him, I lay on my Side, so that my Face was parallel to his, and he stood but three Yards off: However, I have had him since many Times in my Hand, and therefore cannot be deceived in the Description. His Dress was very plain and simple, the Fashion of it between the *Asiatick* and the *European*; but he had on his Head a light Helmet of Gold, adorned with Jewels, and a Plume on the Crest. He held his Sword drawn in his Hand, to defend himself, if I should happen to break loose; it was almost three Inches long, the Hilt and Scabbard were Gold enriched with Diamonds. His Voice was shrill, but very clear and articulate, and I could distinctly hear it when I stood up. The Ladies and Courtiers were all most magnificently clad, so that the Spot they stood upon seemed to resemble a Petticoat spread on the Ground, embroidered with Figures of Gold and Silver. His Imperial Majesty spoke often to me, and I returned Answers, but neither of us could understand a Syllable. There were several of his Priests and Lawyers present (as I conjectured by their Habits) who were commanded to address themselves to me, and I spoke to them in as many Languages as I had the least Smattering of, which were *High* and *Low Dutch*, *Latin*, *French*, *Spanish*, *Italian*, and *Lingua Franca*; but all to no purpose. After about two Hours the Court retired, and I was left with a strong Guard, to prevent the Impertinence, and probably the Malice of the Rabble, who were very impatient to croud about me as near as they durst; and some of them had the Impudence to shoot their Arrows at me as I sate on the Ground by the Door of my House; whereof one very narrowly missed my left Eye. But the Colonel ordered six of the Ringleaders to be seized, and thought no Punishment so proper as to deliver them bound into my Hands, which some of his Soldiers accordingly did, pushing them forwards with the But-ends of their Pikes into my Reach: I took them all in my right Hand, put five of them into my Coat-pocket; and as to the sixth, I made a Countenance as if I would eat him alive. The poor Man squalled terribly, and the Colonel and his Officers were in much Pain, especially when they saw me take out my Penknife: But I soon put them out of Fear; for, looking mildly, and immediately cutting the Strings he was bound with, I set him gently on the Ground, and away he ran. I treated the rest in the same Manner, taking them one by one out of my Pocket; and I observed, both the Soldiers and People were highly obliged at this Mark of my Clemency, which was represented very much to my Advantage at Court.

Towards Night I got with some Difficulty into my House, where I lay on the Ground, and continued to do so about a Fortnight; during which time the Emperor gave Orders to have a Bed prepared for me. Six Hundred Beds of the common Measure were brought in Carriages, and worked up in my House; an Hundred and Fifty of their Beds sown together made up the Breadth and Length, and these were four double, which however kept me but very indifferently from the Hardness of the Floor, that was of smooth Stone. By the same Computation they provided me with Sheets, Blankets, and Coverlets, tolerable enough for one who had been so long enured to Hardships as I.

As the News of my Arrival spread through the Kingdom, it brought prodigious Numbers of rich, idle, and curious People to see me; so that the Villages were almost emptied, and great Neglect of Tillage and Houshold Affairs must have ensued, if his Imperial Majesty had not provided by several Proclamations and Orders of State against this Inconveniency. He directed that those, who had already beheld me, should return home, and not presume to come within fifty Yards of my House, without Licence from Court; whereby the Secretaries of State got considerable Fees.

IN the mean time, the Emperor held frequent Councils to debate what Course should be taken with me; and I was afterwards assured by a particular Friend, a Person of great Quality, and who was as much in the *Secret* as any; that the Court was under many Difficulties concerning me. They apprehended my breaking loose; that my Diet would be very expensive, and might cause a Famine. Sometimes they determined to starve me, or at least to shoot me in the Face and Hands with poisoned Arrows, which would soon dispatch me: But again they considered, that the Stench of so large a Carcase might produce a Plague in the Metropolis, and probably spread through the whole Kingdom. In the midst of these Consultations, several Officers of the Army went to the Door of the great Council-Chamber; and two of them being admitted, gave an Account of my Behaviour to the six Criminals above-mentioned; which made so favourable an Impression in the Breast of his Majesty, and the whole Board, in my Behalf, that an Imperial Commission was issued out, obliging all the Villages nine hundred Yards round the City, to deliver in every Morning six Beeves, forty Sheep, and other Victuals for my Sustenance; together with a proportionable Quantity of Bread and Wine, and other Liquors: For the due Payment of which his Majesty gave Assignments upon his Treasury. For this Prince lives chiefly upon his own Demesnes; seldom, except upon great Occasions raising any Subsidies upon his Subjects, who are bound to attend him in his Wars at their own Expence. An Establishment was also made of Six Hundred Persons to be my Domesticks, who had Board-Wages allowed for their Maintenance, and Tents built for them very conveniently on each side of my Door. It was likewise ordered, that three hundred Taylors should make me a Suit of Cloaths after the Fashion of the Country: That, six of his Majesty's greatest Scholars should be employed to instruct me in their Language: And, lastly, that the Emperor's Horses, and those of the Nobility, and Troops of Guards, should be exercised in my Sight, to accustom themselves to me. All these Orders were duly put in Execution; and in about three Weeks I made a great Progress in Learning their Language; during which Time, the Emperor frequently honoured me with his Visits, and was pleased to assist my Masters in teaching me. We began already to converse together in some Sort; and the first Words I learnt, were to express my Desire, that he would please to give me my Liberty; which I every Day repeated on my Knees. His Answer, as I could apprehend, was, that this must be a Work of Time, not to be thought on without the Advice of his Council; and that first I must *Lumos Kelmin pesso desmar lon Emposo*; that is, *Swear a Peace with him and his Kingdom.* However, that I should be used with all Kindness; and he advised me to acquire by my Patience and discreet Behaviour, the good Opinion of himself and his Subjects. He desired I would not take it ill, if he gave Orders to certain proper Officers to search me; for probably I might carry about me several Weapons, which must needs be dangerous Things, if they answered the Bulk of so prodigious a Person. I said, his Majesty should be satisfied, for I was ready to strip my self, and turn up my Pockets before him. This I delivered, part in Words, and part in Signs. He replied, that by the Laws of the Kingdom, I must be searched by two of his Officers: That he knew this could not be done without my Consent and Assistance; that he had so good an Opinion of my Generosity and Justice, as to trust their Persons in my Hands: That whatever they took from me should be returned when I left the Country, or paid for at the Rate which I would set upon them. I took up the two Officers in my Hands, put them first into my Coat-Pockets, and then into every other Pocket about me, except my two Fobs, and another secret Pocket which I had no Mind should be searched, wherein I had some little Necessaries of no Consequence to any but my self. In one of my Fobs there was a Silver Watch, and in the other a small Quantity of Gold in a Purse. These Gentlemen, having Pen, Ink, and Paper about them, made an exact Inventory of every thing they saw; and when they had done, desired I would set them down, that they might deliver it to the Emperor. This Inventory I afterwards translated into *English*, and is Word for Word as follows.

IMPRIMIS, In the right Coat-Pocket of the *Great Man Mountain* (for so I interpret the Words *Quinbus Flestrin*) after the strictest Search, we found only one great Piece of coarse Cloth, large enough to be a Foot-Cloth for your Majesty's chief Room of State. In the left Pocket, we saw a huge Silver Chest, with a Cover of the same Metal, which we, the Searchers, were not able to lift. We desired it should be opened; and one of us stepping into it, found himself up to the mid Leg in a sort of Dust, some part whereof flying up to our Faces, set us both a sneezing for several Times together. In his right Waistcoat-Pocket, we found a pro-digious Bundle of white thin Substances, folded one over another, about the Bigness of three Men, tied with a strong Cable, and marked with black Figures; which we humbly conceive to be Writings; every Letter almost half as large as the Palm of our Hands. In the left there was a sort of Engine, from the Back of which were extended twenty long Poles, resembling the Pallisado's before your Majesty's Court; wherewith we conjecture the *Man Mountain* combs his Head; for we did not always trouble him with Ques-tions, because we found it a great Difficulty to make him understand us. In the large Pocket on the right Side of his middle Cover, (so I translate the Word *Ranfu-Lo*, by which they meant my Breeches) we saw a hollow Pillar of Iron, about the Length of a Man, fastened to a strong Piece of Timber, larger than the Pillar; and upon one side of the Pillar were huge Pieces of Iron sticking out, cut into strange Figures; which we know not what to make of. In the left Pocket, another Engine of the same kind. In the smaller Pocket on the right Side, were several round flat Pieces of white and red Metal, of different Bulk: Some of the white, which seemed to be Silver, were so large and heavy, that my Comrade and I could hardly lift them. In the left Pocket were two black Pillars irregularly shaped: we could not, without Difficulty, reach the Top of them as we stood at the Bottom of his Pocket: One of them was covered, and seemed all of a Piece; but at the upper End of the other, there ap-peared a white round Substance, about twice the bigness of our Heads. Within each of these was inclosed a prodigious

Plate of Steel; which, by our Orders, we obliged him to shew us, because we apprehended they might be dangerous Engines. He took them out of their Cases, and told us, that in his own Country his Practice was to shave his Beard with one of these, and to cut his Meat with the other. There were two Pockets which we could not enter: These he called his Fobs; they were two large Slits cut into the Top of his middle Cover, but squeezed close by the Pressure of his Belly. Out of the right Fob hung a great Silver Chain, with a wonderful kind of Engine at the Bottom. We directed him to draw out whatever was at the End of that Chain; which appeared to be a Globe, half Silver, and half of some transparent Metal: For on the transparent Side we saw certain strange Figures circularly drawn, and thought we could touch them, until we found our Fingers stopped with that lucid Substance. He put this Engine to our Ears, which made an incessant Noise like that of a Water-Mill. And we conjecture it is either some unknown Animal, or the God that he worships: But we are more inclined to the latter Opinion, because he assured us (if we understood him right, for he expressed himself very imperfectly) that he seldom did any Thing without consulting it. He called it his Oracle, and said it pointed out the Time for every Action of his Life. From the left Fob he took out a Net almost large enough for a Fisherman, but contrived to open and shut like a Purse, and served him for the same Use: We found therein several massy Pieces of yellow Metal, which if they be of real Gold, must be of immense Value.

HAVING thus, in Obedience to your Majesty's Commands, diligently searched all his Pockets; we observed a Girdle about his Waist made of the Hyde of some prodigious Animal; from which, on the left Side, hung a Sword of the Length of five Men; and on the right, a Bag or Pouch divided into two Cells; each Cell capable of holding three of your Majesty's Subjects. In one of these Cells were several Globes or Balls of a most ponderous Metal, about the Bigness of our Heads, and required a strong Hand to lift them: The other Cell contained a Heap of certain black Grains, but of no great Bulk or Weight, for we could hold about fifty of them in the Palms of our Hands.

THIS is an exact Inventory of what we found about the Body of the *Man Mountain*; who used us with great Civility, and due Respect to your Majesty's Commission. Signed and Sealed on the fourth Day of the eighty ninth Moon of your Majesty's auspicious Reign.

Clefren Frelock, Marsi Frelock.

WHEN this Inventory was read over to the Emperor, he directed me to deliver up the several Particulars. He first called for my Scymiter, which I took out, Scabbard and all. In the mean time he ordered three thousand of his choicest Troops, who then attended him, to surround me at a Distance, with their Bows and Arrows just ready to discharge: But I did not observe it; for my Eyes were wholly fixed upon his Majesty. He then desired me to draw my Scymiter, which, although it had got some Rust by the Sea-Water, was in most Parts exceeding bright. I did so, and immediately all the Troops gave a Shout between Terror and Surprize; for the Sun shone clear, and the Reflexion dazzled their Eyes, as I waved the Scymiter to and fro in my Hand. His Majesty, who is a most magnanimous Prince, was less daunted than I could expect; he ordered me to return it into the Scabbard, and cast it on the Ground as gently as I could, about six Foot from the End of my Chain. The next Thing he demanded was one of the hollow Iron Pillars, by which he meant my Pocket-Pistols. I drew it out, and at his Desire, as well as I could, expressed to him the Use of it, and charging it only with Powder, which by the Closeness of my Pouch, happened to escape wetting in the Sea, (an Inconvenience that all prudent Mariners take special Care to provide against) I first cautioned the Emperor not to be afraid; and then I let it off in the Air. The Astonishment here was much greater than at the Sight of my Scymiter. Hundreds fell down as if they had been struck dead; and even the Emperor, although he stood his Ground, could not recover himself in some time. I delivered up both my Pistols in the same Manner as I had done my Scymiter, and

then my Pouch of Powder and Bullets; begging him that
the former might be kept from Fire; for it would kindle
with the smallest Spark, and blow up his Imperial Palace
into the Air. I likewise delivered up my Watch, which the
Emperor was very curious to see; and commanded two of
his tallest Yeomen of the Guards to bear it on a Pole upon
their Shoulders, as Dray-men in *England* do a Barrel of
Ale. He was amazed at the continual Noise it made, and
the Motion of the Minute-hand, which he could easily discern; for their Sight is much more acute than ours: He
asked the Opinions of his learned Men about him, which
were various and remote, as the Reader may well imagine
without my repeating; although indeed I could not very
perfectly understand them. I then gave up my Silver and
Copper Money, my Purse with nine large Pieces of Gold,
and some smaller ones; my Knife and Razor, my Comb
and Silver Snuff-Box, my Handkerchief and Journal Book.
My Scymiter, Pistols, and Pouch, were conveyed in Carriages to his Majesty's Stores; but the rest of my Goods
were returned me.

I HAD, as I before observed, one private Pocket which
escaped their Search, wherein there was a Pair of Spectacles
(which I sometimes use for the Weakness of my Eyes) a
Pocket Perspective, and several other little Conveniences;
which being of no Consequence to the Emperor, I did not
think my self bound in Honour to discover; and I apprehended they might be lost or spoiled if I ventured them out
of my Possession.

CHAPTER III.

THE AUTHOR DIVERTS THE EMPEROR AND HIS NOBILITY
OF BOTH SEXES, IN A VERY UNCOMMON MANNER. THE
DIVERSIONS OF THE COURT OF LILLIPUT DESCRIBED. THE
AUTHOR HATH HIS LIBERTY GRANTED HIM UPON CERTAIN
CONDITIONS.

My Gentleness and good Behaviour had gained so far on the Emperor and his Court, and indeed upon the Army and People in general, that I began to conceive Hopes of getting my Liberty in a short Time. I took all possible Methods to cultivate this favourable Disposition. The Natives came by Degrees to be less apprehensive of any Danger from me. I would sometimes lie down, and let five or six of them dance on my Hand. And at last the Boys and Girls would venture to come and play at Hide and Seek in my Hair. I had now made a good Progress in understanding and speaking their Language. The Emperor had a mind one Day to entertain me with several of the Country Shows; wherein they exceed all Nations I have known, both for Dexterity and Magnificence. I was diverted with none so much as that of the Rope-Dancers, performed upon a slender white Thread, extended about two Foot, and twelve Inches from the Ground. Upon which, I shall desire Liberty, with the Reader's Patience, to enlarge a little.

This Diversion is only practised by those Persons, who are Candidates for great Employments, and high Favour, at Court. They are trained in this Art from their Youth, and are not always of noble Birth, or liberal Education. When a great Office is vacant, either by Death or Disgrace, (which often happens) five or six of those Candidates petition the Emperor to entertain his Majesty and the Court with a Dance on the Rope; and whoever jumps the highest without falling, succeeds in the Office. Very often the chief Ministers themselves are commanded to shew their Skill,

and to convince the Emperor that they have not lost their
Faculty. *Flimnap*, the Treasurer, is allowed to cut a Caper
on the strait Rope, at least an Inch higher than any other
Lord in the whole Empire. I have seen him do the Summer-
set several times together, upon a Trencher fixed on the
Rope, which is no thicker than a common Packthread
in *England*. My Friend *Reldresal*, principal Secretary for
private Affairs, is, in my Opinion, if I am not partial, the
second after the Treasurer; the rest of the great Officers are
much upon a Par.

THESE Diversions are often attended with fatal Accidents,
whereof great Numbers are on Record. I my self have seen
two or three Candidates break a Limb. But the Danger
is much greater, when the Ministers themselves are commanded to shew their Dexterity: For, by contending to excel themselves and their Fellows, they strain so far, that there
is hardly one of them who hath not received a Fall; and
some of them two or three. I was assured, that a Year or
two before my Arrival, *Flimnap* would have infallibly broke
his Neck, if one of the *King's Cushions*, that accidentally
lay on the Ground, had not weakened the Force of his Fall.

THERE is likewise another Diversion, which is only shewn
before the Emperor and Empress, and first Minister, upon
particular Occasions. The Emperor lays on a Table three
fine silken Threads of six Inches long. One is Blue, the
other Red, and the third Green. These Threads are proposed as Prizes, for those Persons whom the Emperor hath
a mind to distinguish by a peculiar Mark of his Favour.
The Ceremony is performed in his Majesty's great Chamber
of State; where the Candidates are to undergo a Tryal of
Dexterity very different from the former; and such as I have
not observed the least Resemblance of in any other Country
of the old or the new World. The Emperor holds a Stick
in his Hands, both Ends parallel to the Horizon, while the
Candidates advancing one by one, sometimes leap over the
Stick, sometimes creep under it backwards and forwards
several times, according as the Stick is advanced or depressed. Sometimes the Emperor holds one End of the
Stick, and his first Minister the other; sometimes the Minis-

ter has it entirely to himself. Whoever performs his Part with most Agility, and holds out the longest in *leaping* and *creeping*, is rewarded with the Blue-coloured Silk; the Red is given to the next, and the Green to the third, which they all wear girt twice round about the Middle; and you see few great Persons about this Court, who are not adorned with one of these Girdles.

Cf: Gawain & the Green Knight

THE Horses of the Army, and those of the Royal Stables, having been daily led before me, were no longer shy, but would come up to my very Feet, without starting. The Riders would leap them over my Hand as I held it on the Ground; and one of the Emperor's Huntsmen, upon a large Courser, took my Foot, Shoe and all; which was indeed a prodigious Leap. I had the good Fortune to divert the Emperor one Day, after a very extraordinary Manner. I desired he would order several Sticks of two Foot high, and the Thickness of an ordinary Cane, to be brought me; whereupon his Majesty commanded the Master of his Woods to give Directions accordingly; and the next Morning six Wood-men arrived with as many Carriages, drawn by eight Horses to each. I took nine of these Sticks, and fixing them firmly in the Ground in a Quadrangular Figure, two Foot and a half square; I took four other Sticks, and tyed them parallel at each Corner, about two Foot from the Ground; and then I fastened my Handkerchief to the nine Sticks that stood erect; and extended it on all Sides, till it was as tight as the Top of a Drum; and the four parallel Sticks rising about five Inches higher than the Handkerchief, served as Ledges on each Side. When I had finished my Work, I desired the Emperor to let a Troop of his best Horse, Twenty-four in Number, come and exercise upon this Plain. His Majesty approved of the Proposal, and I took them up one by one in my Hands, ready mounted and armed, with the proper Officers to exercise them. As soon as they got into Order, they divided into two Parties, performed mock Skirmishes, discharged blunt Arrows, drew their Swords, fled and pursued, attacked and retired; and in short discovered the best military Discipline I ever beheld. The parallel Sticks secured them and their Horses from falling over the Stage; and the Emperor was so much delighted, that he ordered this Entertainment to be repeated several Days; and once was pleased to be lifted up, and give the Word of Command; and, with great Difficulty, persuaded even the Empress her self to let me hold her in her close Chair, within two Yards of the Stage, from whence she was able to take a full View of the whole Performance. It was my good Fortune that no ill Accident happened in these Entertainments; only once a fiery Horse that belonged to one of the Captains, pawing with his Hoof struck a Hole in my Handkerchief, and his Foot slipping, he overthrew his Rider and himself; but I immediately relieved them both: For covering the Hole with one Hand, I set down the Troop with the other, in the same Manner as I took them up. The Horse that fell was strained in the left Shoulder, but the Rider got no Hurt, and I repaired my Handkerchief as well as I could: However, I would not trust to the Strength of it any more in such dangerous Enterprizes.

ABOUT two or three Days before I was set at Liberty, as I was entertaining the Court with these Kinds of Feats, there arrived an Express to inform his Majesty, that some of his Subjects riding near the Place where I was first taken up, had seen a great black Substance lying on the Ground, very oddly shaped, extending its Edges round as wide as his Majesty's Bedchamber, and rising up in the Middle as high as a Man. That it was no living Creature, as they at first apprehended; for it lay on the Grass without Motion, and some of them had walked round it several Times: That by mounting upon each others Shoulders, they had got to the Top, which was flat and even; and, stamping upon it, they found it was hollow within: That they humbly conceived it might be something belonging to the *Man-Mountain*; and if his Majesty pleased, they would undertake to bring it with only five Horses. I presently knew what they meant; and was glad at Heart to receive this Intelligence. It seems, upon my first reaching the Shore, after our Shipwreck, I was in such Confusion, that before I came to the Place where I went to sleep, my Hat, which I had fastened with a String to my Head while I was rowing, and had stuck on all the Time I was swimming, fell off after I came to Land; the String, as I conjecture, breaking by some Accident which I never observed, but thought my Hat had been lost at Sea. I intreated his Imperial Majesty to give Orders it might be brought to me as soon as possible, describing to him the Use and the Nature of it: And the next Day the Waggoners arrived with it, but not in a very good Condition; they had bored two Holes in the Brim, within an Inch and a half of the Edge, and fastened two Hooks in the Holes; these Hooks were tied by a long Cord to the Harness, and thus my Hat was dragged along for above half an *English* Mile: but the Ground in that Country being extremely smooth and level, it received less Damage than I expected.

Two Days after this Adventure, the Emperor having ordered that Part of his Army, which quarters in and about his Metropolis, to be in a Readiness, took a fancy of diverting himself in a very singular Manner. He desired I would stand like a *Colossus*, with my Legs as far asunder as I conveniently could. He then commanded his General (who was an old experienced Leader, and a great Patron of mine) to draw up the Troops in close Order, and march them under me; the Foot by Twenty-four in a Breast, and the Horse by Sixteen, with Drums beating, Colours flying, and Pikes advanced. This Body consisted of three Thousand Foot, and a Thousand Horse. His Majesty gave Orders, upon Pain of Death, that every Soldier in his March should observe the strictest Decency, with regard to my Person; which, however, could not prevent some of the younger Officers from turning up their Eyes as they passed under me. And, to confess the Truth, my Breeches were at that Time in so ill a Condition, that they afforded some Opportunities for Laughter and Admiration.

I HAD sent so many Memorials and Petitions for my Liberty, that his Majesty at length mentioned the Matter first in the Cabinet, and then in a full Council; where it was opposed by none, except *Skyresh Bolgolam*, who was pleased, without any Provocation, to be my mortal Enemy. But it was carried against him by the whole Board, and confirmed by the Emperor. That Minister was *Galbet*, or Admiral of the Realm; very much in his Master's Confidence, and a Person well versed in Affairs, but of a morose and sour Complection. However, he was at length persuaded to comply; but prevailed that the Articles and Conditions upon which I should be set free, and to which I must swear, should be drawn up by himself. These Articles were brought to me by *Skyresh Bolgolam* in Person, attended by two under Secretaries, and several Persons of Distinction. After they were read, I was demanded to swear to the Performance of them; first in the Manner of my own Country, and afterwards in the Method prescribed by their Laws; which was to hold my right Foot in my left Hand, to place the middle Finger of my right Hand on the Crown of my Head, and my Thumb on the Tip of my right Ear. But, because the Reader may perhaps be curious to have some Idea of the Style and Manner of Expression peculiar to that People, as well as to know the Articles upon which I recovered my Liberty; I have made a Translation of the whole Instrument, Word for Word, as near as I was able; which I here offer to the Publick.

GOLBASTO MOMAREN EVLAME GURDILO SHEFIN MULLY ULLY GUE, most Mighty Emperor of *Lilliput*, Delight and Terror of the Universe, whose Dominions extend five Thousand Blustrugs, (about twelve Miles in Circumference) to the Extremities of the Globe: Monarch of all Monarchs: Taller than the Sons of Men; whose Feet press down to the Center, and whose Head strikes against the Sun: At whose Nod the Princes of the Earth shake their Knees; pleasant as the Spring, comfortable as the Summer, fruitful as Autumn, dreadful as Winter. His most sublime Majesty proposeth to the *Man-Mountain*, lately arrived at our Celestial Dominions, the following Articles, which by a solemn Oath he shall be obliged to perform.

FIRST, The *Man-Mountain* shall not depart from our Dominions, without our Licence under our Great Seal.

SECONDLY, He shall not presume to come into our Metropolis, without our express Order; at which time, the Inhabitants shall have two Hours Warning, to keep within their Doors.

THIRDLY, The said *Man-Mountain* shall confine his Walks to our principal high Roads; and not offer to walk or lie down in a Meadow, or Field of Corn.

FOURTHLY, As he walks the said Roads, he shall take the utmost Care not to trample upon the Bodies of any of our loving Subjects, their Horses, or Carriages; nor take any of our said Subjects into his Hands, without their own Consent.

FIFTHLY, If an Express require extraordinary Dispatch; the *Man-Mountain* shall be obliged to carry in his Pocket the Messenger and Horse, a six Days Journey once in every Moon, and return the said Messenger back (if so required) safe to our Imperial Presence.

SIXTHLY, He shall be our Ally against our Enemies in the Island of *Blefuscu*, and do his utmost to destroy their Fleet, which is now preparing to invade Us.

SEVENTHLY, That the said *Man-Mountain* shall, at his Times of Leisure, be aiding and assisting to our Workmen, in helping to raise certain great Stones, towards covering the Wall of the principal Park, and other our Royal Buildings.

EIGHTHLY, That the said *Man-Mountain* shall, in two Moons Time, deliver in an exact survey of the Circumference of our Dominions, by a Computation of his own Paces round the Coast.

LASTLY, That upon his solemn Oath to observe all the above Articles, the said *Man-Mountain* shall have a daily Allowance of Meat and Drink, sufficient for the Support of 1728 of our Subjects; with free Access to our Royal Person, and other Marks of our Favour. Given at our Palace at *Belfaborac* the Twelfth Day of the Ninety-first Moon of our Reign.

I swore and subscribed to these Articles with great Chearfulness and Content, although some of them were not so honourable as I could have wished; which proceeded wholly from the Malice of *Skyresh Bolgolam* the High Admiral: Whereupon my Chains were immediately unlocked, and I was at full Liberty: The Emperor himself, in Person, did me the Honour to be by at the whole Ceremony. I made my Acknowledgments, by prostrating myself at his Majesty's Feet: But he commanded me to rise; and after many gracious Expressions, which, to avoid the Censure of Vanity, I shall not repeat; he added, that he hoped I should prove a useful Servant, and well deserve all the Favours he had already conferred upon me, or might do for the future.

The Reader may please to observe, that in the last Article for the Recovery of my Liberty, the Emperor stipulates to allow me a Quantity of Meat and Drink, sufficient for the Support of 1728 *Lilliputians*. Some time after, asking a Friend at Court how they came to fix on that determinate Number; he told me, that his Majesty's Mathematicians, having taken the Height of my Body by the Help of a Quadrant, and finding it to exceed theirs in the Proportion of Twelve to One, they concluded from the Similarity of their Bodies, that mine must contain at least 1728 of theirs, and consequently would require as much Food as was necessary to support that Number of *Lilliputians*. By which, the Reader may conceive an Idea of the Ingenuity of that People, as well as the prudent and exact Oeconomy of so great a Prince.

CHAPTER IV.

MILDENDO, THE METROPOLIS OF LILLIPUT, DESCRIBED, TOGETHER WITH THE EMPEROR'S PALACE. A CONVERSATION BETWEEN THE AUTHOR AND A PRINCIPAL SECRETARY, CONCERNING THE AFFAIRS OF THAT EMPIRE. THE AUTHOR'S OFFERS TO SERVE THE EMPEROR IN HIS WARS.

THE first Request I made after I had obtained my Liberty, was, that I might have Licence to see *Mildendo*, the Metropolis; which the Emperor easily granted me, but with a special Charge to do no Hurt, either to the Inhabitants, or their Houses. The People had Notice by Proclamation of my Design to visit the Town. The Wall which encompassed it, is two Foot and an half high, and at least eleven Inches broad, so that a Coach and Horses may be driven very safely round it; and it is flanked with strong Towers at ten Foot Distance. I stept over the great *Western* Gate, and passed very gently, and sideling through the two principal Streets, only in my short Waistcoat, for fear of damaging the Roofs and Eves of the Houses with the Skirts of my Coat. I walked with the utmost Circumspection, to avoid treading on any Stragglers, who might remain in the Streets, although the Orders were very strict, that all People should keep in their Houses, at their own Peril. The Garret Windows and Tops of Houses were so crowded with Spectators, that I thought in all my Travels I had not seen a more populous Place. The City is an exact Square, each Side of the Wall being five Hundred Foot long. The two great Streets which run cross and divide it into four Quarters, are five Foot wide. The Lanes and Alleys which I could not enter, but only viewed them as I passed, are from Twelve to Eighteen Inches. The Town is capable of holding five Hundred Thousand Souls. The Houses are from three to five Stories. The Shops and Markets well provided.

THE Emperor's Palace is in the Center of the City, where the two great Streets meet. It is inclosed by a Wall of two Foot high, and Twenty Foot distant from the Buildings. I had his Majesty's Permission to step over this Wall; and the Space being so wide between that and the Palace, I could easily view it on every Side. The outward Court is a Square of Forty Foot, and includes two other Courts: In the inmost are the Royal Apartments, which I was very desirous to see, but found it extremely difficult; for the great Gates, from one Square into another, were but Eighteen Inches high, and seven Inches wide. Now the Buildings of the outer Court were at least five Foot high; and it was impossible for me to stride over them, without infinite Damage to the Pile, although the Walls were strongly built of hewn Stone, and four Inches thick. At the same time, the Emperor had a great Desire that I should see the Magnificence of his Palace: But this I was not able to do till three Days after, which I spent in cutting down with my Knife some of the largest Trees in the Royal Park, about an Hundred Yards distant from the City. Of these Trees I made two Stools, each about three Foot high, and strong enough to bear my Weight. The People having received Notice a second time, I went again through the City to the Palace, with my two Stools in my Hands. When I came to the Side of the outer Court, I stood upon one Stool, and took the other in my Hand: This I lifted over the Roof, and gently set it down on the Space between the first and second Court, which was eight Foot wide. I then stept over the Buildings very conveniently from one Stool to the other, and drew up the first after me with a hooked Stick. By this Contrivance I got into the inmost Court; and lying down upon my Side, I applied my Face to the Windows of the middle Stories, which were left open on Purpose, and discovered the most splendid Apartments that can be imagined. There I saw the Empress, and the young Princes in their several Lodgings, with their chief Attendants about them. Her Imperial Majesty was pleased to smile very graciously upon me and gave me out of the Window her Hand to kiss.

But I shall not anticipate the Reader with farther Descriptions of this Kind, because I reserve them for a greater Work, which is now almost ready for the Press; containing a general Description of this Empire, from its first Erection, through a long Series of Princes, with a particular Account of their Wars and Politicks, Laws, Learning, and Religion; their Plants and Animals, their peculiar Manners and Customs, with other Matters very curious and useful; my chief Design at present being only to relate such Events and Transactions as happened to the Publick, or to my self, during a Residence of about nine Months in that Empire.

One Morning, about a Fortnight after I had obtained my Liberty, *Reldresal*, Principal Secretary (as they style him) of private Affairs, came to my House, attended only by one Servant. He ordered his Coach to wait at a Distance, and desired I would give him an Hour's Audience; which I readily consented to, on Account of his Quality, and Personal Merits, as well as of the many good Offices he had done me during my Sollicitations at Court. I offered to lie down, that he might the more conveniently reach my Ear; but he chose rather to let me hold him in my Hand during our Conversation. He began with Compliments on my Liberty; said, he might pretend to some Merit in it; but, however, added, that if it had not been for the present Situation of things at Court, perhaps I might not have obtained it so soon. For, *said he*, as flourishing a Condition as we appear to be in to Foreigners, we labour under two mighty Evils; a violent Faction at home, and the Danger of an Invasion by a most potent Enemy from abroad. As to the first, you are to understand, that for above seventy Moons past, there have been two struggling Parties in this Empire, under the Names of *Tramecksan*, and *Slamecksan*, from the high and low Heels on their Shoes, by which they distinguish themselves.

It is alledged indeed, that the high Heels are most agreeable to our ancient Constitution: But however this be, his Majesty hath determined to make use of only low Heels in the Administration of the Government, and all Offices in the Gift of the Crown; as you cannot but observe; and

(Lowheels)

Whig

Tory

(High heels)

particularly, that his Majesty's Imperial Heels are lower at least by a *Drurr* than any of his Court; (*Drurr* is a Measure about the fourteenth Part of an Inch.) The Animosities between these two Parties run so high, that they will neither eat nor drink, nor talk with each other. We compute the *Tramecksan*, or High-Heels, to exceed us in Number; but the Power is wholly on our Side. We apprehend his Imperial Highness, the Heir to the Crown, to have some Tendency towards the High-Heels; at least we can plainly discover one of his Heels higher than the other; which gives him a Hobble in his Gait. Now, in the midst of these intestine Disquiets, we are threatened with an Invasion from the Island of *Blefuscu*, which is the other great Empire of the Universe, almost as large and powerful as this of his Majesty. For as to what we have heard you affirm, that there are other Kingdoms and States in the World, inhabited by human Creatures as large as your self, our Philosophers are in much Doubt; and would rather conjecture that you dropt from the Moon, or one of the Stars; because it is certain, that an hundred Mortals of your Bulk, would, in a short Time, destroy all the Fruits and Cattle of his Majesty's Dominions. Besides, our Histories of six Thousand Moons make no Mention of any other Regions, than the two great Empires of *Lilliput* and *Blefuscu*. Which two mighty Powers have, as I was going to tell you, been engaged in a most obstinate War for six and thirty Moons past. It began upon the following Occasion. It is allowed on all Hands, that the primitive Way of breaking Eggs before we eat them, was upon the larger End: But his present Majesty's Grand-father, while he was a Boy, going to eat an Egg, and breaking it according to the ancient Practice, happened to cut one of his Fingers. Whereupon the Emperor his Father, published an Edict, commanding all his Subjects, upon great Penalties, to break the smaller End of their Eggs. The People so highly resented this Law, that our Histories tell us, there have been six Rebellions raised on that Account; wherein one Emperor lost his Life, and another his Crown. These civil Commotions were constantly fomented by the Monarchs of *Blefuscu*; and when

they were quelled, the Exiles always fled for Refuge to that
Empire. It is computed, that eleven Thousand Persons
have, at several Times, suffered Death, rather than submit
to break their Eggs at the smaller End. Many hundred large
Volumes have been published upon this Controversy: But
the Books of the *Big-Endians* have been long forbidden,
and the whole Party rendred incapable by Law of holding
Employments. During the Course of these Troubles, the
Emperors of *Blefuscu* did frequently expostulate by their
Ambassadors, accusing us of making a Schism in Religion,
by offending against a fundamental Doctrine of our great
Prophet *Lustrog*, in the fifty-fourth Chapter of the *Brundre-
cal*, (which is their *Alcoran*.) This, however, is thought to
be a meer Strain upon the Text: For the Words are these;
*That all true Believers shall break their Eggs at the con-
venient End*: and which is the convenient End, seems, in my
humble Opinion, to be left to every Man's Conscience, or
at least in the Power of the chief Magistrate to determine.
Now the *Big-Endian* Exiles have found so much Credit
in the Emperor of *Blefuscu's* Court; and so much private
Assistance and Encouragement from their Party here at
home, that a bloody War hath been carried on between the
two Empires for six and thirty Moons with various Success;
during which Time we have lost Forty Capital Ships, and
a much greater Number of smaller Vessels, together with
thirty thousand of our best Seamen and Soldiers; and the
Damage received by the Enemy is reckoned to be somewhat
greater than ours. However, they have now equipped a
numerous Fleet, and are just preparing to make a Descent
upon us: And his Imperial Majesty, placing great Confidence in your Valour and Strength, hath commanded me to
lay this Account of his Affairs before you.

I DESIRED the Secretary to present my humble Duty to the
Emperor, and to let him know, that I thought it would not
become me, who was a Foreigner, to interfere with Parties;
but I was ready, with the Hazard of my Life, to defend his
Person and State against all Invaders.

CHAPTER V.

THE AUTHOR BY AN EXTRAORDINARY STRATAGEM
PREVENTS AN INVASION. A HIGH TITLE OF HONOUR IS
CONFERRED UPON HIM. AMBASSADORS ARRIVE FROM
THE EMPEROR OF BLEFUSCU, AND SUE FOR PEACE. THE
EMPRESS'S APARTMENT ON FIRE BY AN ACCIDENT;
THE AUTHOR INSTRUMENTAL IN SAVING
THE REST OF THE PALACE.

THE Empire of *Blefuscu*, is an Island situated to the
North North-East Side of *Lilliput*, from whence it is
parted only by a Channel of eight Hundred Yards
wide. I had not yet seen it, and upon this Notice of an
intended Invasion, I avoided appearing on that Side of the
Coast, for fear of being discovered by some of the Enemies
Ships, who had received no Intelligence of me; all intercourse between the two Empires having been strictly forbidden during the War, upon Pain of Death; and an
Embargo laid by our Emperor upon all Vessels whatsoever.
I communicated to his Majesty a Project I had formed of
seizing the Enemies whole Fleet; which, as our Scouts assured us, lay at Anchor in the Harbour ready to sail with
the first fair Wind. I consulted the most experienced Seamen, upon the Depth of the Channel, which they had often
plummed; who told me, that in the Middle at high Water
it was seventy *Glumgluffs* deep, which is about six Foot of
European Measure; and the rest of it fifty *Glumgluffs* at
most. I walked to the North-East Coast over against *Blefuscu*; where, lying down behind a Hillock, I took out my
small Pocket Perspective Glass, and viewed the Enemy's
Fleet at Anchor, consisting of about fifty Men of War, and
a great Number of Transports: I then came back to my
House, and gave Order (for which I had a Warrant) for a
great Quantity of the strongest Cable and Bars of Iron.
The Cable was about as thick as Packthread, and the Bars

of the Length and Size of a Knitting-Needle. I trebled the Cable to make it stronger; and for the same Reason I twisted three of the Iron Bars together, binding the Extremities into a Hook. Having thus fixed fifty Hooks to as many Cables, I went back to the North-East Coast, and putting off my Coat, Shoes, and Stockings, walked into the Sea in my Leathern Jerken, about half an Hour before high Water. I waded with what Haste I could, and swam in the Middle about thirty Yards until I felt the Ground; I arrived at the Fleet in less than half an Hour. The Enemy was so frighted when they saw me, that they leaped out of their Ships, and swam to Shore; where there could not be fewer than thirty thousand Souls. I then took my Tackling, and fastning a Hook to the Hole at the Prow of each, I tyed all the Cords together at the End. While I was thus employed, the Enemy discharged several Thousand Arrows, many of which stuck in my Hands and Face; and besides the excessive Smart, gave me much Disturbance in my Work. My greatest Apprehension was for my Eyes, which I should have infallibly lost, if I had not suddenly thought of an Expedient. I kept, among other little Necessaries, a Pair of Spectacles in a private Pocket, which, as I observed before, had escaped the Emperor's Searchers. These I took out, and fastened as strongly as I could upon my Nose; and thus armed went on boldly with my Work in spight of the Enemy's Arrows; many of which struck against the Glasses of my Spectacles, but without any other Effect, further than a little to discompose them. I had now fastened all the Hooks, and taking the Knot in my Hand, began to pull; but not a Ship would stir, for they were all too fast held by their Anchors; so that the boldest Part of my Enterprize remained. I therefore let go the Cord, and leaving the Hooks fixed to the Ships, I resolutely cut with my Knife the Cables that fastened the Anchors; receiving above two hundred Shots in my Face and Hands: Then I took up the knotted End of the Cables to which my Hooks were tyed; and with great Ease drew fifty of the Enemy's largest Men of War after me.

THE *Blefuscudians*, who had not the least Imagination of

what I intended, were at first confounded with Astonishment. They had seen me cut the Cables, and thought my Design was only to let the Ships run a-drift, or fall foul on each other: But when they perceived the whole Fleet moving in Order, and saw me pulling at the End; they set up such a Scream of Grief and Dispair, that it is almost impossible to describe or conceive. When I had got out of Danger, I stopt a while to pick out the Arrows that stuck in my Hands and Face, and rubbed on some of the same Ointment that was given me at my first Arrival, as I have formerly mentioned. I then took off my Spectacles, and waiting about an Hour until the Tyde was a little fallen, I waded through the Middle with my Cargo, and arrived safe at the Royal Port of *Lilliput*.

THE Emperor and his whole Court stood on the Shore, expecting the Issue of this great Adventure. They saw the Ships move forward in a large Half-Moon, but could not discern me, who was up to my Breast in Water. When I advanced to the Middle of the Channel, they were yet more in Pain because I was under Water to my Neck. The Emperor concluded me to be drowned, and that the Enemy's Fleet was approaching in a hostile Manner: But he was soon eased of his Fears; for the Channel growing shallower every Step I made, I came in a short Time within Hearing; and holding up the End of the Cable by which the Fleet was fastened, I cryed in a loud Voice, *Long live the most puissant Emperor of Lilliput!* This great Prince received me at my Landing with all possible Encomiums, and created me a *Nardac* upon the Spot, which is the highest Title of Honour among them.

HIS Majesty desired I would take some other Opportunity of bringing all the rest of his Enemy's Ships into his Ports. And so unmeasurable is the Ambition of Princes, that he seemed to think of nothing less than reducing the whole Empire of *Blefuscu* into a Province, and governing it by a Viceroy; of destroying the *Big-Endian* Exiles, and compelling that People to break the smaller End of their Eggs; by which he would remain sole Monarch of the whole World. But I endeavoured to divert him from this Design, by many Arguments drawn from the Topicks of Policy as well as Justice: And I plainly protested, that I would never be an Instrument of bringing a free and brave People into Slavery: And when the Matter was debated in Council, the wisest Part of the Ministry were of my Opinion.

This open bold Declaration of mine was so opposite to the Schemes and Politicks of his Imperial Majesty, that he could never forgive me: He mentioned it in a very artful Manner at Council, where, I was told, that some of the wisest appeared, at least by their Silence, to be of my Opinion; but others, who were my secret Enemies, could not forbear some Expressions, which by a Side-wind reflected on me. And from this Time began an Intrigue between his Majesty, and a Junta of Ministers maliciously bent against me, which broke out in less than two Months, and had like to have ended in my utter Destruction. Of so little Weight are the greatest Services to Princes, when put into the Balance with a Refusal to gratify their Passions.

About three Weeks after this Exploit, there arrived a solemn Embassy from *Blefuscu*, with humble Offers of a Peace; which was soon concluded upon Conditions very advantageous to our Emperor; wherewith I shall not trouble the Reader. There were six Ambassadors, with a Train of about five Hundred Persons; and their Entry was very magnificent, suitable to the Grandeur of their Master, and the Importance of their Business. When their Treaty was finished, wherein I did them several good Offices by the Credit I now had, or at least appeared to have at Court; their Excellencies, who were privately told how much I had been their Friend, made me a Visit in Form. They began with many Compliments upon my Valour and Generosity; invited me to that Kingdom in the Emperor their Master's Name; and desired me to shew them some Proofs of my prodigious Strength, of which they had heard so many Wonders; wherein I readily obliged them, but shall not interrupt the Reader with the Particulars.

When I had for some time entertained their Excellencies to their infinite Satisfaction and Surprize, I desired they would do me the Honour to present my most humble Respects to the Emperor their Master, the Renown of whose Virtues had so justly filled the whole World with Admiration, and whose Royal Person I resolved to attend before I returned to my own Country. Accordingly, the next time I had the Honour to see our Emperor, I desired his general Licence to wait on the *Blefuscudian* Monarch, which he was pleased to grant me, as I could plainly perceive, in a very cold Manner; but could not guess the Reason, till I had a Whisper from a certain Person, that *Flimnap* and *Bolgolam* had represented my Intercourse with those Ambassadors, as a Mark of Disaffection, from which I am sure my Heart was wholly free. And this was the first time I began to conceive some imperfect Idea of Courts and Ministers.

IT is to be observed, that these Ambassadors spoke to me by an Interpreter; the Languages of both Empires differing as much from each other as any two in *Europe*, and each Nation priding itself upon the Antiquity, Beauty, and Energy of their own Tongues, with an avowed Contempt for that of their Neighbour: Yet our Emperor standing upon the Advantage he had got by the Seizure of their Fleet, obliged them to deliver their Credentials, and make their Speech in the *Lilliputian* Tongue. And it must be confessed, that from the great Intercourse of Trade and Commerce between both Realms; from the continual Reception of Exiles, which is mutual among them; and from the Custom in each Empire to send their young Nobility and richer Gentry to the other, in order to polish themselves, by seeing the World, and understanding Men and Manners; there are few Persons of Distinction, or Merchants, or Seamen, who dwell in the Maritime Parts, but what can hold Conversation in both Tongues; as I found some Weeks after, when I went to pay my Respects to the Emperor of *Blefuscu*, which in the Midst of great Misfortunes, through the Malice of my Enemies, proved a very happy Adventure to me, as I shall relate in its proper Place.

THE Reader may remember, that when I signed those Articles upon which I recovered my Liberty, there were some which I disliked upon Account of their being too servile, neither could any thing but an extreme Necessity have forced me to submit. But being now a *Nardac*, of the highest Rank in that Empire, such Offices were looked upon as below my Dignity; and the Emperor (to do him Justice) never once mentioned them to me. However, it was not long before I had an Opportunity of doing his Majesty, at least, as I then thought, a most signal Service. I was alarmed at Midnight with the Cries of many Hundred People at my Door; by which being suddenly awaked, I was in some Kind of Terror. I heard the Word *Burglum* repeated incessantly; several of the Emperor's Court making their Way through the Croud, intreated me to come immediately to the Palace, where her Imperial Majesty's Apartment was on fire, by the Carelessness of a Maid of Honour, who fell asleep while she was reading a Romance. I got up in an Instant; and Orders being given to clear the Way before me; and it being likewise a Moon-shine Night, I made a shift to get to the Palace without trampling on any of the People. I found they had already applied Ladders to the Walls of the Apartment, and were well provided with Buckets, but the Water was at some Distance. These Buckets were about the Size of a large Thimble, and the poor People supplied me with them as fast as they could; but the Flame was so violent, that they did little Good. I might easily have stifled it with my Coat, which I unfortunately left behind me for haste, and came away only in my Leathern Jerkin. The Case seemed wholly desperate and deplorable; and this magnificent Palace would have infallibly been burnt down to the Ground, if, by a Presence of Mind, unusual to me, I had not suddenly thought of an Expedient. I had the Evening before drank plentifully of a most delicious Wine, called *Glimigrim*, (the *Blefuscudians* call it *Flunec*, but ours is esteemed the better Sort) which is very diuretick. By the luckiest Chance in the World, I had not discharged myself of any Part of it. The Heat I had contracted by coming very near the Flames, and by my labouring to quench them, made the Wine begin to operate by Urine; which I voided in such a Quantity, and applied so well to the proper Places, that in three Minutes the Fire was wholly extinguished; and the rest of that noble Pile, which had cost so many Ages in erecting, preserved from Destruction.

It was now Day-light, and I returned to my House, without waiting to congratulate with the Emperor; because, although I had done a very eminent Piece of Service, yet I could not tell how his Majesty might resent the Manner by which I had performed it: For, by the fundamental Laws of the Realm, it is Capital in any Person, of what Quality soever, to make water within the Precincts of the Palace. But I was a little comforted by a Message from his Majesty, that he would give Orders to the Grand Justiciary for passing my Pardon in Form; which, however, I could not obtain. And I was privately assured, that the Empress conceiving the greatest Abhorrence of what I had done, removed to the most distant Side of the Court, firmly resolved that those Buildings should never be repaired for her Use; and, in the Presence of her chief Confidents, could not forbear vowing Revenge.

CHAPTER VI.

OF THE INHABITANTS OF LILLIPUT; THEIR LEARNING, LAWS, AND CUSTOMS. THE MANNER OF EDUCATING THEIR CHILDREN. THE AUTHOR'S WAY OF LIVING IN THAT COUNTRY. HIS VINDICATION OF A GREAT LADY.

ALTHOUGH I intend to leave the Description of this Empire to a particular Treatise, yet in the mean time I am content to gratify the curious Reader with some general Ideas. As the common Size of the Natives is somewhat under six Inches, so there is an exact Proportion in all other Animals, as well as Plants and Trees: For Instance, the tallest Horses and Oxen are between four and five Inches in Height, the Sheep an Inch and a half, more or less; their Geese about the Bigness of a Sparrow; and so the several Gradations downwards, till you come to the smallest, which, to my Sight, were almost invisible; but Nature hath adapted the Eyes of the *Lilliputians* to all Objects proper for their View: They see with great Exactness, but at no great Distance. And to show the Sharpness of their Sight towards Objects that are near, I have been much pleased with observing a Cook pulling a Lark, which was not so large as a common Fly; and a young Girl threading an invisible Needle with invisible Silk. Their tallest Trees are about seven Foot high; I mean some of those in the great Royal Park, the Tops whereof I could but just reach with my Fist clinched. The other Vegetables are in the same Proportion: But this I leave to the Reader's Imagination.

I SHALL say but little at present of their Learning, which for many Ages hath flourished in all its Branches among them: But their Manner of Writing is very peculiar; being neither from the Left to the Right, like the *Europeans*; nor from the Right to the Left, like the *Arabians*; nor from up to down, like the *Chinese*; nor from down to up, like the *Cascagians*; but aslant from one Corner of the Paper to the other, like Ladies in *England*.

THEY bury their Dead with their Heads directly downwards; because they hold an Opinion, that in eleven Thousand Moons they are all to rise again; in which Period, the Earth (which they conceive to be flat) will turn upside down, and by this Means they shall, at their Resurrection, be found ready standing on their Feet. The Learned among them confess the Absurdity of this Doctrine; but the Practice still continues, in Compliance to the Vulgar.

THERE are some Laws and Customs in this Empire very peculiar; and if they were not so directly contrary to those of my own dear Country, I should be tempted to say a little in their Justification. It is only to be wished, that they were as well executed. The first I shall mention, relateth to Informers. All Crimes against the State, are punished here with the utmost Severity; but if the Person accused make his Innocence plainly to appear upon his Tryal, the Accuser is immediately put to an ignominious Death; and out of his Goods or Lands, the innocent Person is quadruply recom-

pensed for the Loss of his Time, for the Danger he underwent, for the Hardship of his Imprisonment, and for all the
Charges he hath been at in making his Defence. Or, if that
Fund be deficient, it is largely supplyed by the Crown. The
Emperor doth also confer on him some publick Mark of
his Favour; and Proclamation is made of his Innocence
through the wholly City.

THEY look upon Fraud as a greater Crime than Theft,
and therefore seldom fail to punish it with Death: For
they alledge, that Care and Vigilance, with a very common
Understanding, may preserve a Man's Goods from Thieves;
but Honesty hath no Fence against superior Cunning: And
since it is necessary that there should be a perpetual Intercourse of buying and selling, and dealing upon Credit;
where Fraud is permitted or connived at, or hath no Law
to punish it, the honest Dealer is always undone, and the
Knave gets the Advantage. I remember when I was once
interceeding with the King for a Criminal who had wronged
his Master of a great Sum of Money, which he had received
by Order, and ran away with; and happening to tell his
Majesty, by way of Extenuation, that it was only a Breach
of Trust; the Emperor thought it monstrous in me to offer,
as a Defence, the greatest Aggravation of the Crime: And
truly, I had little to say in Return, farther than the common
Answer, that different Nations had different Customs; for,
I confess, I was heartily ashamed.

ALTHOUGH we usually call Reward and Punishment, the
two Hinges upon which all Government turns; yet I could
never observe this Maxim to be put in Practice by any
Nation except that of *Lilliput*. Whoever can there bring
sufficient Proof that he hath strictly observed the Laws of
his Country for Seventy-three Moons, hath a Claim to certain Privileges, according to his Quality and Condition of
Life, with a proportionable Sum of Money out of a Fund
appropriated for that Use: He likewise acquires the Title of
Snilpall, or *Legal*, which is added to his Name, but doth not
descend to his Posterity. And these People thought it a
prodigious Defect of Policy among us, when I told them
that our Laws were enforced only by Penalties, without

any Mention of Reward. It is upon this account that the Image of Justice, in their Courts of Judicature, is formed with six Eyes, two before, as many behind, and on each Side one, to signify Circumspection; with a Bag of Gold open in her right Hand, and a Sword sheathed in her left, to shew she is more disposed to reward than to punish.

In chusing Persons for all Employments, they have more Regard to good Morals than to great Abilities: For, since Government is necessary to Mankind, they believe that the common Size of human Understandings, is fitted to some Station or other; and that Providence never intended to make the Management of publick Affairs a Mystery, to be comprehended only by a few Persons of sublime Genius, of which there seldom are three born in an Age: But, they suppose Truth, Justice, Temperance, and the like, to be in every Man's Power; the Practice of which Virtues, assisted by Experience and a good Intention, would qualify any Man for the Service of his Country, except where a Course of Study is required. But they thought the Want of Moral Virtues was so far from being supplied by superior Endowments of the Mind, that Employments could never be put into such dangerous Hands as those of Persons so qualified; and at least, that the Mistakes committed by Ignorance in a virtuous Disposition, would never be of such fatal Consequence to the Publick Weal, as the Practices of a Man, whose Inclinations led him to be corrupt, and had great Abilities to manage, to multiply, and defend his Corruptions.

In like Manner, the Disbelief of a Divine Providence renders a Man uncapable of holding any publick Station: For, since Kings avow themselves to be the Deputies of Providence, the *Lilliputians* think nothing can be more absurd than for a Prince to employ such Men as disown the Authority under which he acteth.

In relating these and the following Laws, I would only be understood to mean the original Institutions, and not the most scandalous Corruptions into which these People are fallen by the degenerate Nature of Man. For as to that infamous Practice of acquiring great Employments by dancing on the Ropes, or Badges of Favour and Distinction by leaping over Sticks, and creeping under them; the Reader is to observe, that they were first introduced by the Grandfather of the Emperor now reigning; and grew to the present Height, by the gradual Increase of Party and Faction.

INGRATITUDE is among them a capital Crime, as we read it to have been in some other Countries: For they reason thus; that whoever makes ill Returns to his Benefactor, must needs be a common Enemy to the rest of Mankind, from whom they have received no Obligation; and therefore such a Man is not fit to live.

THEIR Notions relating to the Duties of Parents and Children differ extremely from ours. For, since the Conjunction of Male and Female is founded upon the great Law of Nature, in order to propagate and continue the Species; the *Lilliputians* will needs have it, that Men and Women are joined together like other Animals, by the Motives of Concupiscence; and that their Tenderness towards their Young, proceedeth from the like natural Principle: For which Reason they will never allow, that a Child is under any Obligation to his Father for begetting him, or to his Mother for bringing him into the World; which, considering the Miseries of human Life, was neither a Benefit in itself, nor intended so by his Parents, whose Thoughts in their Love-encounters were otherwise employed. Upon these, and the like Reasonings, their Opinion is, that Parents are the last of all others to be trusted with the Education of their own Children: And therefore they have in every Town publick Nurseries, where all Parents, except Cottagers and Labourers, are obliged to send their Infants of both Sexes to be reared and educated when they come to the Age of twenty Moons; at which Time they are supposed to have some Rudiments of Docility. These Schools are of several Kinds, suited to different Qualities, and to both Sexes. They have certain Professors well skilled in preparing Children for such a Condition of Life as befits the Rank of their Parents, and their own Capacities as well as Inclinations. I shall first say something of the Male Nurseries, and then of the Female.

THE Nurseries for Males of Noble or Eminent Birth, are provided with grave and learned Professors, and their several Deputies. The Clothes and Food of the Children are plain and simple. They are bred up in the Principles of Honour, Justice, Courage, Modesty, Clemency, Religion, and Love of their Country: They are always employed in some Business, except in the Times of eating and sleeping, which are very short, and two Hours for Diversions, consisting of bodily Exercises. They are dressed by Men until four Years of Age, and then are obliged to dress themselves, although their Quality be ever so great; and the Women Attendants, who are aged proportionably to ours at fifty, perform only the most menial Offices. They are never suffered to converse with Servants, but go together in small or greater Numbers to take their Diversions, and always in the Presence of a Professor, or one of his Deputies; whereby they avoid those early bad Impressions of Folly and Vice to which our Children are subject. Their Parents are suffered to see them only twice a Year; the Visit is not to last above an Hour; they are allowed to kiss the Child at Meeting and Parting; but a Professor, who always standeth by on those Occasions, will not suffer them to whisper, or use any fondling Expressions, or bring any Presents of Toys, Sweet-meats, and the like.

THE Pension from each Family for the Education and Entertainment of a Child, upon Failure of due Payment, is levyed by the Emperor's Officers.

THE Nurseries for Children of ordinary Gentlemen, Merchants, Traders, and Handicrafts, are managed proportionably after the same Manner; only those designed for Trades, are put out Apprentices at seven Years old; whereas those of Persons of Quality continue in their Exercises until Fifteen, which answers to One and Twenty with us: But the Confinement is gradually lessened for the last three Years.

IN the Female Nurseries, the young Girls of Quality are educated much like the Males, only they are dressed by orderly Servants of their own Sex, but always in the Presence of a Professor or Deputy, until they come to dress themselves, which is at five Years old. And if it be found that these Nurses ever presume to entertain the Girls with frightful or foolish Stories, or the common Follies practised by Chamber-Maids among us; they are publickly whipped thrice about the City, imprisoned for a Year, and banished for Life to the most desolate Parts of the Country. Thus the young Ladies there are as much ashamed of being Cowards and Fools, as the Men; and despise all personal Ornaments beyond Decency and Cleanliness; neither did I perceive any Difference in their Education, made by their Difference of Sex, only that the Exercises of the Females were not altogether so robust; and that some Rules were given them relating to domestick Life, and a smaller Compass of Learning was enjoyed them: For, their Maxim is, that among People of Quality, a Wife should be always a reasonable and agreeable Companion, because she cannot always be young. When the Girls are twelve Years old, which among them is the marriageable Age, their Parents or Guardians take them home, with great Expressions of Gratitude to the Professors, and seldom without Tears of the young Lady and her Companions.

In the Nurseries of Females of the meaner Sort, the Children are instructed in all Kinds of Works proper for their Sex, and their several Degrees: Those intended for Apprentices are dismissed at seven Years old, the rest are kept to eleven.

The meaner Families who have Children at these Nurseries, are obliged, besides their annual Pension, which is as low as possible, to return to the Steward of the Nursery a small Monthly Share of their Gettings, to be a Portion for the Child; and therefore all Parents are limited in their Expences by the Law. For the *Lilliputians* think nothing can be more unjust, than that People, in Subservience to their own Appetites, should bring Children into the World, and leave the Burthen of supporting them on the Publick. As to Persons of Quality, they give Security to appropriate a certain Sum for each Child, suitable to their Condition; and these Funds are always managed with good Husbandry, and the most exact Justice.

The Cottagers and Labourers keep their Children at

home, their Business being only to till and cultivate the Earth; and therefore their Education is of little Consequence to the Publick; but the Old and Diseased among them are supported by Hospitals: For begging is a Trade unknown in this Empire.

AND here it may perhaps divert the curious Reader, to give some Account of my Domestick, and my Manner of living in this Country, during a Residence of nine Months and thirteen Days. Having a Head mechanically turned, and being likewise forced by Necessity, I had made for myself a Table and Chair convenient enough, out of the largest Trees in the Royal Park. Two hundred Sempstresses were employed to make me Shirts, and Linnen for my Bed and Table, all of the strongest and coarsest kind they could get; which, however, they were forced to quilt together in several Folds; for the thickest was some Degrees finer than Lawn. Their Linnen is usually three Inches wide, and three Foot make a Piece. The Sempstresses took my Measure as I lay on the Ground, one standing at my Neck, and another at my Mid-Leg, with a strong Cord extended, that each held by the End, while the third measured the Length of the Cord with a Rule of an Inch long. Then they measured my right Thumb, and desired no more; for by a mathematical Computation, that twice round the Thumb is once round the Wrist, and so on to the Neck and the Waist; and by the Help of my old Shirt, which I displayed on the Ground before them for a Pattern, they fitted me exactly. Three hundred Taylors were employed in the same Manner to make me Clothes; but they had another Contrivance for taking my Measure. I kneeled down, and they raised a Ladder from the Ground to my Neck; upon this Ladder one of them mounted, and let fall a Plum-Line from my Collar to the Floor, which just answered the Length of my Coat; but my Waist and Arms I measured myself. When my Cloaths were finished, which was done in my House, (for the largest of theirs would not have been able to hold them) they looked like the Patch-work made by the Ladies in *England*, only that mine were all of a Colour.

I HAD three hundred Cooks to dress my Victuals, in little

convenient Huts built about my House, where they and their Families lived, and prepared me two Dishes a-piece. I took up twenty Waiters in my Hand, and placed them on the Table; an hundred more attended below on the Ground, some with Dishes of Meat, and some with Barrels of Wine, and other Liquors, slung on their Shoulders; all which the Waiters above drew up as I wanted, in a very ingenious Manner, by certain Cords, as we draw the Bucket up a Well in *Europe*. A Dish of their Meat was a good Mouthful, and a Barrel of their Liquor a reasonable Draught. Their Mutton yields to ours, but their Beef is excellent. I have had a Sirloin so large, that I have been forced to make three Bits of it; but this is rare. My Servants were astonished to see me eat it Bones and all, as in our Country we do the Leg of a Lark. Their Geese and Turkeys I usually eat at a Mouthful, and I must confess they far exceed ours. Of their smaller Fowl I could take up twenty or thirty at the End of my Knife.

ONE Day his Imperial Majesty being informed of my Way of living, desired that himself, and his Royal Consort, with the young Princes of the Blood of both Sexes, might have the Happiness (as he was pleased to call it) of dining with me. They came accordingly, and I placed them upon Chairs of State on my Table, just over against me, with their Guards about them. *Flimnap* the Lord High Treasurer attended there likewise, with his white Staff; and I observed he often looked on me with a sour Countenance, which I would not seem to regard, but eat more than usual, in Honour to my dear Country, as well as to fill the Court with Admiration. I have some private Reasons to believe, that this Visit from his Majesty gave *Flimnap* an Opportunity of doing me ill Offices to his Master. That Minister had always been my secret Enemy, although he outwardly caressed me more than was usual to the Moroseness of his Nature. He represented to the Emperor the low Condition of his Treasury; that he was forced to take up Money at great Discount; that Exchequer Bills would not circulate under nine *per Cent.* below Par; that I had cost his Majesty about a Million and a half of *Sprugs*, (their greatest Gold

Coin, about the Bigness of a Spangle;) and upon the whole, that it would be adviseable in the Emperor to take the first fair Occasion of dismissing me.

I AM here obliged to vindicate the Reputation of an excellent Lady, who was an innocent Sufferer upon my Account. The Treasurer took a Fancy to be jealous of his Wife, from the Malice of some evil Tongues, who informed him that her Grace had taken a violent Affection for my Person; and the Court-Scandal ran for some Time that she once came privately to my Lodging. This I solemnly declare to be a most infamous Falshood, without any Grounds, farther than that her Grace was pleased to treat me with all innocent Marks of Freedom and Friendship. I own she came often to my House, but always publickly, nor ever without three more in the Coach, who were usually her Sister, and young Daughter, and some particular Acquaintance; but this was common to many other Ladies of the Court. And I still appeal to my Servants round, whether they at any Time saw a Coach at my Door without knowing what Persons were in it. On those Occasions, when a Servant had given me Notice, my Custom was to go immediately to the Door; and after paying my Respects, to take up the Coach and two Horses very carefully in my Hands, (for if there were six Horses, the Postillion always unharnessed four) and place them on a Table, where I had fixed a moveable Rim quite round, of five Inches high, to prevent Accidents. And I have often had four Coaches and Horses at once on my Table full of Company, while I sat in my Chair leaning my Face towards them; and when I was engaged with one Sett, the Coachmen would gently drive the others round my Table. I have passed many an Afternoon very agreeably in these Conversations: But I defy the Treasurer, or his two Informers, (I will name them, and let them make their best of it) *Clustril* and *Drunlo*, to prove that any Person ever came to me *incognito*, except the Secretary *Reldresal*, who was sent by express Command of his Imperial Majesty, as I have before related. I should not have dwelt so long upon this Particular, if it had not been a Point wherein the Reputation of a great Lady is so nearly

concerned; to say nothing of my own; although I had the
Honour to be a *Nardac*, which the Treasurer himself is not;
for all the World knows he is only a *Clumglum*, a Title inferior by one Degree, as that of a Marquess is to a Duke
in *England*; yet I allow he preceded me in right of his Post.
These false Informations, which I afterwards came to the
Knowledge of, by an Accident not proper to mention, made
the Treasurer shew his Lady for some Time an ill Countenance, and me a worse: For although he were at last unde-
ceived and reconciled to her, yet I lost all Credit with him;
and found my Interest decline very fast with the Emperor
himself, who was indeed too much governed by that
Favourite.

CHAPTER VII.

THE AUTHOR BEING INFORMED OF A DESIGN TO ACCUSE HIM OF HIGH TREASON, MAKES HIS ESCAPE TO BLEFUSCU. HIS RECEPTION THERE.

BEFORE I proceed to give an Account of my leaving
this Kingdom, it may be proper to inform the Reader
of a private Intrigue which had been for two Months
forming against me.

I HAD been hitherto all my Life a Stranger to Courts,
for which I was unqualified by the Meanness of my Condition. I had indeed heard and read enough of the Dispositions of great Princes and Ministers; but never expected to
have found such terrible Effects of them in so remote a
Country, governed, as I thought, by very different Maxims
from those in *Europe*.

WHEN I was just preparing to pay my Attendance on the
Emperor of *Blefuscu*; a considerable Person at Court (to
whom I had been very serviceable at a time when he lay
under the highest Displeasure of his Imperial Majesty)
came to my House very privately at Night in a close Chair,
and without sending his Name, desired Admittance: The

Chair-men were dismissed; I put the Chair, with his Lordship in it, into my Coat-Pocket; and giving Orders to a
trusty Servant to say I was indisposed and gone to sleep, I
fastened the Door of my House, placed the Chair on the
Table, according to my usual Custom, and sat down by it.
After the common Salutations were over, observing his
Lordship's Countenance full of Concern; and enquiring
into the Reason, he desired I would hear him with Patience,
in a Matter that highly concerned my Honour and my Life.
His Speech was to the following Effect, for I took Notes of
it as soon as he left me.

You are to know, said he, that several Committees of
Council have been lately called in the most private Manner
on your Account: And it is but two Days since his Majesty
came to a full Resolution.

You are very sensible that *Skyris Bolgolam* (*Galbet*, or
High Admiral) hath been your mortal Enemy almost ever
since your Arrival. His original Reasons I know not; but
his Hatred is much increased since your great Success
against *Blefuscu*, by which his Glory, as Admiral, is obscured. This Lord, in Conjunction with *Flimnap* the High
Treasurer, whose Enmity against you is notorious on Account of his Lady; *Limtoc* the General, *Lalcon* the Chamberlain, and *Balmuff* the grand Justiciary, have prepared
Articles of Impeachment against you, for Treason, and
other capital Crimes.

This Preface made me so impatient, being conscious of
my own Merits and Innocence, that I was going to interrupt; when he intreated me to be silent; and thus proceeded.

Out of Gratitude for the Favours you have done me, I
procured Information of the whole Proceedings, and a
Copy of the Articles, wherein I venture my Head for your
Service.

Articles of Impeachment against Quinbus Flestrin,
(*the* Man-Mountain.)

ARTICLE I.

WHEREAS, by a Statute made in the Reign of his Imperial Majesty *Calin Deffar Plune*, it is enacted, That whoever shall make water within the Precincts of the Royal Palace, shall be liable to the Pains and Penalties of High Treason: Notwithstanding, the said *Quinbus Flestrin*, in open Breach of the said Law, under Colour of extinguishing the Fire kindled in the Apartment of his Majesty's most dear Imperial Consort, did maliciously, traitorously, and devilishly, by discharge of his Urine, put out the said Fire kindled in the said Apartment, lying and being within the Precincts of the said Royal Palace; against the Statute in that Case provided, &c. against the Duty, &c.

ARTICLE II.

THAT the said *Quinbus Flestrin* having brought the Imperial Fleet of *Blefuscu* into the Royal Port, and being afterwards commanded by his Imperial Majesty to seize all the other Ships of the said Empire of *Blefuscu*, and reduce that Empire to a Province, to be governed by a Vice-Roy from hence; and to destroy and put to death not only all the *Big-Endian Exiles*, but likewise all the People of that Empire, who would not immediately forsake the *Big-Endian* Heresy: He the said *Flestrin*, like a false Traitor against his most Auspicious, Serene, Imperial Majesty, did petition to be excused from the said Service, upon Pretence of Unwillingness to force the Consciences, or destroy the Liberties and Lives of an innocent People.

ARTICLE III.

THAT, whereas certain Embassadors arrived from the Court of *Blefuscu* to sue for Peace in his Majesty's Court:

He the said *Flestrin* did, like a false Traitor, aid, abet, comfort, and divert the said Embassadors; although he knew them to be Servants to a Prince who was lately an open Enemy to his Imperial Majesty, and in open War against his said Majesty.

ARTICLE IV.

THAT the said *Quinbus Flestrin*, contrary to the Duty of a faithful Subject, is now preparing to make a Voyage to the Court and Empire of *Blefuscu*, for which he hath received only verbal Licence from his Imperial Majesty; and under Colour of the said Licence, doth falsly and traitorously intend to take the said Voyage, and thereby to aid, comfort, and abet the Emperor of *Blefuscu*, so late an Enemy, and in open War with his Imperial Majesty aforesaid.

THERE are some other Articles, but these are the most important, of which I have read you an Abstract.

IN the several Debates upon this Impeachment, it must be confessed that his Majesty gave many Marks of his great *Lenity*; often urging the Services you had done him, and endeavouring to extenuate your Crimes. The Treasurer and Admiral insisted that you should be put to the most painful and ignominious Death, by setting Fire on your House at Night; and the General was to attend with Twenty Thousand Men armed with poisoned Arrows, to shoot you on the Face and Hands. Some of your Servants were to have private Orders to strew a poisonous Juice on your Shirts and Sheets, which would soon make you tear your own Flesh, and die in the utmost Torture. The General came into the same Opinion; so that for a long time there was a Majority against you. But his Majesty resolving, if possible, to spare your Life, at last brought off the Chamberlain.

UPON this Incident, *Reldresal*, principal Secretary for private Affairs, who always approved himself your true Friend, was commanded by the Emperor to deliver his Opinion, which he accordingly did; and therein justified the good Thoughts you have of him. He allowed your Crimes to be great; but that still there was room for Mercy, the most commendable Virtue in a Prince, and for which his Majesty was so justly celebrated. He said, the Friendship between you and him was so well known to the World, that perhaps the most honourable Board might think him partial: However, in Obedience to the Command he had received, he would freely offer his Sentiments. That if his Majesty, in Consideration of your Services, and pursuant to his own merciful Disposition, would please to spare your Life, and only give order to put out both your Eyes; he humbly conceived, that by this Expedient, Justice might in some measure be satisfied, and all the World would applaud the *Lenity* of the Emperor, as well as the fair and generous Proceedings of those who have the Honour to be his Counsellors. That the Loss of your Eyes would be no Impediment to your bodily Strength, by which you might still be useful to his Majesty. That Blindness is an Addition to Courage, by concealing Dangers from us; that the Fear you had for your Eyes, was the greatest Difficulty in bringing over the Enemy's Fleet; and it would be sufficient for you to see by the Eyes of the Ministers, since the greatest Princes do no more.

THIS Proposal was received with the utmost Disapprobation by the whole Board. *Bolgolam*, the Admiral, could not preserve his Temper; but rising up in Fury, said, he wondered how the Secretary durst presume to give his Opinion for preserving the Life of a Traytor: That the Services you had performed, were, by all true Reasons of State, the great Aggravation of your Crimes; that you, who were able to extinguish the Fire, by discharge of Urine in her Majesty's Apartment (which he mentioned with Horror) might, at another time, raise an Inundation by the same Means, to drown the whole Palace; and the same Strength which enabled you to bring over the Enemy's Fleet, might serve, upon the first Discontent, to carry it back: That he had good Reasons to think you were a *Big-Endian* in your Heart; and as Treason begins in the Heart before it appears in Overt-Acts; so he accused you as a Traytor on that Account, and therefore insisted you should be put to death.

THE Treasurer was of the same Opinion; he shewed to what Streights his Majesty's Revenue was reduced by the Charge of maintaining you, which would soon grow insupportable: That the Secretary's Expedient of putting out your Eyes, was so far from being a Remedy against this Evil, that it would probably increase it; as it is manifest from the common Practice of blinding some Kind of Fowl, after which they fed the faster, and grew sooner fat: That his sacred Majesty, and the Council, who are your Judges, were in their own Consciences fully convinced of your Guilt; which was a sufficient Argument to condemn you to death, without the *formal Proofs required by the strict Letter of the Law*.

BUT his Imperial Majesty fully determined against capital Punishment, was graciously pleased to say, that since the Council thought the Loss of your Eyes too easy a Censure, some other may be inflicted hereafter. And your Friend the Secretary humbly desiring to be heard again, in Answer to what the Treasurer had objected concerning the great Charge his Majesty was at in maintaining you; said, that his Excellency, who had the sole Disposal of the Emperor's Revenue, might easily provide against this Evil, by gradually lessening your Establishment; by which, for want of sufficient Food, you would grow weak and faint, and lose your Appetite, and consequently decay and consume in a few Months; neither would the Stench of your Carcass be then so dangerous, when it should become more than half diminished; and immediately upon your Death, five or six Thousand of his Majesty's Subjects might, in two or three Days, cut your Flesh from your Bones, take it away by Cart-loads, and bury it in distant Parts to prevent Infection; leaving the Skeleton as a Monument of Admiration to Posterity.

THUS by the great Friendship of the Secretary, the whole Affair was compromised. It was strictly enjoined, that the Project of starving you by Degrees should be kept a Secret; but the Sentence of putting out your Eyes was entered on the Books; none dissenting except *Bolgolam* the Admiral, who being a Creature of the Empress, was perpetually insti-

gated by her Majesty to insist upon your Death; she having
born perpetual Malice against you, on Account of that infamous and illegal Method you took to extinguish the Fire
in her Apartment.

IN three Days your Friend the Secretary will be directed
to come to your House, and read before you the Articles
of Impeachment; and then to signify the great *Lenity* and
Favour of his Majesty and Council; whereby you are only
condemned to the Loss of your Eyes, which his Majesty
doth not question you will gratefully and humbly submit
to; and Twenty of his Majesty's Surgeons will attend, in
order to see the Operation well performed, by discharging
very sharp pointed Arrows into the Balls of your Eyes, as
you lie on the Ground.

I LEAVE to your Prudence what Measures you will take;
and to avoid Suspicion, I must immediately return in as
private a Manner as I came.

HIS Lordship did so, and I remained alone, under many
Doubts and Perplexities of Mind.

IT was a Custom introduced by this Prince and his Ministry, (very different, as I have been assured, from the Practices of former Times) that after the Court had decreed any
cruel Execution, either to gratify the Monarch's Resentment, or the Malice of a Favourite; the Emperor always
made a Speech to his whole Council, expressing his *great
Lenity and Tenderness, as Qualities known and confessed
by all the World.* This Speech was immediately published
through the Kingdom; nor did any thing terrify the People
so much as those Encomiums on his Majesty's Mercy;
because it was observed, that the more these Praises were
enlarged and insisted on, the more *inhuman* was the Punishment, and the *Sufferer more innocent.* Yet, as to myself, I
must confess, having never been designed for a Courtier,
either by my Birth or Education, I was so ill a Judge of
Things, that I could not discover the *Lenity* and Favour of
this Sentence; but conceived it (perhaps erroneously) rather
to be rigorous than gentle. I sometimes thought of standing my Tryal; for although I could not deny the Facts alledged in the several Articles, yet I hoped they would admit

of some Extenuations. But having in my Life perused many
State-Tryals, which I ever observed to terminate as the
Judges thought fit to direct; I durst not rely on so dangerous
a Decision, in so critical a Juncture, and against such powerful Enemies. Once I was strongly bent upon Resistance:
For while I had Liberty, the whole Strength of that Empire
could hardly subdue me, and I might easily with Stones pelt
the Metropolis to Pieces: But I soon rejected that Project
with Horror, by remembering the Oath I had made to the
Emperor, the Favours I received from him, and the high
Title of *Nardac* he conferred upon me. Neither had I so
soon learned the Gratitude of Courtiers, to persuade myself
that his Majesty's *present Severities acquitted me of all past
Obligations*.

AT last I fixed upon a Resolution, for which it is probable
I may incur some Censure, and not unjustly; for I con-
fess I owe the preserving my Eyes, and consequently my
Liberty, to my own great Rashness and Want of Experience:
Because if I had then known the Nature of Princes and
Ministers, which I have since observed in many other
Courts, and their Methods of treating Criminals less ob-
noxious than myself; I should with great Alacrity and
Readiness have submitted to so *easy* a Punishment. But
hurried on by the Precipitancy of Youth; and having his
Imperial Majesty's Licence to pay my Attendance upon the
Emperor of *Blefuscu*; I took this Opportunity, before the
three Days were elapsed, to send a Letter to my Friend
the Secretary, signifying my Resolution of setting out that
Morning for *Blefuscu*, pursuant to the Leave I had got; and
without waiting for an Answer, I went to that Side of the
Island where our Fleet lay. I seized a large Man of War,
tied a Cable to the Prow, and lifting up the Anchors, I stript
myself, put my Cloaths (together with my Coverlet, which
I carryed under my Arm) into the Vessel; and drawing it
after me, between wading and swimming, arrived at the
Royal Port of *Blefuscu*, where the People had long expected
me: They lent me two Guides to direct me to the Capital
City, which is of the same Name; I held them in my Hands
until I came within two Hundred Yards of the Gate; and

desired them to signify my Arrival to one of the Secretaries, and let him know, I there waited his Majesty's Commands. I had an Answer in about an Hour, that his Majesty, attended by the Royal Family, and great Officers of the Court, was coming out to receive me. I advanced a Hundred Yards; the Emperor, and his Train, alighted from their Horses, the Empress and Ladies from their Coaches; and I did not perceive they were in any Fright or Concern. I lay on the Ground to kiss his Majesty's and the Empress's Hand. I told his Majesty, that I was come according to my Promise, and with the Licence of the Emperor my Master, to have the Honour of seeing so mighty a Monarch, and to offer him any Service in my Power, consistent with my Duty to my own Prince; not mentioning a Word of my Disgrace, because I had hitherto no regular Information of it, and might suppose myself wholly ignorant of any such Design; neither could I reasonably conceive that the Emperor would discover the Secret while I was out of his Power: Wherein, however, it soon appeared I was deceived.

I SHALL not trouble the Reader with the particular Account of my Reception at this Court, which was suitable to the Generosity of so great a Prince; nor of the Difficulties I was in for want of a House and Bed, being forced to lie on the Ground, wrapt up in my Coverlet.

CHAPTER VIII.

THE AUTHOR, BY A LUCKY ACCIDENT, FINDS MEANS TO LEAVE BLEFUSCU; AND, AFTER SOME DIFFICULTIES, RETURNS SAFE TO HIS NATIVE COUNTRY.

THREE Days after my Arrival, walking out of Curiosity to the North-East Coast of the Island; I observed, about half a League off, in the Sea, somewhat that looked like a Boat overturned: I pulled off my Shoes and Stockings, and wading two or three Hundred Yards, I found the Object to approach nearer by Force of the Tide; and then plainly saw it to be a real Boat, which I supposed might, by some Tempest, have been driven from a Ship. Whereupon I returned immediately towards the City, and desired his Imperial Majesty to lend me Twenty of the tallest Vessels he had left after the Loss of his Fleet, and three Thousand Seamen under the Command of his Vice-Admiral. This Fleet sailed round, while I went back the shortest Way to the Coast where I first discovered the Boat; I found the Tide had driven it still nearer; the Seamen were all provided with Cordage, which I had beforehand twisted to a sufficient Strength. When the Ships came up, I stript myself, and waded till I came within an Hundred Yards of the Boat; after which I was forced to swim till I got up to it. The Seamen threw me the End of the Cord, which I fastened to a Hole in the fore-part of the Boat, and the other End to a Man of War: But I found all my Labour to little Purpose; for being out of my Depth, I was not able to work. In this Necessity, I was forced to swim behind, and push the Boat forwards as often as I could, with one of my Hands; and the Tide favouring me, I advanced so far, that I could just hold up my Chin and feel the Ground. I rested two or three Minutes, and then gave the Boat another Shove, and so on till the Sea was no higher than my Arm-pits. And now the most laborious Part being over, I took out my other Cables which were stowed in one of the Ships, and fastening them first to the Boat, and then to nine of the Vessels which attended me; the Wind being favourable, the Seamen towed, and I shoved till we arrived within forty Yards of the Shore; and waiting till the Tide was out, I got dry to the Boat, and by the Assistance of two Thousand Men, with Ropes and Engines, I made a shift to turn it on its Bottom, and found it was but little damaged.

I SHALL not trouble the Reader with the Difficulties I was under by the Help of certain Paddles, which cost me ten Days making, to get my Boat to the Royal Port of *Blefuscu*; where a mighty Concourse of People appeared upon my Arrival, full of Wonder at the Sight of so prodigious a Vessel. I told the Emperor, that my good Fortune had thrown this Boat in my Way, to carry me to some Place from whence I might return into my native Country; and begged his Majesty's Orders for getting Materials to fit it up; together with his Licence to depart; which, after some kind Expostulations, he was pleased to grant.

I DID very much wonder, in all this Time, not to have heard of any Express relating to me from our Emperor to the Court of *Blefuscu*. But I was afterwards given privately to understand, that his Imperial Majesty, never imagining I had the least Notice of his Designs, believed I was only gone to *Blefuscu* in Performance of my Promise, according to the Licence he had given me, which was well known at our Court; and would return in a few Days when that Ceremony was ended. But he was at last in pain at my long absence; and, after consulting with the Treasurer, and the rest of that Cabal; a Person of Quality was dispatched with the Copy of the Articles against me. This Envoy had Instructions to represent to the Monarch of *Blefuscu*, the great *Lenity* of his Master, who was content to punish me no further than with the Loss of my Eyes: That I had fled from Justice, and if I did not return in two Hours, I should be deprived of my Title of *Nardac*, and declared a Traitor. The Envoy further added; that in order to maintain the Peace and Amity between both Empires, his Master expected, that his Brother of *Blefuscu* would give Orders to have me sent back to *Lilliput*, bound Hand and Foot, to be punished as a Traitor.

THE Emperor of *Blefuscu* having taken three Days to consult, returned an Answer consisting of many Civilities and Excuses. He said, that as for sending me bound, his Brother knew it was impossible; that although I had deprived him of his Fleet, yet he owed great Obligations to me for many good Offices I had done him in making the Peace. That however, both their Majesties would soon be made easy; for I had found a prodigious Vessel on the Shore, able to carry me on the Sea, which he had given order to fit up with my own Assistance and Direction; and he hoped in a few Weeks both Empires would be freed from so insupportable an Incumbrance.

WITH this Answer the Envoy returned to *Lilliput*, and the Monarch of *Blefuscu* related to me all that had past; offering me at the same time (but under the strictest Confidence) his gracious Protection, if I would continue in his Service; wherein although I believed him sincere, yet I resolved never more to put any Confidence in Princes or Ministers, where I could possibly avoid it; and therefore, with all due Acknowledgments for his favourable Intentions, I humbly begged to be excused. I told him, that since Fortune, whether good or evil, had thrown a Vessel in my Way; I was resolved to venture myself in the Ocean, rather than be an Occasion of Difference between two such mighty Monarchs. Neither did I find the Emperor at all displeased; and I discovered by a certain Accident, that he was very glad of my Resolution, and so were most of his Ministers.

THESE Considerations moved me to hasten my Departure somewhat sooner than I intended; to which the Court, impatient to have me gone, very readily contributed. Five hundred Workmen were employed to make two Sails to my Boat, according to my Directions, by quilting thirteen fold of their strongest Linnen together. I was at the Pains of making Ropes and Cables, by twisting ten, twenty or thirty of the thickest and strongest of theirs. A great Stone that I happened to find, after a long Search by the Seashore, served me for an Anchor. I had the Tallow of three hundred Cows for greasing my Boat, and other Uses. I was at incredible Pains in cutting down some of the largest Timber Trees for Oars and Masts, wherein I was, however, much assisted by his Majesty's Ship-Carpenters, who helped me in smoothing them, after I had done the rough Work.

IN about a Month, when all was prepared, I sent to receive his Majesty's Commands, and to take my leave. The Emperor and Royal Family came out of the Palace; I lay down on my Face to kiss his Hand, which he very graciously gave me; so did the Empress, and young Princes of the Blood. His Majesty presented me with fifty Purses of two hundred *Sprugs* a-piece, together with his Picture at full length, which I put immediately into one of my Gloves, to keep it from being hurt. The Ceremonies at my Departure were too many to trouble the Reader with at this time.

I STORED the Boat with the Carcasses of an hundred Oxen, and three hundred Sheep, with Bread and Drink proportionable, and as much Meat ready dressed as four hundred Cooks could provide. I took with me six Cows and two Bulls alive, with as many Yews and Rams, intending to carry them into my own Country and propagate the Breed. And to feed them on board, I had a good Bundle of Hay, and a Bag of Corn. I would gladly have taken a Dozen of the Natives; but this was a thing the Emperor would by no Means permit; and besides a diligent Search into my Pockets, his Majesty engaged my Honour not to carry away any of his Subjects, although with their own Consent and Desire.

HAVING thus prepared all things as well as I was able; I set sail on the Twenty-fourth Day of *September* 1701, at six in the Morning; and when I had gone about four Leagues to the Northward, the Wind being at South-East; at six in the Evening, I descryed a small Island about half a League to the North West. I advanced forward, and cast Anchor on the Lee-side of the Island, which seemed to be uninhabited. I then took some Refreshment, and went to my Rest. I slept well, and as I conjecture at least six Hours; for I found the Day broke in two Hours after I awaked. It was a clear Night; I eat my Breakfast before the Sun was up; and heaving Anchor, the Wind being favourable, I steered the same Course that I had done the Day before, wherein I was directed by my Pocket-Compass. My Intention was to reach, if possible, one of those Islands, which I had reason to believe lay to the North-East of *Van Diemen's* Land. I discovered nothing all that Day; but upon the next, about three in the Afternoon, when I had by my Computation made Twenty-four Leagues from *Blefuscu*, I descryed a Sail steering to the South-East; my Course was due East. I hailed her, but could get no Answer; yet I found I gained upon her, for the Wind slackened. I made all the Sail I could, and in half an Hour she spyed me, then hung out her Antient, and discharged a Gun. It is not easy to express the Joy I was in upon the unexpected Hope of once more seeing my beloved Country, and the dear Pledges I had left in it. The Ship slackned her Sails, and I came up with her between five and six in the Evening, *September* 26; but my Heart leapt within me to see her *English* Colours. I put my Cows and Sheep into my Coat-Pockets, and got on board with all my little Cargo of Provisions. The Vessel was an *English* Merchant-man, returning from *Japan* by the *North* and *South Seas*; the Captain, Mr. *John Biddel* of *Deptford*, a very civil Man, and an excellent Sailor. We were now in the Latitude of 30 Degrees South; there were about fifty Men in the Ship; and here I met an old Comrade of mine, one *Peter Williams*, who gave me a good Character to the Captain. This Gentleman treated me with Kindness, and desired I would let him know what Place I came from last, and whither I was bound; which I did in few Words; but he thought I was raving, and that the Dangers I underwent had disturbed my Head; whereupon I took my black Cattle and Sheep out of my Pocket, which, after great Astonishment, clearly convinced him of my Veracity. I then shewed him the Gold given me by the Emperor of *Blefuscu*, together with his Majesty's Picture at full Length, and some other Rarities of that Country. I gave him two Purses of two Hundred *Sprugs* each, and promised, when we arrived in *England*, to make him a Present of a Cow and a Sheep big with Young.

I SHALL not trouble the Reader with a particular Account of this Voyage; which was very prosperous for the most Part. We arrived in the *Downs* on the 13th of *April* 1702. I had only one Misfortune, that the Rats on board carried away one of my Sheep; I found her Bones in a Hole, picked clean from the Flesh. The rest of my Cattle I got safe on Shore, and set them a grazing in a Bowling-Green at *Greenwich*, where the Fineness of the Grass made them feed very heartily, although I had always feared the contrary: Neither could I possibly have preserved them in so long a Voyage, if the Captain had not allowed me some of his best Bisket, which rubbed to Powder, and mingled with Water, was their constant Food. The short Time I continued in *Eng-*

land, I made a considerable Profit by shewing my Cattle to many Persons of Quality, and others: And before I began my second Voyage, I sold them for six Hundred Pounds. Since my last Return, I find the Breed is considerably increased, especially the Sheep; which I hope will prove much to the Advantage of the Woollen Manufacture, by the Fineness of the Fleeces.

I STAYED but two Months with my Wife and Family; for my insatiable Desire of seeing foreign Countries would suffer me to continue no longer. I left fifteen Hundred Pounds with my Wife, and fixed her in a good House at *Redriff.* My remaining Stock I carried with me, Part in Money, and Part in Goods, in Hopes to improve my Fortunes. My eldest Uncle, *John,* had left me an Estate in Land, near *Epping,* of about Thirty Pounds a Year; and I had a long Lease of the *Black-Bull* in *Fetter-Lane,* which yielded me as much more: So that I was not in any Danger of leaving my Family upon the Parish. My Son *Johnny,* named so after his Uncle, was at the Grammar School, and a towardly Child. My Daughter *Betty* (who is now well married, and has Children) was then at her Needle-Work. I took Leave of my Wife, and Boy and Girl, with Tears on both Sides; and went on board the *Adventure,* a Merchant-Ship of three Hundred Tons, bound for *Surat,* Captain *John Nicholas* of *Liverpool,* Commander. But my Account of this Voyage must be referred to the second Part of my Travels.

The End of the First Part.

D

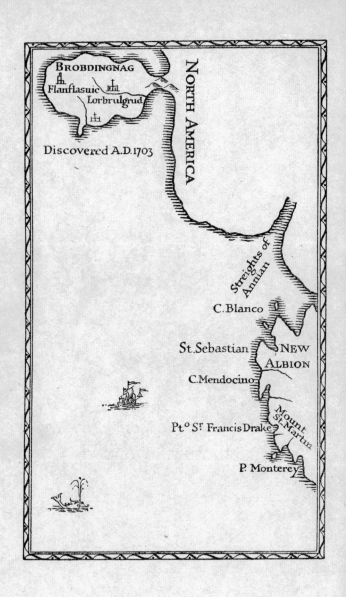

PART II.

A VOYAGE TO BROBDINGNAG

CHAPTER I.

A GREAT STORM DESCRIBED. THE LONG BOAT SENT TO
FETCH WATER. THE AUTHOR GOES WITH IT TO DISCOVER
THE COUNTRY. HE IS LEFT ON SHOAR, IS SEIZED BY ONE
OF THE NATIVES, AND CARRIED TO A FARMER'S HOUSE.
HIS RECEPTION THERE, WITH SEVERAL ACCIDENTS THAT
HAPPENED THERE. A DESCRIPTION OF THE INHABITANTS.

HAVING been condemned by Nature and Fortune
to an active and restless Life; in two Months after
my Return, I again left my native Country, and
took Shipping in the *Downs* on the 20th Day of *June* 1702,
in the *Adventure*, Capt. *John Nicholas*, a *Cornish* Man,
Commander, bound for *Surat*. We had a very prosperous
Gale till we arrived at the *Cape* of *Good-hope*, where we
landed for fresh Water; but discovering a Leak we un-
shipped our Goods, and wintered there; for the Captain
falling sick of an Ague, we could not leave the *Cape* till the
End of *March*. We then set sail, and had a good Voyage
till we passed the *Streights* of *Madagascar*; but having got
Northward of that Island, and to about five Degrees South
Latitude, the Winds, which in those Seas are observed to
blow a constant equal Gale between the North and West,
from the Beginning of *December* to the Beginning of *May*,
on the 19th of *April* began to blow with much greater Violence, and more Westerly than usual; continuing so for
twenty Days together, during which time we were driven a
little to the East of the *Molucca* Islands, and about three
Degrees Northward of the Line, as our Captain found by
an Observation he took the 2d of *May*, at which time the

Wind ceased, and it was a perfect Calm, whereat I was not a little rejoyced. But he being a Man well experienced in the Navigation of those Seas, bid us all prepare against a Storm, which accordingly happened the Day following: For a Southern Wind, called the Southern *Monsoon*, began to set in.

FINDING it was like to overblow, we took in our Spritsail, and stood by to hand the Fore-sail; but making foul Weather, we looked the Guns were all fast, and handed the Missen. The Ship lay very broad off, so we thought it better spooning before the Sea, than trying or hulling. We reeft the Foresail and set him, we hawled aft the Fore-sheet; the Helm was hard a Weather. The Ship wore bravely. We belay'd the Foredown-hall; but the Sail was split, and we hawl'd down the Yard, and got the Sail into the Ship, and unbound all the things clear of it. It was a very fierce Storm; the Sea broke strange and dangerous. We hawl'd off upon the Lanniard of the Wipstaff, and helped the Man at Helm. We would not get down our Top-Mast, but let all stand, because she scudded before the Sea very well, and we knew that the Top-Mast being aloft, the Ship was the wholesomer, and made better way through the Sea, seeing we had Sea room. When the Storm was over, we set Fore-sail and Main-sail, and brought the Ship too. Then we set the Missen, Maintop-Sail and the Foretop-Sail. Our Course was East North-east, the Wind was at South-west. We got the Star-board Tack aboard, we cast off our Weather-braces and Lifts; we set in the Lee-braces, and hawl'd forward by the Weather-bowlings, and hawl'd them tight, and belayed them, and hawl'd over the Missen Tack to Windward, and kept her full and by as near as she would lye.

DURING this Storm, which was followed by a strong Wind West South-west, we were carried by my Computation about five hundred Leagues to the East, so that the oldest Sailor on Board could not tell in what part of the World we were. Our Provisions held out well, our Ship was staunch, and our Crew all in good Health; but we lay in the utmost Distress for Water. We thought it best to hold on the same Course rather than turn more Northerly, which might have brought us to the North-west Parts of great *Tartary*, and into the frozen Sea.

ON the 16*th* Day of *June* 1703, a Boy on the Top-mast discovered Land. On the 17*th* we came in full View of a great Island or Continent, (for we knew not whether) on the South-side whereof was a small Neck of Land jutting out into the Sea, and a Creek too shallow to hold a Ship of above one hundred Tuns. We cast Anchor within a League of this Creek, and our Captain sent a dozen of his Men well armed in the Long Boat, with Vessels for Water if any could be found. I desired his leave to go with them, that I might see the Country, and make what Discoveries I could. When we came to Land we saw no River or Spring, nor any Sign of Inhabitants. Our Men therefore wandered on the Shore to find out some fresh Water near the Sea, and I walked alone about a Mile on the other Side, where I observed the Country all barren and rocky. I now began to be weary, and seeing nothing to entertain my Curiosity, I returned gently down towards the Creek; and the Sea being full in my View, I saw our Men already got into the Boat, and rowing for Life to the Ship. I was going to hollow after them, although it had been to little purpose, when I observed a huge Creature walking after them in the Sea, as fast as he could: He waded not much deeper than his Knees, and took prodigious strides: But our Men had the start of him half a League, and the Sea thereabouts being full of sharp pointed Rocks, the Monster was not able to overtake the Boat. This I was afterwards told, for I durst not stay to see the Issue of that Adventure; but run as fast as I could the Way I first went; and then climbed up a steep Hill, which gave me some Prospect of the Country. I found it fully cultivated; but that which first surprized me was the Length of the Grass, which in those Grounds that seemed to be kept for Hay, was above twenty Foot high.

I FELL into a high Road, for so I took it to be, although it served to the Inhabitants only as a foot Path through a Field of Barley. Here I walked on for sometime, but could see little on either Side, it being now near Harvest, and the Corn rising at least forty Foot. I was an Hour walking to the end of this Field; which was fenced in with a Hedge of at least one hundred and twenty Foot high, and the Trees so lofty that I could make no Computation of their Altitude. There was a Stile to pass from this Field into the next: It had four Steps, and a Stone to cross over when you came to the utmost. It was impossible for me to climb this Stile, because every Step was six Foot high, and the upper Stone above twenty. I was endeavouring to find some Gap in the Hedge; when I discovered one of the Inhabitants in the next Field advancing towards the Stile, of the same Size with him whom I saw in the Sea pursuing our Boat. He appeared as Tall as an ordinary Spire-steeple; and took about ten Yards at every Stride, as near as I could guess. I was struck with the utmost Fear and Astonishment, and ran to hide my self in the Corn, from whence I saw him at the Top of the Stile, looking back into the next Field on the right Hand; and heard him call in a Voice many Degrees louder than a speaking Trumpet; but the Noise was so High in the Air, that at first I certainly thought it was Thunder. Whereupon seven Monsters like himself came towards him with Reaping-Hooks in their Hands, each Hook about the largeness of six Scythes. These People were not so well clad as the first, whose Servants or Labourers they seemed to be. For, upon some Words he spoke, they went to reap the Corn in the Field where I lay. I kept from them at as great a Distance as I could, but was forced to move with extream Difficulty; for the Stalks of the Corn were sometimes not above a Foot distant, so that I could hardly squeeze my Body betwixt them. However, I made a shift to go forward till I came to a part of the Field where the Corn had been laid by the Rain and Wind: Here it was impossible for me to advance a step; for the Stalks were so interwoven that I could not creep through, and the Beards of the fallen Ears so strong and pointed, that they pierced through my Cloaths into my Flesh. At the same time I heard the Reapers not above an hundred Yards behind me. Being quite dispirited with Toil, and wholly overcome by Grief and Despair, I lay down between two Ridges, and heartily wished I might there end my Days. I bemoaned my desolate Widow, and

Fatherless Children: I lamented my own Folly and Wilfulness in attempting a second Voyage against the Advice of all my Friends and Relations. In this terrible Agitation of Mind I could not forbear thinking of *Lilliput*, whose Inhabitants looked upon me as the greatest Prodigy that ever appeared in the World; where I was able to draw an Imperial Fleet in my Hand, and perform those other Actions which will be recorded for ever in the Chronicles of that Empire, while Posterity shall hardly believe them, although attested by Millions. I reflected what a Mortification it must prove to me to appear as inconsiderable in this Nation, as one single *Lilliputian* would be among us. But, this I conceived was to be the least of my Misfortunes: For, as human Creatures are observed to be more Savage and cruel in Proportion to their Bulk; what could I expect but to be a Morsel in the Mouth of the first among these enormous Barbarians who should happen to seize me? Undoubtedly Philosophers are in the Right when they tell us, that nothing is great or little otherwise than by Comparison: It might have pleased Fortune to let the *Lilliputians* find some Nation, where the People were as diminutive with respect to them, as they were to me. And who knows but that even this prodigious Race of Mortals might be equally overmatched in some distant Part of the World, whereof we have yet no Discovery?

Scared and confounded as I was, I could not forbear going on with these Reflections; when one of the Reapers approaching within ten Yards of the Ridge where I lay, made me apprehend that with the next Step I should be squashed to Death under his Foot, or cut in two with his Reaping Hook. And therefore when he was again about to move, I screamed as loud as Fear could make me. Whereupon the huge Creature trod short, and looking round about under him for some time, at last espied me as I lay on the Ground. He considered a while with the Caution of one who endeavours to lay hold on a small dangerous Animal in such a Manner that it shall not be able either to scratch or to bite him; as I my self have sometimes done with a *Weasel* in *England*. At length he ventured to take me up behind by the middle between his Fore-finger and Thumb, and brought me within three Yards of his Eyes, that he might behold my Shape more perfectly. I guessed his Meaning; and my good Fortune gave me so much Presence of Mind, that I resolved not to struggle in the least as he held me in the Air above sixty Foot from the Ground; although he grievously pinched my Sides, for fear I should slip through his Fingers. All I ventured was to raise my Eyes towards the Sun, and place my Hands together in a supplicating Posture, and to speak some Words in an humble melancholy Tone, suitable to the Condition I then was in. For, I apprehended every Moment that he would dash me against the Ground, as we usually do any little hateful Animal which we have a Mind to destroy. But my good Star would have it, that he appeared pleased with my Voice and Gestures, and began to look upon me as a Curiosity; much wondering to hear me pronounce articulate Words, although he could not understand them. In the mean time I was not able to forbear Groaning and shedding Tears, and turning my Head towards my Sides; letting him know, as well as I could, how cruelly I was hurt by the Pressure of his Thumb and Finger. He seemed to apprehend my Meaning; for, lifting up the Lappet of his Coat, he put me gently into it, and immediately ran along with me to his Master, who was a substantial Farmer, and the same Person I had first seen in the Field.

THE Farmer having (as I supposed by their Talk) received such an Account of me as his Servant could give him, took a piece of a small Straw, about the Size of a walking Staff, and therewith lifted up the Lappets of my Coat; which it seems he thought to be some kind of Covering that Nature had given me. He blew my Hairs aside to take a better View of my Face. He called his Hinds about him, and asked them (as I afterwards learned) whether they had ever seen in the Fields any little Creature that resembled me. He then placed me softly on the Ground upon all four; but I got immediately up, and walked slowly backwards and forwards, to let those People see I had no Intent to run away. They all sate down in a Circle about me, the better to observe my Motions. I pulled off my Hat, and made a low Bow towards the Farmer: I fell on my Knees, and lifted up my Hands and Eyes, and spoke several Words as loud as I could: I took a Purse of Gold out of my Pocket, and humbly presented it to him. He received it on the Palm of his Hand, then applied it close to his Eye, to see what it was, and afterwards turned it several times with the Point of a Pin, (which he took out of his Sleeve,) but could make nothing of it. Whereupon I made a Sign that he should place his Hand on the Ground: I then took the Purse, and opening it, poured all the Gold into his Palm. There were six *Spanish*-Pieces of four Pistoles each, besides twenty or thirty smaller Coins. I saw him wet the Tip of his little Finger upon his Tongue, and take up one of my largest Pieces, and then another; but he seemed to be wholly ignorant what they were. He made me a Sign to put them again into my Purse, and the Purse again into my Pocket; which after offering to him several times, I thought it best to do.

The Farmer by this time was convinced I must be a rational Creature. He spoke often to me, but the Sound of his Voice pierced my Ears like that of a Water-Mill; yet his Words were articulate enough. I answered as loud as I could in several Languages; and he often laid his Ear within two Yards of me, but all in vain, for we were wholly unintelligible to each other. He then sent his Servants to their Work, and taking his Handkerchief out of his Pocket, he doubled and spread it on his Hand, which he placed flat on the Ground with the Palm upwards, making me a Sign to step into it, as I could easily do, for it was not above a Foot in thickness. I thought it my part to obey; and for fear of falling, laid my self at full Length upon the Handkerchief, with the Remainder of which he lapped me up to the Head for further Security; and in this Manner carried me home to his House. There he called his Wife, and shewed me to her; but she screamed and ran back as Women in *England* do at the Sight of a Toad or a Spider. However, when she had a while seen my Behaviour, and how well I observed the Signs her Husband made, she was soon reconciled, and by Degrees grew extreamly tender of me.

IT was about twelve at Noon, and a Servant brought in Dinner. It was only one substantial Dish of Meat (fit for the plain Condition of an Husband-Man) in a Dish of about four and twenty Foot Diameter. The Company were the Farmer and Wife, three Children, and an old Grandmother: When they were sat down, the Farmer placed me at some Distance from him on the Table, which was thirty Foot high from the Floor. I was in a terrible Fright, and kept as far as I could from the Edge, for fear of falling. The Wife minced a bit of Meat, then crumbled some Bread on a Trencher, and placed it before me. I made her a low Bow, took out my Knife and Fork, and fell to eat; which gave them exceeding Delight. The Mistress sent her Maid for a small Dram-cup, which held about two Gallons; and filled it with Drink: I took up the Vessel with much difficulty in both Hands, and in a most respectful Manner drank to her Lady-ship's Health, expressing the Words as loud as I could in *English*; which made the Company laugh so heartily, that I was almost deafened with the Noise. This Liquour tasted like a small Cyder, and was not unpleasant. Then the Master made me a Sign to come to his Trencher side; but as I walked on the Table, being in great surprize all the time, as the indulgent Reader will easily conceive and excuse, I happened to stumble against a Crust, and fell flat on my Face, but received no hurt. I got up immediately, and observing the good People to be in much Concern, I took my Hat (which I held under my Arm out of good Manners) and waving it over my Head, made three Huzza's, to shew I had got no Mischief by the Fall. But advancing forwards toward my Master (as I shall henceforth call him) his youngest Son who sate next him, an arch Boy of about ten Years old, took me up by the Legs, and held me so high in the Air, that I trembled every Limb; but his Father snatched me from him; and at the same time gave him such a Box on the left Ear, as would have felled an *European* Troop of Horse to the Earth; ordering him to be taken from the Table. But, being afraid the Boy might owe me a Spight; and well remembring how mischievous all Children among us naturally are to Sparrows, Rabbits, young Kittens, and Puppy-Dogs; I fell on my Knees, and pointing to the Boy, made my Master understand, as well as I could, that I desired his Son might be pardoned. The Father complied, and the Lad took his Seat again; whereupon I went to him and kissed his Hand, which my Master took, and made him stroak me gently with it.

In the Midst of Dinner my Mistress's favourite Cat leapt into her Lap. I heard a Noise behind me like that of a Dozen Stocking-Weavers at work; and turning my Head, I found it proceeded from the Purring of this Animal, who seemed to be three Times larger than an Ox, as I computed by the View of her Head, and one of her Paws, while her Mistress was feeding and stroaking her. The Fierceness of this Creature's Countenance altogether discomposed me; although I stood at the further End of the Table, above fifty Foot off; and although my Mistress held her fast for fear she might give a Spring, and seize me in her Talons. But it happened there was no Danger; for the Cat took not the least Notice of me when my Master placed me within three Yards of her. And as I have been always told, and found true by Experience in my Travels, that flying, or discovering Fear before a fierce Animal, is a certain Way to make it pursue or attack you; so I resolved in this dangerous Juncture to shew no Manner of Concern. I walked with Intrepidity five or six Times before the very Head of the Cat, and came within half a Yard of her; whereupon she drew her self back, as if she were more afraid of me: I had less Apprehension concerning the Dogs, whereof three or four came into the Room, as it is usual in Farmers Houses; one of which was a Mastiff equal in Bulk to four Elephants, and a Grey-hound somewhat taller than the Mastiff, but not so large.

When Dinner was almost done, the Nurse came in with a Child of a Year old in her Arms; who immediately spyed me, and began a Squall that you might have heard from *London-Bridge* to *Chelsea*; after the usual Oratory of Infants, to get me for a Play-thing. The Mother out of pure

Indulgence took me up, and put me towards the Child, who presently seized me by the Middle, and got my Head in his Mouth, where I roared so loud that the Urchin was frighted, and let me drop; and I should infallibly have broke my Neck, if the Mother had not held her Apron under me. The Nurse to quiet her Babe made use of a Rattle, which was a Kind of hollow Vessel filled with great Stones, and fastned by a Cable to the Child's Waist: But all in vain, so that she was forced to apply the last Remedy by giving it suck. I must confess no Object ever disgusted me so much as the Sight of her monstrous Breast, which I cannot tell what to compare with, so as to give the curious Reader an Idea of its Bulk, Shape and Colour. It stood prominent six Foot, and could not be less than sixteen in Circumference. The Nipple was about half the Bigness of my Head, and the Hue both of that and the Dug so varified with Spots, Pimples and Freckles, that nothing could appear more nauseous: For I had a near Sight of her, she sitting down the more conveniently to give Suck, and I standing on the Table. This made me reflect upon the fair Skins of our *English* Ladies, who appear so beautiful to us, only because they are of our own Size, and their Defects not to be seen but through a magnifying Glass, where we find by Experiment that the smoothest and whitest Skins look rough and coarse, and ill coloured.

I REMEMBER when I was at *Lilliput*, the Complexions of those diminutive People appeared to me the fairest in the World: And talking upon this Subject with a Person of Learning there, who was an intimate Friend of mine; he said, that my Face appeared much fairer and smoother when he looked on me from the Ground, than it did upon a nearer View when I took him up in my Hand, and brought him close; which he confessed was at first a very shocking Sight. He said, he could discover great Holes in my Skin; that the Stumps of my Beard were ten Times stronger than the Bristles of a Boar; and my Complexion made up of several Colours altogether disagreeable: Although I must beg Leave to say for my self, that I am as fair as most of my Sex and Country, and very little Sunburnt by all my Travels.

On the other Side, discoursing of the Ladies in that Emperor's Court, he used to tell me, one had Freckles, another too wide a Mouth, a third too large a Nose; nothing of which I was able to distinguish. I confess this Reflection was obvious enough; which, however, I could not forbear, lest the Reader might think those vast Creatures were actually deformed: For I must do them Justice to say they are a comely Race of People; and particularly the Features of my Master's Countenance, although he were but a Farmer, when I beheld him from the Height of sixty Foot, appeared very well proportioned.

WHEN Dinner was done, my Master went out to his Labourers; and as I could discover by his Voice and Gesture, gave his Wife a strict Charge to take Care of me. I was very much tired and disposed to sleep, which my Mistress perceiving, she put me on her own Bed, and covered me with a clean white Handkerchief, but larger and coarser than the Main Sail of a Man of War.

I SLEPT about two Hours, and dreamed I was at home with my Wife and Children, which aggravated my Sorrows when I awaked and found my self alone in a vast Room, between two and three Hundred Foot wide, and above two Hundred high; lying in a Bed twenty Yards wide. My Mistress was gone about her houshold Affairs, and had locked me in. The Bed was eight Yards from the Floor. Some natural Necessities required me to get down: I durst not presume to call, and if I had, it would have been in vain with such a Voice as mine at so great a Distance from the Room where I lay, to the Kitchen where the Family kept. While I was under these Circumstances, two Rats crept up the Curtains, and ran smelling backwards and forwards on the Bed: One of them came up almost to my Face; whereupon I rose in a Fright, and drew out my Hanger to defend my self. These horrible Animals had the Boldness to attack me on both Sides, and one of them held his Fore-feet at my Collar; but I had the good Fortune to rip up his Belly before he could do me any Mischief. He fell down at my Feet; and the other seeing the Fate of his Comrade, made his Escape, but not without one good Wound on the Back, which I gave him as he fled, and made the Blood run trickling from him. After this Exploit I walked gently to and fro on the Bed, to recover my Breath and Loss of Spirits. These Creatures were of the Size of a large Mastiff, but infinitely more nimble and fierce; so that if I had taken off my Belt before I went to sleep, I must have infallibly been torn to Pieces and devoured. I measured the Tail of the dead Rat, and found it to be two Yards long, wanting an Inch; but it went against my Stomach to drag the Carcass off the Bed, where it lay still bleeding; I observed it had yet some Life, but with a strong Slash cross the Neck, I thoroughly dispatched it.

Soon after, my Mistress came into the Room, who seeing me all bloody, ran and took me up in her Hand. I pointed to the dead *Rat*, smiling and making other Signs to shew I was not hurt; whereat she was extremely rejoyced, calling the Maid to take up the dead *Rat* with a Pair of Tongs, and throw it out of the Window. Then she set me on a Table, where I shewed her my Hanger all bloody, and wiping it on the Lappet of my Coat, returned it to the Scabbard. I was pressed to do more than one Thing, which another could not do for me; and therefore endeavoured to make my Mistress understand that I desired to be set down on the Floor; which after she had done, my Bashfulness would not suffer me to express my self farther than by pointing to the Door, and bowing several Times. The good Woman with much Difficulty at last perceived what I would be at; and taking me up again in her Hand, walked into the Garden where she set me down. I went on one Side about two Hundred Yards; and beckoning to her not to look or follow me, I hid my self between two Leaves of Sorrel, and there discharged the Necessities of Nature.

I hope, the gentle Reader will excuse me for dwelling on these and the like Particulars; which however insignificant they may appear to grovelling vulgar Minds, yet will certainly help a Philosopher to enlarge his Thoughts and Imagination, and apply them to the Benefit of publick as well as private Life; which was my sole Design in presenting this and other Accounts of my Travels to the World; wherein

I have been chiefly studious of Truth, without affecting any Ornaments of Learning, or of Style. But the whole Scene of this Voyage made so strong an Impression on my Mind, and is so deeply fixed in my Memory, that in committing it to Paper, I did not omit one material Circumstance: However, upon a strict Review, I blotted out several Passages of less Moment which were in my first Copy, for fear of being censured as tedious and trifling, whereof Travellers are often, perhaps not without Justice, accused.

CHAPTER II.

A DESCRIPTION OF THE FARMER'S DAUGHTER. THE AUTHOR CARRIED TO A MARKET-TOWN, AND THEN TO THE METROPOLIS. THE PARTICULARS OF HIS JOURNEY.

My Mistress had a Daughter of nine Years old, a Child of towardly Parts for her Age, very dextrous at her Needle, and skilful in dressing her Baby. Her Mother and she contrived to fit up the Baby's Cradle for me against Night: The Cradle was put into a small Drawer of a Cabinet, and the Drawer placed upon a hanging Shelf for fear of the *Rats*. This was my Bed all the Time I stayed with those People, although made more convenient by Degrees, as I began to learn their Language, and make my Wants known. This young Girl was so handy, that after I had once or twice pulled off my Cloaths before her, she was able to dress and undress me, although I never gave her that Trouble when she would let me do either my self. She made me seven Shirts, and some other Linnen of as fine Cloth as could be got, which indeed was coarser than Sackcloth; and these she constantly washed for me with her own Hands. She was likewise my School-Mistress to teach me the Language: When I pointed to any thing, she told me the Name of it in her own Tongue, so that in a few Days I was able to call for whatever I had a mind to. She was very good natured, and not above forty Foot high, being little for her Age. She gave me the Name of *Grildrig*, which the Family took up, and afterwards the whole Kingdom. The Word imports what the *Latins* call *Nanunculus*, the *Italians Homunceletino*, and the *English Mannikin*. To her I chiefly owe my Preservation in that Country: We never parted while I was there; I called her my *Glumdalclitch*, or little Nurse: And I should be guilty of great Ingratitude if I omitted this honourable Mention of her Care and Affection towards me, which I heartily wish it lay in my Power to re-quite as she deserves, instead of being the innocent but un-happy Instrument of her Disgrace, as I have too much Reason to fear.

It now began to be known and talked of in the Neigh-bourhood, that my Master had found a strange Animal in the Fields, about the Bigness of a *Splacknuck*, but exactly shaped in every Part like a human Creature; which it like-wise imitated in all its Actions; seemed to speak in a little Language of its own, had already learned several Words of theirs, went erect upon two Legs, was tame and gentle, would come when it was called, do whatever it was bid, had the finest Limbs in the World, and a Complexion fairer than a Nobleman's Daughter of three Years old. Another Farmer who lived hard by, and was a particular Friend of my Master, came on a Visit on Purpose to enquire into the Truth of this Story. I was immediately produced, and placed upon a Table; where I walked as I was commanded, drew my Hanger, put it up again, made my Reverence to my Master's Guest, asked him in his own Language how he did, and told him he was welcome; just as my little Nurse had instructed me. This Man, who was old and dim-sighted, put on his Spectacles to behold me better, at which I could not forbear laughing very heartily; for his Eyes appeared like the Full-Moon shining into a Chamber at two Windows. Our People, who discovered the Cause of my Mirth, bore me Company in Laughing; at which the old Fellow was Fool enough to be angry and out of Counten-ance. He had the Character of a great Miser; and to my Misfortune he well deserved it by the cursed Advice he gave my Master, to shew me as a Sight upon a Market-Day in the next Town, which was half an Hour's Riding, about two and twenty Miles from our House. I guessed there was some Mischief contriving, when I observed my Master and his Friend whispering long together, sometimes pointing at me; and my Fears made me fancy that I overheard and understood some of their Words. But, the next Morning *Glumdalclitch* my little Nurse told me the whole Matter, which she had cunningly picked out from her Mother. The poor Girl laid me on her Bosom, and fell a weeping with Shame and Grief. She apprehended some Mischief would happen to me from rude vulgar Folks, who might squeeze me to Death, or break one of my Limbs by taking me in their Hands. She had also observed how modest I was in my Nature, how nicely I regarded my Honour; and what an Indignity I should conceive it to be exposed for Money as a publick Spectacle to the meanest of the People. She said, her *Papa* and *Mamma* had promised that *Grildrig* should be hers; but now she found they meant to serve her as they did last Year, when they pretended to give her a Lamb; and yet, as soon as it was fat, sold it to a Butcher. For my own Part, I may truly affirm that I was less concerned than my Nurse. I had a strong Hope which never left me, that I should one Day recover my Liberty; and as to the Ignominy of being carried about for a Monster, I considered my self to be a perfect Stranger in the Country; and that such a Misfortune could never be charged upon me as a Reproach if ever I should return to *England*; since the King of *Great Britain* himself, in my Condition, must have undergone the same Distress.

My Master, pursuant to the Advice of his Friend, carried me in a Box the next Market-Day to the neighbouring Town; and took along with him his little Daughter my Nurse upon a Pillion behind me. The Box was close on every Side, with a little Door for me to go in and out, and a few Gimlet-holes to let in Air. The Girl had been so careful to put the Quilt of her Baby's Bed into it, for me to lye down on. However, I was terribly shaken and discomposed in this Journey, although it were but of half an Hour. For the Horse went about forty Foot at every Step; and trotted so high, that the Agitation was equal to the rising and falling of a Ship in a great Storm, but much more frequent: Our Journey was somewhat further than from *London* to St. *Albans.* My Master alighted at an Inn which he used to frequent; and after consulting a while with the Inn-keeper, and making some necessary Preparations, he hired the *Grultrud,* or Cryer, to give Notice through the Town, of a strange Creature to be seen at the Sign of the Green *Eagle,* not so big as a *Splacknuck,* (an Animal in that Country very finely shaped, about six Foot long) and in every Part of the Body resembling an human Creature; could speak several Words, and perform an Hundred diverting Tricks.

I WAS placed upon a Table in the largest Room of the Inn, which might be near three Hundred Foot square. My little Nurse stood on a low Stool close to the Table, to take care of me, and direct what I should do. My Master, to avoid a Croud, would suffer only Thirty People at a Time to see me. I walked about on the Table as the Girl commanded; she asked me Questions as far as she knew my Understanding of the Language reached, and I answered them as loud as I could. I turned about several Times to the Company, paid my humble Respects, said they were welcome; and used some other Speeches I had been taught. I took up a Thimble filled with Liquor, which *Glumdalclitch* had given me for a Cup, and drank their Health. I drew out my Hanger, and flourished with it after the Manner of Fencers in *England.* My Nurse gave me Part of a Straw, which I exercised as a Pike, having learned the Art in my Youth. I was that Day shewn to twelve Sets of Company; and as often forced to go over again with the same Fopperies, till I was half dead with Weariness and Vexation. For, those who had seen me, made such wonderful Reports, that the People were ready to break down the Doors to come in. My Master for his own Interest would not suffer any one to touch me, except my Nurse; and, to prevent Danger, Benches were set round the Table at such a Distance, as put me out of every Body's Reach. However, an unlucky School-Boy aimed a Hazel-Nut directly at my

Head, which very narrowly missed me; otherwise, it came with so much Violence, that it would have infallibly knocked out my Brains; for it was almost as large as a small Pumpion: But I had the Satisfaction to see the young Rogue well beaten, and turned out of the Room.

My Master gave publick Notice, that he would shew me again the next Market-Day: And in the mean time, he prepared a more convenient Vehicle for me, which he had Reason enough to do; for I was so tired with my first Journey, and with entertaining Company eight Hours together, that I could hardly stand upon my Legs, or speak a Word. It was at least three Days before I recovered my Strength; and that I might have no rest at home, all the neighbouring Gentlemen from an Hundred Miles round, hearing of my Fame, came to see me at my Master's own House. There could not be fewer than thirty Persons with their Wives and Children; (for the Country is very populous;) and my Master demanded the Rate of a full Room whenever he shewed me at Home, although it were only to a single Family. So that for some time I had but little Ease every Day of the Week, (except *Wednesday*, which is their Sabbath) although I were not carried to the Town.

My Master finding how profitable I was like to be, resolved to carry me to the most considerable Cities of the Kingdom. Having therefore provided himself with all things necessary for a long Journey, and settled his Affairs at Home; he took Leave of his Wife; and upon the 17*th* of *August* 1703, about two Months after my Arrival, we set out for the Metropolis, situated near the Middle of that Empire, and about three Thousand Miles distance from our House: My Master made his Daughter *Glumdalclitch* ride behind him. She carried me on her Lap in a Box tied about her Waist. The Girl had lined it on all Sides with the softest Cloth she could get, well quilted underneath; furnished it with her Baby's Bed, provided me with Linnen and other Necessaries; and made every thing as convenient as she could. We had no other Company but a Boy of the House, who rode after us with the Luggage.

My Master's Design was to shew me in all the Towns

by the Way, and to step out of the Road for Fifty or an Hundred Miles, to any Village or Person of Quality's House where he might expect Custom. We made easy Journies of not above seven or eight Score Miles a Day: For *Glumdalclitch*, on Purpose to spare me, complained she was tired with the trotting of the Horse. She often took me out of my Box at my own Desire, to give me Air, and shew me the Country; but always held me fast by Leading-strings. We passed over five or six Rivers many Degrees broader and deeper than the *Nile* or the *Ganges*; and there was hardly a Rivulet so small as the *Thames* at *London-Bridge*. We were ten Weeks in our Journey; and I was shewn in Eighteen large Towns, besides many Villages and private Families.

On the 26th Day of *October*, we arrived at the Metropolis, called in their Language *Lorbrulgrud*, or *Pride of the Universe*. My Master took a Lodging in the principal Street of the City, not far from the Royal Palace; and put out Bills in the usual Form, containing an exact Description of my Person and Parts. He hired a large Room between three and four Hundred Foot wide. He provided a Table sixty Foot in Diameter, upon which I was to act my Part; and pallisadoed it round three Foot from the Edge, and as many high, to prevent my falling over. I was shewn ten Times a Day to the Wonder and Satisfaction of all People. I could now speak the Language tolerably well; and perfectly understood every Word that was spoken to me. Besides, I had learned their Alphabet, and could make a shift to explain a Sentence here and there; for *Glumdalclitch* had been my Instructer while we were at home, and at leisure Hours during our Journey. She carried a little Book in her Pocket, not much larger than a *Sanson's Atlas*; it was a common Treatise for the use of young Girls, giving a short Account of their Religion; out of this she taught me my Letters, and interpreted the Words.

CHAPTER III.

THE AUTHOR SENT FOR TO COURT. THE QUEEN BUYS HIM OF HIS MASTER THE FARMER, AND PRESENTS HIM TO THE KING. HE DISPUTES WITH HIS MAJESTY'S GREAT SCHOLARS. AN APARTMENT AT COURT PROVIDED FOR THE AUTHOR. HE IS IN HIGH FAVOUR WITH THE QUEEN. HE STANDS UP FOR THE HONOUR OF HIS OWN COUNTRY. HIS QUARRELS WITH THE QUEEN'S DWARF.

THE frequent Labours I underwent every Day, made in a few Weeks a very considerable Change in my Health: The more my Master got by me, the more unsatiable he grew. I had quite lost my Stomach, and was almost reduced to a Skeleton. The Farmer observed it; and concluding I soon must die, resolved to make as good a Hand of me as he could. While he was thus reasoning and resolving with himself; a *Slardral*, or Gentleman Usher, came from Court, commanding my Master to bring me immediately thither for the Diversion of the Queen and her Ladies. Some of the latter had already been to see me; and reported strange Things of my Beauty, Behaviour, and good Sense. Her Majesty and those who attended her, were beyond Measure delighted with my Demeanor. I fell on my Knees, and begged the Honour of kissing her Imperial Foot; but this Gracious Princess held out her little Finger towards me (after I was set on a Table) which I embraced in both my Arms, and put the Tip of it, with the utmost Respect, to my Lip. She made me some general Questions about my Country and my Travels, which I answered as distinctly and in as few Words as I could. She asked, whether I would be content to live at Court. I bowed down to the Board of the Table, and humbly answered, that I was my Master's Slave; but if I were at my own Disposal, I should be proud to devote my Life to her Majesty's Service. She then asked my Master whether he were willing to sell me at a good Price. He, who apprehended I could not live a Month, was ready enough to part with me; and demanded a Thousand Pieces of Gold; which were ordered him on the Spot, each Piece being about the Bigness of eight Hundred Moydores: But, allowing for the Proportion of all Things between that Country and *Europe*, and the high Price of Gold among them; was hardly so great a Sum as a Thousand Guineas would be in *England*. I then said to the Queen; since I was now her Majesty's most humble Creature and Vassal, I must beg the Favour, that *Glumdalclitch*, who had always tended me with so much Care and Kindness, and understood to do it so well, might be admitted into her Service, and continue to be my Nurse and Instructor. Her Majesty agreed to my Petition; and easily got the Farmer's Consent, who was glad enough to have his Daughter preferred at Court: And the poor Girl herself was not able to hide her Joy. My late Master withdrew, bidding me farewell, and saying he had left me in a good Service; to which I replyed not a Word, only making him a slight Bow.

THE Queen observed my Coldness; and when the Farmer was gone out of the Apartment, asked me the Reason. I made bold to tell her Majesty, that I owed no other Obligation to my late Master, than his not dashing out the Brains of a poor harmless Creature found by Chance in his Field; which Obligation was amply recompenced by the Gain he had made in shewing me through half the Kingdom, and the Price he had now sold me for. That the Life I had since led, was laborious enough to kill an Animal of ten Times my Strength. That my Health was much impaired by the continual Drudgery of entertaining the Rabble every Hour of the Day; and that if my Master had not thought my Life in Danger, her Majesty perhaps would not have got so cheap a Bargain. But as I was out of all fear of being ill treated under the Protection of so great and good an Empress, the Ornament of Nature, the Darling of the World, the Delight of her Subjects, the Phœnix of the Creation; so, I hoped my late Master's Apprehensions would appear to be groundless; for I already found my Spirits to revive by the Influence of her most August Presence.

THIS was the Sum of my Speech, delivered with great Improprieties and Hesitation; the latter Part was altogether framed in the Style peculiar to that People, whereof I learned some Phrases from *Glumdalclitch*, while she was carrying me to Court.

THE Queen giving great Allowance for my Defectiveness in speaking, was however surprised at so much Wit and good Sense in so diminutive an Animal. She took me in her own Hand, and carried me to the King, who was then retired to his Cabinet. His Majesty, a Prince of much Gravity, and austere Countenance, not well observing my Shape at first View, asked the Queen after a cold Manner, how long it was since she grew fond of a *Splacknuck*; for such it seems he took me to be, as I lay upon my Breast in her Majesty's right Hand. But this Princess, who hath an infinite deal of Wit and Humour, set me gently on my Feet upon the Scrutore; and commanded me to give His Majesty an Account of my self, which I did in a very few Words; and *Glumdalclitch*, who attended at the Cabinet Door, and could not endure I should be out of her Sight, being admitted; confirmed all that had passed from my Arrival at her Father's House.

THE King, although he be as learned a Person as any in his Dominions; and had been educated in the Study of Philosophy, and particularly Mathematicks; yet when he observed my Shape exactly, and saw me walk erect, before I began to speak, conceived I might be a piece of Clockwork, (which is in that Country arrived to a very great Perfection) contrived by some ingenious Artist. But, when he heard my Voice, and found what I delivered to be regular and rational, he could not conceal his Astonishment. He was by no means satisfied with the Relation I gave him of the Manner I came into his Kingdom; but thought it a Story concerted between *Glumdalclitch* and her Father, who had taught me a Sett of Words to make me sell at a higher Price. Upon this Imagination he put several other Questions to me, and still received rational Answers, no otherwise defective than by a Foreign Accent, and an imperfect Knowledge in the Language; with some rustick Phrases which I had learned at the Farmer's House, and did not suit the polite Style of a Court.

His Majesty sent for three great Scholars who were then in their weekly waiting (according to the Custom in that Country.) These Gentlemen, after they had a while examined my Shape with much Nicety, were of different Opinions concerning me. They all agreed that I could not be produced according to the regular Laws of Nature; because I was not framed with a Capacity of preserving my Life, either by Swiftness, or climbing of Trees, or digging Holes in the Earth. They observed by my Teeth, which they viewed with great Exactness, that I was a carnivorous Animal; yet most Quadrupeds being an Overmatch for me; and Field-Mice, with some others, too nimble, they could not imagine how I should be able to support my self, unless I fed upon Snails and other Insects; which they offered by many learned Arguments to evince that I could not possibly do. One of them seemed to think that I might be an Embrio, or abortive Birth. But this Opinion was rejected by the other two, who observed my Limbs to be perfect and finished; and that I had lived several Years, as it was manifested from my Beard; the Stumps whereof they plainly discovered through a Magnifying-Glass. They would not allow me to be a Dwarf, because my Littleness was beyond all Degrees of Comparison; for the Queen's favourite Dwarf, the smallest ever known in that Kingdom, was near thirty Foot high. After much Debate, they concluded unanimously that I was only *Relplum Scalcath*, which is interpreted literally *Lusus Naturæ*; a Determination exactly agreeable to the Modern Philosophy of *Europe*: whose Professors, disdaining the old Evasion of *occult Causes*, whereby the Followers of *Aristotle* endeavour in vain to disguise their Ignorance; have invented this wonderful Solution of all Difficulties, to the unspeakable Advancement of human Knowledge.

After this decisive Conclusion, I entreated to be heard a Word or two. I applied my self to the King, and assured His Majesty, that I came from a Country which abounded with several Millions of both Sexes, and of my own Stature;

where the Animals, Trees, and Houses were all in Proportion; and where by Consequence I might be as able to defend my self, and to find Sustenance, as any of his Majesty's Subjects could do here; which I took for a full Answer to those Gentlemens Arguments. To this they only replied with a Smile of Contempt; saying, that the Farmer had instructed me very well in my Lesson. The King, who had a much better Understanding, dismissing his learned Men, sent for the Farmer, who by good Fortune was not yet gone out of Town: Having therefore first examined him privately, and then confronted him with me and the young Girl; his Majesty began to think that what we told him might possibly be true. He desired the Queen to order, that a particular Care should be taken of me; and was of Opinion, that *Glumdalclitch* should still continue in her Office of tending me, because he observed we had a great Affection for each other. A convenient Apartment was provided for her at Court; she had a sort of Governess appointed to take care of her Education, a Maid to dress her, and two other Servants for menial Offices; but, the Care of me was wholly appropriated to her self. The Queen commanded her own Cabinet-maker to contrive a Box that might serve me for a Bed-chamber, after the Model that *Glumdalclitch* and I should agree upon. This Man was a most ingenious Artist; and according to my Directions, in three Weeks finished for me a wooden Chamber of sixteen Foot square, and twelve High; with Sash Windows, a Door, and two Closets, like a *London* Bed-chamber. The Board that made the Cieling was to be lifted up and down by two Hinges, to put in a Bed ready furnished by her Majesty's Upholsterer; which *Glumdalclitch* took out every Day to air, made it with her own Hands, and letting it down at Night, locked up the Roof over me. A Nice Workman, who was famous for little Curiosities, undertook to make me two Chairs, with Backs and Frames, of a Substance not unlike Ivory; and two Tables, with a Cabinet to put my Things in. The Room was quilted on all Sides, as well as the Floor and the Cieling, to prevent any Accident from the Carelessness of those who carried me; and to break the Force of a Jolt when I went in a Coach. I desired a Lock for my Door to prevent Rats and Mice from coming in: The Smith after several Attempts made the smallest that was ever seen among them; for I have known a larger at the Gate of a Gentleman's House in *England*. I made a shift to keep the Key in a Pocket of my own, fearing *Glumdalclitch* might lose it. The Queen likewise ordered the thinnest Silks that could be gotten, to make me Cloaths; not much thicker than an *English* Blanket, very cumbersome till I was accustomed to them. They were after the Fashion of the Kingdom, partly resembling the *Persian*, and partly the *Chinese*; and are a very grave decent Habit.

THE Queen became so fond of my Company, that she could not dine without me. I had a Table placed upon the same at which her Majesty eat, just at her left Elbow; and a Chair to sit on. *Glumdalclitch* stood upon a Stool on the Floor, near my Table, to assist and take Care of me. I had an entire set of Silver Dishes and Plates, and other Necessaries, which in Proportion to those of the Queen, were not much bigger than what I have seen in a *London* Toy-shop, for the Furniture of a Baby-house: These my little Nurse kept in her Pocket, in a Silver Box, and gave me at Meals as I wanted them; always cleaning them her self. No Person dined with the Queen but the two Princesses Royal; the elder sixteen Years old, and the younger at that time thirteen and a Month. Her Majesty used to put a Bit of Meat upon one of my Dishes, out of which I carved for my self; and her Diversion was to see me eat in Miniature. For the Queen (who had indeed but a weak Stomach) took up at one Mouthful, as much as a dozen *English* Farmers could eat at a Meal, which to me was for some time a very nauseous Sight. She would craunch the Wing of a Lark, Bones and all, between her Teeth, although it were nine Times as large as that of a full grown Turkey; and put a Bit of Bread in her Mouth, as big as two twelve-penny Loves. She drank out of a Golden Cup, above a Hogshead at a Draught. Her Knives were twice as long as a Scythe set strait upon the Handle. The Spoons, Forks, and other Instruments were all in the same Proportion. I remember when *Glumdalclitch* carried me out of Curiosity to see some of the Tables at Court, where ten or a dozen of these enormous Knives and Forks were lifted up together; I thought I had never till then beheld so terrible a Sight.

It is the Custom, that every *Wednesday*, (which as I have before observed, was their Sabbath) the King and Queen, with the Royal Issue of both Sexes, dine together in the Apartment of his Majesty; to whom I was now become a Favourite; and at these Times my little Chair and Table were placed at his left Hand before one of the Salt-sellers. This Prince took a Pleasure in conversing with me; enquiring into the Manners, Religion, Laws, Government, and Learning of *Europe*, wherein I gave him the best Account I was able. His Apprehension was so clear, and his Judgment so exact, that he made very wise Reflexions and Observations upon all I said. But, I confess, that after I had been a little too copious in talking of my own beloved Country; of our Trade, and Wars by Sea and Land, of our Schisms in Religion, and Parties in the State; the Prejudices of his Education prevailed so far, that he could not forbear taking me up in his right Hand, and stroaking me gently with the other; after an hearty Fit of laughing, asked me whether I were a *Whig* or a *Tory*. Then turning to his first Minister, who waited behind him with a white Staff, near as tall as the Main-mast of the Royal *Sovereign*; he observed, how contemptible a Thing was human Grandeur, which could be mimicked by such diminutive Insects as I: And yet, said he, I dare engage, those Creatures have their Titles and Distinctions of Honour; they contrive little Nests and Burrows, that they call Houses and Cities; they make a Figure in Dress and Equipage; they love, they fight, they dispute, they cheat, they betray. And thus he continued on, while my Colour came and went several Times, with Indignation to hear our noble Country, the Mistress of Arts and Arms, the Scourge of *France*, the Arbitress of *Europe*, the Seat of Virtue, Piety, Honour and Truth, the Pride and Envy of the World, so contemptuously treated.

But, as I was not in a Condition to resent Injuries, so, upon mature Thoughts, I began to doubt whether I were injured or no. For, after having been accustomed several

Months to the Sight and Converse of this People, and observed every Object upon which I cast my Eyes, to be of proportionable Magnitude; the Horror I had first conceived from their Bulk and Aspect was so far worn off, that if I then beheld a Company of *English* Lords and Ladies in their Finery and Birth-day Cloaths, acting their several Parts in the most courtly Manner of Strutting, and Bowing and Prating; to say the Truth, I should have been strongly tempted to laugh as much at them as this King and his Grandees did at me. Neither indeed could I forbear smiling at my self, when the Queen used to place me upon her Hand towards a Looking-Glass, by which both our Persons appeared before me in full View together; and there could nothing be more ridiculous than the Comparison: So that I really began to imagine my self dwindled many Degrees below my usual Size.

NOTHING angred and mortified me so much as the Queen's Dwarf, who being of the lowest Stature that was ever in that Country, (for I verily think he was not full Thirty Foot high) became so insolent at seeing a Creature so much beneath him, that he would always affect to swagger and look big as he passed by me in the Queen's Antichamber, while I was standing on some Table talking with the Lords or Ladies of the Court; and he seldom failed of a smart Word or two upon my Littleness; against which I could only revenge my self by calling him *Brother*, challenging him to wrestle; and such Repartees as are usual in the Mouths of *Court Pages*. One Day at Dinner, this malicious little Cubb was so nettled with something I had said to him, that raising himself upon the Frame of her Majesty's Chair, he took me up by the Middle, as I was sitting down, not thinking any Harm, and let me drop into a large Silver Bowl of Cream; and then ran away as fast as he could. I fell over Head and Ears, and if I had not been a good Swimmer, it might have gone very hard with me; for *Glumdalclitch* in that Instant happened to be at the other End of the Room; and the Queen was in such a Fright, that she wanted Presence of Mind to assist me. But my little Nurse ran to my Relief; and took me out, after I had swallowed above a

Quart of Cream. I was put to Bed; however I received no other Damage than the Loss of a Suit of Cloaths, which was utterly spoiled. The Dwarf was soundly whipped, and as a further Punishment, forced to drink up the Bowl of Cream, into which he had thrown me; neither was he ever restored to Favour: For, soon after the Queen bestowed him to a Lady of high Quality; so that I saw him no more, to my very great Satisfaction; for I could not tell to what Extremitys such a malicious Urchin might have carried his Resentment.

He had before served me a scurvy Trick, which set the Queen a laughing, although at the same time she were heartily vexed, and would have immediately cashiered him, if I had not been so generous as to intercede. Her Majesty had taken a Marrow-bone upon her Plate; and after knocking out the Marrow, placed the Bone again in the Dish erect as it stood before; the Dwarf watching his Opportunity, while *Glumdalclitch* was gone to the Side-board, mounted the Stool that she stood on to take care of me at Meals; took me up in both Hands, and squeezing my Legs together, wedged them into the Marrow-bone above my Waist; where I stuck for some time, and made a very ridiculous Figure. I believe it was near a Minute before any one knew what was become of me; for I thought it below me to cry out. But, as Princes seldom get their Meat hot, my Legs were not scalded, only my Stockings and Breeches in a sad Condition. The Dwarf at my Entreaty had no other Punishment than a sound whipping.

I was frequently raillied by the Queen upon Account of my Fearfulness; and she used to ask me whether the People of my Country were as great Cowards as my self. The Occasion was this. The Kingdom is much pestered with Flies in Summer; and these odious Insects, each of them as big as a *Dunstable* Lark, hardly gave me any Rest while I sat at Dinner, with their continual Humming and Buzzing about my Ears. They would sometimes alight upon my Victuals, and leave their loathsome Excrement or Spawn behind, which to me was very visible, although not to the Natives of that Country, whose large Opticks were not so

acute as mine in viewing smaller Objects. Sometimes they
would fix upon my Nose or Forehead, where they stung
me to the Quick, smelling very offensively; and I could
easily trace that viscous Matter, which our Naturalists tell
us enables those Creatures to walk with their Feet upwards
upon a Cieling. I had much ado to defend my self against
these detestable Animals, and could not forbear starting
when they came on my Face. It was the common Practice
of the Dwarf to catch a Number of these Insects in his
Hand, as School-boys do among us, and let them out suddenly under my Nose, on Purpose to frighten me, and divert
the Queen. My Remedy was to cut them in Pieces with my
Knife as they flew in the Air; wherein my Dexterity was
much admired.

I REMEMBER one Morning when *Glumdalclitch* had set me
in my Box upon a Window, as she usually did in fair Days
to give me Air, (for I durst not venture to let the Box be
hung on a Nail out of the Window, as we do with Cages in
England) after I had lifted up one of my Sashes, and sat
down at my Table to eat a Piece of Sweet-Cake for my
Breakfast; above twenty Wasps, allured by the Smell, came
flying into the Room, humming louder than the Drones
of as many Bagpipes. Some of them seized my Cake, and
carried it piecemeal away; others flew about my Head and
Face, confounding me with the Noise, and putting me in
the utmost Terror of their Stings. However I had the Courage to rise and draw my Hanger, and attack them in the
Air. I dispatched four of them, but the rest got away; and
I presently shut my Window. These Insects were as large
as Partridges; I took out their Stings, found them an Inch
and a half long, and as sharp as Needles. I carefully preserved them all, and having since shewn them with some
other Curiosities in several Parts of *Europe*; upon my Return to *England* I gave three of them to *Gresham College*,
and kept the fourth for my self.

CHAPTER IV.

THE COUNTRY DESCRIBED. A PROPOSAL FOR CORRECT-
ING MODERN MAPS. THE KING'S PALACE, AND SOME
ACCOUNT OF THE METROPOLIS. THE AUTHOR'S WAY OF
TRAVELLING. THE CHIEF TEMPLE DESCRIBED.

I NOW intend to give the Reader a short Description
of this Country, as far as I travelled in it, which was not
above two thousand Miles round *Lorbrulgrud* the Metropolis. For, the Queen, whom I always attended, never
went further when she accompanied the King in his Progresses; and there staid till his Majesty returned from viewing his Frontiers. The whole Extent of this Prince's Dominions reacheth about six thousand Miles in Length, and
from three to five in Breadth. From whence I cannot but
conclude, that our Geographers of *Europe* are in a great
Error, by supposing nothing but Sea between *Japan* and
California: For it was ever my Opinion, that there must be
a Balance of Earth to counterpoise the great Continent of
Tartary; and therefore they ought to correct their Maps
and Charts, by joining this vast Tract of Land to the
North-west Parts of *America*; wherein I shall be ready to
lend them my Assistance.

THE Kingdom is a Peninsula, terminated to the North-
east by a Ridge of Mountains thirty Miles high which are
altogether impassable by Reason of the Volcanoes upon the
Tops. Neither do the most Learned know what sort of
Mortals inhabit beyond those Mountains, or whether they
be inhabited at all. On the three other Sides it is bounded
by the Ocean. There is not one Sea-port in the whole Kingdom; and those Parts of the Coasts into which the Rivers
issue, are so full of pointed Rocks, and the Sea generally so
rough, that there is no venturing with the smallest of their
Boats; so that these People are wholly excluded from any
Commerce with the rest of the World. But the large Rivers

are full of Vessels, and abound with excellent Fish; for they seldom get any from the Sea, because the Sea-fish are of the same Size with those in *Europe*, and consequently not worth catching; whereby it is manifest, that Nature in the Production of Plants and Animals of so extraordinary a Bulk, is wholly confined to this Continent; of which I leave the Reasons to be determined by Philosophers. However, now and then they take a Whale that happens to be dashed against the Rocks, which the common People feed on heartily. These Whales I have known so large that a Man could hardly carry one upon his Shoulders; and sometimes for Curiosity they are brought in Hampers to *Lorbrulgrud*: I saw one of them in a Dish at the King's Table, which passed for a Rarity; but I did not observe he was fond of it; for I think indeed the Bigness disgusted him, although I have seen one somewhat larger in *Greenland*.

THE Country is well inhabited, for it contains fifty one Cities, near an hundred walled Towns, and a great Number of Villages. To satisfy my curious Reader, it may be sufficient to describe *Lorbrulgrud*. This City stands upon almost two equal Parts on each Side the River that passes through. It contains above eighty thousand Houses. It is in Length three *Glonglungs* (which make about fifty four English Miles) and two and a half in Breadth, as I measured it myself in the Royal Map made by the King's Order, which was laid on the Ground on purpose for me, and extended an hundred Feet; I paced the Diameter and Circumference several times Bare-foot, and computing by the Scale, measured it pretty exactly.

THE King's Palace is no regular Edifice, but an Heap of Buildings about seven Miles round: The chief Rooms are generally two hundred and forty Foot high, and broad and long in Proportion. A Coach was allowed to *Glumdalclitch* and me, wherein her Governess frequently took her out to see the Town, or go among the Shops; and I was always of the Party, carried in my Box; although the Girl at my own Desire would often take me out, and hold me in her Hand, that I might more conveniently view the Houses and the People as we passed along the Streets. I reckoned our

Coach to be about a Square of *Westminster-Hall*, but not altogether so high; however, I cannot be very exact. One Day the Governess ordered our Coachman to stop at several Shops; where the Beggars watching their Opportunity, crouded to the Sides of the Coach, and gave me the most horrible Spectacles that ever an *European* Eye beheld. There was a Woman with a Cancer in her Breast, swelled to a monstrous Size, full of Holes, in two or three of which I could have easily crept, and covered my whole Body. There was a Fellow with a Wen in his Neck, larger than five Woolpacks; and another with a couple of wooden Legs, each about twenty Foot high. But, the most hateful Sight of all was the Lice crawling on their Cloaths: I could see distinctly the Limbs of these Vermin with my naked Eye, much better than those of an *European* Louse through a Microscope; and their Snouts with which they rooted like Swine. They were the first I had ever beheld; and I should have been curious enough to dissect one of them, if I had proper Instruments (which I unluckily left behind me in the Ship) although indeed the Sight was so nauseous, that it perfectly turned my Stomach.

BESIDE the large Box in which I was usually carried, the Queen ordered a smaller one to be made for me, of about twelve Foot Square, and ten high, for the Convenience of Travelling; because the other was somewhat too large for *Glumdalclitch's* Lap, and cumbersom in the Coach; it was made by the same Artist, whom I directed in the whole Contrivance. This travelling Closet was an exact Square with a Window in the Middle of three of the Squares, and each Window was latticed with Iron Wire on the outside, to prevent Accidents in long Journeys. On the fourth Side, which had no Window, two strong Staples were fixed, through which the Person that carried me, when I had a Mind to be on Horseback, put in a Leathern Belt, and buckled it about his Waist. This was always the Office of some grave trusty Servant in whom I could confide, whether I attended the King and Queen in their Progresses, or were disposed to see the Gardens, or pay a Visit to some great Lady or Minister of State in the Court, when *Glumdalclitch*

E

happened to be out of Order: For I soon began to be known and esteemed among the greatest Officers, I suppose more upon Account of their Majesty's Favour, than any Merit of my own. In Journeys, when I was weary of the Coach, a Servant on Horseback would buckle my Box, and place it on a Cushion before him; and there I had a full Prospect of the Country on three Sides from my three Windows. I had in this Closet a Field-Bed and a Hammock hung from the Cieling, two Chairs and a Table, neatly screwed to the Floor, to prevent being tossed about by the Agitation of the Horse or the Coach. And having been long used to Sea-Voyages, those Motions, although sometimes very violent, did not much discompose me.

WHENEVER I had a Mind to see the Town, it was always in my Travelling-Closet; which *Glumdalclitch* held in her Lap in a kind of open Sedan, after the Fashion of the Country, born by four Men, and attended by two others in the Queen's Livery. The People who had often heard of me, were very curious to croud about the Sedan; and the Girl was complaisant enough to make the Bearers stop, and to take me in her Hand that I might be more conveniently seen.

I WAS very desirious to see the chief Temple, and particularly the Tower belonging to it, which is reckoned the highest in the Kingdom. Accordingly one Day my Nurse carried me thither, but I may truly say I came back disappointed; for, the Height is not above three thousand Foot, reckoning from the Ground to the highest Pinnacle top; which allowing for the Difference between the Size of these People, and us in *Europe*, is no great matter for Admiration, nor at all equal in Proportion, (if I rightly remember) to *Salisbury* Steeple. But, not to detract from a Nation to which during my Life I shall acknowledge myself extremely obliged; it must be allowed, that whatever this famous Tower wants in Height, is amply made up in Beauty and Strength. For the Walls are near an hundred Foot thick, built of hewn Stone, whereof each is about forty Foot square, and adorned on all Sides with Statues of Gods and

Emperors cut in Marble larger than the Life, placed in their several Niches. I measured a little Finger which had fallen down from one of these Statues, and lay unperceived among some Rubbish; and found it exactly four Foot and an Inch in Length. *Glumdalclitch* wrapped it up in a Handkerchief, and carried it home in her Pocket to keep among other Trinkets, of which the Girl was very fond, as Children at her Age usually are.

THE King's Kitchen is indeed a noble Building, vaulted at Top, and about six hundred Foot high. The great Oven is not so wide by ten Paces as the Cupola at St. *Paul's*: For I measured the latter on purpose after my Return. But if I should describe the Kitchen-grate, the prodigious Pots and Kettles, the Joints of Meat turning on the Spits, with many other Particulars; perhaps I should be hardly believed; at least a severe Critick would be apt to think I enlarged a little, as Travellers are often suspected to do. To avoid which Censure, I fear I have run too much into the other Extream; and that if this Treatise should happen to be translated into the Language of *Brobdingnag*, (which is the general Name of that Kingdom) and transmitted thither; the King and his People would have Reason to complain; that I had done them an Injury by a false and diminutive Representation.

HIS Majesty seldom keeps above six hundred Horses in his Stables: They are generally from fifty four to sixty Foot high. But, when he goes abroad on solemn Days, he is attended for State by a Militia Guard of five hundred Horse, which indeed I thought was the most splendid Sight that could be ever beheld, till I saw part of his Army in Battalia; whereof I shall find another Occasion to speak.

CHAPTER V.

SEVERAL ADVENTURES THAT HAPPENED TO THE AUTHOR.
THE EXECUTION OF A CRIMINAL. THE AUTHOR SHEWS
HIS SKILL IN NAVIGATION.

I SHOULD have lived happy enough in that Country, if
my Littleness had not exposed me to several ridiculous
and troublesome Accidents; some of which I shall venture to relate. *Glumdalclitch* often carried me into the Gardens of the Court in my smaller Box, and would sometimes
take me out of it and hold me in her Hand, or set me down
to walk. I remember, before the Dwarf left the Queen, he
followed us one Day into those Gardens; and my Nurse
having set me down, he and I being close together, near
some Dwarf Apple-trees, I must need shew my Wit by a
silly Allusion between him and the Trees, which happens
to hold in their Language as it doth in ours. Whereupon,
the malicious Rogue watching his Opportunity, when I was
walking under one of them, shook it directly over my Head,
by which a dozen Apples, each of them near as large as a
Bristol Barrel, came tumbling about my Ears; one of them
hit me on the Back as I chanced to stoop, and knocked me
down flat on my Face, but I received no other Hurt; and
the Dwarf was pardoned at my Desire, because I had given
the Provocation.

ANOTHER Day, *Glumdalclitch* left me on a smooth Grass-
plot to divert my self while she walked at some Distance
with her Governess. In the mean time, there suddenly fell
such a violent Shower of Hail, that I was immediately by
the Force of it struck to the Ground: And when I was
down, the Hail-stones gave me such cruel Bangs all over
the Body, as if I had been pelted with Tennis-Balls; however I made a Shift to creep on all four, and shelter my self
by lying flat on my Face on the Lee-side of a Border of

Lemmon Thyme; but so bruised from Head to Foot, that I could not go abroad in ten Days. Neither is this at all to be wondered at; because Nature in that Country observing the same Proportion through all her Operations, a Hailstone is near Eighteen Hundred Times as large as one in *Europe*; which I can assert upon Experience, having been so curious to weigh and measure them.

But, a more dangerous Accident happened to me in the same Garden, when my little Nurse, believing she had put me in a secure Place, which I often entreated her to do, that I might enjoy my own Thoughts; and having left my Box at home to avoid the Trouble of carrying it, went to another Part of the Gardens with her Governess and some Ladies of her Acquaintance. While she was absent and out of hearing, a small white Spaniel belonging to one of the chief Gardiners, having got by Accident into the Garden, happened to range near the Place where I lay. The Dog following the Scent, came directly up, and taking me in his Mouth, ran strait to his Master, wagging his Tail, and set me gently on the Ground. By good Fortune he had been so well taught, that I was carried between his Teeth without the least Hurt, or even tearing my Cloaths. But, the poor Gardiner, who knew me well, and had a great Kindness for me, was in a terrible Fright. He gently took me up in both his Hands, and asked me how I did; but I was so amazed and out of Breath, that I could not speak a Word. In a few Minutes I came to my self, and he carried me safe to my little Nurse, who by this time had returned to the Place where she left me, and was in cruel Agonies when I did not appear, nor answer when she called; she severely reprimanded the Gardiner on Account of his Dog. But, the Thing was hushed up, and never known at Court; for the Girl was afraid of the Queen's Anger; and truly as to my self, I thought it would not be for my Reputation that such a Story should go about.

This Accident absolutely determined *Glumdalclitch* never to trust me abroad for the future out of her Sight. I had been long afraid of this Resolution; and therefore concealed from her some little unlucky Adventures that happened in those Times when I was left by my self. Once a Kite hovering over the Garden, made a Stoop at me, and if I had not resolutely drawn my Hanger, and run under a thick Espalier, he would have certainly carried me away in his Talons. Another time, walking to the Top of a fresh Mole-hill, I fell to my Neck in the Hole through which that Animal had cast up the Earth; and coined some Lye not worth remembring, to excuse my self for spoiling my Cloaths. I likewise broke my right Shin against the Shell of a Snail, which I happened to stumble over, as I was walking alone, and thinking on poor *England*.

I CANNOT tell whether I were more pleased or mortified to observe in those solitary Walks, that the smaller Birds did not appear to be at all afraid of me; but would hop about within a Yard Distance, looking for Worms, and other Food, with as much Indifference and Security as if no Creature at all were near them. I remember, a Thrush had the Confidence to snatch out of my Hand with his Bill, a Piece of Cake that *Glumdalclitch* had just given me for my Breakfast. When I attempted to catch any of these Birds, they would boldly turn against me, endeavouring to pick my Fingers, which I durst not venture within their Reach; and then they would hop back unconcerned to hunt for Worms or Snails, as they did before. But, one Day I took a thick Cudgel, and threw it with all my Strength so luckily at a Linnet, that I knocked him down, and seizing him by the Neck with both my Hands, ran with him in Triumph to my Nurse. However, the Bird who had only been stunned, recovering himself, gave me so many Boxes with his Wings on both Sides of my Head and Body, although I held him at Arms Length, and was out of the Reach of his Claws, that I was twenty Times thinking to let him go. But I was soon relieved by one of our Servants, who wrung off the Bird's Neck; and I had him next Day for Dinner by the Queen's Command. This Linnet, as near as I can remember, seemed to be somewhat larger than an *English* Swan.

THE Maids of Honour often invited *Glumdalclitch* to their Apartments, and desired she would bring me along with her, on Purpose to have the Pleasure of seeing and touching me. They would often strip me naked from Top to Toe, and lay me at full Length in their Bosoms; wherewith I was much disgusted; because, to say the Truth, a very offensive Smell came from their Skins; which I do not mention or intend to the Disadvantage of those excellent Ladies, for whom I have all Manner of Respect: But, I conceive, that my Sense was more acute in Proportion to my Littleness; and that those illustrious Persons were no more disagreeable to their Lovers, or to each other, than People of the same Quality are with us in *England*. And, after all, I found their natural Smell was much more supportable than when they used Perfumes, under which I immediately swooned away. I cannot forget, that an intimate Friend of mine in *Lilliput* took the Freedom in a warm Day, when I had used a good deal of Exercise, to complain of a strong Smell about me; although I am as little faulty that way as most of my Sex: But I suppose, his Faculty of Smelling was as nice with regard to me, as mine was to that of this People. Upon this Point, I cannot forbear doing Justice to the Queen my Mistress, and *Glumdalclitch* my Nurse; whose Persons were as sweet as those of any Lady in *England*.

THAT which gave me most Uneasiness among these Maids of Honour, when my Nurse carried me to visit them, was to see them use me without any Manner of Ceremony, like a Creature who had no Sort of Consequence. For, they would strip themselves to the Skin, and put on their Smocks in my Presence, while I was placed on their Toylet directly before their naked Bodies; which, I am sure, to me was very far from being a tempting Sight, or from giving me any other Motions than those of Horror and Disgust. Their Skins appeared so coarse and uneven, so variously coloured when I saw them near, with a Mole here and there as broad as a Trencher, and Hairs hanging from it thicker than Pack-threads; to say nothing further concerning the rest of their Persons. Neither did they at all scruple while I was by, to discharge what they had drunk, to the Quantity of at least two Hogsheads, in a Vessel that held above three Tuns. The handsomest among these Maids of Honour, a pleasant frolicksome Girl of sixteen, would sometimes set me astride upon one of her Nipples; with many other Tricks, wherein the Reader will excuse me for not being over particular. But, I was so much displeased, that I entreated *Glumdalclitch* to contrive some Excuse for not seeing that young Lady any more.

ONE Day, a young Gentleman who was Nephew to my Nurse's Governess, came and pressed them both to see an Execution. It was of a Man who had murdered one of that Gentleman's intimate Acquaintance. *Glumdalclitch* was prevailed on to be of the Company, very much against her Inclination, for she was naturally tender hearted: And, as for my self, although I abhorred such Kind of Spectacles; yet my Curiosity tempted me to see something that I thought must be extraordinary. The Malefactor was fixed in a Chair upon a Scaffold erected for the Purpose; and his Head cut off at one Blow with a Sword of about forty Foot long. The Veins and Arteries spouted up such a prodigious Quantity of Blood, and so high in the Air, that the great *Jet d'Eau* at *Versailles* was not equal for the Time it lasted; and the Head when it fell on the Scaffold Floor, gave such a Bounce, as made me start, although I were at least an *English* Mile distant.

THE Queen, who often used to hear me talk of my Sea-Voyages, and took all Occasions to divert me when I was melancholy, asked me whether I understood how to handle a Sail or an Oar; and whether a little Exercise of Rowing might not be convenient for my Health. I answered, that I understood both very well. For although my proper Employment had been to be Surgeon or Doctor to the Ship; yet often upon a Pinch, I was forced to work like a common Mariner. But, I could not see how this could be done in their Country, where the smallest Wherry was equal to a first Rate Man of War among us; and such a Boat as I could manage, would never live in any of their Rivers: Her Majesty said, if I would contrive a Boat, her own Joyner should make it, and she would provide a Place for me to sail in. The Fellow was an ingenious Workman, and by my Instructions in ten Days finished a Pleasure-Boat with all its Tackling, able conveniently to hold eight *Europeans*. When it was finished, the Queen was so delighted, that she ran with it in her Lap to the King, who ordered it to be put in a Cistern full of Water, with me in it, by way of Tryal; where I could not manage my two Sculls or little Oars for want of Room. But, the Queen had before contrived another Project. She ordered the Joyner to make a wooden Trough of three Hundred Foot long, fifty broad, and eight deep; which being well pitched to prevent leaking, was placed on the Floor along the Wall, in an outer Room of the Palace. It had a Cock near the Bottom, to let out the Water when it began to grow stale; and two Servants could easily fill it in half an Hour. Here I often used to row for my Diversion, as well as that of the Queen and her Ladies, who thought themselves agreeably entertained with my Skill and Agility. Sometimes I would put up my Sail, and then my Business was only to steer, while the Ladies gave me a Gale with their Fans; and when they were weary, some of the Pages would blow my Sail forward with their Breath, while I shewed my Art by steering Starboard or Larboard as I pleased. When I had done, *Glumdalclitch* always carried back my Boat into her Closet, and hung it on a Nail to dry.

IN this Exercise I once met an Accident which had like to have cost me my Life. For, one of the Pages having put my Boat into the Trough; the Governess who attended *Glumdalclitch*, very officiously lifted me up to place me in the Boat; but I happened to slip through her Fingers, and should have infallibly fallen down forty Foot upon the Floor, if by the luckiest Chance in the World, I had not been stop'd by a Corking-pin that stuck in the good Gentlewoman's Stomacher; the Head of the Pin passed between my Shirt and the Waistband of my Breeches; and thus I was held by the Middle in the Air, till *Glumdalclitch* ran to my Relief.

ANOTHER time, one of the Servants, whose Office it was to fill my Trough every third Day with fresh Water; was so careless to let a huge Frog (not perceiving it) slip out of his Pail. The Frog lay concealed till I was put into my Boat, but then seeing a resting Place, climbed up, and made it lean so much on one Side, that I was forced to balance it with all my Weight on the other, to prevent overturning. When the Frog was got in, it hopped at once half the Length of the Boat, and then over my Head, backwards and forwards, dawbing my Face and Cloaths with its odious Slime. The Largeness of its Features made it appear the most deformed Animal that can be conceived. However, I desired *Glumdalclitch* to let me deal with it alone. I banged it a good while with one of my Sculls, and at last forced it to leap out of the Boat.

But, the greatest Danger I ever underwent in that Kingdom, was from a Monkey, who belonged to one of the Clerks of the Kitchen. *Glumdalclitch* had locked me up in her Closet, while she went somewhere upon Business, or a Visit. The Weather being very warm, the Closet Window was left open, as well as the Windows and the Door of my bigger Box, in which I usually lived, because of its Largeness and Conveniency. As I sat quietly meditating at my Table, I heard something bounce in at the Closet Window, and skip about from one Side to the other; whereat, although I were much alarmed, yet I ventured to look out, but not stirring from my Seat; and then I saw this frolicksome Animal, frisking and leaping up and down, till at last he came to my Box, which he seemed to view with great Pleasure and Curiosity, peeping in at the Door and every Window. I retreated to the farther Corner of my Room, or Box; but the Monkey looking in at every Side, put me into such a Fright, that I wanted Presence of Mind to conceal my self under the Bed, as I might easily have done. After some time spent in peeping, grinning, and chattering, he at last espyed me; and reaching one of his Paws in at the Door, as a Cat does when she plays with a Mouse, although I often shifted Place to avoid him; he at length seized the Lappet of my Coat (which being made of that Country Silk, was very thick and strong) and dragged me out. He took me up in his right Fore-foot, and held me as a Nurse doth a Child she is going to suckle; just as I have seen the same Sort of Creature do with a Kitten in

Europe: And when I offered to struggle, he squeezed me
so hard, that I thought it more prudent to submit. I have
good Reason to believe that he took me for a young one of
his own Species, by his often stroaking my Face very gently
with his other Paw. In these Diversions he was interrupted
by a Noise at the Closet Door, as if some Body were opening it; whereupon he suddenly leaped up to the Window
at which he had come in, and thence upon the Leads and
Gutters, walking upon three Legs, and holding me in the
fourth, till he clambered up to a Roof that was next to ours.
I heard *Glumdalclitch* give a Shriek at the Moment he was
carrying me out. The poor Girl was almost distracted: That
Quarter of the Palace was all in an Uproar; the Servants
ran for Ladders; the Monkey was seen by Hundreds in the
Court, sitting upon the Ridge of a Building, holding me
like a Baby in one of his Fore-Paws, and feeding me with
the other, by cramming into my Mouth some Victuals he
had squeezed out of the Bag on one Side of his Chaps,
and patting me when I would not eat; whereat many of
the Rabble below could not forbear laughing; neither do I
think they justly ought to be blamed; for without Question,
the Sight was ridiculous enough to every Body but my self.
Some of the People threw up Stones, hoping to drive the
Monkey down; but this was strictly forbidden, or else very
probably my Brains had been dashed out.

THE Ladders were now applied, and mounted by several
Men; which the Monkey observing, and finding himself almost encompassed; not being able to make Speed enough
with his three Legs, let me drop on a Ridge-Tyle, and made
his Escape. Here I sat for some time five Hundred Yards
from the Ground, expecting every Moment to be blown
down by the Wind, or to fall by my own Giddiness, and
come tumbling over and over from the Ridge to the Eves.
But an honest Lad, one of my Nurse's Footmen, climbed
up, and putting me into his Breeches Pocket, brought me
down safe.

I WAS almost choaked with the filthy Stuff the Monkey
had crammed down my Throat; but, my dear little Nurse
picked it out of my Mouth with a small Needle; and then

I fell a vomiting, which gave me great Relief. Yet I was so weak and bruised in the Sides with the Squeezes given me by this odious Animal, that I was forced to keep my Bed a Fortnight. The King, Queen, and all the Court, sent every Day to enquire after my Health; and her Majesty made me several Visits during my Sickness. The Monkey was killed, and an Order made that no such Animal should be kept about the Palace.

When I attended the King after my Recovery, to return him Thanks for his Favours, he was pleased to railly me a good deal upon this Adventure. He asked me what my Thoughts and Speculations were while I lay in the Monkey's Paw; how I liked the Victuals he gave me, his Manner of Feeding; and whether the fresh Air on the Roof had sharpened my Stomach. He desired to know what I would have done upon such an Occasion in my own Country. I told his Majesty, that in *Europe* we had no Monkies, except such as were brought for Curiosities from other Places, and so small, that I could deal with a Dozen of them together, if they presumed to attack me. And as for that monstrous Animal with whom I was so lately engaged, (it was indeed as large as an Elephant) if my Fears had suffered me to think so far as to make Use of my Hanger (looking fiercely, and clapping my Hand upon the Hilt as I spoke) when he poked his Paw into my Chamber, perhaps I should have given him such a Wound, as would have made him glad to withdraw it with more Haste than he put it in. This I delivered in a firm Tone, like a Person who was jealous lest his Courage should be called in Question. However, my Speech produced nothing else besides a loud Laughter; which all the Respect due to his Majesty from those about him, could not make them contain. This made me reflect, how vain an Attempt it is for a Man to endeavour doing himself Honour among those who are out of all Degree of Equality or Comparison with him. And yet I have seen the Moral of my own Behaviour very frequent in *England* since my Return; where a little contemptible Varlet, without the least Title to Birth, Person, Wit, or common Sense, shall presume to look with Importance, and put himself upon a Foot with the greatest Persons of the Kingdom.

I WAS every Day furnishing the Court with some ridiculous Story; and *Glumdalclitch*, although she loved me to Excess, yet was arch enough to inform the Queen, whenever I committed any Folly that she thought would be diverting to her Majesty. The Girl who had been out of Order, was carried by her Governess to take the Air about an Hour's Distance, or thirty Miles from Town. They alighted out of the Coach near a small Foot-path in a Field; and *Glumdalclitch* setting down my travelling Box, I went out of it to walk. There was a Cow-dung in the Path, and I must needs try my Activity by attempting to leap over it. I took a Run, but unfortunately jumped short, and found my self just in the Middle up to my Knees. I waded through with some Difficulty, and one of the Footmen wiped me as clean as he could with his Handkerchief; for I was filthily bemired, and my Nurse confined me to my Box until we returned home; where the Queen was soon informed of what had passed, and the Footmen spread it about the Court; so that all the Mirth, for some Days, was at my Expence.

CHAPTER [VI].

SEVERAL CONTRIVANCES OF THE AUTHOR TO PLEASE
THE KING AND QUEEN. HE SHEWS HIS SKILL IN MUSICK.
THE KING ENQUIRES INTO THE STATE OF EUROPE, WHICH
THE AUTHOR RELATES TO HIM. THE KING'S
OBSERVATIONS THEREON.

I USED to attend the King's Levee once or twice a Week, and had often seen him under the Barber's Hand, which indeed was at first very terrible to behold. For, the Razor was almost twice as long as an ordinary Scythe. His Majesty, according to the Custom of the Country, was only shaved twice a Week. I once prevailed on the Barber

to give me some of the Suds or Lather, out of which I picked
Forty or Fifty of the strongest Stumps of Hair, I then took
a Piece of fine Wood, and cut it like the Back of a Comb,
making several Holes in it at equal Distance, with as small
a Needle as I could get from *Glumdalclitch*. I fixed in the
Stumps so artificially, scraping and sloping them with my
Knife towards the Points, that I made a very tolerable
Comb; which was a seasonable Supply, my own being so
much broken in the Teeth, that it was almost useless:
Neither did I know any Artist in that Country so nice and
exact, as would undertake to make me another.

AND this puts me in mind of an Amusement wherein I
spent many of my leisure Hours. I desired the Queen's
Woman to save for me the Combings of her Majesty's
Hair, whereof in time I got a good Quantity; and consulting with my Friend the Cabinet-maker, who had received
general Orders to do little Jobbs for me; I directed him to
make two Chair-frames, no larger than those I had in my
Box, and then to bore little Holes with a fine Awl round
those Parts where I designed the Backs and Seats; through
these Holes I wove the strongest Hairs I could pick out,
just after the Manner of Cane-chairs in *England*. When
they were finished, I made a Present of them to her Majesty,
who kept them in her Cabinet, and used to shew them for
Curiosities; as indeed they were the Wonder of every one
who beheld them. The Queen would have had me sit upon
one of these Chairs, but I absolutely refused to obey her;
protesting I would rather dye a Thousand Deaths than
place a dishonourable Part of my Body on those precious
Hairs that once adorned her Majesty's Head. Of these
Hairs (as I had always a Mechanical Genius) I likewise
made a neat little Purse about five Foot long, with her
Majesty's Name decyphered in Gold Letters; which I gave
to *Glumdalclitch*, by the Queen's Consent. To say the Truth,
it was more for Shew than Use, being not of Strength to
bear the Weight of the larger Coins; and therefore she kept
nothing in it, but some little Toys that Girls are fond of.

THE King, who delighted in Musick, had frequent Consorts at Court, to which I was sometimes carried, and set in

my Box on a Table to hear them: But, the Noise was so great, that I could hardly distinguish the Tunes. I am confident, that all the Drums and Trumpets of a Royal Army, beating and sounding together just at your Ears, could not equal it. My Practice was to have my Box removed from the Places where the Performers sat, as far as I could; then to shut the Doors and Windows of it, and draw the Window-Curtains; after which I found their Musick not disagreeable.

I HAD learned in my Youth to play a little upon the Spinet; *Glumdalclitch* kept one in her Chamber, and a Master attended twice a Week to teach her: I call it a Spinet, because it somewhat resembled that Instrument, and was play'd upon in the same Manner. A Fancy came into my Head, that I would entertain the King and Queen with an *English* Tune upon this Instrument. But this appeared extremely difficult: For, the Spinet was near sixty Foot long, each Key being almost a Foot wide; so that, with my Arms extended, I could not reach to above five Keys; and to press them down required a good smart stroak with my Fist, which would be too great a Labour, and to no purpose. The Method I contrived was this. I prepared two round Sticks about the Bigness of common Cudgels; they were thicker at one End than the other; and I covered the thicker End with a Piece of a Mouse's Skin, that by rapping on them, I might neither Damage the Tops of the Keys, nor interrupt the Sound. Before the Spinet, a Bench was placed about four Foot below the Keys, and I was put upon the Bench. I ran sideling upon it that way and this, as fast as I could, banging the proper Keys with my two Sticks; and made a shift to play a Jigg to the great Satisfaction of both their Majesties: But, it was the most violent Exercise I ever underwent, and yet I could not strike above sixteen Keys, nor, consequently, play the Bass and Treble together, as other Artists do; which was a great Disadvantage to my Performance.

THE King, who as I before observed, was a Prince of excellent Understanding, would frequently order that I should be brought in my Box, and set upon the Table in his Closet. He would then command me to bring one of my Chairs out of the Box, and sit down within three Yards Distance upon the Top of the Cabinet; which brought me almost to a Level with his Face. In this Manner I had several Conversations with him. I one Day took the Freedom to tell his Majesty, that the Contempt he discovered towards *Europe*, and the rest of the World, did not seem answerable to those excellent Qualities of Mind, that he was Master of. That, Reason did not extend itself with the Bulk of the Body: On the contrary, we observed in our Country, that the tallest Persons were usually least provided with it. That among other Animals, Bees and Ants had the Reputation of more Industry, Art, and Sagacity than many of the larger Kinds. And that, as inconsiderable as he took me to be, I hoped I might live to do his Majesty some signal Service. The King heard me with Attention; and began to conceive a much better Opinion of me than he had ever before. He desired I would give him as exact an Account of the Government of *England* as I possibly could; because, as fond as Princes commonly are of their own Customs (for so he conjectured of other Monarchs by my former Discourses) he should be glad to hear of any thing that might deserve Imitation.

IMAGINE with thy self, courteous Reader, how often I then wished for the Tongue of *Demosthenes* or *Cicero*, that might have enabled me to celebrate the Praises of my own dear native Country in a Style equal to its Merits and Felicity.

I BEGAN my Discourse by informing his Majesty, that our Dominions consisted of two Islands, which composed three mighty Kingdoms under one Sovereign, besides our Plantations in *America*. I dwelt long upon the Fertility of our Soil, and the Temperature of our Climate. I then spoke at large upon the Constitution of an *English* Parliament, partly made up of an illustrious Body called the House of Peers, Persons of the noblest Blood, and of the most ancient and ample Patrimonies. I described that extraordinary Care always taken of their Education in Arts and Arms, to qualify them for being Counsellors born to the King and Kingdom; to have a Share in the Legislature, to be

Members of the highest Court of Judicature from whence there could be no Appeal; and to be Champions always ready for the Defence of their Prince and Country by their Valour, Conduct and Fidelity. That these were the Ornament and Bulwark of the Kingdom; worthy Followers of their most renowned Ancestors, whose Honour had been the Reward of their Virtue; from which their Posterity were never once known to degenerate. To these were joined several holy Persons, as part of that Assembly, under the Title of Bishops; whose peculiar Business it is, to take care of Religion, and of those who instruct the People therein. These were searched and sought out through the whole Nation, by the Prince and wisest Counsellors, among such of the Priesthood, as were most deservedly distinguished by the Sanctity of their Lives, and the Depth of their Erudition; who were indeed the spiritual Fathers of the Clergy and the People.

THAT, the other Part of the Parliament consisted of an Assembly called the House of Commons; who were all principal Gentlemen, *freely* picked and culled out by the People themselves, for their great Abilities, and Love of their Country, to represent the Wisdom of the whole Nation. And, these two Bodies make up the most august Assembly in *Europe*; to whom, in Conjunction with the Prince, the whole Legislature is committed.

I THEN descended to the Courts of Justice, over which the Judges, those venerable Sages and Interpreters of the Law, presided, for determining the disputed Rights and Properties of Men, as well as for the Punishment of Vice, and Protection of Innocence. I mentioned the prudent Management of our Treasury; the Valour and Atchievements of our Forces by Sea and Land. I computed the Number of our People, by reckoning how many Millions there might be of each Religious Sect, or Political Party among us. I did not omit even our Sports and Pastimes, or any other Particular which I thought might redound to the Honour of my Country. And, I finished all with a brief historical Account of Affairs and Events in *England* for about an hundred Years past.

THIS Conversation was not ended under five Audiences, each of several Hours; and the King heard the whole with great Attention; frequently taking Notes of what I spoke, as well as Memorandums of what Questions he intended to ask me.

WHEN I had put an End to these long Discourses, his Majesty in a sixth Audience consulting his Notes, proposed many Doubts, Queries, and Objections, upon every Article. He asked, what Methods were used to cultivate the Minds and Bodies of our young Nobility; and in what kind of Business they commonly spent the first and teachable Part of their Lives. What Course was taken to supply that Assembly, when any noble Family became extinct. What Qualifications were necessary in those who are to be created new Lords: Whether the Humour of the Prince, a Sum of Money to a Court-Lady, or a Prime Minister; or a Design of strengthening a Party opposite to the publick Interest, ever happened to be Motives in those Advancements. What Share of Knowledge these Lords had in the Laws of their Country, and how they came by it, so as to enable them to decide the Properties of their Fellow-Subjects in the last Resort. Whether they were always so free from Avarice, Partialities, or Want, that a Bribe, or some other sinister View, could have no Place among them. Whether those holy Lords I spoke of, were constantly promoted to that Rank upon Account of their Knowledge in religious Matters, and the Sanctity of their Lives; had never been Compliers with the Times, while they were common Priests; or slavish prostitute Chaplains to some Nobleman, whose Opinions they continued servilely to follow after they were admitted into that Assembly.

HE then desired to know, what Arts were practised in electing those whom I called Commoners. Whether, a Stranger with a strong Purse might not influence the vulgar Voters to chuse him before their own Landlords, or the most considerable Gentleman in the Neighbourhood. How it came to pass, that People were so violently bent upon getting into this Assembly, which I allowed to be a great Trouble and Expence, often to the Ruin of their Families, without any Salary or Pension: Because this appeared such an exalted Strain of Virtue and publick Spirit, that his Majesty seemed to doubt it might possibly not be always sincere: And he desired to know, whether such zealous Gentlemen could have any Views of refunding themselves for the Charges and Trouble they were at, by sacrificing the publick Good to the Designs of a weak and vicious Prince, in Conjunction with a corrupted Ministry. He multiplied his Questions, and sifted me thoroughly upon every Part of this Head; proposing numberless Enquiries and Objections, which I think it not prudent or convenient to repeat.

UPON what I said in relation to our Courts of Justice, his Majesty desired to be satisfied in several Points: And, this I was the better able to do, having been formerly almost ruined by a long Suit in Chancery, which was decreed for me with Costs. He asked, what Time was usually spent in determining between Right and Wrong; and what Degree of Expence. Whether Advocates and Orators had Liberty to plead in Causes manifestly known to be unjust, vexatious, or oppressive. Whether Party in Religion or Politicks were observed to be of any Weight in the Scale of Justice. Whether those pleading Orators were Persons educated in the general Knowledge of Equity; or only in provincial, national, and other local Customs. Whether they or their Judges had any Part in penning those Laws, which they assumed the Liberty of interpreting and glossing upon at their Pleasure. Whether they had ever at different Times pleaded for and against the same Cause, and cited Precedents to prove contrary Opinions. Whether they were a rich or a poor Corporation. Whether they received any pecuniary Reward for pleading or delivering their Opinions. And particularly whether they were ever admitted as Members in the lower Senate.

HE fell next upon the Management of our Treasury; and said, he thought my Memory had failed me, because I computed our Taxes at about five or six Millions a Year; and when I came to mention the Issues, he found they sometimes amounted to more than double; for, the Notes he had taken were very particular in this Point; because he hoped, as he told me, that the Knowledge of our Conduct might be useful to him; and he could not be deceived in his Calculations. But, if what I told him were true, he was still at a Loss how a Kingdom could run out of its Estate like a private Person. He asked me, who were our Creditors? and, where we found Money to pay them? He wondered to hear me talk of such chargeable and extensive Wars; that, certainly we must be a quarrelsome People, or live among very bad Neighbours; and that our Generals must needs be richer than our Kings. He asked, what Business we had out of our own Islands, unless upon the Score of Trade or Treaty, or to defend the Coasts with our Fleet. Above all, he was amazed to hear me talk of a mercenary standing Army in the Midst of Peace, and among a free People. He said, if we were governed by our own Consent in the Persons of our Representatives, he could not imagine of whom we were afraid, or against whom we were to fight; and would hear my Opinion, whether a private Man's House might not better be defended by himself, his Children, and Family; than by half a Dozen Rascals picked up at a Venture in the Streets, for small Wages, who might get an Hundred Times more by cutting their Throats.

He laughed at my odd Kind of Arithmetick (as he was pleased to call it) in reckoning the Numbers of our People by a Computation drawn from the several Sects among us in Religion and Politicks. He said, he knew no Reason, why those who entertain Opinions prejudicial to the Publick, should be obliged to change, or should not be obliged to conceal them. And, as it was Tyranny in any Government to require the first, so it was Weakness not to enforce the second: For, a Man may be allowed to keep Poisons in his Closet, but not to vend them about as Cordials.

He observed, that among the Diversions of our Nobility and Gentry, I had mentioned Gaming. He desired to know at what Age this Entertainment was usually taken up, and when it was laid down. How much of their Time it employed; whether it ever went so high as to affect their Fortunes. Whether mean vicious People, by their Dexterity in that Art, might not arrive at great Riches, and sometimes keep our very Nobles in Dependance, as well as habituate them to vile Companions; wholly take them from the Improvement of their Minds, and force them by the Losses they received, to learn and practice that infamous Dexterity upon others.

HE was perfectly astonished with the historical Account I gave him of our Affairs during the last Century; protesting it was only an Heap of Conspiracies, Rebellions, Murders, Massacres, Revolutions, Banishments; the very worst Effects that Avarice, Faction, Hypocrisy, Perfidiousness, Cruelty, Rage, Madness, Hatred, Envy, Lust, Malice, and Ambition could produce.

HIS Majesty in another Audience, was at the Pains to recapitulate the Sum of all I had spoken; compared the Questions he made, with the Answers I had given; then taking me into his Hands, and stroaking me gently, delivered himself in these Words, which I shall never forget, nor the Manner he spoke them in. My little Friend *Grildrig*; you have made a most admirable Panegyrick upon your Country. You have clearly proved that Ignorance, Idleness, and Vice are the proper Ingredients for qualifying a Legislator. That Laws are best explained, interpreted, and applied by those whose Interest and Abilities lie in perverting, confounding, and eluding them. I observe among you some Lines of an Institution, which in its Original might have been tolerable; but these half erased, and the rest wholly blurred and blotted by Corruptions. It doth not appear from all you have said, how any one Perfection is required towards the Procurement of any one Station among you; much less that Men are ennobled on Account of their Virtue, that Priests are advanced for their Piety or Learning, Soldiers for their Conduct or Valour, Judges for their Integrity, Senators for the Love of their Country, or Counsellors for their Wisdom. As for yourself (continued the King) who have spent the greatest Part of your Life in travelling; I am well disposed to hope you may hitherto have escaped many Vices of your Country. But, by what I have gathered from your own Relation, and the Answers I have with much Pains wringed and extorted from you;

I cannot but conclude the Bulk of your Natives, to be the most pernicious Race of little odious Vermin that Nature ever suffered to crawl upon the Surface of the Earth.

CHAPTER VII.

THE AUTHOR'S LOVE OF HIS COUNTRY. HE MAKES A PROPOSAL OF MUCH ADVANTAGE TO THE KING; WHICH IS REJECTED. THE KING'S GREAT IGNORANCE IN POLITICKS. THE LEARNING OF THAT COUNTRY VERY IMPERFECT AND CONFINED. THEIR LAWS, AND MILITARY AFFAIRS, AND PARTIES IN THE STATE.

NOTHING but an extreme Love of Truth could have hindered me from concealing this Part of my Story. It was in vain to discover my Resentments, which were always turned into Ridicule: And I was forced to rest with Patience, while my noble and most beloved Country was so injuriously treated. I am heartily sorry as any of my Readers can possibly be, that such an Occasion was given: But this Prince happened to be so curious and inquisitive upon every Particular, that it could not consist either with Gratitude or good Manners to refuse giving him what Satisfaction I was able. Yet thus much I may be allowed to say in my own Vindication; that I artfully eluded many of his Questions; and gave to every Point a more favourable turn by many Degrees than the strictness of Truth would allow. For, I have always born that laudable Partiality to my own Country, which *Dionysius Halicarnassensis* with so much Justice recommends to an Historian. I would hide the Frailties and Deformities of my Political Mother, and place her Virtues and Beauties in the most advantageous Light. This was my sincere Endeavour in those many Discourses I had with that mighty Monarch, although it unfortunately failed of Success.

BUT, great Allowances should be given to a King who

lives wholly secluded from the rest of the World, and must therefore be altogether unacquainted with the Manners and Customs that most prevail in other Nations: The want of which Knowledge will ever produce many *Prejudices*, and a certain *Narrowness of Thinking*; from which we and the politer Countries of *Europe* are wholly exempted. And it would be hard indeed, if so remote a Prince's Notions of Virtue and Vice were to be offered as a Standard for all Mankind.

To confirm what I have now said, and further to shew the miserable Effects of a *confined Education*; I shall here insert a Passage which will hardly obtain Belief. In hopes to ingratiate my self farther into his Majesty's Favour, I told him of an Invention discovered between three and four hundred Years ago, to make a certain Powder; into an heap of which the smallest Spark of Fire falling, would kindle the whole in a Moment, although it were as big as a Mountain; and make it all fly up in the Air together, with a Noise and Agitation greater than Thunder. That, a proper Quantity of this Powder rammed into an hollow Tube of Brass or Iron, according to its Bigness, would drive a Ball of Iron or Lead with such Violence and Speed, as nothing was able to sustain its Force. That, the largest Balls thus discharged, would not only Destroy whole Ranks of an Army at once; but batter the strongest Walls to the Ground; sink down Ships with a thousand Men in each, to the Bottom of the Sea; and when linked together by a Chain, would cut through Masts and Rigging; divide Hundreds of Bodies in the Middle, and lay all Waste before them. That we often put this Powder into large hollow Balls of Iron, and discharged them by an Engine into some City we were besieging; which would rip up the Pavement, tear the Houses to Pieces, burst and throw Splinters on every Side, dashing out the Brains of all who came near. That I knew the Ingredients very well, which were Cheap, and common; I understood the Manner of compounding them, and could direct his Workmen how to make those Tubes of a Size proportionable to all other Things in his Majesty's Kingdom; and the largest need not be above two hundred Foot long;

twenty or thirty of which Tubes, charged with the proper Quantity of Powder and Balls, would batter down the Walls of the strongest Town in his Dominions in a few Hours; or destroy the whole Metropolis, if ever it should pretend to dispute his absolute Commands. This I humbly offered to his Majesty, as a small Tribute of Acknowledgment in return of so many Marks that I had received of his Royal Favour and Protection.

THE King was struck with Horror at the Description I had given of those terrible Engines, and the Proposal I had made. He was amazed how so impotent and groveling an Insect as I (these were his Expressions) could entertain such inhuman Ideas, and in so familiar a Manner as to appear wholly unmoved at all the Scenes of Blood and Desolation, which I had painted as the common Effects of those destructive Machines; whereof he said, some evil Genius, Enemy to Mankind, must have been the first Contriver. As for himself, he protested, that although few Things delighted him so much as new Discoveries in Art or in Nature; yet he would rather lose Half his Kingdom than be privy to such a Secret; which he commanded me, as I valued my Life, never to mention any more.

A STRANGE Effect of *narrow Principles* and *short Views!* that a Prince possessed of every Quality which procures Veneration, Love and Esteem; of strong Parts, great Wisdom and profound Learning; endued with admirable Talents for Government, and almost adored by his Subjects; should from a *nice unnecessary Scruple*, whereof in *Europe* we can have no Conception, let slip an Opportunity put into his Hands, that would have made him absolute Master of the Lives, the Liberties, and the Fortunes of his People. Neither do I say this with the least Intention to detract from the many Virtues of that excellent King; whose Character I am sensible will on this Account be very much lessened in the Opinion of an *English* Reader: But, I take this Defect among them to have risen from their Ignorance; by not having hitherto reduced *Politicks* into a *Science*, as the more acute Wits of *Europe* have done. For, I remember very well, in a Discourse one Day with the King; when

I happened to say, there were several thousand Books among us written upon the *Art of Government*; it gave him (directly contrary to my Intention) a very mean Opinion of our Understandings. He professed both to abominate and despise all *Mystery*, *Refinement*, and *Intrigue*, either in a Prince or a Minister. He could not tell what I meant by *Secrets of State*, where an Enemy or some Rival Nation were not in the Case. He confined the Knowledge of governing within very *narrow Bounds*; to common Sense and Reason, to Justice and Lenity, to the Speedy Determination of Civil and criminal Causes; with some other obvious Topicks which are not worth considering. And, he gave it for his Opinion; that whoever could make two Ears of Corn, or two Blades of Grass to grow upon a Spot of Ground where only one grew before; would deserve better of Mankind, and do more essential Service to his Country, than the whole Race of Politicians put together.

THE Learning of this People is very defective; consisting only in Morality, History, Poetry and Mathematicks; wherein they must be allowed to excel. But, the last of these is wholly applied to what may be useful in Life; to the Improvement of Agriculture and all mechanical Arts; so that among us it would be little esteemed. And as to Ideas, Entities, Abstractions and Transcendentals, I could never drive the least Conception into their Heads.

No Law of that Country must exceed in Words the Number of Letters in their Alphabet; which consists only of two and twenty. But indeed, few of them extend even to that Length. They are expressed in the most plain and simple Terms, wherein those People are not Mercurial enough to discover above one Interpretation. And, to write a Comment upon any Law, is a capital Crime. As to the Decision of civil Causes, or Proceedings against Criminals, their Precedents are so few, that they have little Reason to boast of any extraordinary Skill in either.

THEY have had the Art of Printing, as well as the *Chinese*, Time out of Mind. But their Libraries are not very large; for that of the King's, which is reckoned the largest, doth not amount to above a thousand Volumes; placed in a

Gallery of twelve hundred Foot long; from whence I had Liberty to borrow what Books I pleased. The Queen's Joyner had contrived in one of *Glumdalclitch's* Rooms a Kind of wooden Machine five and twenty Foot high, formed like a standing Ladder; the Steps were each fifty Foot long: It was indeed a moveable Pair of Stairs, the lowest End placed at ten Foot Distance from the Wall of the Chamber. The Book I had a Mind to read was put up leaning against the Wall. I first mounted to the upper Step of the Ladder, and turning my Face towards the Book, began at the Top of the Page, and so walking to the Right and Left about eight or ten Paces according to the Length of the Lines, till I had gotten a little below the Level of my Eyes; and then descending gradually till I came to the Bottom: After which I mounted again, and began the other Page in the same Manner, and so turned over the Leaf, which I could easily do with both my Hands, for it was as thick and stiff as a Paste-board, and in the largest Folio's not above eighteen or twenty Foot long.

THEIR Stile is clear, masculine, and smooth, but not Florid; for they avoid nothing more than multiplying unnecessary Words, or using various Expressions. I have perused many of their Books, especially those in History and Morality. Among the latter I was much diverted with a little old Treatise, which always lay in *Glumdalclitch's* Bed-chamber, and belonged to her Governess, a grave elderly Gentlewoman, who dealt in Writings of Morality and Devotion. The Book treats of the Weakness of Human kind; and is in little Esteem except among Women and the Vulgar. However, I was curious to see what an Author of that Country could say upon such a Subject. This Writer went through all the usual Topicks of *European* Moralists; shewing how diminutive, contemptible, and helpless an Animal was Man in his own Nature; how unable to defend himself from the Inclemencies of the Air, or the Fury of wild Beasts: How much he was excelled by one Creature in Strength, by another in Speed, by a third in Foresight, by a fourth in Industry. He added, that Nature was degenerated in these latter declining Ages of the World, and could now

produce only small abortive Births in Comparison of those
in ancient Times. He said, it was very reasonable to think,
not only that the Species of Men were originally much
larger, but also that there must have been Giants in former
Ages; which, as it is asserted by History and Tradition, so
it hath been confirmed by huge Bones and Sculls casually
dug up in several Parts of the Kingdom, far exceeding the
common dwindled Race of Man in our Days. He argued,
that the very Laws of Nature absolutely required we should
have been made in the Beginning, of a Size more large and
robust, not so liable to Destruction from every little Accident of a Tile falling from an House, or a Stone cast from
the Hand of a Boy, or of being drowned in a little Brook.
From this Way of Reasoning the Author drew several
moral Applications useful in the Conduct of Life, but needless here to repeat. For my own Part, I could not avoid
reflecting, how universally this Talent was spread of drawing Lectures in Morality, or indeed rather Matter of Discontent and repining, from the Quarrels we raise with
Nature. And, I believe upon a strict Enquiry, those Quarrels
might be shewn as ill-grounded among us, as they are
among that People.

As to their military Affairs; they boast that the King's
Army consists of an hundred and seventy six thousand
Foot, and thirty two thousand Horse: If that may be called
an Army, which is made up of Tradesmen in the several
Cities, and Farmers in the Country, whose Commanders
are only the Nobility and Gentry, without Pay or Reward.
They are indeed perfect enough in their Exercises; and
under very good Discipline, wherein I saw no great Merit:
For, how should it be otherwise, where every Farmer is
under the Command of his own Landlord, and every Citizen under that of the principal Men in his own City, chosen
after the Manner of *Venice* by *Ballot*?

I HAVE often seen the Militia of *Lorbrulgrud* drawn out
to Exercise in a great Field near the City, of twenty Miles
Square. They were in all not above twenty five thousand
Foot, and six thousand Horse; but it was impossible for me
to compute their Number, considering the Space of Ground

they took up. A *Cavalier* mounted on a large Steed might be about Ninety Foot high. I have seen this Whole Body of Horse upon the Word of Command draw their Swords at once, and brandish them in the Air. Imagination can Figure nothing so Grand, so surprising and so astonishing. It looked as if ten thousand Flashes of Lightning were darting at the same time from every Quarter of the Sky.

I WAS curious to know how this Prince, to whose Dominions there is no Access from any other Country, came to think of Armies, or to teach his People the Practice of military Discipline. But I was soon informed, both by Conversation, and Reading their Histories. For, in the Course of many Ages they have been troubled with the same Disease, to which the whole Race of Mankind is Subject; the Nobility often contending for Power, the People for Liberty, and the King for absolute Dominion. All which, however happily tempered by the Laws of that Kingdom, have been sometimes violated by each of the three Parties; and have more than once occasioned Civil Wars, the last whereof was happily put an End to by this Prince's Grandfather in a general Composition; and the Militia then settled with common Consent hath been ever since kept in the strictest Duty.

CHAPTER VIII.

THE KING AND QUEEN MAKE A PROGRESS TO THE FRONTIERS. THE AUTHOR ATTENDS THEM. THE MANNER IN WHICH HE LEAVES THE COUNTRY VERY PARTICULARLY RELATED. HE RETURNS TO ENGLAND.

I HAD always a strong Impulse that I should some time recover my Liberty, although it were impossible to conjecture by what Means, or to form any Project with the least Hope of succeeding. The Ship in which I sailed was the first ever known to be driven within Sight of that Coast; and the King had given strict Orders, that if at any Time another appeared, it should be taken ashore, and with all its Crew and Passengers brought in a Tumbril to *Lorbrul-grud*. He was strongly bent to get me a Woman of my own Size, by whom I might propagate the Breed: But I think I should rather have died than undergone the Disgrace of leaving a Posterity to be kept in Cages like tame Canary Birds; and perhaps in time sold about the Kingdom to Persons of Quality for Curiosities. I was indeed treated with much Kindness; I was the Favourite of a great King and Queen, and the Delight of the whole Court; but it was upon such a Foot as ill became the Dignity of human Kind. I could never forget those domestick Pledges I had left behind me. I wanted to be among People with whom I could converse upon even Terms; and walk about the Streets and Fields without Fear of being trod to Death like a Frog or young Puppy. But, my Deliverance came sooner than I expected, and in a Manner not very common: The whole Story and Circumstances of which I shall faithfully relate.

I HAD now been two Years in this Country; and, about the Beginning of the third, *Glumdalclitch* and I attended the King and Queen in Progress to the South Coast of the Kingdom. I was carried as usual in my Travelling-Box, which, as I have already described, was a very convenient Closet of twelve Foot wide. I had ordered a Hammock to be fixed by silken Ropes from the four Corners at the Top; to break the Jolts, when a Servant carried me before him on Horseback, as I sometimes desired; and would often sleep in my Hammock while we were upon the Road. On the Roof of my Closet, set not directly over the Middle of the Hammock, I ordered the Joyner to cut out a Hole of a Foot square to give me Air in hot Weather as I slept; which Hole I shut at pleasure with a Board that drew backwards and forwards through a Groove.

WHEN we came to our Journey's End, the King thought proper to pass a few Days at a Palace he hath near *Flan-flasnic*, a City within eighteen *English* Miles of the Sea-side. *Glumdalclitch* and I were much fatigued: I had gotten a small Cold; but the poor Girl was so ill as to be confined to her Chamber. I longed to see the Ocean, which must be the only Scene of my Escape, if ever it should happen. I pretended to be worse than I really was; and desired leave to take the fresh Air of the Sea, with a Page whom I was very fond of, and who had sometimes been trusted with me. I shall never forget with what Unwillingness *Glumdal-clitch* consented; nor the strict Charge she gave the Page to be careful of me; bursting at the same time into a Flood of Tears, as if she had some Foreboding of what was to happen. The Boy took me out in my Box about Half an Hour's Walk from the Palace, towards the Rocks on the Sea-shore. I ordered him to set me down; and lifting up one of my Sashes, cast many a wistful melancholy Look towards the Sea. I found myself not very well; and told the Page that I had a Mind to take a Nap in my Hammock, which I hoped would do me good. I got in, and the Boy shut the Window close down, to keep out the Cold. I soon fell asleep: And all I can conjecture is, that while I slept, the Page, thinking no Danger could happen, went among the Rocks to look for Birds Eggs; having before observed him from my Window searching about, and picking up one or two in the Clefts. Be that as it will; I found my self suddenly awaked with a violent Pull upon the Ring which was fastned at the Top of my Box for the Conveniency of Carriage. I felt the Box raised very high in the Air, and then born forward with prodigious Speed. The first Jolt had like to have shaken me out of my Hammock; but after-wards the Motion was easy enough. I called out several times as loud as I could raise my Voice, but all to no pur-pose. I looked towards my Windows, and could see noth-ing but the Clouds and Sky. I heard a Noise just over my Head like the clapping of Wings; and then began to per-ceive the woful Condition I was in; that some Eagle had got the Ring of my Box in his Beak, with an Intent to let it fall on a Rock, like a Tortoise in a Shell, and then pick out my Body and devour it. For the Sagacity and Smell of this Bird enable him to discover his Quarry at a great Dis-tance, although better concealed than I could be within a two Inch Board.

IN a little time I observed the Noise and flutter of Wings

to encrease very fast; and my Box was tossed up and down like a Sign-post in a windy Day. I heard several Bangs or Buffets, as I thought, given to the Eagle (for such I am certain it must have been that held the Ring of my Box in his Beak) and then all on a sudden felt my self falling perpendicularly down for above a Minute; but with such incredible Swiftness that I almost lost my Breath. My Fall was stopped by a terrible Squash, that sounded louder to my Ears than the Cataract of *Niagara*; after which I was quite in the Dark for another Minute, and then my Box began to rise so high that I could see Light from the Tops of my Windows. I now perceived that I was fallen into the Sea. My Box, by the Weight of my Body, the Goods that were in, and the broad Plates of Iron fixed for Strength at the four Corners of the Top and Bottom, floated about five Foot deep in Water. I did then, and do now suppose, that the Eagle which flew away with my Box was pursued by two or three others, and forced to let me drop while he was defending himself against the Rest, who hoped to share in the Prey. The Plates of Iron fastned at the Bottom of the Box, (for those were the strongest) preserved the Balance while it fell; and hindred it from being broken on the Surface of the Water. Every Joint of it was well grooved, and the Door did not move on Hinges, but up and down like a Sash; which kept my Closet so tight that very little Water came in. I got with much Difficulty out of my Hammock, having first ventured to draw back the Slip board on the Roof already mentioned, contrived on purpose to let in Air; for want of which I found my self almost stifled.

How often did I then wish my self with my dear *Glumdalclitch*, from whom one single Hour had so far divided me ! And I may say with Truth, that in the midst of my own Misfortune, I could not forbear lamenting my poor Nurse, the Grief she would suffer for my Loss, the Displeasure of the Queen, and the Ruin of her Fortune. Perhaps many Travellers have not been under greater Difficulties and Distress than I was at this Juncture; expecting every Moment to see my Box dashed in Pieces, or at least overset by the first violent Blast, or a rising Wave. A Breach in one single

Pane of Glass would have been immediate Death: Nor could any thing have preserved the Windows but the strong Lattice Wires placed on the outside against Accidents in Travelling. I saw the Water ooze in at several Crannies, although the Leaks were not considerable; and I endeavoured to stop them as well as I could. I was not able to lift up the Roof of my Closet, which otherwise I certainly should have done, and sat on the Top of it, where I might at least preserve myself from being shut up, as I may call it, in the Hold. Or, if I escaped these Dangers for a Day or two, what could I expect but a miserable Death of Cold and Hunger! I was four Hours under these Circumstances, expecting and indeed wishing every Moment to be my last.

I HAVE already told the Reader, that there were two strong Staples fixed upon the Side of my Box which had no Window, and into which the Servant, who used to carry me on Horseback, would put a Leathern Belt, and buckle it about his Waist. Being in this disconsolate State, I heard, or at least thought I heard some kind of grating Noise on that Side of my Box where the Staples were fixed; and soon after I began to fancy that the Box was pulled, or towed along in the Sea; for I now and then felt a sort of tugging, which made the Waves rise near the Tops of my Windows, leaving me almost in the Dark. This gave me some faint Hopes of Relief, although I were not able to imagine how it could be brought about. I ventured to unscrew one of my Chairs, which were always fastned to the Floor; and having made a hard shift to screw it down again directly under the Slipping-board that I had lately opened; I mounted on the Chair, and putting my Mouth as near as I could to the Hole, I called for Help in a loud Voice, and in all the Languages I understood. I then fastned my Handkerchief to a Stick I usually carried, and thrusting it up the Hole, waved it several times in the Air; that if any Boat or Ship were near, the Seamen might conjecture some unhappy Mortal to be shut up in the Box.

I FOUND no Effect from all I could do, but plainly perceived my Closet to be moved along; and in the Space of an Hour, or better, that Side of the Box where the Staples were, and had no Window, struck against something that was hard. I apprehended it to be a Rock, and found my self tossed more than ever. I plainly heard a Noise upon the Cover of my Closet, like that of a Cable, and the grating of it as it passed through the Ring. I then found my self hoisted up by Degrees at least three Foot higher than I was before. Whereupon, I again thrust up my Stick and Handkerchief, calling for Help till I was almost hoarse. In return to which, I heard a great Shout repeated three times, giving me such Transports of Joy as are not to be conceived but by those who feel them. I now heard a trampling over my Head; and somebody calling through the Hole with a loud Voice in the *English* Tongue: *If there be any Body below, let them speak*. I answered, I was an *Englishman*, drawn by ill Fortune into the greatest Calamity that ever any Creature underwent; and begged, by all that was moving, to be delivered out of the Dungeon I was in. The Voice replied, I was safe, for my Box was fastned to their Ship; and the Carpenter should immediately come, and saw an Hole in the Cover, large enough to pull me out. I answered, that was needless, and would take up too much Time; for there was no more to be done, but let one of the Crew put his Finger into the Ring, and take the Box out of the Sea into the Ship, and so into the Captain's Cabbin. Some of them upon hearing me talk so wildly, thought I was mad; others laughed; for indeed it never came into my Head, that I was now got among People of my own Stature and Strength. The Carpenter came, and in a few Minutes sawed a Passage about four Foot square; then let down a small Ladder, upon which I mounted, and from thence was taken into the Ship in a very weak Condition.

THE Sailors were all in Amazement, and asked me a thousand Questions, which I had no Inclination to answer. I was equally confounded at the Sight of so many Pigmies; for such I took them to be, after having so long accustomed my Eyes to the monstrous Objects I had left. But the Captain, Mr. *Thomas Wilcocks*, an honest worthy *Shropshire* Man, observing I was ready to faint, took me into his Cabbin, gave me a Cordial to comfort me, and made me

F

turn in upon his own Bed; advising me to take a little Rest, of which I had great need. Before I went to sleep I gave him to understand, that I had some valuable Furniture in my Box too good to be lost; a fine Hammock, an handsome Field-Bed, two Chairs, a Table and a Cabinet: That my Closet was hung on all Sides, or rather quilted with Silk and Cotton: That if he would let one of the Crew bring my Closet into his Cabbin, I would open it before him, and shew him my Goods. The Captain hearing me utter these Absurdities, concluded I was raving: However, (I suppose to pacify me) he promised to give Order as I desired; and going upon Deck, sent some of his Men down into my Closet, from whence (as I afterwards found) they drew up all my Goods, and stripped off the Quilting; but the Chairs, Cabinet and Bed-sted being screwed to the Floor, were much damaged by the Ignorance of the Seamen, who tore them up by Force. Then they knocked off some of the Boards for the Use of the Ship; and when they had got all they had a Mind for, let the Hulk drop into the Sea, which by Reason of many Breaches made in the Bottom and Sides, sunk *to rights.* And indeed I was glad not to have been a Spectator of the Havock they made; because I am confident it would have sensibly touched me, by bringing former Passages into my Mind, which I had rather forget.

I SLEPT some Hours, but perpetually disturbed with Dreams of the Place I had left, and the Dangers I had escaped. However, upon waking I found my self much recovered. It was now about eight a Clock at Night, and the Captain ordered Supper immediately, thinking I had already fasted too long. He entertained me with great Kindness, observing me not to look wildly, or talk inconsistently; and when we were left alone, desired I would give him a Relation of my Travels, and by what Accident I came to be set adrift in that monstrous wooden Chest. He said, that about twelve a Clock at Noon, as he was looking through his Glass, he spied it at a Distance, and thought it was a Sail, which he had a Mind to make; being not much out of his Course, in hopes of buying some Biscuit, his own beginning to fall short. That, upon coming nearer,

and finding his Error, he sent out his Long-boat to discover
what I was; that his Men came back in a Fright, swearing
they had seen a swimming House. That he laughed at their
Folly, and went himself in the Boat, ordering his Men to
take a strong Cable along with them. That the Weather
being calm, he rowed round me several times, observed my
Windows, and the Wire Lattices that defended them. That
he discovered two Staples upon one Side, which was all
of Boards, without any Passage for Light. He then commanded his Men to row up to that Side; and fastning a
Cable to one of the Staples, ordered his Men to tow my
Chest (as he called it) towards the Ship. When it was there,
he gave Directions to fasten another Cable to the Ring
fixed in the Cover, and to raise up my Chest with Pullies,
which all the Sailors were not able to do above two or three
Foot. He said, they saw my Stick and Handkerchief thrust
out of the Hole, and concluded, that some unhappy Man
must be shut up in the Cavity. I asked whether he or the
Crew had seen any prodigious Birds in the Air about the
Time he first discovered me: To which he answered, that
discoursing this Matter with the Sailors while I was asleep,
one of them said he had *observed* three Eagles flying towards the North; but remarked nothing of their being larger
than the usual Size; which I suppose must be imputed to
the great Height they were at: And he could not guess the
Reason of my Question. I then asked the Captain how far
he reckoned we might be from Land; he said, by the best
Computation he could make, we were at least an hundred
Leagues. I assured him, that he must be mistaken by almost half; for I had not left the Country from whence I
came, above two Hours before I dropt into the Sea. Whereupon he began again to think that my Brain was disturbed,
of which he gave me a Hint, and advised me to go to Bed
in a Cabin he had provided. I assured him I was well refreshed with his good Entertainment and Company, and
as much in my Senses as ever I was in my Life. He then
grew serious, and desired to ask me freely whether I were
not troubled in Mind by the Consciousness of some enormous Crime, for which I was punished at the Command of

some Prince, by exposing me in that Chest; as great Criminals in other Countries have been forced to Sea in a leaky Vessel without Provisions: For, although he should be sorry to have taken so ill a Man into his Ship, yet he would engage his Word to set me safe on Shore in the first Port where we arrived. He added, that his Suspicions were much increased by some very absurd Speeches I had delivered at first to the Sailors, and afterwards to himself, in relation to my Closet or Chest, as well as by my odd Looks and Behaviour while I was at Supper.

I BEGGED his Patience to hear me tell my Story; which I faithfully did from the last Time I left *England*, to the Moment he first discovered me. And, as Truth always forceth its Way into rational Minds; so, this honest worthy Gentleman, who had some Tincture of Learning, and very good Sense, was immediately convinced of my Candor and Veracity. But, further to confirm all I had said, I entreated him to give Order that my Cabinet should be brought, of which I kept the Key in my Pocket, (for he had already informed me how the Seamen disposed of my Closet) I opened it in his Presence, and shewed him the small Collection of Rarities I made in the Country from whence I had been so strangely delivered. There was the Comb I had contrived out of the Stumps of the King's Beard; and another of the same Materials, but fixed into a paring of her Majesty's Thumb-nail, which served for the Back. There was a Collection of Needles and Pins from a Foot to half a Yard long. Four Wasp-Stings, like Joyners Tacks: Some Combings of the Queen's Hair: A Gold Ring which one Day she made me a Present of in a most obliging Manner, taking it from her little Finger, and throwing it over my Head like a Collar. I desired the Captain would please to accept this Ring in Return of his Civilities; which he absolutely refused. I shewed him a Corn that I had cut off with my own Hand from a Maid of Honour's Toe; it was about the Bigness of a *Kentish* Pippin, and grown so hard, that when I returned to *England*, I got it hollowed into a Cup and set in Silver. Lastly, I desired him to see the Breeches I had then on, which were made of a Mouse's Skin.

I COULD force nothing on him but a Footman's Tooth, which I observed him to examine with great Curiosity, and found he had a Fancy for it. He received it with abundance of Thanks, more than such a Trifle could deserve. It was drawn by an unskilful Surgeon in a Mistake from one of *Glumdalclitch's* Men, who was afflicted with the Tooth-ach; but it was as sound as any in his Head. I got it cleaned, and put it into my Cabinet. It was about a Foot long, and four Inches in Diameter.

THE Captain was very well satisfied with this plain Relation I had given him; and said, he hoped when we returned to *England*, I would oblige the World by putting it in Paper, and making it publick. My Answer was, that I thought we were already over-stocked with Books of Travels: That nothing could now pass which was not extra-ordinary; wherein I doubted, some Authors less consulted Truth than their own Vanity or Interest, or the Diversion of ignorant Readers. That my Story could contain little besides common Events, without those ornamental Descrip-tions of strange Plants, Trees, Birds, and other Animals; or the barbarous Customs and Idolatry of savage People, with which most Writers abound. However, I thanked him for his good Opinion, and promised to take the Matter into my Thoughts.

He said, he wondered at one Thing very much; which was, to hear me speak so loud; asking me whether the King or Queen of that Country were thick of Hearing. I told him it was what I had been used to for above two Years past; and that I admired as much at the Voices of him and his Men, who seemed to me only to whisper, and yet I could hear them well enough. But, when I spoke in that Country, it was like a Man talking in the Street to another looking out from the Top of a Steeple, unless when I was placed on a Table, or held in any Person's Hand. I told him, I had likewise observed another Thing; that when I first got into the Ship, and the Sailors stood all about me, I thought they were the most little contemptible Creatures I had ever be-held. For, indeed, while I was in that Prince's Country, I could never endure to look in a Glass after my Eyes had been accustomed to such prodigious Objects; because the Comparison gave me so despicable a Conceit of my self. The Captain said, that while we were at Supper, he observed me to look at every thing with a Sort of Wonder; and that I often seemed hardly able to contain my Laughter; which he knew not well how to take, but imputed it to some Disorder in my Brain. I answered, it was very true; and I wondered how I could forbear, when I saw his Dishes of the Size of a Silver Three-pence, a Leg of Pork hardly a Mouthful, a Cup not so big as a Nutshell: And so I went on, describing the rest of his Houshold stuff and Provisions after the same Manner. For although the Queen had ordered a little Equipage of all Things necessary for me while I was in her Service; yet my Ideas were wholly taken up with what I saw on every Side of me; and I winked at my own Littleness, as People do at their own Faults. The Captain understood my Raillery very well, and merrily replied with the old *English* Proverb, that he doubted, my Eyes were bigger than my Belly; for he did not observe my Stomach so good, although I had fasted all Day: And continuing in his Mirth, protested he would have gladly given an Hundred Pounds to have seen my Closet in the Eagle's Bill, and afterwards in its Fall from so great an Height into the Sea; which would certainly have been a most astonishing Object, worthy to have the Description of it transmitted to future Ages: And the Comparison of *Phaeton* was so obvious, that he could not forbear applying it, although I did not much admire the Conceit.

THE Captain having been at *Tonquin*, was in his Return to *England* driven North Eastward to the Latitude of 44 Degrees, and of Longitude 143. But meeting a Trade Wind two Days after I came on board him, we sailed Southward a long Time, and coasting *New-Holland*, kept our Course West-south-west, and then South-south-west till we doubled the *Cape of Good-hope*. Our Voyage was very prosperous, but I shall not trouble the Reader with a Journal of it. The Captain called in at one or two Ports, and sent in his Longboat for Provisions and fresh Water; but I never went out of the Ship till we came into the *Downs*, which was on the

3d Day of *June* 1706, about nine Months after my Escape. I offered to leave my Goods in Security for Payment of my Freight; but the Captain protested he would not receive one Farthing. We took kind Leave of each other; and I made him promise he would come to see me at my House in *Redriff*. I hired a Horse and Guide for five Shillings, which I borrowed of the Captain.

As I was on the Road; observing the Littleness of the Houses, the Trees, the Cattle and the People, I began to think my self in *Lilliput*. I was afraid of trampling on every Traveller I met; and often called aloud to have them stand out of the Way; so that I had like to have gotten one or two broken Heads for my Impertinence.

WHEN I came to my own House, for which I was forced to enquire, one of the Servants opening the Door, I bent down to go in (like a Goose under a Gate) for fear of striking my Head. My Wife ran out to embrace me, but I stooped lower than her Knees, thinking she could otherwise never be able to reach my Mouth. My Daughter kneeled to ask me Blessing, but I could not see her till she arose; having been so long used to stand with my Head and Eyes erect to above Sixty Foot; and then I went to take her up with one Hand, by the Waist. I looked down upon the Servants, and one or two Friends who were in the House, as if they had been Pigmies, and I a Giant. I told my Wife, she had been too thrifty; for I found she had starved herself and her Daughter to nothing. In short, I behaved my self so unaccountably, that they were all of the Captain's Opinion when he first saw me; and concluded I had lost my Wits. This I mention as an Instance of the great Power of Habit and Prejudice.

IN a little Time I and my Family and Friends came to a right Understanding: But my Wife protested I should never go to Sea any more; although my evil Destiny so ordered, that she had not Power to hinder me; as the Reader may know hereafter. In the mean Time, I here conclude the second Part of my unfortunate Voyages.

The End of the Second Part.

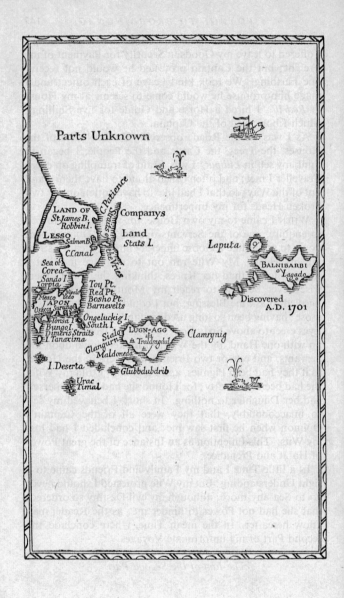

Parts Unknown

Land of
St. James B.
Robbin I.

Companys

Land
Stats I.

LESSO

Salmon B.

C. Canal

Sea of
Corea

Sando I.
Torpta

Meaco
Ninsto
Yedo

JAPON
Osacca Surughag

Tonsa I.
Bungo I.
Dimeris Straits
I. Tanaxima

Toy Pt.
Red Pt.
Bosho Pt.
Barnevelts

Ongeluckig I.
South I.

Sial

Glangurni
Maldoneda

I. Deserta

Glubbdubdrib

Urac
Timal

Laputa

BALNIBARBI
o Lagado

Discovered
A.D. 1701

LUGN-AGG
th Traldragdul

Clamrgnig

PART III.

A VOYAGE TO LAPUTA, BAL-
NIBARBI, LUGGNAGG,
GLUBBDUBDRIB,
AND JAPAN.

CHAPTER I.

THE AUTHOR SETS OUT ON HIS THIRD VOYAGE. IS TAKEN
BY PYRATES. THE MALICE OF A DUTCHMAN. HIS
ARRIVAL AT AN ISLAND. HE IS RECEIVED INTO LAPUTA.

I HAD not been at home above ten Days, when Captain
William Robinson, a *Cornish* Man, Commander of the
Hopewell, a stout Ship of three Hundred Tuns, came
to my House. I had formerly been Surgeon of another Ship
where he was Master, and a fourth Part Owner, in a Voyage
to the *Levant*. He had always treated me more like a
Brother than an inferior Officer; and hearing of my Arrival
made me a Visit, as I apprehended only out of Friendship,
for nothing passed more than what is usual after long Absence. But repeating his Visits often, expressing his Joy to
find me in good Health, asking whether I were now settled
for Life, adding that he intended a Voyage to the *East-Indies*,
in two Months, at last he plainly invited me, although with
some Apologies, to be Surgeon of the Ship. That I should
have another Surgeon under me, besides our two Mates;
that my Sallary should be double to the usual Pay; and that
having experienced my Knowledge in Sea-Affairs to be at
least equal to his, he would enter into any Engagement to

follow my Advice, as much as if I had Share in the Command.

HE said so many other obliging things, and I knew him to be so honest a Man, that I could not reject his Proposal; the Thirst I had of seeing the World, notwithstanding my past Misfortunes, continuing as violent as ever. The only Difficulty that remained, was to persuade my Wife, whose Consent however I at last obtained, by the Prospect of Advantage she proposed to her Children.

WE set out the 5th Day of *August*, 1706, and arrived at Fort St. *George*, the 11th of *April* 1707. We stayed there three Weeks to refresh our Crew, many of whom were sick. From thence we went to *Tonquin*, where the Captain resolved to continue some time; because many of the Goods he intended to buy were not ready, nor could he expect to be dispatched in several Months. Therefore in hopes to defray some of the Charges he must be at, he bought a Sloop, loaded it with several Sorts of Goods, wherewith the *Tonquinese* usually trade to the neighbouring Islands; and putting Fourteen Men on Board, whereof three were of the Country, he appointed me Master of the Sloop, and gave me Power to traffick, while he transacted his Affairs at *Tonquin*.

WE had not sailed above three Days, when a great Storm arising, we were driven five Days to the North-North-East, and then to the East; after which we had fair Weather, but still with a pretty strong Gale from the West. Upon the tenth Day we were chased by two Pyrates, who soon overtook us; for my Sloop was so deep loaden, that she sailed very slow; neither were we in a Condition to defend our selves.

WE were boarded about the same Time by both the Pyrates, who entered furiously at the Head of their Men; but finding us all prostrate upon our Faces, (for so I gave Order,) they pinioned us with strong Ropes, and setting a Guard upon us, went to search the Sloop.

I OBSERVED among them a *Dutchman*, who seemed to be of some Authority, although he were not Commander of either Ship. He knew us by our Countenances to be *Eng-*

lishmen, and jabbering to us in his own Language, swore we should be tyed Back to Back, and thrown into the Sea. I spoke *Dutch* tolerably well; I told him who we were, and begged him in Consideration of our being Christians and Protestants, of neighbouring Countries, in strict Alliance, that he would move the Captains to take some Pity on us. This inflamed his Rage; he repeated his Threatnings, and turning to his Companions, spoke with great Vehemence, in the *Japanese* Language, as I suppose; often using the Word *Christianos*.

THE largest of the two Pyrate Ships was commanded by a *Japanese* Captain, who spoke a little *Dutch*, but very imperfectly. He came up to me, and after several Questions, which I answered in great Humility, he said we should not die. I made the Captain a very low Bow, and then turning to the *Dutchman*, said, I was sorry to find more Mercy in a Heathen, than in a Brother Christian. But I had soon Reason to repent those foolish Words; for that malicious Reprobate, having often endeavoured in vain to persuade both the Captains that I might be thrown into the Sea, (which they would not yield to after the Promise made me, that I should not die) however prevailed so far as to have a Punishment inflicted on me, worse in all human Appearance than Death it self. My Men were sent by an equal Division into both the Pyrate-Ships, and my Sloop new manned. As to my self, it was determined that I should be set a-drift, in a small Canoe, with Paddles and a Sail, and four Days Provisions; which last the *Japanese* Captain was so kind to double out of his own Stores, and would permit no Man to search me. I got down into the Canoe, while the *Dutchman* standing upon the Deck, loaded me with all the Curses and injurious Terms his Language could afford.

ABOUT an Hour before we saw the Pyrates, I had taken an Observation, and found we were in the Latitude of 46 N. and of Longitude 183. When I was at some Distance from the Pyrates, I discovered by my Pocket-Glass several Islands to the South-East. I set up my Sail, the Wind being fair, with a Design to reach the nearest of those Islands, which I made a Shift to do in about three Hours. It was all rocky; however I got many Birds Eggs; and striking Fire, I kindled some Heath and dry Sea Weed, by which I roasted my Eggs. I eat no other Supper, being resolved to spare my Provisions as much as I could. I passed the Night under the Shelter of a Rock, strowing some Heath under me, and slept pretty well.

THE next Day I sailed to another Island, and thence to a third and fourth, sometimes using my Sail, and sometimes my Paddles. But not to trouble the Reader with a particular Account of my Distresses; let it suffice, that on the 5th Day, I arrived at the last Island in my Sight, which lay South-South-East to the former.

THIS Island was at a greater Distance than I expected, and I did not reach it in less than five Hours. I encompassed it almost round before I could find a convenient Place to land in, which was a small Creek, about three Times the Wideness of my Canoe. I found the Island to be all rocky, only a little intermingled with Tufts of Grass, and sweet smelling Herbs. I took out my small Provisions, and after having refreshed myself, I secured the Remainder in a Cave, whereof there were great Numbers. I gathered Plenty of Eggs upon the Rocks, and got a Quantity of dry Sea-weed, and parched Grass, which I designed to kindle the next Day, and roast my Eggs as well as I could. (For I had about me my Flint, Steel, Match, and Burning-glass.) I lay all Night in the Cave where I had lodged my Provisions. My Bed was the same dry Grass and Sea-weed which I intended for Fewel. I slept very little; for the Disquiets of my Mind prevailed over my Wearyness, and kept me awake. I considered how impossible it was to preserve my Life, in so desolate a Place; and how miserable my End must be. Yet I found my self so listless and desponding, that I had not the Heart to rise; and before I could get Spirits enough to creep out of my Cave, the Day was far advanced. I walked a while among the Rocks, the Sky was perfectly clear, and the Sun so hot, that I was forced to turn my Face from it: When all on a Sudden it became obscured, as I thought, in a Manner very different from what happens by the Interposition of a Cloud. I turned back, and perceived a vast

Opake Body between me and the Sun, moving forwards towards the Island: It seemed to be about two Miles high, and hid the Sun six or seven Minutes, but I did not observe the Air to be much colder, or the Sky more darkned, than if I had stood under the Shade of a Mountain. As it approached nearer over the Place where I was, it appeared to be a firm Substance, the Bottom flat, smooth, and shining very bright from the Reflexion of the Sea below. I stood upon a Height about two Hundred Yards from the Shoar, and saw this vast Body descending almost to a Parallel with me, at less than an *English* Mile Distance. I took out my Pocket-Perspective, and could plainly discover Numbers of People moving up and down the Sides of it, which appeared to be sloping, but what those People were doing, I was not able to distinguish.

THE natural Love of Life gave me some inward Motions of Joy; and I was ready to entertain a Hope, that this Adventure might some Way or other help to deliver me from the desolate Place and Condition I was in. But, at the same Time, the Reader can hardly conceive my Astonishment, to behold an Island in the Air, inhabited by Men, who were able (as it should seem) to raise, or sink, or put it into a progressive Motion, as they pleased. But not being, at that Time, in a Disposition to philosophise upon this Phæ-nomenon, I rather chose to observe what Course the Island would take; because it seemed for a while to stand still. Yet soon after it advanced nearer; and I could see the Sides of it, encompassed with several Gradations of Galleries and Stairs, at certain Intervals, to descend from one to the other. In the lowest Gallery, I beheld some People fishing with long Angling Rods, and others looking on. I waved my Cap, (for my Hat was long since worn out,) and my Hand-kerchief towards the Island; and upon its nearer Approach, I called and shouted with the utmost Strength of my Voice; and then looking circumspectly, I beheld a Crowd gathered to that Side which was most in my View. I found by their pointing towards me and to each other, that they plainly discovered me, although they made no Return to my Shout-ing: But I could see four or five Men running in great Haste

up the Stairs to the Top of the Island, who then disappeared. I happened rightly to conjecture, that these were
sent for Orders to some Person in Authority upon this Occasion.

THE Number of People increased; and in less than Half
an Hour, the Island was moved and raised in such a Manner,
that the lowest Gallery appeared in a Parallel of less than
an Hundred Yards Distance from the Height where I stood.
I then put my self into the most supplicating Postures, and
spoke in the humblest Accent, but received no Answer.
Those who stood nearest over-against me, seemed to be
Persons of Distinction, as I supposed by their Habit. They
conferred earnestly with each other, looking often upon
me. At length one of them called out in a clear, polite,
smooth Dialect, not unlike in Sound to the *Italian*; and
therefore I returned an Answer in that Language, hoping
at least that the Cadence might be more agreeable to his
Ears. Although neither of us understood the other, yet my
Meaning was easily known, for the People saw the Distress
I was in.

THEY made Signs for me to come down from the Rock,
and go towards the Shoar, which I accordingly did; and
the flying Island being raised to a convenient Height, the
Verge directly over me, a Chain was let down from the
lowest Gallery, with a Seat fastned to the Bottom, to which
I fixed my self, and was drawn up by Pullies.

CHAPTER II.

THE HUMOURS AND DISPOSITIONS OF THE LAPUTIANS
DESCRIBED. AN ACCOUNT OF THEIR LEARNING. OF THE
KING AND HIS COURT. THE AUTHOR'S RECEPTION THERE.
THE INHABITANTS SUBJECT TO FEARS AND DISQUIETUDES.
AN ACCOUNT OF THE WOMEN.

AT my alighting I was surrounded by a Crowd of
People, but those who stood nearest seemed to be
of better Quality. They beheld me with all the Marks
and Circumstances of Wonder; neither indeed was I much
in their Debt; having never till then seen a Race of Mortals
so singular in their Shapes, Habits, and Countenances.
Their Heads were all reclined to the Right, or the Left; one
of their Eyes turned inward, and the other directly up to
the Zenith. Their outward Garments were adorned with
the Figures of Suns, Moons, and Stars, interwoven with
those of Fiddles, Flutes, Harps, Trumpets, Guittars, Harpsi-
cords, and many more Instruments of Musick, unknown
to us in *Europe*. I observed here and there many in the
Habit of Servants, with a blown Bladder fastned like a Flail
to the End of a short Stick, which they carried in their
Hands. In each Bladder was a small Quantity of dried
Pease, or little Pebbles, (as I was afterwards informed.)
With these Bladders they now and then flapped the Mouths
and Ears of those who stood near them, of which Practice
I could not then conceive the Meaning. It seems, the Minds
of these People are so taken up with intense Speculations,
that they neither can speak, or attend to the Discourses of
others, without being rouzed by some external Taction
upon the Organs of Speech and Hearing; for which Reason,
those Persons who are able to afford it, always keep a
Flapper, (the Original is *Climenole*) in their Family, as one
of their Domesticks; nor ever walk abroad or make Visits
without him. And the Business of this Officer is, when two

or more Persons are in Company, gently to strike with his
Bladder the Mouth of him who is to speak, and the Right
Ear of him or them to whom the Speaker addresseth himself. This *Flapper* is likewise employed diligently to attend
his Master in his Walks, and upon Occasion to give him
a soft Flap on his Eyes; because he is always so wrapped
up in Cogitation, that he is in manifest Danger of falling
down every Precipice, and bouncing his Head against every
Post; and in the Streets, of jostling others, or being jostled
himself into the Kennel.

It was necessary to give the Reader this Information,
without which he would be at the same Loss with me, to
understand the Proceedings of these People, as they conducted me up the Stairs, to the Top of the Island, and
from thence to the Royal Palace. While we were ascending, they forgot several Times what they were about, and
left me to my self, till their Memories were again rouzed
by their *Flappers*; for they appeared altogether unmoved
by the Sight of my foreign Habit and Countenance, and by
the Shouts of the Vulgar, whose Thoughts and Minds were
more disengaged.

At last we entered the Palace, and proceeded into the
Chamber of Presence; where I saw the King seated on his
Throne, attended on each Side by Persons of prime Quality.
Before the Throne, was a large Table filled with Globes and
Spheres, and Mathematical Instruments of all Kinds. His
Majesty took not the least Notice of us, although our Entrance were not without sufficient Noise, by the Concourse
of all Persons belonging to the Court. But, he was then
deep in a Problem, and we attended at least an Hour, before he could solve it. There stood by him on each Side, a
young Page, with Flaps in their Hands; and when they saw
he was at Leisure, one of them gently struck his Mouth,
and the other his Right Ear; at which he started like one
awaked on the sudden, and looking towards me, and the
Company I was in, recollected the Occasion of our coming,
whereof he had been informed before. He spoke some
Words; whereupon immediately a young Man with a Flap
came up to my Side, and flapt me gently on the Right Ear;

but I made Signs as well as I could, that I had no Occasion for such an Instrument; which as I afterwards found, gave his Majesty and the whole Court a very mean Opinion of my Understanding. The King, as far as I could conjecture, asked me several Questions, and I addressed my self to him in all the Languages I had. When it was found, that I could neither understand nor be understood, I was conducted by his Order to an Apartment in his Palace, (this Prince being distinguished above all his Predecessors for his Hospitality to Strangers,) where two Servants were appointed to attend me. My Dinner was brought, and four Persons of Quality, whom I remembered to have seen very near the King's Person, did me the Honour to dine with me. We had two Courses, of three Dishes each. In the first Course, there was a Shoulder of Mutton, cut into an Æquilateral Triangle; a Piece of Beef into a Rhomboides; and a Pudding into a Cycloid. The second Course was two Ducks, trussed up into the Form of Fiddles; Sausages and Puddings resembling Flutes and Haut-boys, and a Breast of Veal in the Shape of a Harp. The Servants cut our Bread into Cones, Cylinders, Parallelograms, and several other Mathematical Figures.

While we were at Dinner, I made bold to ask the Names of several Things in their Language; and those noble Persons, by the Assistance of their *Flappers*, delighted to give me Answers, hoping to raise my Admiration of their great Abilities, if I could be brought to converse with them. I was soon able to call for Bread, and Drink, or whatever else I wanted.

After Dinner my Company withdrew, and a Person was sent to me by the King's Order, attended by a *Flapper*. He brought with him Pen, Ink, and Paper, and three or four Books; giving me to understand by Signs, that he was sent to teach me the Language. We sat together four Hours, in which Time I wrote down a great Number of Words in Columns, with the Translations over against them. I likewise made a Shift to learn several short Sentences. For my Tutor would order one of my Servants to fetch something, to turn about, to make a Bow, to sit, or stand, or walk, and the like. Then I took down the Sentence in Writing. He shewed me also in one of his Books, the Figures of the Sun, Moon, and Stars, the Zodiack, the Tropics and Polar Circles, together with the Denominations of many Figures of Planes and Solids. He gave me the Names and Descriptions of all the Musical Instruments, and the general Terms of Art in playing on each of them. After he had left me, I placed all my Words with their Interpretations in alphabetical Order. And thus in a few Days, by the Help of a very faithful Memory, I got some Insight into their Language.

THE Word, which I interpret the *Flying* or *Floating Island*, is in the Original *Laputa*; whereof I could never learn the true Etymology. *Lap* in the old obsolete Language signifieth *High*, and *Untuh* a *Governor*; from which they say by Corruption was derived *Laputa* from *Lapuntuh*. But I do not approve of this Derivation, which seems to be a little strained. I ventured to offer to the Learned among them a Conjecture of my own, that *Laputa* was *quasi Lap outed*; *Lap* signifying properly the dancing of the Sun Beams in the Sea; and *outed* a Wing, which however I shall not obtrude, but submit to the judicious Reader.

THOSE to whom the King had entrusted me, observing how ill I was clad, ordered a Taylor to come next Morning, and take my Measure for a Suit of Cloths. This Operator did his Office after a different Manner from those of his Trade in *Europe*. He first took my Altitude by a Quadrant, and then with Rule and Compasses, described the Dimensions and Out-Lines of my whole Body; all which he entred upon Paper, and in six Days brought my Cloths very ill made, and quite out of Shape, by happening to mistake a Figure in the Calculation. But my Comfort was, that I observed such Accidents very frequent, and little regarded.

DURING my Confinement for want of Cloaths, and by an Indisposition that held me some Days longer, I much enlarged my Dictionary; and when I went next to Court, was able to understand many Things the King spoke, and to return him some Kind of Answers. His Majesty had given Orders, that the Island should move North-East and by

East, to the vertical Point over *Lagado,* the Metropolis of the whole Kingdom, below upon the firm Earth. It was about Ninety Leagues distant, and our Voyage lasted four Days and an Half. I was not in the least sensible of the progressive Motion made in the Air by the Island. On the second Morning, about Eleven o'Clock, the King himself in Person, attended by his Nobility, Courtiers, and Officers, having prepared all their Musical Instruments, played on them for three Hours without Intermission; so that I was quite stunned with the Noise; neither could I possibly guess the Meaning, till my Tutor informed me. He said, that the People of their Island had their Ears adapted to hear the Musick of the Spheres, which always played at certain Periods; and the Court was now prepared to bear their Part in whatever Instrument they most excelled.

IN our Journey towards *Lagado* the Capital City, his Majesty ordered that the Island should stop over certain Towns and Villages, from whence he might receive the Petitions of his Subjects. And to this Purpose, several Packthreads were let down with small Weights at the Bottom. On these Packthreads the People strung their Petitions, which mounted up directly like the Scraps of Paper fastned by School-boys at the End of the String that holds their Kite. Sometimes we received Wine and Victuals from below, which were drawn up by Pullies.

THE Knowledge I had in Mathematicks gave me great Assistance in acquiring their Phraseology, which depended much upon that Science and Musick; and in the latter I was not unskilled. Their Ideas are perpetually conversant in Lines and Figures. If they would, for Example, praise the Beauty of a Woman, or any other Animal, they describe it by Rhombs, Circles, Parallelograms, Ellipses, and other Geometrical Terms; or else by Words of Art drawn from Musick, needless here to repeat. I observed in the King's Kitchen all Sorts of Mathematical and Musical Instruments, after the Figures of which they cut up the Joynts that were served to his Majesty's Table.

THEIR Houses are very ill built, the Walls bevil, without one right Angle in any Apartment; and this Defect ariseth from the Contempt they bear for practical Geometry; which they despise as vulgar and mechanick, those Instructions they give being too refined for the Intellectuals of their Workmen; which occasions perpetual Mistakes. And although they are dextrous enough upon a Piece of Paper, in the Management of the Rule, the Pencil, and the Divider, yet in the common Actions and Behaviour of Life, I have not seen a more clumsy, awkward, and unhandy People, nor so slow and perplexed in their Conceptions upon all other Subjects, except those of Mathematicks and Musick. They are very bad Reasoners, and vehemently given to Opposition, unless when they happen to be of the right Opinion, which is seldom their Case. Imagination, Fancy, and Invention, they are wholly Strangers to, nor have any Words in their Language by which those Ideas can be expressed; the whole Compass of their Thoughts and Mind, being shut up within the two forementioned Sciences.

Most of them, and especially those who deal in the Astronomical Part, have great Faith in judicial Astrology, although they are ashamed to own it publickly. But, what I chiefly admired, and thought altogether unaccountable, was the strong Disposition I observed in them towards News and Politicks; perpetually enquiring into publick Affairs, giving their Judgments in Matters of State; and passionately disputing every Inch of a Party Opinion. I have indeed observed the same Disposition among most of the Mathematicians I have known in *Europe*; although I could never discover the least Analogy between the two Sciences; unless those People suppose, that because the smallest Circle hath as many Degrees as the largest, therefore the Regulation and Management of the World require no more Abilities than the handling and turning of a Globe. But, I rather take this Quality to spring from a very common Infirmity of human Nature, inclining us to be more curious and conceited in Matters where we have least Concern, and for which we are least adapted either by Study or Nature.

These People are under continual Disquietudes, never enjoying a Minute's Peace of Mind; and their Disturbances proceed from Causes which very little affect the rest of Mortals. Their Apprehensions arise from several Changes they dread in the Celestial Bodies. For Instance; that the Earth by the continual Approaches of the Sun towards it, must in Course of Time be absorbed or swallowed up. That the Face of the Sun will by Degrees be encrusted with its own Effluvia, and give no more Light to the World. That, the Earth very narrowly escaped a Brush from the Tail of the last Comet, which would have infallibly reduced it to Ashes; and that the next, which they have calculated for One and Thirty Years hence, will probably destroy us. For, if in its Perihelion it should approach within a certain Degree of the Sun, (as by their Calculations they have Reason to dread) it will conceive a Degree of Heat ten Thousand Times more intense than that of red hot glowing Iron; and in its Absence from the Sun, carry a blazing Tail Ten Hundred Thousand and Fourteen Miles long; through which if the Earth should pass at the Distance of one Hundred Thousand Miles from the *Nucleus*, or main Body of the Comet, it must in its Passage be set on Fire, and reduced to Ashes. That the Sun daily spending its Rays without any Nutriment to supply them, will at last be wholly consumed and annihilated; which must be attended with the Destruction of this Earth, and of all the Planets that receive their Light from it.

THEY are so perpetually alarmed with the Apprehensions of these and the like impending Dangers, that they can neither sleep quietly in their Beds, nor have any Relish for the common Pleasures or Amusements of Life. When they meet an Acquaintance in the Morning, the first Question is about the Sun's Health; how he looked at his Setting and Rising, and what Hopes they have to avoid the Stroak of the approaching Comet. This Conversation they are apt to run into with the same Temper that Boys discover, in delighting to hear terrible Stories of Sprites and Hobgoblins, which they greedily listen to, and dare not go to Bed for fear.

THE Women of the Island have Abundance of Vivacity; they contemn their Husbands, and are exceedingly fond of

Strangers, whereof there is always a considerable Number
from the Continent below, attending at Court, either upon
Affairs of the several Towns and Corporations, or their own
particular Occasions; but are much despised, because they
want the same Endowments. Among these the Ladies chuse
their Gallants: But the Vexation is, that they act with too
much Ease and Security; for the Husband is always so
wrapped in Speculation, that the Mistress and Lover may
proceed to the greatest Familiarities before his Face, if he
be but provided with Paper and Implements, and without
his *Flapper* at his Side.

THE Wives and Daughters lament their Confinement to
the Island, although I think it the most delicious Spot of
Ground in the World; and although they live here in the
greatest Plenty and Magnificence, and are allowed to do
whatever they please: They long to see the World, and take
the Diversions of the Metropolis, which they are not allowed
to do without a particular Licence from the King; and this
is not easy to be obtained, because the People of Quality
have found by frequent Experience, how hard it is to persuade their Women to return from below. I was told, that
a great Court Lady, who had several Children, is married
to the prime Minister, the richest Subject in the Kingdom,
a very graceful Person, extremely fond of her, and lives in
the finest Palace of the Island; went down to *Lagado*, on
the Pretence of Health, there hid her self for several Months,
till the King sent a Warrant to search for her; and she was
found in an obscure Eating-House all in Rags, having
pawned her Cloths to maintain an old deformed Footman,
who beat her every Day, and in whose Company she was
taken much against her Will. And although her Husband
received her with all possible Kindness, and without the
least Reproach; she soon after contrived to steal down
again with all her Jewels, to the same Gallant, and hath not
been heard of since.

THIS may perhaps pass with the Reader rather for an
European or *English* Story, than for one of a Country so
remote. But he may please to consider, that the Caprices
of Womankind are not limited by any Climate or Nation;

and that they are much more uniform than can be easily imagined.

IN about a Month's Time I had made a tolerable Proficiency in their Language, and was able to answer most of the King's Questions, when I had the Honour to attend him. His Majesty discovered not the least Curiosity to enquire into the Laws, Government, History, Religion, or Manners of the Countries where I had been; but confined his Questions to the State of Mathematicks, and received the Account I gave him, with great Contempt and Indifference, though often rouzed by his *Flapper* on each Side.

CHAPTER III.

A PHÆNOMENON SOLVED BY MODERN PHILOSOPHY AND ASTRONOMY. THE LAPUTIANS GREAT IMPROVEMENTS IN THE LATTER. THE KING'S METHOD OF SUPPRESSING INSURRECTIONS.

I DESIRED Leave of this Prince to see the Curiosities of the Island; which he was graciously pleased to grant, and ordered my Tutor to attend me. I chiefly wanted to know to what Cause in Art or in Nature, it owed its several Motions; whereof I will now give a philosophical Account to the Reader.

THE flying or floating Island is exactly circular; its Diameter 7837 Yards, or about four Miles and an Half, and consequently contains ten Thousand Acres. It is three Hundred Yards thick. The Bottom, or under Surface, which appears to those who view it from below, is one even regular Plate of Adamant, shooting up to the Height of about two Hundred Yards. Above it lye the several Minerals in their usual Order; and over all is a Coat of rich Mould ten or twelve Foot deep. The Declivity of the upper Surface, from the Circumference to the Center, is the natural Cause why all the Dews and Rains which fall upon the Island, are conveyed in small Rivulets towards the Middle, where they are emptied into four large Basons, each of about Half a Mile in Circuit, and two Hundred Yards distant from the Center. From these Basons the Water is continually exhaled by the Sun in the Day-time, which effectually prevents their overflowing. Besides, as it is in the Power of the Monarch to raise the Island above the Region of Clouds and Vapours, he can prevent the falling of Dews and Rains whenever he pleases. For the highest Clouds cannot rise above two Miles, as Naturalists agree, at least they were never known to do so in that Country.

AT the Center of the *Island* there is a Chasm about fifty Yards in Diameter, from whence the Astronomers descend into a large Dome, which is therefore called *Flandona Gagnole*, or the *Astronomers Cave*; situated at the Depth of an Hundred Yards beneath the upper Surface of the Adamant. In this Cave are Twenty Lamps continually burning, which from the Reflection of the Adamant cast a strong Light into every Part. The Place is stored with great Variety of Sextants, Quadrants, Telescopes, Astrolabes, and other Astronomical Instruments. But the greatest Curiosity, upon which the Fate of the Island depends, is a Load-stone of a prodigious Size, in Shape resembling a Weaver's Shuttle. It is in Length six Yards, and in the thickest Part at least three Yards over. This Magnet is sustained by a very strong Axle of Adamant, passing through its Middle, upon which it plays, and is poized so exactly that the weakest Hand can turn it. It is hooped round with an hollow Cylinder of Adamant, four Foot deep, as many thick, and twelve Yards in Diameter, placed horizontally, and supported by Eight Adamantine Feet, each Six Yards high. In the Middle of the Concave Side there is a Groove Twelve Inches deep, in which the Extremities of the Axle are lodged, and turned round as there is Occasion.

THIS Stone cannot be moved from its Place by any Force, because the Hoop and its Feet are one continued Piece with that Body of Adamant which constitutes the Bottom of the Island.

By Means of this Load-stone, the Island is made to rise and fall, and move from one Place to another. For, with respect to that Part of the Earth over which the Monarch presides, the Stone is endued at one of its Sides with an attractive Power, and at the other with a repulsive. Upon placing the Magnet erect with its attracting End towards the Earth, the Island descends; but when the repelling Extremity points downwards, the Island mounts directly upwards. When the Position of the Stone is oblique, the Motion of the Island is so too. For in this Magnet the Forces always act in Lines parallel to its Direction.

By this oblique Motion the Island is conveyed to different Parts of the Monarch's Dominions. To explain the Manner of its Progress, let *A B* represent a Line drawn cross the Dominions of *Balnibarbi*; let the Line *c d* represent the Load-stone, of which let *d* be the repelling End, and *c* the attracting End, the Island being over *C*; let the Stone be placed in the Position *c d* with its repelling End downwards; then the Island will be driven upwards obliquely towards *D*. When it is arrived at *D*, let the Stone be turned upon its Axle till its attracting End points towards *E*, and then the Island will be carried obliquely towards *E*; where if the Stone be again turned upon its Axle till it stands in the Position *E F*, with its repelling Point downwards, the Island will rise obliquely towards *F*, where by directing the attracting End towards *G*, the Island may be carried to *G*, and from *G* to *H*, by turning the Stone, so as to make its repelling Extremity point directly downwards. And thus by changing the Situation of the Stone as often as there is Occasion, the Island is made to rise and fall by Turns in an oblique Direction; and by those alternate Risings and Fallings (the Obliquity being not considerable) is conveyed from one Part of the Dominions to the other.

But it must be observed, that this Island cannot move beyond the Extent of the Dominions below; nor can it rise above the Height of four Miles. For which the Astronomers (who have written large Systems concerning the Stone) assign the following Reason: That the Magnetick Virtue does not extend beyond the Distance of four Miles, and that the

Mineral which acts upon the Stone in the Bowels of the Earth, and in the Sea about six Leagues distant from the Shoar, is not diffused through the whole Globe, but terminated with the Limits of the King's Dominions: And it was easy from the great Advantage of such a superior Situation, for a Prince to bring under his Obedience whatever Country lay within the Attraction of that Magnet.

WHEN the Stone is put parallel to the Plane of the Horizon, the Island standeth still; for in that Case, the Extremities of it being at equal Distance from the Earth, act with equal Force, the one in drawing downwards, the other in pushing upwards; and consequently no Motion can ensue.

THIS Load-stone is under the Care of certain Astronomers, who from Time to Time give it such Positions as the Monarch directs. They spend the greatest Part of their Lives in observing the celestial Bodies, which they do by the Assistance of Glasses, far excelling ours in Goodness. For, although their largest Telescopes do not exceed three Feet, they magnify much more than those of a Hundred with us, and shew the Stars with greater Clearness. This Advantage hath enabled them to extend their Discoveries much farther than our Astronomers in *Europe*. They have made a Catalogue of ten Thousand fixed Stars, whereas the largest of ours do not contain above one third Part of that Number. They have likewise discovered two lesser Stars, or *Satellites*, which revolve about *Mars*; whereof the innermost is distant from the Center of the primary Planet exactly three of his Diameters, and the outermost five; the former revolves in the Space of ten Hours, and the latter in Twenty-one and an Half; so that the Squares of their periodical Times, are very near in the same Proportion with the Cubes of their Distance from the Center of *Mars*; which evidently shews them to be governed by the same Law of Gravitation, that influences the other heavenly Bodies.

THEY have observed Ninety-three different Comets, and settled their Periods with great Exactness. If this be true, (and they affirm it with great Confidence) it is much to be wished that their Observations were made publick; whereby the Theory of Comets, which at present is very lame and defective, might be brought to the same Perfection with other Parts of Astronomy.

THE King would be the most absolute Prince in the Universe, if he could but prevail on a Ministry to join with him; but these having their Estates below on the Continent, and considering that the Office of a Favourite hath a very uncertain Tenure, would never consent to the enslaving their Country.

IF any Town should engage in Rebellion or Mutiny, fall into violent Factions, or refuse to pay the usual Tribute; the King hath two Methods of reducing them to Obedience. The first and the mildest Course is by keeping the Island hovering over such a Town, and the Lands about it; whereby he can deprive them of the Benefit of the Sun and the Rain, and consequently afflict the Inhabitants with Dearth and Diseases. And if the Crime deserve it, they are at the same time pelted from above with great Stones, against which they have no Defence, but by creeping into Cellars or Caves, while the Roofs of their Houses are beaten to Pieces. But if they still continue obstinate, or offer to raise Insurrections; he proceeds to the last Remedy, by letting the Island drop directly upon their Heads, which makes a universal Destruction both of Houses and Men. However, this is an Extremity to which the Prince is seldom driven, neither indeed is he willing to put it in Execution; nor dare his Ministers advise him to an Action, which as it would render them odious to the People, so it would be a great Damage to their own Estates that lie all below; for the Island is the King's Demesn.

BUT there is still indeed a more weighty Reason, why the Kings of this Country have been always averse from executing so terrible an Action, unless upon the utmost Necessity. For if the Town intended to be destroyed should have in it any tall Rocks, as it generally falls out in the larger Cities; a Situation probably chosen at first with a View to prevent such a Catastrophe: Or if it abound in high Spires or Pillars of Stone, a sudden Fall might endanger the Bottom or under Surface of the Island, which although it consist as I have said, of one entire Adamant two hundred Yards thick, might happen to crack by too great a Choque, or burst by approaching too near the Fires from the Houses below; as the Backs both of Iron and Stone will often do in our Chimneys. Of all this the People are well apprized, and understand how far to carry their Obstinacy, where their Liberty or Property is concerned. And the King, when he is highest provoked, and most determined to press a City to Rubbish, orders the Island to descend with great Gentleness, out of a Pretence of Tenderness to his People, but indeed for fear of breaking the Adamantine Bottom; in which Case it is the Opinion of all their Philosophers, that the Load-stone could no longer hold it up, and the whole Mass would fall to the Ground.

By a fundamental Law of this Realm, neither the King nor either of his two elder Sons, are permitted to leave the Island; nor the Queen till she is past Child-bearing.

CHAPTER IV.

THE AUTHOR LEAVES LAPUTA, IS CONVEYED TO BALNI-BARBI, ARRIVES AT THE METROPOLIS. A DESCRIPTION OF THE METROPOLIS AND THE COUNTRY ADJOINING. THE AUTHOR HOSPITABLY RECEIVED BY A GREAT LORD. HIS CONVERSATION WITH THAT LORD.

ALTHOUGH I cannot say that I was ill treated in this Island, yet I must confess I thought my self too much neglected, not without some Degree of Contempt. For neither Prince nor People appeared to be curious in any Part of Knowledge, except Mathematicks and Musick, wherein I was far their inferior, and upon that Account very little regarded.

On the other Side, after having seen all the Curiosities of the Island, I was very desirous to leave it, being heartily weary of those People. They were indeed excellent in two Sciences for which I have great Esteem, and wherein I am

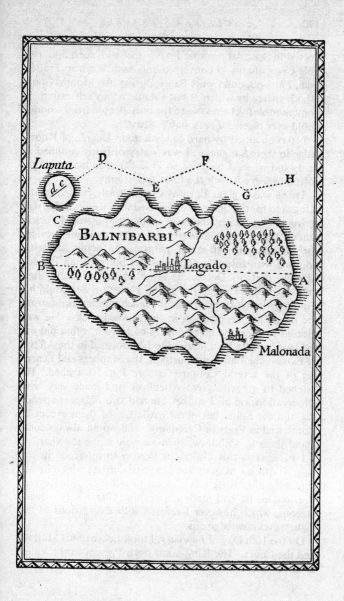

not unversed; but at the same time so abstracted and involved in Speculation, that I never met with such disagreeable Companions. I conversed only with Women, Tradesmen, *Flappers*, and Court-Pages, during two Months of my Abode there; by which at last I rendered my self extremely contemptible; yet these were the only People from whom I could ever receive a reasonable Answer.

I HAD obtained by hard Study a good Degree of Knowledge in their Language: I was weary of being confined to an Island where I received so little Countenance; and resolved to leave it with the first Opportunity.

THERE was a great Lord at Court, nearly related to the King, and for that Reason alone used with Respect. He was universally reckoned the most ignorant and stupid Person among them. He had performed many eminent Services for the Crown, had great natural and acquired Parts, adorned with Integrity and Honour; but so ill an Ear for Musick, that his Detractors reported he had been often known to beat Time in the wrong Place; neither could his Tutors without extreme Difficulty teach him to demonstrate the most easy Proposition in the Mathematicks. He was pleased to shew me many Marks of Favour, often did me the Honour of a Visit, desired to be informed in the Affairs of *Europe*, the Laws and Customs, the Manners and Learning of the several Countries where I had travelled. He listened to me with great Attention, and made very wise Observations on all I spoke. He had two *Flappers* attending him for State, but never made use of them except at Court, and in Visits of Ceremony; and would always command them to withdraw when we were alone together.

I INTREATED this illustrious Person to intercede in my Behalf with his Majesty for Leave to depart; which he accordingly did, as he was pleased to tell me, with Regret: For, indeed he had made me several Offers very advantageous, which however I refused with Expressions of the highest Acknowledgment.

ON the 16th Day of *February*, I took Leave of his Majesty and the Court. The King made me a Present to the Value of about two Hundred Pounds *English*; and my Protector his Kinsman as much more, together with a Letter of Recommendation to a Friend of his in *Lagado*, the Metropolis: The Island being then hovering over a Mountain about two Miles from it, I was let down from the lowest Gallery, in the same Manner as I had been taken up.

THE Continent, as far as it is subject to the Monarch of the *Flying Island*, passeth under the general Name of *Balnibarbi*; and the Metropolis, as I said before, is called *Lagado*. I felt some little Satisfaction in finding my self on firm Ground. I walked to the City without any Concern, being clad like one of the Natives, and sufficiently instructed to converse with them. I soon found out the Person's House to whom I was recommended; presented my Letter from his Friend the Grandee in the Island, and was received with much Kindness. This great Lord, whose Name was *Munodi*, ordered me an Apartment in his own House, where I continued during my Stay, and was entertained in a most hospitable Manner.

THE next Morning after my Arrival he took me in his Chariot to see the Town, which is about half the Bigness of *London*; but the Houses very strangely built, and most of them out of Repair. The People in the Streets walked fast, looked wild, their Eyes fixed, and were generally in Rags. We passed through one of the Town Gates, and went about three Miles into the Country, where I saw many Labourers working with several Sorts of Tools in the Ground, but was not able to conjecture what they were about; neither did I observe any Expectation either of Corn or Grass, although the Soil appeared to be excellent. I could not forbear admiring at these odd Appearances both in Town and Country; and I made bold to desire my Conductor, that he would be pleased to explain to me what could be meant by so many busy Heads, Hands and Faces, both in the Streets and the Fields, because I did not discover any good Effects they produced; but on the contrary, I never knew a Soil so unhappily cultivated, Houses so ill contrived and so ruinous, or a People whose Countenances and Habit expressed so much Misery and Want.

THIS Lord *Munodi* was a Person of the first Rank, and

had been some Years Governor of *Lagado*; but by a Cabal of Ministers was discharged for Insufficiency. However the King treated him with Tenderness, as a well-meaning Man, but of a low contemptible Understanding.

WHEN I gave that free Censure of the Country and its Inhabitants, he made no further Answer than by telling me, that I had not been long enough among them to form a Judgment; and that the different Nations of the World had different Customs; with other common Topicks to the same Purpose. But when we returned to his Palace, he asked me how I liked the Building, what Absurdities I observed, and what Quarrel I had with the Dress or Looks of his Domesticks. This he might safely do; because every Thing about him was magnificent, regular and polite. I answered, that his Excellency's Prudence, Quality, and Fortune, had exempted him from those Defects which Folly and Beggary had produced in others. He said, if I would go with him to his Country House about Twenty Miles distant, where his Estate lay, there would be more Leisure for this Kind of Conversation. I told his Excellency, that I was entirely at his Disposal; and accordingly we set out next Morning.

DURING our Journey, he made me observe the several Methods used by Farmers in managing their Lands; which to me were wholly unaccountable: For except in some very few Places, I could not discover one Ear of Corn, or Blade of Grass. But, in three Hours travelling, the Scene was wholly altered; we came into a most beautiful Country; Farmers Houses at small Distances, neatly built, the Fields enclosed, containing Vineyards, Corn-grounds and Meadows. Neither do I remember to have seen a more delightful Prospect. His Excellency observed my Countenance to clear up; he told me with a Sigh, that there his Estate began, and would continue the same till we should come to his House. That his Countrymen ridiculed and despised him for managing his Affairs no better, and for setting so ill an Example to the Kingdom; which however was followed by very few, such as were old and wilful, and weak like himself.

WE came at length to the House, which was indeed a

noble Structure, built according to the best Rules of ancient Architecture. The Fountains, Gardens, Walks, Avenues, and Groves were all disposed with exact Judgment and Taste. I gave due Praises to every Thing I saw, whereof his Excellency took not the least Notice till after Supper; when, there being no third Companion, he told me with a very melancholy Air, that he doubted he must throw down his Houses in Town and Country, to rebuild them after the present Mode; destroy all his Plantations, and cast others into such a Form as modern Usage required; and give the same Directions to all his Tenants, unless he would submit to incur the Censure of Pride, Singularity, Affectation, Ignorance, Caprice; and perhaps encrease his Majesty's Displeasure.

THAT the Admiration I appeared to be under, would cease or diminish when he had informed me of some Particulars, which probably I never heard of at Court, the People there being too much taken up in their own Speculations, to have Regard to what passed here below.

THE Sum of his Discourse was to this Effect. That about Forty Years ago, certain Persons went up to *Laputa*, either upon Business or Diversion; and after five Months Continuance, came back with a very little Smattering in Mathematicks, but full of Volatile Spirits acquired in that Airy Region. That these Persons upon their Return, began to dislike the Management of every Thing below; and fell into Schemes of putting all Arts, Sciences, Languages, and Mechanics upon a new Foot. To this End they procured a Royal Patent for erecting an Academy of PROJECTORS in *Lagado*: And the Humour prevailed so strongly among the People, that there is not a Town of any Consequence in the Kingdom without such an Academy. In these Colleges, the Professors contrive new Rules and Methods of Agriculture and Building, and new Instruments and Tools for all Trades and Manufactures, whereby, as they undertake, one Man shall do the Work of Ten; a Palace may be built in a Week, of Materials so durable as to last for ever without repairing. All the Fruits of the Earth shall come to Maturity at whatever Season we think fit to chuse, and increase an Hundred

G

Fold more than they do at present; with innumerable other happy Proposals. The only Inconvenience is, that none of these Projects are yet brought to Perfection; and in the mean time, the whole Country lies miserably waste, the Houses in Ruins, and the People without Food or Cloaths. By all which, instead of being discouraged, they are Fifty Times more violently bent upon prosecuting their Schemes, driven equally on by Hope and Despair: That, as for himself, being not of an enterprizing Spirit, he was content to go on in the old Forms; to live in the Houses his Ancestors had built, and act as they did in every Part of Life without Innovation. That, some few other Persons of Quality and Gentry had done the same; but were looked on with an Eye of Contempt and ill Will, as Enemies to Art, ignorant, and ill Commonwealths-men, preferring their own Ease and Sloth before the general Improvement of their Country.

His Lordship added, that he would not by any further Particulars prevent the Pleasure I should certainly take in viewing the grand Academy, whither he was resolved I should go. He only desired me to observe a ruined Building upon the Side of a Mountain about three Miles distant, of which he gave me this Account. That he had a very convenient Mill within Half a Mile of his House, turned by a Current from a large River, and sufficient for his own Family as well as a great Number of his Tenants. That, about seven Years ago, a Club of those Projectors came to him with Proposals to destroy this Mill, and build another on the Side of that Mountain, on the long Ridge whereof a long Canal must be cut for a Repository of Water, to be conveyed up by Pipes and Engines to supply the Mill: Because the Wind and Air upon a Height agitated the Water, and thereby made it fitter for Motion: And because the Water descending down a Declivity would turn the Mill with half the Current of a River whose Course is more upon a Level. He said, that being then not very well with the Court, and pressed by many of his Friends, he complyed with the Proposal; and after employing an Hundred Men for two Years, the Work miscarryed, the Projectors went off, laying the Blame intirely upon him; railing at him ever since, and putting others upon the same Experiment, with equal Assurance of Success, as well as equal Disappointment.

In a few Days we came back to Town; and his Excellency, considering the bad Character he had in the Academy, would not go with me himself, but recommended me to a Friend of his to bear me Company thither. My Lord was pleased to represent me as a great Admirer of Projects, and a Person of much Curiosity and easy Belief; which indeed was not without Truth; for I had my self been a Sort of Projector in my younger Days.

CHAPTER V.

THE AUTHOR PERMITTED TO SEE THE GRAND ACADEMY
OF LAGADO. THE ACADEMY LARGELY DESCRIBED.
THE ARTS WHEREIN THE PROFESSORS
EMPLOY THEMSELVES.

THIS Academy is not an entire single Building, but a Continuation of several Houses on both Sides of a Street; which growing waste, was purchased and applyed to that Use.

I WAS received very kindly by the Warden, and went for many Days to the Academy. Every Room hath in it one or more Projectors; and I believe I could not be in fewer than five Hundred Rooms.

THE first Man I saw was of a meagre Aspect, with sooty Hands and Face, his Hair and Beard long, ragged and singed in several Places. His Clothes, Shirt, and Skin were all of the same Colour. He had been Eight Years upon a Project for extracting Sun-Beams out of Cucumbers, which were to be put into Vials hermetically sealed, and let out to warm the Air in raw inclement Summers. He told me, he did not doubt in Eight Years more, that he should be able to supply the Governors Gardens with Sun-shine at a reasonable Rate; but he complained that his Stock was low, and intreated me to give him something as an Encouragement to Ingenuity, especially since this had been a very dear Season for Cucumbers. I made him a small Present, for my Lord had furnished me with Money on purpose, because he knew their Practice of begging from all who go to see them.

I WENT into another Chamber, but was ready to hasten back, being almost overcome with a horrible Stink. My Conductor pressed me forward, conjuring me in a Whisper to give no Offence, which would be highly resented; and therefore I durst not so much as stop my Nose. The Projector of this Cell was the most ancient Student of the Academy. His Face and Beard were of a pale Yellow; his Hands and Clothes dawbed over with Filth. When I was presented to him, he gave me a very close Embrace, (a Compliment I could well have excused.) His Employment from his first coming into the Academy, was an Operation to reduce human Excrement to its original Food, by separating the several Parts, removing the Tincture which it receives from the Gall, making the Odour exhale, and scumming off the Saliva. He had a weekly Allowance from the Society, of a Vessel filled with human Ordure, about the Bigness of a *Bristol* Barrel.

I SAW another at work to calcine Ice into Gunpowder; who likewise shewed me a Treatise he had written concerning the Malleability of Fire, which he intended to publish.

THERE was a most ingenious Architect who had contrived a new Method for building Houses, by beginning at the Roof, and working downwards to the Foundation; which he justified to me by the like Practice of those two prudent Insects the Bee and the Spider.

THERE was a Man born blind, who had several Apprentices in his own Condition: Their Employment was to mix Colours for Painters, which their Master taught them to distinguish by feeling and smelling. It was indeed my Misfortune to find them at that Time not very perfect in their Lessons; and the Professor himself happened to be generally mistaken: This Artist is much encouraged and esteemed by the whole Fraternity.

IN another Apartment I was highly pleased with a Projector, who had found a Device of plowing the Ground with Hogs, to save the Charges of Plows, Cattle, and Labour. The Method is this: In an Acre of Ground you bury at six Inches Distance, and eight deep, a Quantity of Acorns, Dates, Chesnuts, and other Masts or Vegetables whereof these Animals are fondest; then you drive six Hundred or more of them into the Field, where in a few Days they will root up the whole Ground in search of their Food, and make it fit for sowing, at the same time manuring it with their Dung. It is true, upon Experiment they found the Charge and Trouble very great, and they had little or no Crop. However, it is not doubted that this Invention may be capable of great Improvement.

I WENT into another Room, where the Walls and Ceiling were all hung round with Cobwebs, except a narrow Passage for the Artist to go in and out. At my Entrance he called aloud to me not to disturb his Webs. He lamented the fatal Mistake the World had been so long in of using Silk-Worms, while we had such plenty of domestick Insects, who infinitely excelled the former, because they understood how to weave as well as spin. And he proposed farther, that by employing Spiders, the Charge of dying Silks would be wholly saved; whereof I was fully convinced when he shewed me a vast Number of Flies most beautifully coloured, wherewith he fed his Spiders; assuring us, that the Webs would take a Tincture from them; and as he had them of all Hues, he hoped to fit every Body's Fancy, as soon as he could find proper Food for the Flies, of certain Gums, Oyls, and other glutinous Matter, to give a Strength and Consistence to the Threads.

THERE was an Astronomer who had undertaken to place a Sun-Dial upon the great Weather-Cock on the Town-House, by adjusting the annual and diurnal Motions of the Earth and Sun, so as to answer and coincide with all accidental Turnings of the Wind.

I WAS complaining of a small Fit of the Cholick; upon

which my Conductor led me into a Room, where a great
Physician resided, who was famous for curing that Disease by contrary Operations from the same Instrument.
He had a large Pair of Bellows, with a long slender Muzzle
of Ivory. This he conveyed eight Inches up the Anus, and
drawing in the Wind, he affirmed he could make the Guts
as lank as a dried Bladder. But when the Disease was more
stubborn and violent, he let in the Muzzle while the Bellows
was full of Wind, which he discharged into the Body of the
Patient ; then withdrew the Instrument to replenish it, clapping his Thumb strongly against the Orifice of the Funda-
ment; and this being repeated three or four Times, the ad-
ventitious Wind would rush out, bringing the noxious along
with it (like Water put into a Pump) and the Patient recovers. I saw him try both Experiments upon a Dog, but
could not discern any Effect from the former. After the
latter, the Animal was ready to burst, and made so violent
a Discharge, as was very offensive to me and my Companions. The Dog died on the Spot, and we left the Doctor
endeavouring to recover him by the same Operation.

I visited many other Apartments, but shall not trouble
my Reader with all the Curiosities I observed, being studious of Brevity.

I had hitherto seen only one Side of the Academy, the
other being appropriated to the Advancers of speculative
Learning; of whom I shall say something when I have mentioned one illustrious Person more, who is called among
them *the universal Artist*. He told us, he had been Thirty
Years employing his Thoughts for the Improvement of
human Life. He had two large Rooms full of wonderful
Curiosities, and Fifty Men at work. Some were condensing
Air into a dry tangible Substance, by extracting the Nitre,
and letting the aqueous or fluid Particles percolate: Others
softening Marble for Pillows and Pin-cushions; others petri-
fying the Hoofs of a living Horse to preserve them from
foundring. The Artist himself was at that Time busy upon
two great Designs: The first, to sow Land with Chaff,
wherein he affirmed the true seminal Virtue to be contained,
as he demonstrated by several Experiments which I was not

skilful enough to comprehend. The other was, by a certain Composition of Gums, Minerals, and Vegetables outwardly applied, to prevent the Growth of Wool upon two young Lambs; and he hoped in a reasonable Time to propagate the Breed of naked Sheep all over the Kingdom.

WE crossed a Walk to the other Part of the Academy, where, as I have already said, the Projectors in speculative Learning resided.

THE first Professor I saw was in a very large Room, with Forty Pupils about him. After Salutation, observing me to look earnestly upon a Frame, which took up the greatest Part of both the Length and Breadth of the Room; he said, perhaps I might wonder to see him employed in a Project for improving speculative Knowledge by practical and mechanical Operations. But the World would soon be sensible of its Usefulness; and he flattered himself, that a more noble exalted Thought never sprang in any other Man's Head. Every one knew how laborious the usual Method is of attaining to Arts and Sciences; whereas by his Contrivance, the most ignorant Person at a reasonable Charge, and with a little bodily Labour, may write Books in Philosophy, Poetry, Politicks, Law, Mathematicks and Theology, without the least Assistance from Genius or Study. He then led me to the Frame, about the Sides whereof all his Pupils stood in Ranks. It was Twenty Foot square, placed in the Middle of the Room. The Superficies was composed of several Bits of Wood, about the Bigness of a Dye, but some larger than others. They were all linked together by slender Wires. These Bits of Wood were covered on every Square with Papers pasted on them; and on these Papers were written all the Words of their Language in their several Moods, Tenses, and Declensions, but without any Order. The Professor then desired me to observe, for he was going to set his Engine at work. The Pupils at his Command took each of them hold of an Iron Handle, whereof there were Forty fixed round the Edges of the Frame; and giving them a sudden Turn, the whole Disposition of the Words was entirely changed. He then commanded Six and Thirty of the Lads to read the several Lines softly as they appeared

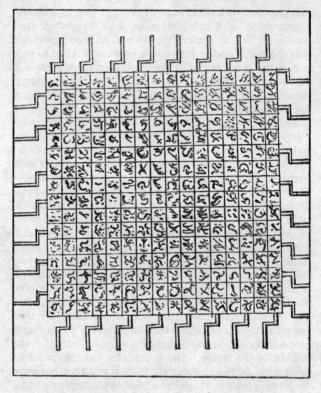

upon the Frame; and where they found three or four Words together that might make Part of a Sentence, they dictated to the four remaining Boys who were Scribes. This Work was repeated three or four Times, and at every Turn the Engine was so contrived, that the Words shifted into new Places, as the square Bits of Wood moved upside down.

SIX Hours a-Day the young Students were employed in this Labour; and the Professor shewed me several Volumes in large Folio already collected, of broken Sentences, which he intended to piece together; and out of those rich Materials to give the World a compleat Body of all Arts and Sciences;

which however might be still improved, and much ex-
pedited, if the Publick would raise a Fund for making and
employing five Hundred such Frames in *Lagado*, and oblige
the Managers to contribute in common their several Collections.

HE assured me, that this Invention had employed all his
Thoughts from his Youth; that he had emptyed the whole
Vocabulary into his Frame, and made the strictest Compu-
tation of the general Proportion there is in Books between
the Numbers of Particles, Nouns, and Verbs, and other
Parts of Speech.

I MADE my humblest Acknowledgments to this illustrious
Person for his great Communicativeness; and promised if
ever I had the good Fortune to return to my native Country,
that I would do him Justice, as the sole Inventor of this
wonderful Machine; the Form and Contrivance of which
I desired Leave to delineate upon Paper as in the Figure
here annexed. I told him, although it were the Custom of
our Learned in *Europe* to steal Inventions from each other,
who had thereby at least this Advantage, that it became a
Controversy which was the right Owner; yet I would take
such Caution, that he should have the Honour entire without a Rival.

WE next went to the School of Languages, where three
Professors sat in Consultation upon improving that of their
own Country.

THE first Project was to shorten Discourse by cutting
Polysyllables into one, and leaving out Verbs and Parti-
ciples; because in Reality all things imaginable are but
Nouns.

THE other, was a Scheme for entirely abolishing all Words
whatsoever: And this was urged as a great Advantage in
Point of Health as well as Brevity. For, it is plain, that
every Word we speak is in some Degree a Diminution of
our Lungs by Corrosion; and consequently contributes to
the shortning of our Lives. An Expedient was therefore
offered, that since Words are only Names for *Things*, it
would be more convenient for all Men to carry about them,
such *Things* as were necessary to express the particular Busi-

ness they are to discourse on. And this Invention would
certainly have taken Place, to the great Ease as well as
Health of the Subject, if the Women in Conjunction with
the Vulgar and Illiterate had not threatned to raise a Rebellion, unless they might be allowed the Liberty to speak
with their Tongues, after the Manner of their Forefathers:
Such constant irreconcileable Enemies to Science are the
common People. However, many of the most Learned and
Wise adhere to the new Scheme of expressing themselves by
Things; which hath only this Inconvenience attending it;
that if a Man's Business be very great, and of various Kinds,
he must be obliged in Proportion to carry a greater Bundle
of *Things* upon his Back, unless he can afford one or two
strong Servants to attend him. I have often beheld two of
those Sages almost sinking under the Weight of their Packs,
like Pedlars among us; who when they met in the Streets
would lay down their Loads, open their Sacks, and hold
Conversation for an Hour together; then put up their Implements, help each other to resume their Burthens, and
take their Leave.

But, for short Conversations a Man may carry Implements in his Pockets and under his Arms, enough to supply
him, and in his House he cannot be at a Loss; therefore the
Room where Company meet who practice this Art, is full
of all *Things* ready at Hand, requisite to furnish Matter for
this Kind of artificial Converse.

Another great Advantage proposed by this Invention,
was, that it would serve as an universal Language to be
understood in all civilized Nations, whose Goods and Utensils are generally of the same Kind, or nearly resembling,
so that their Uses might easily be comprehended. And thus,
Embassadors would be qualified to treat with foreign
Princes or Ministers of State, to whose Tongues they were
utter Strangers.

I was at the Mathematical School, where the Master
taught his Pupils after a Method scarce imaginable to us in
Europe. The Proposition and Demonstration were fairly
written on a thin Wafer, with Ink composed of a Cephalick
Tincture. This the Student was to swallow upon a fasting

Stomach, and for three Days following eat nothing but Bread and Water. As the Wafer digested, the Tincture mounted to his Brain, bearing the Proposition along with it. But the Success hath not hitherto been answerable, partly by some Error in the *Quantum* or Composition, and partly by the Perverseness of Lads; to whom this Bolus is so nauseous, that they generally steal aside, and discharge it upwards before it can operate; neither have they been yet persuaded to use so long an Abstinence as the Prescription requires.

CHAPTER VI.

A FURTHER ACCOUNT OF THE ACADEMY. THE AUTHOR
PROPOSETH SOME IMPROVEMENTS, WHICH ARE
HONOURABLY RECEIVED.

IN the School of political Projectors I was but ill entertained; the Professors appearing in my Judgment wholly out of their Senses; which is a Scene that never fails to make me melancholy. These unhappy People were proposing Schemes for persuading Monarchs to chuse Favourites upon the Score of their Wisdom, Capacity and Virtue; of teaching Ministers to consult the publick Good; of rewarding Merit, great Abilities, and eminent Services; of instructing Princes to know their true Interest, by placing it on the same Foundation with that of their People: Of chusing for Employments Persons qualified to exercise them; with many other wild impossible Chimæras, that never entered before into the Heart of Man to conceive; and confirmed in me the old Observation, that there is nothing so extravagant and irrational which some Philosophers have not maintained for Truth.

BUT, however I shall so far do Justice to this Part of the Academy, as to acknowledge that all of them were not so visionary. There was a most ingenious Doctor who seemed to be perfectly versed in the whole Nature and System of

Government. This illustrious Person had very usefully employed his Studies in finding out effectual Remedies for all Diseases and Corruptions, to which the several Kinds of publick Administration are subject by the Vices or Infirmities of those who govern, as well as by the Licentiousness of those who are to obey. For Instance: Whereas all Writers and Reasoners have agreed, that there is a strict universal Resemblance between the natural and the political Body; can there be any thing more evident, than that the Health of both must be preserved, and the Diseases cured by the same Prescriptions? It is allowed, that Senates and great Councils are often troubled with redundant, ebullient, and other peccant Humours; with many Diseases of the Head, and more of the Heart; with strong Convulsions, with grievous Contractions of the Nerves and Sinews in both Hands, but especially the Right: With Spleen, Flatus, Vertigoes and Deliriums; with scrophulous Tumours full of fœtid purulent Matter; with sower frothy Ructations; with Canine Appetites and Crudeness of Digestion; besides many others needless to mention. This Doctor therefore proposed, that upon the meeting of a Senate, certain Physicians should attend at the three first Days of their sitting, and at the Close of each Day's Debate, feel the Pulses of every Senator; after which having maturely considered, and consulted upon the Nature of the several Maladies, and the Methods of Cure; they should on the fourth Day return to the Senate-House, attended by their Apothecaries stored with proper Medicines; and before the Members sat, administer to each of them Lenitives, Aperitives, Abstersives, Corrosives, Restringents, Palliatives, Laxatives, Cephalalgicks, Ictericks, Apophlegmaticks, Acousticks, as their several Cases required; and according as these Medicines should operate, repeat, alter, or omit them at the next Meeting.

THIS Project could not be of any great Expence to the Publick; and might in my poor Opinion, be of much Use for the Dispatch of Business in those Countries where Senates have any Share in the legislative Power; beget Unanimity, shorten Debates, open a few Mouths which are now closed, and close many more which are now open; curb the Petulancy of the Young, and correct the Positiveness of the Old; rouze the Stupid, and damp the Pert.

AGAIN; Because it is a general Complaint that the Favourites of Princes are troubled with short and weak Memories; the same Doctor proposed, that whoever attended a first Minister, after having told his Business with the utmost Brevity, and in the plainest Words; should at his Departure give the said Minister a Tweak by the Nose, or a Kick in the Belly, or tread on his Corns, or lug him thrice by both Ears, or run a Pin into his Breech, or pinch his Arm black and blue; to prevent Forgetfulness: And at every Levee Day repeat the same Operation, till the Business were done or absolutely refused.

HE likewise directed, that every Senator in the great Council of a Nation, after he had delivered his Opinion, and argued in the Defence of it, should be obliged to give his Vote directly contrary; because if that were done, the Result would infallibly terminate in the Good of the Publick.

WHEN Parties in a State are violent, he offered a wonderful Contrivance to reconcile them. The Method is this. You take an Hundred Leaders of each Party; you dispose them into Couples of such whose Heads are nearest of a Size; then let two nice Operators saw off the *Occiput* of each Couple at the same Time, in such a Manner that the Brain may be equally divided. Let the *Occiputs* thus cut off be interchanged, applying each to the Head of his opposite Party-man. It seems indeed to be a Work that requireth some Exactness; but the Professor assured us, that if it were dextrously performed, the Cure would be infallible. For he argued thus; that the two half Brains being left to debate the Matter between themselves within the Space of one Scull, would soon come to a good Understanding, and produce that Moderation as well as Regularity of Thinking, so much to be wished for in the Heads of those, who imagine they came into the World only to watch and govern its Motion: And as to the Difference of Brains in Quantity or Quality, among those who are Directors in Faction; the

Doctor assured us from his own Knowledge, that it was a perfect Trifle.

I HEARD a very warm Debate between two Professors, about the most commodious and effectual Ways and Means of raising Money without grieving the Subject. The first affirmed, the justest Method would be to lay a certain Tax upon Vices and Folly; and the Sum fixed upon every Man, to be rated after the fairest Manner by a Jury of his Neighbours. The second was of an Opinion directly contrary; to tax those Qualities of Body and Mind for which Men chiefly value themselves; the Rate to be more or less according to the Degrees of excelling; the Decision whereof should be left entirely to their own Breast. The highest Tax was upon Men, who are the greatest Favourites of the other Sex; and the Assessments according to the Number and Natures of the Favours they have received; for which they are allowed to be their own Vouchers. Wit, Valour, and Politeness were likewise proposed to be largely taxed, and collected in the same Manner, by every Person giving his own Word for the Quantum of what he possessed. But, as to Honour, Justice, Wisdom and Learning, they should not be taxed at all; because, they are Qualifications of so singular a Kind, that no Man will either allow them in his Neighbour, or value them in himself.

THE Women were proposed to be taxed according to their Beauty and Skill in Dressing; wherein they had the same Privilege with the Men, to be determined by their own Judgment. But Constancy, Chastity, good Sense, and good Nature were not rated, because they would not bear the Charge of Collecting.

To keep Senators in the Interest of the Crown, it was proposed that the Members should raffle for Employments; every Man first taking an Oath, and giving Security that he would vote for the Court, whether he won or no; after which the Losers had in their Turn the Liberty of raffling upon the next Vacancy. Thus, Hope and Expectation would be kept alive; none would complain of broken Promises, but impute their Disappointments wholly to Fortune, whose Shoulders are broader and stronger than those of a Ministry.

ANOTHER Professor shewed me a large Paper of Instructions for discovering Plots and Conspiracies against the Government. He advised great Statesmen to examine into the Dyet of all suspected Persons; their Times of eating; upon which Side they lay in Bed; with which Hand they wiped their Posteriors; to take a strict View of their Excrements, and from the Colour, the Odour, the Taste, the Consistence, the Crudeness, or Maturity of Digestion, form a Judgment of their Thoughts and Designs: Because Men are never so serious, thoughtful, and intent, as when they are at Stool; which he found by frequent Experiment: For in such Conjunctures, when he used merely as a Trial to consider which was the best Way of murdering the King, his Ordure would have a Tincture of Green; but quite different when he thought only of raising an Insurrection, or burning the Metropolis.

THE whole Discourse was written with great Acuteness, containing many Observations both curious and useful for Politicians, but as I conceived not altogether compleat. This I ventured to tell the Author, and offered if he pleased to supply him with some Additions. He received my Proposition with more Compliance than is usual among Writers, especially those of the Projecting Species; professing he would be glad to receive farther Information.

I TOLD him, that in the Kingdom of *Tribnia*, by the Natives called *Langden*, where I had long sojourned, the Bulk of the People consisted wholly of Discoverers, Witnesses, Informers, Accusers, Prosecutors, Evidences, Swearers; together with their several subservient and subaltern Instruments; all under the Colours, the Conduct, and pay of Ministers and their Deputies. The Plots in that Kingdom are usually the Workmanship of those Persons who desire to raise their own Characters of profound Politicians; to restore new Vigour to a crazy Administration; to stifle or divert general Discontents; to fill their Coffers with Forfeitures; and raise or sink the Opinion of publick Credit, as either shall best answer their private Advantage. It is first agreed and settled among them, what suspected Persons shall be accused of a Plot: Then, effectual Care is taken to secure all their Letters and other Papers, and put the Owners in Chains. These Papers are delivered to a Set of Artists very dextrous in finding out the mysterious Meanings of Words, Syllables and Letters. For Instance, they can decypher a Close-stool to signify a Privy-Council; a Flock of Geese, a Senate; a lame Dog, an Invader; the Plague, a standing Army; a Buzard, a Minister; the Gout, a High Priest; a Gibbet, a Secretary of State; a Chamber pot, a Committee of Grandees; a Sieve, a Court Lady; a Broom, a Revolution; a Mouse-trap, an Employment; a bottomless Pit, the Treasury; a Sink, a C[our]t; a Cap and Bells, a Favourite; a broken Reed, a Court of Justice; an empty Tun, a General; a running Sore, the Administration.

WHEN this Method fails, they have two others more effectual; which the Learned among them call Acrosticks, and Anagrams. *First*, they can decypher all initial Letters into political Meanings: Thus, *N*, shall signify a Plot; *B*, a Regiment of Horse; *L*, a Fleet at Sea. Or, *secondly*, by transposing the Letters of the Alphabet, in any suspected Paper, they can lay open the deepest Designs of a discontented Party. So for Example, if I should say in a Letter to a Friend, *Our Brother* Tom *hath just got the Piles*; a Man of Skill in this Art would discover how the same Letters which compose that Sentence, may be analysed into the following Words; *Resist, —— a Plot is brought home —— The Tour*. And this is the Anagrammatick Method.

THE Professor made me great Acknowledgments for communicating these Observations, and promised to make honourable mention of me in his Treatise.

I SAW nothing in this Country that could invite me to a longer Continuance; and began to think of returning home to *England*.

CHAPTER V[II].

THE AUTHOR LEAVES LAGADO, ARRIVES AT MALDONADA.
NO SHIP READY. HE TAKES A SHORT VOYAGE TO GLUBB-
DUBDRIB. HIS RECEPTION BY THE GOVERNOR.

THE Continent of which this Kingdom is a part, extends itself, as I have Reason to believe, Eastward
to that unknown Tract of *America*, Westward of *California*, and North to the Pacifick Ocean, which is not above
an hundred and fifty Miles from *Lagado*; where there is a
good Port and much Commerce with the great Island of
Luggnagg; situated to the North-West about 29 Degrees
North Latitude, and 140 Longitude. This Island of *Luggnagg* stands South Eastwards of *Japan*, about an hundred
Leagues distant. There is a strict Alliance between the
Japanese Emperor and the King of *Luggnagg*, which affords
frequent Opportunities of sailing from one Island to the
other. I determined therefore to direct my Course this Way,
in order to my Return to *Europe*. I hired two Mules with a
Guide to shew me the Way, and carry my small Baggage.
I took leave of my noble Protector, who had shewn me
so much Favour, and made me a generous Present at my
Departure.

My Journey was without any Accident or Adventure
worth relating. When I arrived at the Port of *Maldonada*,
(for so it is called) there was no Ship in the Harbour bound
for *Luggnagg*, nor like to be in some Time. The Town is
about as large as *Portsmouth*. I soon fell into some Acquaintance, and was very hospitably received. A Gentleman of Distinction said to me, that since the Ships bound
for *Luggnagg* could not be ready in less than a Month, it
might be no disagreeable Amusement for me to take a Trip
to the little Island of *Glubbdubdrib*, about five Leagues off
to the South-West. He offered himself and a Friend to

accompany me, and that I should be provided with a small convenient Barque for the Voyage.

GLUBBDUBDRIB, as nearly as I can interpret the Word, signifies the Island of *Sorcerers* or *Magicians*. It is about one third as large as the Isle of *Wight*, and extreamly fruitful: It is governed by the Head of a certain Tribe, who are all Magicians. This Tribe marries only among each other; and the eldest in Succession is Prince or Governor. He hath a noble Palace, and a Park of about three thousand Acres, surrounded by a Wall of hewn Stone twenty Foot high. In this Park are several small Inclosures for Cattle, Corn and Gardening.

THE Governor and his Family are served and attended by Domesticks of a Kind somewhat unusual. By his Skill in Necromancy, he hath Power of calling whom he pleaseth from the Dead, and commanding their Service for twenty four Hours, but no longer; nor can he call the same Persons up again in less than three Months, except upon very extraordinary Occasions.

WHEN we arrived at the Island, which was about Eleven in the Morning, one of the Gentlemen who accompanied me, went to the Governor, and desired Admittance for a Stranger, who came on purpose to have the Honour of attending on his Highness. This was immediately granted, and we all three entered the Gate of the Palace between two Rows of Guards, armed and dressed after a very antick Manner, and something in their Countenances that made my Flesh creep with a Horror I cannot express. We passed through several Apartments between Servants of the same Sort, ranked on each Side as before, till we came to the Chamber of Presence, where after three profound Obeysances, and a few general Questions, we were permitted to sit on three Stools near the lowest Step of his Highness's Throne. He understood the Language of *Balnibarbi*, although it were different from that of his Island. He desired me to give him some Account of my Travels; and to let me see that I should be treated without Ceremony, he dismissed all his Attendants with a Turn of his Finger, at which to my great Astonishment they vanished in an Instant, like

Visions in a Dream, when we awake on a sudden. I could not recover myself in some Time, till the Governor assured me that I should receive no Hurt; and observing my two Companions to be under no Concern, who had been often entertained in the same Manner, I began to take Courage; and related to his Highness a short History of my several Adventures, yet not without some Hesitation, and frequently looking behind me to the Place where I had seen those domestick Spectres. I had the Honour to dine with the Governor, where a new Set of Ghosts served up the Meat, and waited at Table. I now observed myself to be less terrified than I had been in the Morning. I stayed till Sun-set, but humbly desired his Highness to excuse me for not accepting his Invitation of lodging in the Palace. My two Friends and I lay at a private House in the Town adjoining, which is the Capital of this little Island; and the next Morning we returned to pay our Duty to the Governor, as he was pleased to command us.

AFTER this Manner we continued in the Island for ten Days, most Part of every Day with the Governor, and at Night in our Lodging. I soon grew so familiarized to the Sight of Spirits, that after the third or fourth Time they gave me no Emotion at all; or if I had any Apprehensions left, my Curiosity prevailed over them. For his Highness the Governor ordered me to call up whatever Persons I would chuse to name, and in whatever Numbers among all the Dead from the Beginning of the World to the present Time, and command them to answer any Questions I should think fit to ask; with this Condition, that my Questions must be confined within the Compass of the Times they lived in. And one Thing I might depend upon, that they would certainly tell me Truth; for Lying was a Talent of no Use in the lower World.

I MADE my humble Acknowledgments to his Highness for so great a Favour. We were in a Chamber, from whence there was a fair Prospect into the Park. And because my first Inclination was to be entertained with Scenes of Pomp and Magnificence, I desired to see *Alexander* the Great, at the Head of his Army just after the Battle of *Arbela*;

which upon a Motion of the Governor's Finger immediately appeared in a large Field under the Window, where we stood. *Alexander* was called up into the Room: It was with great Difficulty that I understood his *Greek*, and had but little of my own. He assured me upon his Honour that he was not poisoned, but dyed of a Fever by excessive Drinking.

Next I saw *Hannibal* passing the *Alps*, who told me he had not a Drop of Vinegar in his Camp.

I saw *Cæsar* and *Pompey* at the Head of their Troops just ready to engage. I saw the former in his last great Triumph. I desired that the Senate of *Rome* might appear before me in one large Chamber, and a modern Representative, in Counterview, in another. The first seemed to be an Assembly of Heroes and Demy-Gods; the other a Knot of Pedlars, Pick-pockets, Highwaymen and Bullies.

The Governor at my Request gave the Sign for *Cæsar* and *Brutus* to advance towards us. I was struck with a profound Veneration at the Sight of *Brutus*; and could easily discover the most consummate Virtue, the greatest Intrepidity, and Firmness of Mind, the truest Love of his Country, and general Benevolence for Mankind in every Lineament of his Countenance. I observed with much Pleasure, that these two Persons were in good Intelligence with each other; and *Cæsar* freely confessed to me, that the greatest Actions of his own Life were not equal by many Degrees to the Glory of taking it away. I had the Honour to have much Conversation with *Brutus*; and was told that his Ancestor *Junius, Socrates, Epaminondas, Cato* the Younger, Sir *Thomas More* and himself, were perpetually together: A *Sextumvirate* to which all the Ages of the World cannot add a Seventh.

It would be tedious to trouble the Reader with relating what vast Numbers of illustrious Persons were called up, to gratify that insatiable Desire I had to see the World in every Period of Antiquity placed before me. I chiefly fed my Eyes with beholding the Destroyers of Tyrants and Usurpers, and the Restorers of Liberty to oppressed and injured Nations. But it is impossible to express the Satisfaction I received in my own Mind, after such a Manner as to make it a suitable Entertainment to the Reader.

CHAPTER VIII.

A FURTHER ACCOUNT OF GLUBBDUBDRIB. ANTIENT AND MODERN HISTORY CORRECTED.

HAVING a Desire to see those Antients, who were most renowned for Wit and Learning, I set apart one Day on purpose. I proposed that *Homer* and *Aristotle* might appear at the Head of all their Commentators; but these were so numerous, that some Hundreds were forced to attend in the Court and outward Rooms of the Palace. I knew and could distinguish those two Heroes at first Sight, not only from the Croud, but from each other. *Homer* was the taller and comelier Person of the two, walked very erect for one of his Age, and his Eyes were the most quick and piercing I ever beheld. *Aristotle* stooped much, and made use of a Staff. His Visage was meager, his Hair lank and thin, and his Voice hollow. I soon discovered, that both of them were perfect Strangers to the rest of the Company, and had never seen or heard of them before. And I had a Whisper from a Ghost, who shall be nameless, that these Commentators always kept in the most distant Quarters from their Principals in the lower World, through a Consciousness of Shame and Guilt, because they had so horribly misrepresented the Meaning of those Authors to Posterity. I introduced *Didymus* and *Eustathius* to *Homer*, and prevailed on him to treat them better than perhaps they deserved; for he soon found they wanted a Genius to enter into the Spirit of a Poet. But *Aristotle* was out of all Patience with the Account I gave him of *Scotus* and *Ramus*, as I presented them to him; and he asked them whether the rest of the Tribe were as great Dunces as themselves.

I THEN desired the Governor to call up *Descartes* and *Gassendi*, with whom I prevailed to explain their Systems to *Aristotle*. This great Philosopher freely acknowledged his own Mistakes in Natural Philosophy, because he proceeded in many things upon Conjecture, as all Men must do; and he found, that *Gassendi*, who had made the Doctrine of *Epicurus* as palatable as he could, and the *Vortices* of *Descartes*, were equally exploded. He predicted the same Fate to *Attraction*, whereof the present Learned are such zealous Asserters. He said, that new Systems of Nature were but new Fashions, which would vary in every Age; and even those who pretend to demonstrate them from Mathematical Principles, would flourish but a short Period of Time, and be out of Vogue when that was determined.

I SPENT five Days in conversing with many others of the antient Learned. I saw most of the first *Roman* Emperors. I prevailed on the Governor to call up *Eliogabalus's* Cooks to dress us a Dinner; but they could not shew us much of their Skill, for want of Materials. A *Helot* of *Agesilaus* made us a Dish of *Spartan* Broth, but I was not able to get down a second Spoonful.

THE two Gentlemen who conducted me to the Island were pressed by their private Affairs to return in three Days, which I employed in seeing some of the modern Dead, who had made the greatest Figure for two or three Hundred Years past in our own and other Countries of *Europe*; and having been always a great Admirer of old illustrious Families, I desired the Governor would call up a Dozen or two of Kings with their Ancestors in order, for eight or nine Generations. But my Disappointment was grievous and unexpected. For, instead of a long Train with Royal Diadems, I saw in one Family two Fidlers, three spruce Courtiers, and an *Italian* Prelate. In another, a Barber, an Abbot, and two Cardinals. I have too great a Veneration for crowned Heads to dwell any longer on so nice a Subject: But as to Counts, Marquesses, Dukes, Earls, and the like, I was not so scrupulous. And I confess it was not without some Pleasure that I found my self able to trace the particular Features, by which certain Families are distinguished up to their Originals. I could plainly discover from whence one Family derives a long Chin; why a second hath abounded with Knaves for two Generations, and Fools for two more; why a third happened to be crack-brained, and a fourth to be Sharpers. Whence it came, what *Polydore Virgil* says of a certain great House, *Nec Vir fortis, nec Fæmina Casta.* How Cruelty, Falshood, and Cowardice grew to be Characteristicks by which certain Families are distinguished as much as by their Coat of Arms. Who first brought the Pox into a noble House, which hath lineally descended in scrophulous Tumours to their Posterity. Neither could I wonder at all this, when I saw such an Interruption of Lineages by Pages, Lacqueys, Valets, Coachmen, Gamesters, Fidlers, Players, Captains, and Pickpockets.

I WAS chiefly disgusted with modern History. For having strictly examined all the Persons of greatest Name in the Courts of Princes for an Hundred Years past, I found how the World had been misled by prostitute Writers, to ascribe the greatest Exploits in War to Cowards, the wisest Counsel to Fools, Sincerity to Flatterers, *Roman* Virtue to Betrayers of their Country, Piety to Atheists, Chastity to Sodomites, Truth to Informers. How many innocent and excellent Persons had been condemned to Death or Banishment, by the practising of great Ministers upon the Corruption of Judges, and the Malice of Factions. How many Villains had been exalted to the highest Places of Trust, Power, Dignity, and Profit: How great a Share in the Motions and Events of Courts, Councils, and Senates might be challenged by Bawds, Whores, Pimps, Parasites, and Buffoons: How low an Opinion I had of human Wisdom and Integrity, when I was truly informed of the Springs and Motives of great Enterprizes and Revolutions in the World, and of the contemptible Accidents to which they owed their Success.

HERE I discovered the Roguery and Ignorance of those who pretend to write *Anecdotes,* or secret History; who send so many Kings to their Graves with a Cup of Poison; will repeat the Discourse between a Prince and chief Minister, where no Witness was by; unlock the Thoughts and Cabinets

of Embassadors and Secretaries of State; and have the perpetual Misfortune to be mistaken. Here I discovered the
true Causes of many great Events that have surprized the
World: How a Whore can govern the Back-stairs, the Back-
stairs a Council, and the Council a Senate. A General confessed in my Presence that he got a Victory purely by the
Force of Cowardice and ill Conduct: And an Admiral, that
for want of proper Intelligence, he beat the Enemy to whom
he intended to betray the Fleet. Three Kings protested to
me, that in their whole Reigns they did never once prefer
any Person of Merit, unless by Mistake or Treachery of
some Minister in whom they confided: Neither would they
do it if they were to live again; and they shewed with great
Strength of Reason, that the Royal Throne could not be
supported without Corruption; because, that positive, confident, restive Temper, which Virtue infused into Man, was
a perpetual Clog to publick Business.

I HAD the Curiosity to enquire in a particular Manner,
by what Method great Numbers had procured to themselves high Titles of Honour, and prodigious Estates; and
I confined my Enquiry to a very modern Period: However,
without grating upon present Times, because I would be
sure to give no Offence even to Foreigners (for I hope the
Reader need not be told that I do not in the least intend
my own Country in what I say upon this Occasion) a great
Number of Persons concerned were called up, and upon a
very slight Examination, discovered such a Scene of Infamy, that I cannot reflect upon it without some Serious-
ness. Perjury, Oppression, Subornation, Fraud, Pandarism,
and the like *Infirmities* were amongst the most excusable
Arts they had to mention; and for these I gave, as it was
reasonable, due Allowance. But when some confessed, they
owed their Greatness and Wealth to Sodomy or Incest;
others to the prostituting of their own Wives and Daughters;
others to the betraying their Country or their Prince; some
to poisoning, more to the perverting of Justice in order to
destroy the Innocent: I hope I may be pardoned if these
Discoveries inclined me a little to abate of that profound
Veneration which I am naturally apt to pay to Persons of

high Rank, who ought to be treated with the utmost Respect due to their sublime Dignity, by us their Inferiors.

I HAD often read of some great Services done to Princes and States, and desired to see the Persons by whom those Services were performed. Upon Enquiry I was told, that their Names were to be found on no Record, except a few of them whom History hath represented as the vilest Rogues and Traitors. As to the rest, I had never once heard of them. They all appeared with dejected Looks, and in the meanest Habit; most of them telling me they died in Poverty and Disgrace, and the rest on a Scaffold or a Gibbet.

AMONG others there was one Person whose Case appeared a little singular. He had a Youth about Eighteen Years old standing by his Side. He told me, he had for many Years been Commander of a Ship; and in the Sea Fight at *Actium*, had the good Fortune to break through the Enemy's great Line of Battle, sink three of their Capital Ships, and take a fourth, which was the sole Cause of *Antony*'s Flight, and of the Victory that ensued: That the Youth standing by him, his only Son, was killed in the Action. He added, that upon the Confidence of some Merit, the War being at an End, he went to *Rome*, and solicited at the Court of *Augustus* to be preferred to a greater Ship, whose Commander had been killed; but without any regard to his Pretensions, it was given to a Boy who had never seen the Sea, the Son of a *Libertina*, who waited on one of the Emperor's Mistresses. Returning back to his own Vessel, he was charged with Neglect of Duty, and the Ship given to a favourite Page of *Publicola* the Vice-Admiral; whereupon he retired to a poor Farm, at a great Distance from *Rome*, and there ended his Life. I was so curious to know the Truth of this Story, that I desired *Agrippa* might be called, who was Admiral in that Fight. He appeared, and confirmed the whole Account, but with much more Advantage to the Captain, whose Modesty had extenuated or concealed a great Part of his Merit.

I WAS surprized to find Corruption grown so high and so quick in that Empire, by the Force of Luxury so lately introduced; which made me less wonder at many parallel

Cases in other Countries, where Vices of all Kinds have reigned so much longer, and where the whole Praise as well as Pillage hath been engrossed by the chief Commander, who perhaps had the least Title to either.

As every Person called up made exactly the same Appearance he had done in the World, it gave me melancholy Reflections to observe how much the Race of human Kind was degenerate among us, within these Hundred Years past. How the Pox under all its Consequences and Denominations had altered every Lineament of an *English* Countenance; shortened the Size of Bodies, unbraced the Nerves, relaxed the Sinews and Muscles, introduced a sallow Complexion, and rendered the Flesh loose and *rancid*.

I DESCENDED so low as to desire that some *English* Yeomen of the old Stamp, might be summoned to appear; once so famous for the Simplicity of their Manners, Dyet and Dress; for Justice in their Dealings; for their true Spirit of Liberty; for their Valour and Love of their Country. Neither could I be wholly unmoved after comparing the Living with the Dead, when I considered how all these pure native Virtues were prostituted for a Piece of Money by their Grand-children; who in selling their Votes, and managing at Elections have acquired every Vice and Corruption that can possibly be learned in a Court.

CHAPTER IX.

THE AUTHOR'S RETURN TO MALDONADA. SAILS TO THE KINGDOM OF LUGGNAGG. THE AUTHOR CONFINED. HE IS SENT FOR TO COURT. THE MANNER OF HIS ADMITTANCE. THE KING'S GREAT LENITY TO HIS SUBJECTS.

THE Day of our Departure being come, I took leave of his Highness the Governor of *Glubbdubdrib*, and returned with my two Companions to *Maldonada*, where after a Fortnight's waiting, a Ship was ready to sail for *Luggnagg*. The two Gentlemen and some others were so generous and kind as to furnish me with Provisions, and see me on Board. I was a Month in this Voyage. We had one violent Storm, and were under a Necessity of steering Westward to get into the Trade-Wind, which holds for above sixty Leagues. On the 21st of *April*, 1708, we sailed in the River of *Clumegnig*, which is a Sea-port Town, at the South-East Point of *Luggnagg*. We cast Anchor within a League of the Town, and made a Signal for a Pilot. Two of them came on Board in less than half an Hour, by whom we were guided between certain Shoals and Rocks, which are very dangerous in the Passage, to a large Basin, where a Fleet may ride in Safety within a Cable's Length of the Town-Wall.

SOME of our Sailors, whether out of Treachery or Inadvertence, had informed the Pilots that I was a Stranger and a great Traveller, whereof these gave Notice to a Custom-House Officer, by whom I was examined very strictly upon my landing. This Officer spoke to me in the Language of *Balnibarbi*, which by the Force of much Commerce is generally understood in that Town, especially by Seamen, and those employed in the Customs. I gave him a short Account of some Particulars, and made my Story as plausible and consistent as I could; but I thought it necessary to disguise my Country, and call my self a *Hollander*; because my Intentions were for *Japan*, and I knew the *Dutch* were the only *Europeans* permitted to enter into that Kingdom. I therefore told the Officer, that having been shipwrecked on the Coast of *Balnibarbi*, and cast on a Rock, I was received up into *Laputa*, or the flying Island (of which he had often heard) and was now endeavouring to get to *Japan*, from whence I might find a Convenience of returning to my own Country. The Officer said, I must be confined till he could receive Orders from Court, for which he would write immediately, and hoped to receive an Answer in a Fortnight. I was carried to a convenient Lodging, with a Centry placed at the Door; however I had the Liberty of a large Garden, and was treated with Humanity enough, being maintained all the Time at the King's Charge. I was invited by several Persons, chiefly out of Curiosity, because it was reported

I came from Countries very remote, of which they had never heard.

I HIRED a young Man who came in the same Ship to be an Interpreter; he was a Native of *Luggnagg*, but had lived some Years at *Maldonada*, and was a perfect Master of both Languages. By his Assistance I was able to hold a Conversation with those that came to visit me; but this consisted only of their Questions and my Answers.

THE Dispatch came from Court about the Time we expected. It contained a Warrant for conducting me and my Retinue to *Traldragdubh* or *Trildrogdrib*, (for it is pronounced both Ways as near as I can remember) by a Party of Ten Horse. All my Retinue was that poor Lad for an Interpreter, whom I persuaded into my Service. At my humble Request we had each of us a Mule to ride on. A Messenger was dispatched half a Day's Journey before us, to give the King Notice of my Approach, and to desire that his Majesty would please to appoint a Day and Hour, when it would be his gracious Pleasure that I might have the Honour to *lick the Dust before his Footstool.* This is the Court Style, and I found it to be more than Matter of Form: For upon my Admittance two Days after my Arrival, I was commanded to crawl upon my Belly, and lick the Floor as I advanced; but on account of my being a Stranger, Care was taken to have it so clean that the Dust was not offensive. However, this was a peculiar Grace, not allowed to any but Persons of the highest Rank, when they desire an Admittance: Nay, sometimes the Floor is strewed with Dust on purpose, when the Person to be admitted happens to have powerful Enemies at Court: And I have seen a great Lord with his Mouth so crammed, that when he had crept to the proper Distance from the Throne, he was not able to speak a Word. Neither is there any Remedy, because it is capital for those who receive an Audience to spit or wipe their Mouths in his Majesty's Presence. There is indeed another Custom, which I cannot altogether approve of. When the King hath a Mind to put any of his Nobles to Death in a gentle indulgent Manner; he commands to have the Floor strowed with a certain brown

Powder, of a deadly Composition, which being licked up infallibly kills him in twenty-four Hours. But in Justice to this Prince's great Clemency, and the Care he hath of his Subjects Lives, (wherein it were much to be wished that the Monarchs of *Europe* would imitate him) it must be mentioned for his Honour, that strict Orders are given to have the infected Parts of the Floor well washed after every such Execution; which if his Domesticks neglect, they are in Danger of incurring his Royal Displeasure. I my self heard him give Directions, that one of his Pages should be whipt, whose Turn it was to give Notice about washing the Floor after an Execution, but maliciously had omitted it; by which Neglect a young Lord of great Hopes coming to an Audience, was unfortunately poisoned, although the King at that Time had no Design against his Life. But this good Prince was so gracious, as to forgive the Page his Whipping, upon Promise that he would do so no more, without special Orders.

To return from this Digression; when I had crept within four Yards of the Throne, I raised my self gently upon my Knees, and then striking my Forehead seven Times against the Ground, I pronounced the following Words, as they had been taught me the Night before, *Ickpling Gloffthrobb Squutserumm blhiop Mlashnalt Zwin tnodbalkguffh Slhiophad Gurdlubh Asht.* This is the Compliment established by the Laws of the Land for all Persons admitted to the King's Presence. It may be rendered into *English* thus: *May your cælestial Majesty out-live the Sun, eleven Moons and an half.* To this the King returned some Answer, which although I could not understand, yet I replied as I had been directed; *Fluft drin Yalerick Dwuldum prastrad mirplush,* which properly signifies, *My Tongue is in the Mouth of my Friend*; and by this Expression was meant that I desired leave to bring my Interpreter; whereupon the young Man already mentioned was accordingly introduced; by whose Intervention I answered as many Questions as his Majesty could put in above an Hour. I spoke in the *Balnibarbian* Tongue, and my Interpreter delivered my Meaning in that of *Luggnagg.*

THE King was much delighted with my Company, and ordered his *Bliffmarklub* or High Chamberlain to appoint a Lodging in the Court for me and my Interpreter, with a daily Allowance for my Table, and a large Purse of Gold for my common Expences.

I STAYED three Months in this Country out of perfect Obedience to his Majesty, who was pleased highly to favour me, and made me very honourable Offers. But I thought it more consistent with Prudence and Justice to pass the Remainder of my Days with my Wife and Family.

CHAPTER X.

THE LUGGNUGGIANS COMMENDED. A PARTICULAR DE-
SCRIPTION OF THE STRULDBRUGS, WITH MANY CON-
VERSATIONS BETWEEN THE AUTHOR AND SOME EMINENT
PERSONS UPON THAT SUBJECT.

THE *Luggnuggians* are a polite and generous People, and although they are not without some Share of that Pride which is peculiar to all *Eastern* Countries, yet they shew themselves courteous to Strangers, especially such who are countenanced by the Court. I had many Acquaintance among Persons of the best Fashion, and being always attended by my Interpreter, the Conversation we had was not disagreeable.

ONE Day in much good Company, I was asked by a Person of Quality, whether I had seen any of their *Struldbrugs* or *Immortals*. I said I had not; and desired he would explain to me what he meant by such an Appellation, applyed to a mortal Creature. He told me, that sometimes, although very rarely, a Child happened to be born in a Family with a red circular Spot in the Forehead, directly over the left Eye-brow, which was an infallible Mark that it should never dye. The Spot, as he described it, was about the Compass of a Silver Threepence, but in the Course of Time grew larger, and changed its Colour; for at Twelve Years old it became green, so continued till Five and Twenty, then turned to a deep blue; at Five and Forty it grew coal black, and as large as an *English* Shilling; but never admitted any farther Alteration. He said these Births were so rare, that he did not believe there could be above Eleven Hundred *Struldbrugs* of both Sexes in the whole Kingdom, of which he computed about Fifty in the Metropolis, and among the rest a young Girl born about three Years ago. That, these Productions were not peculiar to any Family, but a meer Effect of Chance; and the Children of the *Struldbruggs* themselves, were equally mortal with the rest of the People.

I FREELY own myself to have been struck with inexpressible Delight upon hearing this Account: And the Person who gave it me happening to understand the *Balnibarbian* Language, which I spoke very well, I could not forbear breaking out into Expressions perhaps a little too extravagant. I cryed out as in a Rapture; Happy Nation, where every Child hath at least a Chance for being immortal! Happy People who enjoy so many living Examples of antient Virtue, and have Masters ready to instruct them in the Wisdom of all former Ages! But, happiest beyond all Comparison are those excellent *Struldbruggs*, who being born exempt from that universal Calamity of human Nature, have their Minds free and disingaged, without the Weight and Depression of Spirits caused by the continual Apprehension of Death. I discovered my Admiration that I had not observed any of these illustrious Persons at Court; the black Spot on the Fore-head, being so remarkable a Distinction, that I could not have easily overlooked it: And it was impossible that his Majesty, a most judicious Prince, should not provide himself with a good Number of such wise and able Counsellors. Yet perhaps the Virtue of those Reverend Sages was too strict for the corrupt and libertine Manners of a Court. And we often find by Experience, that young Men are too opinionative and volatile to be guided by the sober Dictates of their Seniors. However, since the King was pleased to allow me Access to his Royal Person, I was resolved upon the very first Occasion to deliver my Opinion to him on this Matter freely, and at large by the Help of my Interpreter; and whether he would please to take my Advice or no, yet in one Thing I was determined, that his Majesty having frequently offered me an Establishment in this Country, I would with great Thankfulness accept the Favour, and pass my Life here in the Conversation of those superiour Beings the *Struldbruggs*, if they would please to admit me.

THE Gentleman to whom I addressed my Discourse, because (as I have already observed) he spoke the Language of *Balnibarbi*, said to me with a Sort of a Smile, which usually ariseth from Pity to the Ignorant, that he was glad of any Occasion to keep me among them, and desired my Permission to explain to the Company what I had spoke. He did so; and they talked together for some time in their own Language, whereof I understood not a Syllable, neither could I observe by their Countenances what Impression my Discourse had made on them. After a short Silence, the same Person told me, that his Friends and mine (so he thought fit to express himself) were very much pleased with the judicious Remarks I had made on the great Happiness and Advantages of immortal Life; and they were desirous to know in a particular Manner, what Scheme of Living I should have formed to myself, it it had fallen to my Lot to have been born a *Struldbrugg*.

I ANSWERED, it was easy to be eloquent on so copious and delightful a Subject, especially to me who have been often apt to amuse myself with Visions of what I should do if I were a King, a General, or a great Lord: And upon this very Case I had frequently run over the whole System how I should employ myself, and pass the Time if I were sure to live for ever.

THAT, if it had been my good Fortune to come into the World a *Struldbrugg*; as soon as I could discover my own Happiness by understanding the Difference between Life and Death, I would first resolve by all Arts and Methods whatsoever to procure myself Riches: In the Pursuit of which, by Thrift and Management, I might reasonably expect in about two Hundred Years, to be the wealthiest Man in the Kingdom. In the second Place, I would from my earliest Youth apply myself to the Study of Arts and Sciences, by which I should arrive in time to excel all others in Learning. Lastly, I would carefully record every Action and Event of Consequence that happened in the Publick, impartially draw the Characters of the several Successions of Princes, and great Ministers of State; with my own Observations on every Point. I would exactly set down the several Changes in Customs, Languages, Fashions of Dress, Dyet and Diversions. By all which Acquirements, I should be a living Treasury of Knowledge and Wisdom, and certainly become the Oracle of the Nation.

I WOULD never marry after Threescore, but live in an hospitable Manner, yet still on the saving Side. I would entertain myself in forming and directing the Minds of hopeful young Men, by convincing them from my own Remembrance, Experience and Observation, fortified by numerous Examples, of the Usefulness of Virtue in publick and private Life. But, my choise and constant Companions should be a Sett of my own immortal Brotherhood, among whom I would elect a Dozen from the most ancient down to my own Contemporaries. Where any of these wanted Fortunes, I would provide them with convenient Lodges round my own Estate, and have some of them always at my Table, only mingling a few of the most valuable among you Mortals, whom Length of Time would harden me to lose with little or no Reluctance, and treat your Posterity after the same Manner; just as a Man diverts himself with the annual Succession of Pinks and Tulips in his Garden, without regretting the Loss of those which withered the preceding Year.

THESE *Struldbruggs* and I would mutually communicate our Observations and Memorials through the Course of Time; remark the several Gradations by which Corruption steals into the World, and oppose it in every Step, by giving perpetual Warning and Instruction to Mankind; which, added to the strong Influence of our own Example, would probably prevent that continual Degeneracy of human Nature, so justly complained of in all Ages.

ADD to all this, the Pleasure of seeing the various Revolu-

H

tions of States and Empires; the Changes in the lower and upper World; antient Cities in Ruins, and obscure Villages become the Seats of Kings. Famous Rivers lessening into shallow Brooks; the Ocean leaving one Coast dry, and overwhelming another: The Discovery of many Countries yet unknown. Barbarity over-running the politest Nations, and the most barbarous becoming civilized. I should then see the Discovery of the *Longitude*, the *perpetual Motion*, the *universal Medicine*, and many other great Inventions brought to the utmost Perfection.

WHAT wonderful Discoveries should we make in Astronomy, by outliving and confirming our own Predictions; by observing the Progress and Returns of Comets, with the Changes of Motion in the Sun, Moon and Stars.

I ENLARGED upon many other Topicks, which the natural Desire of endless Life and sublunary Happiness could easily furnish me with. When I had ended, and the Sum of my Discourse had been interpreted as before, to the rest of the Company, there was a good Deal of Talk among them in the Language of the Country, not without some Laughter at my Expence. At last the same Gentleman who had been my Interpreter, said, he was desired by the rest to set me right in a few Mistakes, which I had fallen into through the common Imbecility of human Nature, and upon that Allowance was less answerable for them. That, this Breed of *Struldbruggs* was peculiar to their Country, for there were no such People either in *Balnibarbi* or *Japan*, where he had the Honour to be Embassador from his Majesty, and found the Natives in both those Kingdoms very hard to believe that the Fact was possible; and it appeared from my Astonishment when he first mentioned the Matter to me, that I received it as a Thing wholly new, and scarcely to be credited. That in the two Kingdoms above-mentioned, where during his Residence he had conversed very much, he observed long Life to be the universal Desire and Wish of Mankind. That, whoever had one Foot in the Grave, was sure to hold back the other as strongly as he could. That the oldest had still Hopes of living one Day longer, and looked on Death as the greatest Evil, from which Nature always prompted him to retreat; only in this Island of *Lugg-nagg*, the Appetite for living was not so eager, from the continual Example of the *Struldbruggs* before their Eyes.

THAT the System of Living contrived by me was unreasonable and unjust, because it supposed a Perpetuity of Youth, Health, and Vigour, which no Man could be so foolish to hope, however extravagant he might be in his Wishes. That, the Question therefore was not whether a Man would chuse to be always in the Prime of Youth, attended with Prosperity and Health; but how he would pass a perpetual Life under all the usual Disadvantages which old Age brings along with it. For although few Men will avow their Desires of being immortal upon such hard Conditions, yet in the two Kingdoms beforementioned of *Balnibarbi* and *Japan*, he observed that every Man desired to put off Death for sometime longer, let it approach ever so late; and he rarely heard of any Man who died willingly, except he were incited by the Extremity of Grief or Torture. And he appealed to me whether in those Countries I had travelled as well as my own, I had not observed the same general Disposition.

AFTER this Preface, he gave me a particular Account of the *Struldbruggs* among them. He said they commonly acted like Mortals, till about Thirty Years old, after which by Degrees they grew melancholy and dejected, increasing in both till they came to Fourscore. This he learned from their own Confession; for otherwise there not being above two or three of that Species born in an Age, they were too few to form a general Observation by. When they came to Fourscore Years, which is reckoned the Extremity of living in this Country, they had not only all the Follies and Infirmities of other old Men, but many more which arose from the dreadful Prospect of never dying. They were not only opinionative, peevish, covetous, morose, vain, talkative; but uncapable of Friendship, and dead to all natural Affection, which never descended below their Grand-children. Envy and impotent Desires, are their prevailing Passions. But those Objects against which their Envy seems principally directed, are the Vices of the younger Sort, and the

Deaths of the old. By reflecting on the former, they find
themselves cut off from all Possibility of Pleasure; and
whenever they see a Funeral, they lament and repine that
others are gone to an Harbour of Rest, to which they themselves never can hope to arrive. They have no Remembrance of any thing but what they learned and observed in
their Youth and middle Age, and even that is very imperfect: And for the Truth or Particulars of any Fact, it is safer
to depend on common Traditions than upon their best Re-
collections. The least miserable among them, appear to be
those who turn to Dotage, and entirely lose their Memories;
these meet with more Pity and Assistance, because they
want many bad Qualities which abound in others.

IF a *Struldbrugg* happen to marry one of his own Kind,
the Marriage is dissolved of Course by the Courtesy of the
Kingdom, as soon as the younger of the two comes to be
Fourscore. For the Law thinks it a reasonable Indulgence,
that those who are condemned without any Fault of their
own to a perpetual Continuance in the World, should not
have their Misery doubled by the Load of a Wife.

As soon as they have compleated the Term of Eighty
Years, they are looked on as dead in Law; their Heirs immediately succeed to their Estates, only a small Pittance is
reserved for their Support; and the poor ones are maintained at the publick Charge. After that Period they are
held incapable of any Employment of Trust or Profit;
they cannot purchase Lands, or take Leases, neither are
they allowed to be Witnesses in any Cause, either Civil or
Criminal, not even for the Decision of Meers and Bounds.

AT Ninety they lose their Teeth and Hair; they have at
that Age no Distinction of Taste, but eat and drink whatever they can get, without Relish or Appetite. The Diseases
they were subject to, still continue without encreasing or
diminishing. In talking they forget the common Appellation of Things, and the Names of Persons, even of those
who are their nearest Friends and Relations. For the same
Reason they never can amuse themselves with reading, because their Memory will not serve to carry them from the
Beginning of a Sentence to the End; and by this Defect

they are deprived of the only Entertainment whereof they might otherwise be capable.

THE Language of this Country being always upon the Flux, the *Struldbruggs* of one Age do not understand those of another; neither are they able after two Hundred Years to hold any Conversation (farther than by a few general Words) with their Neighbours the Mortals; and thus they lye under the Disadvantage of living like Foreigners in their own Country.

THIS was the Account given me of the *Struldbruggs*, as near as I can remember. I afterwards saw five or six of different Ages, the youngest not above two Hundred Years old, who were brought to me at several Times by some of my Friends; but although they were told that I was a great Traveller, and had seen all the World, they had not the least Curiosity to ask me a Question; only desired I would give them *Slumskudask*, or a Token of Remembrance; which is a modest Way of begging, to avoid the Law that strictly forbids it, because they are provided for by the Publick, although indeed with a very scanty Allowance.

THEY are despised and hated by all Sorts of People: When one of them is born, it is reckoned ominous, and their Birth is recorded very particularly; so that you may know their Age by consulting the Registry, which however hath not been kept above a Thousand Years past, or at least hath been destroyed by Time or publick Disturbances. But the usual Way of computing how old they are, is, by asking them what Kings or great Persons they can remember, and then consulting History; for infallibly the last Prince in their Mind did not begin his Reign after they were Fourscore Years old.

THEY were the most mortifying Sight I ever beheld; and the Women more horrible than the Men. Besides the usual Deformities in extreme old Age, they acquired an additional Ghastliness in Proportion to their Number of Years, which is not to be described; and among half a Dozen I soon distinguished which was the eldest, although there were not above a Century or two between them.

THE Reader will easily believe, that from what I had

heard and seen, my keen Appetite for Perpetuity of Life was much abated. I grew heartily ashamed of the pleasing Visions I had formed; and thought no Tyrant could invent a Death into which I would not run with Pleasure from such a Life. The King heard of all that had passed between me and my Friends upon this Occasion, and raillied me very pleasantly; wishing I would send a Couple of *Struldbruggs* to my own Country, to arm our People against the Fear of Death; but this it seems is forbidden by the fundamental Laws of the Kingdom; or else I should have been well content with the Trouble and Expence of transporting them.

To keep up pretence of true story

I COULD not but agree, that the Laws of this Kingdom relating to the *Struldbruggs*, were founded upon the strongest Reasons, and such as any other Country would be under the Necessity of enacting in the like Circumstances. Otherwise, as Avarice is the necessary Consequent of old Age, those Immortals would in time become Proprietors of the whole Nation, and engross the Civil Power; which, for want of Abilities to manage, must end in the Ruin of the Publick.

CHAPTER XI.

THE AUTHOR LEAVES LUGGNAGG AND SAILS TO JAPAN. FROM THENCE HE RETURNS IN A DUTCH SHIP TO AMSTERDAM, AND FROM AMSTERDAM TO ENGLAND.

I THOUGHT this Account of the *Struldbruggs* might be some Entertainment to the Reader, because it seems to be a little out of the common Way; at least, I do not remember to have met the like in any Book of Travels that hath come to my Hands: And if I am deceived, my Excuse must be, that it is necessary for Travellers, who describe the same Country, very often to agree in dwelling on the same Particulars, without deserving the Censure of having borrowed or transcribed from those who wrote before them. THERE is indeed a perpetual Commerce between this

Kingdom and the great Empire of *Japan*; and it is very probable that the *Japanese* Authors may have given some Account of the *Struldbruggs*; but my Stay in *Japan* was so short, and I was so entirely a Stranger to the Language, that I was not qualified to make any Enquiries. But I hope the *Dutch* upon this Notice will be curious and able enough to supply my Defects.

His Majesty having often pressed me to accept some Employment in his Court, and finding me absolutely determined to return to my Native Country; was pleased to give me his Licence to depart; and honoured me with a Letter of Recommendation under his own Hand to the Emperor of *Japan*. He likewise presented me with four Hundred forty-four large Pieces of Gold (this Nation delighting in even Numbers) and a red Diamond which I sold in *England* for Eleven Hundred Pounds.

On the 6th Day of *May*, 1709, I took a solemn Leave of his Majesty, and all my Friends. This Prince was so gracious as to order a Guard to conduct me to *Glanguenstald*, which is a Royal Port to the *South-West* Part of the Island. In six Days I found a Vessel ready to carry me to *Japan*; and spent fifteen Days in the Voyage. We landed at a small Port-Town called *Xamoschi*, situated on the *South-East* Part of *Japan*. The Town lies on the *Western* Part, where there is a narrow Streight, leading *Northward* into a long Arm of the Sea, upon the *North-West* Part of which *Yedo* the Metropolis stands. At landing I shewed the Custom-House Officers my Letter from the King of *Luggnagg* to his Imperial Majesty: They knew the Seal perfectly well; it was as broad as the Palm of my Hand. The Impression was, *A King lifting up a lame Beggar from the Earth*. The Magistrates of the Town hearing of my Letter, received me as a publick Minister; they provided me with Carriages and Servants, and bore my Charges to *Yedo*, where I was admitted to an Audience, and delivered my Letter; which was opened with great Ceremony, and explained to the Emperor by an Interpreter, who gave me Notice of his Majesty's Order, that I should signify my Request; and whatever it were, it should be granted for

the sake of his Royal Brother of *Luggnagg*. This Inter-
preter was a Person employed to transact Affairs with the
Hollanders: He soon conjectured by my Countenance that
I was an *European*, and therefore repeated his Majesty's
Commands in *Low-Dutch*, which he spoke perfectly well.
I answered, (as I had before determined) that I was a *Dutch*
Merchant, shipwrecked in a very remote Country, from
whence I travelled by Sea and Land to *Luggnagg*, and then
took Shipping for *Japan*, where I knew my Countrymen
often traded, and with some of these I hoped to get an
Opportunity of returning into *Europe*: I therefore most
humbly entreated his Royal Favour to give Order, that I
should be conducted in Safety to *Nangasac*. To this I added
another Petition, that for the sake of my Patron the King
of *Luggnagg*, his Majesty would condescend to excuse my
performing the Ceremony imposed on my Countrymen, of
trampling upon the Crucifix; because I had been thrown
into his Kingdom by my Misfortunes, without any Intention of trading. When this latter Petition was interpreted
to the Emperor, he seemed a little surprised; and said, he
believed I was the first of my Countrymen who ever made
any Scruple in this Point; and that he began to doubt
whether I were a real *Hollander* or no; but rather suspected
I must be a CHRISTIAN. However, for the Reasons I had
offered, but chiefly to gratify the King of *Luggnagg*, by an
uncommon Mark of his Favour, he would comply with the
singularity of my Humour; but the Affair must be managed
with Dexterity, and his Officers should be commanded to
let me pass as it were by Forgetfulness. For he assured me,
that if the Secret should be discovered by my Countrymen,
the *Dutch*, they would cut my Throat in the Voyage. I returned my Thanks by the Interpreter for so unusual a
Favour; and some Troops being at that Time on their
March to *Nangasac*, the Commanding Officer had Orders
to convey me safe thither, with particular Instructions about
the Business of the *Crucifix*.

ON the 9th Day of *June*, 1709, I arrived at *Nangasac*,
after a very long and troublesome Journey. I soon fell into
Company of some *Dutch* Sailors belonging to the *Amboyna*

of *Amsterdam*, a stout Ship of 450 Tuns. I have lived long in *Holland*, pursuing my Studies at *Leyden*, and I spoke *Dutch* well: The Seamen soon knew from whence I came last; they were curious to enquire into my Voyages and Course of Life. I made up a Story as short and probable as I could, but concealed the greatest Part. I knew many Persons in *Holland*; I was able to invent Names for my Parents, whom I pretended to be obscure People in the Province of *Guelderland*. I would have given the Captain (one *Theodorus Vangrult*) what he pleased to ask for my Voyage to *Holland*; but, understanding I was a Surgeon, he was contented to take half the usual Rate, on Condition that I would serve him in the Way of my Calling. Before we took Shipping, I was often asked by some of the Crew, whether I had performed the Ceremony above-mentioned? I evaded the Question by general Answers, that I had satisfied the Emperor and Court in all Particulars. However, a malicious Rogue of a Skipper went to an Officer, and pointing to me, told him, I had not yet *trampled on the Crucifix*: But the other, who had received Instructions to let me pass, gave the Rascal twenty Strokes on the Shoulders with a Bamboo; after which I was no more troubled with such Questions.

NOTHING happened worth mentioning in this Voyage. We sailed with a fair Wind to the *Cape of Good Hope*, where we staid only to take in fresh Water. On the 16th of *April* we arrived safe at *Amsterdam*, having lost only three Men by Sickness in the Voyage, and a fourth who fell from the Fore-mast into the Sea, not far from the Coast of *Guinea*. From *Amsterdam* I soon after set sail for *England* in a small Vessel belonging to that City.

ON the [2]0th of *April*, 1710, we put in at the *Downs*. I landed the next Morning, and saw once more my Native Country after an Absence of five Years and six Months compleat. I went strait to *Redriff*, whither I arrived the same Day at two in the Afternoon, and found my Wife and Family in good Health.

The End of the Third Part.

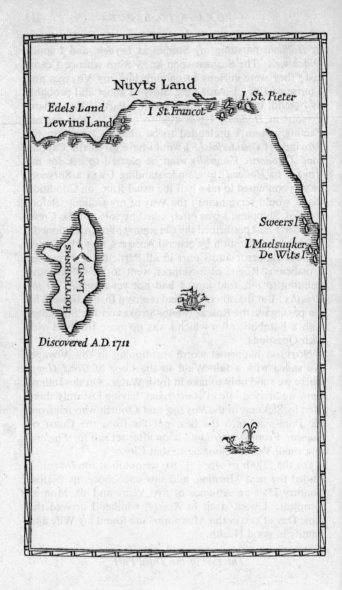

Nuyts Land

Edels Land
Lewins Land

I. St. Francot

I. St. Pieter

Sweers I.

I. Maelsuyker

De Wits I.

HOUTHNHMS LAND

Discovered A.D. 1711

PART IV.

A VOYAGE TO THE COUNTRY OF THE HOUYHNHNMS.

CHAPTER I.

THE AUTHOR SETS OUT AS CAPTAIN OF A SHIP. HIS MEN
CONSPIRE AGAINST HIM, CONFINE HIM A LONG TIME TO
HIS CABBIN, SET HIM ON SHORE IN AN UNKNOWN LAND.
HE TRAVELS UP INTO THE COUNTRY. THE YAHOOS,
A STRANGE SORT OF ANIMAL, DESCRIBED. THE AUTHOR
MEETS TWO HOUYHNHNMS.

I CONTINUED at home with my Wife and Children
about five Months in a very happy Condition, if I could
have learned the Lesson of knowing when I was well.
I left my poor Wife big with Child, and accepted an advantageous Offer made me to be Captain of the *Adventure*,
a stout Merchant-man of 350 Tuns: For I understood
Navigation well, and being grown weary of a Surgeon's
Employment at Sea, which however I could exercise upon
Occasion, I took a skilful young Man of that Calling, one
Robert Purefoy, into my Ship. We set sail from *Portsmouth*
upon the 7th Day of *September*, 1710; on the 14th we met
with Captain *Pocock* of *Bristol*, at *Tenariff*, who was going
to the Bay of *Campeachy*, to cut Logwood. On the 16th
he was parted from us by a Storm: I heard since my Re-
turn, that his Ship foundered, and none escaped, but one
Cabbin-Boy. He was an honest Man, and a good Sailor,
but a little too positive in his own Opinions, which was the
Cause of his Destruction, as it hath been of several others.
For if he had followed my Advice, he might at this Time

215

have been safe at home with his Family as well as my
self.

I HAD several Men died in my Ship of Calentures, so that
I was forced to get Recruits out of *Barbadoes*, and the *Lee-
ward Islands*, where I touched by the Direction of the Merchants who employed me; which I had soon too much
Cause to repent; for I found afterwards that most of them
had been Buccaneers. I had fifty Hands on Board; and
my Orders were, that I should trade with the *Indians* in
the *South-Sea*, and make what Discoveries I could. These
Rogues whom I had picked up, debauched my other Men,
and they all formed a Conspiracy to seize the Ship and
secure me; which they did one Morning, rushing into my
Cabbin, and binding me Hand and Foot, threatening to
throw me overboard, if I offered to stir. I told them, I was
their Prisoner, and would submit. This they made me swear
to do, and then unbound me, only fastening one of my Legs
with a Chain near my Bed; and placed a Centry at my
Door with his Piece charged, who was commanded to shoot
me dead if I attempted my Liberty. They sent me down
Victuals and Drink, and took the Government of the Ship
to themselves. Their Design was to turn Pirates, and
plunder the *Spaniards*, which they could not do, till they
got more Men. But first they resolved to sell the Goods in
the Ship, and then go to *Madagascar* for Recruits, several
among them having died since my Confinement. They
sailed many Weeks, and traded with the *Indians*; but I knew
not what Course they took, being kept close Prisoner in
my Cabbin, and expecting nothing less than to be murdered, as they often threatened me.

UPON the 9th Day of *May*, 1711, one *James Welch* came
down to my Cabbin; and said he had Orders from the
Captain to set me ashore. I expostulated with him, but in
vain; neither would he so much as tell me who their new
Captain was. They forced me into the Long-boat, letting
me put on my best Suit of Cloaths, which were as good as
new, and a small Bundle of Linnen, but no Arms except
my Hanger; and they were so civil as not to search my
Pockets, into which I conveyed what Money I had, with

some other little Necessaries. They rowed about a League; and then set me down on a Strand. I desired them to tell me what Country it was: They all swore, they knew no more than my self, but said, that the Captain (as they called him) was resolved, after they had sold the Lading, to get rid of me in the first Place where they discovered Land. They pushed off immediately, advising me to make haste, for fear of being overtaken by the Tide; and bade me farewell.

IN this desolate Condition I advanced forward, and soon got upon firm Ground, where I sat down on a Bank to rest my self, and consider what I had best to do. When I was a little refreshed, I went up into the Country, resolving to deliver my self to the first Savages I should meet; and purchase my Life from them by some Bracelets, Glass Rings, and other Toys, which Sailors usually provide themselves with in those Voyages, and whereof I had some about me: The Land was divided by long Rows of Trees, not regularly planted, but naturally growing; there was great Plenty of Grass, and several Fields of Oats. I walked very circumspectly for fear of being surprised, or suddenly shot with an Arrow from behind, or on either Side. I fell into a beaten Road, where I saw many Tracks of human Feet, and some of Cows, but most of Horses. At last I beheld several Animals in a Field, and one or two of the same Kind sitting in Trees. Their Shape was very singular, and deformed, which a little discomposed me, so that I lay down behind a Thicket to observe them better. Some of them coming forward near the Place where I lay, gave me an Opportunity of distinctly marking their Form. Their Heads and Breasts were covered with a thick Hair, some frizzled and others lank; they had Beards like Goats, and a long Ridge of Hair down their Backs, and the fore Parts of their Legs and Feet; but the rest of their Bodies were bare, so that I might see their Skins, which were of a brown Buff Colour. They had no Tails, nor any Hair at all on their Buttocks, except about the *Anus*; which, I presume Nature had placed there to defend them as they sat on the Ground; for this Posture they used, as well as lying down, and often stood on their hind Feet. They climbed high Trees, as nimbly as a Squirrel, for they had strong extended Claws before and behind, terminating on sharp Points, hooked. They would often spring, and bound, and leap with prodigious Agility. The Females were not so large as the Males; they had long lank Hair on their Heads, and only a Sort of Down on the rest of their Bodies, except about the *Anus*, and *Pudenda*. Their Dugs hung between their fore Feet, and often reached almost to the Ground as they walked. The Hair of both Sexes was of several Colours, brown, red, black and yellow. Upon the whole, I never beheld in all my Travels so disagreeable an Animal, or one against which I naturally conceived so strong an Antipathy. So that thinking I had seen enough, full of Contempt and Aversion, I got up and pursued the beaten Road, hoping it might direct me to the Cabbin of some *Indian*. I had not gone far when I met one of these Creatures full in my Way, and coming up directly to me. The ugly Monster, when he saw me, distorted several Ways every Feature of his Visage, and stared as at an Object he had never seen before; then approaching nearer, lifted up his fore Paw, whether out of Curiosity or Mischief, I could not tell: But I drew my Hanger, and gave him a good Blow with the flat Side of it; for I durst not strike him with the Edge, fearing the Inhabitants might be provoked against me, if they should come to know, that I had killed or maimed any of their Cattle. When the Beast felt the Smart, he drew back, and roared so loud, that a Herd of at least forty came flocking about me from the next Field, howling and making odious Faces; but I ran to the Body of a Tree, and leaning my Back against it, kept them off, by waving my Hanger. Several of this cursed Brood getting hold of the Branches behind, leaped up into the Tree, from whence they began to discharge their Excrements on my Head: However, I escaped pretty well, by sticking close to the Stem of the Tree, but was almost stifled with the Filth, which fell about me on every Side.

In the Midst of this Distress, I observed them all to run away on a sudden as fast as they could; at which I ventured to leave the Tree, and pursue the Road, wondering what it was that could put them into this Fright. But looking on my Left-Hand, I saw a Horse walking softly in the Field; which my Persecutors having sooner discovered, was the Cause of their Flight. The Horse started a little when he came near me, but soon recovering himself, looked full in my Face with manifest Tokens of Wonder: He viewed my Hands and Feet, walking round me several times. I would have pursued my Journey, but he placed himself directly in the Way, yet looking with a very mild Aspect, never offering the least Violence. We stood gazing at each other for some time; at last I took the Boldness, to reach my Hand towards his Neck, with a Design to stroak it; using the common Style and Whistle of Jockies when they are going to handle a strange Horse. But, this Animal seeming to receive my Civilities with Disdain, shook his Head, and bent his Brows, softly raising up his Left Fore-Foot to remove my Hand. Then he neighed three or four times, but in so different a Cadence, that I almost began to think he was speaking to himself in some Language of his own.

WHILE He and I were thus employed, another Horse came up; who applying himself to the first in a very formal Manner, they gently struck each others Right Hoof before, neighing several times by Turns, and varying the Sound, which seemed to be almost articulate. They went some Paces off, as if it were to confer together, walking Side by Side, backward and forward, like Persons deliberating upon some Affair of Weight; but often turning their Eyes towards me, as it were to watch that I might not escape. I was amazed to see such Actions and Behaviour in Brute Beasts; and concluded with myself, that if the Inhabitants of this Country were endued with a proportionable Degree of Reason, they must needs be the wisest People upon Earth. This Thought gave me so much Comfort, that I resolved to go forward untill I could discover some House or Village, or meet with any of the Natives; leaving the two Horses to discourse together as they pleased. But the first, who was a Dapple-Grey, observing me to steal off, neighed after me in so expressive a Tone, that I fancied myself to understand what he meant; whereupon I turned back, and came near him, to expect his farther Commands; but concealing my Fear as much as I could; for I began to be in some Pain, how this Adventure might terminate; and the Reader will easily believe I did not much like my present Situation.

THE two Horses came up close to me, looking with great Earnestness upon my Face and Hands. The grey Steed rubbed my Hat all round with his Right Fore-hoof, and discomposed it so much, that I was forced to adjust it better, by taking it off, and settling it again; whereat both he and his Companion (who was a brown Bay) appeared to be much surprized; the latter felt the Lappet of my Coat, and finding it to hang loose about me, they both looked with new Signs of Wonder. He stroked my Right Hand, seeming to admire the Softness, and Colour; but he squeezed it so hard between his Hoof and his Pastern, that I was forced to roar; after which they both touched me with all possible Tenderness. They were under great Perplexity about my Shoes and Stockings, which they felt very often, neighing to each other, and using various Gestures, not unlike those of a Philospher, when he would attempt to solve some new and difficult Phænomenon.

UPON the whole, the Behaviour of these Animals was so orderly and rational, so acute and judicious, that I at last concluded, they must needs be Magicians, who had thus metamorphosed themselves upon some Design; and seeing a Stranger in the Way, were resolved to divert themselves with him; or perhaps were really amazed at the Sight of a Man so very different in Habit, Feature and Complexion from those who might probably live in so remote a Climate. Upon the Strength of this Reasoning, I ventured to address them in the following Manner: Gentlemen, if you be Conjurers, as I have good Cause to believe, you can understand any Language; therefore I make bold to let your Worships know, that I am a poor distressed *Englishman*, driven by his Misfortunes upon your Coast; and I entreat one of you, to let me ride upon his Back, as if he were a real Horse, to some House or Village, where I can be relieved. In return of which Favour, I will make you a Present of this Knife and Bracelet, (taking them out of my Pocket.) The two

Creatures stood silent while I spoke, seeming to listen with great Attention; and when I had ended, they neighed frequently towards each other, as if they were engaged in serious Conversation. I plainly observed, that their Language expressed the Passions very well, and the Words might with little Pains be resolved into an Alphabet more easily than the *Chinese*.

I COULD frequently distinguish the Word *Yahoo*, which was repeated by each of them several times; and although it were impossible for me to conjecture what it meant, yet while the two Horses were busy in Conversation, I endeavoured to practice this Word upon my Tongue; and as soon as they were silent, I boldly pronounced *Yahoo* in a loud Voice, imitating, at the same time, as near as I could, the Neighing of a Horse; at which they were both visibly surprized, and the Grey repeated the same Word twice, as if he meant to teach me the right Accent, wherein I spoke after him as well as I could, and found myself perceivably to improve every time, although very far from any Degree of Perfection. Then the Bay tried me with a second Word, much harder to be pronounced; but reducing it to the *English Orthography*, may be spelt thus, *Houyhnhym*. I did not succeed in this so well as the former, but after two or three farther Trials, I had better Fortune; and they both appeared amazed at my Capacity.

AFTER some farther Discourse, which I then conjectured might relate to me, the two Friends took their Leaves, with the same Compliment of striking each other's Hoof; and the Grey made me Signs that I should walk before him; wherein I thought it prudent to comply, till I could find a better Director. When I offered to slacken my Pace, he would cry *Hhuun, Hhuun*; I guessed his Meaning, and gave him to understand, as well as I could, that I was weary, and not able to walk faster; upon which, he would stand a while to let me rest.

CHAPTER II.

THE AUTHOR CONDUCTED BY A HOUYHNHNM TO HIS
HOUSE. THE HOUSE DESCRIBED. THE AUTHOR'S RECEP-
TION. THE FOOD OF THE HOUYHNHNMS. THE AUTHOR
IN DISTRESS FOR WANT OF MEAT, IS AT LAST RELIEVED.
HIS MANNER OF FEEDING IN THAT COUNTRY.

HAVING travelled about three Miles, we came to a
long Kind of Building, made of Timber, stuck in
the Ground, and wattled a-cross; the Roof was
low, and covered with Straw. I now began to be a little
comforted; and took out some Toys, which Travellers
usually carry for Presents to the Savage *Indians* of *America*
and other Parts, in hopes the People of the House would be
thereby encouraged to receive me kindly. The Horse made
me a Sign to go in first; it was a large Room with a smooth
Clay Floor, and a Rack and Manger extending the whole
Length on one Side. There were three Nags, and two
Mares, not eating, but some of them sitting down upon
their Hams, which I very much wondered at; but wondered
more to see the rest employed in domestick Business: The
last seemed but ordinary Cattle; however this confirmed
my first Opinion, that a People who could so far civilize
brute Animals, must needs excel in Wisdom all the Nations
of the World. The Grey came in just after, and thereby
prevented any ill Treatment, which the others might have
given me. He neighed to them several times in a Style of
Authority, and received Answers.

BEYOND this Room there were three others, reaching the
Length of the House, to which you passed through three
Doors, opposite to each other, in the Manner of a Vista:
We went through the second Room towards the third; here
the Grey walked in first, beckoning me to attend: I waited
in the second Room, and got ready my Presents, for the
Master and Mistress of the House: They were two Knives,

three Bracelets of false Pearl, a small Looking Glass and a
Bead Necklace. The Horse neighed three or four Times,
and I waited to hear some answers in a human Voice, but
I heard no other Returns than in the same Dialect, only one
of two a little shriller than his. I began to think that this
House must belong to some Person of great Note among
them, because there appeared so much Ceremony before
I could gain Admittance. But, that a Man of Quality should
be served all by Horses, was beyond my Comprehension.
I feared my Brain was disturbed by my Sufferings and Mis-
fortunes: I roused my self, and looked about me in the
Room where I was left alone; this was furnished as the
first, only after a more elegant Manner. I rubbed my Eyes
often, but the same Objects still occurred. I pinched my
Arms and Sides, to awake my self, hoping I might be in a
Dream. I then absolutely concluded, that all these Appear-
ances could be nothing else but Necromancy and Magick.
But I had no Time to pursue these Reflections; for the
Grey Horse came to the Door, and made me a Sign to fol-
low him into the third Room; where I saw a very comely
Mare, together with a Colt and Fole, sitting on their
Haunches, upon Mats of Straw, not unartfully made, and
perfectly neat and clean.

THE Mare soon after my Entrance, rose from her Mat,
and coming up close, after having nicely observed my
Hands and Face, gave me a most contemptuous Look; then
turning to the Horse, I heard the Word *Yahoo* often repeated betwixt them; the meaning of which Word I could
not then comprehend, although it were the first I had
learned to pronounce; but I was soon better informed, to
my everlasting Mortification: For the Horse beckoning to
me with his Head, and repeating the Word *Hhuun, Hhuun*,
as he did upon the Road, which I understood was to attend
him, led me out into a kind of Court, where was another
Building at some Distance from the House. Here we
entered, and I saw three of those detestable Creatures,
which I first met after my landing, feeding upon Roots, and
the Flesh of some Animals, which I afterwards found to be
that of Asses and Dogs, and now and then a Cow dead by

Accident or Disease. They were all tied by the Neck with strong Wyths, fastened to a Beam; they held their Food between the Claws of their fore Feet, and tore it with their Teeth.

THE Master Horse ordered a Sorrel Nag, one of his Servants, to untie the largest of these Animals, and take him into a Yard. The Beast and I were brought close together; and our Countenances diligently compared, both by Master and Servant, who thereupon repeated several Times the Word *Yahoo.* My Horror and Astonishment are not to be described, when I observed, in this abominable Animal, a perfect human Figure; the Face of it indeed was flat and broad, the Nose depressed, the Lips large, and the Mouth wide: But these Differences are common to all savage Nations, where the Lineaments of the Countenance are distorted by the Natives suffering their Infants to lie grovelling on the Earth, or by carrying them on their Backs, nuzzling with their Face against the Mother's Shoulders. The Fore-feet of the *Yahoo* differed from my Hands in nothing else, but the Length of the Nails, the Coarseness and Brownness of the Palms, and the Hairiness on the Backs. There was the same Resemblance between our Feet, with the same Differences, which I knew very well, although the Horses did not, because of my Shoes and Stockings; the same in every Part of our Bodies, except as to Hairiness and Colour, which I have already described.

THE great Difficulty that seemed to stick with the two Horses, was, to see the rest of my Body so very different from that of a *Yahoo*, for which I was obliged to my Cloaths, whereof they had no Conception: The Sorrel Nag offered me a Root, which he held (after their Manner, as we shall describe in its proper Place) between his Hoof and Pastern; I took it in my Hand, and having smelt it, returned it to him again as civilly as I could. He brought out of the *Yahoo's* Kennel a Piece of Ass's Flesh, but it smelt so offensively that I turned from it with loathing; he then threw it to the *Yahoo*, by whom it was greedily devoured. He afterwards shewed me a Wisp of Hay, and a Fettlock full of Oats; but I shook my Head, to signify that neither of these were Food for me. And indeed, I now apprehended, that I must absolutely starve, if I did not get to some of my own Species: For as to those filthy *Yahoos*, although there were few greater Lovers of Mankind, at that time, than myself; yet I confess I never saw any sensitive Being so detestable on all Accounts; and the more I came near them, the more hateful they grew, while I stayed in that Country. This the Master Horse observed by my Behaviour, and therefore sent the *Yahoo* back to his Kennel. He then put his Fore-hoof to his Mouth, at which I was much surprized, although he did it with Ease, and with a Motion that appear'd perfectly natural; and made other Signs to know what I would eat; but I could not return him such an Answer as he was able to apprehend; and if he had understood me, I did not see how it was possible to contrive any way for finding myself Nourishment. While we were thus engaged, I observed a Cow passing by; whereupon I pointed to her, and expressed a Desire to let me go and milk her. This had its Effect; for he led me back into the House, and ordered a Mare-servant to open a Room, where a good Store of Milk lay in Earthen and Wooden Vessels, after a very orderly and cleanly Manner. She gave me a large Bowl full, of which I drank very heartily, and found myself well refreshed.

About Noon I saw coming towards the House a Kind of Vehicle, drawn like a Sledge by four *Yahoos*. There was in it an old Steed, who seemed to be of Quality; he alighted with his Hind-feet forward, having by Accident got a Hurt in his Left Fore-foot. He came to dine with our Horse, who received him with great Civility. They dined in the best Room, and had Oats boiled in Milk for the second Course, which the old Horse eat warm, but the rest cold. Their Mangers were placed circular in the Middle of the Room, and divided into several Partitions, round which they sat on their Haunches upon Bosses of Straw. In the Middle was a large Rack with Angles answering to every Partition of the Manger. So that each Horse and Mare eat their own Hay, and their own Mash of Oats and Milk, with much Decency and Regularity. The Behaviour of the young Colt and Fole appeared very modest; and that of the Master and

Mistress extremely chearful and complaisant to their Guest.
The Grey ordered me to stand by him; and much Discourse
passed between him and his Friend concerning me, as I
found by the Stranger's often looking on me, and the frequent Repetition of the Word *Yahoo*.

I HAPPENED to wear my Gloves; which the Master Grey
observing, seemed perplexed; discovering Signs of Wonder
what I had done to my Fore-feet; he put his Hoof three or
four times to them, as if he would signify, that I should
reduce them to their former Shape, which I presently did,
pulling off both my Gloves, and putting them into my
Pocket. This occasioned farther Talk, and I saw the Company was pleased with my Behaviour, whereof I soon found
the good Effects. I was ordered to speak the few Words I
understood; and while they were at Dinner, the Master
taught me the Names for Oats, Milk, Fire, Water, and some
others; which I could readily pronounce after him; having
from my Youth a great Facility in learning Languages.

WHEN Dinner was done, the Master Horse took me aside,
and by Signs and Words made me understand the Concern
he was in, that I had nothing to eat. Oats in their Tongue
are called *Hlunnh*. This Word I pronounced two or three
times; for although I had refused them at first, yet upon
second Thoughts, I considered that I could contrive to make
a Kind of Bread, which might be sufficient with Milk to
keep me alive, till I could make my Escape to some other
Country, and to Creatures of my own Species. The Horse
immediately ordered a white Mare-servant of his Family
to bring me a good Quantity of Oats in a Sort of wooden
Tray. These I heated before the Fire as well as I could, and
rubbed them till the Husks came off, which I made a shift
to winnow from the Grain; I ground and beat them between two Stones, then took Water, and made them into
a Paste or Cake, which I toasted at the Fire, and eat warm
with Milk. It was at first a very insipid Diet, although
common enough in many Parts of *Europe*, but grew tolerable by Time; and having been often reduced to hard Fare
in my Life, this was not the first Experiment I had made
how easily Nature is satisfied. And I cannot but observe,

that I never had one Hour's Sickness, while I staid in this
Island. It is true, I sometimes made a shift to catch a
Rabbet, or Bird, by Springes made of *Yahoos* Hairs; and
I often gathered wholesome Herbs, which I boiled, or eat
as Salades with my Bread; and now and then, for a Rarity,
I made a little Butter, and drank the Whey. I was at first
at a great Loss for Salt; but Custom soon reconciled the
Want of it; and I am confident that the frequent Use of Salt
among us is an Effect of Luxury, and was first introduced
only as a Provocative to Drink; except where it is necessary
for preserving of Flesh in long Voyages, or in Places remote
from great Markets. For we observe no Animal to be fond
of it but Man: And as to myself, when I left this Country,
it was a great while before I could endure the Taste of it
in any thing that I eat.

THIS is enough to say upon the Subject of my Dyet,
wherewith other Travellers fill their Books, as if the Readers
were personally concerned, whether we fare well or ill.
However, it was necessary to mention this Matter, lest the
World should think it impossible that I could find Sustenance for three Years in such a Country, and among such
Inhabitants.

WHEN it grew towards Evening, the Master Horse ordered
a Place for me to lodge in; it was but Six Yards from the
House, and separated from the Stable of the *Yahoos*. Here
I got some Straw, and covering myself with my own Cloaths,
slept very sound. But I was in a short time better accommo-
dated, as the Reader shall know hereafter, when I come to
treat more particularly about my Way of living.

CHAPTER III.

THE AUTHOR STUDIOUS TO LEARN THE LANGUAGE, THE
HOUYHNHNM HIS MASTER ASSISTS IN TEACHING HIM.
THE LANGUAGE DESCRIBED. SEVERAL HOUYHNHNMS OF
QUALITY COME OUT OF CURIOSITY TO SEE THE AUTHOR.
HE GIVES HIS MASTER A SHORT ACCOUNT OF HIS VOYAGE.

My principal Endeavour was to learn the Language,
which my Master (for so I shall henceforth call
him) and his Children, and every Servant of his
House were desirous to teach me. For they looked upon
it as a Prodigy, that a brute Animal should discover such
Marks of a rational Creature. I pointed to every thing, and
enquired the Name of it, which I wrote down in my *Journal
Book* when I was alone, and corrected my bad Accent, by
desiring those of the Family to pronounce it often. In this
Employment, a Sorrel Nag, one of the under Servants, was
very ready to assist me.

IN speaking, they pronounce through the Nose and
Throat, and their Language approaches nearest to the *High
Dutch* or *German*, of any I know in *Europe*; but is much
more graceful and significant. The Emperor *Charles* V.
made almost the same Observation, when he said, That
if he were to speak to his Horse, it should be in *High
Dutch*.

THE Curiosity and Impatience of my Master were so
great, that he spent many Hours of his Leisure to instruct
me. He was convinced (as he afterwards told me) that I
must be a *Yahoo*, but my Teachableness, Civility and Cleanliness astonished him; which were Qualities altogether so
opposite to those Animals. He was most perplexed about
my Cloaths, reasoning sometimes with himself, whether
they were a Part of my Body; for I never pulled them
off till the Family were asleep, and got them on before
they waked in the Morning. My Master was eager to learn

from whence I came; how I acquired those Appearances of
Reason, which I discovered in all my Actions; and to know
my Story from my own Mouth, which he hoped he should
soon do by the great Proficiency I made in learning and
pronouncing their Words and Sentences. To help my Memory, I formed all I learned into the *English* Alphabet, and
writ the Words down with the Translations. This last, after
some time, I ventured to do in my Master's Presence. It
cost me much Trouble to explain to him what I was doing;
for the Inhabitants have not the least Idea of Books or
Literature.

In about ten Weeks time I was able to understand most
of his Questions; and in three Months could give him some
tolerable Answers. He was extremely curious to know from
what Part of the Country I came, and how I was taught to
imitate a rational Creature; because the *Yahoos*, (whom he
saw I exactly resembled in my Head, Hands and Face, that
were only visible,) with some Appearance of Cunning, and
the strongest Disposition to Mischief, were observed to be
the most unteachable of all Brutes. I answered; that I came
over the Sea, from a far Place, with many others of my own
Kind, in a great hollow Vessel made of the Bodies of Trees:
That, my Companions forced me to land on this Coast,
and then left me to shift for myself. It was with some Difficulty, and by the Help of many Signs, that I brought him
to understand me. He replied, That I must needs be mistaken, or that I *said the thing which was not*. (For they have
no Word in their Language to express Lying or Falshood.)
He knew it was impossible that there could be a Country
beyond the Sea, or that a Parcel of Brutes could move a
wooden Vessel whither they pleased upon Water. He was
sure no *Houyhnhnm* alive could make such a Vessel, or
would trust *Yahoos* to manage it.

The Word *Houyhnhnm*, in their Tongue, signifies a
Horse; and in its Etymology, *the Perfection of Nature*. I
told my Master, that I was at a Loss for Expression, but
would improve as fast as I could; and hoped in a short time
I should be able to tell him Wonders: He was pleased to
direct his own Mare, his Colt and Fole, and the Servants

of the Family to take all Opportunities of instructing me;
and every Day for two or three Hours, he was at the same
Pains himself: Several Horses and Mares of Quality in the
Neighbourhood came often to our House, upon the Report spread of a wonderful *Yahoo*, that could speak like a
Houyhnhnm, and seemed in his Words and Actions to discover some Glimmerings of Reason. These delighted to
converse with me; they put many Questions, and received
such Answers, as I was able to return. By all which Advantages, I made so great a Progress, that in five Months
from my Arrival, I understood whatever was spoke, and
could express myself tolerably well.

THE *Houyhnhnms* who came to visit my Master, out of a
Design of seeing and talking with me, could hardly believe
me to be a right *Yahoo*, because my Body had a different
Covering from others of my Kind. They were astonished
to observe me without the usual Hair or Skin, except on my
Head, Face and Hands: but I discovered that Secret to my
Master, upon an Accident, which happened about a Fort-
night before.

I HAVE already told the Reader, that every Night when
the Family were gone to Bed, it was my Custom to strip
and cover myself with my Cloaths: It happened one Morning early, that my Master sent for me, by the Sorrel Nag,
who was his Valet; when he came, I was fast asleep, my
Cloaths fallen off on one Side, and my Shirt above my
Waste. I awaked at the Noise he made, and observed him
to deliver his Message in some Disorder; after which he
went to my Master, and in a great Fright gave him a very
confused Account of what he had seen: This I presently
discovered; for going as soon as I was dressed, to pay my
Attendance upon his Honour, he asked me the Meaning of
what his Servant had reported; that I was not the same
Thing when I slept as I appeared to be at other times; that
his Valet assured him, some Part of me was white, some
yellow, at least not so white, and some brown.

I HAD hitherto concealed the Secret of my Dress, in order
to distinguish myself as much as possible, from that cursed
Race of *Yahoos*; but now I found it in vain to do so any

longer. Besides, I considered that my Cloaths and Shoes would soon wear out, which already were in a declining Condition, and must be supplied by some Contrivance from the Hides of *Yahoos*, or other Brutes; whereby the whole Secret would be known. I therefore told my Master, that in the Country from whence I came, those of my Kind always covered their Bodies with the Hairs of certain Animals prepared by Art, as well for Decency, as to avoid Inclemencies of Air both hot and cold; of which, as to my own Person I would give him immediate Conviction, if he pleased to command me; only desiring his Excuse, if I did not expose those Parts that Nature taught us to conceal. He said, my Discourse was all very strange, but especially the last Part; for he could not understand why Nature should teach us to conceal what Nature had given. That neither himself nor Family were ashamed of any Parts of their Bodies; but however I might do as I pleased. Whereupon, I first unbuttoned my Coat, and pulled it off. I did the same with my Waste-coat; I drew off my Shoes, Stockings and Breeches. I let my Shirt down to my Waste, and drew up the Bottom, fastening it like a Girdle about my Middle to hide my Nakedness.

MY Master observed the whole Performance with great Signs of Curiosity and Admiration. He took up all my Cloaths in his Pastern, one Piece after another, and examined them diligently; he then stroaked my Body very gently, and looked round me several Times; after which he said, it was plain I must be a perfect *Yahoo*; but that I differed very much from the rest of my Species, in the Whiteness, and Smoothness of my Skin, my want of Hair in several Parts of my Body, the Shape and Shortness of my Claws behind and before, and my Affectation of walking continually on my two hinder Feet. He desired to see no more; and gave me leave to put on my Cloaths again, for I was shuddering with Cold.

I EXPRESSED my Uneasiness at his giving me so often the Appellation of *Yahoo*, an odious Animal, for which I had so utter an Hatred and Contempt. I begged he would forbear applying that Word to me, and take the same Order in his Family, and among his Friends whom he suffered to see me. I requested likewise, that the Secret of my having a false Covering to my Body might be known to none but himself, at least as long as my present Cloathing should last: For as to what the Sorrel Nag his Valet had observed, his Honour might command him to conceal it.

ALL this my Master very graciously consented to; and thus the Secret was kept till my Cloaths began to wear out, which I was forced to supply by several Contrivances, that shall hereafter be mentioned. In the mean Time, he desired I would go on with my utmost Diligence to learn their Language, because he was more astonished at my Capacity for Speech and Reason, than at the Figure of my Body, whether it were covered or no; adding, that he waited with some Impatience to hear the Wonders which I promised to tell him.

FROM thenceforward he doubled the Pains he had been at to instruct me; he brought me into all Company, and made them treat me with Civility, because, as he told them privately, this would put me into good Humour, and make me more diverting.

EVERY Day when I waited on him, beside the Trouble he was at in teaching, he would ask me several Questions concerning my self, which I answered as well as I could; and by those Means he had already received some general Ideas, although very imperfect. It would be tedious to relate the several Steps, by which I advanced to a more regular Conversation: But the first Account I gave of my self in any Order and Length, was to this Purpose:

THAT, I came from a very far Country, as I already had attempted to tell him, with about fifty more of my own Species; that we travelled upon the Seas, in a great hollow Vessel made of Wood, and larger than his Honour's House. I described the Ship to him in the best Terms I could; and explained by the Help of my Handkerchief displayed, how it was driven forward by the Wind. That, upon a Quarrel among us, I was set on Shoar on this Coast, where I walked forward without knowing whither, till he delivered me from the Persecution of those execrable *Yahoos*. He asked me,

Who made the Ship, and how it was possible that the *Houyhnhnms* of my Country would leave it to the Management of Brutes? My Answer was, that I durst proceed no farther in my Relation, unless he would give me his Word and Honour that he would not be offended; and then I would tell him the Wonders I had so often promised. He agreed; and I went on by assuring him, that the Ship was made by Creatures like myself, who in all the Countries I had travelled, as well as in my own, were the only governing, rational Animals; and that upon my Arrival hither, I was as much astonished to see the *Houyhnhnms* act like rational Beings, as he or his Friends could be in finding some Marks of Reason in a Creature he was pleased to call a *Yahoo*; to which I owned my Resemblance in every Part, but could not account for their degenerate and brutal Nature. I said farther, That if good Fortune ever restored me to my native Country, to relate my Travels hither, as I resolved to do; every Body would believe that I *said the Thing which was not*; that I invented the Story out of my own Head: And with all possible Respect to Himself, his Family, and Friends, and under his Promise of not being offended, our Countrymen would hardly think it probable, that a *Houyhnhnm* should be the presiding Creature of a Nation, and a *Yahoo* the Brute.

CHAPTER IV.

THE HOUYHNHNMS NOTION OF TRUTH AND FALSHOOD.
THE AUTHOR'S DISCOURSE DISAPPROVED BY HIS MASTER.
THE AUTHOR GIVES A MORE PARTICULAR ACCOUNT OF
HIMSELF, AND THE ACCIDENTS OF HIS VOYAGE.

MY Master heard me with great Appearances of Uneasiness in his Countenance; because *Doubting* or *not believing*, are so little known in this Country, that the Inhabitants cannot tell how to behave themselves under such Circumstances. And I remember in frequent Discourses with my Master concerning the Nature of Manhood, in other Parts of the World; having Occasion to talk of *Lying*, and *false Representation*, it was with much Difficulty that he comprehended what I meant; although he had otherwise a most acute Judgment. For he argued thus; That the Use of Spech was to make us understand one another, and to receive Information of Facts; now if any one *said the Thing which was not*, these Ends were defeated; because I cannot properly be said to understand him; and I am so far from receiving Information, that he leaves me worse than in Ignorance; for I am led to believe a Thing *Black* when it is *White*, and *Short* when it is *Long*. And these were all the Notions he had concerning that Faculty of *Lying*, so perfectly well understood, and so universally practised among human Creatures.

To return from this Digression; when I asserted that the *Yahoos* were the only governing Animals in my Country, which my Master said was altogether past his Conception, he desired to know, whether we had *Houyhnhnms* among us, and what was their Employment: I told him, we had great Numbers; that in Summer they grazed in the Fields, and in Winter were kept in Houses, with Hay and Oats, where *Yahoo* Servants were employed to rub their Skins smooth, comb their Manes, pick their Feet, serve them with Food, and make their Beds. I understand you well, said my Master; it is now very plain from all you have spoken, that whatever Share of Reason the *Yahoos* pretend to, the *Houyhnhnms* are your Masters; I heartily wish our *Yahoos* would be so tractable. I begged his Honour would please to excuse me from proceeding any farther, because I was very certain that the Account he expected from me would be highly displeasing. But he insisted in commanding me to let him know the best and the worst: I told him he should be obeyed. I owned, that the *Houyhnhnms* among us, whom we called *Horses*, were the most generous and comely Animal we had; that they excelled in Strength and Swiftness; and when they belonged to Persons of Quality, employed in Travelling, Racing, and drawing Chariots, they were treated with much Kindness and Care, till they fell into Diseases, or became foundered in the Feet; but then they were sold, and used to all kind of Drudgery till they died; after which their Skins were stripped and sold for what they were worth, and their Bodies left to be devoured by Dogs and Birds of Prey. But the common Race of Horses had not so good Fortune, being kept by Farmers and Carriers, and other mean People, who put them to greater Labour, and feed them worse. I described as well as I could, our Way of Riding; the Shape and Use of a Bridle, a Saddle, a Spur, and a Whip; of Harness and Wheels. I added, that we fastened Plates of a certain hard Substance called *Iron* at the Bottom of their Feet, to preserve their Hoofs from being broken by the Stony Ways on which we often travelled.

My Master, after some Expressions of great Indignation, wondered how we dared to venture upon a *Houyhnhnm's* Back; for he was sure, that the weakest Servant in his House would be able to shake off the strongest *Yahoo*; or by lying down, and rouling upon his Back, squeeze the Brute to Death. I answered, That our Horses were trained up from three or four Years old to the several Uses we intended them for; That if any of them proved intolerably vicious, they were employed for Carriages; that they were severely beaten while they were young for any mischievous Tricks: That the Males, designed for the common Use of Riding or Draught, were generally *castrated* about two Years after their Birth, to take down their Spirits, and make them more tame and gentle: That they were indeed sensible of Rewards and Punishments; but his Honour would please to consider, that they had not the least Tincture of Reason any more than the *Yahoos* in this Country.

It put me to the Pains of many Circumlocutions to give my Master a right Idea of what I spoke; for their Language doth not abound in Variety of Words, because their Wants and Passions are fewer than among us. But it is impossible to express his noble Resentment at our savage Treatment of the *Houyhnhnm* Race; particularly after I had explained the Manner and Use of *Castrating* Horses among us, to hinder them from propagating their Kind, and to render them more servile. He said, if it were possible there could be any Country where *Yahoos* alone were endued with Reason, they certainly must be the governing Animal, because Reason will in Time always prevail against Brutal Strength. But, considering the Frame of our Bodies, and especially of mine, he thought no Creature of equal Bulk was so ill-contrived, for employing that Reason in the common Offices of Life; whereupon he desired to know whether those among whom I lived, resembled me or the *Yahoos* of his Country. I assured him, that I was as well shaped as most of my Age; but the younger and the Females were much more soft and tender, and the Skins of the latter generally as white as Milk. He said, I differed indeed from other *Yahoos*, being much more cleanly, and not altogether so deformed; but in point of real Advantage, he thought I differed for the worse. That my Nails were of no Use either to my fore or hinder Feet: As to my fore Feet, he could not properly call them by that Name, for he never observed me to walk upon them; that they were too soft to bear the Ground; that I generally went with them uncovered, neither was the Covering I sometimes wore on them, of the same Shape, or so strong as that on my Feet behind. That I could not walk with any Security; for if either of my hinder Feet slipped, I must inevitably fall. He then began to find fault with other Parts of my Body; the Flatness of my Face, the Prominence of my Nose, my Eyes placed directly in Front, so that I could not look on either Side without turning my Head: That I was not able to feed my self, without lifting one of my fore Feet to my Mouth: And therefore Nature had placed those Joints to answer that Necessity. He knew not what could be the Use of those several Clefts and Divisions in my Feet behind; that these were too soft to bear the Hardness and Sharpness of Stones without a Covering made from the Skin of some other Brute; that my whole Body wanted a Fence against Heat and Cold, which I was forced to put on and off every Day with Tediousness and Trouble. And lastly, that he observed every Animal in this Country naturally to abhor the *Yahoos*, whom the

Weaker avoided, and the Stronger drove from them. So that supposing us to have the Gift of Reason, he could not see how it were possible to cure that natural Antipathy which every Creature discovered against us; nor consequently, how we could tame and render them serviceable. However, he would (as he said) debate the Matter no farther, because he was more desirous to know my own Story, the Country, where I was born, and the several Actions and Events of my Life before I came hither.

I ASSURED him, how extreamly desirous I was that he should be satisfied in every Point; but I doubted much, whether it would be possible for me to explain my self on several Subjects whereof his Honour could have no Conception, because I saw nothing in his Country to which I could resemble them. That however, I would do my best, and strive to express my self by Similitudes, humbly desiring his Assistance when I wanted proper Words; which he was pleased to promise me.

I SAID, my Birth was of honest Parents, in an Island called *England*, which was remote from this Country, as many Days Journey as the strongest of his Honour's Servants could travel in the Annual Course of the Sun. That I was bred a Surgeon, whose Trade it is to cure Wounds and Hurts in the Body, got by Accident or Violence. That my Country was governed by a Female Man, whom we called a *Queen*. That I left it to get Riches, whereby I might maintain my self and Family when I should return. That in my last Voyage, I was Commander of the Ship and had about fifty *Yahoos* under me, many of which died at Sea, and I was forced to supply them by others picked out from several Nations. That our Ship was twice in Danger of being sunk; the first Time by a great Storm, and the second, by striking against a Rock. Here my Master interposed, by asking me, How I could persuade Strangers out of different Countries to venture with me, after the Losses I had sustained, and the Hazards I had run. I said, they were Fellows of desperate Fortunes, forced to fly from the Places of their Birth, on Account of their Poverty or their Crimes. Some were undone by Law-suits; others spent all they had in Drinking,

I

Whoring and Gaming; others fled for Treason; many for Murder, Theft, Poysoning, Robbery, Perjury, Forgery, Coining false Money; for committing Rapes or Sodomy; for flying from their Colours, or deserting to the enemy; and most of them had broken Prison. None of these durst return to their native Countries for fear of being hanged, or of starving in a Jail; and therefore were under a Necessity of seeking a Livelihood in other Places.

During this Discourse, my Master was pleased often to interrupt me. I had made Use of many Circumlocutions in describing to him the Nature of the several Crimes, for which most of our Crew had been forced to fly their Country. This Labour took up several Days Conversation before he was able to comprehend me. He was wholly at a Loss to know what could be the Use or Necessity of practising those Vices. To clear up which I endeavoured to give him some Ideas of the Desire of Power and Riches; of the terrible Effects of Lust, Intemperance, Malice, and Envy. All this I was forced to define and describe by putting of Cases, and making Suppositions. After which, like one whose Imagination was struck with something never seen or heard of before, he would lift up his Eyes with Amazement and Indignation. Power, Government, War, Law, Punishment, and a Thousand other Things had no Terms, wherein that Language could express them; which made the Difficulty almost insuperable to give my Master any Conception of what I meant: But being of an excellent Understanding, much improved by Contemplation and Converse, he at last arrived at a competent Knowledge of what human Nature in our Parts of the World is capable to perform; and desired I would give him some particular Account of that Land, which we call *Europe*, especially, of my own Country.

CHAPTER V.

THE AUTHOR AT HIS MASTER'S COMMANDS INFORMS HIM
OF THE STATE OF ENGLAND. THE CAUSES OF WAR
AMONG THE PRINCES OF EUROPE. THE AUTHOR BEGINS
TO EXPLAIN THE ENGLISH CONSTITUTION.

T H E Reader may please to observe, that the following
Extract of many Conversations I had with my Master,
contains a Summary of the most material Points,
which were discoursed at several times for above two Years;
his Honour often desiring fuller Satisfaction as I farther
improved in the *Houyhnhnm* Tongue. I laid before him, as
well as I could, the whole State of *Europe*; I discoursed of
Trade and Manufactures, of Arts and Sciences; and the
Answers I gave to all the Questions he made, as they arose
upon several Subjects, were a Fund of Conversation not to
be exhausted. But I shall here only set down the Substance
of what passed between us concerning my own Country,
reducing it into Order as well as I can, without any Regard
to Time or other Circumstances, while I strictly adhere to
Truth. My only Concern is, that I shall hardly be able to
do Justice to my Master's Arguments and Expressions;
which must needs suffer by my Want of Capacity, as well
as by a Translation into our barbarous *English*.

IN Obedience therefore to his Honour's Commands, I
related to him the *Revolution* under the Prince of *Orange*;
the long War with *France* entered into by the said Prince,
and renewed by his Successor the present Queen; wherein
the greatest Powers of *Christendom* were engaged, and
which still continued: I computed at his Request, that
about a Million of *Yahoos* might have been killed in the
whole Progress of it; and perhaps a Hundred or more
Cities taken, and five times as many Ships burnt or sunk.

HE asked me what were the usual Causes or Motives that
made one Country go to War with another. I answered,

they were innumerable; but I should only mention a few of the chief. Sometimes the Ambition of Princes, who never think they have Land or People enough to govern: Sometimes the Corruption of Ministers, who engage their Master in a War in order to stifle or divert the Clamour of the Subjects against their evil Administration. Difference in Opinions hath cost many Millions of Lives: For Instance, whether *Flesh* be Bread, or *Bread* be *Flesh*: Whether the Juice of a certain *Berry* be *Blood* or *Wine*: Whether *Whistling* be a Vice or a Virtue: Whether it be better to *kiss a Post*, or throw it into the Fire: What is the best Colour for a *Coat*, whether *Black*, *White*, *Red* or *Grey*; and whether it should be *long* or *short*, *narrow* or *wide*, *dirty* or *clean*; with many more. Neither are any Wars so furious and bloody, or of so long Continuance, as those occasioned by Difference in Opinion, especially if it be in things indifferent.

Sometimes the Quarrel between two Princes is to decide which of them shall dispossess a Third of his Dominions, where neither of them pretend to any Right. Sometimes one Prince quarrelleth with another, for fear the other should quarrel with him. Sometimes a War is entered upon, because the Enemy is too *strong*, and sometimes because he is too *weak*. Sometimes our Neighbours *want* the *Things* which we *have*, or *have* the Things which we want; and we both fight, till they take ours or give us theirs. It is a very justifiable Cause of War to invade a Country after the People have been wasted by Famine, destroyed by Pestilence, or embroiled by Factions amongst themselves. It is justifiable to enter into a War against our nearest Ally, when one of his Towns lies convenient for us, or a Territory of Land, that would render our Dominions round and compact. If a Prince send Forces into a Nation, where the People are poor and ignorant, he may lawfully put half of them to Death, and make Slaves of the rest, in order to civilize and reduce them from their barbarous Way of Living. It is a very kingly, honourable, and frequent Practice, when one Prince desires the Assistance of another to secure him against an Invasion, that the Assistant, when he hath driven out the Invader, should seize on the Dominions

himself, and kill, imprison or banish the Prince he came to
relieve. Allyance by Blood or Marriage, is a sufficient Cause
of War between Princes; and the nearer the Kindred is, the
greater is their Disposition to quarrel: *Poor* Nations are
hungry, and *rich* Nations are *proud*; and Pride and Hunger
will ever be at Variance. For these Reasons, the Trade of a
Soldier is held the most honourable of all others: Because
a *Soldier* is a *Yahoo* hired to kill in cold Blood as many of
his own Species, who have never offended him, as possibly
he can.

THERE is likewise a Kind of beggarly Princes in *Europe*,
not able to make War by themselves, who hire out their
Troops to richer Nations for so much a Day to each Man;
of which they keep three Fourths to themselves, and it is
the best Part of their Maintenance; such are those in many
Northern Parts of *Europe*.

WHAT you have told me, (said my Master) upon the Subject of War, doth indeed discover most admirably the
Effects of that Reason you pretend to: However, it is happy
that the *Shame* is greater than the *Danger*; and that Nature
hath left you utterly uncapable of doing much Mischief:
For your Mouths lying flat with your Faces, you can hardly
bite each other to any Purpose, unless by Consent. Then,
as to the Claws upon your Feet before and behind, they
are so short and tender, that one of our *Yahoos* would drive
a Dozen of yours before him. And therefore in recounting
the Numbers of those who have been killed in Battle, I cannot but think that you have *said the Thing which is not*.

I COULD not forbear shaking my Head and smiling a little
at his Ignorance. And, being no Stranger to the Art of War,
I gave him a Description of Cannons, Culverins, Muskets,
Carabines, Pistols, Bullets, Powder, Swords, Bayonets,
Battles, Sieges, Retreats, Attacks, Undermines, Counter-
mines, Bombardments, Sea-fights; Ships sunk with a Thou-
sand Men; twenty Thousand killed on each Side; dying
Groans, Limbs flying in the Air: Smoak, Noise, Confusion,
trampling to Death under Horses Feet: Flight, Pursuit,
Victory; Fields strewed with Carcases left for Food to
Dogs, and Wolves, and Birds of Prey; Plundering, Strip-

ping, Ravishing, Burning and Destroying. And, to set forth
the Valour of my own dear Countrymen, I assured him, that
I had seen them blow up a Hundred Enemies at once in a
Siege, and as many in a Ship; and beheld the dead Bodies
drop down in Pieces from the Clouds, to the great Diversion of all the Spectators.

I WAS going on to more Particulars, when my Master
commanded me Silence. He said, whoever understood the
Nature of *Yahoos* might easily believe it possible for so vile
an Animal, to be capable of every Action I had named, if
their Strength and Cunning equalled their Malice. But, as
my Discourse had increased his Abhorrence of the whole
Species, so he found it gave him a Disturbance in his Mind,
to which he was wholly a Stranger before. He thought his
Ears being used to such abominable Words, might by Degrees admit them with less Detestation. That, although he
hated the *Yahoos* of this Country, yet he no more blamed
them for their odious Qualities, than he did a *Gnnayh* (a
Bird of Prey) for its Cruelty, or a sharp Stone for cutting
his Hoof. But, when a Creature pretending to Reason,
could be capable of such Enormities, he dreaded lest the
Corruption of that Faculty might be worse than Brutality
itself. He seemed therefore confident, that instead of
Reason, we were only possessed of some Quality fitted to
increase our natural Vices; as the Reflection from a troubled
Stream returns the Image of an ill-shapen Body, not only
larger, but more *distorted.*

HE added, That he had heard too much upon the Subject
of War, both in this, and some former Discourses. There
was another Point which a little perplexed him at present.
I had said, that some of our Crew left their Country on
Account of being ruined by *Law*: That I had already explained the Meaning of the Word; but he was at a Loss
how it should come to pass, that the *Law* which was intended for *every* Man's Preservation, should be any Man's
Ruin. Therefore he desired to be farther satisfied what
I meant by *Law,* and the Dispensers thereof, according
to the present Practice in my own Country: Because he
thought, Nature and Reason were sufficient Guides for a

reasonable Animal, as we pretended to be, in shewing us what we ought to do, and what to avoid.

I ASSURED his Honour, that *Law* was a Science wherein I had not much conversed, further than by employing Advocates, in vain, upon some Injustices that had been done me. However, I would give him all the Satisfaction I was able.

I SAID there was a Society of Men among us, bred up from their Youth in the Art of proving by Words multiplied for the Purpose, that *White* is *Black*, and *Black* is *White*, according as they are paid. To this Society all the rest of the People are Slaves.

FOR Example. If my Neighbour hath a mind to my *Cow*, he hires a Lawyer to prove that he ought to have my *Cow* from me. I must then hire another to defend my Right; it being against all Rules of *Law* that any Man should be allowed to speak for himself. Now in this Case, I who am the true Owner lie under two great Disadvantages. First, my Lawyer being practiced almost from his Cradle in defending Falshood; is quite out of his Element when he would be an Advocate for Justice, which as an Office unnatural, he always attempts with great Awkwardness, if not with Ill-will. The second Disadvantage is, that my Lawyer must proceed with great Caution: Or else he will be reprimanded by the Judges, and abhorrèd by his Brethren, as one who would lessen the Practice of the Law. And therefore I have but two Methods to preserve my *Cow*. The first is, to gain over my Adversary's Lawyer with a double Fee; who will then betray his Client, by insinuating that he hath Justice on his Side. The second Way is for my Lawyer to make my Cause appear as unjust as he can; by allowing the *Cow* to belong to my Adversary; and this if it be skilfully done, will certainly bespeak the Favour of the Bench.

Now, your Honour is to know, that these Judges are Persons appointed to decide all Controversies of Property, as well as for the Tryal of Criminals; and picked out from the most dextrous Lawyers who are grown old or lazy: And having been byassed all their Lives against Truth and Equity, lie under such a fatal Necessity of favouring Fraud,

Perjury and Oppression; that I have known some of them to have refused a large Bribe from the Side where Justice lay, rather than injure the *Faculty*, by doing any thing unbecoming their Nature or their Office.

IT is a Maxim among these Lawyers, that whatever hath been done before, may legally be done again: And therefore they take special Care to record all the Decisions formerly made against common Justice and the general Reason of Mankind. These, under the Name of *Precedents*, they produce as Authorities to justify the most iniquitous Opinions; and the Judges never fail of directing accordingly.

IN pleading, they studiously avoid entering into the *Merits* of the Cause; but are loud, violent and tedious in dwelling upon all *Circumstances* which are not to the Purpose. For Instance, in the Case already mentioned: They never desire to know what Claim or Title my Adversary hath to my *Cow*; but whether the said *Cow* were Red or Black; her Horns long or short; whether the Field I graze her in be round or square; whether she were milked at home or abroad; what Diseases she is subject to, and the like. After which they consult *Precedents*, adjourn the Cause, from Time to Time, and in Ten, Twenty, or Thirty Years come to an Issue.

IT is likewise to be observed, that this Society hath a peculiar Cant and Jargon of their own, that no other Mortal can understand, and wherein all their Laws are written, which they take special Care to multiply; whereby they have wholly confounded the very Essence of Truth and Falshood, of Right and Wrong; so that it will take Thirty Years to decide whether the Field, left me by my Ancestors for six Generations, belong to me, or to a Stranger three Hundred Miles off.

IN the Tryal of Persons accused for Crimes against the State, the Method is much more short and commendable: The Judge first sends to sound the Disposition of those in Power; after which he can easily hang or save the Criminal, strictly preserving all the Forms of Law.

HERE my Master interposing, said it was a Pity, that Creatures endowed with such prodigious Abilities of Mind

as these Lawyers, by the Description I gave of them must
certainly be, were not rather encouraged to be Instructors
of others in Wisdom and Knowledge. In Answer to which,
I assured his Honour, that in all Points out of their own
Trade, they were usually the most ignorant and stupid
Generation among us, the most despicable in common Conversation, avowed Enemies to all Knowledge and Learning;
and equally disposed to pervert the general Reason of Mankind, in every other Subject of Discourse, as in that of their
own Profession.

CHAPTER VI.

A CONTINUATION OF THE STATE OF ENGLAND, UNDER
QUEEN ANNE. THE CHARACTER OF A FIRST MINISTER IN
THE COURTS OF EUROPE.

M Y Master was yet wholly at a Loss to understand
what Motives could incite this Race of Lawyers
to perplex, disquiet, and weary themselves by engaging in a Confederacy of Injustice, merely for the Sake of
injuring their Fellow-Animals; neither could he comprehend what I meant in saying they did it for *Hire*. Whereupon I was at much Pains to describe to him the Use of
Money, the Materials it was made of, and the Value of the
Metals: That when a *Yahoo* had got a great Store of this
precious Substance, he was able to purchase whatever he
had a mind to; the finest Cloathing, the noblest Houses,
great Tracts of Land, the most costly Meats and Drinks;
and have his Choice of the most beautiful Females. Therefore since *Money* alone, was able to perform all these Feats,
our *Yahoos* thought, they could never have enough of it to
spend or to save, as they found themselves inclined from
their natural Bent either to Profusion or Avarice. That,
the rich Man enjoyed the Fruit of the poor Man's Labour,
and the latter were a Thousand to One in Proportion to the
former. That the Bulk of our People was forced to live miserably, by labouring every Day for small Wages to make a few

live plentifully. I enlarged myself much on these and many other Particulars to the same Purpose: But his Honour was still to seek: For he went upon a Supposition that all Animals had a Title to their Share in the Productions of the Earth; and especially those who presided over the rest. Therefore he desired I would let him know, what these costly Meats were, and how any of us happened to want them. Whereupon I enumerated as many Sorts as came into my Head, with the various Methods of dressing them, which could not be done without sending Vessels by Sea to every Part of the World, as well for Liquors to drink, as for Sauces, and innumerable other Conveniencies. I assured him, that this whole Globe of Earth must be at least three Times gone round, before one of our better Female *Yahoos* could get her Breakfast, or a Cup to put it in. He said, That must needs be a miserable Country which cannot furnish Food for its own Inhabitants. But what he chiefly wondered at, was how such vast Tracts of Ground as I described, should be wholly without *Fresh-water*, and the People put to the Necessity of sending over the Sea for Drink. I replied, that *England* (the dear Place of my Nativity) was computed to produce three Times the Quantity of Food, more than its Inhabitants are able to consume, as well as Liquors extracted from Grain, or pressed out of the Fruit of certain Trees, which made excellent Drink; and the same Proportion in every other Convenience of Life. But, in order to feed the Luxury and Intemperance of the Males, and the Vanity of the Females, we sent away the greatest Part of our necessary Things to other Countries, from whence in Return we brought the Materials of Diseases, Folly, and Vice, to spend among ourselves. Hence it follows of Necessity, that vast Numbers of our People are compelled to seek their Livelihood by Begging, Robbing, Stealing, Cheating, Pimping, Forswearing, Flattering, Suborning, Forging, Gaming, Lying, Fawning, Hectoring, Voting, Scribling, Stargazing, Poysoning, Whoring, Canting, Libelling, Free-thinking, and the like Occupations: Every one of which Terms, I was at much Pains to make him understand.

THAT, *Wine* was not imported among us from foreign Countries, to supply the Want of Water or other Drinks, but because it was a Sort of Liquid which made us merry, by putting us out of our Senses; diverted all melancholy Thoughts, begat wild extravagant Imaginations in the Brain, raised our Hopes, and banished our Fears; suspended every Office of Reason for a Time, and deprived us of the Use of our Limbs, untill we fell into a profound Sleep; although it must be confessed, that we always awaked sick and dispirited; and that the Use of this Liquor filled us with Diseases, which made our Lives uncomfortable and short.

BUT beside all this, the Bulk of our People supported themselves by furnishing the Necessities or Conveniencies of Life to the Rich, and to each other. For Instance, when I am at home and dressed as I ought to be, I carry on my Body the Workmanship of an Hundred Tradesmen; the Building and Furniture of my House employ as many more; and Five Times the Number to adorn my Wife.

I WAS going on to tell him of another Sort of People, who get their Livelihood by attending the Sick; having upon some Occasions informed his Honour that many of my Crew had died of Diseases. But here it was with the utmost Difficulty, that I brought him to apprehend what I meant. He could easily conceive, that a *Houyhnhnm* grew weak and heavy a few Days before his Death; or by some Accident might hurt a Limb. But that Nature, who worketh all things to Perfection, should suffer any Pains to breed in our Bodies, he thought impossible; and desired to know the Reason of so unaccountable an Evil. I told him, we fed on a Thousand Things which operated contrary to each other; that we eat when we were not hungry, and drank without the Provocation of Thirst: That we sat whole Nights drinking strong Liquors without eating a Bit; which disposed us to Sloth, enflamed our Bodies, and precipitated or prevented Digestion. That, prostitute Female *Yahoos* acquired a certain Malady, which bred Rottenness in the Bones of those, who fell into their Embraces: That this and many other Diseases, were propagated from Father to Son;

so that great Numbers come into the World with complicated Maladies upon them: That, it would be endless to
give him a Catalogue of all Diseases incident to human
Bodies; for they could not be fewer than five or six Hundred,
spread over every Limb, and Joynt: In short, every Part,
external and intestine, having Diseases appropriated to
each. To remedy which, there was a Sort of People bred
up among us, in the Profession or Pretence of curing the
Sick. And because I had some Skill in the Faculty, I would
in Gratitude to his Honour, let him know the whole Mystery
and Method by which they proceed.

THEIR Fundamental is, that all Diseases arise from *Repletion*; from whence they conclude, that a great *Evacuation*
of the Body is necessary, either through the natural Passage,
or upwards at the Mouth. Their next Business is, from
Herbs, Minerals, Gums, Oyls, Shells, Salts, Juices, Sea-
weed, Excrements, Barks of Trees, Serpents, Toads, Frogs,
Spiders, dead Mens Flesh and Bones, Birds, Beasts and
Fishes, to form a Composition for Smell and Taste the most
abominable, nauseous and detestable, that they can possibly contrive, which the Stomach immediately rejects with
Loathing: And this they call a *Vomit*. Or else from the same
Store-house, with some other poysonous Additions, they
command us to take in at the Orifice *above* or *below*, (just
as the Physician then happens to be disposed) a Medicine
equally annoying and disgustful to the Bowels; which relaxing the Belly, drives down all before it: And this they
call a *Purge*, or a *Clyster*. For Nature (as the Physicians
alledge) having intended the superior anterior Orifice only
for the *Intromission* of Solids and Liquids, and the inferior
Posterior for Ejection; these Artists ingeniously considering that in all Diseases Nature is forced out of her Seat;
therefore to replace her in it, the Body must be treated in
a Manner directly contrary, by interchanging the Use of
each Orifice; forcing Solids and Liquids in at the *Anus*, and
making Evacuations at the Mouth.

BUT, besides real Diseases, we are subject to many that
are only imaginary, for which the Physicians have invented
imaginary Cures; these have their several Names, and so

have the Drugs that are proper for them; and with these our Female *Yahoos* are always infested.

ONE great Excellency in this Tribe is their Skill at *Prognosticks*, wherein they seldom fail; their Predictions in real Diseases, when they rise to any Degree of Malignity, generally portending *Death*, which is always in their Power, when Recovery is not: And therefore, upon any unexpected Signs of Amendment, after they have pronounced their Sentence, rather than be accused as false Prophets, they know how to approve their Sagacity to the World by a seasonable Dose.

THEY are likewise of special Use to Husbands and Wives, who are grown weary of their Mates; to eldest Sons, to great Ministers of State, and often to Princes.

I HAD formerly upon Occasion discoursed with my Master upon the Nature of *Government* in general, and particularly of our own *excellent Constitution*, deservedly the Wonder and Envy of the whole World. But having here accidentally mentioned a *Minister of State*; he commanded me some Time after to inform him, what Species of *Yahoo* I particularly meant by that Appellation.

I TOLD him, that a *First* or *Chief Minister of State*, whom I intended to describe, was a Creature wholly exempt from Joy and Grief, Love and Hatred, Pity and Anger; at least makes use of no other Passions but a violent Desire of Wealth, Power, and Titles: That he applies his Words to all Uses, except to the Indication of his Mind; That he never tells a *Truth*, but with an Intent that you should take it for a *Lye*; nor a *Lye*, but with a Design that you should take it for a *Truth*; That those he speaks worst of behind their Backs, are in the surest way to Preferment; and whenever he begins to praise you to others or to your self, you are from that Day forlorn. The worst Mark you can receive is a *Promise*, especially when it is confirmed with an Oath; after which every wise Man retires, and gives over all Hopes.

THERE are three Methods by which a Man may rise to be Chief Minister: The first is, by knowing how with Prudence to dispose of a Wife, a Daughter, or a Sister: The second, by betraying or undermining his Predecessor: And the third

is, by a *furious Zeal* in publick Assemblies against the Corruptions of the Court. But a wise Prince would rather chuse
to employ those who practise the last of these Methods;
because such Zealots prove always the most obsequious
and subservient to the Will and Passions of their Master.
That, these *Ministers* having all Employments at their Disposal, preserve themselves in Power by bribing the Majority
of a Senate or great Council; and at last by an Expedient
called an *Act of Indemnity* (whereof I described the Nature
to him) they secure themselves from After-reckonings, and
retire from the Publick, laden with the Spoils of the Nation.

THE Palace of a *Chief Minister*, is a Seminary to breed up
others in his own Trade: The Pages, Lacquies, and Porter,
by imitating their Master, become *Ministers of State* in their
several Districts, and learn to excel in the three principal
Ingredients, of *Insolence*, *Lying*, and *Bribery*. Accordingly,
they have a *Subaltern* Court paid to them by Persons of the
best Rank; and sometimes by the Force of Dexterity and
Impudence, arrive through several Gradations to be Successors to their Lord.

HE is usually governed by a decayed Wench, or favourite
Footman, who are the Tunnels through which all Graces
are conveyed, and may properly be called, *in the last Resort*,
the Governors of the Kingdom.

ONE Day, my Master, having heard me mention the
Nobility of my Country, was pleased to make me a Compliment which I could not pretend to deserve: That, he was
sure, I must have been born of some Noble Family, because
I far exceeded in Shape, Colour, and Cleanliness, all the
Yahoos of his Nation, although I seemed to fail in Strength,
and Agility, which must be imputed to my different Way
of Living from those other Brutes; and besides, I was not
only endowed with the Faculty of Speech, but likewise with
some Rudiments of Reason, to a Degree, that with all his
Acquaintance I passed for a Prodigy.

HE made me observe, that among the *Houyhnhnms*, the
White, the *Sorrel*, and the *Iron-grey*, were not so exactly
shaped as the *Bay*, the *Dapple-grey*, and the *Black*; nor
born with equal Talents of Mind, or a Capacity to improve

them; and therefore continued always in the Condition of Servants, without ever aspiring to match out of their own Race, which in that Country would be reckoned monstrous and unnatural.

I MADE his Honour my most humble Acknowledgements for the good Opinion he was pleased to conceive of me; but assured him at the same Time, that my Birth was of the lower Sort, having been born of plain, honest Parents, who were just able to give me a tolerable Education: That, *Nobility* among us was altogether a different Thing from the Idea he had of it; That, our young *Noblemen* are bred from their Childhood in Idleness and Luxury; that, as soon as Years will permit, they consume their Vigour, and contract odious Diseases among lewd Females; and when their Fortunes are almost ruined, they marry some Woman of mean Birth, disagreeable Person, and unsound Constitution, merely for the sake of Money, whom they hate and despise. That, the Productions of such Marriages are generally scrophulous, rickety or deformed Children; by which Means the Family seldom continues above three Generations, unless the Wife take Care to provide a healthy Father among her Neighbours, or Domesticks, in order to improve and continue the Breed. That, a weak diseased Body, a meager Countenance, and sallow Complexion, are the true Marks of *noble Blood*; and a healthy robust Appearance is so disgraceful in a Man of Quality, that the World concludes his real Father to have been a Groom or a Coachman. The Imperfections of his Mind run parallel with those of his Body; being a Composition of Spleen, Dulness, Ignorance, Caprice, Sensuality and Pride.

WITHOUT the Consent of this illustrious Body, no Law can be enacted, repealed, or altered: And these Nobles have likewise the Decision of all our Possessions without Appeal. *

---

* On the evidence of a direction, in a contemporary hand, in a copy of Motte's first edition (for an analysis of which *v. Rev. of Eng. Studies. III.* 12. 1927. pp. 470–3) it has been suggested that these three lines are misplaced and should be inserted after the second paragraph on p. 125 (Part II. ch. 6). There appears to be insufficient evidence to justify the emendation. [ED.]

CHAPTER VII.

THE AUTHOR'S GREAT LOVE OF HIS NATIVE COUNTRY.
HIS MASTER'S OBSERVATIONS UPON THE CONSTITUTION
AND ADMINISTRATION OF ENGLAND, AS DESCRIBED BY
THE AUTHOR, WITH PARALLEL CASES AND COMPARISONS.
HIS MASTER'S OBSERVATIONS UPON HUMAN NATURE.

THE Reader may be disposed to wonder how I could prevail on my self to give so free a Representation of my own Species, among a Race of Mortals who were already too apt to conceive the vilest Opinion of Human Kind, from that entire Congruity betwixt me and their *Yahoos*. But I must freely confess, that the many Virtues of those excellent *Quadrupeds* placed in opposite View to human Corruptions, had so far opened my Eyes, and enlarged my Understanding, that I began to view the Actions and Passions of Man in a very different Light; and to think the Honour of my own Kind not worth managing; which, besides, it was impossible for me to do before a Person of so acute a Judgment as my Master, who daily convinced me of a thousand Faults in my self, whereof I had not the least Perception before, and which with us would never be numbered even among human Infirmities. I had likewise learned from his Example an utter Detestation of all Falsehood or Disguise; and *Truth* appeared so amiable to me, that I determined upon sacrificing every thing to it.

LET me deal so candidly with the Reader, as to confess, that there was yet a much stronger Motive for the Freedom I took in my Representation of Things. I had not been a Year in this Country, before I contracted such a Love and Veneration for the Inhabitants, that I entered on a firm Resolution never to return to human Kind, but to pass the rest of my Life among these admirable *Houyhnhnms* in the Contemplation and Practice of every Virtue; where I could have no Example or Incitement to Vice. But it was decreed by Fortune, my perpetual Enemy, that so great a Felicity should not fall to my Share. However, it is now some Comfort to reflect, that in what I said of my Countrymen, I *extenuated* their Faults as much as I durst before so strict an Examiner; and upon every Article, gave as *favourable* a Turn as the Matter would bear. For, indeed, who is there alive that will not be swayed by his Byass and Partiality to the Place of his Birth?

I HAVE related the Substance of several Conversations I had with my Master, during the greatest Part of the Time I had the Honour to be in his Service; but have indeed for Brevity sake omitted much more than is here set down.

WHEN I had answered all his Questions, and his Curiosity seemed to be fully satisfied; he sent for me one Morning early, and commanding me to sit down at some Distance, (an Honour which he had never before conferred upon me) He said, he had been very seriously considering my whole Story, as far as it related both to my self and my Country: That, he looked upon us as a Sort of Animals to whose Share, by what Accident he could not conjecture, some small Pittance of *Reason* had fallen, whereof we made no other Use than by its Assistance to aggravate our *natural* Corruptions, and to acquire new ones which Nature had not given us. That, we disarmed our selves of the few Abilities she had bestowed; had been very successful in multiplying our original Wants, and seemed to spend our whole Lives in vain Endeavours to supply them by our own Inventions. That, as to my self, it was manifest I had neither the Strength or Agility of a common *Yahoo*; that I walked infirmly on my hinder Feet; had found out a Contrivance to make my Claws of no Use or Defence, and to remove the Hair from my Chin, which was intended as a Shelter from the Sun and the Weather. Lastly, That I could neither run with Speed, nor climb Trees like my *Brethren* (as he called them) the *Yahoos* in this Country.

THAT, our Institutions of *Government* and *Law* were plainly owing to our gross Defects in *Reason*, and by consequence, in *Virtue*; because *Reason* alone is sufficient to govern a *Rational* Creature; which was therefore a

Character we had no Pretence to challenge, even from the Account I had given of my own People; although he manifestly perceived, that in order to favour them, I had concealed many Particulars, and often *said the Thing which was not*.

HE was the more confirmed in this Opinion, because he observed, that as I agreed in every Feature of my Body with other *Yahoos*, except where it was to my real Disadvantage in point of Strength, Speed and Activity, the Shortness of my Claws, and some other Particulars where Nature had no Part; so, from the Representation I had given him of our Lives, our Manners, and our Actions, he found as near a Resemblance in the Disposition of our Minds. He said, the *Yahoos* were known to hate one another more than they did any different Species of Animals; and the Reason usually assigned, was, the Odiousness of their own Shapes, which all could see in the rest, but not in themselves. He had therefore begun to think it not unwise in us to *cover* our Bodies, and by that Invention, conceal many of our Deformities from each other, which would else be hardly supportable. But, he now found he had been mistaken; and that the Dissentions of those Brutes in his Country were owing to the same Cause with ours, as I had described them. For, if (said he) you throw among five *Yahoos* as much Food as would be sufficient for fifty, they will, instead of eating peaceably, fall together by the Ears, each single one impatient to *have all to it self*; and therefore a Servant was usually employed to stand by while they were feeding abroad, and those kept at home were tied at a Distance from each other. That, if a Cow died of Age or Accident, before a *Houyhnhnm* could secure it for his own *Yahoos*, those in the Neighbourhood would come in Herds to seize it, and then would ensue such a Battle as I had described, with terrible Wounds made by their Claws on both Sides, although they seldom were able to kill one another, for want of such convenient Instruments of Death as we had invented. At other Times the like Battles have been fought between the *Yahoos* of several Neighbourhoods without any visible Cause: Those of one District watching all Oppor-

tunities to surprise the next before they are prepared.
But if they find their Project hath miscarried, they return
home, and for want of Enemies, engage in what I call a
Civil War among themselves.

THAT, in some Fields of his Country, there are certain
shining Stones of several Colours, whereof the *Yahoos* are
violently fond; and when Part of these *Stones* are fixed in
the Earth, as it sometimes happeneth, they will dig with
their Claws for whole Days to get them out, and carry them
away, and hide them by Heaps in their Kennels; but still
looking round with great Caution, for fear their Comrades
should find out their Treasure. My Master said, he could
never discover the Reason of this unnatural Appetite, or
how these *Stones* could be of any Use to a *Yahoo*; but now
he believed it might proceed from the same Principle of
Avarice, which I had ascribed to Mankind. That he had
once, by way of Experiment, privately removed a Heap of
these *Stones* from the Place where one of his *Yahoos* had
buried it: Whereupon, the sordid Animal missing his Treasure, by his loud lamenting brought the whole Herd to the
Place, there miserably howled, then fell to biting and tearing the rest; began to pine away, would neither eat nor
sleep, nor work, till he ordered a Servant privately to convey the *Stones* into the same Hole, and hide them as before;
which when his *Yahoo* had found, he presently recovered
his Spirits and good Humour; but took Care to remove
them to a better hiding Place; and hath ever since been a
very serviceable Brute.

MY Master farther assured me, which I also observed
my self; That in the Fields where these *shining Stones*
abound, the fiercest and most frequent Battles are fought,
occasioned by perpetual Inroads of the neighbouring
Yahoos.

HE said, it was common when two *Yahoos* discovered
such a *Stone* in a Field, and were contending which of them
should be the Proprietor, a third would take the Advantage, and carry it away from them both; which my Master
would needs contend to have some Resemblance with our
Suits at Law; wherein I thought it for our Credit not to

undeceive him; since the Decision he mentioned was much more equitable than many Decrees among us: Because the Plaintiff and Defendant there lost nothing beside the *Stone* they contended for; whereas our *Courts of Equity*, would never have dimissed the Cause while either of them had any thing left.

My Master continuing his Discourse, said, There was nothing that rendered the *Yahoos* more odious, than their undistinguished Appetite to devour every thing that came in their Way, whether Herbs, Roots, Berries, corrupted Flesh of Animals, or all mingled together: And it was peculiar in their Temper, that they were fonder of what they could get by Rapine or Stealth at a greater Distance, than much better Food provided for them at home. If their Prey held out, they would eat till they were ready to burst, after which Nature had pointed out to them a certain *Root* that gave them a general Evacuation.

There was also another Kind of *Root* very *juicy*, but something rare and difficult to be found, which the *Yahoos* fought for with much Eagerness, and would suck it with great Delight: It produced the same Effects that Wine hath upon us. It would make them sometimes hug, and sometimes tear one another; they would howl and grin, and chatter, and roul, and tumble, and then fall asleep in the Mud.

I did indeed observe, that the *Yahoos* were the only Animals in this Country subject to any Diseases; which however, were much fewer than Horses have among us, and contracted not by any ill Treatment they meet with, but by the Nastiness and Greediness of that sordid Brute. Neither has their Language any more than a general Appellation for those Maladies; which is borrowed from the Name of the Beast, and called *Hnea Yahoo*, or the *Yahoo's-Evil*; and the Cure prescribed is a Mixture of *their own Dung* and *Urine*, forcibly put down the *Yahoo's* Throat. This I have since often known to have been taken with Success: And do here freely recommend it to my Countrymen, for the publick Good, as an admirable Specifick against all Diseases produced by Repletion.

As to Learning, Government, Arts, Manufactures, and the like; my Master confessed he could find little or no Resemblance between the *Yahoos* of that Country and those in ours. For, he only meant to observe what Parity there was in our Natures. He had heard indeed some curious *Houyhnhnms* observe, that in most Herds there was a Sort of ruling *Yahoo*, (as among us there is generally some leading or principal Stag in a Park) who was always more *deformed* in Body, and *mischievous in Disposition*, than any of the rest. That, this *Leader* had usually a Favourite as *like himself* as he could get, whose Employment was to *lick his Master's Feet and Posteriors, and drive the Female* Yahoos *to his Kennel*; for which he was now and then rewarded with a Piece of Ass's Flesh. This *Favourite* is hated by the whole Herd; and therefore to protect himself, keeps always *near the Person of his Leader*. He usually continues in Office till a worse can be found; but the very Moment he is discarded, his Successor, at the Head of all the *Yahoos* in that District, Young and Old, Male and Female, come in a Body, and discharge their Excrements upon him from Head to Foot. But how far this might be applicable to our *Courts* and *Favourites*, and *Ministers of State*, my Master said I could best determine.

I DURST make no Return to this malicious Insinuation, which debased human Understanding below the Sagacity of a common *Hound*, who hath Judgment enough to distinguish and follow the Cry of the *ablest Dog in the Pack*, without being ever mistaken.

MY Master told me, there were some Qualities remarkable in the *Yahoos*, which he had not observed me to mention, or at least very slightly, in the Accounts I had given him of human Kind. He said, those Animals, like other Brutes, had their Females in common; but in this they differed, that the She-*Yahoo* would admit the Male, while she was pregnant; and that the Hees would quarrel and fight with the Females as fiercely as with each other. Both which Practices were such Degrees of infamous Brutality, that no other sensitive Creature ever arrived at.

ANOTHER Thing he wondered at in the *Yahoos*, was their

strange Disposition to Nastiness and Dirt; whereas there appears to be a natural Love of Cleanliness in all other Animals. As to the two former Accusations, I was glad to let them pass without any Reply, because I had not a Word to offer upon them in Defence of my Species, which otherwise I certainly had done from my own Inclinations. But I could have easily vindicated human Kind from the Imputation of Singularity upon the last Article, if there had been any *Swine* in that Country, (as unluckily for me there were not) which although it may be a *sweeter Quadruped* than a *Yahoo*, cannot I humbly conceive in Justice pretend to more Cleanliness; and so his Honour himself must have owned, if he had seen their filthy Way of feeding, and their Custom of wallowing and sleeping in the Mud.

My Master likewise mentioned another Quality, which his Servants had discovered in several *Yahoos*, and to him was wholly unaccountable. He said, a Fancy would sometimes take a *Yahoo*, to retire into a Corner, to lie down and howl, and groan, and spurn away all that came near him, although he were young and fat, and wanted neither Food nor Water; nor did the Servants imagine what could possibly ail him. And the only Remedy they found was to set him to hard Work, after which he would infallibly come to himself. To this I was silent out of Partiality to my own Kind; yet here I could plainly discover the true Seeds of *Spleen*, which only seizeth on the *Lazy*, the *Luxurious*, and the *Rich*; who, if they were forced to undergo the *same Regimen*, I would undertake for the Cure.

His Honour had farther observed, that a Female-*Yahoo* would often stand behind a Bank or a Bush, to gaze on the young Males passing by, and then appear, and hide, using many antick Gestures and Grimaces; at which time it was observed, that she had a most *offensive Smell*; and when any of the Males advanced, would slowly retire, looking often back, and with a counterfeit Shew of Fear, run off into some convenient Place where she knew the Male would follow her.

At other times, if a Female Stranger came among them, three or four of her own Sex would get about her, and stare and chatter, and grin, and smell her all over; and then turn off with Gestures that seemed to express Contempt and Disdain.

PERHAPS my Master might refine a little in these Speculations, which he had drawn from what he observed himself, or had been told by others; However, I could not reflect without some Amazement, and much Sorrow, that the Rudiments of *Lewdness*, *Coquetry*, *Censure*, and *Scandal*, should have Place by Instinct in Womankind.

I EXPECTED every Moment, that my Master would accuse the *Yahoos* of those unnatural Appetites in both Sexes, so common among us. But Nature it seems hath not been so expert a Schoolmistress; and these politer Pleasures are entirely the Productions of Art and Reason, on our Side of the Globe.

CHAPTER VIII.

THE AUTHOR RELATETH SEVERAL PARTICULARS OF THE YAHOOS. THE GREAT VIRTUES OF THE HOUYHNHNMS. THE EDUCATION AND EXERCISE OF THEIR YOUTH. THEIR GENERAL ASSEMBLY.

As I ought to have understood human Nature much better than I supposed it possible for my Master to do, so it was easy to apply the Character he gave of the *Yahoos* to myself and my Countrymen; and I believed I could yet make farther Discoveries from my own Observation. I therefore often begged his Honour to let me go among the Herds of *Yahoos* in the Neighbourhood; to which he always very graciously consented, being perfectly convinced that the Hatred I bore those Brutes would never suffer me to be corrupted by them; and his Honour ordered one of his Servants, a strong Sorrel Nag, very honest and good-natured, to be my Guard; without whose Protection I durst not undertake such Adventures. For I have already told the Reader how much I was pestered by those odious Animals upon my first Arrival. I afterwards failed very narrowly three or four times of falling into their Clutches, when I happened to stray at any Distance without my Hanger. And I have Reason to believe, they had some Imagination that I was of their own Species, which I often assisted myself, by stripping up my Sleeves, and shewing my naked Arms and Breast in their Sight, when my Protector was with me: At which times they would approach as near as they durst, and imitate my Actions after the Manner of Monkeys, but ever with great Signs of Hatred; as a tame *Jack Daw* with Cap and Stockings, is always persecuted by the wild ones, when he happens to be got among them.

THEY are prodigiously nimble from their Infancy; however, I once caught a young Male of three Years old, and endeavoured by all Marks of Tenderness to make it quiet; but the little Imp fell a squalling, and scratching, and biting with such Violence, that I was forced to let it go; and it was high time, for a whole Troop of old ones came about us at the Noise; but finding the Cub was safe, (for away it ran) and my Sorrel Nag being by, they durst not venture near us. I observed the young Animal's Flesh to smell very rank, and the Stink was somewhat between a *Weasel* and a *Fox*, but much more disagreeable. I forgot another Circumstance, (and perhaps I might have the Reader's Pardon, if it were wholly omitted) that while I held the odious Vermin in my Hands, it voided its filthy Excrements of a yellow liquid Substance, all over my Cloaths; but by good Fortune there was a small Brook hard by, where I washed myself as clean as I could; although I durst not come into my Master's Presence, until I were sufficiently aired.

BY what I could discover, the *Yahoos* appear to be the most unteachable of all Animals, their Capacities never reaching higher than to draw or carry Burthens. Yet I am of Opinion, this Defect ariseth chiefly from a perverse, restive Disposition. For they are cunning, malicious, treacherous and revengeful. They are strong and hardy, but of a cowardly Spirit, and by Consequence insolent, abject, and cruel. It is observed, that the *Red-haired* of both Sexes are more libidinous and mischievous than the rest, whom yet they much exceed in Strength and Activity.

THE *Houyhnhnms* keep the *Yahoos* for present Use in Huts not far from the House; but the rest are sent abroad to certain Fields, where they dig up Roots, eat several Kinds of Herbs, and search about for Carrion, or sometimes catch *Weasels* and *Luhimuhs* (a Sort of *wild Rat*) which they greedily devour. Nature hath taught them to dig deep Holes with their Nails on the Side of a rising Ground, wherein they lie by themselves; only the Kennels of the Females are larger, sufficient to hold two or three Cubs.

THEY swim from their Infancy like Frogs, and are able to continue long under Water, where they often take Fish, which the Females carry home to their Young. And upon this Occasion, I hope the Reader will pardon my relating an odd Adventure.

BEING one Day abroad with my Protector the Sorrel Nag, and the Weather exceeding hot, I entreated him to let me bathe in a River that was near. He consented, and I immediately stripped myself stark naked, and went down softly into the Stream. It happened that a young Female *Yahoo* standing behind a Bank, saw the whole Proceeding; and inflamed by Desire, as the Nag and I conjectured, came running with all Speed, and leaped into the Water within five Yards of the Place where I bathed. I was never in my Life so terribly frighted; the Nag was grazing at some Distance, not suspecting any Harm: She embraced me after a most fulsome Manner; I roared as loud as I could, and the Nag came galloping towards me, whereupon she quitted her Grasp, with the utmost Reluctancy, and leaped upon the opposite Bank, where she stood gazing and howling all the time I was putting on my Cloaths.

THIS was Matter of Diversion to my Master and his Family, as well as of Mortification to my self. For now I could no longer deny, that I was a real *Yahoo*, in every Limb and Feature, since the Females had a natural Propensity to me as one of their own Species: Neither was the Hair of this Brute of a Red Colour, (which might have been some

Excuse for an Appetite a little irregular) but black as a Sloe, and her Countenance did not make an Appearance altogether so hideous as the rest of the Kind; for, I think, she could not be above Eleven Years old.

HAVING already lived three Years in this Country, the Reader I suppose will expect, that I should, like other Travellers, give him some Account of the Manners and Customs of its Inhabitants, which it was indeed my principal Study to learn.

As these noble *Houyhnhnms* are endowed by Nature with a general Disposition to all Virtues, and have no Conceptions or Ideas of what is evil in a rational Creature; so their grand Maxim is, to cultivate *Reason*, and to be wholly governed by it. Neither is *Reason* among them a Point problematical as with us, where Men can argue with Plausibility on both Sides of a Question; but strikes you with immediate Conviction; as it must needs do where it is not mingled, obscured, or discoloured by Passion and Interest. I remember it was with extreme Difficulty that I could bring my Master to understand the Meaning of the Word *Opinion*, or how a Point could be disputable; because *Reason* taught us to affirm or deny only where we are certain; and beyond our Knowledge we cannot do either. So that Controversies, Wranglings, Disputes, and Positiveness in false or dubious Propositions, are Evils unknown among the *Houyhnhnms*. In the like Manner when I used to explain to him our several Systems of *Natural Philosophy*, he would laugh that a Creature pretending to *Reason*, should value itself upon the Knowledge of other Peoples Conjectures, and in Things, where that Knowledge, if it were certain, could be of no Use. Wherein he agreed entirely with the Sentiments of *Socrates*, as *Plato* delivers them; which I mention as the highest Honour I can do that Prince of Philosophers. I have often since reflected what Destruction such a Doctrine would make in the Libraries of *Europe*; and how many Paths to Fame would be then shut up in the Learned World.

FRIENDSHIP and *Benevolence* are the two principal Virtues among the *Houyhnhnms*; and these not confined to particular Objects, but universal to the whole Race. For, a Stranger from the remotest Part, is equally treated with the nearest Neighbour, and where-ever he goes, looks upon himself as at home. They preserve *Decency* and *Civility* in the highest Degrees, but are altogether ignorant of *Ceremony*. They have no Fondness for their Colts or Foles; but the Care they take in educating them proceedeth entirely from the Dictates of *Reason*. And, I observed my Master to shew the same Affection to his Neighbour's Issue that he had for his own. They will have it that *Nature* teaches them to love the whole Species, and it is *Reason* only that maketh a Distinction of Persons, where there is a superior Degree of Virtue.

WHEN the Matron *Houyhnhnms* have produced one of each Sex, they no longer accompany with their Consorts, except they lose one of their Issue by some Casualty, which very seldom happens: But in such a Case they meet again; or when the like Accident befalls a Person, whose Wife is past bearing, some other Couple bestows on him one of their own Colts, and then go together a second Time, until the Mother be pregnant. This Caution is necessary to prevent the Country from being overburthened with Numbers. But the Race of inferior *Houyhnhnms* bred up to be Servants is not so strictly limited upon this Article; these are allowed to produce three of each Sex, to be Domesticks in the Noble Families.

IN their Marriages they are exactly careful to chuse such Colours as will not make any disagreeable Mixture in the Breed. *Strength* is chiefly valued in the Male, and *Comeliness* in the Female; not upon the Account of *Love*, but to preserve the Race from degenerating: For, where a Female happens to excel in *Strength*, a Consort is chosen with regard to *Comeliness*. Courtship, Love, Presents, Joyntures, Settlements, have no Place in their Thoughts; or Terms whereby to express them in their Language. The young Couple meet and are joined, merely because it is the Determination of their Parents and Friends: It is what they see done every Day; and they look upon it as one of the necessary Actions in a reasonable Being. But the Violation

of Marriage, or any other Unchastity, was never heard of:
And the married Pair pass their Lives with the same Friendship, and mutual Benevolence that they bear to all others
of the same Species, who come in their Way; without Jealousy, Fondness, Quarrelling, or Discontent.

IN educating the Youth of both Sexes, their Method is
admirable, and highly deserveth our Imitation. These are
not suffered to taste a Grain of *Oats*, except upon certain
Days, till Eighteen Years old; nor *Milk*, but very rarely;
and in Summer they graze two Hours in the Morning, and
as many in the Evening, which their Parents likewise observe; but the Servants are not allowed above half that
Time; and a great Part of the Grass is brought home, which
they eat at the most convenient Hours, when they can be
best spared from Work.

TEMPERANCE, *Industry*, *Exercise* and *Cleanliness*, are the
Lessons equally enjoyned to the young ones of both Sexes:
And my Master thought it monstrous in us to give the
Females a different Kind of Education from the Males, except in some Articles of Domestick Management; whereby,
as he truly observed, one Half of our Natives were good for
nothing but bringing Children into the World: And to trust
the Care of their Children to such useless Animals, he said
was yet a greater Instance of Brutality.

BUT the *Houyhnhnms* train up their Youth to Strength,
Speed, and Hardiness, by exercising them in running Races
up and down steep Hills, or over hard stony Grounds; and
when they are all in a Sweat, they are ordered to leap over
Head and Ears into a Pond or a River. Four times a Year
the Youth of certain Districts meet to shew their Proficiency
in Running, and Leaping, and other Feats of Strength or
Agility; where the Victor is rewarded with a Song made in
his or her Praise. On this Festival the Servants drive a Herd
of *Yahoos* into the Field, laden with Hay, and Oats, and
Milk for a Repast to the *Houyhnhnms*; after which, these
Brutes are immediately driven back again, for fear of being
noisome to the Assembly.

EVERY fourth Year, at the *Vernal Equinox*, there is a Representative Council of the whole Nation, which meets in a

Plain about twenty Miles from our House, and continueth about five or six Days. Here they inquire into the State and Condition of the several Districts; whether they abound or be deficient in Hay or Oats, or Cows or *Yahoos*? And where-ever there is any Want (which is but seldom) it is immediately supplied by unanimous Consent and Contribution. Here likewise the Regulation of Children is settled: As for instance, if a *Houyhnhnm* hath two Males, he changeth one of them with another who hath two Females: And when a Child hath been lost by any Casualty, where the Mother is past Breeding, it is determined what Family in the District shall breed another to supply the Loss.

CHAPTER IX.

A GRAND DEBATE AT THE GENERAL ASSEMBLY OF THE HOUYHNHNMS; AND HOW IT WAS DETERMINED. THE LEARNING OF THE HOUYHNHNMS. THEIR BUILDINGS. THEIR MANNER OF BURIALS. THE DEFECTIVENESS OF THEIR LANGUAGE.

O N E of these Grand Assemblies was held in my time, about three Months before my Departure, whither my Master went as the Representative of our District. In this Council was resumed their old Debate, and indeed, the only Debate that ever happened in their Country; whereof my Master after his Return gave me a very particular Account.

THE Question to be debated, was, Whether the *Yahoos* should be exterminated from the Face of the Earth. One of the *Members* for the Affirmative offered several Arguments of great Strength and Weight; alledging, That, as the *Yahoos* were the most filthy, noisome, and deformed Animal which Nature ever produced, so they were the most restive and indocible, mischievous and malicious: They would privately suck the Teats of the *Houyhnhnms* Cows; kill and devour their Cats, trample down their Oats and Grass, if they were not continually watched; and commit a Thousand other Extravagancies. He took Notice of a general Tradition, that *Yahoos* had not been always in their Country: But, that many Ages ago, two of these Brutes appeared together upon a Mountain; whether produced by the Heat of the Sun upon corrupted Mud and Slime, or from the Ooze and Froth of the Sea, was never known. That these *Yahoos* engendered, and their Brood in a short time grew so numerous as to over-run and infest the whole Nation. That the *Houyhnhnms* to get rid of this Evil, made a general Hunting, and at last inclosed the whole Herd; and destroying the Older, every *Houyhnhnm* kept two young Ones in a Kennel, and brought them to such a Degree of Tameness, as an Animal so savage by Nature can be capable of acquiring; using them for Draught and Carriage. That, there seemed to be much Truth in this Tradition, and that those Creatures could not be *Ylnhniamshy* (or *Aborigines* of the Land) because of the violent Hatred the *Houyhnhnms* as well as all other Animals, bore them; which although their evil Disposition sufficiently deserved, could never have arrived at so high a Degree, if they had been *Aborigines*, or else they would have long since been rooted out. That, the Inhabitants taking a Fancy to use the Service of the *Yahoos*, had very imprudently neglected to cultivate the Breed of *Asses*, which were a comely Animal, easily kept, more tame and orderly, without any offensive Smell, strong enough for Labour, although they yield to the other in Agility of Body; and if their Braying be no agreeable Sound, it is far preferable to the horrible Howlings of the *Yahoos*.

SEVERAL others declared their Sentiments to the same Purpose; when my Master proposed an Expedient to the Assembly, whereof he had indeed borrowed the Hint from me. He approved of the Tradition, mentioned by the *Honourable Member*, who spoke before; and affirmed, that the two *Yahoos* said to be first seen among them, had been driven thither over the Sea; that coming to Land, and being forsaken by their Companions, they retired to the Mountains, and degenerating by Degrees, became in Process of Time, much more savage than those of their own Species in the Country from whence these two Originals came. The Reason of his Assertion was, that he had now in his Possession, a certain wonderful *Yahoo*, (meaning myself) which most of them had heard of, and many of them had seen. He then related to them, how he first found me; that, my Body was all covered with an artificial Composure of the Skins and Hairs of other Animals: That, I spoke in a Language of my own; and had thoroughly learned theirs: That, I had related to him the Accidents which brought me thither: That, when he saw me without my Covering, I was an exact *Yahoo* in every Part, only of a whiter Colour, less hairy, and with shorter Claws. He added, how I had endeavoured to persuade him, that in my own and other Countries the *Yahoos* acted as the governing, rational Animal, and held the *Houyhnhnms* in Servitude: That, he observed in me all the Qualities of a *Yahoo*, only a little more civilized by some Tincture of Reason; which however was in a Degree as far inferior to the *Houyhnhnm* Race, as the *Yahoos* of their Country were to me: That, among other things, I mentioned a Custom we had of *castrating Houyhnhnms* when they were young, in order to render them tame; that the Operation was easy and safe; that it was no Shame to learn Wisdom from Brutes, as Industry is taught by the Ant, and Building by the Swallow. (For so I translate the Word *Lyhannh*, although it be a much larger Fowl) That, this Invention might be practiced upon the younger *Yahoos* here, which, besides rendering them tractable and fitter for Use, would in an Age put an End to the whole Species without destroying Life. That, in the mean time the *Houyhnhnms* should be *exhorted* to cultivate the Breed of Asses, which, as they are in all respects more valuable Brutes; so they have this Advantage, to be fit for Service at five Years old, which the others are not till Twelve.

THIS was all my Master thought fit to tell me at that Time, of what passed in the Grand Council. But he was pleased to conceal one Particular, which related personally to myself, whereof I soon felt the unhappy Effect, as the

Reader will know in its proper Place, and from whence I date all the succeeding Misfortunes of my Life.

THE *Houyhnhnms* have no Letters, and consequently, their Knowledge is all traditional. But there happening few Events of any Moment among a People so well united, naturally disposed to every Virtue, wholly governed by Reason, and cut off from all Commerce with other Nations; the historical Part is easily preserved without burthening their Memories. I have already observed, that they are subject to no Diseases, and therefore can have no Need of Physicians. However, they have excellent Medicines composed of Herbs, to cure accidental Bruises and Cuts in the Pastern or Frog of the Foot by sharp Stones, as well as other Maims and Hurts in the several Parts of the Body.

THEY calculate the Year by the Revolution of the Sun and the Moon, but use no Subdivisions into Weeks. They are well enough acquainted with the Motions of those two Luminaries, and understand the Nature of *Eclipses*; and this is the utmost Progress of their *Astronomy*.

IN *Poetry* they must be allowed to excel all other Mortals; wherein the Justness of their Similes, and the Minuteness, as well as Exactness of their Descriptions, are indeed inimitable. Their Verses abound very much in both of these; and usually contain either some exalted Notions of Friendship and Benevolence, or the Praises of those who were Victors in Races, and other bodily Exercises. Their Buildings, although very rude and simple, are not inconvenient, but well contrived to defend them from all Injuries of Cold and Heat. They have a Kind of Tree, which at Forty Years old loosens in the Root, and falls with the first Storm; it grows very strait, and being pointed like Stakes with a sharp Stone, (for the *Houyhnhnms* know not the Use of Iron) they stick them erect in the Ground about ten Inches asunder, and then weave in Oat-straw, or sometimes Wattles betwixt them. The Roof is made after the same Manner, and so are the Doors.

THE *Houyhnhnms* use the hollow Part between the Pastern and the Hoof of their Fore-feet, as we do our Hands, and this with greater Dexterity, than I could at first imagine.

I have seen a white Mare of our Family thread a Needle (which I lent her on Purpose) with that Joynt. They milk their Cows, reap their Oats, and do all the Work whch requires Hands, in the same Manner. They have a Kind of hard Flints, which by grinding against other Stones, they form into Instruments, that serve instead of Wedges, Axes, and Hammers. With Tools made of these Flints, they likewise cut their Hay, and reap their Oats, which there groweth naturally in several Fields: The *Yahoos* draw home the Sheaves in Carriages, and the Servants tread them in certain covered Hutts, to get out the Grain, which is kept in Stores. They make a rude Kind of earthen and wooden Vessels, and bake the former in the Sun.

IF they can avoid Casualties, they die only of old Age, and are buried in the obscurest Places that can be found, their Friends and Relations expressing neither Joy nor Grief at their Departure; nor does the dying Person discover the least Regret that he is leaving the World, any more than if he were upon returning home from a Visit to one of his Neighbours: I remember, my Master having once made an Appointment with a Friend and his Family to come to his House upon some Affair of Importance; on the Day fixed, the Mistress and her two Children came very late; she made two Excuses, first for her Husband, who, as she said, happened that very Morning to *Lhnuwnh*. The Word is strongly expressive in their Language, but not easily rendered into *English*; it signifies, *to retire to his first Mother*. Her Excuse for not coming sooner, was, that her Husband dying late in the Morning, she was a good while consulting her Servants about a convenient Place where his Body should be laid; and I observed she behaved herself at our House, as chearfully as the rest: She died about three Months after.

THEY live generally to Seventy or Seventy-five Years, very seldom to Fourscore: Some Weeks before their Death they feel a gradual Decay, but without Pain. During this time they are much visited by their Friends, because they cannot go abroad with their usual Ease and Satisfaction. However, about ten Days before their Death, which they seldom fail

K

in computing, they return the Visits that have been made by those who are nearest in the Neighbourhood, being carried in a convenient Sledge drawn by *Yahoos*; which Vehicle they use, not only upon this Occasion, but when they grow old, upon long Journeys, or when they are lamed by any Accident. And therefore when the dying *Houyhnhnms* return those Visits, they take a solemn Leave of their Friends, as if they were going to some remote Part of the Country, where they designed to pass the rest of their Lives.

I KNOW not whether it may be worth observing, that the *Houyhnhnms* have no Word in their Language to express any thing that is *evil*, except what they borrow from the Deformities or ill Qualities of the *Yahoos*. Thus they denote the Folly of a Servant, an Omission of a Child, a Stone that cuts their Feet, a Continuance of foul or unseasonable Weather, and the like, by adding to each the Epithet of *Yahoo*. For Instance, *Hhnm Yahoo, Whnaholm Yahoo, Ynlhmndwihlma Yahoo*, and an ill contrived House, *Ynholmhnmrohlnw Yahoo*.

I COULD with great Pleasure enlarge farther upon the Manners and Virtues of this excellent People; but intending in a short time to publish a Volume by itself expressly upon that Subject, I refer the Reader thither. And in the mean time, proceed to relate my own sad Catastrophe.

CHAPTER X.

THE AUTHOR'S OECONOMY AND HAPPY LIFE AMONG THE
HOUYHNHNMS. HIS GREAT IMPROVEMENT IN VIRTUE, BY
CONVERSING WITH THEM. THEIR CONVERSATIONS. THE
AUTHOR HATH NOTICE GIVEN HIM BY HIS MASTER THAT
HE MUST DEPART FROM THE COUNTRY. HE FALLS INTO
A SWOON FOR GRIEF, BUT SUBMITS. HE CONTRIVES AND
FINISHES A CANOO, BY THE HELP OF A FELLOW-SERVANT,
AND PUTS TO SEA AT A VENTURE.

I HAD settled my little Oeconomy to my own Heart's
Content. My Master had ordered a Room to be made
for me after their Manner, about six Yards from the
House; the Sides and Floors of which I plaistered with
Clay, and covered with Rush-mats of my own contriving:
I had beaten Hemp, which there grows wild, and made of it
a Sort of Ticking: This I filled with the Feathers of several
Birds I had taken with Springes made of *Yahoos* Hairs;
and were excellent Food. I had worked two Chairs with
my Knife, the Sorrel Nag helping me in the grosser and
more laborious Part. When my Cloaths were worn to Rags,
I made my self others with the Skins of Rabbets, and of a
certain beautiful Animal about the same Size, called *Nnuh-
noh*, the Skin of which is covered with a fine Down. Of
these I likewise made very tolerable Stockings. I soaled my
Shoes with Wood which I cut from a Tree, and fitted to the
upper Leather, and when this was worn out, I supplied it
with the Skins of *Yahoos*, dried in the Sun. I often got
Honey out of hollow Trees, which I mingled with Water,
or eat it with my Bread. No Man could more verify the
Truth of these two Maxims, *That, Nature is very easily satisfied*; and, *That, Necessity is the Mother of Invention.* I enjoyed perfect Health of Body, and Tranquility of Mind; I
did not feel the Treachery or Inconstancy of a Friend, nor
the Injuries of a secret or open Enemy. I had no Occasion

of bribing, flattering or pimping, to procure the Favour of any great Man, or of his Minion. I wanted no Fence against Fraud or Oppression: Here was neither Physician to destroy my Body, nor Lawyer to ruin my Fortune: No Informer to watch my Words and Actions, or forge Accusations against me for Hire: Here were no Gibers, Censurers, Backbiters, Pick-pockets, Highwaymen, House-breakers, Attorneys, Bawds, Buffoons, Gamesters, Politicians, Wits, Spleneticks, tedious Talkers, Controvertists, Ravishers, Murderers, Robbers, Virtuoso's; no Leaders or Followers of Party and Faction; no Encouragers to Vice, by Seducement or Examples: No Dungeon, Axes, Gibbets, Whipping posts, or Pillories; No cheating Shop-keepers or Mechanicks: No Pride, Vanity or Affectation: No Fops, Bullies, Drunkards, strolling Whores, or Poxes: No ranting, lewd, expensive Wives: No stupid, proud Pedants: No importunate, over-bearing, quarrelsome, noisy, roaring, empty, conceited, swearing Companions: No Scoundrels raised from the Dust upon the Merit of their Vices; or Nobility thrown into it on account of their Virtues: No Lords, Fidlers, Judges or Dancing-Masters.

I HAD the Favour of being admitted to several *Houyhnhnms*, who came to visit or dine with my Master; where his Honour graciously suffered me to wait in the Room, and listen to their Discourse. Both he and his Company would often descend to ask me Questions, and receive my Answers. I had also sometimes the Honour of attending my Master in his Visits to others. I never presumed to speak, except in answer to a Question; and then I did it with inward Regret, because it was a Loss of so much Time for improving my self: But I was infinitely delighted with the Station of an humble Auditor in such Conversations, where nothing passed but what was useful, expressed in the fewest and most significant Words: Where (as I have already said) the greatest *Decency* was observed, without the least Degree of Ceremony; where no Person spoke without being pleased himself, and pleasing his Companions: Where there was no Interruption, Tediousness, Heat, or Difference of Sentiments. They have a Notion, That when People are met together, a short Silence doth much improve Conversation: This I found to be true; for during those little Intermissions of Talk, new Ideas would arise in their Minds, which very much enlivened the Discourse. Their Subjects are generally on Friendship and Benevolence; on Order and Oeconomy; sometimes upon the visible Operations of Nature, or ancient Traditions; upon the Bounds and Limits of Virtue; upon the unerring Rules of Reason; or upon some Determinations, to be taken at the next great Assembly; and often upon the various Excellencies of *Poetry*. I may add, without Vanity, that my Presence often gave them sufficient Matter for Discourse, because it afforded my Master an Occasion of letting his Friends into the History of me and my Country, upon which they were all pleased to discant in a Manner not very advantageous to human Kind; and for that Reason I shall not repeat what they said: Only I may be allowed to observe, That his Honour, to my great Admiration, appeared to understand the Nature of *Yahoos* much better than my self. He went through all our Vices and Follies, and discovered many which I had never mentioned to him; by only supposing what Qualities a *Yahoo* of their Country, with a small Proportion of Reason, might be capable of exerting: And concluded, with too much Probability, how vile as well as miserable such a Creature must be.

I FREELY confess, that all the little Knowledge I have of any Value, was acquired by the Lectures I received from my Master, and from hearing the Discourses of him and his Friends; to which I should be prouder to listen, than to dictate to the greatest and wisest Assembly in *Europe*. I admired the Strength, Comeliness and Speed of the Inhabitants; and such a Constellation of Virtues in such amiable Persons produced in me the highest Veneration. At first, indeed, I did not feel that natural Awe which the *Yahoos* and all other Animals bear towards them; but it grew upon me by Degrees, much sooner than I imagined, and was mingled with a respectful Love and Gratitude, that they would condescend to distinguish me from the rest of my Species.

When I thought of my Family, my Friends, my Country-men, or human Race in general, I considered them as they really were, *Yahoos* in Shape and Disposition, perhaps a little more civilized, and qualified with the Gift of Speech; but making no other Use of Reason, than to improve and multiply those Vices, whereof their Brethren in this Country had only the Share that Nature allotted them. When I hap-pened to behold the Reflection of my own Form in a Lake or Fountain, I turned away my Face in Horror and detesta-tion of my self; and could better endure the Sight of a common *Yahoo*, than of my own Person. By conversing with the *Houyhnhnms*, and looking upon them with Delight, I fell to imitate their Gait and Gesture, which is now grown into a Habit; and my Friends often tell me in a blunt Way, that *I trot like a Horse*; which, however, I take for a great Compliment: Neither shall I disown, that in speaking I am apt to fall into the Voice and manner of the *Houyhnhnms*, and hear my self ridiculed on that Account without the least Mortification.

In the Midst of this Happiness, when I looked upon my self to be fully settled for Life, my Master sent for me one Morning a little earlier than his usual Hour. I observed by his Countenance that he was in some Perplexity, and at a Loss how to begin what he had to speak. After a short Silence, he told me, he did not know how I would take what he was going to say: That, in the last general As-sembly, when the Affair of the *Yahoos* was entered upon, the Representatives had taken Offence at his keeping a *Yahoo* (meaning my self) in his Family more like a *Houyhnhnm* than a Brute Animal. That, he was known frequently to converse with me, as if he could receive some Advantage or Pleasure in my Company: That, such a Practice was not agreeable to Reason or Nature, or a thing ever heard of before among them. The Assembly did there-fore *exhort* him, either to employ me like the rest of my Species, or command me to swim back to the Place from whence I came. That, the first of these Expedients was utterly rejected by all the *Houyhnhnms*, who had ever seen me at his House or their own: For, they alledged, That because I had some Rudiments of Reason, added to the natural Pravity of those Animals, it was to be feared, I might be able to seduce them into the woody and mountainous Parts of the Country, and bring them in Troops by Night to destroy the *Houyhnhnms* Cattle, as being naturally of the ravenous Kind, and averse from Labour.

MY Master added, That he was daily pressed by the *Houyhnhnms* of the Neighbourhood to have the Assembly's *Exhortation* executed, which he could not put off much longer. He doubted, it would be impossible for me to swim to another Country; and therefore wished I would contrive some Sort of Vehicle resembling those I had described to him, that might carry me on the Sea; in which Work I should have the Assistance of his own Servants, as well as those of his Neighbours. He concluded, that for his own Part he could have been content to keep me in his Service as long as I lived; because he found I had cured myself of some bad Habits and Dispositions, by endeavouring, as far as my inferior Nature was capable, to imitate the *Houyhnhnms*.

I SHOULD here observe to the Reader, that a Decree of the general Assembly in this Country, is expressed by the Word *Hnhloayn*, which signifies an *Exhortation*; as near as I can render it: For they have no Conception how a rational Creature can be *compelled*, but only advised, or *exhorted*; because no Person can disobey Reason, without giving up his Claim to be a rational Creature.

I WAS struck with the utmost Grief and Despair at my Master's Discourse; and being unable to support the Agonies I was under, I fell into a Swoon at his Feet: When I came to myself, he told me, that he concluded I had been dead. (For these People are subject to no such Imbecillities of Nature) I answered, in a faint Voice, that Death would have been too great an Happiness; that although I could not blame the Assembly's *Exhortation*, or the Urgency of his Friends; yet in my weak and corrupt Judgment, I thought it might consist with Reason to have been less rigorous. That, I could not swim a League, and probably the nearest Land to theirs might be distant above an

Hundred: That, many Materials, necessary for making a small Vessel to carry me off, were wholly wanting in this Country, which however, I would attempt in Obedience and Gratitude to his Honour, although I concluded the thing to be impossible, and therefore looked on myself as already devoted to Destruction. That, the certain Prospect of an unnatural Death, was the least of my Evils: For, supposing I should escape with Life by some strange Adventure, how could I think with Temper, of passing my Days among *Yahoos*, and relapsing into my old Corruptions, for want of Examples to lead and keep me within the Paths of Virtue. That, I knew too well upon what solid Reasons all the Determinations of the wise *Houyhnhnms* were founded, not to be shaken by Arguments of mine, a miserable *Yahoo*; and therefore after presenting him with my humble Thanks for the Offer of his Servants Assistance in making a Vessel, and desiring a reasonable Time for so difficult a Work, I told him, I would endeavour to preserve a wretched Being; and, if ever I returned to *England*, was not without Hopes of being useful to my own Species, by celebrating the Praises of the renowned *Houyhnhnms*, and proposing their Virtues to the Imitation of Mankind.

My Master in a few Words made me a very gracious Reply, allowed me the Space of two *Months* to finish my Boat; and ordered the Sorrel Nag, my Fellow-Servant, (for so at this Distance I may presume to call him) to follow my Instructions, because I told my Master, that his Help would be sufficient, and I knew he had a Tenderness for me.

In his Company my first Business was to go to that Part of the Coast, where my rebellious Crew had ordered me to be set on Shore. I got upon a Height, and looking on every Side into the Sea, fancied I saw a small Island, towards the *North-East*: I took out my Pocket-glass, and could then clearly distinguish it about five Leagues off, as I computed; but it appeared to the Sorrel Nag to be only a blue Cloud: For, as he had no Conception of any Country beside his own, so he could not be as expert in distinguishing remote Objects at Sea, as we who so much converse in that Element.

AFTER I had discovered this Island, I considered no farther; but resolved, it should, if possible, be the first Place of my Banishment, leaving the Consequence to Fortune.

I RETURNED home, and consulting with the Sorrel Nag, we went into a Copse at some Distance, where I with my Knife, and he with a sharp Flint fastened very artificially, after their Manner, to a wooden Handle, cut down several Oak Wattles about the Thickness of a Walking-staff, and some larger Pieces. But I shall not trouble the Reader with a particular Description of my own Mechanicks: Let it suffice to say, that in six Weeks time, with the Help of the Sorrel Nag, who performed the Parts that required most Labour, I finished a Sort of *Indian* Canoo; but much larger, covering it with the Skins of *Yahoos*, well stitched together, with hempen Threads of my own making. My Sail was likewise composed of the Skins of the same Animal; but I made use of the youngest I could get; the older being too tough and thick; and I likewise provided myself with four Paddles. I laid in a Stock of boiled Flesh, of Rabbets and Fowls; and took with me two Vessels, one filled with Milk, and the other with Water.

I TRIED my Canoo in a large Pond near my Master's House, and then corrected in it what was amiss; stopping all the Chinks with *Yahoos* Tallow, till I found it stanch, and able to bear me, and my Freight. And when it was as compleat as I could possibly make it, I had it drawn on a Carriage very gently by *Yahoos*, to the Sea-side, under the Conduct of the Sorrel Nag, and another Servant.

WHEN all was ready, and the Day came for my Departure, I took Leave of my Master and Lady, and the whole Family, my Eyes flowing with Tears, and my Heart quite sunk with Grief. But his Honour, out of Curiosity, and perhaps (if I may speak it without Vanity) partly out of Kindness, was determined to see me in my Canoo; and got several of his neighbouring Friends to accompany him. I was forced to wait above an Hour for the Tide, and then observing the Wind very fortunately bearing towards the Island, to which I intended to steer my Course, I took a second Leave of my Master: But as I was going to prostrate myself to kiss his

Hoof, he did me the Honour to raise it gently to my Mouth. I am not ignorant how much I have been censured for mentioning this last Particular. Detractors are pleased to think it improbable, that so illustrious a Person should descend to give so great a Mark of Distinction to a Creature so inferior as I. Neither have I forgot, how apt some Travellers are to boast of extraordinary Favours they have received. But, if these Censurers were better acquainted with the noble and courteous Disposition of the *Houyhnhnms*, they would soon change their Opinion.

I PAID my Respects to the rest of the *Houyhnhnms* in his Honour's Company; then getting into my Canoo, I pushed off from Shore.

CHAPTER XI.

THE AUTHOR'S DANGEROUS VOYAGE. HE ARRIVES AT NEW-HOLLAND, HOPING TO SETTLE THERE. IS WOUNDED WITH AN ARROW BY ONE OF THE NATIVES. IS SEIZED AND CARRIED BY FORCE INTO A PORTUGUEZE SHIP. THE GREAT CIVILITIES OF THE CAPTAIN. THE AUTHOR ARRIVES AT ENGLAND.

I BEGAN this desperate Voyage on *February* 15, 1714/5, at 9 o'Clock in the Morning. The Wind was very favourable; however, I made use at first only of my Paddles; but considering I should soon be weary, and that the Wind might probably chop about, I ventured to set up my little Sail; and thus, with the Help of the Tide, I went at the Rate of a League and a Half an Hour, as near as I could guess. My Master and his Friends continued on the Shoar, till I was almost out of Sight; and I often heard the Sorrel Nag (who always loved me) crying out, *Hnuy illa nyha maiah Yahoo*, Take Care of thy self, gentle *Yahoo*.

MY Design was, if possible, to discover some small Island uninhabited, yet sufficient by my Labour to furnish me with Necessaries of Life, which I would have thought a greater

Happiness than to be first Minister in the politest Court of *Europe*; so horrible was the Idea I conceived of returning to live in the Society and under the Government of *Yahoos*. For in such a Solitude as I desired, I could at least enjoy my own Thoughts, and reflect with Delight on the Virtues of those inimitable *Houyhnhnms*, without any Opportunity of degenerating into the Vices and Corruptions of my own Species.

The Reader may remember what I related when my Crew conspired against me, and confined me to my Cabbin. How I continued there several Weeks, without knowing what Course we took; and when I was put ashore in the Long-boat, how the Sailors told me with Oaths, whether true or false, that they knew not in what Part of the World we were. However, I did then believe us to be about ten Degrees *Southward* of the *Cape of Good Hope*, or about 45 Degrees *Southern* Latitude, as I gathered from some general Words I overheard among them, being I supposed to the *South-East* in their intended Voyage to *Madagascar*. And although this were but little better than Conjecture, yet I resolved to steer my Course *Eastward*, hoping to reach the *South-West* Coast of *New-Holland*, and perhaps some such Island as I desired, lying *Westward* of it. The Wind was full West, and by six in the Evening I computed I had gone *Eastward* at least eighteen Leagues; when I spied a very small Island about half a League off, which I soon reached. It was nothing but a Rock with one Creek, naturally arched by the Force of Tempests. Here I put in my Canoo, and climbing a Part of the Rock, I could plainly discover Land to the *East*, extending from *South* to *North*. I lay all Night in my Canoo; and repeating my Voyage early in the Morning, I arrived in seven Hours to the *South-East* Point of *New-Holland*. This confirmed me in the Opinion I have long entertained, that the *Maps* and *Charts* place this Country at least three Degrees more to the *East* than it really is; which Thought I communicated many Years ago to my worthy Friend Mr. *Herman Moll*, and gave him my Reasons for it, although he hath rather chosen to follow other Authors.

I saw no Inhabitants in the Place where I landed; and being unarmed, I was afraid of venturing far into the Country. I found some Shell-Fish on the Shore, and eat them raw, not daring to kindle a Fire, for fear of being discovered by the Natives. I continued three Days feeding on Oysters and Limpits, to save my own Provisions; and I fortunately found a Brook of excellent Water, which gave me great Relief.

On the fourth Day, venturing out early a little too far, I saw twenty or thirty Natives upon a Height, not above five hundred Yards from me. They were stark naked, Men, Women and Children round a Fire, as I could discover by the Smoke. One of them spied me, and gave Notice to the rest; five of them advanced towards me, leaving the Women and Children at the Fire. I made what haste I could to the Shore, and getting into my Canoo, shoved off: The Savages observing me retreat, ran after me; and before I could get far enough into the Sea, discharged an Arrow, which wounded me deeply on the Inside of my left Knee (I shall carry the Mark to my Grave.) I apprehended the Arrow might be poisoned; and paddling out of the Reach of their Darts (being a calm Day) I made a shift to suck the Wound, and dress it as well as I could.

I was at a Loss what to do, for I durst not return to the same Landing-place, but stood to the *North*, and was forced to paddle; for the Wind, although very gentle, was against me, blowing *North-West*. As I was looking about for a secure Landing-place, I saw a Sail to the *North North-East*, which appearing every Minute more visible, I was in some Doubt, whether I should wait for them or no; but at last my Detestation of the *Yahoo* Race prevailed; and turning my Canoo, I sailed and paddled together to the *South*, and got into the same Creek from whence I set out in the Morning; choosing rather to trust my self among these *Barbarians* than live with *European Yahoos*. I drew up my Canoo as close as I could to the Shore, and hid my self behind a Stone by the little Brook, which, as I have already said, was excellent Water.

The Ship came within half a League of this Creek, and

sent out her Long-Boat with Vessels to take in fresh Water (for the Place it seems was very well known) but I did not observe it until the Boat was almost on Shore; and it was too late to seek another Hiding-Place. The Seamen at their landing observed my Canoo, and rummaging it all over, easily conjectured that the Owner could not be far off. Four of them well armed searched every Cranny and Lurking-hole, till at last they found me flat on my Face behind the Stone. They gazed a while in Admiration at my strange uncouth Dress; my Coat made of Skins, my wooden-soaled Shoes, and my furred Stockings; from whence, however, they concluded I was not a Native of the Place, who all go naked. One of the Seamen in *Portugueze* bid me rise, and asked who I was. I understood that Language very well, and getting upon my Feet, said, I was a poor *Yahoo*, banished from the *Houyhnhnms*, and desired they would please to let me depart. They admired to hear me answer them in their own Tongue, and saw by my Complection I must be an *European*; but were at a Loss to know what I meant by *Yahoos* and *Houyhnhnms*, and at the same Time fell a laughing at my strange Tone in speaking, which resembled the Neighing of a Horse. I trembled all the while betwixt Fear and Hatred: I again desired Leave to depart, and was gently moving to my Canoo; but they laid hold on me, desiring to know what Country I was of? whence I came? with many other Questions. I told them, I was born in *England*, from whence I came about five Years ago, and then their Country and ours was at Peace. I therefore hoped they would not treat me as an Enemy, since I meant them no Harm, but was a poor *Yahoo*, seeking some desolate Place where to pass the Remainder of his unfortunate Life.

WHEN they began to talk, I thought I never heard or saw any thing so unnatural; for it appeared to me as monstrous as if a Dog or a Cow should speak in *England*, or a *Yahoo* in *Houyhnhnm-Land*. The honest *Portugueze* were equally amazed at my strange Dress, and the odd Manner of delivering my Words, which however they understood very well. They spoke to me with great Humanity, and said they were sure their Captain would carry me *gratis* to *Lisbon*, from whence I might return to my own Country; that two of the Seamen would go back to the Ship, to inform the Captain of what they had seen, and receive his Orders; in the mean Time, unless I would give my solemn Oath not to fly, they would secure me by Force. I thought it best to comply with their Proposal. They were very curious to know my Story, but I gave them very little Satisfaction; and they all conjectured, that my Misfortunes had impaired my Reason. In two Hours the Boat, which went loaden with Vessels of Water, returned with the Captain's Commands to fetch me on Board. I fell on my Knees to preserve my Liberty; but all was in vain, and the Men having tied me with Cords, heaved me into the Boat, from whence I was taken into the Ship, and from thence into the Captain's Cabbin.

His Name was *Pedro de Mendez*; he was a very courteous and generous Person; he entreated me to give some Account of my self, and desired to know what I would eat or drink; said, I should be used as well as himself, and spoke so many obliging Things, that I wondered to find such Civilities from a *Yahoo*. However, I remained silent and sullen; I was ready to faint at the very Smell of him and his Men. At last I desired something to eat out of my own Canoo; but he ordered me a Chicken and some excellent Wine, and then directed that I should be put to Bed in a very clean Cabbin. I would not undress my self, but lay on the Bed-cloaths; and in half an Hour stole out, when I thought the Crew was at Dinner; and getting to the Side of the Ship, was going to leap into the Sea, and swim for my Life, rather than continue among *Yahoos*. But one of the Seamen prevented me, and having informed the Captain, I was chained to my Cabbin.

After Dinner *Don Pedro* came to me, and desired to know my Reason for so desperate an Attempt; assured me he only meant to do me all the Service he was able; and spoke so very movingly, that at last I descended to treat him like an Animal which had some little Portion of Reason. I gave him a very short Relation of my Voyage; of the

Conspiracy against me by my own Men; of the Country where they set me on Shore, and of my five Years Residence there. All which he looked upon as if it were a Dream or a Vision; whereat I took great Offence: For I had quite forgot the Faculty of Lying, so peculiar to *Yahoos* in all Countries where they preside, and consequently the Disposition of suspecting Truth in others of their own Species. I asked him, Whether it were the Custom of his Country to *say the Thing that was not*? I assured him I had almost forgot what he meant by Falshood; and if I had lived a thousand Years in *Houyhnhnmland*, I should never have heard a Lie from the meanest Servant. That I was altogether indifferent whether he believed me or no; but however, in return for his Favours, I would give so much Allowance to the Corruption of his Nature, as to answer any Objection he would please to make; and he might easily discover the Truth.

THE Captain, a wise Man, after many Endeavours to catch me tripping in some Part of my Story, at last began to have a better Opinion of my Veracity. But he added, that since I professed so inviolable an Attachment to Truth, I must give him my Word of Honour to bear him Company in this Voyage without attempting any thing against my Life; or else he would continue me a Prisoner till we arrived at *Lisbon*. I gave him the Promise he required; but at the same time protested that I would suffer the greatest Hardships rather than return to live among *Yahoos*.

OUR Voyage passed without any considerable Accident. In Gratitude to the Captain I sometimes sate with him at his earnest Request, and strove to conceal my Antipathy against human Kind, although it often broke out; which he suffered to pass without Observation. But the greatest Part of the Day, I confined myself to my Cabbin, to avoid seeing any of the Crew. The Captain had often intreated me to strip myself of my savage Dress, and offered to lend me the best Suit of Cloaths he had. This I would not be prevailed on to accept, abhorring to cover myself with any thing that had been on the Back of a *Yahoo*. I only desired he would lend me two clean Shirts, which having been washed since he wore them, I believed would not so much defile me. These I changed every second Day, and washed them myself.

WE arrived at *Lisbon, Nov.* 5, 1715. At our landing, the Captain forced me to cover myself with his Cloak, to prevent the Rabble from crouding about me. I was conveyed to his own House; and at my earnest Request, he led me up to the highest Room backwards. I conjured him to conceal from all Persons what I had told him of the *Houyhnhnms*; because the least Hint of such a Story would not only draw Numbers of People to see me, but probably put me in Danger of being imprisoned, or burnt by the *Inquisition.* The Captain persuaded me to accept a Suit of Cloaths newly made; but I would not suffer the Taylor to take my Measure; however, Don *Pedro* being almost of my Size, they fitted me well enough. He accoutred me with other Necessaries all new, which I aired for Twenty-four Hours before I would use them.

THE Captain had no Wife, nor above three Servants, none of which were suffered to attend at Meals; and his whole Deportment was so obliging, added to very good *human* Understanding, that I really began to tolerate his Company. He gained so far upon me, that I ventured to look out of the back Window. By Degrees I was brought into another Room, from whence I peeped into the Street, but drew my Head back in a Fright. In a Week's Time he seduced me down to the Door. I found my Terror gradually lessened, but my Hatred and Contempt seemed to increase. I was at last bold enough to walk the Street in his Company, but kept my Nose well stopped with Rue, or sometimes with Tobacco.

IN ten Days, Don *Pedro*, to whom I had given some Account of my domestick Affairs, put it upon me as a Point of Honour and Conscience, that I ought to return to my native Country, and live at home with my Wife and Children. He told me, there was an *English* Ship in the Port just ready to sail, and he would furnish me with all things necessary. It would be tedious to repeat his Arguments, and my Contradictions. He said, it was altogether impossible to find such a solitary Island as I had desired to live in;

but I might command in my own House, and pass my time in a Manner as recluse as I pleased.

I COMPLIED at last, finding I could not do better. I left *Lisbon* the 24th Day of *November*, in an *English* Merchantman, but who was the Master I never inquired. Don *Pedro* accompanied me to the Ship, and lent me Twenty Pounds. He took kind Leave of me, and embraced me at parting; which I bore as well as I could. During this last Voyage I had no Commerce with the Master, or any of his Men; but pretending I was sick kept close in my Cabbin. On the Fifth of *December*, 1715, we cast Anchor in the *Downs* about Nine in the Morning, and at Three in the Afternoon I got safe to my House at *Redriff*.

MY Wife and Family received me with great Surprize and Joy, because they concluded me certainly dead; but I must freely confess, the Sight of them filled me only with Hatred, Disgust and Contempt; and the more, by reflecting on the near Alliance I had to them. For, although since my unfortunate Exile from the *Houyhnhnm* Country, I had compelled myself to tolerate the Sight of *Yahoos*, and to converse with Don *Pedro de Mendez*; yet my Memory and Imaginations were perpetually filled with the Virtues and Ideas of those exalted *Houyhnhnms*. And when I began to consider, that by copulating with one of the *Yahoo*-Species, I had become a Parent of more; it struck me with the utmost Shame, Confusion and Horror.

As soon as I entered the House, my Wife took me in her Arms, and kissed me; at which, having not been used to the Touch of that odious Animal for so many Years, I fell in a Swoon for almost an Hour. At the Time I am writing, it is five Years since my last Return to *England*: During the first Year I could not endure my Wife or Children in my Presence, the very Smell of them was intolerable; much less could I suffer them to eat in the same Room. To this Hour they dare not presume to touch my Bread, or drink out of the same Cup; neither was I ever able to let one of them take me by the Hand. The first Money I laid out was to buy two young Stone-Horses, which I keep in a good Stable, and next to them the Groom is my greatest Favourite; for

I feel my Spirits revived by the Smell he contracts in the Stable. My Horses understand me tolerably well; I converse with them at least four Hours every Day. They are Strangers to Bridle or Saddle; they live in great Amity with me, and Friendship to each other.

CHAPTER XII.

THE AUTHOR'S VERACITY. HIS DESIGN IN PUBLISHING THIS WORK. HIS CENSURE OF THOSE TRAVELLERS WHO SWERVE FROM THE TRUTH. THE AUTHOR CLEARS HIMSELF FROM ANY SINISTER ENDS IN WRITING. AN OBJECTION ANSWERED. THE METHOD OF PLANTING COLONIES. HIS NATIVE COUNTRY COMMENDED. THE RIGHT OF THE CROWN TO THOSE COUNTRIES DESCRIBED BY THE AUTHOR, IS JUSTIFIED. THE DIFFICULTY OF CONQUERING THEM. THE AUTHOR TAKES HIS LAST LEAVE OF THE READER; PROPOSETH HIS MANNER OF LIVING FOR THE FUTURE; GIVES GOOD ADVICE, AND CONCLUDETH.

THUS, gentle Reader, I have given thee a faithful History of my Travels for Sixteen Years, and above Seven Months; wherein I have not been so studious of Ornament as of Truth. I could perhaps like others have astonished thee with strange improbable Tales; but I rather chose to relate plain Matter of Fact in the simplest Manner and Style; because my principal Design was to inform, and not to amuse thee.

It is easy for us who travel into remote Countries, which are seldom visited by *Englishmen* or other *Europeans*, to form Descriptions of wonderful Animals both at Sea and Land. Whereas, a Traveller's chief Aim should be to make Men wiser and better, and to improve their Minds by the bad, as well as good Example of what they deliver concerning foreign Places.

I COULD heartily wish a Law were enacted, that every Traveller, before he were permitted to publish his Voyages, should be obliged to make Oath before the *Lord High Chancellor*, that all he intended to print was absolutely true to the best of his Knowledge; for then the World would no longer be deceived as it usually is, while some Writers, to make their Works pass the better upon the Publick, impose the grossest Falsities on the unwary Reader. I have perused several Books of Travels with great Delight in my younger Days; but, having since gone over most Parts of the Globe, and been able to contradict many fabulous Accounts from my own Observation; it hath given me a great Disgust against this Part of Reading, and some Indignation to see the Credulity of Mankind so impudently abused. Therefore, since my Acquaintance were pleased to think my poor Endeavours might not be unacceptable to my Country; I imposed on myself as a Maxim, never to be swerved from, that I would *strictly adhere to Truth*; neither indeed can I be ever under the least Temptation to vary from it, while I retain in my Mind the Lectures and Example of my noble Master, and the other illustrious *Houyhnhnms*, of whom I had so long the Honour to be an humble Hearer.

> ——*Nec si miserum Fortuna Sinonem*
> *Finxit, vanum etiam, mendacemque improba finget.*

I KNOW very well, how little Reputation is to be got by Writings which require neither Genius nor Learning, nor indeed any other Talent, except a good Memory, or an exact *Journal*. I know likewise, that Writers of Travels, like *Dictionary*-Makers, are sunk into Oblivion by the Weight and Bulk of those who come last, and therefore lie uppermost. And it is highly probable, that such Travellers who shall hereafter visit the Countries described in this Work of mine, may by detecting my Errors, (if there be any) and adding many new Discoveries of their own, jostle me out of Vogue, and stand in my Place; making the World forget that ever I was an Author. This indeed would be too great a Mortification if I wrote for Fame: But, as my

sole Intention was the Publick Good, I cannot be altogether disappointed. For, who can read the Virtues I have
mentioned in the glorious *Houyhnhnms*, without being
ashamed of his own Vices, when he considers himself as the
reasoning, governing Animal of his Country ? I shall say
nothing of those remote Nations where *Yahoos* preside;
amongst which the least corrupted are the *Brobdingnagians*,
whose wise Maxims in Morality and Government, it would
be our Happiness to observe. But I forbear descanting
further, and rather leave the judicious Reader to his own
Remarks and Applications.

I am not a little pleased that this Work of mine can possibly meet with no Censurers: For what Objections can be
made against a Writer who relates only plain Facts that
happened in such distant Countries, where we have not the
least Interest with respect either to Trade or Negotiations ?
I have carefully avoided every Fault with which common
Writers of Travels are often too justly charged. Besides, I
meddle not the least with any *Party*, but write without
Passion, Prejudice, or Ill-will against any Man or Number
of Men whatsoever. I write for the noblest End, to inform
and instruct Mankind, over whom I may, without Breach
of Modesty, pretend to some Superiority, from the Advantages I received by conversing so long among the most accomplished *Houyhnhnms*. I write without any View towards
Profit or Praise. I never suffer a Word to pass that may
look like Reflection, or possibly give the least Offence even
to those who are most ready to take it. So that, I hope, I
may with Justice pronounce myself an Author perfectly
blameless; against whom the Tribes of Answerers, Con-
siderers, Observers, Reflecters, Detecters, Remarkers, will
never be able to find Matter for exercising their Talents.

I confess, it was whispered to me, that I was bound in
Duty as a Subject of *England*, to have given in a Memorial
to a Secretary of State, at my first coming over; because,
whatever Lands are discovered by a Subject, belong to
the Crown. But I doubt, whether our Conquests in the
Countries I treat of, would be as easy as those of *Ferdinando
Cortez* over the naked *Americans*. The *Lilliputians* I think,

are hardly worth the Charge of a Fleet and Army to reduce them; and I question whether it might be prudent or safe to attempt the *Brobdingnagians*: Or, whether an *English* Army would be much at their Ease with the Flying Island over their Heads. The *Houyhnhnms*, indeed, appear not to be so well prepared for War, a Science to which they are perfect Strangers, and especially against missive Weapons. However, supposing myself to be a Minister of State, I could never give my Advice for invading them. Their Prudence, Unanimity, Unacquaintedness with Fear, and their Love of their Country would amply supply all Defects in the military Art. Imagine twenty Thousand of them breaking into the Midst of an *European* Army, confounding the Ranks, overturning the Carriages, battering the Warriors Faces into Mummy, by terrible Yerks from their hinder Hoofs: For they would well deserve the Character given to *Augustus*; *Recalcitrat undique tutus.* But instead of Proposals for conquering that magnanimous Nation, I rather wish they were in a Capacity or Disposition to send a sufficient Number of their Inhabitants for civilizing *Europe*; by teaching us the first Principles of Honour, Justice, Truth, Temperance, publick Spirit, Fortitude, Chastity, Friendship, Benevolence, and Fidelity. The *Names* of all which Virtues are still retained among us in most Languages, and are to be met with in modern as well as ancient Authors; which I am able to assert from my own small Reading.

But, I had another Reason which made me less forward to enlarge his Majesty's Dominions by my Discoveries: To say the Truth, I had conceived a few Scruples with relation to the distributive Justice of Princes upon those Occasions. For Instance, A Crew of Pyrates are driven by a Storm they know not whither; at length a Boy discovers Land from the Top-mast; they go on Shore to rob and plunder; they see an harmless People, are entertained with Kindness, they give the Country a new Name, they take formal Possession of it for the King, they set up a rotten Plank or a Stone for a Memorial, they murder two or three Dozen of the Natives, bring away a Couple more by Force for a Sample, return home, and get their Pardon. Here commences a new

Dominion acquired with a Title by *Divine Right*. Ships are
sent with the first Opportunity; the Natives driven out or
destroyed, their Princes tortured to discover their Gold; a
free Licence given to all Acts of Inhumanity and Lust; the
Earth reeking with the Blood of its Inhabitants: And this
execrable Crew of Butchers employed in so pious an Expedition, is a *modern Colony* sent to convert and civilize
an idolatrous and barbarous People.

BUT this Description, I confess, doth by no means affect
the *British* Nation, who may be an Example to the whole
World for their Wisdom, Care, and Justice in planting
Colonies; the liberal Endowments for the Advancement of
Religion and Learning; their Choice of devout and able
Pastors to propagate *Christianity*; their Caution in stocking
their Provinces with People of sober Lives and Conversations from this the Mother Kingdom; their strict Regard
to the Distribution of Justice, in supplying the Civil Administration through all their Colonies with Officers of the
greatest Abilities, utter Strangers to Corruption: And to
crown all, by sending the most vigilant and virtuous Governors, who have no other Views than the Happiness of the
People over whom they preside, and the Honour of the
King their Master.

BUT, as those Countries which I have described do not
appear to have any Desire of being conquered, and enslaved,
murdered or driven out by Colonies; nor abound either in
Gold, Silver, Sugar or Tobacco; I did humbly conceive they
were by no Means proper Objects of our Zeal, our Valour,
or our Interest. However, if those whom it may concern,
think fit to be of another Opinion, I am ready to depose,
when I shall be lawfully called, That no *European* did ever
visit these Countries before me. I mean, if the Inhabitants
ought to be believed.

BUT, as to the Formality of taking Possession in my
Sovereign's Name, it never came once into my Thoughts;
and if it had, yet as my Affairs then stood, I should perhaps
in point of Prudence and Self-Preservation, have put it off
to a better Opportunity.

HAVING thus answered the *only* Objection that can be

raised against me as a Traveller; I here take a final Leave
of my Courteous Readers, and return to enjoy my own
Speculations in my little Garden at *Redriff*; to apply those
excellent Lessons of Virtue which I learned among the
Houyhnhnms; to instruct the *Yahoos* of my own Family as
far as I shall find them docible Animals; to behold my
Figure often in a Glass, and thus if possible habituate my
self by Time to tolerate the Sight of a human Creature: To
lament the Brutality of *Houyhnhnms* in my own Country,
but always treat their Persons with Respect, for the Sake
of my noble Master, his Family, his Friends, and the whole
Houyhnhnm Race, whom these of ours have the Honour
to resemble in all their Lineaments, however their Intellectuals came to degenerate.

I BEGAN last Week to permit my Wife to sit at Dinner
with me, at the farthest End of a long Table; and to answer
(but with the utmost Brevity) the few Questions I asked
her. Yet the Smell of a *Yahoo* continuing very offensive, I
always keep my Nose well stopt with Rue, Lavender, or
Tobacco-Leaves. And although it be hard for a Man late in
Life to remove old Habits; I am not altogether out of Hopes
in some Time to suffer a Neighbour *Yahoo* in my Company,
without the Apprehensions I am yet under of his Teeth or
his Claws.

MY Reconcilement to the *Yahoo*-kind in general might
not be so difficult, if they would be content with those Vices
and Follies only which Nature hath entitled them to. I am
not in the least provoked at the Sight of a Lawyer, a Pick-
pocket, a Colonel, a Fool, a Lord, a Gamster, a Politician,
a Whoremunger, a Physician, an Evidence, a Suborner, an
Attorney, a Traytor, or the like: This is all according to
the due Course of Things: But, when I behold a Lump of
Deformity, and Diseases both in Body and Mind, smitten
with *Pride*, it immediately breaks all the Measures of my
Patience; neither shall I be ever able to comprehend how
such an Animal and such a Vice could tally together. The
wise and virtuous *Houyhnhnms*, who abound in all Excellencies that can adorn a rational Creature, have no Name
for this Vice in their Language, which hath no Terms to

express any thing that is evil, except those whereby they describe the detestable Qualities of their *Yahoos*; among which they were not able to distinguish this of Pride, for want of thoroughly understanding Human Nature, as it sheweth it self in other Countries, where that Animal presides. But I, who had more Experience, could plainly observe some Rudiments of it among the wild *Yahoos*.

BUT the *Houyhnhnms*, who live under the Government of Reason, are no more proud of the good Qualities they possess, than I should be for not wanting a Leg or an Arm, which no Man in his Wits would boast of, although he must be miserable without them. I dwell the longer upon this Subject from the Desire I have to make the Society of an *English Yahoo* by any Means not insupportable; and therefore I here intreat those who have any Tincture of this absurd Vice, that they will not presume to appear in my Sight.

FINIS

A

TALE

OF A

TUB

SELECTION

A Tale of a Tub was published with *The Battle of the Books*—Swift's spirited contribution to the now forgotten quarrel about the respective merits of the Ancients and the Moderns—on May 10, 1704. Both works were written while Swift was in Sir William Temple's service at Moor Park in Surrey, and contain almost excessive evidence of the heavy reading he indulged in at that time. The *Tale*, itself—the allegory of three brothers, representing respectively the Church of Rome, the Church of England and the Dissenters—is interrupted by alternate chapters or *Digressions*, in which Swift's hatred of pretence and pedantry, and his power of ridicule and satire are brilliantly displayed. The story of the brothers and their strange antics, which incurred for Swift the displeasure of Queen Anne and was the principal reason—aggravated by his lampooning the Duchess of Somerset —for his exclusion from preferment, is no longer of general interest and has therefore been omitted from the following selections. The *Digressions*, however, have been printed in full.

Three editions of the book were printed in 1704, and a fourth in the following year. The fifth edition, with engraved illustrations and notes by Swift and Wotton—the basis of the present text—was published in 1710. This edition was corrected by Swift, though he still preserved his anonymity, and contains an *Apology* by way of reply to the critics of the earlier editions. Though frequently reprinted, neither of the two pieces was included in Swift's collected works during his lifetime. Of none of his writings was he more careful to guard the secret of its authorship. But it is related that at the end of his life he remarked on being handed a copy: " Good God! What a genius I had when I wrote that book !"

NOTE: The marginal references in the original edition have been placed in < > brackets and transferred to the foot of the page in the following selections.

A TALE OF A TUB

TO THE RIGHT HONOURABLE,
JOHN LORD SOMMERS

My Lord,

THO' the Author has written a large Dedication, yet
That being address'd to a Prince, whom I am never
likely to have the Honor of being known to; A
Person, besides, as far as I can observe, not at all regarded,
or thought on by any of our present Writers; And, being
wholly free from that Slavery, which Booksellers usually lie
under, to the Caprices of Authors; I think it a wise Piece
of Presumption, to inscribe these Papers to your Lordship,
and to implore your Lordship's Protection of them. God
and your Lordship know their Faults, and their Merits;
for as to my own Particular, I am altogether a Stranger to
the Matter; And, tho' every Body else should be equally ignorant, I do not fear the Sale of the Book, at all the worse,
upon that Score. Your Lordship's Name on the Front,
in Capital Letters, will at any time get off one Edition:
Neither would I desire any other Help, to grow an Alderman, than a Patent for the sole Priviledge of Dedicating to
your Lordship.

I should now, in right of a Dedicator, give your Lord-
ship a List of your own Virtues, and at the same time,
be very unwilling to offend your Modesty; But, chiefly, I
should celebrate your Liberality towards Men of great
Parts and small Fortunes, and give you broad Hints, that
I mean my self. And, I was just going on in the usual
Method, to peruse a hundred or two of Dedications, and
transcribe an Abstract, to be applied to your Lordship;
But, I was diverted by a certain Accident. For, upon the
Covers of these Papers, I casually observed written in large
Letters, the two following Words, *DETUR, DIGNIS-
SIMO*; which, for ought I knew, might contain some
important Meaning. But, it unluckily fell out, that none of
the Authors I employ, understood *Latin* (tho' I have them

often in pay, to translate out of that Language) I was therefore compelled to have recourse to the Curate of our
Parish, who Englished it thus, *Let it be given to the Worthi-
est*; And his Comment was, that the Author meant, his
Work should be dedicated to the sublimest Genius of the
Age, for Wit, Learning, Judgment, Eloquence and Wisdom.
I call'd at a Poet's Chamber (who works for my Shop) in
an Alley hard by, shewed him the Translation, and desired
his Opinion, who it was that the Author could mean; He
told me, after some Consideration, that Vanity was a
Thing he abhorr'd; but by the Description, he thought
Himself to be the Person aimed at; And, at the same time,
he very kindly offer'd his own Assistance *gratis*, towards
penning a Dedication to Himself. I desired him, however,
to give a second Guess; Why then, said he, It must be I,
or my Lord *Sommers*. From thence I went to several other
Wits of my Acquaintance, with no small Hazard and
Weariness to my Person, from a prodigious Number of
dark, winding Stairs; But found them all in the same Story,
both of your Lordship and themselves. Now, your Lordship is to understand, that this Proceeding was not of my
own Invention; For, I have somewhere heard, it is a Maxim,
that those, to whom every Body allows the second Place,
have an undoubted Title to the First.

This infallibly convinced me, that your Lordship was
the Person intended by the Author. But, being very unacquainted in the Style and Form of Dedications, I employ'd
those Wits aforesaid, to furnish me with Hints and Materials, towards a Panegyrick upon your Lordship's Virtues.

In two Days, they brought me ten Sheets of Paper, fill'd
up on every Side. They swore to me, that they had ran-
sack'd whatever could be found in the Characters of
Socrates, Aristides, Epaminondas, Cato, Tully, Atticus, and
other hard Names, which I cannot now recollect. However,
I have Reason to believe, they imposed upon my Ignorance,
because, when I came to read over their Collections, there
was not a Syllable there, but what I and every body else
knew as well as themselves: Therefore, I grievously suspect
a Cheat; and, that these Authors of mine, stole and tran-

scribed every Word, from the universal Report of Mankind. So that I look upon my self, as fifty Shillings out of Pocket, to no manner of Purpose.

If, by altering the Title, I could make the same Materials serve for another Dedication (as my Betters have done) it would help to make up my Loss: But, I have made several Persons, dip here and there in those Papers, and before they read three Lines, they have all assured me, plainly, that they cannot possibly be applied to any Person besides your Lordship.

I expected, indeed, to have heard of your Lordship's Bravery, at the Head of an Army; Of your undaunted Courage, in mounting a Breach, or scaling a Wall; Or, to have had your Pedigree trac'd in a Lineal Descent from the House of *Austria*; Or, of your wonderful Talent at Dress and Dancing; Or, your Profound Knowledge in *Algebra*, *Metaphysicks*, and the Oriental Tongues. But to ply the World with an old beaten Story of your Wit, and Eloquence, and Learning, and Wisdom, and Justice, and Politeness, and Candor, and Evenness of Temper in all Scenes of Life; Of that great Discernment in Discovering, and Readiness in Favouring deserving Men; with forty other common Topicks: I confess, I have neither Conscience, nor Countenance to do it. Because, there is no Virtue, either of a Publick or Private Life, which some Circumstances of your own, have not often produced upon the Stage of the World; And those few, which for want of Occasions to exert them, might otherwise have pass'd unseen or unobserved by your *Friends*, your *Enemies* have at length brought to Light.

'Tis true, I should be very loth, the Bright Example of your Lordship's Virtues should be lost to After-Ages, both for their sake and your own; but chiefly, because they will be so very necessary to adorn the History of a *late Reign*; And That is another Reason, why I would forbear to make a Recital of them here; Because, I have been told by Wise Men, that as Dedications have run for some Years past, a good Historian will not be apt to have Recourse thither, in search of Characters.

There is one Point, wherein I think we Dedicators would do well to change our Measures; I mean, instead of running on so far, upon the Praise of our Patron's *Liberality*, to spend a Word or two, in admiring their *Patience*. I can put no greater Compliment on your Lordship's, than by giving you so ample an Occasion to exercise it at present. Tho', perhaps, I shall not be apt to reckon much Merit to your Lordship upon that Score, who having been formerly used to tedious Harangues, and sometimes to as little Purpose, will be the readier to pardon this, especially, when it is offered by one, who is with all Respect and Veneration,

> *My* Lord,
> *Your Lordship's Most Obedient,*
> *and most Faithful Servant*,
> The Bookseller.

THE PREFACE

THE Wits of the present Age being so very numerous and penetrating, it seems, the Grandees of *Church* and *State* begin to fall under horrible Apprehensions, lest these Gentlemen, during the intervals of a long Peace, should find leisure to pick Holes in the weak sides of Religion and Government. To prevent which, there has been much Thought employ'd of late upon certain Projects for taking off the Force, and Edge of these formidable Enquirers, from canvasing and reasoning upon such delicate Points. They have at length fixed upon one, which will require some Time as well as Cost, to perfect. Mean while the Danger hourly increasing, by new Levies of Wits all appointed (as there is Reason to fear) with Pen, Ink, and Paper which may at an hours Warning be drawn out into Pamphlets, and other Offensive Weapons, ready for immediate Execution: It was judged of absolute necessity, that some present Expedient be thought on, till the Main

Design can be brought to Maturity. To this End, at a Grand Committee, some Days ago, this important Discovery was made by a certain curious and refined Observer; That Sea-men have a Custom when they meet a *Whale*, to fling him out an empty *Tub*, by way of Amusement, to divert him from laying violent Hands upon the Ship. This Parable was immediately mythologiz'd: The *Whale* was interpreted to be *Hob's Leviathan*, which tosses and plays with all other Schemes of Religion and Government, whereof a great many are hollow, and dry, and empty, and noisy, and wooden, and given to Rotation. This is the *Leviathan* from whence the terrible Wits of our Age are said to borrow their Weapons. The *Ship* in danger, is easily understood to be its old Antitype the *Commonwealth*. But, how to analyze the *Tub*, was a Matter of difficulty; when after long Enquiry and Debate, the literal Meaning was preserved: And it was decreed, that in order to prevent these *Leviathans* from tossing and sporting with the *Commonwealth*, (which of it self is too apt to *fluctuate*) they should be diverted from that Game by a *Tale of a Tub*. And my Genius being conceived to lye not unhappily that way, I had the Honor done me to be engaged in the Performance.

This is the sole Design in publishing the following Treatise, which I hope will serve for an *Interim* of some Months to employ those unquiet Spirits, till the perfecting of that great Work: into the Secret of which, it is reasonable the courteous Reader should have some little Light.

It is intended that a large Academy be erected, capable of containing nine thousand seven hundred forty and three Persons; which by modest Computation is reckoned to be pretty near the current Number of *Wits* in this Island. These are to be disposed into the several Schools of this Academy, and there pursue those Studies to which their Genius most inclines them. The Undertaker himself will publish his Proposals with all convenient speed, to which I shall refer the curious Reader for a more particular Account, mentioning at present only a few of the Principal Schools. There is first, a large *Pederastick* School, with

French and *Italian* Masters. There is also, the *Spelling*
School, *a very spacious Building*: the School of *Looking
Glasses*: The School of *Swearing*: the School of *Criticks*:
the School of *Salivation*: The School of *Hobby-Horses*:
The School of *Poetry* : *The School of *Tops*: The School
of *Spleen*: The School of *Gaming*: with many others too
tedious to recount. No Person to be admitted Member
into any of these Schools, without an Attestation under
two sufficient Persons Hands, certifying him to be a *Wit*.

But, to return. I am sufficiently instructed in the Principal Duty of a Preface, if my Genius were capable of arriv-
at it. Thrice have I forced my Imagination to make the
Tour of my Invention, and thrice it has returned empty;
the latter having been wholly drained by the following
Treatise. Not so, my more successful Brethren the *Moderns*,
who will by no means let slip a Preface or Dedication,
without some notable distinguishing Stroke, to surprize
the Reader at the Entry, and kindle a Wonderful Expectation of what is to ensue. Such was that of a most ingenious
Poet, who solliciting his Brain for something new, compared himself to the *Hangman*, and his Patron to the
Patient: This was †*Insigne, recens, indictum ore alio.*
When I went thro' That necessary and noble ‡Course of
Study, I had the happiness to observe many such egregious
Touches, which I shall not injure the Authors by trans-
planting: Because I have remarked, that nothing is so very
tender as a *Modern* Piece of Wit, and which is apt to suffer
so much in the Carriage. Some things are extreamly witty
to day, or *fasting*, or *in this place*, or *at eight o'clock*, or
over a Bottle, or *spoke by Mr.* What d'y'call'm, or *in a
Summer's Morning*: Any of which, by the smallest Trans-
posal or Misapplication, is utterly annihilate. Thus, *Wit*
has its Walks and Purlieus, out of which it may not stray

---

* *This I think the Author should have omitted, it being of the very
same Nature with the* School of Hobby-Horses, *if one may venture
to censure one who is so severe a Censurer of others, perhaps with
too little Distinction.*

⟨† *Hor.*⟩ Something extraordinary, new and never hit upon
before.

⟨‡ *Reading Prefaces, &c.*⟩

the breadth of an Hair, upon peril of being lost. The _Moderns_ have artfully fixed this _Mercury_, and reduced it to the Circumstances of Time, Place and Person. Such a Jest there is, that will not pass out of _Covent-Garden_; and such a one, that is no where intelligible but at _Hide-Park_ Corner. Now, tho' it sometimes tenderly affects me to consider, that all the towardly Passages I shall deliver in the following Treatise, will grow quite out of date and relish with the first shifting of the present Scene: yet I must need subscribe to the Justice of this Proceeding: because, I cannot imagine why we should be at Expence to furnish Wit for succeeding Ages, when the former have made no sort of Provision for ours; wherein I speak the Sentiment of the very newest, and consequently the most Orthodox Refiners, as well as my own. However, being extreamly sollicitous, that every accomplished Person who has got into the Taste of Wit, calculated for this present Month of _August_, 1697, should descend to the very _bottom_ of all the _Sublime_ throughout this Treatise; I hold fit to lay down this general Maxim. Whatever Reader desires to have a thorow Comprehension of an Author's Thoughts, cannot take a better Method, than by putting himself into the Circumstances and Postures of Life, that the Writer was in, upon every important Passage as it flow'd from his Pen; For this will introduce a Parity and strict Correspondence of Idea's between the Reader and the Author. Now, to assist the diligent Reader in so delicate an Affair, as far as brevity will permit, I have recollected, that the shrewdest Pieces of this Treatise, were conceived in Bed, in a Garret: At other times (for a Reason best known to my self) I thought fit to sharpen my Invention with Hunger; and in general, the whole Work was begun, continued, and ended, under a long Course of Physick, and a great want of Money. Now, I do affirm, it will be absolutely impossible for the candid Peruser to go along with me in a great many bright Passages, unless upon the several Difficulties emergent, he will please to capacitate and prepare himself by these Directions. And this I lay down as my principal _Postulatum_.

L

Because I have profess'd to be a most devoted Servant of all *Modern* Forms: I apprehend some curious *Wit* may object against me, for proceeding thus far in a Preface, without declaiming, according to the Custom, against the Multitude of Writers whereof the whole Multitude of Writers most reasonably complains. I am just come from perusing some hundreds of Prefaces, wherein the Authors do at the very beginning address the gentle Reader concerning this enormous Grievance. Of these I have preserved a few Examples, and shall set them down as near as my Memory has been able to retain them.

One begins thus;

For a Man to set up for a Writer, when the Press swarms with, &c.

Another;

The Tax upon Paper does not lessen the Number of Scriblers, who daily pester, &c.

Another;

When every little Would-be-wit takes Pen in hand, 'tis in vain to enter the Lists, &c.

Another;

To observe what Trash the Press swarms with, &c.

Another;

SIR, *It is meerly in Obedience to your Commands that I venture into the Publick; for who upon a less Consideration would be of a Party with such a Rabble of Scriblers*, &c.

Now, I have two Words in my own Defence, against this Objection. First: I am far from granting the Number of Writers, a Nuisance to our Nation, having strenuously maintained the contrary in several Parts of the following Discourse. Secondly: I do not well understand the Justice of this Proceeding, because I observe many of these polite Prefaces, to be not only from the same Hand, but from those who are most voluminous in their several Productions. Upon which I shall tell the Reader a short Tale.

A Mountebank in Leicester-Fields, *had drawn a huge Assembly about him. Among the rest, a fat unweildy*

Fellow, half stifled in the Press, would be every fit crying out, Lord! what a filthy Crowd is here? Pray, good People, give way a little, Bless me! what a Devil has rak'd this Rabble together: Z——ds, what squeezing is this! Honest Friend, remove your Elbow. At last, a Weaver *that stood next him could hold no longer: A Plague confound you* (said he) *for an over-grown Sloven; and who* (in the Devil's Name) *I wonder, helps to make up the Crowd half so much as yourself? Don't you consider* (with a Pox) *that you take up more room with that Carcass than any five here? Is not the Place as free for us as for you? Bring your own Guts to a reasonable Compass* (and be d——n'd) *and then I'll engage we shall have room enough for us all.*

There are certain common Privileges of a Writer, the Benefit whereof, I hope, there will be no Reason to doubt; Particularly, that where I am not understood, it shall be concluded, that something very useful and profound is couch'd underneath, And again, that whatever word or Sentence is Printed in a different Character, shall be judged to contain something extraordinary either of *Wit* or *Sublime*.

As for the Liberty I have thought fit to take of praising my self, upon some Occasions or none; I am sure it will need no Excuse, if a Multitude of great Examples be allowed sufficient Authority: For it is here to be noted, that *Praise* was originally a Pension paid by the World: but the *Moderns* finding the Trouble and Charge too great in collecting it, have lately bought out the *Fee-Simple*; since which time, the Right of Presentation is wholly in our selves. For this Reason it is, that when an Author makes his own Elogy, he uses a certain form to declare and insist upon his Title, which is commonly in these or the like words, *I speak without Vanity*; which I think plainly shews it to be a Matter of Right and Justice. Now, I do here once for all declare, that in every Encounter of this Nature, thro' the following Treatise, the Form aforesaid is imply'd; which I mention, to save the Trouble of repeating it on so many Occasions.

'Tis a great Ease to my Conscience that I have writ so

elaborate and useful a Discourse without one grain of
Satyr intermixt; which is the sole point wherein I have
taken leave to dissent from the famous Originals of our
Age and Country. I have observ'd some Satyrists to use
the Publick much at the Rate that Pedants do a naughty
Boy ready Hors'd for Discipline: First expostulate the
Case, then plead the Necessity of the Rod, from great
Provocations, and conclude every Period with a Lash.
Now, if I know any thing of Mankind, these Gentlemen
might very well spare their Reproof and Correction: For
there is not, through all Nature, another so callous and
insensible a Member as the *World's Posteriors*, whether
you apply to it the *Toe* or the *Birch*. Besides, most of our
late Satyrists seem to lye under a sort of Mistake, that
because Nettles have the Prerogative to Sting, therefore all
other Weeds must do so too. I make not this Comparison
out of the least Design to detract from these worthy
Writers: For it is well known among *Mythologists*, that
Weeds have the Preeminence over all other Vegetables;
and therefore the first *Monarch* of this Island, whose Taste
and Judgment were so acute and refined, did very wisely
root out the *Roses* from the Collar of the *Order*, and plant
the *Thistles* in their stead as the nobler Flower of the two.
For which Reason it is conjectured by profounder Anti-
quaries, that the Satyrical Itch, so prevalent in this part
of our Island, was first brought among us from beyond
the *Tweed*. Here may it long flourish and abound; May it
survive and neglect the Scorn of the World, with as much
Ease and Contempt as the World is insensible to the Lashes
of it. May their own Dullness, or that of their party, be
no Discouragement for the Authors to proceed; but let
them remember, it is with *Wits* as with *Razors*, which are
never so apt to *cut* those they are employ'd on, as when
they have *lost their Edge*. Besides, those whose Teeth are
too rotten to bite, are best of all others, qualified to revenge
that Defect with their Breath.

I am not like other Men, to envy or undervalue the
Talents I cannot reach; for which Reason I must needs
bear a true Honour to this large eminent Sect of our

British Writers. And I hope, this little Panegyrick will not be offensive to their Ears, since it has the Advantage of being only designed for themselves. Indeed, Nature her self has taken order, that Fame and Honour should be purchased at a better Pennyworth by Satyr, than by any other Productions of the Brain; the World being soonest provoked to *Praise* by *Lashes,* as Men are to *Love.* There is a Problem in an ancient Author, why Dedications, and other Bundles of Flattery run all upon stale musty Topicks, without the smallest Tincture of any thing New; not only to the torment and nauseating of the *Christian* Reader, but (if not suddenly prevented) to the universal spreading of that pestilent Disease, the Lethargy, in this Island: whereas, there is very little Satyr which has not something in it untouch'd before. The Defects of the former are usually imputed to the want of Invention among those who are Dealers in that kind: But, I think, with a great deal of Injustice; the Solution being easy and natural. For, the Materials of Panegyrick being very few in Number, have been long since exhausted: For, as Health is but one Thing, and has been always the same, whereas Diseases are by thousands, besides new and daily Additions; So, all the Virtues that have been ever in Mankind, are to be counted upon a few Fingers, but his Follies and Vices are in-numerable, and Time adds hourly to the Heap. Now, the utmost a poor Poet can do, is to get by heart a List of the Cardinal Virtues, and deal them with his utmost Liberality to his Hero or his Patron: He may ring the Changes as far as it will go, and vary his Phrase till he has talk'd round; but the Reader quickly finds, it is all *Pork, with a little variety of Sawce: For there is no inventing Terms of Art beyond our Idea's; and when Idea's are exhausted, Terms of Art must be so too.

But, tho' the Matter for Panegyrick were as fruitful as the Topicks of Satyr, yet would it not be hard to find out a sufficient Reason, why the latter will be always better received than the first. For, this being bestowed only upon

⟨* *Plutarch.*⟩

one or a few Persons at a time, is sure to raise Envy, and consequently ill words from the rest, who have no share in the Blessing: But Satyr being levelled at all, is never resented for an offence by any, since every individual Person makes bold to understand it of others, and very wisely removes his particular Part of the Burthen upon the shoulders of the World, which are broad enough, and able to bear it. To this purpose, I have sometimes reflected upon the Difference between *Athens* and *England*, with respect to the Point before us. In the *Attick** Commonwealth, it was the Privilege and Birth-right of every Citizen and Poet, to rail aloud and in publick, or to expose upon the Stage by Name, any Person they pleased, tho' of the greatest Figure, whether a *Creon*, an *Hyperbolus*, an *Alcibiades*, or a *Demosthenes*: But on the other side, the least reflecting word let fall against the *People* in general, was immediately caught up, and revenged upon the Authors, however considerable for their Quality or their Merits. Whereas, in *England* it is just the Reverse of all this. Here, you may securely display your utmost *Rhetorick* against Mankind, in the Face of the World; tell them, " *That all are gone astray; That there is none that* " *doth good, no not one; That we live in the very Dregs of* " *Time; That Knavery and Atheism are Epidemick as the* " *Pox; That Honesty is fled with Astræa;* with any other Common places *equally* new and eloquent, which are furnished by the †*Splendida bilis.* And when you have done, the whole Audience, far from being offended, shall return you thanks as a Deliverer of precious and useful Truths. Nay farther; It is but to venture your Lungs, and you may preach in *Convent-Garden* against Foppery and Fornication, and *something else*: Against Pride, and Dissimulation, and Bribery, at W*hite Hall*: You may expose Rapins and Injustice in the *Inns* of *Court* Chappel: And in a *City* Pulpit be as fierce as you please, against Avarice, Hypocrisie and Extortion. 'Tis but a *Ball* bandied to and fro, and every Man carries a *Racket* about Him to strike it

---

from himself among the rest of the Company. But on the other side, whoever should mistake the Nature of things so far, as to drop but a single Hint in publick, How *such a one*, starved half the Fleet, and half-poison'd the rest: How *such a one*, from a true Principle of *Love* and *Honour*, pays no Debts but for *Wenches* and *Play*: How *such a one* has got a Clap and runs out of his Estate: *How *Paris* bribed by *Juno* and *Venus*, loath to offend either Party, slept out the whole Cause on the Bench: Or, how *such an Orator* makes long Speeches in the Senate with much Thought, little Sense, and to no Purpose; whoever, I say, should venture to be thus particular, must expect to be imprisoned for *Scandalum Magnatum*: to have *Challenges* sent him; to be sued for *Defamation*; and to be *brought before the Bar of the House.*

But I forget that I am expatiating on a Subject, wherein I have no concern, having neither a Talent nor an Inclination for Satyr. On the other side, I am so entirely satisfied with the whole present Procedure of human Things, that I have been for some Years preparing Materials towards *A Panegyrick upon the World*, to which I intended to add a Second Part, entituled, *A Modest Defence of the Proceedings of the Rabble in all Ages*. Both these I had Thoughts to Publish by way of Appendix to the following Treatise, but finding my Common-Place-Book fill much slower than I had reason to expect, I have chosen to defer them to another Occasion. Besides, I have been unhappily prevented in that Design, by a certain Domestick Misfortune, in the Particulars whereof, tho' it would be very seasonable, and much in the *Modern* way, to inform the *gentle Reader*, and would also be of great Assistance towards extending this Preface into the Size now in Vogue, which by Rule ought to be *large* in proportion as the subsequent Volume is *small*. Yet I shall now dismiss our impatient Reader from any farther Attendance at the *Porch*; and having duly prepared his Mind by a preliminary Dis-

---

* Juno *and* Venus *are Money and a Mistress, very powerful Bribes to a Judge, if Scandal says true. I remember such Reflexions were cast about that time, but I cannot fix the Person intended here.*

course, shall gladly introduce him to the sublime Mysteries that ensue.

A DIGRESSION CONCERNING CRITICKS

Tho' I have been hitherto as cautious as I could, upon all Occasions, most nicely to follow the Rules and Methods of Writing, laid down by the Example of our illustrious *Moderns*; yet has the unhappy shortness of my Memory led me into an Error, from which I must immediately extricate my self, before I can decently pursue my Principal Subject. I confess with Shame, it was an unpardonable Omission to proceed so far as I have already done, before I had performed the due Discourses, Expostulatory, Supplicatory, or Deprecatory with my *good Lords* the *Criticks*. Towards some Atonement for this grievous Neglect, I do here make humbly bold to present them with a short Account of themselves and their *Art*, by looking into the Original and Pedigree of the Word, as it is generally understood among us, and very briefly considering the antient and present State thereof.

By the Word, *Critick*, at this Day so frequent in all Conversations, there have sometimes been distinguished three very different Species of Mortal Men, according as I have read in *Antient Books and Pamphlets*. For first, by this Term was understood such Persons as invented or drew up Rules for themselves and the World, by observing which, a careful Reader might be able to pronounce upon the productions of the *Learned*, form his Taste to a true Relish of the *Sublime* and the *Admirable*, and divide every Beauty of Matter or of Style from the Corruption that Apes it: In their common perusal of Books, singling out the Errors and Defects, the Nauseous, the Fulsome, the Dull, and the Impertinent, with the Caution of a Man that walks thro' *Edenborough* Streets in a Morning, who is indeed as careful as he can, to watch diligently, and spy out the Filth in his Way, not that he is curious to observe the Colour and Complexion of the Ordure, or take its Dimensions, much less to be padling in, or tasting it: but only with a Design to come out as cleanly as he may. These men seem, tho' very erroneously, to have understood the Appellation of *Critick* in a literal Sence; That one principal part of his Office was to Praise and Acquit; and, that a *Critick*, who sets up to Read, only for an Occasion of Censure and Reproof, is a Creature as barbarous as a *Judge*, who should take up a Resolution to hang all Men that came before him upon a Tryal.

Again; by the word *Critick*, have been meant, the Restorers of Antient Learning from the Worms, and Graves, and Dust of Manuscripts.

Now, the Races of these two have been for some Ages utterly extinct; and besides, to discourse any farther of them would not be at all to my purpose.

The Third, and Noblest Sort, is that of the *TRUE CRI-TICK*, whose Original is the most Antient of all. Every *True Critick* is a Hero born, descending in a direct Line from a Celestial Stem, by *Momus* and *Hybris*, who begat *Zoilus*, who begat *Tigellius*, who begat *Etcætera* the Elder, who begat *B[en]tly*, and *Rym[e]r*, and *W[o]tton*, and *Perrault*, and *Dennis*, who begat *Etcætera* the Younger.

And these are the *Criticks* from whom the Commonwealth of Learning has in all Ages received such immense benefits, that the Gratitude of their Admirers placed their Origine in Heaven, among those of *Hercules*, *Theseus*, *Perseus*, and other great Deservers of Mankind. But Heroick Virtue it self hath not been exempt from the Obloquy of Evil Tongues. For it hath been objected, that those Antient Heroes, famous for their Combating so many Giants, and Dragons, and Robbers, were in their own Persons a greater Nuisance to Mankind, than any of those Monsters they subdued; and therefore, to render their Obligations more Compleat, when all *other* Vermin were destroy'd, should in Conscience have concluded with the same Justice upon themselves: as *Hercules* most generously did, and hath upon that Score, procured to himself more Temples and Votaries than the best of his Fellows, For these Reasons, I suppose, it is why some have conceived, it would be very expedient for the Publick Good of Learning, that every *True Critick*, as soon as he had finished his Task assigned, should immediately deliver himself up to Ratsbane, or Hemp, or some convenient *Altitude*, and that no Man's Pretensions to so illustrious a Character, should by any means be received, before That Operation were performed.

Now, from this Heavenly Descent of *Criticism*, and the close Analogy it bears to *Heroick Virtue*, 'tis easie to Assign the proper Employment of a *True Ancient Genuine Critick*; which is, to travel thro' this vast World of Writings: to pursue and hunt those Monstrous Faults bred within them: to drag out the lurking Errors like *Cacus* from his Den; to multiply them like *Hydra's* Heads; and rake them together like *Augea's* Dung. Or else drive away a sort of *Dangerous Fowl*, who have a perverse Inclination to plunder the best Branches of the *Tree of Knowledge*, like those *Stimphalian* Birds that eat up the Fruit.

These Reasonings will furnish us with an adequate Definition of a true *Critick*; that, He is *a Discoverer and Collector of Writers Faults*. Which may be farther put beyond Dispute by the following Demonstration: That whoever will examine the Writings in all kinds, wherewith this antient Sect has honour'd the World, shall immediately find, from the whole Thread and Tenour of them, that the Idea's of the Authors have been altogether conversant, and taken up with the Faults and Blemishes, and Oversights, and Mistakes of other Writers; and let the Subject treated on be whatever it will, their Imaginations are so entirely possess'd and replete with the Defects of other Pens, that the very Quintessence of what is bad, does of necessity distill into their own: by which means the Whole appears to be nothing else but an *Abstract* of the *Criticisms* themselves have made.

Having thus briefly consider'd the Original and Office of a *Critick*, as the Word is understood in its most noble and universal Acceptation, I proceed to refute the Objections of those who argue from the Silence and Pretermission of

Authors; by which they pretend to prove, that the very
Art of *Criticism*, as now exercised, and by me explained,
is wholly *Modern*; and consequently, that the *Criticks* of
Great Britain and *France*, have no Title to an Original
so Antient and Illustrious as I have deduced. Now, If I
can clearly make out on the contrary, that the most Antient
Writers have particularly described, both the Person and
the Office of a *True Critick*, agreeable to the Definition
laid down by me; their Grand Objection, from the Silence
of Authors, will fall to the Ground.

I confess to have for a long time born a part in this
general Error; from which I should never have acquitted
my self, but thro' the Assistance of our Noble *Moderns*;
whose most edifying Volumes I turn indefatigably over
Night and Day, for the Improvement of my Mind, and
the good of my Country: These have with unwearied
Pains made many useful Searches into the weak sides of
the *Antients*, and given us a comprehensive List of them.*
Besides, they have proved beyond contradiction, that the
very finest Things delivered of old, have been long since
invented, and brought to Light by much later Pens, and
that the noblest Discoveries those *Antients* ever made, of
Art or of Nature, have all been produced by the tran-
scending Genius of the present Age. Which clearly shews,
how little Merit those *Antients* can justly pretend to; and
takes off that blind Admiration paid them by Men in a
Corner, who have the Unhappiness of conversing too little
with *present Things*. Reflecting maturely upon all this,
and taking in the whole Compass of Human Nature, I
easily concluded, that these *Antients*, highly sensible of
their many Imperfections, must needs have endeavoured
from some Passages in their Works, to obviate, soften, or
divert the Censorious Reader, by *Satyr*, or *Panegyrick*
upon the *True Criticks*, in Imitation of their *Masters* the
Moderns. Now, in the Common-Places of †both these, I
was plentifully instructed, by a long Course of useful Study
in *Prefaces* and *Prologues*; and therefore immediately

⟨* *See* Wotton *of Antient and Modern Learning.*⟩
⟨† *Satyr, and Panegyrick upon Criticks.*⟩

resolved to try what I could discover of either, by a diligent Perusal of the most Antient Writers, and especially those who treated of the earliest Times. Here I found to my great Surprize, that although they all entred, upon Occasion, into particular Descriptions of the *True Critick*, according as they were governed by their Fears or their Hopes: yet whatever they touch'd of that kind, was with abundance of Caution, adventuring no farther than *Mythology* and *Hieroglyphick*. This, I suppose, gave ground to superficial Readers, for urging the Silence of Authors, against the Antiquity of the *True Critick*; tho' the *Types* are so apposite, and the Applications so necessary and natural, that it is not easy to conceive, how any Reader of a *Modern Eye* and *Taste* could over-look them. I shall venture from a great Number to produce a few, which I am very confident, will put this Question beyond Dispute.

It well deserves considering, that these *Antient Writers* in treating Enigmatically upon the Subject, have generally fixed upon the very *same Hieroglyph*, varying only the Story according to their Affections or their Wit. For first; *Pausanias* is of Opinion, that the Perfection of Writing correct was entirely owing to the Institution of *Criticks*; and, that he can possibly mean no other than the *True Critick*, is, I think, manifest enough from the following Description. He says, *They were a Race of Men, who delighted to nibble at the Superfluities, and Excrescencies of Books*; *which the Learned at length observing, took Warning of their own Accord, to lop the Luxuriant, the Rotten, the Dead, the Sapless, and the Overgrown Branches from their Works*. But now, all this he cunningly shades under the following Allegory; *that the* *Nauplians *in* Argia, *learned the Art of pruning their Vines, by observing, that when an* ASS *had browsed upon one of them, it thrived the better, and bore fairer Fruit*. But †*Herodotus* holding the very same *Hieroglyph*, speaks much plainer, and almost *in terminis*. He hath been so bold as to tax the *True Criticks*, of Ignorance and Malice; telling us openly, for I think nothing can be plainer, that *in the Western Part of* Libya, *there were* ASSES *with* HORNS: Upon which Relation *Ctesias yet refines, mentioning the very same Animal about *India*, adding, That whereas all other ASSES *wanted a Gall, these horned ones were so redundant in that Part, that their Flesh was not to be eaten because of its extream* Bitterness.

Now, the Reason why those Antient Writers treated this Subject only by Types and Figures, was, because they durst not make open Attacks against a Party so Potent and so Terrible, as the *Criticks* of those Ages were: whose very Voice was so Dreadful, that a Legion of Authors would tremble, and drop their Pens at the Sound; For so †*Herodotus* tells us expressly in another Place, how *a vast Army of* Scythians *was to put to flight in a Panick Terror, by the Braying of an* ASS. From hence it is conjectured by certain profound *Philologers*, that the great Awe and Reverence paid to a *True Critick*, by the Writers of *Britain*, have been derived to Us, from those our *Scythian* Ancestors. In short, this Dread was so universal, that in process of Time, those Authors who had a mind to publish their Sentiments more freely, in describing the *True Criticks* of their several Ages, were forced to leave off the use of the former Hieroglyph, as too nearly approaching the *Prototype*, and invented other Terms instead thereof that were more cautious and mystical; so ‡*Diodorus* speaking to the same purpose, ventures no farther than to say, That *in the Mountains of* Helicon *there grows a certain* Weed, *which bears a Flower of so damned a Scent, as to poison those who offer to smell it.* Lucretius gives exactly the Same Relation,

§ *Est etiam in magnis Heliconis montibus arbos,*
   Floris odore hominem retro consueta necare. Lib. 6.

But *Ctesias*, whom we lately quoted, hath been a great

⟨* Vide *excerpta ex eo apud* Photium.⟩
⟨† *Lib.* 4.⟩   ⟨‡ *Lib.*⟩
§ *Near* Helicon, *and round the Learned Hill,*
   Grown Trees, whose Blossoms with their Odour kill. [Creech.]

deal bolder; He had been used with much severity by the *True Criticks* of his own Age, and therefore could not forbear to leave behind him, at least one deep Mark of his Vengeance against the whole Tribe. His Meaning is so near the surface, that I wonder how it possibly came to be overlook'd by those who deny the Antiquity of *True Criticks*. For pretending to make a Description of many strange Animals about *India*, he hath set down these remarkable Words. *Amongst the rest*, says he, *there is a* Serpent *that wants* Teeth, *and consequently cannot bite, but if its* Vomit (*to which it is much addicted*) *happens to fall upon any Thing, a certain Rotenness or Corruption ensues: These* Serpents *are generally found among the* Mountains *where* Jewels *grow, and they frequently emit a* poisonous Juice *whereof, whoever drinks, that Person's* Brains *flie out of his Nostrils*.

There was also among the *Antients* a sort of *Critick*, not distinguisht in *Specie* from the Former, but in Growth or Degree, who seem to have been only the *Tyro's* or *junior* Scholars; yet, because of their differing Employments, they are frequently mentioned as a Sect by themselves. The usual exercise of these younger Students, was to attend constantly at Theatres, and learn to Spy out the *worst Parts* of the Play, whereof they were obliged carefully to take Note, and render a rational Account, to their Tutors. Flesht at these smaller Sports, like young Wolves, they grew up in Time, to be nimble and strong enough for hunting down large Game. For it hath been observed both among Antients and Moderns, that a *True Critick* hath one Quality in common with a *Whore* and an *Alderman*, never to change his Title or his Nature; that a *Grey Critick* has been certainly a *Green* one, the Perfections and Acquirements of his Age being only the improved Talents of his Youth; like *Hemp*, which some Naturalists inform us, is bad for *Suffocations*, tho' taken but in the Seed. I esteem the Invention, or at least the Refinement of *Prologues*, to have been owing to these younger Proficients, of whom *Terence* makes frequent and honourable mention, under the Name of *Malevoli*.

Now, 'tis certain, the Institution of the *True Criticks*, was of absolute Necessity to the Commonwealth of Learning. For all Human Actions seem to be divided like *Themistocles* and his Company; One Man can *Fiddle*, and another can make *a small Town a great City*, and he that cannot do either one or the other, deserves to be kick'd out of the Creation. The avoiding of which Penalty, has doubtless given the first Birth to the Nation of *Criticks* and withal, an Occasion for their secret Detractors to report; that a *True Critick* is a sort of Mechanick, set up with a Stock and Tools for his Trade, at as little Expence as a *Taylor*; and that there is much Analogy between the Utensils and Abilities of both: That the *Taylor's Hell* is the Type of a Critick's *Common-Place-Book*, and his Wit and Learning held forth by the *Goose*: That it requires at least as many of these, to the making up of one Scholar, as of the others to the Composition of a Man: That the Valour of both is equal, and their *Weapons* near of a Size. Much may be said in answer to these invidious Reflections; and I can positively affirm the first to be a Falshood: For, on the contrary, nothing is more certain, than that it requires greater Layings out, to be free of the *Critick's* Company, than of any other you can name. For, as to be a *true Beggar*, it will cost the richest Candidate every Groat he is worth; so, before one can commence a *True Critick*, it will cost a man all the good Qualities of his Mind; which, perhaps, for a less Purchase, would be thought but an indifferent Bargain.

Having thus amply proved the Antiquity of *Criticism*, and described the Primitive State of it; I shall now examine the present Condition of this Empire, and shew how well it agrees with its antient self. *A certain Author, whose Works have many Ages since been entirely lost, does in his fifth Book and eighth Chapter, say of *Criticks*, that *their Writings are the Mirrors of Learning*. This I understand in a literal Sense, and suppose our Author must mean, that whoever designs to be a perfect Writer,

---

⟨* *A Quotation after the manner of a great Author. Vide* Bently's *Dissertation, &c.*⟩

must inspect into the Books of *Criticks*, and correct his Invention there as in a Mirror. Now, whoever considers that the *Mirrors* of the Antients were made of *Brass*, and *sine Mercurio*, may presently apply the two Principal Qualifications of a *True Modern Critick*, and consequently, must needs conclude, that these have always been, and must be for ever the same. For, *Brass* is an Emblem of Duration, and when it is skilfully burnished, will cast *Reflections* from its own *Superficies*, without any Assistance of *Mercury* from behind. All the other Talents of a *Critick* will not require a particular Mention, being included, or easily deducible to these. However, I shall conclude with three Maxims, which may serve both as Characteristicks to distinguish a *True Modern Critick* from a Pretender, and will be also of admirable Use to those worthy Spirits, who engage in so useful and honourable an Art.

The first is, That *Criticism*, contrary to all other Faculties of the Intellect, is ever held the truest and best, when it is the very *first* Result of the *Critick's* Mind: As Fowlers reckon the first aim for the surest, and seldom fail of missing the Mark, if they stay not for a Second.

Secondly; The *True Criticks* are known by their Talent of swarming about the noblest Writers, to which they are carried meerly by Instinct, as a Rat to the best Cheese, or a Wasp to the fairest Fruit. So, when the *King* is a Horseback, he is sure to be the *dirtiest* Person of the Company, and they that make their Court best, are such as *bespatter* him most.

Lastly; A *True Critick*, in the Perusal of a Book, is like a *Dog* at a Feast, whose Thoughts and Stomach are wholly set upon what the Guests *fling away*, and consequently, is apt to *Snarl* most, when there are the fewest *Bones*.

This much, I think, is sufficient to serve by way of Address to my Patrons, the *True Modern Criticks*, and may very well atone for my past Silence, as well as That which I am like to observe for the future. I hope I have deserved so well of their whole *Body*, as to meet with generous and tender Usage at their *Hands*.

A DIGRESSION IN THE MODERN KIND

WE whom the World is pleased to honor with the Title of *Modern Authors,* should never have been able to compass our great Design of an everlasting Remembrance, and never-dying Fame, if our Endeavours had not been so highly serviceable to the general Good of Mankind. This, *O Universe*, is the Adventurous Attempt of me thy Secretary;

——————Quemvis perferre laborem
Suadet, & inducit noctes vigilare serenas.

To this End, I have some Time since, with a World of Pains and Art, dissected the Carcass of *Humane Nature*, and read many useful Lectures upon the several Parts, both *Containing* and *Contained*; till at last it *smelt* so strong, I could preserve it no longer. Upon which, I have been at a great Expence to fit up all the Bones with exact Contexture, and in due Symmetry; so that I am ready to shew a very compleat Anatomy thereof to all curious *Gentlemen and others*. But not to Digress farther in the midst of a Digression, as I have known some Authors inclose Digressions in one another, like a Nest of Boxes; I do affirm, that having carefully cut up *Humane Nature*, I have found a very strange, new and important Discovery; That the Publick Good of Mankind is performed by two Ways, *Instruction* and *Diversion*. And I have farther proved in my said several Readings, (which, perhaps, the World may one day see, if I can prevail on any Friend to steal a Copy, or on certain Gentlemen of my Admirers, to be very Importunate) that, as Mankind is now disposed, he receives much greater Advantage by being *Diverted* than *Instructed*; His Epidemical Diseases being *Fastidiosity*, *Amorphy*, and *Oscitation*; whereas in the present universal Empire of Wit and Learning, there seems but little Matter left for *Instruction*. However, in Compliance with a Lesson of Great Age and Authority, I have attempted carrying the Point in all its Heights; and accordingly throughout this Divine Treatise, have skilfully kneaded up both together with a *Layer* of *Utile* and a *Layer* of *Dulce*.

When I consider how exceedingly our Illustrious *Moderns* have eclipsed the weak glimmering Lights of the *Antients*, and turned them out of the Road of all fashionable Commerce, to a degree, that our choice *Town-Wits of most refined Accomplishments, are in grave Dispute, whether there have been ever any *Antients* or no: In which Point we are like to receive wonderful Satisfaction from the most useful Labours and Lucubrations of that Worthy *Modern*, Dr B[en]*tly*: I say, when I consider all this, I cannot but bewail, that no famous *Modern* hath ever yet attempted an universal System in a small portable Volume, of all Things that are to be Known, or Believed, or Imagined, or Practised in Life. I am, however, forced to acknowledge, that such an enterprise was thought on some Time ago by a great Philosopher of †*O. Brazile*. The Method he proposed, was by a certain curious *Receipt*, a *Nostrum*, which after his untimely Death, I found among his Papers; and do here out of my great Affection to the *Modern Learned*, present them with it, not doubting, it may one Day encourage some worthy Undertaker.

You take fair correct Copies, well bound in Calfs Skin, and Lettered at the Back, of all Modern Bodies of Arts and Sciences whatsoever, and in what Language you please. These you distil in balneo Mariæ, *infusing* Quintessence of Poppy Q.S. *together with three Pints of* Lethe, *to be had from the Apothecaries. You cleanse away carefully the* Sordes *and* Caput mortuum, *letting all that is volatile evaporate. You preserve only the first Running, which is again to be distilled seventeen times, till what remains will amount to about two Drams. This you keep in a Glass Viol Hermetically sealed, for one and twenty Days. Then you*

---

* *The Learned Person here meant by our Author, hath been endeavouring to annihilate so many Antient Writers, that until he is pleas'd to stop his hand it will be dangerous to affirm, whether there have been ever any Antients in the World.*

† *This is an imaginary Island, of Kin to that which is call'd the* Painters Wives Island, *placed in some unknown part of the Ocean, meerly at the Fancy of the Map-maker.*

begin your Catholick Treatise, taking every Morning fasting,
(*first shaking the Viol*) *three Drops of this* Elixir, *snuffing it
strongly up your Nose. It will dilate it self about the Brain*
(*where there is any*) *in fourteen Minutes, and you immediately perceive in your Head an infinite Number of*
Abstracts, Summaries, Compendiums, Extracts, Collections, Medulla's, Excerpta quædam's, Florilegia's *and the
like, all disposed into great Order, and reducible upon Paper*.

I must needs own, it was by the Assistance of this
Arcanum, that I, tho' otherwise *impar,* have adventured
upon so daring an Attempt; never atchieved or undertaken
before, but by a certain Author called *Homer,* in whom,
tho' otherwise a Person not without some Abilities, and
for an Ancient, of a tolerable Genius; I have discovered
many gross Errors, which are not to be forgiven his very
Ashes, if by chance any of them are left. For whereas, we
are assured, he design'd his Work for a *compleat Body
of all Knowledge Human, Divine, Political, and Mechanick;
it is manifest, he hath wholly neglected some, and been
very imperfect in the rest. For, first of all, as eminent a
Cabbalist as his Disciples would represent Him, his Account of the *Opus magnum* is extreamly poor and deficient;
he seems to have read but very superficially, either *Sendivogius, Behmen,* or †*Anthroposophia Theomagica.* He is
also quite mistaken about the *Sphæra Pyroplastica,* a
neglect not to be attoned for; and (if the Reader will admit
so severe a Censure) *Vix crederem Autorem hunc, unquam
audivisse ignis vocem.* His Failings are not less prominent
in several parts of the *Mechanicks.* For, having read his
Writings with the utmost Application usual among *Modern
Wits,* I could never yet discover the least Direction about
the Structure of that useful Instrument a *Save-all.* For
want of which, if the *Moderns* had not lent their Assistance,

---

⟨* *Homerus omnes res humanas Poematis complexus est.* Xenoph.
in conviv.⟩

† *A Treatise written about fifty Years ago, by a* Welsh *Gentleman
of* Cambridge, *his Name, as I remember, was* Vaughan, *as appears
by the Answer to it, writ by the Learned Dr.* Henry Moor; *it is a
Piece of the most unintelligible Fustian, that, perhaps, was ever publish'd in any Language.*

we might yet have wandred *in the Dark*. But I have still behind, a Fault far more notorious to tax this Author with; I mean, *his gross Ignorance in the *Common Laws of this Realm*, and in the Doctrine as well as Discipline of the Church of *England*. A Defect indeed, for which both he and all the Ancients stand most justly censured by my worthy and ingenious Friend Mr. *W[o]tton*, Batchelor of Divinity, in his incomparable Treatise of *Ancient and Modern Learning*; A Book never to be sufficiently valued, whether we consider the happy Turns and Flowings of the Author's Wit, the great Usefulness of his sublime Discoveries upon the Subject of *Flies* and *Spittle*, or the laborious Eloquence of his Stile. And I cannot forbear doing that Author the Justice of my publick Acknowledgments, for the great *Helps* and *Liftings* I had out of his incomparable Piece, while I was penning this Treatise.

But, besides these Omissions in *Homer* already mentioned, the curious Reader will also observe several Defects in that Author's Writings, for which he is not altogether so accountable. For whereas every Branch of Knowledge has received such wonderful Acquirements since his Age, especially within these last three Years, or thereabouts; it is almost impossible, he could be so very perfect in Modern Discoveries, as his Advocates pretend. We freely acknowledge Him to be the Inventor of the *Compass*, of *Gun-Powder*, and the *Circulation of the Blood*: But, I challenge any of his Admirers to shew me in all his Writings, a compleat Account of the *Spleen*; Does he not also leave us wholly to seek in the Art of *Political Wagering*? What can be more defective and unsatisfactory than his long Dissertation upon *Tea*? and as to his Method of *Salivation without Mercury*, so much celebrated of late, it is to my own Knowledge and Experience, a Thing very little to be relied on.

It was to supply such momentous Defects, that I have been prevailed on after long Sollicitation, to take Pen in

---

* Mr *W[o]tt[o]n* (*to whom our Author never gives any Quarter*) *in his Comparison of Antient and Modern Learning, Numbers Divinity, Law, &c. among those Parts of Knowledge wherein we excel the Antients.*

Hand; and I dare venture to Promise, the Judicious Reader shall find nothing neglected here, that can be of Use upon any Emergency of Life. I am confident to have included and exhausted all that Human Imagination can *Rise* or *Fall* to. Particularly, I recommend to the Perusal of the Learned, certain Discoveries that are wholly untoucht by others; whereof I shall only mention among a great many more; *My New help of Smatterers*, or the *Art of being Deep-learned, and Shallow-read. A curious Invention about Mouse-Traps. An Universal Rule of Reason, or Every Man his own Carver*; Together with a most useful Engine for *catching of Owls*. All which the judicious Reader will find largely treated on, in the several Parts of this Discourse.

I hold my self obliged to give as much Light as is possible, into the Beauties and Excellencies of what I am writing, because it is become the Fashion and Humor most applauded among the first Authors of this Polite and Learned Age, when they would correct the ill Nature of Critical, or inform the Ignorance of Courteous Readers. Besides, there have been several famous Pieces lately published both in Verse and Prose; wherein, if the Writers had not been pleas'd, out of their great Humanity and Affection to the Publick, to give us a nice Detail of the *Sublime*, and the *Admirable* they contain; it is a thousand to one, whether we should ever have discovered one Grain of either. For my own particular, I cannot deny, that whatever I have said upon this Occasion, had been more proper in a Preface, and more agreeable to the Mode, which usually directs it there. But I here think fit to lay hold on that great and honourable Privilege of being the *Last Writer*; I claim an absolute Authority in Right, as the *freshest Modern*, which gives me a Despotick Power over all Authors before me. In the Strength of which Title, I do utterly disapprove and declare against that pernicious Custom, of making the Preface a Bill of Fare to the Book. For I have always lookt upon it as a high Point of Indiscretion in *Monster-mongers* and other *Retailers of strange Sights*; to hang out a fair Large Picture over the Door, drawn after the Life, with a most eloquent

Description underneath: This hath saved me many a Threepence, for my Curiosity was fully satisfied, and I never offered to go in, tho' often invited by the urging and attending Orator, with his last *moving* and *standing* Piece of Rhetorick; *Sir, Upon my Word, we are just going to begin.* Such is exactly the Fate, at this Time, of *Prefaces, Epistles, Advertisements, Introductions, Prolegomena's, Apparatus's, To-the-Reader's.* This Expedient was admirable at first; Our Great *Dryden* has long carried it as far as it would go, and with incredible Success. He has often said to me in Confidence, that the World would never have suspected him to be so great a Poet, if he had not assured them so frequently in his Prefaces, that it was impossible they could either doubt or forget it. Perhaps it may be so; However, I much fear, his Instructions have edify'd out of their Place, and taught Men to grow Wiser in certain Points, where he never intended they should; For it is lamentable to behold, with what a lazy Scorn, many of the yawning Readers in our Age, do now a-days twirl over forty or fifty Pages of *Preface* and *Dedication*, (which is the usual *Modern* Stint) as if it were so much *Latin.* Tho' it must be also allowed on the other Hand that a very considerable Number is known to proceed *Criticks* and *Wits*, by reading nothing else. Into which two Factions, I think, all present Readers may justly be divided. Now, for my self, I profess to be of the former Sort; and therefore having the *Modern* Inclination to expatiate upon the Beauty of my own Productions, and display the bright Parts of my Discourse; I thought best to do it in the Body of the Work, where, as it now lies, it makes a very considerable Addition to the Bulk of the Volume, *a Circumstance by no means to be neglected by a skilful Writer.*

A DIGRESSION IN PRAISE OF DIGRESSIONS

I HAVE sometimes *heard* of an *Iliad* in a *Nut-shell*; but it hath been my Fortune to have much oftner *seen* a *Nut-shell* in an *Iliad.* There is no doubt, that Human Life has received most wonderful Advantages from both; but to which of the two the World is chiefly indebted, I shall leave among the Curious, as a Problem worthy of their utmost Enquiry. For the Invention of the latter, I think the Commonwealth of Learning is chiefly obliged to the great *Modern* Improvement of *Digressions*: The late Refinements in Knowledge, running parallel to those of Dyet in our Nation, which among Men of a judicious Taste, are drest up in Various Compounds, consisting in *Soups* and *Ollio's*, *Fricassées* and *Ragousts*.

'Tis true, there is a sort of morose, detracting, ill-bred People, who pretend utterly to disrelish these polite Innovations: And as to the Similitude from Dyet, they allow the Parallel, but are so bold to pronounce the Example it self, a Corruption and Degeneracy of Taste. They tell us, that the Fashion of jumbling fifty Things together in a Dish, was at first introduced in Compliance to a depraved and *debauched Appetite*, as well as to a *crazy Constitution*; And to see a Man hunting thro' an *Ollio*, after the *Head* and *Brains* of a *Goose*, a *Wigeon*, or a *Woodcock*, is a Sign, he wants a Stomach and Digestion for more substantial Victuals. Farther, they affirm, that *Digressions* in a Book, are like the *Forein Troops* in a *State*, which argue the Nation to want a *Heart* and *Hands* of its own, and often, either *subdue* the *Natives*, or drive them into the most *unfruitful Corners*.

But, after all that can be objected by these supercilious Censors; 'tis manifest, the Society of Writers would quickly be reduced to a very inconsiderable Number, if Men were put upon making Books, with the fatal Confinement of delivering nothing beyond what is to the Purpose. 'Tis acknowledged, that were the Case the same among Us, as with the *Greeks* and *Romans*, when Learning was in its *Cradle*, to be reared and fed, and cloathed by *Invention*; it would be an easy Task to fill up Volumes upon particular Occasions, without farther exspatiating from the Subject, than by moderate Excursions, helping to advance or clear the main Design. But with *Knowledge*, it has fared as with a numerous Army, encamped in a fruitful Country; which for a few Days maintains it self by the Product of the Soyl it is on; Till Provisions being spent, they send to forrage many a Mile, among Friends or Enemies it matters not. Mean while, the neighbouring Fields trampled and beaten down, become barren and dry, affording no Sustenance but Clouds of Dust.

The whole Course of Things, being thus entirely changed between *Us* and the *Antients*; and the *Moderns* wisely sensible of it, we of this Age have discovered a shorter, and more prudent Method, to become *Scholars* and *Wits*, without the Fatigue of *Reading* or of *Thinking*. The most accomplisht Way of using Books at present, is twofold: Either first, to serve them as some Men do *Lords*, learn their *Titles* exactly, and then brag of their Acquaintance. Or Secondly, which is indeed the choicer, the profounder, and politer Method, to get a thorough Insight into the *Index*, by which the whole Book is governed and turned, like *Fishes* by the *Tail*. For, to enter the Palace of Learning at the *great Gate*, requires an Expence of Time and Forms; therefore Men of much Haste and little Ceremony, are content to get in by the *Back-Door*. For, the Arts are all in a *flying* March, and therefore more easily subdued by attacking them in the *Rear*. Thus Physicians discover the State of the whole Body, by consulting only what comes from *Behind*. Thus Men catch Knowledge by throwing their Wit on the *Posteriors* of a Book, as Boys do Sparrows with flinging *Salt* upon their *Tails*. Thus Human Life is best understood by the wise man's Rule of *Regarding the End*. Thus are the Sciences found like *Hercules's* Oxen, by *tracing them Backwards*. Thus are *old Sciences* unravelled like *old Stockings*, by beginning at the *Foot*.

Besides all this, the Army of the Sciences hath been of late, with a world of Martial Discipline, drawn into its *close Order*, so that a View, or a Muster may be taken of it with abundance of Expedition. For this great Blessing we are wholly indebted to *Systems* and *Abstracts*, in which the *Modern* Fathers of Learning, like prudent Usurers, spent their Sweat for the Ease of Us their Children. For *Labor* is the Seed of *Idleness*, and it is the peculiar Happiness of our Noble Age to gather the *Fruit*.

Now the Method of growing Wise, Learned, and *Sublime*, having become so regular an Affair, and so established in all its Forms; the Numbers of Writers must needs have encreased accordingly, and to a Pitch that has made it of absolute Necessity for them to interfere continually with each other. Besides, it is reckoned, that there is not at this present, a sufficient Quantity of new Matter left in Nature, to furnish and adorn any one particular Subject to the Extent of a Volume. This I am told by a very skillful *Computer*, who hath given a full Demonstration of it from Rules of *Arithmetick*.

This, perhaps, may be objected against, by those, who maintain the Infinity of Matter, and therefore, will not allow that any *Species* of it can be exhausted. For Answer to which, let us examine the noblest Branch of *Modern* Wit or Invention, planted and cultivated by the present Age, and, which of all others, hath born the most, and the fairest Fruit. For tho' some Remains of it were left us by the *Antients*, yet have not any of those, as I remember, been translated or compiled into Systems for *Modern* Use. Therefore We may affirm, to our own Honor, that it has in some sort, been both invented, and brought to a Perfection by the same Hands. What I mean, is that highly celebrated Talent among the *Modern* Wits, of deducing Similitudes, Allusions, and Applications, very Surprizing, Agreeable, and Apposite, from the *Pudenda* of either Sex, together with *their proper Uses*. And truly, having observed how little Invention bears any Vogue, besides what is derived into these *Channels*, I have sometimes had a Thought, That the happy Genius of our Age and Country, was prophetically held forth by that antient *typical Description of the *Indian* Pygmies; *whose Stature did not exceed above two Foot*; *Sed quorum pudenda crassa, & ad talos usque pertingentia*. Now, I have been very curious to inspect the late Productions, wherein the Beauties of this kind have most prominently appeared. And altho' this

---

⟨* *Ctesiæ fragm. apud Photium.*⟩

Vein hath bled so freely, and all Endeavours have been used in the Power of Human Breath, to dilate, extend, and keep it open: Like the Scythians, *who had a Custom, and an Instrument, to blow up the Privities of their Mares, that they might yield the more Milk*; Yet I am under an Apprehension, it is near growing dry, and past all Recovery; And that either some new *Fonde* of Wit should, if possible, be provided, or else that we must e'en be content with Repetition here, as well as upon all other Occasions.

This will stand as an uncontestable Argument, that our *Modern* Wits are not to reckon upon the Infinity of Matter, for a constant Supply. What remains therefore, but that our last Recourse must be had to large *Indexes*, and little *Compendiums*; *Quotations* must be plentifully gathered, and bookt in Alphabet; To this End, tho' Authors need be little consulted, yet *Criticks*, and *Commentators*, and *Lexicons* carefully must. But above all, those judicious Collectors of *bright Parts*, and *Flowers*, and *Observanda's* are to be nicely dwelt on; by some called the *Sieves* and *Boulters* of Learning; tho' it is left undetermined, whether they dealt in *Pearls* or Meal; and consequently, whether we are more to value that which *passed thro'*, or what *staid behind*.

By these Methods, in a few Weeks, there starts up many a Writer, capable of managing the profoundest, and most universal Subjects. For, what tho' his *Head* be empty, provided his *Common-place-Book* be full; And if you will bate him but the Circumstances of *Method*, and *Style*, and *Grammar*, and *Invention*; allow him but the common Priviledges of transcribing from others, and digressing from himself, as often as he shall see Occasion; He will desire no more Ingredients towards fitting up a Treatise, that shall make a very comely Figure on a Bookseller's Shelf, there to be preserved neat and clean, for a long Eternity, adorn'd with the Heraldry of its Title, fairly inscribed on a Label; never to be thumb'd or greas'd by Students, nor bound to everlasting Chains of Darkness

---

⟨* *Herodot.* L. 4.⟩

in a Library; But when the Fulness of time is come, shall happily undergo the Tryal of Purgatory in order *to ascend the Sky.*

Without these Allowances, how is it possible, we *Modern* Wits should ever have an Opportunity to introduce our Collections listed under so many thousand Heads of a different Nature? for want of which, the Learned World would be deprived of infinite Delight, as well as Instruction, and we our selves buried beyond Redress in an inglorious and undistinguish Oblivion.

From such Elements as these, I am alive to behold the Day, wherein the Corporation of Authors can out-vie all its Brethren in the *Field.* A Happiness derived to us with a great many others, from our *Scythian* Ancestors; among whom, the Number of *Pens* was so infinite, that the *Grecian Eloquence had no other way of expressing it, than by saying, *That in the Regions, far to the* North, *it was hardly possible for a Man to travel, the very Air was so replete with* Feathers.

The Necessity of this Digression, will easily excuse the Length; and I have chosen for it as proper a Place as I could readily find. If the judicious Reader can assign a fitter, I do here empower him to remove it into any other Corner he pleases.

A DIGRESSION CONCERNING THE ORIGINAL, THE USE AND IMPROVEMENT OF MADNESS IN A COMMONWEALTH

. . . . . IF we take a Survey of the greatest Actions that have been performed in the World, under the Influence of Single Men; which are, *The Establishment of New Empires by Conquest: The Advance and Progress of New Schemes in Philosophy; and the contriving, as well as the propagating of New Religions:* We shall find the Authors of them all,

⟨* *Herodot.* L. 4.⟩

to have been Persons, whose natural Reason hath admitted great Revolutions from their Dyet, their Education, the Prevalency of some certain Temper, together
with the particular Influence of Air and Climate. Besides,
there is something Individual in human Minds, that easily
kindles at the accidental Approach and Collision of certain
Circumstances, which tho' of paltry and mean Appearance,
do often flame out into the greatest Emergencies of Life.
For great Turns are not always given by strong Hands,
but by lucky Adaption, and at proper Seasons; and it is
of no import, where the Fire was kindled, if the Vapor
has once got up into the Brain. For the *upper Region* of
Man, is furnished like the *middle Region* of the Air; The
Materials are formed from Causes of the widest Difference,
yet produce at last the same Substance and Effect. Mists
arise from the Earth, Steams from Dunghils, Exhalations
from the Sea, and Smoak from Fire; yet all Clouds are
the same in Composition, as well as Consequences: and
the Fumes issuing from a Jakes, will furnish as comely
and useful a Vapor, as Incense from an Altar. Thus far,
I suppose, will easily be granted me; and then it will
follow, that as the Face of Nature never produces Rain,
but when it is overcast and disturbed, so Human Understanding, seated in the Brain, must be troubled and overspread by Vapours, ascending from the lower Faculties,
to water the Invention, and render it fruitful. Now, altho'
these Vapours (as it hath been already said) are of as
various Original, as those of the Skies, yet the Crop they
produce, differs both in Kind and Degree, meerly according to the Soil. I will produce two Instances to prove and
Explain what I am now advancing.

    *A certain Great Prince raised a mighty Army, filled
his Coffers with infinite Treasures, provided an invincible
Fleet, and all this, without giving the least Part of his
Design to his greatest Ministers, or his nearest Favourites.
Immediately the whole World was alarmed; the neigh-
bouring Crowns, in trembling Expectations, towards what

---

* *This was* Harry *the Great of* France.

Point the Storm would burst; the small Politicians, every where forming profound Conjectures. Some believed he had laid a Scheme for Universal Monarchy: Others, after much Insight, determined the Matter to be a Project for pulling down the *Pope*, and setting up the *Reformed* Religion, which had once been his own. Some, again, of a deeper Sagacity, sent him into *Asia* to subdue the *Turk*, and recover *Palestine*. In the midst of all these Projects and Preparations; a certain *State-Surgeon*, gathering the Nature of the Disease by these Symptoms, attempted the Cure, at one Blow performed the Operation, broke the Bag, and out flew the *Vapour*; nor did any thing want to render it a compleat Remedy, only, that the Prince unfortunately happened to Die in the Performance. Now, is the Reader exceeding curious to learn, from whence this *Vapour* took its Rise, which had so long set the Nations at a Gaze? What secret Wheel, what hidden Spring could put into Motion so wonderful an Engine? It was afterwards discovered, that the Movement of this whole Machine had been directed by an absent *Female*, whose Eyes had raised a Protuberancy, and before Emission, she was removed into an Enemy's Country. What should an unhappy Prince do in such ticklish Circumstances as these? He tried in vain the Poet's never-failing Receipt of *Corpora quæque*; For,

> *Idque petit corpus mens unde est saucia amore;*
> *Unde feritur, eo tendit, gestitq; coire.* Lucr.

Having to no purpose used all peaceable Endeavours, the collected part of the *Semen*, raised and enflamed, became adust, converted to Choler, turned head upon the spinal Duct, and ascended to the Brain. The very same Principle that influences a *Bully* to break the Windows of a Whore, who has jilted him, naturally stirs up a Great Prince to raise mighty Armies, and dream of nothing but Sieges, Battles, and Victories.

——————— *Teterrima belli*
Causa ———————

————————————————————————
* Ravillac, *who stabb'd* Henry *the Great in his Coach.*

The other *Instance is, what I have read somewhere, in a very antient Author, of a mighty King, who for the space of above thirty Years, amused himself to take and loose Towns; beat Armies, and be beaten; drive Princes out of their Dominions; fright Children from their Bread and Butter; burn, lay waste, plunder, dragoon, massacre Subject and Stranger, Friend and Foe, Male and Female. 'Tis recorded, that the Philosophers of each Country were in grave Dispute, upon Causes Natural, Moral, and Political, to find out where they should assign an original Solution of this Phœnomenon. At last the *Vapour* or *Spirit*, which animated the Hero's Brain, being in perpetual Circulation, seized upon that Region of [the] Human Body, so renown'd for furnishing the †*Zibeta Occidentalis*, and gathering there into a Tumor, left the rest of the World for that Time in Peace. Of such mighty Consequence it is, where those Exhalations fix; and of so little, from whence they proceed. The same Spirits which in their superior Progress would conquer a Kingdom, descending upon the *Anus*, conclude in a *Fistula*.

Let us next examine the great Introducers of new Schemes in Philosophy, and search till we can find, from what Faculty of the Soul the Disposition arises in mortal Man, of taking it into his Head, to advance new Systems with such an eager Zeal, in things agreed on all hands impossible to be known: from what Seeds this Disposition springs, and to what Quality of human Nature these Grand Innovators have been indebted for their Number of Disciples. Because, it is plain, that several of the chief among them, both *Antient* and *Modern*, were usually mistaken by their Adversaries, and indeed, by all, except their own Followers, to have been Persons Crazed, or out of their Wits, having generally proceeded in the common Course of their Words and Actions, by a Method very different

---

* *This is meant of the Present* French *King.*

† Paracelsus, *who was so famous for Chymistry, try'd an Experiment upon human Excrement, to make a Perfume of it, which when he had brought to Perfection, he called* Zibeta Occidentalis, *or* Western-Civet, *the back Parts of Man (according to his Division mention'd by the Author) being the* West.

from the vulgar Dictates of *unrefined* Reason : agreeing for the most Part in their several Models, with their present undoubted Successors in the *Academy* of *Modern Bedlam* (whose Merits and Principles I shall farther examine in due Place.) Of this Kind were *Epicurus, Diogenes, Apollonius, Lucretius, Paracelsus, Des Cartes*, and others; who, if they were now in the World, tied fast, and separate from their Followers, would in this our undistinguishing Age, incur manifest Danger of *Phlebotomy*, and *Whips*, and *Chains*, and *dark Chambers*, and *Straw*. For, what Man in the natural State, or Course of Thinking, did ever conceive it in his Power, to reduce the Notions of all Mankind, exactly to the same Length, and Breadth, and Heighth of his own? Yet this is the first humble and civil Design of all Innovators in the Empire of Reason. *Epicurus*, modestly hoped, that one Time or other, a certain Fortuitous Concourse of all Mens Opinions, after perpetual Justlings, the Sharp with the Smooth, the Light and the Heavy, the Round and the Square, would by certain *Clinanima*, unite in the Notions of *Atoms* and *Void*, as these did in the Originals of all Things. *Cartesius* reckoned to see before he died, the Sentiments of all Philosophers, like so many lesser Stars in his *Romantick* System, rapt and drawn within his own *Vortex*. Now, I would gladly be informed, how it is possible to account for such Imaginations as these in particular Men, without Recourse to my *Phænomenon* of *Vapours*, ascending from the lower Faculties to over-shadow the Brain, and there distilling into Conceptions, for which the Narrowness of our Mother-Tongue has not yet assigned any other Name, besides that of *Madness* or *Phrenzy*. Let us therefore now conjecture how it comes to pass, that none of these great Prescribers, do ever fail providing themselves and their Notions, with a Number of implicite Disciples. And, I think, the Reason is easie to be assigned : For, there is a peculiar *String* in the Harmony of Human Understanding, which in several individuals is exactly of the same Tuning. This, if you can dexterously screw up to its right key, and then strike gently upon it; Whenever you have the Good

Fortune to light among those of the same Pitch, they will by a secret necessary Sympathy, strike exactly at the same time. And in this one Circumstance, lies all the Skill or Luck of the Matter; for if you chance to jar the String among those who are either above or below your own Height, instead of subscribing to your Doctrine, they will tie you fast, call you Mad, and feed you with Bread and Water. It is therefore a Point of the nicest Conduct to distinguish and adapt this noble Talent, with respect to the Differences of Persons and of Times. *Cicero* understood this very well, when writing to a Friend in *England,* with a Caution, among other Matters, to beware of being cheated by our *Hackney-Coachmen* (who, it seems, in those days, were as arrant Rascals as they are now) has these remarkable Words. *Est quod gaudeas te in ista loca venisse, ubi aliquid sapere viderere.* For, to speak a bold Truth, it is a fatal Miscarriage, so ill to order Affairs, as to pass for a *Fool* in one Company, when in another you might be treated as a *Philosopher.* Which I desire *some certain Gentlemen of my Acquaintance,* to lay up in their Hearts, as a very seasonable *Innuendo.*

This, indeed, was the Fatal Mistake of that worthy Gentleman, my most ingenious Friend, Mr. *W[o]tt[o]n*: A Person, in appearance ordain'd for great Designs, as well as Performances; whether you will consider his *Notions* or his *Looks.* Surely, no Man ever advanced into the Publick, with fitter Qualifications of Body and Mind, for the Propagation of a new Religion. Oh, had those happy Talents misapplied to vain Philosophy, been turned into their proper Channels of *Dreams* and *Visions,* where *Distortion* of Mind and Countenance, are of such Sovereign Use; the base detracting World would not then have dared to report, that something is amiss, that his Brain hath undergone an unlucky Shake; which even his Brother *Modernists* themselves, like Ungrates, do whisper so loud, that it reaches up to the very Garret I an now writing in.

Lastly, Whosoever pleases to look into the Fountains

⟨* *Epist. ad Fam. Trebatio.*⟩

of *Enthusiasm*, from whence, in all Ages, have eternally proceeded such fatning Streams, will find the Spring Head to have been as *troubled* and *muddy* as the Current; Of such great Emolument, is a Tincture of this *Vapour*, which the World calls *Madness*, that without its Help, the World would not only be deprived of those two great Blessings, *Conquests* and *Systems*, but even all Mankind would unhappily be reduced to the same Belief in Things Invisible. Now, the former *Postulatum* being held, that it is of no Import from what Originals this *Vapour* proceeds, but either in what *Angles* it strikes and spreads over the Understanding, or upon what *Species* of Brain it ascends; It will be a very delicate Point, to cut the Feather, and divide the several Reasons to a Nice and Curious Reader, how this numerical Difference in the Brain, can produce Effects of so vast a Difference from the same Vapour, as to be the sole Point of Individuation between *Alexander the Great, Jack of Leyden*, and Monsieur *Des Cartes*. The present *Argument* is the most abstracted that ever I engaged in, it strains my Faculties to their highest Stretch; and I desire the Reader to attend with utmost Perpensity; For, I now proceed to unravel this knotty Point.

*There is in Mankind a certain *   *
*   *   *   *   *   *   *   *
*   *   *   *   *   *   *   *
*   *   *   *   *   *   *   *   *Hic multa*
*   *   *   *   *   *   *   *   *desiderantur.*
*   *   *   *   *   *   *   *
*   *   *   *   *   And this I take to be a clear Solution of the Matter.

Having therefore so narrowly past thro' this intricate Difficulty, the Reader will, I am sure, agree with me in the Conclusion; that if the *Moderns* mean by *Madness*, only a Disturbance or Transposition of the Brain, by Force of certain *Vapours* issuing up from the lower Faculties; Then

---

* *Here is another Defect in the Manuscript, but I think the Author did wisely, and that the Matter which thus strained his Faculties, was not worth a Solution; and it were well if all Metaphysical Cobweb Problems were no otherwise answered.*

M

has this *Madness* been the Parent of all those mighty Revolutions, that have happened in *Empire*, in *Philosophy*, and in *Religion*. For, the Brain, in its natural Position and State of Serenity, disposeth its Owner to pass his Life in the common Forms, without any Thought of subduing Multitudes to his own *Power*, his *Reasons* or his *Visions*; and the more he shapes his Understanding by the Pattern of Human Learning, the less he is inclined to form Parties after his particular Notions; because that instructs him in his private Infirmities, as well as in the stubborn Ignorance of the People. But when a Man's Fancy gets *astride* on his Reason, when Imagination is at Cuffs with the Senses, and common Understanding, as well as common Sense, is Kickt out of Doors; the first Proselyte he makes, is Himself, and when that is once compass'd, the Difficulty is not so great in bringing over others; A strong Delusion always operating from *without*, as vigorously as from *within*. For, Cant and Vision are to the Ear and the Eye, the same that Tickling is to the Touch. Those Entertainments and Pleasures we most value in Life, are such as *Dupe* and play the Wag with the Senses. For, if we take an Examination of what is generally understood by *Happiness*, as it has Respect, either to the Understanding or the Senses, we shall find all its Properties and Adjuncts will herd under this short Definition: That, *it is a perpetual Possession of being well Deceived*. And first, with Relation to the Mind or Understanding; 'tis manifest, what mighty Advantages Fiction has over Truth; and the Reason is just at our Elbow; because Imagination can build nobler Scenes, and produce more wonderful Revolutions than Fortune or Nature will be at Expence to furnish. Nor is Mankind so much to blame in his Choice, thus determining him, if we consider that the Debate meerly lies between *Things past*, and *Things conceived*; and so the Question is only this; Whether Things that have Place in the *Imagination*, may not as properly be said to *Exist*, as those that are seated in the *Memory*; which may be justly held in the Affirmative, and very much to the Advantage of the former, since This is acknowledged to be the *Womb* of

Things, and the other allowed to be no more than the *Grave*. Again, if we take this Definition of Happiness, and examine it with Reference to the Senses, it will be acknowledged wonderfully adapt. How fading and insipid do all Objects accost us that are not convey'd in the Vehicle of *Delusion*? How shrunk is every Thing, as it appears in the Glass of Nature? So, that if it were not for the Assistance of Artificial *Mediums*, false Lights, refracted Angles, Varnish, and Tinsel; there would be a mighty Level in the Felicity and Enjoyments of Mortal Men. If this were seriously considered by the World, as I have a certain Reason to suspect it hardly will; Men would no longer reckon among their high Points of Wisdom, the Art of exposing weak Sides, and publishing Infirmities; an Employment in my Opinion, neither better nor worse than that of *Unmasking*, which I think, has never been allowed fair Usage, either in the *World* or the *Play-House*.

In the Proportion that Credulity is a more peaceful Possession of the Mind, than Curiosity, so far preferable is that Wisdom, which converses about the Surface, to that pretended Philosophy which enters into the Depth of Things, and then comes gravely back with Informations and Discoveries, that in the inside they are good for nothing. The two Senses, to which all Objects first address themselves, are the Sight and the Touch; These never examine farther than the Colour, the Shape, the Size, and whatever other Qualities dwell, or are drawn by Art upon the Outward of Bodies; and then comes Reason officiously, with Tools for cutting, and opening, and mangling, and piercing, offering to demonstrate, that they are not of the same consistence quite thro'. Now, I take all this to be the last Degree of perverting Nature; one of whose Eternal Laws it is, to put her best Furniture forward. And therefore, in order to save the Charges of all such expensive Anatomy for the Time to come; I do here think fit to inform the Reader, that in such Conclusions as these, Reason is certainly in the Right; and that in most Corporeal Beings, which have fallen under my Cognizance, the *Outside* hath been infinitely preferable to the *Inn*: Whereof I have been farther convinced from some late Experiments. Last Week I saw a Woman *flay'd*, and you will hardly believe, how much it altered her Person for the worse. Yesterday I ordered the Carcass of a *Beau* to be stript in my Presence; when we were all amazed to find so many unsuspected Faults under one Suit of Cloaths: Then I laid open his *Brain*, his *Heart*, and his *Spleen*; But, I plainly perceived at every Operation, that the farther we proceeded, we found the Defects encrease upon us in Number and Bulk: from all which, I justly formed this Conclusion to my self; That whatever Philosopher or Projector can find out an Art to sodder and patch up the Flaws and Imperfections of Nature, will deserve much better of Mankind, and teach us a more useful Science, than that so much in present Esteem, of widening and exposing them (like him who held *Anatomy* to be the ultimate End of *Physick*.) And he, whose Fortunes and Dispositions have placed him in a convenient Station to enjoy the Fruits of this noble Art; He that can with *Epicurus* content his Ideas with the *Films* and *Images* that fly off upon his Senses from the *Superficies* of Things; Such a Man truly wise, creams off Nature, leaving the Sower and the Dregs, for Philosophy and Reason to lap up. This is the sublime and refined Point of Felicity, called, *the Possession of being well deceived*; The Serene Peaceful State of being a Fool among Knaves.

But to return to *Madness*. It is certain, that according to the System I have above deduced; every *Species* thereof proceeds from a Redundancy of *Vapours*; therefore, as some Kinds of *Phrenzy* give double Strength to the Sinews, so there are of other *Species*, which add Vigor, and Life, and Spirit to the Brain: Now, it usually happens, that these active Spirits, getting Possession of the Brain, resemble those that haunt other waste and empty Dwellings, which for want of Business, either vanish, and carry away a Piece of the House, or else stay at home and fling it all out of the Windows. By which are mystically display'd the two principal Branches of *Madness*, and which some Philosophers not considering so well as I, have mistook to be different in their Causes, over-hastily assigning the first to Deficiency, and the other to Redundance.

I think it therefore manifest, from what I have here advanced, that the main Point of Skill and Address, is to furnish Employment for this Redundancy of *Vapour*, and prudently to adjust the Season of it; by which means it may certainly become of Cardinal and Catholick Emolument in a Commonwealth. Thus one man chusing a proper Juncture, leaps into a Gulph, from whence proceeds a Hero, and is called the Saver of his Country; Another atchieves the same Enterprise, but unluckily timing it, has left the Brand of *Madness*, fixt as a Reproach upon his Memory; Upon so nice a Distinction are we taught to repeat the Name of *Curtius* with Reverence and Love; that of *Empedocles*, with Hatred and Contempt. Thus, also it is usually conceived, that the Elder *Brutus* only personated the *Fool* and *Madman*, for the Good of the Publick: but this was nothing else, than a Redundancy of the same *Vapor*, long misapplied, called by the *Latins*, *Ingenium par negotiis*: Or, (to translate it as nearly as I can) a sort of *Phrenzy*, never in its right Element, till you take it up in Business of the State.

Upon all which, and many other Reasons of equal Weight, though not equally curious; I do here gladly embrace an Opportunity I have long sought for, of Recommending it as a very noble Undertaking to Sir E[dwar]d S[eymou]r, Sir C[hristophe]r M[usgra]ve, Sir J[oh]n B[ow]ls, J[oh]n H[o]w, Esq; and other Patriots concerned, that they would move for Leave to bring in a Bill, for appointing Commissioners to Inspect into *Bedlam*, and the Parts adjacent; who shall be empowered to *send for Persons, Papers, and Records*: to examine into the Merits and Qualifications of every Student and Professor; to observe with utmost Exactness their several Dispositions and Behaviour; by which means, duly distinguishing and adapting their Talents, they might produce admirable Instruments for the several Offices in a State, for the principal

⟨* *Tacit.*⟩

Management of affairs *Ecclesiasticall, Civil* and *Military*; proceeding in such Methods as I shall here humbly propose. And, I hope the Gentle Reader will give some Allowance to my great Solicitudes in this important Affair, upon Account of that high Esteem I have ever born that honourable Society, whereof I had some Time the Happiness to be an unworthy Member.

Is any Student tearing his Straw in piece-meal, Swearing and Blaspheming, biting his Grate, foaming at the Mouth, and emptying his Pispot in the Spectator's Faces? Let the Right Worshipful, the *Commissioners of Inspection*, give him a Regiment of Dragoons, and send him into *Flanders* among the *Rest*. Is another eternally talking, sputtering, gaping, bawling, in a Sound without Period or Article? What wonderful Talents are here mislaid! Let him be furnished immediately with a green Bag and Papers, and *three Pence in his Pocket, and away with Him to *Westminster-Hall*. You will find a Third, gravely taking the Dimensions of his Kennel; A Person of Foresight and Insight, tho' kept quite in the Dark; for why, like *Moses, Ecce* †*cornuta erat ejus facies.* He walks duly in one Pace, intreats your Penny with due Gravity and Ceremony; talks much of hard Times, and Taxes, and the *Whore of Babylon*; Bars up the woodden Window of his Cell constantly at eight a Clock: Dreams of *Fire*, and *Shop-lifters*, and *Court-Customers*, and *Priviledg'd Places*. Now, what a Figure would all these Acquirements amount to, if the Owner were sent into the *City* among his Brethren! Behold a Fourth, in much and deep Conversation with himself, biting his Thumbs at proper Junctures; His Countenance chequered with Business and Design; sometimes walking very fast, with his Eyes nailed to a Paper that he holds in his Hands: A great Saver of Time, somewhat thick of Hearing, very short of Sight, but more of Memory. A Man ever in Haste, a great Hatcher and Breeder of Business, and excellent at the Famous Art of *whispering Nothing.* A

⟨* *A Lawyer's Coach-hire.*⟩
† Cornutus, *is either Horned or Shining, and by this Term*, Moses *is described in the vulgar* Latin *of the Bible.*

huge Idolator of Monosyllables and Procrastination; so ready to *Give* his Word to every Body, that he never *keeps* it. One that has forgot the common *Meaning* of Words, but an admirable Retainer of the *Sound*. Extreamly subject to the *Loosness*, for his *Occasions* are perpetually *calling him away*. If you approach his Grate in his familiar Intervals; *Sir*, says he, *Give me a Penny, and I'll sing you a Song: But give me the Penny first*. (Hence comes the common Saying, and commoner Practice of parting with Money for a *Song*.) What a compleat System of *Court-Skill* is here described in every Branch of it, and all utterly lost with wrong Application? Accost the Hole of another Kennel, first stopping your Nose, you will behold a surley, gloomy, nasty, slovenly Mortal, raking in his own Dung, and dabling in his Urine. The best Part of his Diet, is the Reversion of his own Ordure, which exspiring into Steams, whirls perpetually about, and at last reinfunds. His Complexion is of a dirty Yellow, with a thin scattered Beard, exactly agreeable to that of his Dyet upon its first Declination; like other Insects, who having their Birth and Education in an Excrement, from thence borrow their Colour and their Smell. The Student of this Apartment is very sparing of his Words, but somewhat over-liberal of his Breath; He holds his Hand out ready to receive your Penny, and immediately upon Receipt, withdraws to his former Occupations. Now, is it not amazing to think, the Society of *Warwick-Lane*, should have no more Concern, for the Recovery of so useful a Member, who, if one may judge from these Appearances, would become the greatest Ornament to that Illustrious Body? Another Student struts up fiercely to your Teeth, puffing with his Lips, half squeezing out his Eyes, and very graciously holds out his Hand to kiss. The *Keeper* desires you not to be afraid of this Professor, for he will do you no Hurt: To him alone is allowed the Liberty of the Anti-Chamber, and the *Orator* of the Place gives you to understand, that this solemn Person is a *Taylor* run mad with Pride. This considerable Student is adorned with many other Qualities, upon which, at present, I shall not farther enlarge . . . .

*Heark in your Ear . . . .
I am strangely mistaken, if all his Address, his Motions, and his Airs, would not then be very natural, and in their proper Element.

I shall not descend so minutely, as to insist upon the vast Number of *Beaux, Fidlers, Poets,* and *Politicians,* that the World might recover by such a Reformation. But what is more material, besides the clear Gain redounding to the Commonwealth, by so large an Acquisition of Persons to employ, whose Talents and Acquirements, if I may be so bold to affirm it, are now buried, or at least misapplied: It would be a mighty Advantage accruing to the Publick from this Enquiry, that all these would very much excel, and arrive at great Perfection in their several Kinds; which, I think, is manifest from what I have already shewn; and shall inforce by this one plain Instance; That even, I my self, the Author of these momentous Truths, am a Person, whose Imaginations are hard-mouth'd, and exceedingly disposed to run away with his *Reason,* which I have observed from long Experience, to be a very light Rider, and easily shook off; upon which Account, my Friends will never trust me alone, without a solemn Promise, to vent my Speculations in this, or the like manner, for the universal Benefit of Human kind; which, perhaps, the gentle, courteous, and candid Reader, brimful of that *Modern* Charity and Tenderness, usually annexed to his *Office,* will be very hardly persuaded to believe.

THE AUTHOR'S COMPLIMENT TO THE READERS &c.

It is an unanswerable Argument of a very refined Age, the wonderful Civilities that have passed of late Years, between the Nation of *Authors,* and that of *Readers.* There can hardly †pop out a *Play,* a *Pamphlet,* or a *Poem,* with-

---

I cannot conjecture what the Author means here, or how this Chasm could be fill'd, tho' it is capable of more than one Interpretation.
† *This is litterally true, as we may observe in the Prefaces to most Plays, Poems, &c.*

out a Preface full of Acknowledgement to the World, for the General Reception and Applause they have given it, which the Lord knows where, or when, or how, or from whom it received. In due Deference to so laudable a Custom, I do here return my humble Thanks to *His Majesty*, and both Houses of *Parliament*; To the *Lords* of the King's most honourable Privy-Council, to the Reverend the *Judges*: To the *Clergy* and *Gentry* and *Yeomantry* of this Land: But in a more especial manner, to my worthy Brethren and Friends at *Will's Coffee-House*, and *Gresham-College*, and *Warwick-Lane*, and *Moor-Fields*, and *Scotland-Yard*, and *Westminster-Hall*, and *Guild-Hall*; In short, to all Inhabitants and Retainers whatsoever, either in Court, or Church, or Camp, or City, or Country; for their generous and universal Acceptance of this Divine Treatise. I accept their Approbation, and good Opinion with extream Gratitude, and to the utmost of my poor Capacity, shall take hold of all Opportunities to return the Obligation.

I am also happy, that Fate has flung me into so blessed an Age for the mutual Felicity of *Booksellers* and *Authors*, whom I may safely affirm to be at this Day the two only satisfied Parties in *England*. Ask an *Author* how his last Piece hath succeeded; *Why, truly he thanks his Stars, the World has been very favourable, and he has not the least Reason to complain*: And yet, *By G——, He writ it in a Week at Bits and Starts, when he could steal an Hour from his urgent Affairs*; as it is a hundred to one, you may see farther in the Preface, to which he refers you; and for the rest, to the Bookseller. There you go as a Customer, and make the same Question: *He blesses his God, the Thing takes wonderfully, he is just Printing a Second Edition, and has but three left in his Shop. You beat down the Price: Sir, we shall not differ*; and in hopes of your Custom another Time, lets you have it as reasonable as you please; *And, pray send as many of your Acquaintance as you will, I shall upon your Account furnish them all at the same Rate.*

Now, it is not well enough consider'd, to what Accidents and Occasions the World is indebted for the greatest Part of those noble Writings, which hourly start up to entertain it. If it were not for a *rainy Day, a drunken Vigil, a Fit of the Spleen, a Course of Physick, a sleepy Sunday, an ill Run at Dice, a long Taylor's Bill, a Beggar's Purse, a factious Head, a hot Sun, costive Dyet, Want of Books, and a just Contempt of Learning.* But for these Events, I say, and some Others too long to recite, (especially *a prudent Neglect of taking Brimstone inwardly,*) I doubt, the Number of *Authors,* and of *Writings* would dwindle away to a Degree most woful to behold. To confirm this Opinion, hear the Words of the famous *Troglodyte* Philosopher: *'Tis certain* (said he) *some Grains of Folly are of course annexed, as Part of the Composition of Human Nature, only the Choice is left us, whether we please to wear them* Inlaid *or* Embossed; *And we need not go very far to seek how that is usually determined, when we remember, it is with Human Faculties as with Liquors, the lightest will be ever at the Top.*

There is in this famous Island of *Britain* a certain paultry *Scribbler,* very voluminous, whose Character the Reader cannot wholly be a Stranger to. He deals in a pernicious Kind of Writings, called *Second Parts,* and usually passes under the Name of *The Author of the First.* I easily foresee, that as soon as I lay down my Pen, this nimble *Operator* will have stole it, and treat me as inhumanly as he hath already done Dr. *Bl[ackmo]re, L['Estran]ge,* and many others who shall here be nameless, I therefore fly for Justice and Relief, into the Hands of that great *Rectifier of Saddles,* and *Lover of Mankind,* Dr. *B[en]tly,* begging he will take this enormous Grievance into his most *Modern* Consideration: And if it should so happen, that the *Furniture of an Ass,* in the Shape of a *Second Part,* must for my Sins be clapt, by a Mistake upon my Back, that he will immediately please, in the Presence of the World, to lighten me of the Burthen, and take it home to *his own House,* till the *true Beast* thinks fit to call for it.

In the mean time I do here give this publick Notice, that my Resolutions are, to circumscribe within this Discourse the whole Stock of Matter I have been so many Years providing. Since my *Vein* is once opened, I am content to exhaust it all at a Running, for the peculiar Advantage of my dear Country, and for the universal Benefit of Mankind. Therefore hospitably considering the Number of my Guests, they shall have my whole Entertainment at a Meal; And I scorn to set up the *Leavings* in the Cupboard. What the *Guests* cannot eat may be given to the *Poor*, and the *Dogs under the Table may gnaw the *Bones*; This I understand for a more generous Proceeding, than to turn the Company's Stomach, by inviting them again to morrow to a scurvy Meal of *Scraps*.

If the Reader fairly considers the Strength of what I have advanced in the foregoing Section, I am convinced it will produce a wonderful Revolution in his Notions and Opinions; And he will be abundantly better prepared to receive and to relish the concluding Part of this miraculous Treatise. Readers may be divided into three Classes, the *Superficial*, the *Ignorant*, and the *Learned*: And I have with much Felicity fitted my Pen to the Genius and Advantage of each. The *Superficial* Reader will be strangely provoked to *Laughter*; which clears the Breast and the Lungs, is Soverain against the *Spleen*, and the most innocent of all *Diureticks*. The *Ignorant* Reader (between whom and the former, the Distinction is extreamly nice) will find himself disposed to *Stare*; which is an admirable Remedy for ill Eyes, serves to raise and enliven the Spirits, and wonderfully helps *Perspiration*. But the Reader truly *Learned*, chiefly for whose Benefit I wake, when others sleep, and sleep when others wake, will here find sufficient Matter to employ his Speculations for the rest of his Life. It were much to be wisht, and I do here humbly propose for an Experiment, that every Prince in *Christendom* will take seven of the *deepest Scholars* in his Dominions, and shut them up close for *seven* Years, in *seven* Chambers, with a Command to write *seven* ample Commentaries on this comprehensive Discourse. I shall venture to affirm, that whatever Difference may be found in their several Conjectures, they will be all, without the least Distortion,

---

* *By Dogs, the Author means common injudicious Criticks, as he explains it himself before in his* Digression upon Criticks, *(Page* 316.)

manifestly deduceable from the Text. Mean time, it is my earnest Request, that so useful an Undertaking may be entered upon (if their Majesties please) with all convenient speed; because I have a strong Inclination, before I leave the World, to taste a Blessing, which we *mysterious* Writers can seldom reach, till we have got into our Graves. Whether it is, that *Fame* being a Fruit grafted on the Body, can hardly grow, and much less ripen, till the *Stock* is in the Earth; Or, whether she be a Bird of Prey, and is lured among the rest, to pursue after the Scent of a *Carcass*: Or, whether she conceives, her Trumpet sounds best and farthest, when she stands on a *Tomb*, by the Advantage of a rising Ground, and the Echo of a hollow Vault.

'Tis true, indeed, the Republick of *dark* Authors, after they once found out this excellent Expedient of *Dying*, have been peculiarly happy in the Variety, as well as Extent of their Reputation. For, *Night* being the universal Mother of Things, wise Philosophers hold all Writings to be *fruitful* in the Proportion they are *dark*; And therefore, the **true illuminated* (that is to say, the *Darkest* of all) have met with such numberless Commentators, whose *Scholiastick* Midwifry hath deliver'd them of Meanings, that the Authors themselves, perhaps, never conceived, and yet may very justly be allowed the Lawful Parents of them: †The Words of such Writers being like Seed, which, however scattered at random, when they light upon a fruitful ground, will multiply far beyond either the Hopes or Imagination of the Sower.

And therefore in order to promote so useful a Work, I will here take Leave to glance a few *Innuendo's*, that may be of great Assistance to those sublime Spirits, who shall be appointed to labor in a universal Comment upon this wonderful Discourse. And First, ‡I have couched a very profound Mystery in the Number of 0's multiply'd by *Seven*, and divided by *Nine*. Also, if a devout Brother of

---

⟨* *A name of the* Rosycrucians.⟩
† *Nothing is more frequent than for Commentators to force Interpretation, which the Author never meant.*
‡ *This is what the* Cabbalists *among the Jews have done with the* Bible, *and pretend to find wonderful Mysteries by it.*

the *Rosy Cross* will pray fervently for sixty three Mornings, with a lively Faith, and then transpose certain Letters and Syllables according to Prescription, in the second and fifth Section; they will certainly reveal into a full Receit of the *Opus Magnum.* Lastly, Whoever will be at the Pains to calculate the whole Number of each Letter in this Treatise, and sum up the Difference exactly between the several Numbers, assigning the true natural Cause for every such Difference; the Discoveries in the Product, will plentifully reward his Labour. But then he must beware of **Bythus* and *Sigè*, and be sure not to forget the Qualities of *Acamoth*; *A cujus lacrymis humecta prodit Substantia, à risu lucida, à tristitiâ solida, & à timore mobilis,* wherein †*Eugenius Philalethes* hath committed an unpardonable Mistake.

---

* *I was told by an Eminent Divine, whom I consulted on this Point, that these two Barbarous Words, with that of* Acamoth *and its Qualities, as here set down, are quoted from* Irenæus. *This he discover'd by searching that Antient Writer for another Quotation of our Author, which he has placed in the Title Page, and refers to the Book and Chapter; the Curious were very Inquisitive, whether those Barbarous Words,* Basima Eacabasa, &c. *are really in* Irenæus, *and upon enquiry 'twas found they were a sort of Cant or Jargon of certain Hereticks, and therefore very properly prefix'd to such a Book as this of our Author.*

⟨† *Vid.* Anima magica abscondita.⟩ *To the abovementioned Treatise, called* Anthroposophia Theomagica, *there is another annexed, called* Anima Magica Abscondita, *written by the same Author* Vaughan, *under the Name of* Eugenius Philalethes, *but in neither of those Treatises is there any mention of* Acamoth *or its Qualities, so that this is nothing but Amusement, and a Ridicule of dark, unintelligible Writers; only the Words,* A cujus lacrymis, &c. *are as we have said, transcribed from* Irenæus, *tho' I know not from what part. I believe one of the Authors Designs was to set curious Men a hunting thro' Indexes, and enquiring for Books out of the common Road.*

THE
CONDUCT
OF THE
ALLIES

SELECTION

The Conduct of the Allies, whether judged on its own merits, or by the profound effect it produced on public opinion, is probably the most famous political pamphlet in the English language. Though certain passages in a work of this kind have inevitably lost their interest, the main theme—the folly, waste and expense of war and the desirability of peace—which I have tried to preserve in the following selection, is as fresh and, alas, as pertinent to-day as it was over two hundred years ago. This is not the place to analyse the pamphlet in detail; written in the heat of party conflict, it is at times both inaccurate and exaggerated in its statements. The attack on Marlborough, for example, is grossly unjust. Nor indeed is this the place to discuss the propriety of political factions. Whether or not we agree with the Tories, who had enlisted Swift's services on their side, that the Whig policy of continuing a continental war was ruining the country, we must admit that, in Swift's pen, Harley and his colleagues had a weapon of unparalleled force and directness. Swift's indignation, though not as savage, nor, one might add, as disinterested as it was to become, was never more effective than at this juncture in public affairs.

The story of the writing, publication and revision of the tract is recorded, step by step, in the *Journal to Stella*. A first edition of 1000 copies appeared on November 27, 1711, and was exhausted within two days. Three more editions of the same size were sold by the first week of December. Two more editions, of different format, each of 3000 copies " to be sent into the country " were taken up by the end of January. A seventh edition was called for early in the year. Besides these, at least five Dublin editions are recorded. Certain passages, not included here, were revised by Swift on the advice of Lord Bolingbroke. The definitive text, the basis of Mr C. B. Wheeler's critical edition [Oxford 1916] is that of the seventh edition. But in view of the fact that, apart from a few revisions not affecting the present selection, the first seven editions are verbally almost identical, the text I have chosen to print follows that of the first edition.

The Conduct of the Allies and of the Late Ministry in beginning and carrying on the Present War.

THE PREFACE

I CANNOT sufficiently admire the Industry of a sort of Men, wholly out of Favour with the Prince and People, and openly professing a separate Interest from the Bulk of the Landed Men, who yet are able to raise, at this Juncture, so great a Clamour against a Peace, without offering one single Reason, but what we find in their Ballads. I lay it down for a Maxim, That no reasonable Man, whether Whig or Tory (since it is necessary to use those foolish Terms) can be of Opinion for continuing the War, upon the Foot it now is unless he be a Gainer by it, or hopes it may occasion some new Turn of Affairs at home, to the Advantage of his Party; or lastly, unless he be very ignorant of the Kingdom's Condition, and by what Means we have been reduced to it. Upon the two first Cases, where Interest is concerned, I have nothing to say: But as to the last, I think it highly necessary, that the Publick should be freely and impartially told what Circumstances they are in, after what Manner they have been treated by those whom they trusted so many Years with the Disposal of their Blood and Treasure, and what the Consequences of this Management are like to be upon themselves and their Posterity.

Those who either by Writing or Discourse, have undertaken to defend the Proceedings of the Late Ministry, in the Management of the War, and of the Treaty at Gertruydenburg, have spent time in celebrating the Conduct and Valour of our Leaders and their Troops, in summing up the Victories they have gained, and the Towns they have taken. Then they tell us what high Articles were insisted on by our Ministers *and those of the Confederates, and what Pains both were at in persuading* France *to accept them. But nothing of this can give the least Satisfaction to the just Complaints of the Kingdom. As to the War, our Grievances are, That a greater Load has been laid on Us than was either just or necessary, or than we have been able to bear; that the grossest Impositions have been submitted to for the Advancement of private Wealth and Power, or in order to forward the more dangerous Designs of a* Faction, *to both which a Peace would have put an End; And that the Part of the War which was chiefly our Province, which would have been most beneficial to us, and destructive to the Enemy, was wholly neglected. As to a Peace, We complain of being deluded by a* Mock Treaty; *in which those who Negotiated, took care to make such Demands as they knew were impossible to be complied with, and therefore might securely press every Article as if they were in earnest.*

These are some of the Points I design to treat of in the following Discourse; with several others which I thought it necessary, at this time, for the Kingdom to be informed of. I think I am not mistaken in those Facts I mention; at least not in any Circumstance so material, as to weaken the Consequences I draw from them.

After Ten Years War with perpetual Success, to tell us it is yet impossible to have a good Peace, is very surprising, and seems so different from what hath ever hapned in the World before, that a Man of any Party may be allowed suspecting, we have either been ill used, or have not made the most of our Victories, and might therefore desire to know where the Difficulty lay: Then it is natural to enquire into our present Condition; how long we shall be able to go on at this Rate; what the Consequences may be upon the present and future Ages; and whether a Peace, without that impracticable Point which some People do so much insist on, be really ruinous in it self, or equally so with the Continuance of the War.

THE CONDUCT
OF THE ALLIES, &c.

THE Motives that may engage a wise Prince or State in a War, I take to be one or more of these: Either to check the overgrown Power of some ambitious Neighbour; to recover what hath been unjustly taken from Them; to revenge some Injury They have received; (which all Political casuists allow); to assist some Ally in a just Quarrel; or lastly, to defend Themselves when They are invaded. In all these Cases, the Writers upon Politicks admit a War to be justly undertaken. The last is what hath been usually called *pro aris & focis*; where no Expence or Endeavour can be too great, because all we have is at stake, and consequently, our utmost Force to be exerted; and the Dispute is soon determined, either in Safety or utter Destruction. But in the other four, I believe it will be found, that no Monarch or Commonwealth did ever engage beyond a certain Degree; never proceeding so far as to exhaust the Strength and Substance of their Country by Anticipations and Loans, which in a few Years must put them in a worse Condition than any they could reasonably apprehend from those Evils, for the preventing of which they first entred into the War: Because this would be to run into real infallible Ruin, only in hopes to remove what might perhaps but appear so by a probable Speculation.

And, as a War should be undertaken upon a just and prudent Motive, so it is still more obvious, that a Prince ought maturely to consider the Condition he is in when he enters on it; Whether his Coffers be full, his Revenues clear of Debts, his People numerous and rich by a long Peace and free Trade, not overpressed with many burthensom Taxes; No violent Faction ready to dispute his just Prerogative, and thereby weaken his Authority at home, and lessen his Reputation abroad. For, if the contrary of all this happen to be his Case, he will hardly be persuaded to disturb the World's Quiet and his own, while there is any other way left of preserving the latter with Honour and Safety.

351

Supposing the War to have commenced upon a just Motive; the next Thing to be considered, is, when a Prince ought in Prudence to receive the Overtures of a Peace: Which I take to be, either when the Enemy is ready to yield the Point originally contended for, or when that Point is found impossible to be ever obtained; or when contending any longer, though with Probability of gaining that Point at last, would put such a Prince and his People in a worse Condition that the present Loss of it. All which Considerations are of much greater Force, where a War is managed by an Alliance of many Confederates, which in the variety of Interests, among the several Parties, is liable to so many unforeseen Accidents.

In a Confederate War it ought to be considered, which Party has the deepest share in the Quarrel: For though each may have their Particular Reasons, yet one or two among them will probably be more concerned than the rest, and therefore ought to bear the greatest part of the Burthen, in proportion to their Strength. For Example: Two Princes may be Competitors for a Kingdom, and it will be your Interest to take the Part of Him, who will probably allow you good Conditions of Trade, rather than of the other, who possibly may not. However, that Prince whose Cause you espouse, though never so vigorously, is the Principal in that War, and You, properly speaking, are but a Second. Or a Commonwealth may lie in danger to be over-run by a powerful Neighbour, which in time may produce very bad Consequences upon your Trade and Liberty: 'Tis therefore necessary, as well as prudent, to lend them Assistance, and help them to win a strong secure Frontier; but, as They must in course be the first and greatest Sufferers, so, in Justice, they ought to bear the greatest Weight. If a House be on fire, it behooves all in the Neighbourhood to run with Buckets to quench it; but the Owner is sure to be undone first; and it is not impossible that those at next Door may escape, by a Shower from Heaven, or the stillness of the Weather, or some other favourable Accident.

But, if an Ally, who is not so immediately concerned in

the good or ill Fortune of the War, be so generous, as to contribute more than the Principal Party, and even more in proportion to his Abilities, he ought at least to have his Share in what is conquered from the Enemy: Or, if his Romantick Disposition transports him so far, as to expect little or nothing of this, he might, however hope, that the Principals would make it up in Dignity and Respect; and he would surely think it monstrous to find them inter-medling in his Domestick Affairs, prescribing what Servants he should keep or dismiss, pressing him perpetually with the most unreasonable Demands, and at every turn threatning to break the Alliance, if he will not comply.

*

The Part we have acted in the Conduct of this whole War, with reference to our Allies abroad, and to a prevailing Faction at home, is what I shall now particularly examin; where I presume it will appear, by plain Matters of Fact, that no Nation was ever so long or so scandal-ously abused by the Folly, the Temerity, the Corruption, the Ambition of its domestick Enemies; or treated with so much Insolence, Injustice and Ingratitude by its forein Friends.

This will be manifest by proving the Three following Points.

First, That against all manner of Prudence, or common Reason, we engaged in this War as Principals, when we ought to have acted only as Auxiliaries.

Secondly, That we spent all our Vigour in pursuing that Part of the War which could least answer the End we proposed by beginning of it; and made no Efforts at all where we could have most weakned the Common Enemy, and at the same time enriched our selves.

Lastly, That we suffered each of our Allies to break every Article in those Treaties and Agreements by which they were bound, and to lay the Burthen upon us.

Upon the first of these Points, That we ought to have entred into this War only as Auxiliaries. Let any Man reflect upon our Condition at that time: Just come out of the most tedious, expensive and unsuccessful War that ever *England* had been engaged in; sinking under heavy Debts, of a Nature and Degree never heard of by Us or Our Ancestors; the Bulk of the Gentry and People heartily tired of the War, and glad of a Peace, though it brought no other Advantage but it self: No sudden Prospect of lessening our Taxes, which were grown as necessary to pay our Debts, as to raise Armies: A sort of artificial Wealth of Funds and Stocks in the Hands of those who for Ten Years before had been Plundering the Publick: Many Corruptions in every Branch of our Government, that needed Reformation. Under these Difficulties, from which Twenty Years Peace, and the wisest Management, could hardly recover us, we declare War against *France*, fortified by the Accession and Alliance of those Powers I mentioned before, and which, in the former War, had been Parties in our Confederacy. It is very obvious what a Change must be made in the Balance, by such Weights taken out of Our Scale and put into Theirs; since it was manifest by Ten Years Experience, that *France* without those Additions of Strength, was able to maintain it self against us. So that Human Probability ran with mighty odds on the other side; and in that case, nothing under the most extreme Necessity should force any State to engage in a War.

*

. . We became Principal in a War, in Conjunction with two Allies, whose share in the Quarrel was, beyond all Proportion, greater than Ours. However, I can see no Reason from the Words of the Grand Alliance, by which we were obliged to make those prodigious Expences we have since been at. By what I have always heard and read, I take the *whole Strength of a Nation*, as understood in that Treaty, to be the utmost that a Prince can raise Annually from his Subjects; if he be forced to Mortgage and Borrow, whether at home or abroad, it is not, properly speaking, *his own Strength*, or that of the Nation, but the entire Substance of particular Persons, which not being able to raise out of the annual Income of his Kingdom, he takes upon Security, and can only pay the Interest; and by this Method one Part of the Nation is pawned to the other, with hardly a Possibility left of being ever redeemed.

Surely it would have been enough for us to have suspended the Payment of our Debts contracted in the former War, to have continued our Land and Malt Tax, with those others which have since been mortgaged: These, with some Additions, would have made up such a Sum, as, with prudent Management, might, I suppose, have maintained an hundred thousand Men by Sea and Land; a reasonable Quota in all conscience for that Ally, who apprehended least Danger, and expected least Advantage. Nor can we imagine that either of the Confederates, when the War begun, would have been so unreasonable, as to refuse joyning with us upon such a Foot, and expect that we should every Year go between three and four Millions in Debt (which hath been our Case) because the *French* could hardly have contrived any Offers of a Peace so ruinous to us as such a War. Posterity will be at a loss to conceive what kind of Spirit could possess their Ancestors, who after ten Years Suffering, by the unexampled Politicks of a Nation, maintaining a War by annually Pawning it self; and during a short Peace, while they were looking back with Horror on the heavy Load of Debts they had contracted; universally condemning those pernicious Counsels which had occasioned them; racking their Invention for some Remedies or Expedients to mend their shattered Condition: That these very People, without giving themselves time to breath, should again enter into a more dangerous, chargeable, and extensive War, for the same, or perhaps a greater Period of Time, and without any apparent Necessity. It is obvious in a private Fortune, that whoever annually runs out, and continues the same Expences, must every Year mortgage a greater Quantity of Land than he did before; and as the Debt doubles and trebles upon him, so doth his Inability to pay it. By the same Proportion we have suffered twice as much by this last ten Years War, as we did by the former; and if it were possible to continue it five Years longer at the same rate, it would be as great a Burthen as the whole Twenty. This Computation, so easy and trivial as it is almost a shame to mention, Posterity will think that those who first advised the War, had either not the Sense or the Honesty to consider.

And as we have wasted our Strength and vital Substance in this profuse manner, so we have shamefully misapplied it to Ends at least very different from those for which we undertook the War, and often to effect others which after a Peace we may severely repent. This is the second Article I proposed to examine.

We have now for Ten Years together turned the whole Force and Expence of the War, where the Enemy was best able to hold us at a Bay; where we could propose no manner of Advantage to our selves; where it was highly impolitick to enlarge our Conquests; utterly neglecting that Part which would have saved and gained us many Millions, which the perpetual Maxims of our Government teach us to pursue; which would have soonest weakened the Enemy, and must either have promoted a speedy Peace, or enabled us to continue the War.

Those who are fond of continuing the War cry up our constant Success at a most prodigious rate, and reckon it infinitely greater than in all human Probability we had reason to hope. Ten glorious Campaigns are passed, and now at last, like the sick Man, we are just expiring with all sorts of good Symptoms. Did the Advisers of this War suppose it would continue Ten Years, without expecting the Successes we have had; and yet at the same time determine, that *France* must be reduced, and *Spain* subdued, by employing our whole Strength upon *Flanders*? Did they believe the last War left us in a Condition to furnish such vast Supplies for so long a Period, without involving Us and our Posterity in unextricable Debts? If after such Miraculous *Doings*, we are not yet in a Condition of bringing *France* to our Terms, nor can tell when we shall be so, though we should proceed without any Reverse of Fortune; What could we look for in the ordinary course of Things, but a *Flanders* War of at least Twenty Years longer? Do they indeed think a Town taken for the *Dutch*, is a sufficient Recompence to us for six Millions of Money? which is of so little Consequence to the determining the War, that the *French* may yet hold out a dozen Years more, and afford a Town every Campaign at the same Price.

I say not this, by any means, to detract from the Army or its Leaders. Getting into the Enemy's Lines, passing Rivers, and taking Towns, may be Actions attended with many glorious Circumstances: But when all this brings no real solid Advantage to us, when it hath no other End than to enlarge the Territories of the *Dutch*, and encrease the Fame and Wealth of our *General*, I conclude, however it comes about, that Things are not as they should be; and that surely our Forces and Money might be better employed, both towards reducing our Enemy, and working out some Benefit to our selves. But the Case is still much harder. We are destroying many thousand Lives, exhausting all our Substance, not for our own Interest, which would be but common Prudence; not for a Thing indifferent, which would be sufficient Folly, but perhaps to our own Destruction, which is perfect Madness. We may live to feel the Effects of our Valour more sensibly than all the Consequences we imagine from the Dominions of *Spain* in the Duke of *Anjou*. We have Conquered a noble Territory for the *States*, that will maintain sufficient Troops to Defend it self, feed many hundred thousand Inhabitants, where all Encouragement will be given to introduce and improve Manufactures, which was the only Advantage they wanted; and which, added to their Skill, Industry and Parsimony, will enable them to undersell us in every Market of the World.

*

. . . . . . I have sometimes wondered how it came to pass, that the Style of *Maritime Powers*, by which our Allies, in a sort of contemptuous manner, usually couple us with the *Dutch*, did never put us in mind of the Sea; and while some Politicians were shewing us the way to *Spain* by *Flanders*, others by *Savoy* or *Naples*, that the *West-Indies* should never come into their Heads. With half the Charge we have been at, we might have maintained our original Quota of Forty thousand Men in *Flanders*, and at the same time, by our Fleets and Naval Forces, have so distressed the *Spaniards* in the North and South Seas of *America*, as to prevent any Returns of Mony from thence, except in our own Bottoms. This is what best became us to do as a Maritime Power: This, with any common degree of Success, would soon have compelled *France* to the Necessities of a Peace, and *Spain* to acknowledge the Archduke. But while We, for Ten Years, have been squandring away our Mony upon the Continent, *France* hath been wisely engrossing all the Trade of *Peru*, going directly with their Ships to *Lima*, and other Ports, and there receiving Ingots of Gold and Silver for *French* Goods of little Value; which, beside the mighty Advantage to their Nation at present, may divert the Channel of that Trade for the future, so beneficial to us, who used to receive annually such vast Sums at *Cadiz*, for our Goods sent thence to the *Spanish West-Indies*. All this we tamely saw and suffered, without the least Attempt to hinder it; except what was performed by some private Men at *Bristol*, who inflamed by a true Spirit of Courage and Industry, did, about three Years ago, with a few Vessels, fitted out at their own Charge, make a most successful Voyage into those Parts, took one of the *Aquapulco* Ships, very narrowly mist of the other, and are lately returned laden with unenvied Wealth; to shew us what might have been done with the like Management, by a publick Undertaking. At least we might easily have prevented those great Returns of Mony to *France* and *Spain*, though we could not have taken it our selves. And if it be true, as the Advocates for War would have it, that the *French* are now so impoverished; in what Condition must they have been, if that Issue of Wealth had been stopped?

But great Events often turn upon very small Circumstances. It was the Kingdom's Misfortune, that the Sea was not the Duke of *Marlborough*'s Element, otherwise the whole Force of the War would infallibly have been bestowed there, infinitely to the Advantage of his Country, which would then have gone hand in hand with his own. But it is very truly objected, That if we alone had made such an Attempt as this, *Holland* would have been Jealous; or if we had done it in Conjunction with *Holland*, the House of *Austria* would have been discontented. This hath been the Style of late Years; which whoever introduced among us, they have taught our Allies to speak after them. Otherwise it could hardly enter into any Imagination, that while we are Confederates in a War with those who are to have the whole Profit, and who leave a double share of the Burthen upon Us, we dare not think of any Design, though against the Common Enemy, where there is the least Prospect of doing Good to our own Country, for fear of giving Umbrage and Offence to our Allies; while we are ruining our selves to Conquer Provinces and Kingdoms for Them.

*

It was something singular that the *States* should express their Uneasiness, when they thought we intended to make some Attempt in the *Spanish West-Indies*; because it is agreed between us, that whatever is Conquered there by Us or Them, shall belong to the Conqueror: Which is the only Article that I can call to mind, in all our Treaties or Stipulations, with any view of Interest to this Kingdom; and for that very Reason, I suppose, among others, hath been altogether neglected. Let those who think this too severe a Reflection, examin the whole Management of the present War by Sea and Land with all our Alliances, Treaties, Stipulations and Conventions, and consider, whether the whole does not look as if some particular Care and Industry had been used, to prevent any Benefit or Advantage that might possibly accrue to *Britain*.

This kind of Treatment from our two Principal Allies, hath taught the same Dialect to all the rest; so that there is hardly a petty Prince, whom we half maintain by Subsidies and Pensions, who is not ready, upon every Occasion, to threaten Us, that He will recal His Troops (though they must rob or starve at home) if we refuse to comply with Him in any Demand, however so unreasonable.

Upon the Third Head I shall produce some Instances, to shew how tamely we have suffered each of our Allies to infringe every Article in those Treaties and Stipulations by which they were bound, and to lay the Load upon Us.

*

The Barrier-Treaty between *Great Britain* and *Holland*, was concluded at the *Hague* on the 29th of *October*, in the Year 1709. In this Treaty, neither Her Majesty nor Her Kingdoms have any Interest or Concern, farther than what is mentioned in the Second and the Twentieth Articles: By the former, the States are to assist the Queen in Defending the Act of Succession; and by the other, not to Treat of a Peace till *France* acknowledges the Queen and the Succession of *Hanover*, and promises to remove the *Pretender* out of his Dominions.

As to the first of these, it is certainly for the Safety and Interest of the *States-General*, that the Protestant Succession should be preserved in *England*; because such a Popish Prince as we apprehend, would infallibly join with *France* in the Ruin of that Republick. And the *Dutch* are as much bound to support our Succession, as they are tied to any Part of a Treaty of League Offensive and Defensive, against a Common Enemy, without any separate Benefit upon that Consideration. Her Majesty is in the full peaceable Possession of Her Kingdoms, and of the Hearts of Her People; among whom, hardly one in five hundred are in the Pretender's Interest. And whether the Assistance of the *Dutch*, to preserve a Right so well established, be an Equivalent to those many unreasonable exorbitant Articles in the rest of the Treaty, let the World judge. What an Impression of our Settlement must it give Abroad, to see our Ministers offering such Conditions to the *Dutch*, to prevail on them to be Guarantees of our Acts of Parliament! Neither perhaps is it right, in point of Policy or good Sense, that a Foreign Power should be called in to confirm our Succession by way of Guarantee; but only to acknowledge it. Otherwise we put it out of the Power of our own Legislature to change our Succession, without the Consent of that Prince or State who is Guarantee, how much soever the Necessities of the Kingdom may require it.

*

By the Grand Alliance, which was the Foundation of the present War, the *Spanish Low-Countries* were to be recovered and delivered to the King of *Spain*: But by this Treaty, that Prince is to possess nothing in *Flanders* during the War: and after a Peace, the *States* are to have the Military Command of about twenty Towns with their Dependances, and four hundred thousand Crowns a Year from the King of *Spain* to maintain their Garrisons. By which means they will have the Command of all *Flanders*, from *Newport* on the Sea to *Namur* on the *Maese*, and be entirely Masters of the *Pais de Waas*, the richest part of those Provinces. Further, they have liberty to Garrison any Place they shall think fit in the *Spanish Low-Countries*, whenever there is an Appearance of War; and consequently to put Garrisons into *Ostend*, or where else they please, upon a Rupture with *England*.

By this Treaty likewise, the *Dutch* will, in effect, be entire Masters of all the *Low-Countries*, may impose Duties, Restrictions in Commerce, and Prohibitions at their Pleasure; and in that fertile Country may set up all sorts of Manufactures, particularly the Woollen, by inviting the disobliged Manufacturers in *Ireland*, and the *French* Refugees, who are scattered all over *Germany*. And as this Manufacture encreases abroad, the cloathing People of *England* will be necessitated, for want of Employment, to follow; and in few Years, by help of the low Interest of Mony in *Holland*, *Flanders* may recover that beneficial Trade which we got from them: The Landed Men of *England* will then be forced to re-establish the Staples of Wool abroad; and the *Dutch*, instead of being only the Carriers, will become the original Possessors of those Commodities, with which the greatest Part of the Trade of the World is now carried on. And as they increase their Trade, it is obvious they will enlarge their Strength at Sea, and that ours must lessen in Proportion.

All the Ports in *Flanders* are to be subject to the like Duties the *Dutch* shall lay upon the *Scheld*, which is to be closed on the side of the *States*: Thus all other Nations are, in effect, shut out from Trading with *Flanders*. Yet in the very same Article it is said, that the *States* shall be *favoured in all the Spanish Dominions as much as Great Britain, or as the People most favoured*. We have Conquer'd *Flanders* for them, and are in a worse Condition, as to our Trade there, than before the War began. We have been the great Support of the King of *Spain*, to whom the *Dutch* have hardly contributed any thing at all; and yet *they are to be equally favoured with us in all his Dominions*. Of all this the Queen is under the unreasonable Obligation of being Guarantee, and that they shall possess their Barrier, and their four hundred thousand Crowns a Year, even before a Peace.

It is to be observed, that this Treaty was only Signed by one of our Plenipotentiaries: And I have been told, that the other was heard to say, He would rather lose his Right-hand, than set it to such a Treaty. Had he spoke those Words in due season, and loud enough to be heard on this side the Water, considering the Credit he then had at Court, he might have saved much of his Country's Honour, and got as much to himself: Therefore, if the Report be true, I am inclined to think He only *SAID* it. I have been likewise told, that some very necessary Circumstances were wanting in the Entrance upon this Treaty; but the Ministers here rather chose to sacrifice the Honour of the Crown, and the Safety of their Country, than not ratify what one of their Favourites had transacted.

*

It hath likewise been no small Inconvenience to us, that the *Dutch* are always slow in paying their Subsidies, by which means the weight and pressure of the Payment lies upon the Queen, as well as the Blame, if her Majesty be not very exact; nor will even this always content our Allies. For in *July* 1711, the King of *Spain* was paid all his Subsidies to the first of *January* next; nevertheless he hath since complained for want of Mony; and his Secretary threatned, that if we would not further supply his Majesty, he could not answer for what might happen; although King *Charles* had not at that time, one third of the Troops for which he was paid; and even those he had, were neither Paid nor Cloathed.

I cannot forbear mentioning here another Passage concerning Subsidies, to shew what Opinion Foreigners have of our Easiness, and how much they reckon themselves Masters of our Mony, whenever they think fit to call for it. The Queen was by Agreement to pay Two hundred thousand Crowns a Year to the *Prussian* Troops, the *States* One hundred thousand, and the Emperor only Thirty thousand, for Recruiting, which his Imperial Majesty never paid. Prince *Eugene* happening to pass by *Berlin*, the Ministers of that Court applied themselves to him for Redress in this Particular; and his Highness very frankly promised them, that in Consideration of this Deficiency, *Britain* and the *States* should encrease their Subsidies to Seventy thousand Crowns more between them, and that the Emperor should be punctual for the time to come: This was done by that Prince, without any Orders or Power whatsoever. The *Dutch* very reasonably refused consenting to it; but the *Prussian* Minister here, making his Applications at our Court, prevailed on us to agree to our Proportion, before we could hear what Resolution would be taken in *Holland*. It is therefore to be hoped, that his *Prussian* Majesty, at the end of this War, will not have the same Cause of Complaint, which he had at the Close of the last; that his Military-Chest was emptier by Twenty thousand Crowns, than at the time that War began.

*

When *Portugal* came, as a Confederate into the Grand Alliance, it was stipulated, That the Empire, *England* and *Holland*, should each maintain four Thousand Men of their own Troops in that Kingdom, and pay between them a Million of Pattacoons to the King of *Portugal*, for the Support of twenty eight Thousand *Portugueze*; which number of forty Thousand, was to be the Confederate Army against *Spain* on the Portugal side. This Treaty was ratified by all the Three Powers. But in a short time after, the Emperor declared himself unable to comply with his part of the Agreement, and so left the two Thirds upon Us; who very generously undertook that Burthen, and at the same time two Thirds of the Subsidies for Maintenance of the *Portugueze* Troops. But neither is this the worst Part of the Story: For, although the *Dutch* did indeed send their own particular Quota of four Thousand Men to *Portugal* (which however they would not agree to, but upon Condition, that the other two Thirds should be supplied by us;) yet they never took care to recruit them: For in the year 1706, the *Portugueze*, *British* and *Dutch* Forces, having marched with the Earl of G[*alway*] into *Castile*, and by the noble Conduct of that General being forced to retire into *Valencia*, it was found necessary to raise a new Army on the *Portugal* side; where the Queen hath, at several times, encreased Her Establishment to ten Thousand five Hundred Men, and the *Dutch* never replaced one single Man, nor paid one Peny of their Subsidies to *Portugal* in six Years.

The *Spanish* Army on the side of *Catalonia* is, or ought to be, about fifty Thousand Men (exclusive of *Portugal*): And here the War hath been carried on almost entirely at our Cost. For this whole Army is paid by the Queen, excepting only seven Battalions and fourteen Squadrons of *Dutch* and *Palatines*; and even fifteen Hundred of these are likewise in our Pay; besides the Sums given to King *Charles* for Subsidies and the Maintenance of his Court. Neither are our Troops at *Gibraltar* included within this number. And further, we alone have been at all the Charge of Transporting the Forces first sent from *Genoa* to *Barcelona*; and of all the Imperial Recruits from time to time: And have likewise paid vast Sums as Levy-Mony, for every individual Man and Horse so furnished to Recruit, though the Horses were scarce worth the Price of Transportation. But this hath been almost the constant Misfortune of our Fleet, during the present War; instead of being employed on some Enterprize for the good of the Nation, or even for the Protection of our Trade, to be wholly taken up in Transporting Soldiers.

*

. . . This Treatment, which we have received from our two principal Allies, hath been pretty well copied by most other Princes in the Confederacy, with whom we have any Dealings. For Instance, Seven *Portugueze* Regiments after the Battle of *Almanza*, went off, with the rest of that broken Army, to *Catalonia*; the King of *Portugal* said, he was not able to pay them, while they were out of his Country; the Queen consented therefore to do it Herself, provided the King would raise as many more to supply their Place. This he engaged to do, but never performed. Notwithstanding which, his Subsidies were constantly paid him by my Lord *Godolphin*, for almost four Years, without any Deduction upon Account of those Seven Regiments; directly contrary to the Seventh Article of our Offensive Alliance with that Crown, where it is agreed, that a Deduction shall be made out of those Subsidies, in Proportion to the number of Men wanting in that Complement, which the King is to maintain. But whatever might have been the Reasons for this Proceeding, it seems they are above the Understanding of the present Lord Treasurer; who not entring into those Refinements, of paying the *publick* Mony upon *private* Considerations, hath been so uncourtly as to stop it. This Disappointment, I suppose, hath put the Court of *Lisbon* upon other Expedients of raising the Price of Forage, so as to force us either to lessen our number of Troops, or be at double Expence in maintaining them; and this at a time when their own Product, as well as the Import of Corn, was never greater; And of demanding a Duty upon the Soldiers Cloaths we carry over for those Troops, which have been their sole Defence against an inveterate Enemy; and whose Example might have infused

N

Courage, as well as taught them Discipline, if their Spirits had been capable of receiving either.

*

. . . If all this be true: If, according to what I have affirmed, we began this War contrary to Reason: If, as the other Party themselves, upon all Occasions, acknowledge, the Success we have had was more than we could reasonably expect: If, after all our Success, we have not made that use of it, which in Reason we ought to have done: If we have made weak and foolish Bargains with our Allies, suffered them tamely to break every Article even in those Bargains to our Disadvantage, and allowed them to treat us with Insolence and Contempt, at the very Instant when we were gaining Towns, Provinces, and Kingdoms for them, at the Price of our Ruin, and without any Prospect of Interest to our selves: If we have consumed all our Strength in attacking the Enemy on the strongest side, where (as the old Duke of *Schomberg* expressed it) *to engage with* France, *was to take a Bull by the Horns*; and left wholly unattempted, that part of the War, which could only enable us to continue or to end it. If all this, I say, be our Case, it is a very obvious Question to ask, by what Motives, or what Management, we are thus become the *Dupes* and *Bubbles* of *Europe*? Sure it cannot be owing to the Stupidity arising from the coldness of our Climate, since those among our Allies, who have given us most Reason to complain, are as far removed from the Sun as our selves.

If in laying open the real Causes of our present Misery, I am forced to speak with some Freedom, I think it will require no Apology; Reputation is the smallest Sacrifice Those can make us, who have been the Instruments of our Ruin; because it is That, for which in all Probability they have the least Value. So that in exposing the Actions of such Persons, I cannot be said, properly speaking, to do them an Injury. But as it will be some Satisfaction to the People, to know by whom they have been so long abused; so it may be of great use to us and our Posterity, not to trust the Safety of their Country in the

Hands of those, who act by such Principles, and from such Motives.

I have already observed, that when the Counsels of this War were debated in the late King's time, a certain *Great Man* was then so averse from entring into it, that he rather chose to give up his Employment, and tell the King he could serve him no longer. Upon that Prince's Death, although the Grounds of our Quarrel with *France* had received no manner of Addition, yet this Lord thought fit to alter his Sentiments; for the Scene was quite changed; his Lordship, and the Family with whom he was engaged by so complicated an Alliance, were in the highest Credit possible with the Q[uee]n: The Treasurer's Staff was ready for his Lordship, the Duke was to Command the Army, and the Dutchess by her Employments, and the Favour she was possessed of, to be always nearest her Majesty's Person; by which the whole Power, at home and abroad, would be devolved upon that Family. This was a Prospect so very inviting, that, to confess the Truth, it could not be easily withstood by any who have so keen an Appetite for Wealth or Ambition. By an Agreement subsequent to the Grand Alliance, we were to assist the *Dutch* with Forty thousand Men, all to be Commanded by the D[uke] of M[arlborough]. So that whether this War were prudently begun or not, it is plain, that the true Spring or Motive of it, was the aggrandizing a particular Family, and in short, a War of the *General* and the *Ministry*, and not of the *Prince* or *People*; since those very Persons were against it when they knew the Power, and consequently the Profit, would be in other Hands.

With these Measures fell in all that Sett of People, who are called the *Monied Men*; such as had raised vast Sums by Trading with Stocks and Funds, and Lending upon great Interest and Præmiums; whose perpetual Harvest is War, and whose beneficial way of Traffick must very much decline by a Peace.

In that whole Chain of Encroachments made upon us by the *Dutch*, which I have above deduced, and under those several gross Impositions from other Princes, if any one should ask, why our G[enera]l continued so easy to the last? I know no other way so probable, or indeed so charitable to account for it, as by that unmeasurable Love of Wealth, which his best Friends allow to be his predominant Passion. However, I shall wave any thing that is Personal upon this Subject. I shall say nothing of those great Presents made by several Princes, which the Soldiers used to call Winter-Foraging, and said it was better than that of the Summer; of Two and an half *per Cent.* substracted out of all the Subsidies we pay in those Parts, which amounts to no inconsiderable Sum; and lastly, of the grand Perquisites in a long successful War, which are so amicably adjusted between Him and the *States*.

But when the War was thus begun, there soon fell in other Incidents here at home, which made the Continuance of it necessary for those, who were the chief Advisers. The *Whigs* were at that time out of all Credit or Consideration: The reigning Favourites had always carried what was called the *Tory Principle*, at least as high, as our Constitution could bear; and most others in great Employments, were wholly in the Church-Interest. These last, among whom several were Persons of the greatest Merit, Quality, and Consequence, were not able to endure the many Instances of Pride, Insolence, Avarice and Ambition, which those Favourites began so early to discover, nor to see them presuming to be the sole Dispensers of the Royal Favour. However, their Opposition was to no Purpose; they wrestled with too great a Power, and were soon crushed under it. For, those in Possession finding they could never be quiet in their Usurpations, while others had any Credit, who were at least upon an equal Foot of Merit, began to make Overtures to the discarded *Whigs*, who would be content with any Terms of Accommodation. Thus commenced this *Solemn League and Covenant*, which hath ever since been cultivated with so much Application. The great Traders in Mony were wholly devoted to the *Whigs*, who had first raised them. The Army, the Court, and the Treasury, continued under the old *Despotick* Administration: The *Whigs* were received into Employment, left to manage the Parliament, cry down the Landed Interest, and worry the Church. Mean time, our Allies, who were not ignorant, that all this artificial Structure had no true Foundation in the Hearts of the People, resolved to make their best use of it, as long as it should last. And the General's Credit being raised to a great height at home by our Success in *Flanders*, the *Dutch* began their gradual Impositions; lessening their Quotas, breaking their Stipulations, Garrisoning the Towns we took for them, without supplying their Troops; with many other Infringements: All which we were forced to submit to, because the General was *made easie*; because the Monied Men at home were fond of the War; because the *Whigs* were not yet firmly settled; and because that exorbitant degree of Power, which was built upon a supposed Necessity of employing particular Persons, would go off in a Peace. It is needless to add, that the Emperor, and other Princes, followed the Example of the *Dutch*, and succeeded as well, for the same Reasons.

I have here imputed the Continuance of the War to the mutual Indulgence between our General and Allies, wherein they both so well found their Accounts; to the Fears of the *Mony-changers*, lest their *Tables should be overthrown*; to the Designs of the *Whigs*, who apprehended the Loss of their Credit and Employments in a Peace; and to those at home, who held their immoderate Engrossments of Power and Favour, by no other Tenure, than their own Presumption upon the Necessity of Affairs. The Truth of this will appear indisputable, by considering with what Unanimity and Concert these several Parties acted towards that great End.

When the Vote passed in the House of Lords, against any Peace without *Spain* being restored to the *Austrian* Family, the Earl of W[*harto*]n told the House, That it was indeed impossible and impracticable to recover *Spain*; but however, there were *certain Reasons*, why such a Vote should be made at that time; which Reasons wanted no Explanation: For the General and the Ministry having refused to accept, very Advantagious Offers of a Peace, after the Battle of *Ramellies*, were forced to take in a Set of Men, with a previous Bargain, to skreen them from the Consequences of that Miscarriage. And accordingly upon the first succeeding Opportunity that fell, which was that of the Prince of *Denmark*'s Death, the Chief Leaders of the Party were brought into several great Employments.

So when the Queen was no longer able to bear the Tyranny and Insolence of those ungrateful Servants, who as they *waxed the Fatter*, did but *kick the more*; our two great Allies abroad, and our Stock-jobbers at home, took immediate Alarm; applied the nearest way to the Throne, by Memorials and Messages, jointly directing Her Majesty not to change Her Secretary or Treasurer; who for the true Reasons that these officious Intermedlers demanded their Continuance, ought never to have been admitted into the least Degree of Trust; since what they did was nothing less than betraying the Interest of their Native Country, to those Princes, who in their Turns, were to do what they could to support Them in Power at home.

Thus it plainly appears, that there was a Conspiracy on all sides to go on with those Measures, which must perpetuate the War; and a Comspiracy founded upon the Interest and Ambition of each Party; which begat so firm a Union, that instead of wondring why it lasted so long, I am astonished to think, how it came to be broken. The Prudence, Courage, and Firmness of Her Majesty in all the Steps of that great Change, would, if the Particulars were truly related, make a very shining Part in Her Story: Nor is Her Judgment less to be admired, which directed Her in the Choice of perhaps the only Persons who had Skill, Credit, and Resolution enough to be Her Instruments in overthrowing so many Difficulties.

Some would pretend to lessen the Merit of this, by telling us, that the Rudeness, the Tyranny, the Oppression, the Ingratitude of the late Favourites towards their Mistress, were no longer to be born. They produce Instances to shew, how Her M[ajest]y was pursued through all Her Retreats, particularly at *Windsor*; where, after the Enemy had possessed themselves of every Inch of Ground, they at last attacked and stormed the Castle, forcing the Q[uee]n to fly to an adjoining Cottage, pursuant to the Advice of *Solomon,* who tells us, *It is better to live on the House Tops, than with a scolding Woman in a large House.* They would have it, that such continued ill Usage was enough to enflame the meekest Spirit: They blame the Favourites in point of Policy, and think it nothing extraordinary, that the Queen should be at an end of Her Patience, and resolve to discard them. But I am of another Opinion, and think their Proceedings were right. For nothing is so apt to break even the bravest Spirits, as a continual Chain of Oppressions: One Injury is best defended by a second, and this by a third. By these steps, the old *Masters of the Palace* in *France* became *Masters of the Kingdom*; and by these Steps, a *G[enera]l during Pleasure*, might have grown into a *General for Life*, and a *G[enera]l for Life* into a *King.* So that I still insist upon it as a Wonder, how Her M[ajest]y, thus besieged on all sides, was able to extricate Her self.

*

I had two Reasons for not sooner publishing this Discourse: The first was, Because I would give way to others, who might argue very well upon the same Subject, from general Topicks and Reason, though they might be ignorant of several Facts, which I had the Opportunity to know. The Second was, Because I found it would be necessary, in the course of this Argument, to say something of the State to which this War hath reduced us: At the same time I knew, that such a Discovery ought to be made as late as possible, and at another Juncture would not only be very indiscreet, but might perhaps be dangerous.

It is the Folly of too many, to mistake the Eccho of a *London* Coffee-house for the Voice of the Kingdom. The City Coffee-houses have been for some Years filled with People, whose Fortunes depend upon the *Bank*, *East-India*, or some other Stock: Every new Fund to these, is like a new Mortgage to an Usurer, whose Compassion for a young Heir is exactly the same with that of a Stockjobber to the Landed Gentry. At the Court-End of the Town, the like

Places of Resort are frequented either by Men out of Place, and consequently Enemies to the Present Ministry, or by Officers of the Army: No wonder then, if the general Cry, in all such Meetings, be against any Peace either *with* Spain, or *without*; which, in other Words, is no more than this, That discontented Men desire another Change of Ministry; that Soldiers would be glad to keep their Commissions; and, that the Creditors have Mony still, and would have the Debtors borrow on at the old extorting Rates, while they have any Security to give.

Now, to give the most ignorant Reader some Idea of our present Circumstances, without troubling him or my self with Computations in form: Every body knows, that our Land and Malt Tax amount annually to about Two Millions and an half. All other Branches of the Revenue are mortgaged to pay Interest, for what we have already borrowed. The yearly Charge of the War is usually about Six Millions; to make up which Sum, we are forced to take up, on the Credit of new Funds, about Three Millions and an half. This last Year the computed Charge of the War came to above a Million more, than all the Funds the Parliament could contrive would pay interest for; and so we have been forced to divide a Deficiency of Twelve hundred thousand Pounds among the several Branches of our Expence. This is a Demonstration, that if the War lasts another Campaign, it will be impossible to find Funds for supplying it, without mortgaging the Malt Tax, or by some other Method equally desperate.

If the Peace be made this Winter, we are then to consider, what Circumstances we shall be in towards paying a Debt of about Fifty Millions, which is a fourth Part of the Purchase of the whole Island, if it were to be Sold.

Towards clearing our selves of this monstrous Incumbrance, some of these Annuities will expire or pay off the Principal in Thirty, Forty, or an Hundred Years; the Bulk of the Debt must be lessened gradually by the best Management we can, out of what will remain of the Land and Malt Taxes, after paying Guards and Garrisons, and maintaining and supplying our Fleet in the time of Peace. I have not Skill enough to compute what will be left, after these necessary Charges, towards annually clearing so vast a Debt; but believe it must be very little: However, it is plain that both these Taxes must be continued, as well for supporting the Government, as because we have no other Means for paying off the Principal. And so likewise must all the other Funds remain for paying the Interest. How long a time this must require, how steddy an Administration, and how undisturbed a state of Affairs, both at Home and Abroad, let others determine.

However, some People think all this very reasonable; and that since the Struggle hath been for Peace and Safety, Posterity, who is to partake the Benefit, ought to share in the Expence: As if at the breaking out of this War there had been such a Conjuncture of Affairs, as never happened before, nor would ever happen again. 'Tis wonderful, that our Ancestors, in all their Wars, should never fall under such a Necessity; that we meet no Examples of it, in *Greece* and *Rome*; that no other Nation in *Europe* ever knew any thing like it, except *Spain*, about an Hundred and twenty Years ago; which they drew upon themselves, by their own Folly, and have suffered for it ever since: No doubt, we shall teach Posterity Wisdom, but they will be apt to think the Purchase too dear; and I wish they may stand to the Bargain we have made in their Names.

'Tis easy to entail Debts on succeeding Ages, and to hope they will be able and willing to pay them; but how to insure Peace for any Term of Years, is difficult enough to apprehend. Will Human Nature ever cease to have the same Passions? Princes to entertain Designs of Interest or Ambition, and Occasions of Quarrel to arise? May not we Our selves, by the variety of Events and Incidents which happen in the World, be under a necessity of recovering Towns out of the very Hands of those, for whom we are now ruining Our Country to Take them? Neither can it be said, that those *States*, with whom we may probably differ, will be in as bad a Condition as Ourselves; for, by the Circumstances of our Situation, and the Impositions of our Allies, we are more exhausted, than either they or the Enemy; and by the Nature of our Government, the Corruption of our Manners, and the Opposition of Factions, we shall be more slow in recovering.

It will, no doubt, be a mighty Comfort to our Grandchildren, when they see a few Rags hang up in *Westminster-Hall*, which cost an hundred Millions, whereof they are paying the Arrears, and boasting, as Beggars do, that their Grandfathers were Rich and Great.

I have often reflected on that mistaken Notion of Credit, so boasted of by the Advocates of the late Ministry: Was not all that Credit built upon Funds, raised by the Landed Men, whom they so much hate and despise? Are not the greatest part of those Funds raised from the Growth and Product of Land? Must not the whole Debt be entirely paid, and our Fleets and Garrisons be maintained, by the Land and Malt-Tax, after a Peace? If they call it Credit to run ten Millions in Debt, without Parliamentary Security, by which the Publick is defrauded of almost half, I must think such Credit to be dangerous, illegal, and perhaps treasonable. Neither hath any thing gone further to ruin the Nation, than their boasted Credit. For my own part, when I saw this false Credit sink, upon the Change of the Ministry, I was singular enough to conceive it a good Omen. It seemed, as if the young extravagant Heir had got a new Steward, and was resolved to look into his Estate before things grew desperate, which made the Usurers forbear feeding him with Money, as they used to do.

Since the Monied Men are so fond of War, I should be glad, they would furnish out one Campaign at their own Charge: It is not above six or seven Millions; and I dare engage to make it out, that when they have done this, instead of contributing equal to the Landed Men, they will have their full Principal and Interest, at *6 per Cent.* remaining of all the Money they ever lent to the Government.

Without this Resource, or some other equally miraculous, it is impossible for us to continue the War upon the same Foot. I have already observed, that the last Funds of Interest fell short above a Million, though the Persons most conversant in Ways and Means employed their utmost Invention; so that of necessity we must be still more defective next Campaign. But, perhaps our Allies will make up this Deficiency on our side, by greater Efforts on their own. Quite the contrary; both the Emperor and *Holland* failed this Year in several Articles; and signified to us, some time ago, that they cannot keep up to the same Proportions in the next. We have gained a noble Barrier for the latter, and they have nothing more to demand or desire: The Emperor, however sanguin he may now affect to appear, will, I suppose, be satisfied with *Naples, Sicily, Milan,* and his other Acquisitions, rather than engage in a long hopeless War, for the Recovery of *Spain*, to which his Allies the *Dutch* will neither give their Assistance, nor Consent. So that since we have done their Business; since they have no further Service for our arms, and we have no more Money to give them: And lastly, since we neither desire any Recompence, nor expect any Thanks, we ought, in pity, to be dismissed, and have leave to shift for our selves. They are ripe for a Peace, to enjoy and cultivate what we have conquered for them; and so are we, to recover, if possible, the Effects of their Hardships upon Us. The first Overtures from *France*, are made to *England*, upon safe and honourable Terms: We who bore the Burthen of the War, ought, in reason, to have the greatest share in making the Peace. If we do not hearken to a Peace, others certainly will; and get the Advantage of us there, as they have done in the War. We know the *Dutch* have perpetually threatned us, that they would enter into separate Measures of a Peace; and by the Strength of that Argument, as well as by *other Powerful Motives*, prevailed on those, who were then at the Helm, to comply with them on any Terms, rather than put an end to a War, which every Year brought them such great Accessions to their Wealth and Power. Whoever falls off, a Peace will follow; and then we must be content with such Conditions, as our Allies, out of their great Concern for our Safety and Interest, will please to choose. They have no further occasion for

Fighting; they have gained their Point, and they now tell us, it is *our War*; so that in common Justice, it ought to be *our Peace*.

All we can propose, by the desperate Steps of pawning our Land or Malt-Tax, or erecting a General Excise, is only to raise a Fund of Interest, for running us annually four Millions further in Debt, without any Prospect of ending the War so well, as we can do at present: And when we have sunk the only un-engaged Revenues we had left, our Incumbrances must of necessity remain perpetual.

We have hitherto lived upon *Expedients*, which in time will certainly destroy any Constitution, whether Civil or Natural; and there was no Country in *Christendom* had less Occasion for them, than ours. We have dieted a Healthy Body into a Consumption, by plying it with Physick, instead of Food; Art will help us no longer; and if we cannot recover by letting the Remains of Nature work, we must inevitably die.

What Arts have been used to possess the People with a strong Delusion, that *Britain* must infallibly be ruined, without the Recovery of *Spain* to the House of *Austria*? Making the Safety of a great and powerful Kingdom, as ours was then, to depend upon an Event, which, even after a War of miraculous Successes, proves impracticable. As if Princes and Great Ministers could find no way of settling the Publick Tranquility, without changing the Possessions of Kingdoms, and forcing Sovereigns upon a People against their Inclinations. Is there no Security for the Island of *Britain*, unless a King of *Spain* be Dethroned by the Hands of his Grandfather? Has the Enemy no Cautionary Towns and Sea-Ports, to give us for securing Trade? Can he not deliver us Possession of such Places, as would put him in a worse Condition, whenever he should perfidiously renew the War? The present King of *France* has but few Years to live, by the Course of Nature, and, doubtless, would desire to end his Days in Peace: Grandfathers in private Families are not observed to have great Influence on their Grandsons, and I believe they have much less among Princes. However, when the Authority of a Parent is gone, is it likely that *Philip* will be directed by a Brother, against his own Interest, and that of his Subjects? Have not those two Realms their separate Maxims of Policy, which must operate in Times of Peace? These at least are Probabilities, and cheaper by six Millions a Year than recovering *Spain*, or continuing a War, both which seem absolutely impossible.

But the common Question is, If we must now Surrender *Spain*, what have we been Fighting for all this while? The Answer is ready; We have been Fighting for the Ruin of the Publick Interest, and the Advancement of a Private. We have been fighting to raise the Wealth and Grandeur of a Particular Family; to enrich Usurers and Stock-jobbers; and to cultivate the pernicious Designs of a Faction, by destroying the Landed Interest. The Nation begins now to think these *Blessings* are not worth Fighting for any longer, and therefore desires a Peace.

But the Advocates on the other side cry out, that we might have had a better Peace, than is now in Agitation, above two Years ago. Supposing this to be true, I do assert, that by parity of Reason we must expect one just so much worse, about two Years hence. If those in Power could then have given us a better Peace, more is their Infamy and Guilt, that they did it not; why did they insist upon Conditions, which they were certain would never be granted? We allow it was in their Power to have put a good End to the War, and left the Nation in some hope of recovering it self. And this is what we charge them with as answerable to God, their Country, and Posterity, that the bleeding Condition of their Fellow-Subjects, was a Feather in the Balance with their private Ends.

When we offer to lament the heavy Debts and Poverty of the Nation, 'tis pleasant to hear some Men answer all that can be said, by crying up the Power of *England*, the Courage of *England*, the inexhaustible Riches of *England*. I have heard a Man very sanguine upon this Subject, with a good Employment for Life, and a Hundred thousand Pounds in the Funds, bidding us *Take Courage*, and *Warranting, that all would go well*. This is the Style of Men at Ease, *who lay heavy Burthens upon others, which they will not touch with one of their Fingers.* I have known some People such ill Computers, as to imagine the many Millions in Stocks and Annuities, are so much real Wealth in the Nation; whereas every Farthing of it is entirely lost to us, scattered in *Holland, Germany,* and *Spain*; and the Landed-Men, who now pay the Interest, must at last pay the Principal.

. . . Those who are against any Peace without *Spain,* have, I doubt, been ill informed, as to the low Condition of *France,* and the mighty Consequences of our Successes. As to the first, it must be confessed, that after the Battle of *Ramellies* the *French* were so discouraged with their frequent Losses, and so impatient for a Peace, that their King was resolved to comply on any reasonable Terms. But when his Subjects were informed of our exorbitant Demands, they grew jealous of his Honour, and were unanimous to assist him in continuing the War at any hazard, rather than submit. This fully restored his Authority; and the Supplies he hath received from the *Spanish West-Indies,* which in all are computed, since the War, to amount to Four hundred Millions of Livres, (and all in *Specie*) have enabled him to pay his Troops. Besides, the Money is spent in his own Country; and he hath since waged War in the most thrifty manner, by acting on the Defensive, compounding with us every Campaign for a Town, which costs us fifty times more than it is worth, either as to the Value, or the Consequences. Then he is at no Charge of a Fleet, further than providing Privateers, wherewith his Subjects carry on a Piratical War at their own Expence, and he shares in the Profit; which hath been very considerable to *France,* and of infinite Disadvantage to us, not only by the perpetual Losses we have suffered to an immense Value, but by the general Discouragement of Trade, on which we so much depend. All this considered, with the Circumstances of that Government, where the Prince is Master of the Lives and Fortunes of so mighty a Kingdom, shews that Monarch to be not so sunk in his Affairs, as we have imagined, and have long flattered Ourselves with the Hopes of. For an absolute Government may endure a long War, but it hath generally been ruinous to Free Countries.

Those who are against *any Peace without Spain*, seem likewise to have been mistaken in judging our Victories, and other Successes, to have been of greater Consequence, than they really were.

When our Armies take a Town in *Flanders*, the *Dutch* are immediately put into *Possession*, and we at home make *Bonfires*. I have sometimes pitied the deluded People, to see them squandring away their Fewel to so little purpose. For Example, What is it to Us that *Bouchain* is taken, about which the Warlike Politicians of the Coffee-House make such a Clutter? What though the Garrison surrendered Prisoners of War, and in sight of the Enemy? We are not now in a Condition to be fed with Points of Honour. What Advantage have We, but that of spending three or four Millions more to get another Town for the States, which may open them a new Country for *Contributions*, and increase the Perquisites of the G[enera]l?

In that War of ten Years, under the late King, when our Commanders and Soldiers were raw and unexperienced, in comparison of what they are at present, we lost Battles and Towns, as well as we gained them of late, since those Gentlemen have better learned their Trade; yet we bore up then, as the *French* do now: Nor was there any thing decisive in their Successes: They grew weary, as well as we, and at last consented to a Peace, under which we might have been happy enough, if it had not been followed by that wise *Treaty* of *Partition*, which revived the Flame, that hath lasted ever since. I see nothing else in the modern way of making War, but that the Side, which can hold out longest, will end it with most Advantage. In such a close Country as *Flanders*, where it is carried on by Sieges, the Army, that acts offensively, is at a much greater Expence of Men and Mony; and there is hardly a Town taken in the common Forms, where the Besiegers have not the worse of the Bargain. I never yet knew a Soldier, who would not affirm, that any Town might be Taken, if you were content to be at the Charge. If you will count upon sacrificing so

much Blood and Treasure, the rest is all a regular, established Method, which cannot fail. When the King of
France, in the Times of his Grandeur, sat down before a
Town, his Generals and Engineers would often fix the Day,
when it should Surrender. The Enemy, sensible of all this,
hath for some Years past avoided a Battle, where he hath
so ill succeeded, and taken a surer way to consume us, by
letting our Courage evaporate against Stones and Rubbish,
and sacrificing a single Town to a Campaign, which he can
so much better afford to Lose, than we to Take.

*

There is no doubt, but the present Ministry (provided
they could get over the Obligations of Honour and Conscience) might find their Advantage in advising the Continuance of the War, as well as the last did, though not in
the same Degree, after the Kingdom has been so much
exhausted. They might prolong it, till the Parliament desire
a Peace; and in the mean time leave Them in full Possession
of Power. Therefore it is plain, that their Proceedings at
present, are meant to serve their Country, directly against
their private Interest; whatever Clamor may be raised by
those, who for the vilest Ends, would remove Heaven
and Earth to oppose their Measures. But they think it
infinitely better, to accept such Terms as will secure our
Trade, find a sufficient Barrier for the *States*, give *Reasonable Satisfaction* to the Emperor, and restore the Tranquility of *Europe*, though without adding *Spain* to the
Empire: Rather than go on in a languishing way, upon the
vain Expectation of some improbable Turn, for the Recovery of that Monarchy out of the *Bourbon* Family; and
at last be forced to a worse Peace, by some of the Allies
falling off, upon our utter Inability to continue the War.

AN
ARGUMENT
&c.

THIS " very happy and judicious irony ", as Dr Johnson called it, was probably written in 1708. " I am every day writing by speculations in my chamber ", Swift wrote on September 17, 1708, to Ambrose Philips, in reference, presumably, to this tract and two others :—*A Project for the Advancement of Religion and the Reformation of Manners* [printed 1709] and *The Sentiments of a Church of England Man with Respect to Religion and Government* [first printed in *Miscellanies*, 1711]. Although Swift's sympathies were with the Whigs when he wrote it, it is clear that his opinions were bound sooner or later to force him into opposition. As far as the Church was concerned, Swift was always a Tory.

AN ARGUMENT

To prove that the Abolishing of
CHRISTIANITY IN ENGLAND,
may as Things now stand, be attended with some Inconveniences, and
perhaps not produce those many
good Effects proposed thereby.

Written in the Year, 1708.

I AM very sensible what a Weakness and Presumption it
is, to reason against the general Humor and Disposition
of the World. I remember it was with great Justice, and
a due regard to the Freedom both of the Publick and the
Press, forbidden upon several Penalties to Write, or Discourse, or lay Wagers against the *Union* even before it was
confirmed by Parliament, because that was look'd upon
as a Design, to oppose the Current of the People, which
besides the Folly of it, is a manifest Breach of the Fundamental Law that makes this Majority of Opinion the Voice
of God. In like manner, and for the very same Reasons,
it may perhaps be neither safe nor prudent to argue against
the abolishing of Christianity, at a Juncture when all
Parties seem so unanimously determined upon the Point,
as we cannot but allow from their Actions, their Discourses,
and their Writings. However, I know not how, whether
from the Affectation of Singularity, or the Perverseness of
Human Nature, but so it unhappily falls out, that I cannot
be entirely of this Opinion. Nay though I were sure,
an Order were issued out for my immediate Prosecution
by the Attorney-General, I should still confess that in the

present Posture of our Affairs at home or abroad, I do not yet see the absolute Necessity of extirpating the Christian Religion from among us.

This perhaps may appear too great a Paradox even for our wise and paradoxical Age to endure; therefore I shall handle it with all Tenderness, and with the utmost Deference to that great and profound Majority which is of another Sentiment.

And yet the Curious may please to observe, how much the Genius of a Nation is liable to alter in half an Age. I have heard it affirmed for certain by some very old People, that the contrary Opinion was even in their Memories as much in Vogue as the other is now; And, that a Project for the abolishing of Christianity would then have appeared as singular, and been thought as absurd, as it would be at this time to write or discourse in it's Defence.

Therefore I freely own, that all Appearances are against me. The System of the Gospel after the Fate of other Systems is generally antiquated and exploded; and the Mass or Body of the common People, among whom it seems to have had it's latest Credit, are now grown as much ashamed of it as their Betters. Opinions like Fashions always descending from those of Quality to the middle sort, and thence to the Vulgar, where at length they are dropt and vanish.

But here I would not be mistaken, and must therefore be so bold as to borrow a Distinction from the Writers on the other side, when they make a Difference betwixt Nominal and Real *Trinitarians*. I hope no Reader imagines me so weak to stand up in the Defence of Real Christianity, such as used in Primitive Times (if we may believe the Authors of those Ages) to have an Influence upon Mens Belief and Actions: To offer at the restoring of That would indeed be a wild Project; It would be to dig up Foundations, to destroy at one Blow all the Wit, and half the Learning of the Kingdom; to break the entire Frame and Constitution of Things, to ruin Trade, extinguish Arts and Sciences with the Professors of them; In short, to turn our

Courts, Exchanges, and shops into Deserts; and would be full as absurd as the Proposal of *Horace*, where he advises the *Romans* all in a Body to leave their City, and seek a new Seat in some remote Part of the World, by way of a Cure for the Corruption of their Manners.

Therefore I think this Caution was in it self altogether unnecessary (which I have inserted only to prevent all Possibility of Caviling) since every candid Reader will easily understand my Discourse to be intended only in Defence of Nominal Christianity, the other having been for some time wholly laid aside by general Consent, as utterly inconsistent with all our present Schemes of Wealth and Power.

But why we should therefore cast off the Name and Title of Christians, although the general Opinion and Resolution be so violent for it, I confess I cannot (with submission) apprehend the Consequence necessary. However, since the Undertakers propose such wonderful Advantages to the Nation by this Project, and advance many plausible Objections against the System of Christianity, I shall briefly consider the Strength of both, fairly allow them their greatest Weight, and offer such Answers as I think most reasonable. After which I will beg leave to shew what Inconveniences may possibly happen by such an Innovation, in the present Posture of our Affairs.

First, One great Advantage proposed by the abolishing of Christianity is, That it would very much enlarge and establish Liberty of Conscience, that great Bulwark of our Nation, and of the Protestant Religion, which is still too much limited by Priest-craft, notwithstanding all the good Intentions of the Legislature, as we have lately found by a severe Instance. For it is confidently reported, that two Young Gentlemen of real Hopes, bright Wit, and profound Judgment, who upon a thorough Examination of Causes and Effects, and by the meer Force of natural Abilities, without the least Tincture of Learning, having made a Discovery, that there was no God, and generously communicating their Thoughts for the good of the Publick; were some time ago by an unparalelled Severity, and upon I know not what obsolete Law, broke for Blasphemy. And as it hath been wisely observed, if Persecution once begins no Man alive knows how far it may reach, or where it will end.

In answer to all which, with deference to wiser Judgments, I think this rather shews the Necessity of a Nominal Religion among us. Great Wits love to be free with the highest Objects, and if they cannot be allowed a God to revile or renounce; they will speak Evil of Dignities, abuse the Government, and reflect upon the Ministry, which I am sure few will deny to be of much more pernicious Consequence, according to the saying of *Tiberius, Deorum Offensa Diis curæ*. As to the particular Fact related, I think it is not fair to argue from one Instance, perhaps another cannot be produced, yet (to the Comfort of all those who may be apprehensive of Persecution) Blasphemy we know is freely spoke a Million of times in every Coffee-House and Tavern, or wherever else good Company meet. It must be allowed indeed that to Break an *English* Free-born Officer only for Blasphemy, was, to speak the gentlest of such an Action, a very high strain of absolute Power. Little can be said in Excuse for the General; Perhaps he was afraid it might give Offence to the Allies, among whom, for ought we know, it may be the Custom of the Country to believe a God. But if he argued, as some have done, upon a mistaken Principle, that an Officer who is guilty of speaking Blasphemy, may sometime or other proceed so far as to raise a Mutiny, the Consequence is by no means to be admitted; For, surely, the Commander of an *English* Army is like to be but ill obey'd, whose Soldiers fear and reverence him as little as they do a Deity.

It is further objected against the Gospel System, that it obliges Men to the Belief of Things too difficult for free Thinkers, and such who have shook off the Prejudices that usually cling to a confin'd Education. To which I answer, that Men should be cautious how they raise Objections which reflect upon the Wisdom of the Nation. Is not every body freely allowed to believe whatever he pleases, and to publish his Belief to the World whenever he thinks fit, especially if it serves to strengthen the Party which is in the

Right. Would any indifferent Foreiner, who should read the Trumpery lately written by *Asgill, Tindall, Toland, Coward,* and Forty more, imagine the Gospel to be our Rule of Faith, and to be confirmed by Parliaments. Does any Man either Believe, or say he believes, or desire to have it thought that he says he Believes one Syllable of the Matter, and is any Man worse received upon that Score, or does he find his want of Nominal Faith a disadvantage to him in the Pursuit of any Civil or Military Employment? What if there be an old dormant Statute or two against him, are they not now obsolete, to a degree, that *Empson* and *Dudley* themselves if they were now alive, would find it impossible to put them in Execution?

It is likewise urged, that there are by Computation in this Kingdom above Ten Thousand Parsons, whose Revenues added to those of my Lords the Bishops, would suffice to maintain at least Two Hundred Young Gentlemen of Wit and Pleasure, and Free-thinking, Enemies to Priest-Craft, narrow Principles, Pedantry, and Prejudices, who might be an Ornament to the Court and Town: And then, again, so great a Number of able (bodied) Divines might be a Recruit to our Fleet and Armies. This indeed appears to be a Consideration of some Weight: But then on the other side, several Things deserve to be considered likewise: As, First, Whether it may not be thought necessary that in certain Tracts of Country, like what we call Parishes, there should be one Man at least, of Abilities to Read and Write. Then it seems a wrong Computation, that the Revenues of the Church throughout this Island would be large enough to maintain Two Hundred Young Gentlemen, or even half that Number, after the present refined way of Living, that is, to allow each of them such a Rent, as in the modern Form of Speech, would make them Easy. But still there is in this Project a greater Mischief behind; And we ought to beware of the Woman's Folly, who killed the Hen that every Morning laid her a Golden Egg. For, pray what would become of the Race of Men in the next Age, if we had nothing to trust to besides the Scrophulous consumptive Productions furnished by our

Men of Wit and Pleasure, when having squandred away their Vigor, Health and Estates, they are forced by some disagreeable Marriage to piece up their broken Fortunes, and entail Rottenness and Politeness on their Posterity. Now, here are Ten Thousand Persons reduced by the wise Regulations of *Henry* the Eighth, to the necessity of a low Dyet, and moderate Exercise, who are the only great Restorers of our Breed, without which the Nation would in an Age or two become but one great Hospital.

Another Advantage proposed by the Abolishing of Christianity, is the clear Gain of one Day in Seven, which is now entirely lost, and consequently the Kingdom one Seventh less considerable in Trade, Business, and Pleasure; beside the Loss to the Publick of so many Stately Structures now in the Hands of the Clergy, which might be converted into Play-houses, Exchanges, Market-houses, common Dormitories, and other Publick Edifices.

I hope I shall be forgiven a hard Word if I call this a perfect Cavil. I readily own there hath been an old Custom time out of mind, for People to assemble in the Churches every *Sunday*, and that shops are still frequently shut, in order as it is conceived, to preserve the Memory of that antient Practice; but how this can prove a hindrance to Business or Pleasure, is hard to imagine. What if the Men of Pleasure are forced one Day in the Week to Game at Home instead of the *Chocolate-House*. Are not the *Taverns* and *Coffee-Houses* open? Can there be a more convenient Season for taking a Dose of Physick? Are fewer Claps got upon *Sundays* than other Days? Is not that the chief Day for Traders to Sum up the Accounts of the Week, and for Lawyers to prepare their Briefs? But I would fain know how it can be pretended that the Churches are misapplied. Where are more Appointments and Rendevouzes of Gallantry? Where more Care to appear in the foremost Box with greater Advantage of Dress? Where more Meetings for Business? Where more Bargains driven of all sorts? And where so many Conveniences or Incitements to Sleep?

There is one Advantage greater than any of the foregoing, proposed by the Abolishing of Christianity, that it will utterly extinguish Parties among us, by removing those Factious Distinctions of High and Low Church, of *Whig* and *Tory*, *Presbyterian* and *Church of England*, which are now so many mutual Clogs upon Publick Proceedings, and are apt to prefer the gratifying themselves or depressing their Adversaries, before the most important Interest of the State.

I confess, if it were certain that so great an Advantage would redound to the Nation by this Expedient, I would submit and be silent: But, will any Man say that if the Words, *Whoring*, *Drinking*, *Cheating*, *Lying*, *Stealing*, were by Act of Parliament ejected out of the *English* Tongue and Dictionaries, We should all Awake next Morning Chast and Temperate, Honest and Just, and Lovers of Truth. Is this a fair Consequence? Or if the Physicians would forbid us to pronounce the Words *Pox*, *Gout*, *Rhumatism* and *Stone*, would that Expedient serve like so many *Talismans* to destroy the Diseases themselves? Are Party and Faction rooted in Mens Hearts no deeper than Phrases borrowed from Religion, or founded upon no firmer Principles? And is our Language so poor that we cannot find other Terms to express them? Are Envy, Pride, Avarice and Ambition such ill Nomenclators, that they cannot furnish Appellations for their Owners? Will not *Heydukes* and *Mamalukes*, *Mandarins* and *Patshaws*, or any other Words formed at Pleasure, serve to distinguish those who are in the Ministry from others who would be in it if they could? What, for instance, is easier than to vary the Form of Speech, and instead of the Word, Church, make it a Question in Politicks, Whether the Monument be in Danger? Because Religion was nearest at hand to furnish a few convenient Phrases, is our Invention so barren, we can find no other? Suppose for Argument sake, that the *Tories* favoured *Margarita*, the *Whigs*, Mrs *Tofts*, and the *Trimmers Valentini*, would not *Margaritians*, *Toftians* and *Valentinians* be very tolerable Marks of Distinction? The *Prasini* and *Veneti*, two most virulent Factions in *Italy*, began (if I remember right) by a Distinction

of Colors in Ribbans, which we might do with as Good a
Grace about the Dignity of the *Blew* and the *Green*, and
would serve as properly to divide the Court, the Parlia-
ment, and the Kingdom between them, as any Terms of
Art whatsoever, borrowed from Religion. And therefore
I think there is little Force in this Objection against
Christianity, or Prospect of so great an Advantage as is
proposed in the abolishing of it.

'Tis again objected as a very absurd ridiculous Custom,
that a Set of Men should be suffered, much less employed
and hired, to bawl one Day in Seven against the Lawfulness of those Methods most in use towards the Pursuit
of Greatness, Riches and Pleasure, which are the constant
Practice of all Men alive on the other Six. But this Objection is I think, a little unworthy so refined an Age as ours.
Let us argue this Matter calmly; I appeal to the Breast
of any polite Free Thinker, whether in the Pursuit of
gratifying a predominant Passion, he hath not always felt
a wonderful Incitement, by reflecting it was a Thing forbidden; And therefore we see, in order to cultivate this
Taste, the Wisdom of the Nation hath taken special Care,
that the Ladies should be furnished with Prohibited Silks,
and the Men with Prohibited Wine; And indeed it were
to be wisht, that some other Prohibitions were promoted,
in order to improve the Pleasures of the Town, which for
want of such Expedients begin already, as I am told, to
flag and grow languid, giving way daily to cruel Inroads
from the Spleen.

'Tis likewise proposed as a great Advantage to the
Publick, that if we once discard the System of the Gospel,
all Religion will of course be banished for ever, and consequently along with it, those grievous Prejudices of Education, which under the Names of Virtue, Conscience,
Honor, Justice, and the like, are so apt to disturb the Peace
of human Minds, and the Notions whereof are so hard to
be eradicated by Right Reason or Free Thinking, sometimes during the whole Course of our Lives.

Here first I observe how difficult it is to get rid of a
Phrase which the World is once grown fond of, though

the occasion that first produced it, be entirely taken away. For some Years past, if a Man had but an ill-favoured Nose, the deep Thinkers of the Age would some way or other contrive to impute the Cause to the Prejudice of his Education. From this Fountain are said to be derived all our foolish Notions of Justice, Piety, Love of our Country, all our Opinions of God or a Future State, Heaven, Hell and the like: And there might formerly perhaps have been some Pretence for this Charge. But so effectual Care hath been since taken to remove those Prejudices, by an entire Change in the Methods of Education, that (with Honour I mention it to our Polite Innovators) the Young Gentlemen who are now on the Scene seem to have not the least Tincture left of those Infusions, or String of those Weeds, and by consequence the Reason for abolishing Nominal Christianity upon that Pretext, is wholly ceast.

For the rest, it may perhaps admit a Controversy, whether the banishing all Notions of Religion whatsoever, would be convenient for the Vulgar. Not that I am in the least of Opinion with those who hold Religion to have been the Invention of Politicians, to keep the lower Part of the World in Awe by the fear of Invisible Powers; unless Mankind were then very different from what it is now: For I look upon the Mass or Body of our People here in *England*, to be as Free Thinkers, that is to say, as Stanch Unbelievers, as any of the highest Rank. But I conceive some scattered Notions about a Superior Power to be of singular Use for the Common People, as furnishing excellent Materials to keep Children quiet when they grow peevish, and providing Topicks of Amusement in a tedious Winter Night.

Lastly, 'tis proposed as a singular Advantage, that the abolishing of Christianity will very much contribute to the uniting of *Protestants*, by enlarging the Terms of Communion so as to take in all sorts of *Dissenters*, who are now shut out of the Pale upon Account of a few Ceremonies which all Sides confess to be Things indifferent: That this alone will effectually answer the great Ends of a Scheme for Comprehension, by opening a large noble

Gate, at which all Bodies may enter; whereas the chaffering with *Dissenters*, and dodging about this or t'other Ceremony, is but like opening a few Wickets, and leaving them at jar, by which no more than one can get in at a time, and that, not without stooping, and sideling, and squeezing his Body.

To all this I answer; that there is one darling Inclination of Mankind, which usually affects to be a Retainer to Religion, though she be neither it's Parent, it's Godmother, nor it's Friend; I mean the Spirit of Opposition, that lived long before Christianity, and can easily subsist without it. Let us for instance, examine wherein the Opposition of Sectaries among us consists, we shall find Christianity to have no share in it at all. Does the Gospel any where prescribe a starcht squeezed Countenance, a Stiff formal Gate, a singularity of Manners and Habit, or any affected Forms and Modes of Speech different from the reasonable Part of Mankind? Yet, if Christianity did not lend it's Name, to stand in the Gap, and to employ or divert these Humors, they must of necessity be spent in Contraventions to the Laws of the Land, and Disturbance of the Publick Peace. There is a Portion of Enthusiasm assigned to every Nation, which if it hath not proper Objects to work on, will burst out, and set all into a Flame. If the Quiet of a State can be bought by only flinging Men a few Ceremonies to devour, it is a Purchase no Wise Man would refuse. Let the Mastiffs amuse themselves about a Sheepskin stufft with Hay, provided it will keep them from Worrying the Flock. The Institution of Convents abroad, seems in one Point a strain of great Wisdom, there being few Irregularities in human Passions, which may not have recourse to vent themselves in some of those Orders, which are so many Retreats for the Speculative, the Melancholy, the Proud, the Silent, the Politick and the Morose, to spend themselves, and evaporate the Noxious Particles; for each of whom we in this Island are forced to provide a several Sect of Religion, to keep them Quiet; and whenever Christianity shall be abolished, the Legislature must find some other Expedient to employ and entertain them.

For what imports it how large a Gate you open, if there will be always left a Number who place a Pride and a Merit in not coming in.

Having thus consider'd the most important Objections against Christianity, and the chief Advantages proposed by the Abolishing thereof; I shall now with equal Deference and Submission to wiser Judgments as before, proceed to mention a few Inconveniences that may happen, if the Gospel should be repealed; which perhaps the Projectors may not have sufficiently considered.

And first, I am very sensible how much the Gentlemen of Wit and Pleasure are apt to murmur, and be choqued at the sight of so many daggled-tail Parsons, that happen to fall in their way, and offend their Eyes; but at the same Time these wise Reformers do not consider what an Advantage and Felicity it is, for great Wits to be always provided with Objects of Scorn and Contempt, in order to exercise and improve their Talents, and divert their Spleen from falling on each other or on themselves, especially when all this may be done without the least imaginable Danger to their Persons.

And to urge another Argument of a parallel Nature. If Christianity were once abolished, how would the Free Thinkers, the Strong Reasoners, and the Men of profound Learning, be able to find another Subject so calculated in all Points whereon to display their Abilities. What wonderful Productions of Wit should we be deprived of, from those whose Genius by continual Practice hath been wholly turn'd upon Railery and Invectives against Religion, and would therefore never be able to shine or distinguish themselves upon any other Subject. We are daily complaining of the great decline of Wit among us, and would we take away the greatest, perhaps the only Topick we have left? Who would ever have suspected *Asgil[l]* for a Wit, or *Toland* for a Philosopher, if the inexhaustible Stock of Christianity had not been at hand to provide them with Materials. What other Subject through all Art or Nature could have produced *Tindall* for a profound Author, or furnished him with Readers. It is the wise Choice of the

Subject that alone adorns and distinguishes the Writer. For, had a Hundred such Pens as these been employed on the side of Religion, they would have immediately sunk into Silence and Oblivion.

Nor do I think it wholly groundless, or my Fears altogether imaginary, that the Abolishing of Christianity may perhaps bring the Church in Danger, or at least put the Senate to the Trouble of another Securing Vote. I desire I may not be mistaken; I am far from presuming to affirm or think that the Church is in Danger at present, or as Things now stand, but we know not how soon it may be so when the Christian Religion is repealed. As plausible as this Project seems, there may a dangerous Design lurk under it; Nothing can be more notorious, than that the *Atheists, Deists, Socinians, Anti-Trinitarians,* and other Subdivisions of Free Thinkers, are Persons of little Zeal for the present Ecclesiastical Establishment: Their declared Opinion is for repealing the Sacramental Test, they are very indifferent with regard to Ceremonies, nor do they hold the *Jus Divinum* of Episcopacy. Therefore they may be intended as one Politick step towards altering the Constitution of the Church Established, and setting up *Presbytery* in the stead, which I leave to be further considered by those at the Helm.

In the last Place, I think nothing can be more plain, than that by this Expedient, we shall run into the Evil we chiefly pretend to avoid; and that the Abolishment of the *Christian* Religion, will be the readiest Course we can take to introduce Popery. And I am the more inclined to this Opinion, because we know it has been the constant Practice of the *Jesuits* to send over Emissaries, with Instructions to personate themselves Members of the several prevailing Sects amongst us. So it is recorded, that they have at sundry Times appeared in the Guise *of Presbyterians, Anabaptists, Independents* and *Quakers,* according as any of these were most in Credit; So, since the Fashion hath been taken up of exploding Religion, the *Popish* Missionaries have not been wanting to mix with the Free-Thinkers; among whom, *Toland* the great Oracle of the *Anti-*

Christians is an *Irish* Priest, the Son of an *Irish* Priest; and the most learned and ingenious Author of a Book called the *Rights of the Christian Church*, was in a proper Juncture reconciled to the *Romish* Faith, whose true Son, as appears by a hundred Passages in his Treatise he still continues. Perhaps I could add some others to the Number; but the Fact is beyond Dispute, and the Reasoning they proceed by is right: For supposing Christianity to be extinguished, the People will never be at Ease till they find out some other Method of Worship; which will as infallibly produce Superstition, as this will end in *Popery*.

And therefore, if notwithstanding all I have said, it still be thought necessary to have a Bill brought in for repealing Christianity; I would humbly offer an Amendment; that instead of the Word, Christianity, may be put Religion in general, which I conceive will much better answer all the good Ends proposed by the Projectors of it. For, as long as we leave in being, a God and his Providence, with all the necessary Consequences which curious and inquisitive Men will be apt to draw from such Premises, we do not strike at the Root of the Evil, though we should ever so effectually annihilate the present Scheme of the Gospel; For, of what use is Freedom of Thought, if it will not produce Freedom of Action, which is the sole End, how remote soever in Appearance, of all Objections against Christianity; And therefore, the Free-Thinkers consider it as a sort of Edifice, wherein all the Parts have such a mutual Dependence on each other, that if you happen to pull out one single Nail, the whole Fabrick must fall to the Ground. This was happily exprest by him who had heard of a Text brought for proof of the Trinity, which in an antient Manuscript was differently read; He thereupon immediately took the Hint, and by a sudden Deduction of a long Sorites, most Logically concluded; Why, if it be as you say, I may safely Whore and Drink on, and defy the Parson. From which, and many the like Instances easy to be produced, I think nothing can be more manifest, than that the Quarrel is not against any particular Points of hard digestion in the Christian System, but against Religion in general, which by laying Restraints on human Nature, is supposed the great Enemy to the Freedom of Thought and Action.

Upon the whole, if it shall still be thought for the Benefit of Church and State, that Christianity be abolished; I conceive however, it may be more convenient to defer the Execution to a Time of Peace, and not venture in this Conjuncture to disoblige our Allies, who as it falls out, are all Christians, and many of them, by the Prejudices of their Education, so bigotted, as to place a sort of Pride in the Appellation. If upon being rejected by them, we are to trust to an Alliance with the *Turk*, we shall find our selves much deceived: For, as he is too remote, and generally engaged in War with the *Persian* Emperor, so his People would be more Scandalized at our Infidelity, than our Christian Neighbours. For they are not only strict observers of Religious Worship; but what is worse, believe a God, which is more than is required of us even while we preserve the Name of Christians.

To conclude, Whatever some may think of the great Advantages to Trade by this favourite Scheme, I do very much apprehend, that in Six Months time after the Act is past for the Extirpation of the Gospel, the Bank, and *East-India* Stock, may fall at least One *per Cent*. And since that is Fifty times more than ever the Wisdom of our Age thought fit to venture for the Preservation of Christianity, there is no Reason we should be at so great a Loss meerly for the sake of destroying it.

A
LETTER
TO A
YOUNG
GENTLEMAN

THE advice given by Swift in this letter is remarkably free from the irony which in the circumstances might have been expected of him, and which runs through his *Argument to Prove that the Abolishing of Christianity . . . may . . . be attended with some Inconveniences* [p. 383]. But it does provide evidence, if any is needed, to confirm that Swift, though he respected his calling and demanded a high standard of conduct from its members, had little affection for it himself.

The letter was twice printed in 1721 as a sixpenny pamphlet, " By a Person of Quality ". In the same year it was included in the fourth edition of *Miscellanies in Prose and Verse. Dublin: Printed for S. Fairbrother*, with the title: " A Letter from a Lay-Patron to a Gentleman designing for Holy Orders ". It was reprinted in the first volume of *Miscellanies*, 1727 [unrecorded by Spencer Jackson in his Bibliography], and again in Faulkner's edition, 1735.

A LETTER TO A
YOUNG GENTLEMAN
LATELY ENTER'D INTO
HOLY ORDERS

Dated *January* the 9th, 1719-20.

SIR,

ALTHOUGH it was against my Knowledge or Advice that you entred into Holy Orders, under the present Dispositions of Mankind towards the *Church*, yet since it is now supposed too late to recede (at least according to the general Practice and Opinion) I cannot forbear offering my Thoughts to you upon this new Condition of Life you are engaged in.

I could heartily wish that the Circumstances of your Fortune, had enabled you to have continued some Years longer in the University; at least, 'till you were ten Years standing; to have laid in a competent Stock of human Learning, and some knowledge in Divinity, before you attempted to appear in the World: For I cannot but lament the common Course, which at least nine in ten of those who enter into the Ministry are obliged to run. When they have taken a Degree, and are consequently grown a Burthen to their Friends, who now think themselves fully discharged, they get into Orders as soon as they can, (upon which I shall make no Remarks) first sollicite a Readership, and if they be very fortunate, arrive in time to a Curacy here in Town, or else are sent to be Assistants in the Country, where they probably continue several Years (many of them their whole Lives) with thirty or forty Pounds a Year for their Support, 'till some Bishop, who happens to be not overstock'd with Relations, or attach'd to Favourites, or is content to supply his Diocess without Colonies from *England*, bestows them some inconsiderable Benefice, when 'tis odds they are already encumbred with a numerous Family. I would be glad to know what Intervals of Life such Persons can possibly set apart for Improvement of their Minds; or which way they could be furnish'd with Books, the Library they brought with them from their College being usually not the most numerous, or judiciously chosen. If such Gentlemen arrive to be great Scholars, it must I think be either by Means supernatural, or by a Method altogether out of any Road yet known to the Learned. But I conceive the Fact directly otherwise, and that many of them lose the greatest part of the small Pittance they received at the University.

I take it for granted, that you intend to pursue the beaten Track, and are already desirous to be seen in a Pulpit, only I hope you will think it proper to pass your Quarentine among some of the desolate Churches five Miles round this Town, where you may at least learn to *Read* and to *Speak* before you venture to expose your Parts in a City Congregation; not that these are better Judges, but because, if a Man must needs expose his Folly, it is more safe and discreet to do so, before few Witnesses, and in a scattered Neighbourhood. And you will do well if you can prevail upon some intimate and judicious Friend, to be your constant Hearer, and allow Him with the utmost Freedom to give you notice of whatever he shall find amiss either in your Voice or Gesture; for want of which early Warning, many Clergymen continue Defective; and sometimes Ridiculous to the end of their Lives; neither is it rare to observe among excellent and learned Divines, a certain ungratious Manner, or an unhappy Tone of Voice, which they never have been able to shake off.

I could likewise have been glad if you had applied your self a little more to the Study of the *English* Language, than I fear you have done; the neglect whereof is one of the most general Defects among the Scholars of this Kingdom, who seem to have not the least Conception of a Style, but run on in a flat kind of Phraseology, often mingled with barbarous Terms and Expressions, peculiar to the Nation:

Neither do I perceive that any Person, either finds or acknowledges his Wants upon this Head, or in the least
desires to have them supplied. Proper Words in proper
Places, makes the true Definitions of a Style. But this
would require too ample a Disquisition to be now dwelt
on: However, I shall venture to name one or two Faults,
which are easy to be remedied with a very small portion
of Abilities.

The first is the frequent use of obscure Terms, which by
the Women are called *Hard Words*, and by the better sort
of Vulgar, *Fine Language*. Than which I do not know
a more universal, inexcusable, and unnecessary Mistake
among the Clergy of all Distinctions, but especially the
younger Practitioners. I have been curious enough to take
a List of several hundred Words in a Sermon of a new
Beginner, which not one of his Hearers among a hundred
could possibly understand, neither can I easily call to mind
any Clergyman of my own Acquaintance who is wholly
exempt from this Error, although many of them agree with
me in the dislike of the Thing. But I am apt to put my self
in the place of the Vulgar, and think many Words difficult or obscure, which they will not allow to be so, because
those Words are obvious to Scholars. I believe the Method
observed by the famous Lord *Falkland* in some of his
Writings, would not be an ill one for young Divines: I
was assured by an old Person of Quality who knew him
well, that when he doubted whether a Word were perfectly
intelligible or no, he used to consult one of his Lady's
Chambermaids (not the Waiting-woman, because it was
possible she might be conversant in Romances) and by her
Judgment was guided whether to receive or to reject it.
And if that great Person thought such a Caution necessary
in Treatises offered to the learned World, it will be sure
at least as proper in Sermons, where the meanest Hearer
is supposed to be concerned, and where very often a Lady's
Chambermaid may be allowed to equal half the Congregation, both as to Quality and Understanding. But I know
not how it comes to pass, that Professors in most Arts and
Sciences, are generally the worst qualified to explain their

Meanings to those who are not of their Tribe: A common Farmer shall make you understand in three Words, *that his Foot is out of Joint, or his Collar-bone broken,* wherein a *Surgeon,* after a hundred terms of Art, if you are not a Scholar, shall leave you to seek. It is frequently the same case in Law, Physick, and even many of the meaner Arts.

And upon this Account it is, that among *hard Words,* I number likewise those which are peculiar to Divinity as it is a Science, because I observe several Clergymen otherwise little fond of obscure Terms, yet in their Sermons very liberal of all those which they find in Ecclesiastical Writers, as if it were our Duty to understand them; which I am sure it is not. And I defy the greatest Divine to produce any Law either of God or Man which obliges me to comprehend the meaning of *Omniscience, Omnipresence, Ubiquity, Attribute, Beatifick Vision,* with a thousand others so frequent in Pulpits, any more than that of *Excentrick, Idiosyncracy, Entity,* and the like. I believe I may venture to insist further, that many Terms used in holy Writ, particularly by St. *Paul,* might with more Discretion be changed into plainer Speech, except when they are introduced as part of a Quotation.

I am the more earnest in this Matter, because it is a general Complaint, and the justest in the World. For a Divine has nothing to say to the wisest Congregation of any Parish in this Kingdom, which he may not express in a manner to be understood by the meanest among them. And this Assertion must be true, or else God requires from us more than we are able to perform. However, not to contend whether a Logician might possibly put a Case that would serve for an Exception, I will appeal to any Man of Letters, whether at least nineteen in twenty of those perplexing Words might not be changed into easy ones, such as naturally first occur to ordinary Men, and probably did so at first to those very Gentlemen who are so fond of the former.

We are often reproved by Divines from the Pulpits, on account of our Ignorance in Things Sacred, and perhaps with Justice enough. However, it is not very reasonable for them to expect, that *common Men* should understand Expressions which are never made use of in *common Life*. No Gentleman thinks it safe or prudent to send a Servant with a Message, without repeating it more than once, and endeavouring to put it into Terms brought down to the Capacity of the Bearer: Yet after all this Care, it is frequent for Servants to mistake, and sometimes to occasion Misunderstandings among Friends. Although the common Domesticks, in a Gentlemans Family have more Opportunities of improving their Minds than the ordinary Sort of Tradesmen.

It is usual for Clergymen who are taxed with this learned Defect, to quote Dr. *Tillotson*, and other famous Divines, in their Defence; without considering the Difference between elaborate Discourses upon important Occasions, delivered to Princes or Parliaments, written with a View of being made Publick, and a plain Sermon intended for the middle or lower Size of People. Neither do they seem to remember the many Alterations, Additions and Expungings made by great Authors in those Treatises which they prepare for the Publick. Besides, that excellent Prelate abovementioned, was known to Preach after a much more popular Manner in the City Congregations: And if in those parts of his Works he be any where too obscure for the Understandings of many who may be supposed to have been his Hearers, it ought to be numbred among his Omissions.

The fear of being thought Pedants hath been of pernicious Consequence to young Divines. This hath wholly taken many of them off from their severer Studies in the University, which they have exchanged for Plays, Poems, and Pamphlets, in order to qualify them for Tea-Tables and Coffee-Houses. This they usually call *Polite Conversation*; *knowing the World*; and *Reading Men instead of Books*. These Accomplishments, when applied in the Pulpit, appear by a quaint, terse, florid Style, rounded into Periods and Cadencies, commonly without either Propriety or Meaning. I have listen'd with my utmost Attention for half an Hour to an Orator of this Species, without being able to understand, much less to carry away one single Sentence out of a whole Sermon. Others, to shew that their Studies have not been confined to Sciences, or ancient Authors, will talk in the Style of a Gaming Ordinary, and *White-Fryers*, where I suppose the Hearers can be little edified by the Terms of *Palming*, *Shuffling*, *Biting*, *Bamboozling*, and the like, if they have not been sometimes conversant among Pickpockets and Sharpers. And truly, as they say, a Man is known by his Company, so it should seem, that a Man's Company may be known by his manner of expressing himself, either in publick Assemblies, or private Conversation.

It would be endless to run over the several Defects of Style among us; I shall therefore say nothing of the *Mean* and the *Paultry* (which are usually attended by the *Fustian*) much less of the *Slovenly* or *Indecent*. Two Things I will just warn you against; the first is the Frequency of flat unnecessary Epithets, and the other is the Folly of using old threadbare Phrases, which will often make you go out of your Way to find and apply them, are nauseous to rational Hearers, and will seldom express your Meaning as well as your own natural Words.

Although, as I have already observed, our *English* Tongue is too little cultivated in this Kingdom; yet the Faults are nine in ten owing to Affectation, and not to the Want of Understanding. When a Man's Thoughts are clear, the properest Words will generally offer themselves first, and his own Judgment will direct him in what Order to place them, so as they may be best understood. Where Men err against this Method, it is usually on purpose, and to shew their Learning, their Oratory, their Politeness, or their Knowledge of the World. In short, that Simplicity without which no human Performance can arrive to any great Perfection, is no where more eminently useful than in this.

I have been considering that part of Oratory which relates to the moving of the Passions: This I observe is in Esteem and Practice among some Church Divines, as well as among all the Preachers and Hearers of the Fanatick or Enthusiastick Strain. I will here deliver to you (perhaps with more Freedom than Prudence) my Opinion upon the Point.

The two great Orators of *Greece* and *Rome*, *Demosthenes* and *Cicero*, though each of them a Leader (or as the *Greeks* called it a *Demagogue*) in a popular State, yet seem to differ in their Practice upon this Branch of their Art; the former, who had to deal with a People of much more Politeness, Learning, and Wit, laid the greatest Weight of his Oratory, upon the Strength of his Arguments offered to their Understanding and Reason: Whereas *Tully* considered the Dispositions of a sincere, more ignorant, and less mercurial Nation, by dwelling almost entirely on the pathetick Part.

But the principal Thing to be remembered is, that the constant Design of both these Orators in all their Speeches, was to drive some one particular Point, either the Condemnation or Acquittal of an accused Person, a Persuasive to War, the enforcing of a Law, and the like; which was determined upon the Spot, according as the Oratory on either Side prevailed. And here it was often found of absolute necessity to enflame or cool the Passions of the Audience, especially at *Rome* where *Tully* spoke, and with those Writings young Divines (I mean those among them who read old Authors) are more conversant than with those of *Demosthenes*, who by many Degrees excelled the other at least as an Orator. But I do not see how this Talent of moving the Passions can be of any great Use towards directing Christian Men in the Conduct of their Lives, at least in these Northern Climates, where I am confident, the strongest Eloquence of that Kind will leave few Impressions upon any of our Spirits deep enough to last till the next Morning, or rather to the next Meal.

But what hath chiefly put me out of Conceit with this moving manner of Preaching, is the frequent Disappointment it meets with. I know a Gentleman, who made it a Rule in reading, to skip over all Sentences where he spy'd a Note of Admiration at the End. I believe those Preachers who abound in *Epiphonema*'s, if they look about them, would find one part of their Congregation out of Countenance, and the other asleep, except perhaps an old Female Beggar or two in the Isles, who (if they be sincere) may probably groan at the Sound.

Nor is it a wonder that this Expedient should so often miscarry, which requires so much Art and Genius to arrive at any Perfection in it, as any Man will find, much sooner than learn by consulting *Cicero* himself.

I therefore entreat you to make use of this Faculty (if you are ever so unfortunate as to think you have it) as seldom, and with as much Caution as you can, else I may probably have occasion to say of you as a great Person said of another upon this very Subject. A Lady askt him coming out of Church, whether it were not a very moving Discourse? *Yes*, said he, *I was extreamly sorry, for the Man is my Friend.*

If in Company you offer something for a Jest, and no body seconds you in your own Laughter, or seems to relish what you said, you may condemn their Taste, if you please, and appeal to better Judgments; but in the mean time, it must be agreed you make a very indifferent Figure; and it is at least equally ridiculous to be disappointed in endeavouring to make other Folks grieve, as to make them laugh.

A plain convincing Reason may possibly operate upon the Mind both of a learned and ignorant Hearer as long as they live, and will edify a thousand times more than the Art of wetting the Handkerchiefs of a whole Congregation, if you were sure to attain it.

If your Arguments be strong, in God's Name offer them in as moving a Manner as the Nature of the Subject will probably admit, wherein Reason and good Advice will be your safest Guides; but beware of letting the pathetick part swallow up the Rational: For I suppose, *Philosophers* have long agreed, that Passion should never prevail over Reason.

As I take it, the two principal Branches of Preaching, are first to tell the People what is their Duty, and then to convince them that it is so. The Topicks for both these, we know are brought from *Scripture* and *Reason.* Upon this first, I wish it were often practised to instruct the Hearers in the Limits, Extent, and Compass of every Duty, which requires a good deal of Skill and Judgment: The other Branch is, I think, not so difficult. But what I would offer upon both, is this; that it seems to be in the Power of a reasonable Clergyman, if he will be at the Pains, to make the most ignorant Man comprehend what is his Duty, and to convince him by Argument drawn to the Level of his Understanding, that he ought to perform it.

But I must remember that my Design in this *Paper* was not so much to instruct you in your Business either as a Clergyman or a Preacher, as to warn you against some Mistakes which are obvious to the generality of Mankind as well as to me; and we who are Hearers, may be allowed to have some Opportunities in the Quality of being Standers by. Only perhaps I may now again transgress by desiring you to express the Heads of your Divisions in as few and clear Words as you possibly can, otherwise, I and many thousand others will never be able to retain them, nor consequently to carry away a Syllable of the Sermon.

I shall now mention a Particular wherein your whole Body will be certainly against me, and the Laity almost to a Man on my Side. However it came about, I cannot get over the Prejudice of taking some little Offence at the Clergy for perpetually reading their Sermons; perhaps my frequent hearing of Foreigners, who never make use of Notes, may have added to my Disgust. And I cannot but think, that whatever is read, differs as much from what is repeated without Book, as a Copy does from an Original. At the same time, I am highly sensible what an extream Difficulty it would be upon you to alter this Method, and that, in such a Case, your Sermons would be much less valuable than they are, for want of Time to improve and correct them. I would therefore gladly come to a Compromise with you in this Matter. I knew a Clergyman of some Distinction, who appeared to deliver his Sermon without looking into his Notes, which when I complimented him upon, he assured me he could not repeat six Lines; but his

Method was to write the whole Sermon in a large plain
Hand, with all the Forms of Margin, Paragraph, marked
Page, and the like; then on *Sunday* Morning, took care to
run it over five or six times, which he could do in an Hour;
and when he deliver'd it, by pretending to turn his Face
from one Side to the other, he would (in his own Expression)
pick up the Lines, and cheat his People by making them
believe he had it all by Heart. He farther added, that
whenever he happened by neglect to omit any of these
Circumstances, the Vogue of the *Parish* was, *Our Doctor
gave us but an indifferent Sermon to Day.* Now among us,
many Clergymen act so directly contrary to this Method,
that from a Habit of saving *Time* and *Paper*, which they
acquired at the University, they write in so diminutive a
Manner, with such frequent Blots and Interlineations, that
they are hardly able to go on without perpetual Hesitations
or extemporary Expletives: And I desire to know what can
be more inexcusable, than to see a Divine, and a Scholar,
at a Loss in reading his own Compositions, which it is
supposed he has been preparing with much *Pains* and
Thought for the Instruction of his People. The want of a
little more Care in this Article, is the Cause of much un-
graceful Behaviour. You will observe some Clergymen
with their Heads held down from the beginning to the
end, within an Inch of the Cushion, to read what is hardly
legible; which, besides the untoward Manner, hinders
them from making the best Advantage of their Voice:
Others again have a Trick of popping up and down every
Moment from their *Paper* to the Audience, like an idle
Schoolboy on a Repetition Day.

Let me entreat you therefore to add one half Crown a
Year to the Article of *Paper*; to transcribe your Sermons
in as large and plain a Manner as you can, and either make
no Interlineations, or change the whole Leaf; for we
your Hearers would rather you should be less correct than
perpetually stammering, which I take to be one of the worst
Solecisms in *Rhetorick*: And lastly, read your Sermon once
or twice for a few Days before you preach it: To which
you will probably answer some Years hence, *That it was*

but just finished when the last Bell rung to Church; and I shall readily believe, but not excuse you.

I cannot forbear warning you in the most earnest Manner against endeavouring at Wit in your Sermons, because by the strictest Computation, it is very near a Million to one that you have none; and because too many of your Calling have consequently made themselves everlastingly ridiculous by attempting it. I remember several young Men in this Town, who could never leave the *Pulpit* under half a dozen *Conceits*; and this Faculty adhered to those Gentlemen a longer or shorter Time exactly in proportion to their several Degrees of Dullness: Accordingly, I am told that some of them retain it to this Day. I heartily wish the Brood were at an end.

Before you enter into the common unsufferable Cant of taking all Occasions to disparage the Heathen *Philosophers*, I hope you will differ from some of your Brethren, by first enquiring what those *Philosophers* can say for themselves. The System of Morality to be gathered out of the Writings or Sayings of those ancient Sages, falls undoubtedly very short of that delivered in the Gospel, and wants besides, the divine Sanction which our Saviour gave to His. Whatever is further related by the Evangelists, contains chiefly, Matters of Fact, and consequently of Faith, such as the Birth of Christ, His being the Messiah, His Miracles, His Death, Resurrection, and Ascension. None of which can properly come under the Appellation of human Wisdom, being intended only to make us Wise unto Salvation. And therefore in this Point, nothing can justly be laid to the Charge of the *Philosophers* further than that they were ignorant of certain Facts which happened long after their Death. But I am deceived, if a better Comment could be any where collected, upon the Moral Part of the Gospel, than from the Writings of those excellent Men; even that Divine Precept of loving our Enemies, is at large insisted on by *Plato*, who puts it, as I remember, into the Mouth of *Socrates*. And as to the Reproach of Heathenism, I doubt they had less of it than the corrupted *Jews* in whose Time they lived. For it is a gross piece of Ignorance among us to conceive, that in those polite and learned Ages, even Persons of any tolerable Education, much less the wisest *Philosophers* did acknowledge or worship any more than one Almighty Power under several Denominations, to whom they allowed all those Attributes we ascribe to the Divinity: And as I take it, human Comprehension reacheth no further: Neither did our Saviour think it necessary to explain to us the Nature of God, because I suppose it would be impossible without bestowing on us other Faculties than we possess at present. But the true Misery of the Heathen World appears to be what I before mentioned, the want of a Divine Sanction, without which the Dictates of the Philosophers failed in the Point of Authority, and consequently the Bulk of Mankind lay indeed under a great Load of Ignorance even in the Article of Morality, but the Philosophers themselves did not. Take the Matter in this Light, and it will afford Field enough for a Divine to enlarge on, by shewing the Advantages which the Christian World has over the Heathen, and the absolute Necessity of Divine Revelations, to make the Knowledge of the true God, and the Practice of Virtue more universal in the World.

I am not ignorant how much I differ in this Opinion from some ancient Fathers in the Church, who arguing against the Heathens, made it a Principal Topick to decry their Philosophy as much as they could: Which, I hope, is not altogether our present Case. Besides, it is to be considered, that those Fathers lived in the Decline of *Literature*; and in my Judgment (who should be unwilling to give the least Offence) appear to be rather most excellent, holy Persons, than of transcendent Genius or Learning. Their genuine Writings (for many of them have extremely suffered by spurious Additions) are of admirable use for confirming the Truth of ancient Doctrines and Discipline, by shewing the State and Practice of the Primitive Church. But among such of them as have fallen in my Way, I do not remember any whose Manner of arguing or exhorting I could heartily recommend to the Imitation of a young Divine when he is to speak from the Pulpit. Perhaps I judge too hastily; there being several of them in whose Writings I have made very little Progress, and in others none at all. For I perused only such as were recommended to me, at a Time when I had more Leisure and a better Disposition to read, than have since fallen to my Share.

To return then to the Heathen Philosophers, I hope you will not only give them Quarter, but make their Works a considerable Part of your Study: To these I will venture to add the principal Orators and Historians, and perhaps a few of the Poets: By the reading of which, you will soon discover your Mind and Thoughts to be enlarged, your Imagination extended and refined, your Judgment directed, your Admiration lessened, and your Fortitude encreased: All which Advantages must needs be of excellent Use to a Divine, whose Duty it is to preach and practice the Contempt of human Things.

I would say something concerning Quotations, wherein I think you cannot be too sparing, except from Scripture, and the primitive Writers of the Church. As to the former, when you offer a Text as a Proof or an Illustration, we your Hearers expect to be fairly used, and sometimes think we have reason to complain, especially of you younger Divines, which makes us fear that some of you conceive you have no more to do than turn over a Concordance, and there having found the principal Word, introduce as much of the Verse as will serve your Turn, tho' in Reality it makes nothing for you. I do not altogether disapprove the Manner of interweaving Texts of Scripture through the Stile of your Sermon, wherein however, I have sometimes observed great Instances of Indiscretion and Impropriety, against which I therefore venture to give you a Caution.

As to Quotations from ancient Fathers, I think they are best brought in to confirm some Opinion controverted by those who differ from us: In other Cases we give you full Power to adopt the Sentence for your own, rather than tell us, *As St.* Austin *excellently observes*. But to mention modern Writers by Name, or use the Phrase of *a late excellent Prelate of our Church*, and the like, is altogether intolerable, and for what Reason I know not, makes every rational Hearer ashamed. Of no better a Stamp is your *Heathen Philosopher* and *famous Poet,* and *Roman Historians,* at least in common Congregations, who will rather believe you on your own Word, than on that of *Plato* or *Homer.*

I have lived to see *Greek* or *Latin* almost entirely driven out of the Pulpit, for which I am heartily glad. The frequent Use of the latter was certainly a Remnant of Popery which never admitted Scripture in the vulgar Language; and I wonder, that Practice was never accordingly objected to us by the Fanaticks.

The mention of Quotations puts me in mind of Commonplace-Books, which have been long in use by industrious young Divines, and I hear do still continue so; I know they are very beneficial to Lawyers and Physicians, because they are Collections of Facts or Cases, whereupon a great Part of their several Faculties depend; of these I have seen several, but never yet any written by a Clergyman; only from what I am informed, they generally are Extracts of Theological and Moral Sentences drawn from Ecclesiastical and other Authors, reduced under proper Heads, usually begun, and perhaps finished while the Collectors were young in the Church, as being intended for Materials or Nurseries to stock future Sermons. You will observe the wisest Editors of ancient Authors, when they meet a Sentence worthy of being distinguished, take special Care to have the first word printed in capital Letters, that you may not overlook it. Such, for Example, as *the Inconstancy of Fortune, the Goodness of Peace, the Excellency of Wisdom, the Certainty of Death, That Prosperity makes Men insolent, and Adversity humble;* and the like eternal Truths, which every Plowman knew long enough before *Aristotle* or *Plato* were born. If Theological Common-place-Books be no better filled, I think they had better be laid aside, and I could wish that Men of tolerable Intellectuals would trust their own natural Reason, improved by a general Conversation with Books, to enlarge on Points which they are supposed already to understand. If a rational

Man reads an excellent Author with just Application, he shall find himself extreamly improved, and perhaps insensibly led to imitate that Author's Perfections, altho' in a little Time he should not remember one Word in the Book, nor even the Subject it handled: For Books give the same Turn to our Thoughts and Way of Reasoning, that good and ill Company does to our Behaviour and Conversation; without either loading our Memories, or making us even sensible of the Change. And particularly I have observed in Preaching, that no Men succeed better than those who trust entirely to the Stock or Fund of their own Reason, advanced indeed, but not overlaid by Commerce with Books: Whoever only reads in order to transcribe wise and shining Remarks, without entring into the Genius and Spirit of the Author, as it is probable he will make no very judicious Extract, so he will be apt to trust to that Collection in all his Compositions, and be misled out of the regular Way of thinking, in order to introduce those Materials which he has been at the Pains to gather: And the Product of all this will be found a manifest incoherent Piece of Patchwork.

Some Gentlemen abounding in their University Erudition, are apt to fill their Sermons with Philosophical Terms and Notions of the metaphysical or abstracted Kind, which generally have one Advantage, to be equally understood by the Wise, the Vulgar, and the Preacher himself. I have been better entertained, and more informed by a Chapter in the *Pilgrim's Progress*, than by a long Discourse upon the *Will* and the *Intellect*, and *simple* or *complex Idea's*. Others again, are fond of dilating on *Matter* and *Motion*, talk of the *fortuitous Concourse of Atoms*, of *Theories*, and *Phænomena*; directly against the Advice of St. *Paul*, who yet appears to have been conversant enough in those kind of Studies.

I do not find that you are any where directed in the Canons or Articles, to attempt explaining the Mysteries of the Christian Religion. And indeed since Providence intended there should be Mysteries, I do not see how it can be agreeable to *Piety*, *Orthodoxy* or good *Sense*, to go about such a Work. For, to me there seems to be a manifest Dilemma in the Case: If you explain them, they are Mysteries no longer; if you fail, you have laboured to no Purpose. What I should think most reasonable and safe for you to do upon this Occasion; upon solemn Days to deliver the Doctrine as the Church holds it, and confirm it by Scripture. For my part, having considered the Matter impartially, I can see no great Reason which those Gentlemen you call the *Free-Thinkers* can have for their Clamour against Religious Mysteries; since it is plain, they were not invented by the Clergy, to whom they bring no Profit, nor acquire any Honour. For every Clergyman is ready either to tell us the utmost he knows, or to confess that he does not understand them; neither is it strange that there should be Mysteries in Divinity as well as in the commonest Operations of Nature.

And here I am at a Loss what to say upon the frequent Custom of preaching against *Atheism, Deism, Free-thinking*, and the like, as young Divines are particularly fond of doing, especially when they exercise their Talent in Churches frequented by People of Quality, which as it is but an ill Compliment to the Audience; so I am under some Doubt whether it answers the End.

Because Persons under those Imputations are generally no great Frequenters of Churches, and so the Congregation is but little edify'd for the sake of three or four Fools who are past Grace. Neither do I think it any Part of *Prudence* to perplex the Minds of well-disposed People with Doubts, which probably would never have otherwise come into their Heads. But I am of Opinion, and dare be positive in it, that not one in an hundred of those who pretend to be *Free-Thinkers*, are really so in their Hearts. For there is one Observation which I never knew to fail, and I desire you will examine it in the Course of your Life, that no Gentleman of a liberal Education, and regular in his Morals, did ever profess himself a *Free-Thinker*: Where then are these kind of People to be found? Among the worst part of the Soldiery made up of Pages, younger Brothers of obscure Families, and others of desperate

Fortunes; or else among idle Town Fops; and now and then a drunken 'Squire of the Country. Therefore nothing can be plainer, than that Ignorance and Vice are two Ingredients absolutely necessary in the Composition of those you generally call *Free-Thinkers*, who in propriety of Speech, *are no Thinkers at all*. And since I am in the Way of it, pray consider one Thing farther: As young as you are, you cannot but have already observed, what a violent Run there is among too many weak People against University Education. Be firmly assured, that the whole Cry is made up by those who were either never sent to a College; or through their Irregularities and Stupidity never made the least Improvement while they were there. I have at least forty of the latter Sort now in my Eye; several of them in this Town, whose *Learning, Manners, Temperance, Probity, Good Nature,* and *Politicks,* are all of a Piece. Others of them in the Country, Oppressing their Tenants, tyrannizing over the Neighbourhood, cheating the Vicar, talking Nonsense, and getting Drunk at the Sessions. It is from such Seminaries as these, that the World is provided with the several Tribes and Denominations of *Free-Thinkers*, who, in my Judgment, are not to be reformed by Arguments offered to prove the Truth of the *Christian Religion*, because Reasoning will never make a Man correct an ill Opinion, which by Reasoning he never acquired: For in the Course of Things, Men always grow vicious before they become Unbelievers; but if you could once convince the Town or Country profligate, by Topicks drawn from the View of their own *Quiet, Reputation, Health,* and *Advantage,* their *Infidelity* would soon drop off: This I confess is no easy Task, because it is almost in a literal Sense, to fight with Beasts. Now, to make it clear, that we are to look for no other Original of this *Infidelity* whereof Divines so much complain: It is allowed on all Hands, that the People of *England* are more corrupt in their *Morals* than any other Nation at this Day under the *Sun*: And this Corruption is manifestly owing to other Causes, both *Numerous* and *Obvious,* much more than to the Publication of irreligious

Books, which indeed are but the Consequence of the former. For all the Writers against Christianity since the Revolution have been of the lowest Rank among Men in regard to *Literature*, *Wit*, and good *Sense*, and upon that Account wholly unqualify'd to propagate *Heresies*, unless among a People already abandoned.

In an Age where every Thing disliked by those who think with the Majority is called *Disaffection*, it may perhaps be ill interpreted, when I venture to tell you that this Universal Depravation of *Manners* is owing to the perpetual bandying of *Factions* among us for thirty Years past; when without weighing the *Motives of Justice*, *Law*, *Conscience* or *Honour*, every Man adjusts his *Principles* to those of the *Party* he hath chosen, and among whom he may best find his own account: But by reason of our frequent Vicissitudes, Men who were impatient to be out of Play, have been forced to recant, or at least to reconcile their former Tenets with every new System of Administration. Add to this, that the old fundamental Custom of annual Parliaments being wholly laid aside, and Elections growing chargeable, since Gentlemen found that their Country Seats brought them in less than a Seat in the House, the Voters, *that is to say*, the Bulk of the common People have been universally seduced into *Bribery*, *Perjury*, *Drunkenness*, *Malice*, and *Slanders*.

Not to be further tedious, or rather invidious, these are a few among other Causes which have contributed to the Ruin of our *Morals*, and consequently to the Contempt of *Religion*: For imagine to your self, if you please, a landed Youth whom his Mother would never suffer to look into a Book for fear of spoiling his Eyes, got into Parliament, and observing all Enemies to the Clergy heard with the utmost Applause; what Notions he must imbibe; how readily he will join in the Cry; what an Esteem he will conceive of himself; and what a Contempt he must entertain, not only for his Vicar at home, but for the whole Order.

I therefore again conclude, that the Trade of *Infidelity* hath been taken up only for an Expedient to keep in

Countenance that universal Corruption of *Morals,* which many other Causes first contributed to introduce and to cultivate. And thus, Mr. *Hobbs*'s saying upon Reason may be much more properly apply'd to Religion: That, *if Religion will be against a Man, a Man will be against Religion.* Though after all, I have heard a Profligate offer much stronger arguments against paying his Debts, than ever he was known to do against *Christianity*; indeed the Reason was, because in that Juncture he happened to be closer prest by the *Bailiff* than the *Parson.*

Ignorance may perhaps be the *Mother* of *Superstition*; but *Experience* hath not proved it to be so of *Devotion*: For *Christianity* always made the most easy and quickest Progress in civilized Countries. I mention this because it is affirmed that the Clergy are in most Credit where Ignorance prevails (and surely this Kingdom would be called the *Paradise* of Clergymen if that Opinion were true) for which they instance *England* in the Times of *Popery.* But whoever knows any Thing of three or four Centuries before the Reformation, will find the little Learning then stirring was more equally divided between the *English* Clergy and Laity than it is at present. There were several famous Lawyers in that *Period,* whose Writings are still in the highest Repute, and some *Historians* and *Poets* who were not of the *Church.* Whereas now a days our Education is so corrupted, that you will hardly find a young Person of Quality with the least Tincture of Knowledge, at the same time that the Clergy were never more learned, or so scurvily treated. Here among Us, at least, a Man of Letters out of the three Professions, is almost a Prodigy. And these few who have preserved any Rudiments of Learning are (except perhaps one or two Smatterers) the Clergy's Friends to a Man: And I dare appeal to any Clergyman in this Kingdom, whether the greatest Dunce in his Parish is not always the most proud, wicked, fraudulent, and intractable of his Flock.

I think the Clergy have almost given over perplexing themselves and their Hearers with abstruse Points of Predestination, Election and the like; at least it is time they should; and therefore I shall not trouble you further upon this Head.

I have now said all I could think convenient with Relation to your Conduct in the Pulpit: Your Behaviour in Life is another Scene, upon which I shall readily offer you my Thoughts, if you appear to desire them from me by your Approbation of what I have here Written; if not, I have already troubled you too much.

I am SIR,

Your Affectionate

Friend and Servant,

January 9th,   *A. B.*
1719-20.

A LETTER TO A YOUNG POET

A Letter of Advice to a Young Poet was published for the first time in London and Dublin in 1721. A second edition appeared in the same year, and the letter was included in an unauthorised volume of *Miscellanies. . . . The Fourth Edition. London: Printed in the Year M.DCC.XXII. Price 2s. 6d.* It was not, however, reprinted either in the *Miscellanies* [1727–35] or in Faulkner's collected edition [1735]. It should be read in conjunction with Swift's poem: *On Poetry: A Rapsody* [p. 790].

A LETTER OF
ADVICE TO A YOUNG
POET

together with a Proposal for
the Encouragement of
Poetry in this
Kingdom.

SIR,

As I have always profess'd a Friendship for you, and for that Reason, have been more inquisitive into your Conduct and Studies than is usually agreeable to young Men; so I must own I am not a little pleas'd to find by your last Account, that you have entirely bent your Thoughts to *English Poetry*, with design to make it your Profession and Business. Two Reasons incline me to encourage you in this Study, one, the narrowness of your present Circumstances, the other, the great use of *Poetry* to Mankind and Society, and in every Employment of life. Upon these Views, I cannot but commend your wise Resolution to withdraw so early from other unprofitable and severe Studies, and betake your self to that, which, if you have good Luck, will advance your Fortune, and make you an Ornament to your Friends, and your Country. It may be your Justification and further Encouragement to consider, that *History*, Ancient or Modern, cannot furnish you an instance of one Person, Eminent in any Station, who was not in some measure vers'd in *Poetry*, or at least, a Well wisher to the Professors of it; neither would I dispair to prove, if legally call'd thereto, that it is impossible to be a good *Soldier*, *Divine*, or *Lawyer*, or even so much as an Eminent *Bell-man*, or *Ballad-singer*, without some taste of

Poetry, and a competent Skill in Versification: but I say
the less of this because the renowned Sr. *P. Sidney* has
exhausted the Subject before me in his *Defence of Poesie*,
on which I shall make no other Remark but this, that he
argues there as if he really believed himself.

For my own part, having never made one Verse since I
was at *School*, where I suffered too much for my Blunders
in *Poetry* to have any love to it ever since; I am not able
from any Experience of my own, to give you those instructions you desire, neither will I Declare (for I love to
conceal my Passions) how much I lament my neglect of
Poetry in those Periods of my Life, which were properest
for Improvements in that Ornamental part of Learning;
besides my Age and Infirmities might well excuse me to
you, as being unqualify'd to be your *Writing-Master* with
Spectacles on, and a shaking Hand. However, that I may
not be altogether wanting to you in an Affair of so much
Importance to your Credit and Happiness, I shall here
give you some scatter'd Thoughts upon the Subject, such
as I have gather'd by Reading and Observation.

There is a certain little Instrument, the first of those in
use with Scholars, and the meanest considering the Materials of it, whether it be a Joynt of Wheaten-Straw, (the
old *Arcadian* Pipe) or just three inches of slender Wire,
or a stript Feather, or a Corking-Pin. Furthermore, this
same diminutive Tool, for the posture of it, usually reclines
its Head on the Thumb of the right Hand, sustains the
foremost Finger upon its Breast, and is it self supported
by the second. This is commonly known by the name of
a FESCUE, I shall here therefore condescend to be this
little Elementary Guide, and point out some Particulars
which may be of use to you in your Hornbook of *Poetry*.

In the first place, I am not yet convinc'd, that it is at all
necessary for a modern Poet to *believe in God*, or have
any serious sense of Religion; and in this Article you must
give me leave to suspect your Capacities, because Religion
being what your Mother taught you, you will hardly find
it possible at least not easy, all at once to get over those
early Prejudices, so far as to think it better to be a *great*

Wit than a *good Christian*, tho' herein the general practice is against you, so that if upon Enquiry you find in your self any such Softnesses, owing to the nature of your Education, my Advice is, that you forthwith lay down your Pen, as having no further business with it in the way of *Poetry*; unless you will be content to pass for an *Insipid* or will submit to be hooted at by your Fraternity, or can disguise your Religion as well-bred Men do their Learning, in Complaisance to Company.

For *Poetry*, as it has been manag'd for some Years past, by such as make a Business of it (and of such only I speak here; for I do not call him a Poet that writes for his Diversion, any more than that Gentleman a Fidler who amuses himself with a Violin) I say our *Poetry* of late has been altogether disengag'd from the narrow notions of Virtue and Piety, because it has been found by Experience of our Professors, that the smallest quantity of Religion, like a single drop of Malt-Liquor in Claret, will muddy and discompose the brightest Poetical Genius.

Religion supposes Heaven and Hell, the Word of God and Sacraments and twenty other Circumstances, which taken seriously, are a wonderful check to Wit and Humour, and such as a true Poet cannot possibly give into with a saving to his Poetical License; but yet it is necessary for him, that others shou'd believe those things seriously, that his Wit may be exercised on their *Wisdom*, for so doing: For tho' a Wit need not have Religion, Religion is necessary to a Wit, as an Instrument is to the Hand that plays upon it: And for this the Moderns plead the Example of their great Idol *LUCRETIUS*, who had not been by half so eminent a Poet (as he truly was) but that he stood tip-toe on Religion. *Religio pedibus Subjecta*, and by that rising Ground had the Advantage of all the Poets of his own or following Times, who were not mounted on the same Pedestal.

Besides, it is further to be observed, that PETRONIUS, another of their Favourites, speaking of the Qualifications of a good Poet, insists chiefly on the *Liber Spiritus*; by which, I have been ignorant enough heretofore to suppose he meant, a good Invention, or great compass of Thought, or a sprightly Imagination: But I have learned a better Construction from the Opinion and Practice of the Moderns; and taking it literally for a free Spirit *i.e.* a Spirit or *Mind*, free or *disengag'd* from all Prejudices concerning God, Religion and another World, it is to me a plain Account why our present Sett of Poets are, and hold themselves oblig'd to be, *Free-Thinkers*.

But altho' I cannot recommend Religion upon the Practice of some of our most eminent *English* Poets, yet I can justly advise you, from their Example, to be conversant in the *Scriptures*, and, if possible, to make your self entirely Master of them: In which, however, I intend nothing less than imposing upon you a Task of Piety. Far be it from me to desire you to believe them, or lay any great stress upon their Authority, (in that you may do as you think fit) but to read them as a Piece of necessary Furniture for a *Wit* and a *Poet*; which is a very different View from that of a Christian. For I have made it my Observation that the greatest Wits have been the best Textuaries: Our modern Poets are, to a Man, almost as well read in the Scriptures as some of our Divines, and often abound more with the Phrase. They have read them Historically, Critically, Musically, Comically, Poetically, and every other Way except *Religiously*, and have found their Account in doing so. For the Scriptures are undoubtedly a Fund *of* Wit, and a Subject *for* Wit. You may, according to the modern Practice, be witty *upon* them or *out* of them: And to speak the Truth, but for them, I know not what our *Play-wrights* would do for Images, Allusions, Similitudes, Examples, or even Language it self. Shut up the Sacred Books, and I would be bound our Wit would run down like an Alarm, or fall as the Stocks did, and ruin half the Poets in these Kingdoms. And if that were the Case, how would most of that Tribe, (all, I think, but the *immortal Addison*, who made a better Use of his Bible, and a few more) who dealt so freely in that Fund, rejoice that they had drawn out in time, and left the present Generation of Poets to be the BUBBLES.

But here I must enter one Caution, and desire you to take Notice, that in this Advice of reading the Scriptures, I had not the least Thought concerning your Qualification that Way for Poetical *Orders*; which I mention because I find a Notion of that kind advanc'd by one of our *English* Poets, and is, I suppose, maintained by the rest. He says to *Spencer*, in a pretended Vision.

———— *with Hands laid on ordain me fit*
For the great Cure and Ministry of Wit.

which Passage is, in my Opinion, a notable Allusion to the Scriptures, and making (but reasonable) Allowances for the *small* Circumstance of Profaness, bordering close upon Blasphemy, is *inimitably* fine; besides some useful Discoveries made in it, as, that there are Bishops in Poetry, that these Bishops must ordain young Poets, and with laying on Hands, and that Poetry is a Cure of Souls; and consequently speaking, those who have such Cures ought to be Poets, and too often are so: And indeed, as of old, Poets and Priests were one and the same Function, the Alliance of those ministerial Offices is to this Day happily maintain'd in the same Persons; and this I take to be the only justifiable Reason for that Appellation which they so much affect, I mean the modest Title of DIVINE POETS. However, having never been present at the Ceremony of Ordaining to the Priesthood of Poetry, I own I have no Notion of the Thing, and shall say the less of it here.

The Scriptures then being generally both the Fountain and Subject of modern Wit, I could do no less than give them the Preference in your Reading. After a thorough Acquaintance with them, I would advise you to turn your thoughts to HUMAN LITERATURE, which yet I say, more in Compliance with vulgar Opinions than according to my own Sentiments.

For indeed, nothing has surprised me more than to see the Prejudices of Mankind as to this Matter of human Learning, who have generally thought it necessary to be a good Scholar in order to be a good Poet, than which nothing is falser in Fact, or more contrary to Practice and Experience. Neither will I dispute the Matter, if any Man will undertake to shew me one professed Poet now in being, who is any thing of what may be justly called a *Scholar*, or is the worse *Poet* for that, but perhaps the better, for being so little encumbred with the Pedantry of Learning: 'Tis true, the contrary was the Opinion of our Forefathers, which we of this Age have *Devotion* enough to receive from them on their own Terms, and unexamin'd, but not *Sense* enough to perceive 'twas a gross Mistake in them. So *Horace* has told us.

> *Scribendi recte sapere est & principium et fons,*
> *Rem tibi Socraticae poterunt ostendere chartae.*

But to see the different casts of Mens Heads, some not inferiour to that Poet in Understanding (if you will take their own Word for it,) do see no Consequence in this Rule, and are not ashamed to declare themselves of a contrary Opinion. Do not many Men write well in common Account who have nothing of that Principle? Many are too *Wise* to be Poets, and others too much Poets to be *Wise*. Must a Man, forsooth, be no less than a Philosopher to be a Poet, when it is plain, that some of the greatest *Ideots* of the Age, are our prettiest Performers that way? And for this, I appeal to the Judgment and Observation of Mankind. Sir *Ph. Sidney*'s notable Remark upon this Nation, may not be improper to mention here. He says, *In our Neighbour-Country* Ireland, *where true Learning goes very bare, yet are their Poets held in devout Reverence*; which shews, that Learning is no way necessary either to the making a Poet, or judging of him. And further, to see the Fate of things notwithstanding our Learning here, is as bare as ever, yet are our Poets not held as formerly, in devout Reverence, but are, perhaps, the most contemptible Race of Mortals now in this Kingdom, which is less to be Wonder'd at, than Lamented.

Some of the old Philosophers were Poets (as according to the forementioned Author, *Socrates* and *Plato* were, which however, is what I did not know before) but that does not say, that all Poets are, or that any need be Philosophers, otherwise than as those are so call'd who are a little out at the Elbows. In which sense the great *SHAKESPEAR* might have been a Philosopher; but was no Scholar, yet was an excellent Poet. Neither do I think a late most judicious Critick so much mistaken, as others do, in advancing this Opinion, that *Shakespear had been a worse Poet had he been a better Scholar*: And Sir W^m. *Davenant* is another instance in the same kind. Nor must it be forgotten that *Plato* was an avow'd Enemy to Poets, which is perhaps the Reason why Poets have been always at Enmity with his Profession; and have rejected all Learning and Philosophy for the sake of that one Philosopher. As I take the matter, neither Philosophy, nor any part of Learning, is more necessary to *Poetry,* (which if you will believe the same Author is *the sum of all Learning*) than to know the Theory of Light, and the several Proportions and Diversifications of it in particular Colours is to a good Painter.

Whereas, therefore a certain Author, call'd *Petronius Arbiter*, going upon the same Mistake, has confidently declar'd, that one Ingredient of a good Poet, is, *Mens ingenti literarum flumine inundata*: I do on the contrary, declare that this his Assertion (to speak of it in the softest Terms) is no better than an invidious and unhandsome Reflection on all the *Gentlemen-Poets* of these Times; for with his good leave, much less than a Flood or Inundation will serve the Turn, and to my certain knowledge, some of our greatest Wits in your Poetical way, have not as much real Learning, as would cover a *Sixpence* in the bottom of a *Bason*; nor do I think the worse of them.

For to speak my private Opinion, I am for every Man's working upon his own Materials, and producing only what he can find within himself, which is commonly a better Stock than the owner knows it to be. I think Flowers of Wit ought to spring, as those in a Garden do, from their own Root and Stem, without Foreign Assistance. I would have a Man's Wit rather like a Fountain that feeds it self invisibly, than a River that is supply'd by several Streams from abroad.

Or if it be necessary, as the Case is with some barren Wits, to take in the Thoughts of others, in order to draw forth their own, as dry Pumps will not play till Water is thrown into them; in that Necessity, I would recommend some of the approv'd Standard-Authors of Antiquity for your Perusal, as a Poet and a Wit; because *Maggots* being what you look for, as *Monkeys* do for *Vermin* in their Keepers Heads, you will find they abound in good old Authors, as in rich old Cheese, not in the new; and for that Reason you must have the Classicks, especially the most *Worm-eaten* of them, often in your Hands.

But with this Caution, that you are not to use those Ancients as unlucky Lads do their old Fathers, and make no Conscience of picking their Pockets and pillaging them. Your Business is not to steal *from* them, but to improve *upon* them, and make their Sentiments your own; which is, an effect, of great Judgment, and tho' difficult, yet very possible, without the Scurvy Imputation of Filching: For I humbly conceive, tho' I light my Candle at my Neighbour's Fire, that does not alter the Property, or make the Wyck, the Wax, or the Flame, or the whole Candle, less my own.

Possibly you may think it a very severe Task, to arrive at a competent Knowledge of so many of the Ancients, as excel in their Way; and indeed it would be really so, but for the short and easie Method, lately found out, of Abstracts, Abridgments, and Summaries, &c. which are admirable Expedients for being very learned with little or no *Reading*, and have the same Use, with Burning-Glasses, to collect the diffus'd Rays of Wit and Learning in Authors, and make them point with Warmth and Quickness upon the Reader's Imagination. And to this is nearly related that other modern Device of consulting Indexes, which is to read Books *Hebraically*, and begin where others usually end; and this is a compendious Way of coming to an Acquaintance with Authors: for Authors are to be us'd like *Lobsters*, you must look for the best Meat in the *Tails*, and lay the *Bodies* back again in the Dish. Your cunningest *Thieves* (and what else are *Readers*, who only read to *borrow*, i.e. to *steal*) use to cut off the Portmanteau from behind, without staying to dive into the Pockets of the Owner. Lastly, you are taught thus much in the very Elements of Philosophy, for one of the first Rules in Logick is, *Finis est primus in intentione*.

The learned World is therefore most highly indebted to a late painful and judicious Editor of the Classicks, who has labour'd in that new Way with exceeding Felicity. Every Author by his Management, Sweats under himself, being over-loaded with his own *Index* and carrys, like a North-Country Pedlar, all his Substance and Furniture upon his Back, and with as great Variety of Trifles. To him let all young Students make their Compliments for so much Time and Pains sav'd in the Pursuit of useful Knowledge; for whoever shortens a Road is a Benefactor to the Publick, and to every particular Person who has Occasion to travel that Way.

But to proceed. I have lamented nothing more in my Time than the disuse of some ingenious *little Plays* in fashion, with young Folks, when I was a Boy, and to which the great Facility of that Age, above ours, in Composing was certainly owing; and if any thing has brought a Damp upon the Versification of these Times, we have no further than this to go for the Cause of it. Now could these Sports be happily reviv'd, I am of Opinion your wisest Course would be to apply your Thoughts to them, and never fail to make a Party when you can, in those profitable Diversions. For Example, *Crambo* is of extraordinary Use to good *Rhiming*, and Rhiming is what I have ever accounted the very Essential of a good Poet: And in that Notion I am not singular; for the aforesaid Sir *P. Sidney* has declar'd, that *the chief life of modern Versifying consisteth in the like sounding of Words, which we call Rhime*, which is an Authority, either without Exception, or above any Reply. Wherefore, you are ever to try a good Poem as you would a sound Pipkin, and if it rings well upon the Knuckle, be sure there is no Flaw

P

in it. Verse without Rhime, is Body without a Soul, (for the *chief life consisteth in the Rhime*) or a Bell without a Clapper; which, in Strictness, is no Bell, as being neither of Use nor Delight. And the same ever honoured Knight, with so musical an Ear, had that Veneration for the Tunableness and chiming of Verse, that he speaks of a Poet as one that has *the Reverend Title of a Rhimer*. Our celebrated *Milton* has done these Nations great Prejudice in this Particular, having spoil'd as many *reverend Rhimers* by his Example, as he has made *real Poets*.

For which Reason, I am overjoy'd to hear, that a very ingenious Youth of this Town is now upon the useful Design (for which he is never enough to be commended) of bestowing Rhime upon *Milton's Paradise-Lost*, which will make your Poem, in that only defective, more Heroick and Sonorous than it has hitherto been. I wish the Gentleman Success in the Performance, and, as it is a Work in which a young Man could not be more happily Employ'd, or appear in with greater advantage to his Character, so I am concern'd that it did not fall out to be your Province.

With much the same View, I would recommend to you the witty Play of *Pictures and Motto's*, which will furnish your Imagination with great store of *Images* and suitable *Devices*. We of these Kingdoms have found our account in this Diversion, as little as we Consider or Acknowledge it. For to this we owe our Eminent Felicity in Posies of Rings, Motto's of Snuff-Boxes, the Humours of Sign-Posts with their Elegant Inscriptions, &c. in which kind of Productions, not any Nation in the World, no, not the *Dutch* themselves, will presume to Rival us.

For much the same Reason, it may be proper for you to have some insight into the Play call'd, *What is it like*, as of great use in common Practice to quicken slow Capacities, and improve the quickest: But the chief End of it is, to supply the Fancy with variety of *Similes* for all Subjects. It will teach you to bring things to a likeness, which have not the least imaginable Conformity in Nature, which is properly Creation, and the very business of a *Poet*, as his Name implies; and let me tell you, a good

Poet can no more be without a stock of *Similes* by him, than a *Shoe-Maker* without his *Lasts*. He shou'd have them siz'd, and rang'd, and hung up in order in his Shop, ready for all Customers, and shap'd to the Feet of all sorts of Verse: And here I cou'd more fully (and I long to do it) insist upon the wonderful Harmony and Ressemblance, between a *Poet* and a *Shoe-Maker*, in many Circumstances common to both; such as the binding of their Temples, the Stuff they work upon, and the paring Knife they use, &c. but that I would not digress, nor seem to trifle in so serious a matter.

Now I say, if you apply your self, to these diminutive Sports (not to mention others of equal Ingenuity, such as *Draw-gloves, Cross-purposes, Questions and Commands,* and the rest) it is not to be conceived what Benefit (of Nature) you will find by them, and how they will open the body of your Invention. To these devote your Spare hours, or rather spare all your Hours to them, and then you will act as becomes a Wise Man, and make even Diversion an Improvement; like the inimitable management of the Bee, which does the whole business of Life at once, and at the same time both *Feeds*, and *Works*, and *Diverts* it self.

Your own Prudence will, I doubt not, direct you to take a place every Evening amongst the *Ingenious*, in the Corner of a certain *Coffee-House* in this Town, where you will receive a Turn equally right as to *Wit*, *Religion* and *Politicks*: As likewise to be as frequent at the Play-House, as you can afford, without selling your Books. For in our chast Theatre, even *CATO* himself might sit to the falling of the Curtain: Besides, you will sometimes meet with tolerable Conversation amongst the *Players*, they are such a kind of Men as may pass upon the same Sort of Capacities, for *Wits* off the *Stage*, as they do for fine Gentlemen upon it. Besides that, I have known a Factor deal in as good Ware, and sell as Cheap as the Merchant himself that Employs him.

Add to this, the Expediency of furnishing out your Shelves with a choice collection of Modern *Miscellanies,* in the gayest Edition; and of reading all sorts of Plays, especially the *New*, and above all, those of our own Growth, printed by Subscription, in which Article of *Irish Manufacture*, I readily agree to the late Proposal, and am altogether for *rejecting and renouncing every Thing that comes from* England: To what purpose shou'd we go thither either for *Coals* or *Poetry*, when we have a *Vein* within our selves equally Good and more Convenient. *Lastly,*

A *Common-place-book*, is what a provident Poet cannot subsist without, for this proverbial Reason, that *great Wits have short Memories*; and whereas, on the other hand, *Poets* being *LYARS* by Profession, ought to have good Memories; to reconcile these, a Book of this sort is in the nature of a Supplimental Memory; or a Record of what occurs remarkable in every Days Reading or Conversation: There you enter not only your own original Thoughts, (which a hundred to one, are *few* and *insignificant*) but such of other Men as you think fit to make your own by entring them there. For taking this for a Rule, when an Author is in your Books, you have the same demand upon him for his *Wit*, as a Merchant has for your *Money*, when you are in his.

By these few and easy Prescriptions (with the help of a good *Genius*) 'tis possible you may in a short time arrive at the Accomplishments of a *Poet*, and shine in that Character. As for your manner of Composing and choice of Subjects, I cannot take upon me to be your Director; but I will venture to give you some short Hints, which you may enlarge upon at your Leisure. Let me entreat you then, by no means to lay aside that Notion peculiar to our modern Refiners in *Poetry*, which is, that a *Poet* must never Write or Discourse as the ordinary part of Mankind do, but in Number and Verse, as an *Oracle*, which I mention the rather, because that upon this Principle, I have known Heroicks brought into the Pulpit, and a whole Sermon compos'd and deliver'd in Blank Verse, to the vast Credit of the Preacher, no less than the real Entertainment and great Edification of the Audience.

The Secret of which I take to be this. When the matter of such Discourses is but meer *Clay*, or, as we usually call it, *Sad stuff*, the Preacher, who can afford no better, wisely Molds, and Polishes, and Drys, and Washes this piece of *Earthen-Ware*, and then Bakes it with Poetick Fire, after which it will Ring like any *Pan-crock*, and is a good Dish to set before common Guests, as every Congregation is, that comes so often for Entertainment to one place.

There was a good old Custom in use which our Ancestors had of Invoking the Muses at the entrance of their Poems, I suppose by way of craving a Blessing: This the graceless *Moderns* have in a great measure laid aside, but are not to be followed in that Poetical *Impiety*; for altho' to nice Ears, such Invocations may sound Harsh and Disagreeable (as tuning Instruments is before a Consort) they are equally necessary. Again, You must not fail to dress your Muse in a Forehead-cloath of *Greek* or *Latin*, I mean, you are always to make use of a *quaint Motto* to call your Compositions; for besides that this Artifice bespeaks the Readers Opinion of the Writers Learning, it is otherwise Useful and Commendable. A bright Passage in the Front of a Poem is a good Mark, like a *Star* in a Horse's *Face*, and the Piece will certainly go off the better for it. The *Os magna sonaturum*, which, if I remember right, *Horace* makes one Qualification of a good Poet, may teach you not to Gag your Muse, or stint your Self in Words and Epithets (which cost you nothing) contrary to the practice of some few *out-of-the-way* Writers who use a natural and concise Expression, and affect a Stile like unto a *Shrewsbury-Cake*, *Short* and *Sweet* upon the Palat, they will not afford you a Word more than is necessary to make them intelligible, which is as poor and niggardly, as it would be to set down no more Meat than your Company will be sure to eat up. Words are but Lackies to sense, and will dance Attendance, without Wages or Compulsion. *Verba non invita sequentur.*

Furthermore, When you set about Composing, it may be necessary for your Ease and better *Distillation* of *Wit*, to put on your worst Cloaths, and the worse the better;

for an Author like a *Limbick* will yield the better for having a Rag about him: Besides that, I have observed a Gardiner cut the outward Rind of a Tree, (which is the *Surtout* of it,) to make it bear well: And this is a natural Account of the usual *Poverty* of *POETS*, and is an Argument why *Wits*, of all Men living, ought to be ill Clad. I have always a secret Veneration for any one I observe to be a little out of Repair in his Person, as supposing him either a *Poet* or a *Philosopher*, because the richest Minerals are ever found under the most ragged and withered Surface of Earth.

As for your choice of *Subjects*, I have only to give you this Caution; that as a handsome way of Praising is certainly the most difficult point in Writing or Speaking, I wou'd by no means advise any young Man to make his first Essay in *PANEGYRICK*, besides the danger of it; for a particular Encomium is ever attended with more ill Will, than any general Invective, for which I need give no Reasons; wherefore my Council is, that you use the Point of your *Pen*, not the *Feather*. Let your first Attempt be a *Coup d'Eclat* in the way of *Lible*, *Lampoon* or *Satyr*. Knock down half a score of Reputations, and you will infallibly raise your Own, and so it be with *Wit*, no matter with how little Justice; for Fiction is your Trade.

Every great Genius seems to ride upon Mankind, like *Pyrrhus* on his *Elephant*, and the way to have the absolute ascendant of your resty Nag, and to keep your Seat, is, at your first mounting, to afford him the Whip and Spurs plentifully, after which, you may travail the rest of the Day with great Alacrity. Once kick the World, and the World and you will live together at a reasonable good Understanding. You cannot but know that *these* of your *Profession* have been call'd *Genus irritabile vatum*, and you will find it necessary to qualify your self for that *waspish* Society, by exerting your Talent of *Satyr* upon the first Occasion, and to abandon good Nature, only to prove your self a true *Poet*, which you will allow to be a valuable Consideration: In a word, a young *Robber* is usually entred by a Murder. A young *Hound* is blooded when he comes first into the Field, a young *BULLY* begins with Killing, his Man: And a young *POET* must shew his *Wit* as the other his Courage, by Cutting and Slashing, and laying about Him, and banging Mankind. *Lastly*,

It will be your Wisdom to look out betimes for a good *Service* for your Muse, according to her Skill and Qualifications, whether in the nature of a *Dairy-Maid*, a *Cook*, or *Char-woman*: I mean to hire out your Pen, to a *Party* which will afford you both *Pay* and *Protection*; and when you have to do with the *Press*, (as you will long to be there) take care to bespeak an importunate Friend, to extort your *Productions* with an agreeable Violence; and which, according to the Cue between you, you must surrender *digito male pertinaci*: there is a Decency in this, for it no more becomes an Author in Modesty to have a hand in publishing his own Works, than a Woman in Labour to lay her self.

I wou'd be very loath to give the least umbrage of Offence by what I have here said, as I may do, if I should be thought to insinuate that these Circumstances of good Writing have been unknown to, or not observed by the *Poets* of this Kingdom. I will do my Countrymen the Justice to say, they have Written by the foregoing Rules with great exactness, and so far as hardly to come behind those of their Profession in *England*, in perfection of low Writing. The *Sublime*, indeed, is not so common with us, but ample amends is made for that want in the great abundance of the *Admirable* and *Amazing*, which appears in all our *Compositions*. Our very good Friend (the Knight aforesaid) speaking of the force of *Poetry*, mentions *Rhiming to death, which* (adds he) *is said to be done in* Ireland, and truly, to our Honour, be it spoken, that Power, in a great measure, continues with us to this Day.

I would now offer some poor Thoughts of mine for the Encouragement of *Poetry* in this Kingdom, if I could hope they would be agreeable. I have had many an aking Heart for the ill plight of that noble Profession here, and it has been my late and early Study how to bring it into better Circumstances. And surely, considering what *Monstrous*

WITS in the Poetick way, do almost daily start up and surprize us in this Town; what *prodigious* Genius's we have here (of which I cou'd give Instances without number;) and withal of what great benefit it might be to our Trade to encourage that Science here, (for it is plain our *Linnen-Manufacture* is advanced by the great Waste of *Paper* made by our present set of *Poets*, not to mention other necessary Uses of the same to *Shop-keepers*, especially *Grocers*, *Apothecarries*, and *Pastry-Cooks*; and I might add, but for our *Writers*, the Nation wou'd in a little time, be utterly destitute of *Bum-Fodder*, and must of Necessity import the same from *England* and *Holland*, where they have it in great abundance, by the undefatigable Labour of their own Wits,) I say, these things consider'd, I am humbly of Opinion, it wou'd be worth the Care of our Governours to cherish Gentlemen of the *Quill*, and give them all proper Encouragements here. And since I am upon the Subject, I shall speak my Mind very *freely*, and if I added *sawcily*, it is no more than my Birth-right as a *Briton*.

Seriously then, I have many Years lamented the want of a *Grub-street* in this our large and polite *City*, unless the whole may be called *one*. And this I have accounted an unpardonable Defect in our Constitution, ever since I had any Opinions I could call my own. Every one knows, *Grub-street* is a Market for *Small-Ware* in WIT, and as necessary considering the usual Purgings of *Human Brain*, as the *Nose* is upon a Man's *Face*: And for the same Reasons, we have here a *Court*, a *College*, a *Play-House*, and beautiful *Ladies*, and fine *Gentlemen*, and good *Claret*, and abundance of *Pens*, *Ink* and *Paper* (clear of Taxes) and every other Circumstance to provoke WIT, and yet those whose Province it is, have not yet thought fit to appoint a place for *Evacuations* of it, which is a very hard Case, as may be judg'd by Comparisons.

And truly this Defect has been attended with unspeakable Inconveniences; for not to mention the Prejudice done to the Common-wealth of *Letters*, I am of opinion we suffer in our Health by it: I believe our corrupted Air, and frequent thick *Fogs* are in a great measure owing to the common exposal of our *Wit*, and that with good Management, our Poetical *Vapours* might be carried off in a *common Drain*, and fall into one Quarter of the Town, without Infecting the whole, as the Case is at present, to the great Offence of our *Nobility*, and *Gentry*, and *Others* of nice *Noses*. When Writers of all sizes, like Freemen of the City, are at liberty to throw out their *Filth* and *Excrementious Productions* in every Street as they please, what can the Consequence be, but that the Town must be *Poyson'd* and become such an other *Jakes*, as by report of great Travellers, *EDINBOROUGH* is at Night, a thing well to be consider'd in these pestilent Times.

I am not of the Society for Reformation of Manners, but without that pragmatical Title, I would be glad to see some Amendment in the Matter before us; wherefore I humbly bespeak the Favour of the *Lord Mayor*, the *Court of Aldermen*, and the *Common Council*, together with the whole Circle of *Arts* in this Town, and do recommend this Affair to their most *Political* Consideration, and I perswade my self they will not be wanting in their best Endeavours, when they can serve two such good Ends at once, as both to keep the Town *Sweet*, and encourage *Poetry* in it. Neither do I make any Exceptions as to *Satyrical Poets*, and *Lampoon-Writers*, in Consideration of their Office: For tho' indeed, their Business is to rake into *Kennels*, and gather up the *Filth* of *Streets* and *Families*, (in which Respect, they may be, for ought I know, as necessary to the Town as *SCAVENGERS* or *CHIMNEY SWEEPS*) yet I have observed they too have themselves at the same Time very foul *Cloaths*, and like dirty *Persons* leave more *Filth* and *Nastiness*, than they sweep away.

In a Word, What I would be at (for I love to be plain in matters of Importance to my Country) is, That some *private Street*, or *blind Alley* of this Town may be fitted up at the charge of the Publick, as an Apartment for the *Muses*, (like those at *Rome*, and *Amsterdam*, for their Female Relations) and be wholly consign'd to the uses of our *WITS*, furnish'd compleatly with all Appurtenances, such as *Authors, Supervisors, Presses, Printers, Hawkers, Shops,* and *Ware-Houses,* and abundance of *Garrets,* and every other Impliment and Circumstance of *WIT*: The benefit of which would obviously be this, *viz*. That we should then have a safe *Repository* for our *BEST Productions,* which at present are handed about in *Single Sheets* or *Manuscripts,* and may be altogether lost, (which were a pity) or at best are subject in that loose Dress, like Handsome Women, to great Abuses.

Another Point that cost me some melancholly Reflections, is the present State of the *Play-House,* the Encouragement of which, hath an immediate Influence upon the *Poetry* of the Kingdom: As a good Market improves the Tillage of the Neighbouring Country and enriches the Plough-man, neither do we of this Town seem enough to know or consider the vast Benefit of a *Play-House* to our City and Nation: That *Single-House* is the Fountain of all our *Love, Wit, Dress* and *Gallantry*. It is the School of *Wisdom*; for there we learn to know *What's what,* which however, I cannot say, is always in that place *sound* Knowledge. There our young Folks drop their *Childish Mistakes,* and come first to perceive their Mothers cheat of the *Parsly-Bed*; there too they get rid of *Natural Prejudices,* especially those of *Religion* and *Modesty,* which are great Restraints to a *Free People*. The same is a Remedy for the *Spleen,* and *Blushing,* and several Distempers occasion'd by the Stagnation of the Blood. It is likewise a School of *Common Swearing*; my *young* Master who at first but *minc'd* an Oath, is Taught there to *mouth* it gracefully, and to Swear as he reads *French, ore rotundo*. Prophaneness was before to him in the nature of his best Suit, or *Holy-Day-Cloaths*; but upon frequenting the *Play-House, Swearing, Cursing,* and *Lying,* become like his *Every-day Coat, Waistcoat* and *Breeches*. Now I say, *Common Swearing,* a produce of this *Country,* as plentiful as our Corn, thus cultivated by the *Play-House,* might with Management be of wonderful Advantage to the Nation, as a Projector of the *Swearers Bank* has prov'd at large. *Lastly,* the *Stage* in great measure supports the *Pulpit*; for I know not what our Divines cou'd have to say there against the Corruptions of the Age, but for the *Play-House,* which is the Seminary of them. From which, it is plain, the Publick is a Gainer by the *Play-House,* and consequently ought to Countenance it; and were I worthy to put in my Word, or prescribe to my Betters, I could say in what manner.

I have heard, that a certain Gentleman has great Designs, to serve the Publick in the way of their Diversions, with due Encouragement, (that is) if he can obtain some *Concordatum-Money,* or *Yearly Sallery,* and handsome *Contributions*: And well he deserves the Favours of the Nation; for, to do him Justice, he has an uncommon Skill in Pastimes, having altogether apply'd his Studies that Way, and travell'd full many a League, by Sea and Land, for this his profound Knowledge. With that View alone he has visited all the Courts and Cities in *Europe,* and has been at more Pains than I shall speak of, to take an exact Draught of the *Play-House* at the *Hague,* as a Model for a new one here. But what can a private Man do by himself in so publick an Undertaking? It is not to be doubted, but by his Care and Industry vast Improvements may be made, not only in our *Play-House,* (which is his immediate Province) but in our *Gaming-Ordinaries, Groom-Porter's, Lotteries, Bowling-Greens, Nine-pin-Allies, Bear-Gardens, Cock-pits, Prizes, Puppet* and *Raree-Shews,* and whatever else concerns the elegant Divertisements of this Town. He is truly an *Original Genius,* and I felicitate this our Capital City on his Residence here, where I wish him long to live and flourish for the Good of the Common-wealth.

Once more, If any further Applications shall be made on t'other Side to obtain a Charter for a *Bank* here, I presume to make a Request, that *Poetry* may be a Sharer in that Privelege, being a Fund as real, and to the full as well grounded as our Stocks; but I fear our Neighbours, who envy our *Wit* as much as they do our *Wealth* or *Trade,* will give no Encouragement to either. I believe also, it might be proper to erect a *Corporation* of *Poets* in this

City. I have been idle enough in my time to make a
Computation of Wits here, and do find we have Three
hundred performing *Poets* and upwards, in and about this
Town, reckoning six Score to the Hundred, and allowing
for *Demi's*, like *Pint-Bottles*, including also the several
Denominations of *Imitators*, *Translators*, and *Familiar-
Letter-Writers*, &c. One of these last has lately entertain'd
the Town with an original Piece, and such a one, as I
dare say, the late *British Spectator*, in his *Decline*, would
have called *an excellent Specimen of the true Sublime*, or
a Noble Poem, or *a fine Copy of Verses on a Subject perfectly New*, (the Author himself) and had given it a Place
amongst his latest Lucubrations.

But as I was saying, so many *Poets*, I am confident, are
sufficient to furnish out a CORPORATION in point of
Number. Then, for the several Degrees of subordinate
Members requisite to such a Body, there can be no Want;
for altho' we have not one *Masterly Poet*, yet we abound
with *Wardens* and *Beadles*, having a Multitude of *Poetasters*, *Poetito's*, *Parcel-Poets*, *Poet-Apes*, and *Philo-Poets*,
and many of inferior Attainments in Wit, but strong
Inclinations to it, which are by odds more than all the
rest. Nor shall I ever be at ease, till this Project of mine
(for which I am heartily thankful to my self) shall be
reduced to Practice. I long to see the Day when our *Poets*
will be a regular and distinct Body, and wait upon our
Lord Mayor on Publick Days, like other good Citizens,
in Gowns turn'd up with Green instead of Lawrels, and
when I my self, who make this Proposal, shall be free of
their Company.

To conclude, What if our Government had a Poet
Laureat *here as in* England? What if our University had
a Professor of Poetry *here as in* England? What if our
Lord Mayor had a City-Bard *here as in* England? And to
refine upon *England*, What if every Corporation, Parish,
and Ward in this Town had a Poet in Fee, *as they have
NOT in* England? Lastly, What if every one *so qualify'd*
were obliged to add one more than usual to the Number
of his Domesticks, and besides a *Fool* and a *Chaplain*,

(which are often united in one Person) would retain a
Poet in his Family; for perhaps a Rhimer is as necessary
amongst Servants of a House, as a *Dobben*, with his Bells,
at the Head of a Team: But these things I leave to the
Wisdom of my Superiors.

While I have been directing your Pen, I should not
forget to govern my own, which has already exceeded the
Bounds of a Letter: I must therefore take my Leave
abruptly, and desire you, without further Ceremony, to
believe that I am, Sir,

Your most Humble Servant,

E. F.

December 1,
  1720.

A
LETTER
TO A
VERY
YOUNG
LADY

"THIS letter", says Lord Orrery, "ought to be read by all new-married women, and will be read with pleasure and advantage by the most distinguished and accomplished ladies." It is characteristic of Swift's curious conception of women that he presumed that the counsels he gives in this letter would be acceptable. "The reader", Dr Johnson pronounced, "may be allowed to doubt whether Swift's opinion of female excellence ought implicitly to be admitted, for, if his general thoughts on women were such as he exhibits, a very little sense in a lady would enrapture, and a very little virtue would astonish him." It might be argued that his own Stella enraptured and astonished him in this way.

There is some doubt about the identity of the lady addressed; the most likely recipient would seem to be Elizabeth, wife of George (Nimrod) Rochfort, a well-known Irish sportsman.

The letter was printed for the first time in the second volume of *Miscellanies in Prose and Verse*, 1727. No earlier or separate edition is known.

A LETTER TO
A VERY YOUNG LADY ON
HER MARRIAGE

MADAM,

THE hurry and impertinence of receiving and paying Visits on account of your Marriage, being now over, you are beginning to enter into a Course of Life, where you will want much Advice to divert you from falling into many Errors, Fopperies, and Follies to which your Sex is subject. I have always born an entire Friendship to your Father and Mother; and the Person they have chosen for your Husband, hath been for some Years past my particular Favorite; I have long wished you might come together, because I hoped, that from the goodness of your Disposition, and by following the Council of wise Friends, you might in time make your self worthy of him. Your Parents were so far in the right, that they did not produce you much into the World, whereby you avoided many wrong Steps which others have taken; and have fewer ill Impressions to be removed: But they failed, as it is generally the Case, in too much neglecting to cultivate your Mind; without which it is impossible to acquire or preserve the Friendship and Esteem of a Wise Man, who soon grows weary of acting the Lover and treating his Wife like a Mistress, but wants a reasonable Companion, and a true Friend through every Stage of his Life. It must be therefore your Business to qualify your self for those Offices, wherein I will not fail to be your Director as long as I shall think you deserve it, by letting you know how you are to act, and what you ought to avoid.

And beware of despising or neglecting my Instructions, whereon will depend, not only your making a good figure in the World, but your own real Happiness, as well as that of the Person who ought to be the Dearest to you.

I must therefore desire you in the first place to be very slow in changing the modest behaviour of a Virgin: It is usual in young wives before they have been many Weeks married, to assume a bold, forward Look and manner of Talking; as if they intended to signify in all Companies, that they were no longer Girls, and consequently that their whole Demeanor, before they got a Husband, was all but a Countenance and Constraint upon their Nature: Whereas, I suppose, if the Votes of wise Men were gathered, a very great Majority would be in favour of those Ladies, who after they were entered into that State, rather chose to double their portion of Modesty and Reservedness.

I must likewise warn you strictly against the least degree of Fondness to your Husband before any Witness whatsoever, even before your nearest Relations, or the very Maids of your Chamber. This proceeding is so exceeding odious and disgustful to all who have either good Breeding or good Sense, that they assign two very unamiable Reasons for it; the one is gross Hypocrisy, and the other has too bad a Name to mention. If there is any difference to be made, your Husband is the lowest Person in Company, either at Home or Abroad, and every Gentleman present has a better Claim to all marks of Civility and Distinction from you. Conceal your Esteem and Love in your own Breast, and reserve your kind Looks and Language for Private hours, which are so many in the Four and Twenty, that they will afford time to employ a Passion as exalted as any that was ever described in a *French* Romance.

Upon this Head, I should likewise advise you to differ in Practice from those Ladies who affect abundance of Uneasiness while their Husbands are abroad, start with every Knock at the Door, and ring the Bell incessantly for the Servants to let in their Master; will not eat a bit at Dinner or Supper if the Husband happens to stay out, and receive him at his return with such a Medly of chiding and kindness, and catechising him where he has been, that a Shrew from *Billingsgate* would be a more easy and eligible Companion.

Of the same leaven are those Wives, who when their

Husbands are gone a Journey, must have a Letter every
Post, upon pain of Fits and Hystericks, and a day must
be fixed for their return home without the least allowance
for Business, or Sickness, or Accidents, or Weather: Upon
which, I can only say that in my observation, those Ladies
who were apt to make the greatest clutter upon such occasions, would liberally have paid a Messenger for bringing
them news that their Husbands had broken their Necks on
the Road.

You will perhaps be offended when I advise you to
abate a little of that violent Passion for fine Cloaths, so
predominant in your Sex. It is a little hard, that ours, for
whose sake you wear them, are not admitted to be of your
Council: I may venture to assure you that we will make
an abatement at any time of Four Pounds a yard in a
Brocade, if the Ladies will but allow a suitable addition
of care in the Cleanliness and Sweetness of their Persons:
For, the satyrical part of mankind will needs believe, that
it is not impossible, to be very fine and very filthy; and
that the Capacities of a Lady are sometimes apt to fall
short in cultivating Cleanliness and Finery together. I
shall only add, upon so tender a subject, what a pleasant
Gentleman said concerning a silly Woman of quality;
that nothing could make her supportable but cutting off
her Head, for his Ears were offended by her Tongue, and
his Nose by her Hair and Teeth.

I am wholly at a loss how to advise you in the choice
of Company, which, however, is a point of as great importance as any in your life. If your general acquaintance be
among Ladies who are your equals or superiors, provided
they have nothing of what is commonly called an ill
Reputation, you think you are safe; and this in the style
of the world will pass for Good company. Whereas I am
afraid it will be hard for you to pick out one Female-
acquaintance in this town, from whom you will not be in
manifest danger of contracting some foppery, affectation,
vanity, folly, or vice. Your only safe way of conversing
with them, is by a firm Resolution to proceed in your
practice and behaviour directly contrary to whatever they

shall say or do: And this I take to be a good General Rule, with very few exceptions. For instance, In the doctrines they usually deliver to young-married-women for managing their Husbands; their several accounts of their own Conduct in that particular to recommend it to your imitation; the Reflections they make upon others of their Sex for acting differently; their directions how to come off with Victory upon any dispute or quarrel you may have with your husband; the Arts by which you may discover and practice upon his Weak sides; when to work by flattery and insinuation, when to melt him with tears, and when to engage with a high hand. In these, and a thousand other cases, it will be prudent to retain as many of their lectures in your Memory as you can, and then determine to act in full Opposition to them all.

I hope your Husband will interpose his authority to limit you in the trade of Visiting: Half a dozen fools are in all conscience as many as you should require; and it will be sufficient for you to see them twice a year: For I think the fashion does not exact, that Visits should be paid to Friends.

I advise that your company at home should consist of Men, rather than Women. To say the truth, I never yet knew a tolerable Woman to be fond of her own Sex: I confess, when both are mixt and well chosen, and put their best qualities forward, there may be an intercourse of civility and good-will; which, with the addition of some degree of sense, can make conversation or any amusement agreeable. But a Knot of Ladies, got together by themselves, is a very school of Impertinence and Detraction, and it is well if those be the worst.

Let your Men-acquaintance be of your Husband's choice, and not recommended to you by any She-companions; because they will certainly fix a Coxcomb upon you, and it will cost you some time and pains before you can arrive at the knowledge of distinguishing such a one from a Man of Sense.

Never take a Favourite-waiting-maid into your Cabinet-Council, to entertain you with Histories of those Ladies whom she hath formerly served, of their Diversions and their Dresses; to insinuate how great a Fortune you brought, and how little you are allowed to squander; to appeal to her from your Husband, and to be determined by her Judgment, because you are sure it will be always for you; to receive and discard Servants by her approbation or dislike; to engage you by her insinuations into misunderstandings with your best Friends; to represent all things in false colours, and to be the common Emissary of Scandal.

But the Grand affair of your life will be to gain and preserve the Friendship and Esteem of your Husband. You are married to a Man of good education and learning, of an excellent understanding, and an exact taste. It is true, and it is happy for you, that these Qualities in him are adorned with great Modesty, a most amiable Sweetness of Temper, and an unusual disposition to Sobriety and Virtue: But neither Good-Nature nor Virtue will suffer him to esteem you against his Judgment; and although he is not capable of using you ill, yet you will in time grow a thing indifferent, and perhaps, contemptible; unless you can supply the loss of Youth and Beauty with more durable Qualities. You have but a very few years to be young and handsome in the eyes of the World; and as few months to be so in the eyes of a Husband, who is not a Fool; for I hope you do not still dream of Charms and Raptures, which Marriage ever did, and ever will, put a sudden end to. Besides yours was a match of Prudence and common Good-liking, without any mixture of that ridiculous Passion which has no Being but in Play-Books and Romances.

You must therefore use all endeavours to attain to some degree of those Accomplishments which your Husband most values in other People, and for which he is most valued himself. You must improve your Mind, by closely pursuing such a Method of Study as I shall direct or approve of. You must get a collection of History and Travels which I will recommend to you, and spend some hours every day in reading them, and making extracts from them if your Memory be weak. You must invite Persons of knowledge and understanding to an acquaintance with you, by whose Conversation you may learn to correct your Taste and Judgment; and when you can bring yourself to comprehend and relish the good Sense of others, you will arrive in time to think rightly yourself, and to become a Reasonable and Agreeable Companion. This must produce in your Husband a true Rational Love and Esteem for you, which old Age will not diminish. He will have a regard for your Judgment and Opinion in matters of the greatest weight; you will be able to entertain each other without a Third Person to relieve you by finding Discourse. The endowments of your Mind will even make your Person more agreeable to him; and when you are alone, your Time will not lie heavy upon your hands for want of some trifling Amusement.

As little respect as I have for the generality of your Sex, it hath sometimes moved me with pity, to see the Lady of the House forced to withdraw immediately after Dinner, and this in Families where there is not much drinking; as if it were an established Maxim, that Women are uncapable of all Conversation. In a Room where both Sexes meet, if the Men are discoursing upon any general Subject, the Ladies never think it their business to partake in what passes, but in a separate Club entertain each other, with the price and choice of Lace and Silk, and what Dresses they liked or disapproved at the Church or the Play-house. And when you are among yourselves, how naturally, after the first Complements, do you apply your hands to each others Lappets and Ruffles and Mantua's, as if the whole business of your Lives, and the publick concern of the World, depended upon the Cut or Colour of your Dresses. As Divines say, that some People take more pains to be Damned, than it would cost them to be Saved; so your Sex employs more thought, memory, and application to be Fools, than would serve to make them wise and useful. When I reflect on this, I cannot conceive you to be Human Creatures, but a sort of Species hardly a degree above a Monkey; who has more diverting Tricks than any of you; is an Animal less mischievous and expensive, might in time be a tolerable Critick in Velvet and Brocade, and for ought I know wou'd equally become them.

I would have you look upon Finery as a necessary Folly, as all great Ladies did whom I have ever known: I do not desire you to be out of the fashion, but to be the last and least in it: I expect that your Dress shall be one degree lower than your Fortune can afford; and in your own heart I would wish you to be an utter Contemner of all Distinctions which a finer Petticoat can give you; because it will neither make you richer, handsomer, younger, better natur'd, more vertuous, or wise, than if it hung upon a Peg.

If you are in company with Men of learning, though they happen to discourse of Arts and Sciences out of your compass, yet you will gather more advantage by list'ning to them, than from all the nonsense and frippery of your own Sex; but, if they be Men of Breeding as well as Learning, they will seldom engage in any Conversation where you ought not to be a hearer, and in time have your part. If they talk of the Manners and Customs of the several Kingdoms of *Europe*, of Travels into remote Nations, of the state of their own Country, or of the great Men and Actions of *Greece* and *Rome*; if they give their judgment upon *English* and *French* Writers, either in Verse or Prose, or of the nature and limits of Virtue and Vice, it is a shame for an *English* Lady not to relish such Discourses, not to improve by them, and endeavour by Reading and Information, to have her share in those Entertainments; rather than turn aside, as it is the usual custom, and consult with the Woman who sits next her, about a new Cargo of Fans.

It is a little hard that not one Gentleman's daughter in a thousand should be brought to read or understand her own natural tongue, or be judge of the easiest Books that are written in it: As any one may find, who can have the patience to hear them, when they are disposed to mangle a Play or Novel, where the least word out of the common road is sure to disconcert them; and it is no wonder, when they are not so much as taught to spell in their childhood, nor can ever attain to it in their whole lives. I advise you therefore to read aloud, more or less, every day to your Husband, if he will permit you, or to any other friend, (but not a Female one) who is able to set you right; and as for spelling, you may compass it in time by making Collections from the Books you read.

I know very well that those who are commonly called Learned Women, have lost all manner of Credit by their impertinent Talkativeness and Conceit of themselves; but there is an easy remedy for this, if you once consider, that after all the pains you may be at, you never can arrive in point of learning to the perfection of a School-boy. But the Reading I would advise you to, is only for improvement of your own good Sense, which will never fail of being Mended by Discretion. It is a wrong method, and ill choice of Books, that makes those Learned Ladies just so much worse for what they have read. And therefore it shall be my care to direct you better, a task for which I take my self to be not ill qualified; because I have spent more time, and have had more opportunities than many others, to observe and discover from what sources the various follies of Women are derived.

Pray observe how insignificant things are the common race of Ladies, when they have passed their Youth and Beauty; how contemptible they appear to the Men, and yet more contemptible to the younger part of their own Sex; and have no relief but in passing their afternoons in visits, where they are never acceptable; and their evenings at cards among each other; while the former part of the day is spent in spleen and envy, or in vain endeavours to repair by art and dress the ruins of Time: Whereas I have known Ladies at Sixty, to whom all the polite part of the Court and Town paid their addresses, without any further view than that of enjoying the pleasure of their conversation.

I am ignorant of any one quality that is amiable in a Man, which is not equally so in a Woman: I do not except even Modesty and Gentleness of nature. Nor do I know one vice or folly which is not equally detestable in both.

There is indeed one infirmity which seems to be generally allowed you, I mean that of Cowardice. Yet there should seem to be something very capricious, that when Women profess their admiration for a Colonel or a Captain on account of his Valour, they should fancy it a very graceful becoming quality in themselves to be afraid of their own shadows; to scream in a Barge when the weather is calmest, or in a Coach at the Ring; to run from a Cow at a hundred yards distance; to fall into fits at the sight of a Spider, an Earwig, or a Frog. At least, if Cowardice be a sign of Cruelty, (as it is generally granted) I can hardly think it an accomplishment so desirable as to be thought worth improving by Affectation.

And as the same Virtues equally become both Sexes, so there is no quality whereby Women endeavour to distinguish themselves from Men, for which they are not just so much the worse; except that only of Reservedness; which however, as you generally manage it, is nothing else but Affectation or Hypocrisy. For as you cannot too much discountenance those of our Sex, who presume to take unbecoming Liberties before you; so you ought to be wholly unconstrain'd in the Company of Deserving Men, when you have had sufficient experience of their Discretion.

There is never wanting in this Town, a tribe of bold, swaggering, rattling Ladies, whose Talents pass among Coxcombs for Wit and Humour; their excellency lies in rude choquing Expressions, and what they call *running a Man down*. If a Gentleman in their Company happens to have any Blemish in his Birth or Person, if any misfortune hath befallen his Family or himself, for which he is ashamed, they will be sure to give him broad Hints of it without any Provocation. I would recommend you to the acquaintance of a common Prostitute, rather than to that of such Termagants as these. I have often thought that no Man is obliged to suppose such Creatures to be Women; but to treat them like insolent Rascals disguised in Female Habits, who ought to be stripp'd and kick'd down stairs.

I will add one thing although it be a little out of place, which is to desire that you will learn to value and esteem your Husband for those good Qualities which he really possesseth, and not to fancy others in him which he certainly hath not. For although this latter is generally understood to be a mark of Love, yet it is indeed nothing but Affectation or ill Judgment. It is true, he wants so very few Accomplishments, that you are in no great danger of erring on this side: But my Caution is occasion'd by a Lady of your Acquaintance, married to a very valuable Person, whom yet she is so unfortunate as to be always commending for those Perfections to which he can least pretend.

I can give you no Advice upon the Article of Expence, only I think you ought to be well informed how much your Husband's Revenue amounts to, and be so good a Computer as to keep within it, in that part of the Management which falls to your share; and not to put yourself in the number of those Politick Ladies, who think they gain a great Point when they have teazed their Husbands to buy them a new Equipage, a lac'd Head, or a fine Petticoat, without once considering what long Scores remain unpaid to the Butcher.

I desire you will keep this Letter in your Cabinet, and often examine impartially your whole Conduct by it: And so God bless you, and make you a fair Example to your Sex, and a perpetual Comfort to your Husband and your Parents.

I am, with great Truth and Affection,

Madam,

>*Your most faithful Friend*
>*and humble Servant.*

A
MEDITATION
UPON A
BROOM-STICK

THOUGHTS
ON VARIOUS
SUBJECTS

RESOLUTIONS

A Meditation upon a Broom-Stick is said to have been composed in 1704 and was probably in print before the end of 1708 [*v.* Henley to Swift, Nov. 2, 1708], though the earliest edition known is dated 1710. The frivolous circumstances in which it came to be written are well known. Swift, while chaplain to Lord Berkeley, grew weary of reading aloud to his lady extracts from " the heavenly meditations " of her favourite author Robert Boyle. One day he substituted this " most solemn waggery ", and under cover of a copy of Boyle's works read it, says Tom Sheridan, " with an inflexible gravity of countenance " and " in the same solemn tone he had used in delivering " the original. Lady Berkeley was enraptured, though not, it seems, as mortified as one would expect when the fraud was revealed. According to Sheridan, she had the good sense to laugh at herself, exclaiming: " What a vile trick that rogue played me. But it is his way, he never balks his humour in any thing ". Swift, at this time, was enjoying the happiest days of his life.

" Mr Pope and Dean Swift ", we are told, " being in the country together, had occasion to observe, that if men of contemplative turns were to take notice of the thoughts which suddenly present themselves to their minds, as they were walking in the fields &c, they might find many, perhaps, as well worth preserving, as some of their more deliberate reflexions. They accordingly agreed to write down such involuntary thoughts." Swift, however, had already published a selection of these moral and diverting *obiter dicta*, before he knew Pope, in the volume of *Miscellanies*, 1711. This passage must evidently refer to a new selection, which Swift sent Pope for their joint volumes of *Miscellanies* printed in 1727. Swift's *Thoughts* were collected by Faulkner in the first volume of his *Works*, 1735. Some additional *Thoughts* were printed after Swift's death by Faulkner and Hawksworth in Volume 8 [1746] and Volume 6 [4to. 1755] respectively of their collected editions of Swift's works.

Thoughts on Religion were first printed in Swift's collected works, Volume 8, i. 4to. 1765. Ed. Deane Swift.

Resolutions when I come to be Old, written while Swift was still a young man, were printed for the first time posthumously in the same volume of his collected works as *Thoughts on Religion*. They are reprinted here from the copy, now in the Forster collection, in Swift's handwriting, which was found among his papers after his death by his cousin Mrs Whiteway.

A
MEDITATION
upon a
BROOM-STICK

THIS single Stick, which you now behold Ingloriously lying in that neglected Corner, I once knew in a Flourishing State in A Forest, it was full of Sap, full of Leaves, and full of Boughs; but now, in vain does the busie Art of Man pretend to Vye with Nature, by tying that wither'd Bundle of Twigs to its sapless Trunk; 'tis now at best but the Reverse of what it was, a Tree turn'd upside down, the Branches on the Earth, and the Root in the Air; 'tis now handled by every Dirty Wench, condemn'd to do her Drudgery, and by a Capricious kind of Fate, destin'd to make other Things Clean, and be Nasty it self: At Length, worn to the Stumps in the Service of the Maids, 'tis either thrown out of Doors, or condemn'd to its last use of kindling Fires. When I beheld this, I sigh'd, and said within my self, Surely Man is a Broom-Stick; Nature sent him into the World Strong and Lusty, in a Thriving Condition, wearing his own Hair on his Head, the proper Branches of this Reasoning Vegetable, till the Axe of Intemperance has lopt off his Green Boughs, and left him a wither'd Trunk: He then flies unto Art, and puts on a *Peruque*, valuing himself upon an Unnatural Bundle of Hairs, all cover'd with Powder that never grew on his Head; but now should this our *Broom-Stick* pretend to enter the Scene, proud of those *Birchen* Spoils it never bore, and all cover'd with Dust, tho' the Sweepings of the Finest Lady's Chamber, we should be apt to Ridicule and Despise its Vanity, Partial Judges that we are! of our own Excellencies, and other Men's Faults.

But a *Broom-stick*, perhaps you'll say, is an Emblem of a Tree standing on its Head; and pray what is Man, but a Topsy-turvy Creature, his Animal Faculties perpetually a-Cock-Horse and Rational; His Head where his Heels should be; groveling on the Earth, and yet with all his Faults, he sets up to be an universal Reformer and Corrector of Abuses, a Remover of Grievances, rakes into every Slut's Corner of Nature, bringing hidden Corruptions to the Light, and raises a mighty Dust where there was none before, sharing deeply all the while, in the very same Pollutions he pretends to sweep away: His last Days are spent in Slavery to Women, and generally the least deserving; 'till worn to the Stumps, like his Brother *Bezom*, he's either kickt out of Doors, or made use of to kindle Flames, for others to warm Themselves by.

THOUGHTS ON VARIOUS SUBJECTS

1

WE have just enough Religion to make us hate, but not enough to make us love one another.

2

Reflect on Things past, as Wars, Negotiations, Factions, &c. We enter so little into those Interests, that we wonder how Men could possibly be so busy and concerned for things so Transitory; look on the present Times, we find the same Humor, yet wonder not at all.

3

How is it possible to expect that Mankind will take Advice, when they will not so much as take Warning.

4

I forget whether Advice be among the lost Things which *Ariosto* says are to be found in the Moon; that and Time ought to have been there.

5

No Preacher is listned to but Time, which gives us the same Train and Turn of Thought that elder People have tried in vain to put into our Heads before.

6

In a *Glass-House*, the Workmen often fling in a small quantity of fresh Coals, which seems to disturb the Fire, but very much enlivens it. This seems to allude to a gentle stirring of the Passions that the Mind may not languish.

7

Religion seems to have grown an Infant with Age, and requires miracles to nurse it, as it had in its Infancy.

8

All Fits of Pleasure are ballanced by an equal degree of Pain or Languor; 'tis like Spending this Year, part of the next Years Revenue.

9

When a true Genius appears in the World, you may know him by this Sign, that the Dunces are all in Confederacy against him.

10

'Tis grown a Word of Course for Writers to say, This Critical Age, as Divines say, This Sinful Age.

11

'Tis pleasant to observe how free the Present Age is in laying Taxes on the Next. *Future Ages shall talk of this; This shall be famous to all Posterity;* whereas their Time and Thoughts will be taken up about present Things, as ours are now.

12

There are but Three ways for a Man to revenge himself of the Censure of the World, to despise it, to return the like, or to endeavour to Live so as to avoid it. The First of these is usually pretended, the Last is almost impossible, the universal Practice is for the Second.

13

Herodotus tells us, that in Cold Countries Beasts very seldom have Horns, but in Hot they have very large ones. This might bear a pleasant Application.

14

If a Man would register all his Opinions upon Love, Politicks, Religion, Learning &c. beginning from his Youth, and so go on to Old Age, what a Bundle of Inconsistencies and Contradictions would appear at last.

15

What they do in Heaven, we are ignorant of; what they do not, we are told expresly, That they neither Marry, nor are given in Marriage.

16

Physicians ought not to give their Judgment of Religion, for the same Reason that Butchers are not admitted to be Jurors upon Life and Death.

17

The Reason why so few Marriages are Happy, is because Young Ladies spend their Time in making Nets, not in making Cages.

18

Ambition often puts Men upon doing the meanest Offices; so Climbing is performed in the same Posture with Creeping.

19

Ill Company is like a Dog, who Dirts those most whom he Loves best.

20

Censure is the Tax a Man pays to the Publick for being eminent.

21

Although Men are accus'd for not knowing their own Weakness, yet perhaps as few know their own Strength. It is in Men as in Soils, where sometimes there is a Vein of Gold, which the Owner knows not of.

22

Satyr is reckon'd the easiest of all Wit; but I take it to be otherwise in very bad Times: For it is as hard to satyrize well a Man of distinguish'd Vices, as to praise well a Man of distinguish'd Virtues. It is easy enough to do either to People of moderate Characters.

23

Invention is the Talent of Youth, and Judgment of Age; so that our Judgment grows harder to please, when we have fewer Things to offer it: This goes through the whole Commerce of Life. When we are old, our Friends find it difficult to please us, and are less concern'd whether we be pleas'd or no.

24

No wise Man ever wished to be younger.

25

The Motives of the best Actions will not bear too strict an Enquiry. It is allow'd, that the Cause of most Actions, good or bad, may be resolved into the Love of ourselves: But the Self-Love of some Men inclines them to please others; and the Self-Love of others is wholly employ'd in pleasing themselves. This makes the great Distinction between Virtue and Vice. Religion is the best Motive of all Actions, yet Religion is allow'd to be the highest Instance of Self-Love.

26

When the World has once begun to use us ill, it afterwards continues the same Treatment with less Scruple or Ceremony, as Men do to a Whore.

27

Complaint is the largest Tribute Heaven receives, and the sincerest Part of our Devotion.

28

The common Fluency of Speech in many men, and most Women, is owing to a Scarcity of Matter, and Scarcity of Words; for whoever is a Master of Language, and hath a Mind full of Ideas, will be apt in speaking to hesitate upon the Choice of both; whereas common Speakers have only one Set of Ideas, and one Set of Words to cloath them in; and these are always ready at the Mouth: So People come faster out of a Church when it is almost empty, than when a Crowd is at the Door.

29

Every Man desires to live long; but no Man would be old.

30

Love of Flattery in most Men proceeds from the mean Opinion they have of themselves; in Women from the contrary.

31

Venus, a beautiful good-natur'd Lady, was the Goddess of Love; *Juno*, a terrible Shrew, the Goddess of Marriage; and they were always mortal Enemies.

32

A very little Wit is valued in a Woman, as we are pleas'd with a few Words spoken plain by a Parrot.

33

Old Men and Comets have been reverenc'd for the same

Reason; their long Beards, and Pretences to foretel Events.

34

There is a Story in *Pausanias* of a Plot for betraying of a City discover'd by the Braying of an *Ass*: The Cackling of *Geese* sav'd the *Capitol*; and *Cataline's* Conspiracy was discover'd by a *Whore*. These are the only three Animals, as far as I remember, famous in History for *Evidences* and *Informers*.

35

Most Sorts of Diversion in Men, Children, and other Animals, are an Imitation of Fighting.

36

Augustus meeting an *Ass* with a *lucky Name*, foretold himself good Fortune. I meet many Asses, but none of them have lucky Names.

37

That was excellently observ'd, say I, when I read a Passage in an Author, where his Opinion agrees with mine. When we differ, there I pronounce him to be *mistaken*.

38

As universal a Practice as Lying is, and as easy a one as it seems, I do not remember to have heard three good Lyes in all my Conversation, even from those who were most celebrated in that Faculty.

39

Men are content to be laughed at for their Wit, but not for their Folly.

40

Query, Whether Churches are not Dormitories of the Living as well as the Dead?

41

Sometimes I read a Book with Pleasure, and detest the Author.

42

I never wonder to see Men wicked, but I often wonder to see them not ashamed.

43

Eloquence smooth and cutting is like a Razor whetted with Oil.

44

Jealousy like Fire may shrivel up Horns, but it makes them stink.

45

When a Man pretends Love, but courts for Money, he is like a Juggler, who conjureth away your Shilling, and conveyeth something very undecent under the Hat.

46

Vision is the Art of seeing Things invisible.

47

Whoever live at a different End of the Town from me, I look upon as Persons out of the World, and only myself and the Scene about me to be in it.

48

Since the union of divinity and humanity is the great article of our religion, it is odd to see some clergymen in their writings of divinity wholly devoid of humanity.

49

The death of a private man is generally of so little importance to the world, that it cannot be a thing of great importance in itself; and yet I do not observe from the practice of mankind, that either philosophy or nature have sufficiently armed us against the fears which attend it. Neither do I find any thing able to reconcile us to it, but extreme pain, shame, or despair; for poverty, imprisonment, ill fortune, grief, sickness, and old age, do generally fail.

THOUGHTS ON RELIGION

1

I AM in all opinions to believe according to my own impartial reason; which I am bound to inform and improve,
as far as my capacity and opportunities will permit.

2

It may be prudent in me to act sometimes by other mens
reason, but I can think only by my own.

3

If another man's reason fully convinceth me, it becomes
my own reason.

4

To say a man is bound to believe, is neither true nor sense.

5

You may force men, by interest or punishment, to say or
swear they believe, and to act as if they believed: You
can go no further.

6

Every man, as a member of the common wealth, ought
to be content with the possession of his own opinion in
private, without perplexing his neighbour or disturbing
the public.

7

Violent zeal for truth hath an hundred to one odds to be
either petulancy, ambition, or pride.

8

The want of belief is a defect that ought to be concealed
when it cannot be overcome.

9

God's mercy is over all his works, but divines of all sorts lessen that mercy too much.

10

I look upon myself, in the capacity of a clergyman, to be one appointed by Providence for defending a post assigned me, and for gaining over as many enemies as I can. Although I think my cause is just, yet one great motion is my submitting to the pleasure of Providence, and to the laws of my country.

11

I am not answerable to God for the doubts that arise in my own breast, since they are the consequence of that reason which he hath planted in me, if I take care to conceal those doubts from others, if I use my best endeavours to subdue them, and if they have no influence on the conduct of my life.

12

I never saw, heard, nor read, that the clergy were beloved in any nation where Christianity was the religion of the country. Nothing can render them popular but some degree of persecution.

13

Those fine gentlemen who affect the humour of railing at the clergy, are, I think, bound in honour to turn parsons themselves, and shew us better examples.

14

It is impossible that anything so natural, so necessary, and so universal as death, should ever have been designed by providence as an evil to mankind.

15

Although reason were intended by providence to govern our passions, yet it seems that, in two points of the greatest moment to the being and continuance of the world, God hath intended our passions to prevail over reason. The first is, the propagation of our species, since no wise man ever married from the dictates of reason. The other is, the love of life, which, from the dictates of reason, every man would despise, and wish it at an end, or that it never had a beginning.

RESOLUTIONS WHEN I COME TO BE OLD

WHEN I COME TO BE OLD
1699

Not to marry a young Woman.

Not to keep young Company unless they reely desire it.

Not to be peevish or morose, or suspicious.

Not to scorn present Ways, or Wits, or Fashions, or Men, or War, &c.

Not to be fond of Children, or let them come near me hardly.

Not to tell the same Story over and over to the same People.

Not to be covetous.

Not to neglect decency, or cleenlyness, for fear of falling into Nastyness.

Not to be over severe with young People, but give Allowances for their youthfull follyes, and Weeknesses.

Not to be influenced by, or give ear to knavish tatling servants, or others.

Not to be too free of advise nor trouble any but those that desire it.

To desire some good Friends to inform me wch of these Resolutions I break, or neglect, & wherein; and reform accordingly.

Not to talk much, nor of my self.

Not to boast of my former beauty, or strength, or favor with Ladyes, &c.

Not to hearken to Flatteryes, nor conceive I can be beloved by a young woman. et eos qui hereditatem captant odisse ac vitare.

Not to be positive or opiniatre.

Not to sett up for observing all these Rules, for fear I should observe none.

IRISH
TRACTS

" THE tracts which follow ", to borrow Scott's words, " are a bright record of the unceasing zeal with which Swift continued, through successive years, and indeed until the total decay of his mental powers, to watch over the interests of Ireland—to warn his countrymen of their errors, to laugh them out of their follies, to vindicate their rights against the aggressions of their powerful neighbours; and to be, in the expressive language of Scripture, ' the man set for their watchman, to blow the trumpet and warn the people '."

The earliest of Swift's appeals to the people of Ireland was published in Dublin in 1720, with the title: *A Proposal for the Universal Use of Irish Manufacture, in Cloaths and Furniture of Houses* &c. *Utterly Rejecting and Renouncing Every Thing wearable that comes from England.* This was followed, four years later, by the so-called *Drapier's Letters*, written by Swift in the character of M.B., a linen-draper, to persuade the Irish of the villainy of a scheme, promoted by an English ironmonger named Wood, to coin copper pence and halfpence for circulation in Ireland. The story of how Wood procured the patent for this job is involved, but it is certain that he paid the Duchess of Kendal, the King's mistress, a considerable sum for the privilege. Although Swift's conclusions were frequently drawn from false premisses and Wood's turpitude and intentions exaggerated and misconstrued, the letters, of which the first and the fourth are reprinted here, had an instantaneous and prodigious success. Their publication—particularly that of the fourth letter—was an event of unprecedented importance in the history of Irish nationalism. The whole country, wearied of a foreign yoke, rallied to the support of the draper, and public opinion triumphed over authority, which offered, in vain, rewards for his arrest. The outcry against Wood's coinage produced, besides these letters, innumerable pamphlets and poems, by Swift or inspired by him, not to mention a Drapers Club, which arranged for the publication in 1725 of a volume of collected letters and other pieces. [*v. note* p. 868.]

LORD WHARTON, the subject of "this damned libellous pamphlet", was Viceroy of Ireland, 1708–1710, under the Whig administration of Godolphin. Swift, it should be noted, was an honorary chaplain during his viceroyalty. The pamphlet is dated August 10, 1710, but Elrington Ball [*Correspondence*, I,

188, 233] is probably correct in suggesting that it was written before this date as part of an agreed Tory policy. It is difficult otherwise to explain the violence of Swift's attack on a man, who had perhaps let him down in the matter of the remission of the First Fruits of the Irish Church, and whose private life was certainly not above reproach, but who scarcely merited such a savage castigation. Its bitterness, one cannot help feeling, was due, in part, to disappointed ambition. The pamphlet seems to have been printed privately [i.e. piratically: *v. Journal to Stella.* Dec. 8, 1710] but no edition earlier than the three published by W. Coryton in 1711 has been discovered.

A Short View of Ireland, published in Dublin early in 1728, was reprinted in *The Intelligencer* [No. XV. 1728], according to Sheridan, who contributed a short preface, " merely to save the labour of writing a paper ". It is of particular interest as one of the very rare occasions on which Swift's customary irony broke down under the pressure of savage indignation. It is said to have been reprinted by Nathaniel Mist, " by which his staff got into trouble ". I have not seen a copy of this edition, which is unrecorded by Spencer Jackson.

A Modest Proposal &c., Swift's most sustained piece of irony in prose, was first published in October 1729, and ran through several editions in Dublin and London. It was reprinted in *Miscellanies, the Third* [Fourth] *Volume,* 1732, which Swift, according to Matthew Pilkington, corrected for the press.

An Examination of Certain Abuses &c. was printed in London in the same year [1732] as the Dublin edition, with the title: *City Cries, Vocal and Instrumental, Or An Examination of Certain Abuses* &c.

The lively yet withering piece of irony entitled *A Serious and Useful Scheme to make an Hospital for Incurables,* was first printed anonymously, together with *A Petition of the Footmen in and about Dublin,* in 1733. It was not however included among Swift's collected works until 1814 [*Works.* Ed. Scott. Vol. IX.]. Nichols, Scott's predecessor, had placed it in his " List of spurious productions ". The reason for his having done so is obscure, unless, as Scott conjectures, " it might be interpreted as casting a slur on an hospital erected upon Lazars-hill . . . near Dublin for the reception of persons afflicted with incurable maladies ". Following the London edition, upon which the present text is based, Faulkner printed two others in Dublin in the same year, and in one of these Swift is described as the author on the title-page. Quite apart from internal evidence, this attribution, which Faulkner, of all Swift's publishers, is least likely to have invented, is almost certainly correct. It is confirmed, moreover, by an important preliminary advertisement, in the second Dublin edition, of Faulkner's proposal to publish Swift's collected works.

THE DRAPIER'S FIRST
LETTER

To the Tradesmen, Shop-Keepers, Farmers, and Common People in General, of the King-dom of Ireland.

Brethren, Friends, Countrymen and *Fellow Subjects,*

WHAT I intend now to say to you, is, next to your Duty to God, and the Care of your Salvation, of the greatest Concern to your selves, and your Children, your *Bread* and *Cloathing,* and every common Necessary of Life entirely depend upon it. Therefore I do most earnestly exhort you as *Men,* as *Christians,* as *Parents,* and as *Lovers of your Country,* to read this Paper with the utmost Attention, or get it read to you by others; which that you may do at the less Expence, I have ordered the Printer to sell it at the lowest Rate.

It is a great fault among you, that when a Person writes with no other Intention than *to do you Good, you will not be at the Pains to Read his Advices*: One Copy of this Paper may serve a Dozen of you, which will be less than a Farthing a-piece. It is your Folly that you have no common or general Interest in your View, not even the Wisest among you, neither do you know or enquire, or care who are your Friends, or who are your Enemies.

About three Years ago, a little Book was written, to advise all People to wear the *Manufactures of this our own Dear Country*: It had no other Design, said nothing against the *King* or *Parliament,* or *any Man,* yet the POOR PRINTER was prosecuted two Years, with the utmost Violence, and even some WEAVERS themselves, for whose Sake it was written, being upon the JURY, FOUND

HIM GUILTY. This would be enough to discourage any Man from endeavouring to do you Good, when you will either neglect him or fly in his Face for his Pains, and when he must expect only *Danger to himself* and *Loss of Money*, perhaps to his Ruin.

However I cannot but warn you once more of the manifest Destruction before your Eyes, if you do not behave your selves as you ought.

I will therefore first tell you the *plain Story of the Fact*; and then I will lay before you how you ought to act in common Prudence, and according to the *Laws of your Country*.

The Fact is thus, It having been many Years since COPPER HALF-PENCE or FARTHINGS were last Coined in this *Kingdom*, they have been for some time very scarce, and many *Counterfeits* passed about under the Name of RAPS, several Applications were made to *England*, that we might have Liberty to *Coin New ones*, as in former times we did; but they did not succeed. At last one Mr. WOOD, *a mean ordinary man, a Hard-Ware Dealer*, procured a *Patent* under His MAJESTIES BROAD SEAL to Coin FOURSCORE AND TEN THOUSAND POUNDS in *Copper* for this *Kingdom*, which Patent however did not oblidge any one here to take them, unless they pleased. Now you must know, that the HALF-PENCE and FARTHINGS in *England* pass for very little more than they are worth. And if you should beat them to Pieces, and sell them to the *Brazier* you would not lose above a Penny in a Shilling. But Mr. WOOD made his HALF-PENCE of such *Base Metal*, and so much smaller than the *English* ones, that the Brazier would not give you above a *Penny* of good Money for a *Shilling* of his; so that this Sum of *Fourscore* and *Ten Thousand Pounds* in good Gold and Silver, must be given for TRASH that will not be worth above *Eight* or *Nine Thousand Pounds* real Value. But this is not the Worst, for Mr. WOOD when he pleases may by Stealth send over *another* and *another Fourscore and Ten Thousand Pounds*, and buy *all our Goods for Eleven Parts in Twelve*, under the Value. For Example, if a

Hatter sells a Dozen of *Hatts* for *Five Shillings* a-piece, which amounts to *Three Pounds*, and receives the Payment in Mr. WOOD's Coin, he really receives only the value of *Five Shillings*.

Perhaps you will wonder how such *an ordinary Fellow* as this Mr. WOOD could have so much Interest as to get his MAJESTIES Broad Seal for so great a Sum of bad Money, to be sent to this Poor Country, and that all the *Nobility* and *Gentry* here could not obtain the same Favour, and let us make our own *Half-pence*, as we used to do. Now I will make that Matter very Plain. We are at a great Distance from the *King's Court*, and have no body there to solicite for us, although a great Number of *Lords* and *Squires*, whose Estates are here, and are our Countrymen, spending all their *Lives* and *Fortunes* there. But this same Mr. WOOD was able to attend constantly for his own Interest; he is an ENGLISH MAN and had GREAT FRIENDS, and it seems knew very well *where to give Money*, to those that would speak to OTHERS that could speak to the KING and could tell A FAIR STORY. And HIS MAJESTY, and perhaps the great Lord or Lords who advised him, might think it was for our *Country's Good*; and so, as the Lawyers express it, the KING was deceived in his Grant, which often happens in *all Reigns*. And I am sure if his MAJESTY knew that such a Patent, if it should take Effect according to the Desire of Mr. WOOD, would utterly Ruin this Kingdom which hath given such great Proofs of it's *Loyalty*, he would immediately recall it, and perhaps shew his Displeasure to SOME BODY OR OTHER, *But a Word to the Wise is enough*. Most of you must have heard, with what Anger our *Honourable House of Commons* received an Account of this WOOD's PATENT. There were several *Fine Speeches* made upon it, and plain Proofs that it was all A WICKED CHEAT from the *Bottom to the Top*, and several *Smart Votes* were printed, which that same WOOD had the assurance to answer likewise in *Print*, and in so confident a Way, as if he were *A better Man than Our whole Parliament* put together.

This WOOD, as soon as his *Patent* was passed, or soon after, sends over a great many *Barrels of these HALF-PENCE,* to *Cork* and other *Seaport Towns,* and to get them off offered an *Hundred Pounds* in his *Coin* for *Seventy* or *Eighty* in *Silver*; But the *Collectors* of the KING's Customs very honestly refused to take them, and so did almost every body else. And since the *Parliament* hath condemned them, and desired the KING that they might be stopped, all the *Kingdom* do abominate them.

But WOOD is still working *under hand* to force his HALF-PENCE upon us, and if he can by help of his *Friends* in *England* prevail so far as to get an Order that the *Commissioners* and *Collectors* of the KING's Money shall Receive them, and that the ARMY is to be paid with them, then he thinks *his Work shall be done.* And this is the Difficulty you will be under in such a *Case.* For the common Soldier when he goes to the *Market* or *Ale-house* will offer this Money, and if it be refused, perhaps he will SWAGGER and HECTOR, and *Threaten* to *Beat* the BUTCHER or *Ale-Wife,* or take the Goods by Force, and throw them the bad HALF-PENCE. In this and the like Cases, the *Shop-keeper,* or *Victualer,* or *any other Tradesmen* has no more to do, than to demand ten times the Price of his Goods, if it is to be paid in WOOD's Money; for Example, Twenty Pence of that Money for A QUART OF ALE, and so in all things else, and not part with his Goods till he gets the *Money.*

For suppose you go to an ALE-HOUSE with that base Money, and the Landlord gives you a Quart for Four of these HALF-PENCE, what must the Victualer do? His BREWER will not be paid in that Coin, or if the BREWER should be such a Fool, the *Farmers* will not take it from them for their *Bere,* because they are bound by their Leases to pay their Rents in Good and Lawful Money of *England,* which this is not, nor of *Ireland* neither, and the 'Squire their Landlord* will never be so bewitched to take such *Trash* for his Land, so that it must certainly stop some where or other, and wherever it stops it is the same thing, and we are all undone.

The common weight of these HALF-PENCE are between Four and Five to an *Ounce*, suppose Five, then three Shillings and Four Pence will weigh a Pound, and consequently *Twenty Shillings* will weigh *Six Pound Butter Weight*. Now there are many Hundred *Farmers* who pay Two Hundred Pound a Year Rent. Therefore when one of these Farmers comes with his Half Years Rent, which is one Hundred Pound, it will be at least Six Hundred Pound weight, which is Three Horse Load.

If a '*Squire* has a mind to come to Town to buy Cloaths and Wine and Spices for himself and Family, or perhaps to pass the Winter here; he must bring with him Five or Six Horses loaden with *Sacks* as the Farmers bring their Corn; and when his Lady comes in her Coach to our Shops, it must be followed by a Car loaden with Mr. WOOD's Money. And I hope we shall have the Grace to take it for no more than it is worth.

They say 'SQUIRE CONOLLY has *Sixteen Thousand Pounds a Year*, now if he sends for his *Rent* to Town, *as it is likely he does, he must* have Two *Hundred and Forty Horses* to bring up his *Half Years Rent*, and Two or Three great *Cellars* in his House for Stowage. But what the Bankers will do I cannot tell. For I am assured, that some great Bankers keep by them *Forty Thousand Pounds* in ready Cash to answer all Payments, which Sum, in Mr. WOOD's Money, would require Twelve Hundred Horses to carry it.

For my own Part, I am already resolved what to do; I have a pretty good Shop of *Irish Stuffs* and *Silks*, and instead of taking Mr. WOOD's bad Copper, I intend to Truck with my Neighbours the BUTCHERS, and *Bakers*, and *Brewers*, and the rest, *Goods for Goods*, and the little *Gold* and *Silver* I have, I will keep by me like my *Heart's Blood* till better Times, or till I am just ready to starve, and then I will buy Mr. WOOD's Money as my Father did the Brass Money in K. JAMES's Time, who could buy *Ten Pound* of it with a *Guinea*, and I hope to get as much for a *Pistole*, and so purchase *Bread* from those who will be such Fools as to sell it me.

These HALF-PENCE, if they once pass, will soon be
COUNTERFEIT, because it may be cheaply done, the
Stuff is *so Base*. The DUTCH likewise will probably do the
same thing, and send them over to us to pay for our *Goods*.
And Mr. WOOD will never be at rest but coin on: So that
in some Years we shall have at least five Times Four Score
and Ten Thousand Pounds of this *Lumber*. Now the Current Money of this Kingdom is not reckoned to be above
Four Hundred Thousand Pounds in all, and while there is a
Silver Six-pence left these BLOODSUCKERS will never
be quiet.

When once the *Kingdom* is reduced to such a Condition,
I will tell you what must be the End: The *Gentlemen of
Estates* will all turn off their *Tenants* for want of Payment,
because as I told you before, the *Tenants* are obliged by
their Leases to pay *Sterling* which is Lawful Current Money
of *England*, then they will turn their own *Farmers*, AS
TOO MANY OF THEM DO ALREADY, Run *all* into
Sheep where they can, keeping only such other *Cattle* as are
necessary, then they will be their own *Merchants* and send
their *Wooll* and *Butter* and *Hydes* and *Linnen* beyond Sea
for ready *Money* and *Wine* and *Spices* and *Silks*. They will
keep only a few miserable *Cottiers*. The *Farmers* must *Rob*
or *Beg*, or leave their *Country*. The *Shop-keepers* in this and
every other Town, must *Break* and *Starve*: For it is the
Landed-man that maintains the *Merchant*, and *Shopkeeper*,
and *Handycrafts Man*.

But when the *'Squire* turns *Farmer* and *Merchant* himself,
all the good Money he gets from abroad, he will hoard up
or send for *England*, and keep some poor *Taylor* or *Weaver*
and the like in his own House, who will be glad to get Bread
at any Rate.

I should never have done if I were to tell you all the
Miseries that we shall undergo if we be so *Foolish* and
Wicked as to take this CURSED COYN. It would be very
hard if all *Ireland* should be put into *One Scale*, and *this
sorry Fellow WOOD* into the other, that Mr. *WOOD* should
weigh down *this whole Kingdom*, by which *England* gets
above a Million of good Money every Year clear into their

Pockets, and that is more than the *English* do by *all the World besides.*

But your *great Comfort is,* that as his *MAJESTIES Patent* does not oblige you to take this *Money,* so the *Laws* have not given the *Crown* a Power of forcing the *Subjects* to take what *Money* the *KING* pleases: For then by the same Reason we might be bound to take PEBBLE-STONES or *Cockle-shells* or *Stamped Leather* for *Current Coin,* if ever we should happen to live under an ill PRINCE, who might likewise by the same Power make a *Guinea* pass for Ten Pounds, a *Shilling* for Twenty Shillings, and so on, by which he would in a short Time get all the *Silver* and *Gold* of the *Kingdom* into his own Hands, and leave us nothing but *Brass* or *Leather* or what he pleased. Neither is any Thing reckoned more *Cruel* or *Oppressive* in the *French Government* than their common Practice of calling in all their Money after they have sunk it very low, and then coining it a New at a much higher Value, which however is not the Thousand Part so wicked as this *abominable Project* of Mr. WOOD. For the *French* give their Subjects *Silver* for *Silver* and *Gold* for *Gold,* but *this Fellow* will not so much as give us good *Brass* or *Copper* for our *Gold* and *Silver,* not even a Twelfth Part of their Worth.

Having said thus much, I will now go on to tell you the Judgments of some great *Lawyers* in this Matter, whom I fee'd on purpose for your Sakes, and got their *Opinions* under their *Hands,* that I might be sure I went upon good Grounds.

A Famous Law-Book, *call'd the* Mirrour of Justice, *discoursing of the Articles (or Laws) ordained by our* Antient Kings *declares the Law to be as follows: It was ordained that no* King *of this Realm should* Change, Impair *or* Amend *the* Money *or make any other* Money *than of* Gold *or* Silver *without the Assent of all the Counties, that is, as my Lord* Coke says, *without the Assent of Parliament.**

This Book is very Antient, and of great Authority for the Time in which it was wrote, and with that Character is often quoted by that great Lawyer my Lord *Coke*. By the Law of England, the several Metals are divided into *Lawful* or *true Metal* and *unlawful* or *false Metal*, *the Former comprehends *Silver* or *Gold*; the Latter all *Baser Metals*: That the Former is only to pass in Payments appears by an Act of *Parliament* made the Twentieth Year of *Edward* the First, called the *Statute concerning the Passing of Pence*, †which I give you here as I got it translated into English, for some of our *Laws* at that Time, were, as I am told writ in *Latin*: *Whoever in Buying or Selling presumeth to refuse an Half-penny or Farthing of Lawful Money, bearing the Stamp which it ought to have, let him be seized on as a Contemner of the King's Majesty, and cast into Prison.*

By this *Statute*, no Person is to be reckoned a *Contemner* of the KING'S *Majesty*, and for that Crime to be *committed to Prison*; but he who refuses to accept the KING's Coin made of *Lawful Metal*, by which, as I observed before, *Silver* and *Gold* only are intended.

That this is the true *Construction* of the *Act*, appears not only from the plain Meaning of the Words, but from my Lord *Coke's* Observation upon it. ‡By this Act (says he) it appears, that no Subject can be forc'd to take in *Buying* or *Selling* or other *Payments*, any Money made but of Lawful Metal; that is, of *Silver* or *Gold*.

The Law of *England* gives the KING all Mines of *Gold* and *Silver*, but not the Mines of other *Metals*, the Reason of which *Prerogative* or *Power*, as it is given by my Lord *Coke* is, §because Money can be made of *Gold* and *Silver*, but not of other Metals.

Pursuant to this Opinion *Half-pence* and *Farthings* were antiently made of *Silver*, which is most evident from the Act of *Parliament* of *Henry* the 4th. Chap. 4. by which it is enacted as follows: *Item, for the great Scarcity that is at present within the Realm of England of Half-pence and Farthings of Silver, it is ordained and established that the Third Part of all the* Money *of* Silver Plate *which shall be brought to the* Bullion, *shall be made in* Half-pence *and* Farthings.

(* 2 *Inst.* 576-7.) († 2 *Inst.* 577.)
(‡ 2 *Inst.* 577.) (§ 2 *Inst.* 577.)

This shews that by the Word Half-penny and Farthing of Lawful Money in that Statute concerning the Passing of Pence, *are meant a small Coin in* Half-pence *and* Farthings *of* Silver.

This is further manifest from the Statute of the Ninth Year of *Edward* the 3d. Chap. 3. which Enacts, *That no Sterling* HALF-PENNY *or* FARTHING *be Molten for to make Vessel, nor any other thing by the Gold-smiths, nor others, upon Forfeiture of the* Money *so molten* (*or melted.*)

By another Act in this *King's* Reign *Black Money* was not to be current in *England*; and by an Act made in the Eleventh Year of his Reign Chap. 5. *Galley Half-pence* were not to pass, what kind of *Coin* these were I do not know, but I presume they were made of *Base Metal*, and that these Acts were no New *Laws*, but farther Declarations of the old *Laws* relating to the *Coin*.

Thus the *Law* stands in Relation to *Coin*, nor is there any Example to the contrary, except one in *Davis's Reports*, who tells us that in the time of *Tyrone's* Rebellion QUEEN ELIZABETH ordered *Money* of *Mixt Metal* to be Coined in the Tower of *London*, and sent over hither for Payment of the ARMY, obliging all People to receive it and Commanding that all Silver Money should be taken only as *Bullion*, that is, for as much as it weighed. *Davis* tells us several Particulars in this Matter too long here to trouble you with, and that the *Privy-Council* of this *Kingdom* obliged a *Merchant* in *England* to receive this mixt Money for Goods transmitted hither.

But this Proceeding is rejected by all the best Lawyers as contrary to Law, the *Privy-Council* here having no such Power. And besides it is to be considered, that the *Queen* was then under great Difficulties by a Rebellion in this *Kingdom* assisted from *Spain*, and whatever is done in great Exigences and Dangerous Times should never be an Example to proceed by in Seasons of *Peace* and *Quietness*.

I will now, my Dear Friends to save you the Trouble, set before you in short, what the *Law* obliges you *to do*, and what it does *not* oblige you to.

First, you are oblig'd to take all Money in Payments

which is coin'd by the KING and is of the *English* Standard or Weight, provided it be of *Gold* or *Silver*.

Secondly, you are not obliged to take any Money which is not of *Gold* or *Silver*, no not the HALF-PENCE, or FARTHINGS of *England*, or of any other Country, and it is only for Convenience, or Ease, that you are content to take them, because the Custom of Coining *Silver HALF-PENCE & FARTHINGS* hath long been left off, I will suppose on Account of their being subject to be lost.

Thirdly, much less are you obliged to take those *Vile Half-Pence* of that same WOOD, by which you must lose almost Eleven-Pence in every Shilling.

Therefore my *Friends*, stand to it One and All, refuse this *Filthy Trash*; It is no Treason to Rebel against Mr. WOOD, His MAJESTY in his Patent obliges no body to take these Half-Pence, our GRACIOUS PRINCE hath no so ill Advisers about him; or if he had, yet you see the Laws have not left it in the KING's Power, to force us to take any Coin but what is Lawful, of right Standard *Gold* and *Silver*, therefore you have nothing to fear.

And let me in the next Place apply my self particularly to you who are the poor Sort of *Tradesmen*, perhaps you may think you will not be so great Losers as the Rich, if these *Half-Pence* should pass, because you seldom see any *Silver*, and your *Customers* come to your *Shops* or *Stalls* with nothing but Brass, which you likewise find hard to be got, but you may take my Word, whenever this Money gains Footing among you you will be utterly undone; if you carry these *Half-Pence* to a Shop for *Tobacco* or *Brandy*, or *any other Thing* you want, the *Shopkeeper* will advance his Goods accordingly, or else he must break and leave the *Key under the Door*. Do you think I will sell you a Yard of tenpenny Stuff for Twenty of Mr. WOOD's *Half-Pence*, no, not under Two hundred at least, neither will I be at the Trouble of counting, but weigh them in a Lump; I will tell you one Thing further, that if Mr. WOOD's Project should take, it will ruin even our Beggars. For when I give a Beggar an half-penny, it will quench his Thirst, or go a good way to fill his Belly, but the Twelfth Part of a Half-penny will do him no more Service than if I should give him three Pins out of my Sleeve.

In short these HALF-PENCE are like the accursed Thing *which as the* Scripture *tells us, the* Children of Israel *were forbidden to touch, they will run about like the* Plague *and destroy every one who lays his Hands upon them. I have heard* Scholars *talk of a Man who told a King that he had invented a Way to torment People by putting them into a* Bull of Brass *with Fire under it, but the* Prince *put the Pro-jector first into his own* Brazen Bull *to make the Experiment; this very much resembles the Project of Mr. WOOD, and the like of this may possibly be Mr. WOOD's Fate, that the* Brass *he contrived to torment this* Kingdom *with, may prove his own Torment, and his Destruction at last.*

N.B. The AUTHOR of this Paper is informed by Persons who have made it their Business to be exact in their Observations on the true Value of these HALF-PENCE that any Person may expect to get a Quart of Two Penny Ale for Thirty-six of them.

I desire all Persons may keep this Paper carefully by them to Re-fresh their Memories whenever they shall have farther Notice of Mr. WOOD's Half-Pence, or any other the like Imposture.

THE DRAPIER'S FOURTH LETTER

To the Whole People of Ireland.

My Dear Countrymen,

HAVING already written Three *Letters* upon so disagreeable a Subject as Mr. *Wood* and his *Half-pence*; I conceived my Task was at an End: But I find, that Cordials must be frequently apply'd to weak Constitutions, *Political* as well as *Natural*. A People long used to Hardships, lose by Degrees the very Notions of *Liberty*, they look upon themselves as Creatures at Mercy, and that all Impositions laid on them by a stronger Hand, are, in the Phrase of the *Report, Legal* and *Obligatory*. Hence proceeds that *Poverty* and *Lowness of Spirit*, to which a *Kingdom* may be subject as well as a *Particular Person*. And when *Esau came fainting from the Field at the Point to Die,* it is no wonder that he *Sold his Birth-Right for a Mess of Pottage.*

I thought I had sufficiently shewn to all who could want Instruction, by what Methods they might safely proceed, whenever this *Coyn* should be offered to them: And I believe there hath not been for many Ages an Example of any Kingdom so firmly united in a Point of great Importance, as this of Ours is at present, against that detestable Fraud. But however, it so happens that some weak People begin to be allarmed anew, by Rumours industriously spread. *Wood* prescribes to the News-Mongers in *London* what they are to write. In one of their Papers published here by some obscure Printer (and probably with no good Design) we are told, that *the Papists in* Ireland *have entered into an Association against his Coyn*, although it be notoriously known, that they never once offered to stir in the Matter; so that the Two Houses of Parliament, the Privy Council, the great Number of Corporations, the Lord Mayor and Aldermen of *Dublin*, the Grand-Juries, and Principal Gentlemen of several Counties are stigmatized in a Lump under the Name of *Papists*.

This Impostor and his Crew do likewise give out, that, by refusing to receive his Dross for Sterling, we *dispute the King's Prerogative, are grown Ripe for Rebellion, and ready to shake off the Dependancy of* Ireland *upon the Crown* of England. To countenance which Reports he hath publish'd a Paragraph in another News-Paper, to let us know that *the Lord Lieutenant is ordered to come over immediately to settle his Half-pence*.

I intreat you, my dear Countrymen, not to be under the least Concern upon these and the like Rumours, which are no more than the last Howls of a Dog dissected alive, as I hope he hath sufficiently been. These Calumnies are the only Reserve that is left him. For surely our continued and (almost) unexampled Loyalty will never be called in Question for not suffering our selves to be Robbed of all that we have, by one obscure *Iron-Monger*.

As to disputing the King's *Prerogative*, give me Leave to explain to those who are Ignorant, what the meaning of that word *Prerogative* is.

The Kings of these Realms enjoy several Powers, wherein the Laws have not interposed: So they can make War and Peace without the Consent of Parliament; and this is a very great *Prerogative*. But if the Parliament doth not approve of the War, the King must bear the Charge of it out of his own Purse, and this is as great a Check on the Crown. So the King hath a *Prerogative* to Coin Money without Consent of Parliament. But he cannot compel the Subject to take that Money except it be Sterling, Gold or Silver; because herein he is Limited by Law. Some Princes have indeed extended their *Prerogative* further than the Law allowed them: Wherein however, the Lawyers of Succeeding Ages, as fond as they are of *Precedents*, have never dared to Justifie them. But to say the Truth, it is only of late Times that *Prerogative* hath been fixed and ascertained. For whoever Reads the Histories of *England*, will find that some former Kings, and these none of the worst, have upon several Occasions ventured to controul the Laws with very little Ceremony or Scruple, even later than the Days of Queen *Elizabeth*. In her Reign that pernicious Council of sending *Base Money* hither, very narrowly failed of Losing the Kingdom, being complained of by the Lord Deputy, the Council, and the whole Body of the *English* here: So that soon after her Death it was recalled by her Successor, and Lawful Money paid in Exchange.

Having thus given you some Notion of what is meant by the King's *Prerogative*, as far as a *Tradesman* can be thought capable of Explaining it, I will only add the Opinion of the great Lord *Bacon*; That *as God governs the World by the settled Laws of Nature, which he hath made, and never transcends those Laws but upon High Important Occasions: So among Earthly Princes, those are the Wisest and the Best, who govern by the known Laws of the Country, and seldomest make Use of their* Prerogative.

Now, here you may see that the Vile Accusation of *Wood* and his Accomplices, charging us with *Disputing the King's Prerogative* by refusing his Brass, can have no Place, because compelling the Subject to take any Coin which is not Sterling is no Part of the King's *Prerogative*, and I am very confident if it were so, we should be the last of his People to dispute it, as well from that inviolable Loyalty we have always paid to his Majesty, as from the Treatment we might in such a Case justly expect from some who seem to think, we have neither *Common Sense* nor *Common Senses*. But God be thanked, the Best of them are only our *Fellow Subjects*, and not our *Masters*. One great Merit I am sure we have, which those of *English* Birth can have no Pretence to, That our Ancestors reduced this Kingdom to the Obedience of ENGLAND, for which we have been rewarded with a worse Climate, the Priviledge of being governed by Laws to which we do not consent, a Ruined Trade, a House of *Peers* without *Jurisdiction*, almost an Incapacity for all Employments; and the Dread of *Wood's* Half-pence.

But we are so far from disputing the King's *Prerogative* in Coyning, that we own he has Power to give a Patent to any Man for setting his Royal Image and Superscription upon whatever Materials he pleases, and Liberty to the Patentee to offer them in any Country from *England* to *Japan*, only attended with one small Limitation, That *no body alive is obliged to take them.*

Upon these considerations I was ever against all Recourse to *England* for a Remedy against the present Impending Evil, especially when I observed that the Addresses of Both Houses, after long Expectance, produced nothing but a REPORT altogether in Favour of *Wood*, upon which I made some Observations in a former Letter, and might at least have made as many more. For it is a Paper of as Singular a Nature as I ever beheld.

But I mistake; for before this *Report* was made, His Majesties *Most Gracious Answer* to the House of Lords was sent over and Printed, wherein there are these Words, *Granting the Patent for Coyning Half-pence and Farthings* AGREEABLE TO THE PRACTICE OF HIS ROYAL PREDECESSORS, &c. That King *Charles* 2d. and King *James* 2d. (AND THEY ONLY) did grant Patents for this Purpose is indisputable, and I have shewn it at large. Their Patents were passed under the great Seal of IRELAND by References to IRELAND, the Copper to be Coyned in IRELAND, the Patentee was bound on Demand to receive his Coyn back in IRELAND, and pay Silver and Gold in Return. *Wood's* Patent was made under the great Seal of ENGLAND, the Brass Coyned in ENGLAND, not the least Reference made to IRELAND, the Sum Immense, and the Patentee under no Obligation to receive it again and give good Money for it: This I only mention, because in my private Thoughts I have sometimes made a Query, whether the *Penner* of those Words in his Majesties *Most Gracious Answer*, AGREEABLE TO THE PRACTICE OF HIS ROYAL PREDECESSORS, had maturely considered the several Circumstances, which, in my poor Opinion seem to make a Difference.

Let me now say something concerning the other great Cause of some Peoples Fear, as *Wood* has taught the *London* News-Writer to express it. That *his Excellency the Lord Lieutenant is coming over to settle* Wood's *Half-pence.*

We know very well that the Lords Lieutenants for several Years past have not thought this Kingdom *Worthy the Honour of their Residence*, longer than was absolutely necessary for the King's Business, which consequently *wanted no Speed in the Dispatch*; and therefore it naturally fell into most Mens Thoughts, that a new Governour coming at an *Unusual* Time must portend some *Unusual* Business to be done, especially if the Common Report be true, that the Parliament Prorogued to I know not when, is by a new Summons (revoking that Prorogation) to assemble soon after his Arrival: For which extraordinary Proceeding the Lawyers on tother Side the Water have by great good Fortune found Two *Precedents*.

All this being granted, it can never enter into my Head that so *Little a Creature* as *Wood* could find Credit enough with the King and his Ministers to have the Lord Lieutenant of *Ireland* sent hither in a Hurry upon his Errand.

For let us take the whole Matter nakedly as it lies before us, without the Refinements of some People, with which we have nothing to do. Here is a Patent granted under the great Seal of *England*, upon false Suggestions, to one *William Wood* for Coyning Copper Half-pence for *Ireland*: The *Parliament* here, upon Apprehensions of the worst Consequences from the said Patent, address the King to have it recalled; this is refused, and a Committee of the Privy Council *Report* to his Majesty, that *Wood* has performed the Conditions of his Patent. He then is left to do the best he can with his Half-pence; no Man being obliged to receive them; the People here, being likewise left to themselves, unite as one Man, resolving they will have nothing to do with his Ware. By this plain Account of the Fact it is Manifest, that the King and his Ministry are wholly out of the Case, and the Matter is left to be disputed between him and us. Will any Man therefore attempt to persuade me, that a Lord Lieutenant is to be dispatched over in great Haste before the Ordinary Time, and a Parliament summoned by anticipating a Prorogation, meerly to put an Hundred thousand Pounds into the Pocket of a *Sharper*, by the Ruin of a most Loyal Kingdom.

But supposing all this to be true. By what Arguments could a Lord Lieutenant prevail on the same Parliament which addressed with so much Zeal and Earnestness against this Evil, to pass it into a Law? I am sure their Opinion of *Wood* and his Project is not mended since the last Prorogation; and Supposing those *Methods* should be used which *Detractors* tell us have been sometimes put in Practice for *gaining Votes*. It is well known that in this Kingdom there are few Employments to be given, and if there were more, it is *as well known* to whose Share they must fall.

But because great Numbers of you are altogether Ignorant in the Affairs of your Country, I will tell you some Reasons why there are so few Employments to be disposed of in this Kingdom. All considerable Offices for Life here are possessed by those to whom the Reversions were granted, and these have been generally Followers of the Chief Governours, or Persons who had Interest in the Court of *England*. So the Lord *Berkely* of *Stratton* holds that great Office of *Master of the Rolls*, the Lord *Palmerstown* is *First Remembrancer* worth near 2000*l*. per Ann. One *Dodington* Secretary to the Earl of *Pembroke*, *begged* the Reversion of *Clerk of the Pells* worth 2500*l*. a Year, which he now enjoys by the Death of the Lord *Newtown*. Mr. *Southwell* is Secretary of State, and the Earl of *Burlington* Lord High Treasurer of *Ireland* by Inheritance. These are only a few among many others which I have been told of, but cannot remember. Nay the Reversion of several Employments during Pleasure are granted the same Way. This among many others is a Circumstance whereby the Kingdom of *Ireland* is distinguished from all other Nations upon Earth, and makes it so Difficult an Affair to get into a Civil Employ, that Mr. *Addison* was forced to purchase an old obscure Place, called *Keeper of the Records of* Berminghams *Tower* of Ten Pounds a Year, and to get a Sallery of 400*l*. annexed to it, though all the Records there are not worth Half a Crown, either for Curiosity or Use. And we lately saw a *Favourite Secretary* descend to be *Master of the Revels*, which by his *Credit and Extortion* he hath made *Pretty Considerable*. I say nothing of the Under-Treasurer-ship worth about 8000*l.* a Year, nor the Commissioners of the Revenue, Four of whom generally live in *England*: For I think none of these are granted in Reversion. But the Jest is, that I have known upon Occasion some of these absent Officers as *Keen* against the Interest of *Ireland* as if they had never been indebted to Her for a *Single Groat.*

I confess, I have been sometimes tempted to wish that this Project of *Wood* might succeed, because I reflected with some Pleasure what a *Jolly Crew* it would bring over among us of *Lords* and *'Squires,* and *Pensioners* of *Both Sexes,* and Officers *Civil* and *Military,* where we should live together as merry and sociable as Beggars, only with this one Abatement, that we should neither have *Meat* to feed, nor *Manufactures* to Cloath us, unless we could be content to *Prance* about in *Coats of Mail,* or Eat Brass as Ostritches do Iron.

I return from this Digression to that which gave me the Occasion of making it: And I believe you are now convinced, that if the Parliament of *Ireland* were as Temptible as any *other* Assembly *within a Mile of* Christendom (which God forbid) yet the *Managers* must of Necessity fail for want of *Tools* to work with. But I will yet go one Step further, by Supposing that a Hundred new Employments were erected on purpose to gratify *Compliers;* yet still an insuperable Difficulty would remain; for it happens, I know now how, that *Money* is neither *Whig* nor *Tory,* neither of *Town* nor *Country Party,* and it is not improbable, that a Gentleman would rather chuse to live upon his *own Estate* which brings him *Gold* and *Silver,* than with the Addition of an *Employment,* when his *Rents* and *Sallery* must both be paid in *Wood's* Brass, at above Eighty per Cent. Discount.

For these and many other Reasons, I am confident you need not be under the least Apprehensions from the sudden Expectation of the *Lord Lieutenant,* while we continue in our present Hearty Disposition; to alter which there is no Suitable Temptation can possibly be offered: And if, as I have often asserted from the best Authority, the *Law* hath not left a *Power* in the *Crown* to force any Money except

Sterling upon the Subject, much less can the Crown *devolve* such a *Power* upon *another*.

This I speak with the utmost Respect to the *Person* and *Dignity* of His Excellency the Lord *Carteret*, whose Character hath been given me by a Gentleman that hath known him from his first Appearance in the World: That Gentleman describes Him as a Young Noble Man of great Accomplishments, Excellent Learning, Regular in his Life, and of much Spirit and Vivacity. He hath since, as I have heard, been employed abroad, was Principal Secretary of State, and is now about the 37th Year of his Age appointed Lord Lieutenant of *Ireland*. From such a Governour this Kingdom may reasonably hope for as much Prosperity as, *under so many Discouragements*, it can be capable of Receiving.

It is true indeed, that within the Memory of Man, there have been Governours of so much Dexterity, as to carry Points of Terrible Consequence to this Kingdom, by their Power with *those who were in Office*, and by their Arts in managing or deluding others with *Oaths, Affability*, and even with *Dinners*. If *Wood's* Brass had in those Times been upon the *Anvil*, it is obvious enough to conceive what Methods would have been taken. *Depending* Persons would have been told in plain Terms, that it was a *Service expected from them, under Pain of the Publick Business being put into more complying Hands.* Others would be allured by *Promises*. To the *Country Gentlemen*, besides *Good Words, Burgundy* and *Closeting*. It would perhaps have been hinted how *kindly it would be taken to comply with a Royal Patent, though it were not compulsary*, that if any Inconveniences ensued, it might be made up with other *Graces or Favours hereafter*. That *Gentlemen ought to consider whether it were prudent or safe to disgust* England: They would be desired to *think of some good Bills for encouraging of Trade, and setting the Poor to Work, some further Acts against Popery and for Uniting Protestants*. There would be solemn Engagements that we should *never be troubled with above Fourty thousand Pounds in his Coyn, and all of the best and weightiest Sort, for which we should only give our Manufactures in Exchange, and keep our Gold and Silver at Home*. Perhaps a *seasonable Report of some Invasion would have been spread in the most proper Juncture*, which is a great Smoother of Rubs in Publick Proceedings; and we should have been told that *this was no Time to create Differences when the Kingdom was in Danger*.

These, I say, and the like Methods would in corrupt Times have been taken to let in this Deluge of Brass among us: And I am Confident would even then have not succeeded, much less under the Administration of so Excellent a Person as the Lord *Carteret*, and in a Country where the People of all Ranks, Parties and Denominations are convinced to a Man, that the utter undoing of themselves and their Posterity for ever will be Dated from the Admission of that Execrable Coyn; that if it once enters, it can be no more confined to a small or Moderate Quantity, than the *Plague* can be confined to a few Families, and that no *Equivalent* can be given by any earthly Power, any more than a Dead Carcass can be recovered to Life by a Cordial.

There is one comfortable Circumstance in this Universal Opposition to Mr. *Wood*, that the People sent over hither from *England* to *fill up our Vacancies Ecclesiastical, Civil and Military*, are all on our Side: *Money*, the great *Divider* of the World, hath by a strange Revolution, been the great *Uniter* of a most *Divided* People. Who would leave a Hundred Pounds a Year in *England* (*a Country of Freedom*) to be paid a Thousand in *Ireland* out of *Wood's* Exchequer. The *Gentleman They* have lately made *Primate* would never quit his Seat in an *English* House of Lords, and his Preferments at *Oxford* and *Bristol*, worth Twelve hundred Pounds a Year, for Four times the Denomination here, but not half the Value; therefore I expect to hear he will be as good an *Irish* Man, upon *this Article*, as any of his Brethren, or even of *Us* who have had the *Misfortune* to be born in this Island. For those, who, in the common Phrase, do not *come hither to learn the Language*, would never change a better Country for a Worse, to receive *Brass* instead of *Gold*.

Another Slander spread by *Wood* and his Emissaries is, that by opposing him we discover an Inclination to *shake off our Dependance upon the Crown of* England. Pray observe how Important a Person is this same *William Wood,* and how the Publick Weal of Two Kingdoms is involved in his Private Interest. First, all those who refuse to take his Coyn *are Papists*; for he tells us that *none but Papists are associated against him*; Secondly, They *dispute the King's Prerogative*; Thirdly, *They are Ripe for Rebellion,* and Fourthly, They are going to *shake off their Dependance upon the Crown of* England; That is to say, *they are going to chuse another King:* For there can be no other Meaning in this Expression, however some may pretend to strain it.

And this gives me an Opportunity of Explaining, to those who are Ignorant, another Point, which hath often *Swelled in my Breast.* Those who come over hither to us from *England,* and some *Weak* People among our selves, whenever in Discourse we make mention *of Liberty* and *Property,* shake their Heads, and tell us, that *Ireland* is a *Depending Kingdom,* as if they would seem, by this Phrase, to intend that the People of *Ireland* is in some State of Slavery or Dependance different from those of *England*: Whereas a *Depending Kingdom* is a *Modern Term of Art,* unknown, as I have heard, to all antient *Civilians,* and *Writers upon Government*; and *Ireland* is on the contrary called in some Statutes an *Imperial Crown,* as held only from God; which is as High a Style as any Kingdom is capable of receiving. Therefore by this Expression, a *Depending Kingdom,* there is no more understood than that by a Statute made here in the 33d Year of *Henry* 8th. *The King and his Successors are to be Kings Imperial of this Realm as United and Knit to the Imperial Crown of* England. I have looked over all the *English* and *Irish* Statutes without finding any Law that makes *Ireland depend* upon *England,* any more than *England* does upon *Ireland.* We have indeed obliged our selves to have the *same King with them,* and consequently they are obliged to have *the same King with us.* For the Law was made by *our own Parliament,* and our Ancestors then were not such *Fools (whatever they were in the Preceding Reign)* to bring themselves under I know not what *Dependance,* which is now talked of without any Ground of *Law, Reason* or *Common Sense.*

R

Let whoever think otherwise, I *M. B. Drapier*, desire to be excepted, for I declare, next under God, I *depend* only on the King my Sovereign, and on the Laws of my own Country; and I am so far from *depending* upon the People of *England*, that if they should ever *Rebel* against my Sovereign (which God forbid) I would be ready at the first Command from his Majesty to take Arms against them, as some of *my* Country-men did against *Theirs* at *Preston*. And if such a Rebellion should prove so successful as to fix the *Pretender* on the Throne of *England*, I would venture to transgress that *Statute* so far as to lose every Drop of my Blood to hinder him from being *King* of *Ireland*.

'Tis true indeed, that within the Memory of Man, the Parliaments of *England* have *Sometimes* assumed the Power of binding this Kingdom by Laws enacted there, wherein they were at first openly opposed (as far as *Truth*, *Reason* and *Justice* are capable of *Opposing*) by the Famous Mr. *Molineaux*, an *English* Gentleman born here, as well as by several of the greatest Patriots, and *best Whigs* in *England* But the *Love and Torrent* of Power prevailed. Indeed the Arguments on both sides were invincible; For in *Reason*, all *Government* without the Consent of the *Governed* is the *very Definition of Slavery*: But in *Fact*, *Eleven Men well Armed will certainly subdue one Single Man in his Shirt*. But I have done. For those who have used *Power* to cramp *Liberty* have gone so far as to Resent even the *Liberty* of *Complaining*, altho' a Man upon the Rack was never known to be refused the Liberty of *Roaring* as loud as he thought fit.

And as we are apt to *sink* too *much* under *unreasonable* Fears, so we are too soon inclined to be *Raised* by groundless Hopes (according to the Nature of all *Consumptive* Bodies like ours). Thus, it hath been given about for several Days past, that *Somebody* in *England* empowered a Second *Somebody* to write to a third *Somebody* here to assure us, that we *should no more be troubled with those Half-pence*, And this is Reported to have been done by the *Same Person*, who was said to have Sworn some Months ago, that he would *Ram them down our Throats* (though I doubt they would *stick in our Stomachs*); but which ever of these Reports is True or False, it is no Concern of ours. For *in this Point* we have nothing to do with *English Ministers*, and I should be sorry it lay in their Power to *Redress* this Grievance or to *Enforce* it: For the *Report of the Committee* hath given me a *Surfeit*. The Remedy is wholly in your own Hands, and therefore I have digressed a little in order to refresh and continue that *Spirit* so seasonably raised amongst you, and to let you see that by the Laws of GOD, of NATURE, of NATIONS, and of your own Country, you ARE and OUGHT to be as FREE a People as your Brethren in *England*.

If the Pamphlets published at *London* by *Wood* and his *Journey-men* in Defence of his Cause, were Reprinted here, and that our Country-men could be persuaded to Read them, they would convince you of his wicked Design more than all I shall ever be able to say. In short I make him a perfect *Saint* in Comparison of what he appears to be from the Writings of those whom he *Hires* to Justifie his *Project*. But he is so far *Master of the Field* (*let others guess the Reason*) that no *London* Printer dare publish any Paper written in Favour of *Ireland*, and here no body hath yet been so *bold* as to *Publish* any thing in *Favour* of *him*.

There was a few Days ago a Pamphlet sent me of near 50 Pages Written in Favour of Mr. *Wood* and his Coynage, Printed in *London*, it is not worth answering, because probably it will never be published here: But it gave me an Occasion to reflect upon an Unhappiness we lye under, that the People of *England* are utterly Ignorant of our Case, which however is no wonder, since it is a Point they do not in the least concern themselves about, farther than perhaps as a Subject of Discourse in a Coffee-House when they have nothing else to talk of. For I have Reason to believe that no Minister ever gave himself the Trouble of Reading any Papers Written in our Defence, because I suppose *their Opinions are already determined*, and are formed wholly upon the Reports of *Wood* and his Accomplices; else it would be impossible that any Man could have the Impudence to write such a Pamphlet as I have mentioned.

Our *Neighbours whose Understandings are just upon a Level with Ours* (which perhaps are none of the *Brightest*) have a strong Contempt for most Nations, but especially for *Ireland*: They look upon Us as a Sort of *Savage Irish*, whom our Ancestors conquered several hundred Years ago, and if I should describe the *Britains* to you as they were in *Cæsar's* Time, when they *Painted their Bodies, or cloathed themselves with the Skins of Beasts*, I would act full as reasonably as they do: However they are so far to be excused in Relation to the present Subject, that, hearing only *one Side of the Cause*, and having neither Opportunity nor Curiosity to examine the *Other*, they *believe a Lye* merely for their Ease, and conclude, because Mr. *Wood* pretends to have *Power*, he hath also *Reason* on his Side.

Therefore to let you see how this Case is represented in *England* by *Wood* and his Adherents, I have thought it proper to extract out of that Pamphlet a few of those Notorious Falshoods in Point of *Fact* and *Reasoning* contained therein; the Knowledge whereof will confirm my Country-men in their *Own* Right Sentiments, when they will see by comparing both, how much their *Enemies are in the Wrong*.

First, The Writer, positively asserts, *That Wood's Halfpence were Current among us for several Months with the universal Approbation of all People, without one single Gainsayer, and we all to a Man thought our selves Happy in having them.*

Secondly, He affirms, *That we were drawn into a Dislike of them only by some Cunning Evil designing Men among us, who opposed this Patent of* Wood *to get another for themselves.*

Thirdly, That *those who most declared at first against* Wood's *Patent were the very Men who intended to get another for their own Advantage.*

Fourthly, That *our Parliament and Privy Council, the Lord Mayor and Aldermen of* Dublin, *the Grand-Juries and Merchants, and in short the whole Kingdom, nay the very Dogs* (as he expresseth it) *were fond of those Half-pence, till they were inflamed by those few designing Persons aforesaid.*

Fifthly. He says directly, That *all those who opposed the Half-pence were Papists and Enemies to King* George.

Thus far I am confident the most Ignorant among you can safely swear from your own Knowledge that the Author is a most notorious Lyar in every Article; the direct contrary being so manifest to the whole Kingdom, that if Occasion required, we might get it confirmed *under Five hundred thousand Hands.*

Sixthly, He would persuade us, That *if we sell Five Shillings worth of our Goods or Manufactures for Two Shillings and Four Pence worth of Copper, although the Copper were melted Down, and that we could get Five Shillings in Gold or Silver for the said Goods, yet to take the said Two Shillings and Four Pence in Copper would be greatly for our advantage.*

And Lastly, He makes us a very fair Offer, as empowered by *Wood*, That *if we will take off Two hundred thousand Pounds in his Half-pence for our Goods, and likewise pay him Three per Cent. Interest for Thirty Years, for an Hundred and Twenty thousand Pounds* (at which he computes the Coynage above the Intrinsick Value of the Copper) *for the Loan of his Coyn, he will after that Time give us good Money for what Half-pence will be then left.*

Let me place this offer in as Clear a Light as I can to shew the unsupportable Villany and Impudence of that incorrigible Wretch. First (says he) *I will send Two hundred thousand Pounds of my Coyn into your Country, the Copper I compute to be in Real Value Eighty thousand Pounds, and I charge you with an Hundred and Twenty thousand Pounds for the Coynage; so that you see I lend you an Hundred and Twenty thousand Pounds for Thirty Years, for which you shall pay me Three per Cent. That is to say Three thousand Six hundred Pounds per Ann. which in Thirty Years will amount to an Hundred and Eight thousand Pounds. And when these Thirty Years are expired, return me my Copper and I will give you Good Money for it.*

This is the Proposal made to us by *Wood* in that Pamphlet Written by one of his *Commissioners*; and the Author is supposed to be the same Infamous *Coleby*, one of his *Under-*

Swearers at the *Committee of Council*, who was tryed for *Robbing the Treasury here*, where he was an Under Clerk.

By this Proposal he will first receive Two hundred thousand Pounds, in Goods or Sterling for as much Copper as he Values at Eighty thousand Pounds but in Reality not worth Thirty thousand Pounds. Secondly, He will receive for Interest an Hundred and Eight thousand Pounds. And when our Children come Thirty Years hence to return his Half-pence upon his Executors (for before that Time He will be probably gone to his own Place) those Executors will very reasonably reject them as Raps and Counterfeits, which probably they will be, and Millions of them of his own Coynage.

Methinks I am fond of such a *Dealer* as this who mends every Day upon our Hands, like a *Dutch* Reckoning, where if you dispute the Unreasonableness and Exorbitance of the Bill, the Landlord shall bring it up every Time with new Additions.

Although these and the like Pamphlets publish'd by *Wood* in *London* be altogether unknown here, where no body could Read them without as much *Indignation* as *Contempt* would allow, yet I thought it proper to give you a Specimen how the *Man* employs his Time, where he Rides alone without one Creature to contradict him, while OUR FEW FRIENDS there wonder at our Silence, and the *English* in general, if they think of this Matter at all, impute our Refusal to *Wilfulness* or *Disaffection*, just as *Wood* and his *Hirelings* are pleased to represent.

But although our Arguments are not suffered to be Printed in *England*, yet the Consequence will be of little Moment. Let *Wood* endeavour to *Persuade* the People *There* that we ought to *Receive* his Coyn, and let me *Convince* our People *Here* that they ought to *Reject* it under Pain of our utter Undoing. And then let him do his *Best* and his *Worst*.

Before I conclude, I must beg Leave in all Humility to tell Mr. *Wood*, that he is guilty of great *Indiscresion*, by causing so Honourable a Name as that of Mr. W[alpole] to be mentioned so often, and in such a Manner, upon his

Occasion: A short Paper Printed at *Bristol* and Re-printed here reports Mr. *Wood* to say, that he *wonders at the Impudence and Insolence of the* Irish *in refusing his Coyn,* and *what he will do when Mr.* W[alpole] *comes to Town.* Where, by the Way, he is mistaken, for it is the *True English People* of *Ireland* who refuse it, although we take it for granted that the *Irish* will do so too whenever they are asked. He orders it to be Printed in another Paper, that *Mr.* W[alpole] *will cram this Brass down our Throats*: Sometimes it is given out that we must *either take these Half-pence or eat our Brogues,* And, in another News Letter but of Yesterday, we Read that the same great Man *hath sworn to make us swallow his Coyn in Fire-Balls.*

This brings to my Mind the known Story of a *Scotch*-man, who receiving Sentence of Death, with all the Circumstances of *Hanging, Beheading, Quartering, Embowelling* and the like, cryed out, *What need all this* COOKERY: And I think we have Reason to ask the same Question; for if we believe *Wood,* here is a *Dinner* getting ready for us, and you see the *Bill of Fare,* and I am sorry the Drink was forgot, which might easily be supply'd with *Melted Lead* and *Flaming Pitch.*

What Vile Words are these to put into the Mouth of a great Councellor, in high Trust with his Majesty, and looked upon as a prime Minister. If Mr. *Wood* hath no better a Manner of representing his Patrons, when I come to be a *Great Man,* he shall never be suffered to attend at my *Levee.* This is not the Style of a Great Minister, it savours too much of the *Kettle* and the *Furnace,* and came entirely out of Mr. *Wood's Forge.*

As for the Threat of making us *eat our Brogues,* we need not be in Pain; for if his Coyn should pass, that *Unpolite Covering for the Feet,* would no longer be a *National Reproach*; because then we should have neither *Shoe* nor *Brogue* left in the Kingdom. But here the Falshood of Mr. *Wood* is fairly detected; for I am confident Mr. W[alpole] never heard of a *Brogue* in his whole Life.

As to *Swallowing these Half-pence in Fire-Balls,* it is a Story equally improbable. For to execute this *Operation* the whole Stock of Mr. *Wood's* Coyn and Metal must be melted down and molded into hollow *Balls* with *Wild-fire*, no bigger than a *Reasonable* Throat can be able to swallow. Now the Metal he hath prepared, and already coyned will amount to at least Fifty Millions of Half-pence to be *Swallowed* by a Million and a Half of People; so that allowing Two Half-pence to each *Ball*, there will be about Seventeen *Balls of Wild-fire* a-piece to be swallowed by every Person in this Kingdom, and to administer this Dose, there cannot be conveniently Fewer than Fifty thousand *Operators*, allowing one *Operator* to every Thirty, which, considering the *Squeamishness* of some Stomachs and the *Peevishness* of *Young Children*, is but reasonable. Now, under Correction of better Judgments, I think the Trouble and Charge of such an Experiment would exceed the Profit, and therefore I take this *Report* to be *Spurious*, or at least only a new *Scheme* of Mr. *Wood* himself, which to make it pass the better in *Ireland* he would Father upon a *Minister of State.*

But I will now demonstrate beyond all Contradiction that Mr. W[alpole] is against this Project of Mr. *Wood*, and is an entire Friend to *Ireland*, only by this one invincible Argument, that he has the Universal Opinion of being a Wise Man, an able Minister, and in all his Proceedings pursuing the *True Interest* of the *King* his Master: And that as his *Integrity* is above all *Corruption*, so is his *Fortune* above all *Temptation*. I reckon therefore we are perfectly safe from that *Corner*, and shall never be under the Necessity of Contending with so *Formidable a Power*, but be left to possess our *Brogues* and *Potatoes* in *Peace* as *Remote from Thunder as we are from* Jupiter.

I am,

My Dear Countrymen,

Your Loving Fellow-Subject,

Fellow-Sufferer and Humble

Servant,

Oct. 13. 1724.   M. B.

Selection from

A Short CHARACTER of His Ex. T[homas] E[arl] of Wharton L[ord] L[ieutenant] of I[reland]

T[HOMAS] E[arl] of *W[harton]* L[ord] L[ieutenant] of *I[reland]* by the force of a wonderful Constitution, hath some Years past his grand Climacterick, without any visible effects of Old Age, either on his Body or his Mind, and in spight of a continual prostitution to those Vices which usually wear out both. His Behaviour is in all the Forms of a young Man at five and twenty. Whether he Walks, or Whistles, or Swears, or talks Baudy, or calls Names, he acquits himself in each beyond a Templar of three Years standing. With the same Grace and in the same Stile he will rattle his Coachman in the midst of the Street, where he is Governour of the Kingdom: and all this is without Consequence, because it is in his Character, and what every Body expects. He seems to be but an ill Dissembler and an ill Liar, tho' they are the two Talents he most practices, and most values himself upon. The Ends he has gain'd by Lying, appear to be more owing to the frequency than the Art of them; his Lies being sometimes detected in an Hour, often in a Day, and always in a Week: He tells them freely in mixt Companies, tho' he knows half of those that hear him to be his Enemies, and is sure they will discover them the Moment they leave him. He swears solemnly he loves you and will serve you, and your Back is no sooner turn'd, but he tells those about him, you are a Dog and a Rascal. He goes constantly to Prayers in the Forms of his Place, and will talk Bawdy and Blasphemy at the Chappel-door. He is a Presbyterian in Politicks, and an Atheist in Religion; but he chuses at present to Whore with a *Papist*. In his Commerce with Mankind, his general Rule is to endeavour imposing on their Understandings, for which he has but one Receipt, a composition of Lies and Oaths, and this he applies indifferently to a Freeholder of forty Shillings, and a Privy Councellor, by which the Easie and the Honest are often either deceived or amused; and either way he gains his Point. He will openly take away your Employment to Day, because you are not of his Party; to Morrow he will meet or send for you, as if nothing at all had pass'd, lay his Hands with much Friendliness on your Shoulders, and with the greatest ease and familiarity in the World, tell you that *the Faction* are driving at something in the House; that you must be sure to attend, and to speak to all your Friends to be there, tho' he knows at the same time that you and your Friends are against him in that very Point he mentions: And however absurd, ridiculous, and gross, this may appear, he has often found it successful; some Men having such an awkward Bashfulness they know not how to refuse upon a sudden, and every Man having something to fear or to hope, which often hinders them from driving Things to Extreams with Persons of Power, whatever Provocations they may have receiv'd. He hath sunk his Fortunes by endeavouring to ruin one Kingdom, and hath rais'd them by going far in the Ruin of another. With a good natural Understanding, a great fluency in Speaking, and no ill taste of Wit, he is generally the worst Companion in the World; his Thoughts being wholly taken up between Vice and Politicks, so that Bawdy, Prophaness, and Business fill up his whole Conversation. To gratify himself in the two First, he makes choice of suitable Favourites, whose Talent reaches no higher than to entertain him with all the Lewdness that passes in Town. As for Business, he is said to be very dextrous at that Part of it which turns upon Intrigue, and he seems to have transfer'd the Talents of his Youth for intriguing with Women, into publick Affairs: For, as some vain young Fellows to make a Gallantry appear of Consequence, will chuse to venture their Necks by climbing up a Wall or Window at Midnight to a Common Wench, where they might as freely have gone at the Door and at Noon-day; so his Ex. either to keep himself in Practice, or to advance the Fame of his Politicks, affects the most obscure, troublesome, and winding Paths, even in the commonest Affairs, those which would as well be brought about in the ordinary Forms, or which would proceed of course whether he interven'd or no.

He bears the Gallantries of his L[ad]y with the Indifference of a *Stoick*, and thinks them well recompensed by a return of Children to support his Family, without the fatigues of being a Father.

He has three predominant Passions, which you will seldom observe united in the same Man, as arising from different Dispositions of Mind, and naturally thwarting each other; these are love of Power, love of Money, and love of Pleasure: They ride him sometimes by turns, and sometimes all together: Since he went into that Kingdom, he seems most dispos'd to the Second, and has met with great Success, having gain'd by his Government of under two Years, Five and Forty Thousand Pounds, by the most favourable computation, half in the Regular way, and half in the Prudential.

He was never yet known to refuse or keep a Promise; as I remember he told a Lady, but with an Exception to the Promise he then made, (which was to get her a Pension) yet he broke even that, and I confess, deceiv'd us both. But here, I desire to distinguish between a Promise and a Bargain; for he will be sure to keep the latter, when he has had the fairest Offer.

A SHORT VIEW OF THE
STATE OF IRELAND

I AM assured that it hath for some time been practised
as a method of making Men's Court, when they are
asked about the Rate of Lands, the Abilities of Tenants,
the State of Trade and Manufacture in this Kingdom, and
how their Rents are payed; to Answer, That in their Neighbourhood all things are in a flourishing Condition, the Rent
and Purchase of Land every Day encreasing. And if a
Gentleman happens to be a little more sincere in his Repre-
sentations, besides being looked on as not well affected, he
is sure to have a Dozen Contradictors at his Elbow. I think
it is no manner of Secret why these Questions are so cordially asked, or so obligingly Answered.

But since with Regard to the Affairs of this Kingdom, I
have been using all Endeavours to subdue my Indignation,
to which indeed I am not provoked by any Personal Interest, being not the Owner of one Spot of Ground in the
whole *Island*, I shall only enumerate by Rules generally
known, and never Contradicted, what are the true Causes
of any Countries flourishing and growing Rich, and then
examine what Effects arise from those Causes in the Kingdom of *Ireland*.

The first Cause of a Kingdom's thriving is the Fruitfulness of the Soyl, to produce the Necessaries and Conveniences of Life, not only sufficient for the Inhabitants, but
for Exportation into other Countries.

The Second, is the Industry of the People in Working
up all their Native Commodities to the last degree of
Manufacture.

The Third, is the Conveniency of safe Ports and Havens,
to Carry out their own Goods, as much manufactured, and
bring in those of others, as little manfactured as the Nature
of mutual Commerce will allow.

The Fourth, is, That the Natives should as much as possible, Export and Import their Goods in Vessels of their own Timber, made in their own Country.

The Fifth, is the Liberty of a free Trade in all Foreign Countries, which will permit them, except to those who are in War with their own Prince or State.

The Sixth, is, by being Governed only by Laws made with their own Consent, for otherwise they are not a free People. And therefore all Appeals for Justice, or Applications, for Favour or Preferment to another Country, are so many grievous Impoverishments.

The Seventh, is, by Improvement of Land, encouragement of Agriculture, and thereby encreasing the Number of their People, without which any Country, however Blessed by Nature, must continue Poor.

The Eighth, is the Residence of the Prince, or Chief Administrator of the Civil Power.

The Ninth, is the Concourse of Foreigners for Education, Curiosity or Pleasure, or as to a general Mart of Trade.

The Tenth, is by disposing all Offices of Honour, Profit or Trust, only to the Natives, or at least with very few Exceptions, where Strangers have long Inhabited the Country, and are supposed to Understand, and regard the Interest of it as their own.

The Eleventh is, when the Rents of Lands, and Profits of Employments, are spent in the Country which produced them, and not in another, the former of which will certainly happen, where the Love of our Native Country prevails.

The Twelfth, is by the publick Revenues being all Spent and Employed at Home, except on the Occasions of a Foreign War.

The Thirteenth, is, where the People are not obliged, unless they find it for their own Interest, or Conveniency, to receive any Monies, except of their own Coynage by a publick Mint, after the manner of all Civilized Nations.

The Fourteenth, is a Disposition of a People of a Country to wear their own Manufactures, and Import as few Incitements to Luxury, either in Cloaths, Furniture, Food or Drink, as they possibly can live conveniently without.

There are many other Causes of a Nation's thriving,

which I cannot at present recollect, but without Advantage from at least some of these; after turning my Thoughts a long time, I am not able to discover from whence our Wealth proceeds, and therefore would gladly be better informed. In the mean time, I will here examine what share falls to *Ireland* of these Causes, or of the Effects and Consequences.

It is not my Intention to complain, but barely to relate Facts, and the matter is not of small Importance. For it is allowed, that a Man who lives in a Solitary House far from help, is not Wise in endeavouring to acquire in the Neighbourhood, the Reputation of being Rich, because those who come for Gold, will go off with Pewter and Brass, rather than return empty; and in the common Practice of the World, those who possess most Wealth, make the least Parade, which they leave to others, who have nothing else to bear them out, in shewing their Faces on the *Exchange*.

As to the first Cause of a Nation's Riches, being the Fertility of the Soyl, as well as Temperature of Clymate, we have no Reason to complain; for although the Quantity of unprofitable Land in this Kingdom, reckoning Bog, and Rock, and barren Mountain, be double in Proportion to what it is in England, yet the Native Productions which both Kingdoms deal in, are very near on equality in point of Goodness, and might with the same Encouragement be as well manufactured. I except Mines and Minerals, in some of which however we are only defective in point of Skill and Industry.

In the Second, which is the Industry of the People, our misfortune is not altogether owing to our own Fault, but to a million of Discouragements.

The conveniency of Ports and Havens which Nature bestowed us so liberally is of no more use to us, than a beautiful Prospect to a Man shut up in a Dungeon.

As to Shipping of it's own, this Kingdom is so utterly unprovided, that of all the excellent Timber cut down within these fifty or sixty Years, it can hardly be said that the Nation hath received the Benefit of one valuable House to dwell in, or one Ship to Trade with.

Ireland is the only Kingdom I ever heard or read of either in ancient or modern Story, which was denied the Liberty of exporting their native Commodities and Manufactures wherever they pleased, except to Countries at War with their own Prince or State, yet this Privilege by the Superiority of meer Power is refused us in the most momentous parts of Commerce, besides an Act of Navigation to which we never consented, pinned down upon us, and rigorously executed, and a thousand other enexampled Circumstances as grievous as they are invidious to mention. To go unto the Rest.

It is too well known that we are forced to obey some Laws we never consented to, which is a Condition I must not call by it's true uncontroverted Name for fear of my L[ord] C[hief] J[ustice] *W[hitshed]'s* Ghost with his LIBERTAS ET NATALE SOLUM, written as a Motto on his Coach, as it stood at the Door of the Court, while he was Perjuring himself to betray both. Thus, we are in the Condition of Patients who have Physick sent them by Doctors at a Distance, Strangers to their Constitution, and the nature of their Disease: And thus, we are forced to pay five hundred *per Cent* to decide our Properties, in all which we have likewise the Honour to be distinguished from the whole Race of Mankind.

As to improvement of Land, those few who attempt that or Planting, through Covetousness or want of Skill, generally leave things worse than they were, neither succeeding in Trees nor Hedges, and by running into the fancy of Grazing after the manner of the *Scythians*, are every Day depopulating the Country.

We are so far from having a King to reside among us, that even the Viceroy is generally absent four Fifths of his time in the Government.

No Strangers from other Countries make this a part of their Travels, where they can expect to see nothing but Scenes of Misery and Desolation.

Those who have the Misfortune to be born here, have the least Title to any considerable Employment, to which they are seldom preferred, but upon a Political Consideration.

One third part of the Rents of *Ireland* is spent in *England*, which with the Profit of Employments, Pensions, Appeals, Journeys of Pleasure or Health, Education at the *Inns* of Court, and both Universities, Remittances at Pleasure, the Pay of all Superior Officers in the Army and other Incidents, will amount to a full half of the Income of the whole Kingdom, all clear profit to *England*.

We are denyed the Liberty of Coining Gold, Silver, or even Copper. In the Isle of *Man*, they Coin their own Silver, every petty Prince, Vassal to the *Emperor* can Coin what Money he pleaseth. And in this as in most of the Articles already mentioned, we are an exception to all other States or Monarchies that were ever known in the World.

As to the last, or Fourteenth Article, we take special Care to Act diametrically contrary to it in the whole Course of our Lives. Both Sexes, but expecially the Women despise and abhor to wear any of their own Manufactures, even those which are better made than in other Countries, particularly a sort of Silk Plad, through which the Workmen are forced to run a sort of Gold-thread that it may pass for *Indian*. Even Ale and Potatoes in great quantity are Imported from *England* as well as Corn, and our foreign Trade is little more than Importation of French Wine, for which I am told we pay ready Money.

Now if all this be true, upon which I could easily enlarge, I would be glad to know by what secret method it is that we grow a Rich and Flourishing People, without Liberty, Trade, Manufactures, Inhabitants, Money, or the privilege of Coining; without Industry, Labour or Improvement of Lands, and with more than half of the Rent and Profits of the whole *Kingdom*, Annually exported, for which we receive not a single Farthing: And to make up all this, nothing worth mentioning, except the Linnen of the *North*, a Trade casual, corrupted and at Mercy, and some Butter from *Cork*. If we do flourish, it must be against every Law of Nature and Reason, like the Thorn at *Glassenbury*, that blossoms in the midst of Winter.

Let the worthy *C[ommissione]rs* who come from *England*

ride round the Kingdom, and observe the face of Nature, or the faces of the Natives, the Improvement of the Land, the thriving numerous Plantations, the noble Woods, the abundance and vicinity of Country-Seats, the commodious Farmers-Houses and Barns, the Towns and Villages, where every body is busy and thriving with all kind of Manufactures, the Shops full of Goods wrought to Perfection, and filled with Customers, the comfortable Dyet and Dress, and Dwellings of the People, the vast Numbers of Ships in our Harbours and Docks, and Shipwrights in our Sea-port-Towns. The Roads crouded with Carryers laden with rich Manufactures, the perpetual Concourse to and fro of pompous Equipages.

With what Envy and Admiration would these Gentlemen return from so delightful a Progress? What glorious Reports would they make when they went back to *England*?

But my Heart is too heavy to continue this Irony longer, for it is manifest that whatever Stranger took such a Journey, would be apt to think himself travelling in *Lapland* or *Ysland*, rather than in a Country so favoured by Nature as Ours, both in Fruitfulness of Soyl, and Temperature of Climate. The miserable Dress, and Dyet, and Dwelling of the People. The general Desolation in most parts of the Kingdom. The old Seats of the Nobility and Gentry all in Ruins, and no new Ones in their stead. The Families of Farmers who pay great Rents, living in Filth and Nastiness upon Butter-milk and Potatoes, without a Shoe or Stocking to their Feet, or a House so convenient as an *English* Hog-sty to receive them. These indeed may be comfortable sights to an English Spectator, who comes for a short time only *to learn the Language*, and returns back to his own Country, whither he finds all our Wealth transmitted.

Nostrâ miseriâ magnus es.

There is not one Argument used to prove the Riches of *Ireland*, which is not a logical Demonstration of it's Poverty. The Rise of our Rents is squeesed out of the very Blood and Vitals, and Cloaths, and Dwellings of the

Tenants who live worse than English Beggars. The lowness of Interest in all other Countries a sign of Wealth is in us a proof of misery, there being no Trade to employ any Borrower. Hence alone comes the Dearness of Land, since the Savers have no other way to lay out their Money. Hence the Dearness of Necessaries for Life, because the Tenants cannot afford to pay such extravagant Rates for Land (which they must take, or go a begging) without raising the Price of Cattle, and of Corn, although they should live upon Chaff. Hence our encrease of Buildings in this City, because Workmen have nothing to do but employ one another, and one half of them are infallibly undone. Hence the daily encrease of *Bankers*, who may be a necessary Evil in a Trading-Country, but so ruinous in Ours, who for their private Advantage have sent away all our Silver, and one third of our Gold, so that within three Years past, the running Cash of the Nation, which was about Five hundred thousand Pounds, is now less than two, and must daily diminish unless we have Liberty to Coin, as well as that important Kingdom the Isle of *Man*, and the meanest Prince in the *German Empire*, as I before observed.

I have sometimes thought, that this Paradox of the Kingdom growing Rich, is chiefly owing to those worthy Gentlemen the BANKERS, who, except some Custom-house Officers, Birds of Passage, oppressive thrifty 'Squires, and a few others that shall be Nameless, are the only thriving People among us: And I have often wished that a Law were enacted to hang up half a Dozen *Bankers* every Year, and thereby interpose at least some short Delay, to the further Ruin of *Ireland*.

Ye are idle, ye are idle, answered *Pharaoh* to the *Israelites*, when they complained to his MAJESTY, that they were forced to make Bricks without Straw.

England enjoys every one of those Advantages for enriching a Nation, which I have above enumerated, and into the Bargain, a good Million returned to them every Year without Labour or Hazard, or one Farthing value received on our side. But how long we shall be able to continue the payment, I am not under the least Concern. One thing I know, that *when the Hen is starved to Death, there will be no more Golden Eggs.*

I think it a little unhospitable, and others may call it a subtil piece of Malice, that, because there may be a Dozen Families in this Town, able to entertain their *English* Friends in a generous manner at their Tables, their Guests upon their Return to *England*, shall report that we wallow in Riches and Luxury.

Yet I confess I have known an Hospital, where all the Household-Officers grew Rich, while the Poor for whose sake it was built, were almost starving for want of Food and Raiment.

To Conclude. If *Ireland* be a rich and flourishing Kingdom, it's Wealth and Prosperity must be owing to certain Causes, that are yet concealed from the whole Race of Mankind, and the Effects are equally Invisible. We need not wonder at Strangers when they deliver such Paradoxes, but a Native and Inhabitant of this Kingdom, who gives the same Verdict, must be either ignorant to Stupidity, or a Man-pleaser at the Expence of all Honour, Conscience and Truth.

A MODEST PROPOSAL

for preventing the Children of Poor People from being a Burthen to their Parents, or the Country, and for making them Beneficial to the Publick.

IT is a melancholly Object to those, who walk through this great Town, or travel in the Country, when they see the *Streets*, the *Roads*, and *Cabbin-Doors*, crowded with *Beggars* of the female Sex, followed by three, four, or six Children, *all in Rags*, and importuning every Passenger for an Alms. These *Mothers* instead of being able to work for their honest livelyhood, are forced to employ all their time in Stroling, to beg Sustenance for their *helpless Infants*, who, as they grow up, either turn *Thieves* for want of work, or leave their *dear native Country to fight for the Pretender in Spain*, or sell themselves to the *Barbadoes*.

I think it is agreed by all Parties, that this prodigious number of Children, in the Arms, or on the Backs, or at the *heels* of their *Mothers*, and frequently of their *Fathers*, is *in the present deplorable state of the Kingdom*, a very great additional grievance; and therefore whoever could find out a fair, cheap and easy method of making these Children sound and useful Members of the common-wealth would deserve so well of the publick, as to have his Statue set up for a preserver of the Nation.

But my Intention is very far from being confined to provide only for the Children of *professed Beggars*: It is of a much greater extent, and shall take in the whole number of Infants at a certain Age, who are born of Parents in effect as little able to support them, as those who demand our Charity in the Streets.

512

As to my own part, having turned my thoughts, for many Years, upon this important Subject, and maturely weighed the several *Schemes of other Projectors*, I have always found them grossly mistaken in their computation. It is true a Child, *just dropt from it's Dam*, may be supported by her Milk, for a Solar year with little other Nourishment, at most not above the Value of two Shillings, which the Mother may certainly get, or the Value in *Scraps*, by her lawful Occupation of begging, and it is exactly at one year Old that I propose to provide for them, in such a manner, as, instead of being a Charge upon their *Parents*, or the *Parish*, or *wanting Food and Raiment* for the rest of their Lives, they shall, on the Contrary, contribute to the Feeding and partly to the Cloathing of many Thousands.

There is likewise another great Advantage in my Scheme, that it will prevent those *voluntary Abortions*, and that horrid practice of *Women murdering their Bastard Children*, alas! too frequent among us, Sacrificing the *poor innocent Babes*, I doubt, more to avoid the Expence, than the Shame, which would move Tears and Pity in the most Savage and inhuman breast. (But not in human ones apparently)

The number of Souls in this Kingdom being usually reckoned one Million and a half, Of these I calculate there may be about two hundred thousand Couple whose Wives are Breeders, from which number I Substract thirty Thousand Couples, who are able to maintain their own Children, i.e. 85% are starving although I apprehend there cannot be so many under *the present distresses of the Kingdom*, but this being granted, there will remain an hundred and seventy thousand Breeders. I again Substract fifty Thousand for those Women who miscarry, or whose Children dye by accident, or disease within the Year. There only remain an hundred and twenty thousand Children of poor Parents annually born: The question therefore is, how this number shall be reared, and provided for, which, as I have already said, under the present Situation of Affairs, is utterly impossible by all the methods hitherto proposed, for we can *neither employ them in Handicraft*, or *Agriculture*; we neither build Houses, (I mean in the Country) nor cultivate Land: They can very seldom pick up a Livelyhood *by Stealing* till they arrive at six years Old, except where they are of towardly parts, although, I confess they learn the Rudiments much earlier, during which time, they can however be properly looked upon only as *Probationers*, as I have been informed by a principal Gentleman in the County of *Cavan*, who protested to me, that he never knew above one or two Instances under the Age of six, even in a part of the Kingdom *so renowned for the quickest proficiency in that Art*.

I am assured by our Merchants, that a Boy or Girl, before twelve years Old, is no saleable Commodity, and even when they come to this Age, they will not yield above three Pounds, or three Pounds and half a Crown at most on the Exchange, which cannot turn to Account either to the Parents or the Kingdom, the Charge of Nutriment and Rags having been at least four times that Value.

I shall now therefore humbly propose my own thoughts, which I hope will not be lyable to the least Objection.

I have been assured by a very knowing *American* of my acquaintance in *London*, that a young healthy Child well Nursed is at a year Old a most delicious, nourishing, and wholesome Food, whether *Stewed, Roasted, Baked*, or *Boyled*, and I make no doubt that it will equally serve in a *Fricasie*, or a *Ragoust*.

I do therefore humbly offer it to *publick consideration*, that of the hundred and twenty thousand Children, already computed, twenty thousand may be reserved for Breed, whereof only one fourth part to be Males, which is more than we allow to *Sheep, black Cattle*, or *Swine*, and my reason is that these Children are seldom the Fruits of Marriage, *a Circumstance not much regarded by our Savages*, therefore *one Male* will be sufficient to serve *four Females*. That the remaining hundred thousand may at a year Old be offered in Sale to the *persons of Quality*, and *Fortune*, through the Kingdom, always advising the Mother to let them Suck plentifully in the last Month, so as to render them Plump, and Fat for a good Table. A Child will make two Dishes at an Entertainment for Friends, and when the Family dines alone, the fore or hind Quarter will make a reasonable Dish, and seasoned with a little Pepper or Salt will be very good Boiled on the fourth Day, especially in Winter.

I have reckoned upon a Medium, that a Child just born will weigh 12 pounds, and in a solar Year if tollerably nursed encreaseth to 28 Pound.

I grant this food will be somewhat dear, and therefore very *proper for Landlords,* who, as they have already devoured most of the Parents, seem to have the best Title to the Children.

Infant's flesh will be in Season throughout the Year, but more plentiful in *March,* and a little before and after, for we are told by a grave Author an eminent *French* Physitian, that *Fish being a prolifick Dyet,* there are more Children born in *Roman Catholick Countries* about nine Months after *Lent,* than at any other Season: Therefore reckoning a Year after *Lent,* the Markets will be more glutted than usual, because the number of *Popish Infants,* is at least three to one in this Kingdom, and therefore it will have one other Collateral advantage by lessening the Number of *Papists* among us.

I have already computed the Charge of nursing a Beggars Child (in which list I reckon all *Cottagers, Labourers,* and four fifths of the *Farmers*) to be about two Shillings *per Annum,* Rags included, and I believe no Gentleman would repine to give Ten Shillings for the *Carcass of a good fat Child,* which, as I have said will make four Dishes of excellent Nutritive Meat, when he hath only some particular friend, or his own Family to Dine with him. Thus the Squire will learn to be a good Landlord, and grow popular among his Tenants, the Mother will have Eight Shillings neat profit, and be fit for Work till she produces another Child.

Those who are more thrifty (*as I must confess the Times require*) may flay the Carcass; the Skin of which, Artificially dressed, will make admirable *Gloves for Ladies,* and *Summer Boots for fine Gentlemen.*

As to our City of *Dublin,* Shambles may be appointed for this purpose, in the most convenient parts of it, and

Butchers we may be assured will not be wanting, although I rather recommend buying the Children alive, and dressing them hot from the Knife, as we do *roasting Pigs*.

A very worthy Person, *a true Lover of his Country*, and whose Virtues I highly esteem, was lately pleased, in discoursing on this matter, to offer a refinement upon my Scheme. He said, that many Gentlemen of this Kingdom, having of late destroyed their Deer, he conceived that the want of Venison might be well supplyed by the Bodies of young Lads and Maidens, not exceeding fourteen Years of Age, nor under twelve, so great a Number of both Sexes in every Country being now ready to Starve, for want of Work and Service: And these to be disposed of by their Parents if alive, or otherwise by their nearest Relations. But with due deference to so excellent a friend, and so deserving a Patriot, I cannot be altogether in his Sentiments, for as to the Males, my *American* acquaintance assured me from frequent Experience, that their flesh was generally Tough and Lean, like that of our Schoolboys, by continual exercise, and their Taste disagreeable, and to Fatten them would not answer the Charge. Then as to the Females, it would, I think with humble Submission, *be a loss to the Publick*, because they soon would become Breeders themselves: And besides it is not improbable that some scrupulous People might be apt to Censure such a Practice, (although indeed very unjustly) as a little bordering upon Cruelty, which, I confess, hath always been with me the strongest objection against any Project, however so well intended.

But in order to justify my friend, he confessed, that this expedient was put into his head by the famous *Sallmanaazor*, a Native of the Island *Formosa*, who came from thence to *London*, above twenty Years ago, and in Conversation told my friend, that in his Country when any young Person happened to be put to Death, the Executioner sold the Carcass to *Persons of Quality*, as a prime Dainty, and that, in his Time, the Body of a plump Girl of fifteen, who was crucifyed for an attempt to Poison the Emperor, was sold to his Imperial *Majesty's prime Minister of State*, and other great *Mandarins* of the Court, *in Joints from the Gibbet*, at four hundred Crowns. Neither indeed can I deny, that if the same use were made of several plump young Girls in this Town, who, without one single Groat to their Fortunes, cannot stir abroad without a Chair, and appear at the *Play-House*, and *Assemblies* in Foreign fineries, which they never will Pay for; the Kingdom would not be the worse.

Some Persons of a desponding Spirit are in great concern about that vast Number of poor People, who are aged, diseased, or maimed, and I have been desired to imploy my thoughts what Course may be taken, to ease the Nation of so grievous an Incumbrance. But I am not in the least pain about the matter, because it is very well known, that they are every Day *dying*, and *rotting*, by *cold*, and *famine*, and *filth*, and *vermin*, as fast as can be reasonably expected. And as to the younger Labourers they are now in almost as hopeful a Condition. They cannot get Work, and consequently pine away for want of Nourishment, to a degree, that if at any time they are accidentally hired to common Labour, they have not strength to perform it, and thus the Country and themselves are happily delivered from the Evils to come.

I have too long degressed, and therefore shall return to my subject. I think the advantages by the Proposal which I have made are obvious and many as well as of the highest importance.

For first, as I have already observed, it would greatly lessen *the Number of Papists*, with whom we are Yearly over-run, being the principal Breeders of the Nation, as well as our most dangerous Enemies, and who stay at home on purpose with a design *to deliver the Kingdom to the Pretender*, hoping to take their Advantage by the absence *of so many good Protestants*, who have chosen rather to leave their Country, than stay at home, and pay Tythes against their Conscience, to an *Episcopal Curate*.

Secondly, the poorer Tenants will have something valuable of their own, which by Law may be made lyable to Distress, and help to pay their Landlord's Rent, their Corn and Cattle being already seazed, and *Money a thing un-known*.

Thirdly, Whereas the Maintenance of an hundred thousand Children, from two Years old, and upwards, cannot be computed at less than Ten Shillings a piece *per Annum*, the Nation's Stock will be thereby encreased fifty thousand pounds *per Annum*, besides the profit of a new Dish, introduced to the Tables of all *Gentlemen of Fortune* in the Kingdom, who have any refinement in Taste, and the Money will circulate among our selves, the Goods being entirely of our own Growth and Manufacture.

Fourthly, The constant Breeders, besides the gain of Eight Shillings ster. *per Annum*, by the Sale of their Children, will be rid of the Charge of maintaining them after the first Year.

Fifthly, this food would likewise bring great *Custom to Taverns*, where the Vintners will certainly be so prudent as to procure the best receipts for dressing it to perfection, and consequently have their Houses frequented by all the *fine Gentlemen*, who justly value themselves upon their Knowledge in good *Eating*, and a skillful Cook, who understands how to oblige his Guests will contrive to make it as expensive as they please.

Sixthly, This would be a great Inducement to Marriage, which all wise Nations have either encouraged by Rewards, or enforced by Laws and Penalties. It would encrease the care and tenderness of Mothers towards their Children, when they were sure of a Settlement for Life, to the poor Babes, provided in some sort by the Publick to their Annual profit instead of Expence. We should soon see an honest Emulation among the married Women, *which of them could bring the fattest Child to the Market*, Men would become as fond of their *Wives*, during the Time of their Pregnancy, as they are now of their *Mares* in Foal, their *Cows* in Calf, or *Sows* when they are ready to Farrow, nor offer to Beat or Kick them (as it is too frequent a practice) for fear of a Miscarriage.

Many other advantages might be enumerated: For Instance, the addition of some thousand Carcases in our exportation of Barreled Beef. The Propagation of *Swines Flesh*, and Improvement in the Art of making good *Bacon*, so much wanted among us by the great destruction of *Pigs*, too frequent at our Tables, which are no way comparable in Taste, or Magnificence to a well grown, fat Yearling Child, which Roasted whole will make a considerable Figure at a *Lord Mayor's Feast*, or any other Publick Entertainment. But this, and many others I omit, being studious of Brevity.

Supposing that one thousand Families in this City, would be constant Customers for Infants Flesh, besides others who might have it at *Merry-meetings*, particularly *Weddings* and *Christenings*, I compute that *Dublin* would take off Annually about twenty thousand Carcases, and the rest of the Kingdom (where probably they will be Sold somewhat Cheaper) the remaining eighty thousand.

I can think of no one Objection, that will possibly be raised against this Proposal, unless it should be urged that the Number of People will be thereby much lessened in the Kingdom. This I freely own, and it was indeed one Principal design in offering it to the World. I desire the Reader will observe, that I Calculate my Remedy *for this one individual Kingdom of IRELAND, and for no other that ever was, is, or, I think, ever can be upon Earth.* Therefore let no Man talk to me of other Expedients: *Of taxing our Absentees at five Shillings a pound: Of using neither Cloaths, nor household Furniture, except what is of our own Growth and Manufacture: Of utterly rejecting the Materials and Instruments that promote Foreign Luxury: Of curing the Expenciveness of Pride, Vanity, Idleness, and Gaming in our Women: Of introducing a Vein of Parcimony, Prudence and Temperance: Of learning to Love our Country, wherein we differ even from LAPLANDERS, and the Inhabitants of TOPINAMBOO: Of quitting our Animosities, and Factions, nor Act any longer like the Jews, who were Murdering one another at the very moment their City was taken: Of being a little Cautious not to Sell our Country and Consciences for nothing: Of teaching Landlords to have at least one degree of Mercy towards their Tenants. Lastly of putting a Spirit of Honesty,*

Industry and Skill into our Shopkeepers, who, if a Resolution could now be taken to Buy only our Native Goods, would immediately unite to Cheat and Exact upon us in the Price, the Measure, and the Goodness, nor could ever yet be brought to make one fair Proposal of just dealing, though often and earnestly invited to it.

Therefore I repeat, let no Man talk to me of these and the like Expedients, till he hath at least some Glimpse of Hope, that there will ever be some hearty and sincere Attempt to put them in Practice.

But as to my self, having been wearied out for many Years with offering vain, idle, visionary thoughts, and at length utterly despairing of Success, I fortunately fell upon this Proposal, which as it is wholly new, so it hath something Solid and Real, of no Expence and little Trouble, full in our own Power, and whereby we can incur no Danger in *disobliging England.* For this kind of Commodity will not bear Exportation, the Flesh being of too tender a Consistance, to admit a long continuance in Salt, *although perhaps I could name a Country, which would be glad to Eat up our whole Nation without it.*

After all I am not so violently bent upon my own Opinion, as to reject any Offer, proposed by wise Men, which shall be found equally Innocent, Cheap, Easy and Effectual. But before something of that kind shall be advanced in Contradiction to my Scheme, and offering a better, I desire the Author, or Authors will be pleased maturely to consider two points. *First,* as things now stand, how they will be able to find Food and Raiment for an hundred thousand useless Mouths and Backs. And *Secondly,* there being a round Million of Creatures in human Figure, throughout this Kingdom, whose whole Subsistance put into a common Stock, would leave them in Debt two Million of Pounds *Sterl.* adding those, who are Beggars by Profession, to the Bulk of Farmers, Cottagers and Labourers with their Wives and Children, who are Beggars in Effect; I desire those *Politicians,* who dislike my Overture, and may perhaps be so bold to attempt an Answer, that they will first ask the Parents of these Mortals, whether they would not at this Day think it a great Happiness to have been sold for Food at a year Old, in the manner I prescribe, and thereby have avoided such a perpetual Scene of Misfortunes, as they have since gone through, by the *oppression of Land-lords*, the Impossibility of paying Rent without Money or Trade, the want of common Sustenance, with neither House nor Cloaths to cover them from Inclemences of Weather, and the most inevitable Prospect of intailing the like, or greater Miseries upon their Breed for ever.

I Profess in the sincerity of my Heart that I have not the least personal Interest in endeavouring to promote this necessary Work having no other Motive than the *publick Good of my Country*, by *advancing our Trade, providing for Infants, relieving the Poor, and giving some Pleasure to the Rich*. I have no Children, by which I can propose to get a single Penny; the youngest being nine Years old, and my Wife past Childbearing.

AN EXAMINATION OF CERTAIN ABUSES, CORRUPTIONS, AND ENORMITIES, IN THE CITY OF DUBLIN

NOTHING is held more commendable in all great Cities, especially the Metropolis of a Kingdom, than what the *French* call the *Police*; by which Word is meant the Government thereof, to prevent the many Disorders occasioned by great Numbers of People and Carriages, especially thro' narrow Streets. In this Government our famous City of *Dublin* is said to be very defective, and universally complained of. Many wholesome Laws have been enacted to correct these Abuses, but are ill executed; and many more are wanting, which I hope the united Wisdom of the Nation (whereof so many good Effects have already appeared this Session) will soon take into their most profound Consideration.

As I have been always watchful over the Good of mine own Country, and particularly for that of our renowned City, where (*absit invidia*) I had the Honour to draw my first Breath; I cannot have a Minute's Ease or Patience to forbear enumerating some of the greatest Enormities, Abuses, and Corruptions spread almost through every Part of *Dublin*; and proposing such Remedies as, I hope, the Legislature will approve of.

The narrow Compass to which I have confined myself in this Paper, will allow me only to touch at the most important Defects, and such as I think seem to require the most speedy Redress.

And first, perhaps there was never known a wiser Institution than that of allowing certain Persons of both Sexes, in large and populous Cities, to cry through the Streets many Necessaries of Life; it would be endless to recount the Conveniences which our City enjoys by this useful Invention, and particularly Strangers, forced hither by Business, who reside here but a short time; for, these having usually but little Money, and being wholly ignorant of the Town, might at an easy Price purchase a tolerable Dinner, if the several Criers would pronounce the Names of the Goods they have to sell, in any tolerable Language. And therefore till our Law-makers shall think it proper to interpose so far as to make these Traders pronounce their Words in such Terms, that a plain Christian Hearer may comprehend what is cryed, I would advise all new Comers to look out at their Garret Windows, and there see whether the Thing that is cryed be *Tripes* or *Flummery, Buttermilk* or *Cowheels*. For, as things are now managed, how is it possible for an honest Country-man, just arrived, to find out what is meant; for Instance, by the following Words, with which his Ears are constantly stunned twice a Day, *Muggs, Juggs and Porringers, up in the Garret, and down in the Cellar*. I say, how is it possible for any Stranger to understand that this Jargon is meant as an invitation to buy a Farthing's worth of Milk for his Breakfast or Supper, unless his Curiosity draws him to the Window, or till his Landlady shall inform him? I produce this only as one Instance, among a Hundred much worse, I mean where the Words make a Sound wholly inarticulate, which give so much Disturbance, and so little Information.

The Affirmation solemnly made in the cry of *Herrings*, is directly against all Truth and Probability, *Herrings alive, alive here*; the very Proverb will convince us of this; for what is more frequent in ordinary Speech, than to say of some Neighbour for whom the Passing-Bell rings, that *he is dead as a Herring*. And, pray how is it possible, that a Herring, which as Philosophers observe, cannot live longer than one Minute, three Seconds and a half out of Water, should bear a Voyage in open Boats from *Howth* to *Dublin*, be tossed into twenty Hands, and preserve its Life in Sieves for several Hours? Nay, we have Witnesses ready to produce, that many Thousands of these Herrings, so impudently asserted to be alive, have been a Day and a Night upon dry Land. But this is not the worst. What can we think of those impious Wretches, who dare in the Face of the Sun, vouch the very same affirmative of their *Salmon*, and cry, *Salmon alive, alive*; whereas, if you call the Woman who cryes it, she is not asham'd to turn back her Mantle, and show you this individual Salmon cut into a dozen Pieces. I have given good Advice to these infamous Disgracers of their Sex and Calling, without the least appearance of Remorse, and fully against the Conviction of their own Consciences. I have mentioned this Grievance to several of our Parish Ministers, but all in vain; so that it must continue till the Government shall think fit to interpose.

There is another Cry, which, from the strictest Observation I can make, appears to be very modern, and it is that of *Sweet-hearts*, and is plainly intended for a Reflection upon the Female Sex, as if there were at present so great a Dearth of Lovers, that the Women instead of receiving Presents from Men, were now forced to offer Money, to purchase *Sweet-hearts*. Neither am I sure, that this Cry doth not glance at some Disaffection against the Government; insinuating, that while so many of our Troops are engaged in foreign Service, and such a great Number of our gallant Officers constantly reside in *England*, the Ladies are forced to take up with Parsons and Attornies: But, this is a most unjust Reflection, as may soon be proved by any Person who frequents the Castle, our publick Walks, our Balls and Assemblies, where the Crowds of *Toupees* were never known to swarm as they do at present.

There is a Cry, peculiar to this City, which I do not remember to have been used in *London*, or at least, not in the same Terms that it hath been practised by both Parties, during each of their Power; but, very unjustly by the *Tories*. While these were at the Helm, they grew daily more and more impatient to put all true *Whigs* and *Hanoverians* out of Employments. To effect which, they hired certain ordinary Fellows, with large Baskets on their Shoulders, to call aloud at every House, *Dirt to carry out*; giving that Denomination to our whole Party, as if they would signify, that the Kingdom could never be *cleansed*, till we were *swept*

from the Earth like *Rubbish*. But, since that happy Turn of
Times, when we were so *miraculously* preserved by just an
Inch, from *Popery*, *Slavery*, *Massacre*, and the *Pretender*;
I must own it Prudence in us, still to go on with the same
Cry, which hath ever since been so effectually observed,
that the true *political Dirt* is wholly removed, and thrown
on its proper Dunghills, there to corrupt, and be no more
heard of.

But, to proceed to other Enormities: Every Person who
walks the Streets, must needs observe the immense Number
of human Excrements at the Doors and Steps of waste
Houses, and at the Sides of every dead Wall; for which the
disaffected Party have assigned a very false and malicious
Cause. They would have it, that these Heaps were laid
there privately by *British Fundaments*, to make the World
believe, that our *Irish* Vulgar do daily eat and drink; and,
consequently, that the Clamour of Poverty among us, must
be false, proceeding only from *Jacobites* and *Papists*. They
would confirm this, by pretending to observe, that a *British
Anus* being more narrowly perforated than one of our own
Country; and many of these Excrements upon a strict View
appearing Cople-crown'd, with a Point like a Cone or Pyra-
mid, are easily distinguish'd from the *Hibernian*, which lie
much flatter, and with less continuity. I communicated this
Conjecture to an eminent Physician, who is well versed
in such profound Speculations; and at my Request was
pleased to make Trial with each of his Fingers, by thrusting
them into the *Anus* of several Persons of both Nations, and
professed he could find no such Difference between them
as those ill-disposed People alledge. On the contrary, he
assured me, that much the greater Number of narrow Cavi-
ties were of *Hibernian* Origin. This I only mention to shew
how ready the Jacobites are to lay hold of any Handle to
express their Malice against the Government. I had almost
forgot to add, that my Friend the Physician could, by smelling each Finger, distinguish the *Hibernian* Excrement from
the *British*, and was not above twice mistaken in an Hundred Experiments; upon which he intends very soon to
publish a learned Dissertation.

s

There is a Diversion in this City, which usually begins among the Butchers, but is often continued by a Succession of other People, through many Streets. It is call'd the COSSING *of a Dog*; and I may justly number it among our Corruptions. The Ceremony is thus: A strange Dog happens to pass through a Flesh-Market: Whereupon an expert Butcher immediately cries in a loud Voice, and the proper Tone, *Coss*, *Coss*, several Times: The same Word is repeated by the People. The Dog, who perfectly understands the Term of Art, and consequently the Danger he is in, immediately flies. The People, and even his own *Brother Animals* pursue; the Pursuit and Cry attend him perhaps half a Mile; he is well worried in his Flight, and sometimes hardly escapes. This, our Ill-wishers of the *Jacobite* Kind, are pleased to call a *Persecution*; and affirm, that it always falls upon Dogs of the *Tory* Principle. But, we can well defend ourselves, by justly alledging that when they were uppermost, they treated our *Dogs* full as inhumanly: As to my own Part, who have in former Times often attended these *Processions*, although I can very well distinguish between a *Whig* and *Tory Dog*; yet I never carried my Resentments very far upon a *Party Principle*, except it were against certain malicious *Dogs*, who most discovered their Malice against us in the *worst of Times*. And, I remember too well, that in the wicked Ministry of the Earl of *Oxford*, a large Mastiff of our Party being unmercifully *cossed*, ran, without thinking, between my Legs, as I was coming up *Fishamble-street*; and, as I am of low Stature, with very short Legs, bore me riding backwards down the Hill, for above two Hundred Yards: And, altho' I made use of his Tail for a Bridle, holding it fast with both my Hands, and clung my Legs as close to his Sides as I could, yet we both came down together into the Middle of the Kennel; where after rowling three or four Times over each other, I got up with much ado, amidst the Shouts and Huzzas of a Thousand malicious *Jacobites*: I cannot, indeed, but gratefully acknowledge, that for this and many other Services and Sufferings, I have been since more than over-paid.

This Adventure may, perhaps, have put me out of Love

with the Diversion of *Cossing*, which I confess my self an Enemy to, unless we could always be sure of distinguishing *Tory Dogs*; whereof great Numbers have since been so prudent, as entirely to change their Principles, and are now justly esteemed the best *Worriers* of their former Friends.

I am assured, and partly know, that all the Chimney-Sweepers Boys, where Members of P[arliamen]t chiefly lodge, are hired by *our Enemies* to sculk in the Tops of Chimneys, with their Heads no higher than will just permit them to look round; and at the usual Hours when Members are going to the House, if they see a Coach stand near the Lodging of any *loyal* Member, they call *Coach, Coach*, as loud as they can bawl, just at the Instant when the Footman begins to give the same Call. And this is chiefly done on those Days, when any Point of Importance is to be debated. This Practice may be of very dangerous Consequence. For, these Boys are all hired by Enemies to the Government; and thus, by the Absence of a few Members for a few Minutes, a Question may be carried against the *true Interest* of the Kingdom, and very probably, not without an Eye towards the *Pretender*.

I have not observed the Wit and Fancy of this Town, so much employed in any one Article, as that of contriving Variety of Signs to hang over Houses, where *Punch* is to be sold. The Bowl is represented full of Punch, the Ladle stands erect in the Middle, supported sometimes by one, and sometimes by two Animals, whose Feet rest upon the Edge of the Bowl. These Animals are sometimes one black *Lyon*, and sometimes a Couple; sometimes a single *Eagle*, and sometimes a spread one, and we often meet a *Crow*, a *Swan*, a *Bear*, or a *Cock*.

Now, I cannot find how any of these Animals, either separate, or in Conjunction, are properly speaking, either fit Emblems or Embellishments, to advance the Sale of Punch. Besides, it is agreed among Naturalists, that no Brute can endure the Taste of strong Liquor, except where he hath been used to it from his Infancy: And, consequently, it is against all the Rules of Hieroglyph, to assign those Animals as Patrons, or Protectors of *Punch*. For, in that Case, we ought to suppose, that the Host keeps always ready the real Bird, or Beast, whereof the Picture hangs over his Door, to entertain his Guest; which, however, to my Knowledge, is not true in Fact. For not one of those Birds is a proper Companion for a *Christian*, as to aiding and assisting in making the *Punch*. For the Birds, as they are drawn upon the Sign, are much more likely to mute, or shed their Feathers into the Liquor. Then, as to the *Bear*, he is too terrible, awkward, and slovenly a Companion to converse with; neither are any of them all, handy enough to fill Liquor to the Company: I do, therefore, vehemently suspect a *Plot* intended against the Government, by these Devices. For, although the *Spread-Eagle* be the Arms of *Germany*, upon which Account it may possibly be a lawful *Protestant* Sign; yet I, who am very suspicious of fair Out-sides, in a Matter which so nearly concerns our Welfare, cannot but call to Mind, that the *Pretender's* Wife is said to be of *German* Birth: And that many *Popish* Princes, in so vast an Extent of Land, are reported to excel both at making and drinking Punch. Besides, it is plain, that the *Spread-Eagle* exhibits to us the perfect Figure of a *Cross*, which is a Badge of *Popery*. Then, as to the *Cock*, he is well known to represent the *French* Nation, our old and dangerous Enemy. The *Swan*, who must of Necessity cover the entire Bowl with his Wings, can be no other than the *Spaniard*, who endeavours to engross all the Treasures of the *Indies* to himself. The *Lyon* is indeed, the common Emblem of Royal Power, as well as the Arms of *England*; but to paint him black, is perfect *Jacobitism*, and a manifest Type of those who blacken the Actions of the best Princes. It is not easy to distinguish, whether that other Fowl painted over the Punch-Bowl, be a *Crow* or *Raven*? It is true, they have both been held ominous Birds; but I rather take it to be the former; because it is the Disposition of a *Crow*, to pick out the Eyes of other Creatures; and often even of *Christians*, after they are dead; and is therefore drawn here, with a Design to put the *Jacobites* in Mind of their old Practice, first to lull us a-sleep, (which is an Emblem of Death) and then to blind our Eyes, that we may not see their dangerous Practices against the State.

To speak my private Opinion, the least offensive Picture in the whole Sett, seems to be the *Bear*; because he represents *Ursa Major*, or the *Great Bear*, who presides over the *North*, where the *Reformation* first began, and which, next to *Britain*, (including *Scotland* and the North of *Ireland*) is the great Protector of the *Protestant* Religion. But, however, in those Signs where I observe the *Bear* to be *chained*, I can't help surmising a *Jacobite* Contrivance, by which these Traytors hint an earnest Desire of using all *true Whigs*, as their Predecessors did the primitive Christians; I mean, to represent us as *Bears*, and then hallow their *Tory-Dogs* to bait us to Death.

Thus I have given a fair Account of what I dislike, in all those Signs set over those Houses that invite us to *Punch*: I own it was a Matter that did not need explaining, being so very obvious to the most common Understanding. Yet, I know not how it happens, but methinks there seems a fatal Blindness, to overspread our corporeal Eyes, as well as our intellectual; and I heartily wish, I may be found a false Prophet. For, these are not bare Suspicions, but manifest Demonstrations.

Therefore, away with those *Popish*, *Jacobite*, and idolatrous Gew-gaws. And I heartily wish a Law were enacted, under severe Penalties, against drinking any *Punch* at all. For nothing is easier, than to prove it a disaffected Liquor. The chief Ingredients, which are Brandy, Oranges, and Lemons, are all sent us from *Popish* Countries; and nothing remains of *Protestant* Growth but Sugar and Water. For, as to Biscuit, which formerly was held a necessary Ingredient, and is truly *British*, we find it is entirely rejected.

But I will put the Truth of my Assertion, past all Doubt: I mean, that this Liquor is by one important Innovation, grown of ill Example, and dangerous Consequence to the Publick. It is well known, that, by the true original Institution of making *Punch*, left us by Captain *Ratcliff*, the Sharpness is only occasioned by the Juice of Lemons, and so con-

tinued till after the happy *Revolution*. Oranges, alas! are a
meer Innovation, and in a Manner *but of Yesterday*. It was
the Politicks of *Jacobites* to introduce them gradually: And,
to what Intent? The Thing speaks it self. It was cunningly
to shew their Virulence against his sacred Majesty King
William, of ever glorious and immortal Memory. But of late,
(to shew how fast Disloyalty increaseth) they came from
one to two, and then to three Oranges; nay, at present we
often find Punch made all with Oranges, and not one single
Lemon. For the *Jacobites*, before the Death of that immortal Prince, had, by a Superstition, formed a private
Prayer, that, as they *squeezed* the *Orange*, so might that
Protestant King be *squeezed* to Death: According to that
known Sorcery described by *Virgil, Limus ut hic durescit,
& hæc ut cera liquescit*, &c. And, thus the *Romans*, when
they sacrificed an Ox, used this Kind of Prayer. *As I knock
down this Ox, so may thou, O* Jupiter, *knock down our
Enemies*. In like Manner, after King *William's* Death,
whenever a *Jacobite squeezed* an *Orange*, he had a mental
Curse upon the *glorious Memory*, and a hearty Wish for
Power to *squeeze* all his Majesty's Friends to Death, as he
squeezed that *Orange*, which bore one of his Titles, as he
was Prince of *Orange*. This I do affirm for Truth; many
of that Faction having confess'd it to me, under an *Oath of
Secrecy*; which, however, I thought it my Duty not to keep,
when I saw my dear Country in Danger. But, what better
can be expected from an *impious* Sett of Men, who never
scruple to drink CONFUSION to all *true Protestants*, under
the Name of *Whigs*? a most unchristian and inhuman Practice, which, to our great Honour and Comfort, was *never*
charged upon us, even by our most malicious Detractors.

The Sign of two *Angels*, hovering in the Air, and with
their right Hands supporting a *Crown*, is met with in several
Parts of this City; and hath often given me great Offence:
For, whether by the Unskilfulness, or dangerous Principles
of the Painters, (although I have good Reasons to suspect
the latter) those *Angels* are usually drawn with such horrid
Countenances, that they give great Offence to every loyal
Eye, and equal Cause of Triumph to the *Jacobites*, being a

most infamous Reflection upon our most able and excellent Ministry.

I now return to that great Enormity of City *Cries*; most of which we have borrowed from *London*. I shall consider them only in a *political* View, as they nearly affect the Peace and Safety of both Kingdoms; and having been originally contrived by wicked *Machiavels*, to bring in *Popery, Slavery*, and *Arbitrary Power*, by defeating the *Protestant* Succession, and introducing the *Pretender*, ought, in Justice, to be here laid open to the World.

About two or three Months after the happy *Revolution*, all Persons who possess any Employment, or Office, in Church or State, were obliged by an Act of Parliament, to take the Oaths to King *William* and Queen *Mary*: And a great Number of disaffected Persons, refusing to take the said Oaths, from a pretended Scruple of Conscience, but really from a Spirit of *Popery* and Rebellion, they contrived a Plot, to make the swearing to those Princes odious in the Eyes of the People. To this End, they hired certain Women of ill Fame, but loud shrill Voices, under Pretence of selling Fish, to go through the Streets, with Sieves on their Heads, and cry, *buy my Soul, buy my Soul*; plainly insinuating, that all those who swore to King *William*, were just ready to sell their *Souls* for an Employment. This Cry was revived at the Death of Queen *Anne*, and, I hear, still continues in *London*, with great Offence to all *true Protestants*; but, to our great Happiness, seems to be almost dropt in Dublin.

But, because I altogether contemn the Displeasure and Resentment of *High-flyers, Tories*, and *Jacobites*, whom I look upon to be *worse even than profest Papists*, I do here declare, that those Evils which I am going to mention, were all brought upon us in the *worst of Times*, under the late Earl of *Oxford's Administration*, during the four last Years of Queen *Anne's* Reign. *That wicked Minister was universally known to be a Papist in his Heart. He was of a most avaricious Nature, and is said to have dyed worth four Millions, sterl. besides his vast Expences in Building, Statues, Gold Plate, Jewels, and other costly Rarities. He was of a mean obscure Birth, from the very Dregs of the People, and so illiterate, that he could hardly read a Paper at the Council Table. I forbear to touch at his open, prophane, profligate Life; because I desire not to rake into the Ashes of the Dead, and therefore I shall observe this wise Maxim:* De mortuis nil nisi bonum.

This flagitious Man, in order to compass his black Designs, employ'd certain wicked Instruments (which great Statesmen are never without) to adapt several *London* Cries, in such a Manner as would best answer his Ends. And, whereas it was upon Grounds grievously suspected, that all *Places* at Court were sold to the highest Bidder: Certain Women were employed by his Emissaries, to carry *Fish* in Baskets on their Heads, and bawl thro' the Streets, *buy my fresh Places.* I must, indeed, own that other Women used the same Cry, who were innocent of this wicked Design, and really sold their Fish of that Denomination to get an honest Livelyhood; but the rest, who were in the *Secret*, although they carried *Fish* in their Sieves or Baskets, to save Appearances; yet they had likewise, a certain Sign, somewhat resembling that of the *Free-Masons*, which the Purchasers of *Places* knew well enough, and were directed by the Women whither they were to resort, and make their Purchase. And, I remember very well, how oddly it look't, when we observed many Gentlemen finely drest, about the Court-end of the Town, and as far as *York-Buildings*, where the Lord Treasurer *Oxford* dwelt, calling the Women who cry'd *buy my fresh Places*, and talking to them in the Corner of a Street, after they understood each other's Sign; but we never could observe that any Fish was bought.

Some Years before the fine Cries last mentioned, the *Duke* of *Savoy* was reported to have made certain Overtures to the Court of *England*, for admitting his eldest Son by the Dutchess of *Orleans's* Daughter, to succeed to the Crown, as next Heir, upon the *Pretender's* being rejected, and that Son was immediately to turn *Protestant*. It was confidently reported, that great Numbers of People disaffected to the then *Illustrious* but now *Royal* House of *Hanover*, were in those Measures. Whereupon, another Sett of Women were hired by the *Jacobite* Leaders, to cry through the whole Town, *buy my* Savoys, *dainty* Savoys, *curious* Savoys. But, I cannot directly charge the late Earl of *Oxford* with this *Conspiracy*, because he was not then chief Minister. However, the wicked Cry still continues in *London*, and was brought over hither, where it remains to this Day, and is in my humble Opinion, a very offensive Sound to every true Protestant, who is old enough to remember those *dangerous* Times.

During the Ministry of that corrupt and *Jacobite* Earl abovementioned, the secret pernicious Design of those in Power, was to sell *Flanders* to *France*; the Consequence of which, must have been the infallible Ruin of the *States-General*, and would have open'd the Way for *France* to obtain that universal Monarchy, after which they have so long aspired; to which the *British* Dominions must next, after *Holland*, have been compelled to submit. And the *Protestant* Religion would be rooted out of the World.

A Design of this vast Importance, after long Consultation among the *Jacobite* Grandees, with the Earl of *Oxford* at their Head, was at last determin'd to be carried on by the same Method with the former; it was therefore again put in Practice; but the Conduct of it was chiefly left to chosen Men, whose Voices were louder and stronger than those of the other Sex. And upon this Occasion, was first instituted in *London*, that famous Cry of FLOUNDERS. But the Cryers were particularly directed to pronounce the Word *Flaunders*, and not *Flounders*. For, the Country which we now by Corruption call *Flanders*, is in it's true Orthography spelt *Flaunders*, as may be obvious to all who read old *English* Books. I say, from hence begun that thundring Cry, which hath ever since stunned the Ears of all *London*, made so many Children fall into Fits, and Women miscarry; *come buy my fresh* Flaunders, *curious* Flaunders, *charming* Flaunders, *alive, alive, ho*; which last Words can with no Propriety of Speech, be apply'd to Fish manifestly dead, (as I observed before in *Herrings* and *Salmon*) but very justly to ten Provinces, which contain many Millions of living *Christians*. And the Application is still closer, when we consider that all the People were to be taken like *Fishes* in a Net; and, by Assistance of the *Pope*, who sets up to be the *universal Fisher of Men*, the whole innocent Nation, was, according to our common Expression, to be *laid as flat as a* Flounder.

I remember, my self, a particular Cryer of *Flounders* in *London*, who arrived at so much Fame for the Loudness of his Voice, that he had the Honour to be mentioned upon that Account, in a Comedy. He hath disturbed me many a Morning, before he came within Fifty Doors of my Lodging. And, although I were not in those Days so fully apprized of the Designs, which our common Enemy had then in Agitation, yet, I know not how, by a secret Impulse, young as I was, I could not forbear conceiving a strong Dislike against the Fellow; and often said to my self, This Cry seems to be forged in the Jesuites School: Alas, poor *England*! I am grievously mistaken if there be not some *Popish* Plot at the Bottom. I communicated my Thoughts to an intimate Friend, who reproached me with being too visionary in my Speculations. But, it proved afterwards, that I conjectured right. And I have often since reflected, that if the wicked Faction could have procured only a Thousand Men, of as strong Lungs as the Fellow I mentioned, none can tell how terrible the Consequences might have been, not only to these two Kingdoms, but over all *Europe*, by selling *Flanders* to *France*. And yet these Cries continue unpunished, both in *London* and *Dublin*, although I confess, not with equal Vehemency or Loudness, because the Reason for contriving this desperate Plot, is, to our great Felicity, wholly ceased.

It is well known, that the Majority of the *British* House of Commons in the last Years of Queen *Anne's* Reign, were in their Hearts directly opposite to the Earl of *Oxford's* pernicious Measures; which put him under the Necessity of bribing them with Sallaries. Whereupon he had again Recourse to his old Politicks. And accordingly, his Emissaries were very busy in employing certain artful Women of no good Life or Conversation, (as it was fully proved before Justice P[eyto]n) to cry that Vegetable commonly called

Sollary, through the Town. These Women differed from the common Cryers of that Herb, by some private Mark which I could never learn; but the Matter was notorious enough, and sufficiently talked of, and about the same Period was the Cry of *Sollary* brought over into this Kingdom. But since there is not at this present, the least Occasion to suspect the Loyalty of our Cryers upon that Article, I am content that it may still be tolerated.

I shall mention but one Cry more, which hath any Reference to Politicks; but is indeed, of all others the most insolent, as well as treasonable, under our present happy Establishment. I mean that of *Turnups*; not of *Turnips*, according to the best Orthography, but absolutely *Turnups*. Although this Cry be of an older Date than some of the preceding Enormities; for it began soon after the Revolution; yet was it never known to arrive at so great an Height, as during the Earl of *Oxford's* Power. Some People, (whom I take to be private Enemies) are, indeed, as ready as my self to profess their Disapprobation of this Cry, on Pretence that it began by the Contrivance of certain old Procuresses, who kept Houses of ill Fame, where lewd Women met to draw young Men into Vice. And this they pretend to prove by some Words in the Cry; because, after the Cryer had bawled out *Turnups, ho, buy my dainty Turnups*, he would sometimes add the two following Verses.

> *Turn up the Mistress, and turn up the Maid,*
> *And turn up the Daughter, and be not afraid.*

This, say some political Sophists, plainly shews that there can be nothing further meant in this infamous Cry, than an Invitation to Lewdness, which indeed, ought to be severely punished in all well regulated Governments; but cannot be fairly interpreted as a Crime of State. But, I hope, we are not so weak and blind to be deluded at this Time of Day, with such poor Evasions. I could, if it were proper, demonstrate the very Time when those two Verses were composed, and name the Author, who was no other than the famous Mr. *Swan*, so well known for his Talent at Quibbling, and was as virulent a *Jacobite* as any in *England*. Neither could he deny the Fact, when he was taxed for it in my Presence by Sir *Harry Dutton-Colt*, and Colonel *Davenport*, at the *Smyrna* Coffee-House, on the 10th of *June*, 1701. Thus it appears to a Demonstration, that those Verses were only a Blind to conceal the most dangerous Designs of that Party, who from the first Years after the happy Revolution, used a Cant Way of talking in their Clubs after this Manner: We hope, to see the Cards shuffled once more, and another King T U R N U P Trump: And, when shall we meet over a Dish of TURNUPS? The same Term of Art was used in their Plots against the Government, and in their treasonable Letters writ in Cyphers, and decyphered by the famous Dr. *Wallis*, as you may read in the Tryals of those Times. This I thought fit to set forth at large, and in so clear a Light, because the *Scotch* and *French* Authors have given a very different Account of the Word TURNUP, but whether out of Ignorance or Partiality I shall not decree; because I am sure, the Reader is convinced by my Discovery. It is to be observed, that this Cry was sung in a particular Manner by Fellows in Disguise, to give Notice where those Traytors were to meet, in Order to concert their villanous Designs.

I have no more to add upon this Article, than an humble Proposal, that those who cry this Root at present in our Streets of *Dublin*, may be compelled by the Justices of the Peace, to pronounce *Turnip*, and not *Turnup*; for, I am afraid, we have still too many Snakes in our Bosom; and it would be well if their Cellars were sometimes searched, when the Owners least expect it; for I am not out of Fear that *latet anguis in Herba*.

Thus, we are zealous in Matters of small Moment, while we neglect those of the highest Importance. I have already made it manifest, that all these Cries were contrived in the worst of Times, under the Ministry of that desperate Statesman, *Robert* late Earl of *Oxford*, and for that very Reason ought to be rejected with Horror, as begun in the Reign of *Jacobites*, and may well be number'd among the Rags of Popery and Treason: Or if it be thought proper, that these Cries must continue, surely they ought to be only trusted in the Hands of true Protestants, who have given Security to the Government.

[Having already spoken of many abuses relating to sign-posts, I cannot here omit one more, because it plainly relates to politics; and is, perhaps, of more dangerous consequence than any of the city cries, because it directly tends to destroy the succession. It is the sign of his present Majesty King George the Second, to be met with in many streets; and yet I happen to be not only the first, but the only, discoverer of this audacious instance of Jacobitism. And I am confident, that, if the justices of the peace would please to make a strict inspection, they might find, in all such houses, before which those signs are hung up in the manner I have observed, that the landlords were malignant Papists, or, which is worse, notorious Jacobites. Whoever views these signs, may read, over his Majesty's head, the following letters and ciphers, G.R. II., which plainly signifies George, King the Second, and not King George the Second, or George the Second, King; but laying the point after the letter G, by which the owner of the house manifestly shows, that he renounces his allegiance to King George the Second, and allows him to be only the second king, *inuendo*, that the Pretender is the first king; and looking upon King George to be only a kind of second king, or viceroy, till the Pretender shall come over and seize the kingdom. I appeal to all mankind, whether this be a strained or forced interpretation of the inscription, as it now stands in almost every street; whether any decipherer would make the least doubt or hesitation to explain it as I have done; whether any other Protestant country would endure so public an instance of treason in the capital city from such vulgar conspirators; and, lastly, whether Papists and Jacobites of great fortunes and quality may not probably stand behind the curtain in this dangerous, open, and avowed design against the government. But I have performed my duty; and leave the reforming of these abuses to the wisdom, the vigilance, the loyalty, and activity of my superiors.]

A SERIOUS AND
Useful Scheme, to make an Hospital for Incurables, of Universal Benefit to all His Majesty's Subjects

THERE is not any thing which contributes more to the Reputation of particular Persons, or to the Honour of a Nation in general, than erecting and endowing proper *Edifices*, for the Reception of those who labour under different Kinds of Distress. The Diseased and Unfortunate are thereby delivered from the Misery of wanting Assistance; and others, are delivered from the Misery of beholding them.

It is certain, that the *Genius* of the People of *England* is strongly turned to publick Charities; and, to so noble a Degree, that almost in every part of this Great and Opulent *City*, and also in many of the adjacent Villages, we meet with a great Variety of *Hospitals*, supported by the generous Contributions of private Families, as well as by the Liberality of the Publick. Some, for Seamen, worn out in the Service of their Country; and others, for infirm disabled Soldiers: Some, for the Maintenance of Tradesmen decayed; and others, for their Widows, and Orphans: Some, for the Service of those who linger under tedious Distempers; and others, for such as are deprived of their Reason.

But I find, upon nice Inspection, that there is one Kind of Charity, almost totally disregarded, which, nevertheless, appears to me of so excellent a Nature, as to be at present more wanted, and better calculated for the Ease, Quietness, and Felicity of this whole Kingdom, than any other can possibly be. I mean,

An Hospital for Incurables.

I must indeed confess, that an Endowment of this Nature would prove a very large, and perpetual Expence. However, I have not the least Diffidence, that I shall be able effectually to convince the World, that my present Scheme for such an *Hospital,* is very practicable; and must be very desirable by every one, who hath the Interest of his *Country,* or his fellow Creatures, *really* at Heart.

It is observable, that altho' the *Bodies* of human Creatures be affected with an infinite Variety of Disorders, which elude the Power of Medicine, and are often found to be incurable; yet their *Minds* are also overrun with an equal Variety, which no Skill, no Power, no Medicine can alter or amend. And I think, that out of regard to the publick Peace and Emolument, as well as the Repose of many pious and valuable Families, this latter Species of *Incurables* ought principally to engage our Attention and Beneficence.

I believe, an *Hospital* for such *Incurables,* will be universally allowed necessary, if we only consider, what Numbers of absolute Incurables, every *Profession, Rank,* and *Degree* would perpetually produce, which, at present, are only national Grievances, and of which we can have no other effectual Method to purge the Kingdom.

For Instance; let any Man seriously consider, what Numbers there are of incurable *Fools,* incurable *Knaves,* incurable *Scolds,* incurable *Scriblers* (beside my self) incurable *Coxcombs,* incurable *Infidels,* incurable *Liers,* incurable *Whores* in all Places of publick Resort:— Not to mention the incurably *Vain,* incurably *Envious,* incurably *Proud,* incurably *Affected,* incurably *Impertinent,* and ten thousand other *Incurables,* which I must of Necessity pass over in Silence, lest I should swell this Essay into a Volume. And without Doubt, every unprejudiced Person will agree, that out of meer Christian Charity, the Publick ought to be eased as much as possible, of this troublesome and intolerable Variety of *Incurables.*

And first; under the Denomination of incurable Fools, we may reasonably expect, that such an *Hospital* would be furnished with considerable Numbers of the Growth of our own *Universities*; who, at present, appear in various Professions in the World, under the venerable Titles of *Physicians*, *Barristers*, and *Ecclesiasticks*.

And, as those *antient Seminaries* have been for some Years past, accounted little better than Nurseries of such sort of Incurables, it should seem highly commendable to make some kind of Provision for them; because, it is more than probable, that if they are to be supported by their own particular Merit in their several Callings, they must necessarily acquire but a very indifferent Maintenance.

I would not, willingly, be here suspected, to cast Reflections on any Order of Men, as if I thought, that small Gains from the Profession of any *Art* or *Science*, were always an undoubted Sign of an equally small Degree of Understanding: For, I profess my self to be somewhat inclined to a very opposite Opinion; having frequently observed, that, at the *Bar*, the *Pulse*, and the *Pulpit*, those who have the least Learning or Sense to plead, meet generally with the largest Share of Promotion and Profit. Of which many Instances might be produced; but the Publick seems to want no Conviction in this Particular.

Under the same Denomination we may further expect a large and ridiculous Quantity of *old rich Widows*; whose eager and impatient Appetites inflame them with extravagant Passions, for *Fellows* of a very different Age and Complexion from themselves: Who purchase Contempt and Aversion with good Jointures; and being loaded with Years, Infirmities, and probably ill Humour, are forced to *bribe* into their Embraces, such whose Fortunes, and Characters, are equally desperate.

Besides, our Collection of incurable *Fools*, would receive an incredible Addition from every one of the following Articles.

From young *extravagant Heirs*; who are just of a competent Age, to become the Bubbles of *Jockeys*, *Sportsmen*, *Gamesters*, *Bullies*, *Sharpers*, *Courtezans*, and such sort of *honourable Pick-pockets*.

From *Misers*; who half starve themselves, to feed the Prodigality of their *Heirs*: And who proclaim to the World how unworthy they are of possessing Estates, by the wretched and ridiculous Methods they take to enjoy them.

From *contentious People*, of all Conditions; who are content to waste the greatest part of their *own* Fortunes at Law, to be the Instruments of impoverishing *others*.

From those, who have any Confidence in *Professions* of Friendship, before Trial; or any Dependance on the *Fidelity* of a *Mistress*.

From young illiterate *Squires*, who travel abroad to import *Lewdness, Conceit, Arrogance, Vanity* and *Foppery*; of which Commodities there seems to be so great an Abundance at Home.

From young *Clergymen*; who contrive, by Matrimony, to acquire a Family, before they have obtained the necessary Means to maintain one.

From those who have considerable Estates in *different* Kingdoms, and yet are so incurably stupid, as to spend their whole Incomes in *This*.

These, and several other Articles which might be mentioned, would afford us a perpetual Opportunity of easing the Publick, by having an *Hospital* for the Accommodation of such Incurables: Who, at present, either by the over Fondness of near Relations, or the Indolence of the Magistrates, are permitted to walk abroad, and appear in the most crowded Places of this City, as if they were indeed *reasonable Creatures*.

I had almost forgot to hint, that under this Article, there is a modest Probability, that many of the *Clergy* would be found properly qualified for Admittance into the *Hospital*, who might serve in the Capacity of *Chaplains*, and save the unnecessary Expence of Sallaries.

To these *Fools*, in order succeed, such as may justly be included under the extensive Denomination of incurable *Knaves*; of which our several *Inns of Court* would constantly afford us abundant Supplies.

I think indeed, that, of this Species of Incurables, there ought to be a certain limited Number annually admitted; which Number, neither any Regard to the Quiet or Benefit of the Nation, nor any other charitable or Publick-spirited

Reason, should tempt us to exceed; because, if all were to be admitted on such a Foundation, who might be reputed *incurable* of *this Distemper*; and if it were possible for the *Publick* to find any Place large enough for their Reception; I have not the least Doubt, that all our *Inns* which are at this Day so crowded, would in a short Time be emptied of their Inhabitants; and the *Law*, that *beneficial Craft*, want hands to conduct it.

I tremble to think what Herds of *Attornies, Sollicitors, Pettifoggers, Scriveners, Usurers, Hackney-Clerks, Pick-pockets, Pawn-Brokers, Jaylors,* and *Justices* of the *Peace,* would hourly be driven to such an *Hospital*: And what Disturbance it might also create in several noble and wealthy Families.

What unexpected Distress might it prove to several Men of Fortune and Quality, to be suddenly deprived of their *rich Stewards,* in whom they had for many Years reposed the utmost Confidence, and to find them irrecoverably lodged among such a Collection of *Incurables*?

How many *Orphans* might then expect to see their *Guardians* hurried away to the *Hospital*; and how many greedy *Executors* find Reason to lament the want of Opportunity to pillage?

Would not *Exchange-Alley* have cause to mourn for the Loss of its *Stock-Jobbers* and *Brokers*; and the *Charitable Corporation,* for the Confinement of many of its *Directors*?

Might not *Westminster-Hall,* as well as all the *Gaming-Houses* in this great City, be entirely unpeopled; and the Professors of Art in each of those Assemblies, become useless in their Vocations, by being deprived of all future Opportunity to be dishonest?

In short, it might put the whole Kingdom into Confusion and Disorder; and, we should find, that the entire Revenues of this Nation would be scarce able to support so great a Number of Incurables, in *this way,* as would appear qualified for Admission into our Hospital.

For, if we only consider, how this Kingdom swarms with *Quadrille-Tables,* and *Gaming-Houses* both publick and private; and also, how each of those Houses (as well as

Westminster-Hall aforesaid) swarms with *Knaves* who are anxious to win, or *Fools* who have any thing to lose; we may soon be convinced, how necessary it will be to limit the Number of Incurables, comprehended under those Titles, lest the Foundation should prove insufficient to maintain any others beside them.

However, if by this Scheme of mine, the Nation can be eased of 20 or 30 thousand such *Incurables*, I think it ought to be esteemed somewhat beneficial, and worthy of the Attention of the Publick.

The next sort, for whom I would gladly provide, and who for several Generations have proved insupportable Plagues and Grievances to the good People of *England*, are those, who may properly be admitted under the Character of incurable *Scolds*.

I own this to be a Distemper of so desperate a Nature, that few *Females* can be found, willing to own themselves any way addicted to it: And yet, it is thought, that there is scarce a single *Parson, Prentice, Alderman, Squire,* or *Husband,* who would not solemnly avouch the very Reverse.

I could wish, indeed, that the Word, SCOLD, might be changed for some more gentle Term, of equal Signification; because, I am convinced, that the very *Name* is as offensive to *Female* Ears, as the Effects of that incurable Distemper is, to the Ears of the *Men*: Which to be sure is inexpressible.

And, that it hath been always customary to honour the very same kind of Actions with different Appellations, only to avoid giving Offence, is evident to common Observation.

For Instance; How many *Lawyers, Attornies, Solicitors, Under-Sheriffs,* intriguing *Chamber-Maids,* and *Counter-Officers,* are continually guilty of *Extortion, Bribery, Oppression,* and many other profitable *Knaveries,* to drain the Purses of those, with whom they are any way concerned? and yet, all these different Expedients to raise a Fortune, pass generally under the milder Names of *Fees, Perquisites, Vails, Presents, Gratuities,* and such like; altho', in strictness

of Speech they should be called, *Robbery*, and consequently
be rewarded with a *Gibbet*.

Nay, how many *honourable* Gentlemen might be enumerated, who keep *open Shop* to make a Trade of Iniquity; who
teach the *Law* to wink whenever Power or Profit appears
in her way; and contrive to grow rich by the *Vice*, the *Con-
tention*, or the *Follies* of Mankind; and who, nevertheless,
instead of being branded with the harsh-sounding Names,
of *Knaves*, *Pilferers*, or *publick Oppressors*, (as they justly
merit) are only distinguished by the Title of *Justices of the
Peace*; in which single Term all those several Appellations
are generally thought to be implied.

But to proceed. When first I determined to prepare this
Scheme for the Use and Inspection of the publick; I intended to examine one whole *Ward* in this City, that my
Computation of the Number of incurable *Scolds*, might be
more perfect and exact. But I found it impossible to finish
my Progress through more than one *Street*.

I made my first Application to a wealthy *Citizen* in *Corn-
hill*, Common-Council-Man for his *Ward*: to whom I
hinted, that if he knew e'er an incurable *Scold* in the Neighbourhood, I had some Hope to provide for her in such a
manner, as to hinder her from being further troublesome.
He referred me with great Delight to his next Door Friend;
yet, whispered me, that with much greater Ease and Pleasure he could furnish me out of his own Family—; and
begged the Preference.

His next Door Friend owned readily that his *Wife's*
Qualifications were not misrepresented, and that he would
chearfully contribute to promote so useful a Scheme; but,
positively asserted, that it would be of small Service, to rid
the Neighbourhood of *one Woman*, while such Multitudes
would remain all equally insupportable.

By which Circumstance I conjectured, that the Quantity
of these *Incurables* in *London*, *Westminster* and *Southwark*,
would be very considerable; and that a generous Contribution might reasonably be expected, for such an *Hospital* as
I am recommending.

Besides, the Number of these *Female Incurables* would

probably be very much increased by additional Quantities of OLD MAIDS; who, being wearied with concealing their ill Humour, for *one Half* of their Lives, are impatient to give it full Vent in the *other*. For, *old Maids*, like old thin-bodied *Wines*, instead of growing more agreeable by Years, are observed, for the most part, to become intolerably *sharp, sour, and useless*.

Under this Denomination also, we may expect to be furnished with as large a Collection of *old Batchelors*, especially those who have Estates, and but a moderate Degree of Understanding. For, an *old* wealthy *Batchelor*, being perpetually surrounded with a set of *Flatterers, Cousins, poor Dependents*, and *Would-be-Heirs*, who for their own Views submit to his Perverseness and Caprice; becomes insensibly infected with this *scolding* Malady, which generally proves incurable, and renders him disagreeable to his *Friends*, and a fit Subject for Ridicule to his *Enemies*.

As to the incurable *Scriblers*, (of which Society I have the Honour to be a Member) they probably are innumerable; and, of Consequence, it will be absolutely impossible to provide for one tenth Part of their Fraternity. However, as this set of *Incurables*, are generally more plagued with Poverty than any other, it will be a double Charity to admit them on the Foundation. A Charity to the World, to whom they are a common Pest and Nusance; and, a Charity to themselves, to relieve them from *Want, Contempt, Kicking*, and several other Accidents of that Nature, to which they are continually liable.

Grubstreet itself would then have reason to rejoice, to see so many of its half-starv'd Manufacturers amply provided for; and the whole Tribe of *meagre Incurables*, would probably shout for Joy, at being delivered from the *Tyranny* and *Garrets*, of Printers, Publishers, and Booksellers.

What a mixed Multitude of *Ballad-Writers, Ode-Makers, Translators, Farce - Compounders, Opera - Mongers, Biographers, Pamphleteers*, and *Journalists*, would appear crowding to the Hospital; not unlike the Brutes resorting to the Ark before the Deluge. And what an universal Satisfaction would such a Sight afford to all, except *Pastry-*

Cooks, Grocers, Chandlers, and *Tobacco-Retailers,* to whom alone the Writings of those Incurables were any way profitable?

I have often been amazed to observe, what a Variety of incurable *Coxcombs* are to be met with, between St. *James's* and *Limehouse,* at every Hour of the Day; as numerous as *Welsh Parsons,* and equally contemptible. How they swarm in all *Coffee-Houses, Theatres, publick-Walks,* and *private Assemblies;* how they are incessantly employed in cultivating Intrigues, and every kind of irrational Pleasure: How industrious they seem to mimick the Appearance of *Monkeys,* as *Monkeys* are emulous to imitate the Gestures of *Men*: And from such Observations I concluded, that to confine the greatest part of those Incurables, who are so many *living Burlesques* of human Nature, would be of eminent Service to this Nation; and I am persuaded, that I am far from being singular in that Opinion.

As for the incurable *Infidels* and *Liers,* I shall range them under the same Article, and would willingly appoint them the same Apartment in the Hospital; because, there is a much nearer Resemblance between them, than is generally imagined.

Have they not an equal Delight in imposing Falsities on the Publick; and seem they not equally desirous to be thought of more Sagacity and Importance than others? Do they not both report, what both know to be false; and both confidently assert what they are conscious is most liable to Contradiction?

The Parallel might easily be carried on much further, if the intended Shortness of this Essay would admit it. However, I cannot forbear taking notice, with what immense Quantities of incurable *Liers,* his Majesty's Kingdoms are overrun; what Offence and Prejudice they are to the *Publick*; what inconceivable Injury to private Persons; and what a Necessity there is, for an *Hospital,* to relieve the Nation from the *Curse* of so many Incurables.

This Distemper appears almost in as many different Shapes, as there are Persons afflicted with it; and in every Individual, is always beyond the Power of Medicine.

Some LIE for their Interest, such as *Fish-Mongers, Flatterers, Pimps, Lawyers, Fortune-Hunters,* and *Fortune-Tellers,* and others LIE for their Entertainment, as *Maids, Wives, Widows,* and all other Tea-Table Attendants.

Some LIE out of *Vanity,* as *Poets, Painters, Players, Fops, Military Officers,* and all those who frequent the *Levees* of the *Great*: And others LIE out of *Ill-nature,* as *old Maids, &c.*

Some LIE out of *Custom,* as *Lovers, Coxcombs, Footmen, Sailors, Mechanicks, Merchants,* and *Chamber-Maids*; and others LIE out of Complaisance or Necessity, as *Courtiers, Chaplains, etc.* In short, it were endless to enumerate them all, but this Sketch may be sufficient to give us some small imperfect Idea of their Numbers.

As to the remaining Incurables, we may reasonably conclude, that they bear at least an equal Proportion to those already mentioned; but with Regard to the incurable *Wh[or]es* in this Kingdom, I must particularly observe, that such of them as are *publick,* and make it their Profession, have proper Hospitals for their Reception already, if we could find *Magistrates* without Passions, or *Officers* without an incurable Itch to a *Bribe.* And, such of them as are *private,* and make it their Amusement, I should be unwilling to disturb for two Reasons.

First; because, it might probably afflict many *Noble, Wealthy, Contented,* and *Unsuspecting Husbands,* by convincing them of their own Dishonour, and the unpardonable Disloyalty of their *Wives*: And secondly; because it will be for ever impossible to confine a *Woman* from being guilty of any kind of Misconduct, when once she is firmly resolved to attempt it.

From all which Observations every reasonable Man must infallibly be convinced, that an Hospital for the Support of these different kinds of Incurables, would be extremely beneficial to these Kingdoms. I think therefore, that nothing further is wanting, but to demonstrate to the Publick, that such a *Scheme* is very practicable; both by having an undoubted Method to raise an annual Income, at least sufficient to make the Experiment; (which is the way of founding all *Hospitals*) and by having also a strong Probability, that such an *Hospital* would be supported by perpetual Benefactions; which, in very few Years, might enable us to increase the Number of *Incurables*, to 9 tenths more, than we can reasonably venture on at first.

A Computation of the daily and annual Expences of an Hospital *to be erected for Incurables.*

p. Day.

Incurable Fools, are almost infinite; However at first I would have only 20 thousand admitted; and allowing to each Person but one Shilling *per* Day for Maintenance, which is as low as possible, the daily Expence for this Article will be ⎱ 1000

Incurable Knaves, are, if possible, more numerous, including *Foreigners*, especially IRISHMEN. Yet I would limit the Number of these to about 30 thousand; which would amount to ⎱ 1500

Incurable Scolds, would be plentifully supplied from almost every Family in the Kingdom. And indeed, to make this Hospital of any real Benefit, we cannot admit fewer, even at first, than 30 thousand, including the *Ladies* of *Billingsgate,* and *Leaden-Hall Market*, which is ⎱ 1500

The incurable Scriblers, are undoubtedly a very considerable Society, and of that Denomination, I would admit at least 40 thousand; because it is to be supposed, that such Incurables will be found in greatest Distress for a daily Maintenance. And, if we had not great Encouragement to hope, that many of that Class would properly be admitted among the *incurable Fools*, I should strenuously intercede to have 10 or 20 thousand more added. But their allowed Number will amount to ⎱ 2000

Incurable Coxcombs, are very numerous: And considering what Numbers are annually imported from *France* and *Italy*, we cannot admit fewer than 10 thousand, which will be ⎱ 500 *p. Day.*

Incurable Infidels, (as they affect to be called) should be received into the Hospital to the Number of 10 thousand: However, if it should accidentally happen, to grow into a Fashion to be *Believers*, it is probable, that the great part of them, would, in a very short time, be dismissed from the Hospital, as perfectly cured. Their Expence would be } 500

Incurable Liers, are infinite in all Parts of the Kingdom: And making Allowance for *Citizen's Wives*, *Mercer's Prentices*, *News-Writers*, *old Maids*, and *Flatterers*, we cannot possibly allow a smaller Number, than 30 thousand, which will amount to } 1500

The *Incurably Envious*, are in vast Quantities throughout this whole Nation. Nor can it reasonably be expected, that their Numbers should lessen, while *Fame* and *Honours* are heaped upon some particular Persons, as the publick Reward of their Superior Accomplishments; while others, who are equally excellent, in their own Opinions, are constrained to live unnoticed and contemned. And as it would be impossible to provide for all those who are possessed with this Distemper, I should consent to admit only 20 thousand at first by way of Experiment, amounting to } 1000

Of the *Incurably Vain*, *Affected*, and *Impertinent*, I should at least admit 10 thousand. Which Number I am confident will appear very inconsiderable, if we include all Degrees of *Females* from the *Dutchess* to the *Chamber-Maid*; all *Poets*, who have had a little Success, especially in the *Dramatick* Way; and all *Players*, who have met with a small Degree of *Approbation*. Amounting only to } 500

By which plain Computation it is evident, that two hundred thousand Persons will be daily provided for, and the Allowance for maintaining this Collection of Incurables, may be seen in the following Account.

p. Day.

	Fools, being 20,000 at one Shilling each	}	1000
	Knaves at 30,000 Ditto		1500
	Scolds 30,000		1500
For the Incurable	*Scriblers* 40,000		2000
	Coxcombs 10,000		500
	Infidels 10,000		500
	Liers 30,000		1500
For the Incurably	*Envious* 20,000		1000
	Vain 10,000		500

Total maintain'd   200,000   Tot. Ex. 10,000

From whence it appears, that the daily Expence will amount to such a Sum, as in 365 Days comes to   *M. Th. H.* 3,650,000

And I am fully satisfied, that a Sum, much greater than this, may easily be raised, with all possible Satisfaction to the *Subject*, and without interfering in the least with the Revenues of the *Crown*.

In the first place, a large Proportion of this Sum might be raised by the voluntary Contribution of the Inhabitants.

The computed Number of People in *Great Britain*, is very little less than eight *Millions*; of which, upon a most moderate Computation, we may account one half to be Incurables. And, as all those different Incurables, whether acting in the Capacity of *Friends, Acquaintances, Wives, Husbands, Daughters, Counsellors, Parents, Old-Maids,* or *Old-Batchelors,* are inconceivable Plagues to all those with whom they happen to be concerned; and as there is no Hope of being eased of such Plagues, except by such an *Hospital,* which by Degrees might be enlarged to contain them all: I think, it cannot be doubted, that at least 3 *Millions* and an Half of People, out of the remaining Proportion, would be found both able and desirous, to contribute so small a Sum as 20 Shillings *per Annum,* for the Quiet of the Kingdom, the Peace of private Families, and the Credit of the Nation in general. And this Contribution would amount to very near our requisite Sum.

Nor can this by any means be esteemed a wild Conjecture; For, where is there a *Man* of common *Sense, Honesty,* or *Good-Nature,* who would not gladly propose even a much greater Sum, to be freed from a *Scold,* a *Knave,* a *Fool,* a *Lier,* a *Coxcomb* conceitedly repeating the Compositions of *others,* or a vain impertinent *Poet* repeating his *own*?

In the next Place, it may justly be supposed, that many young *Noblemen, Knights, Squires,* and extravagant *Heirs,* with very large Estates, would be confined in our *Hospital.* And I would propose, that the annual Income of every particular *Incurable's* Estate, should be appropriated to the Use of the House. But, besides these, there will undoubtedly be many *old Misers, Aldermen, Justices, Directors* of Companies, *Templers,* and *Merchants* of all Kinds, whose Personal Fortunes are immense, and who should proportionably pay to the *Hospital.*

Yet, lest by being here misunderstood, I should seem to propose an unjust or oppressive *Scheme,* I shall further explain my Design.

Suppose, for instance, a young *Nobleman,* possessed of 10 or 20 thousand Pounds *per Annum,* should accidentally be confined there, as an Incurable: I would have only such a Proportion of his Estate, applied to the Support of the *Hospital,* as he himself would spend, if he were at Liberty. And after his Death, the Profits of the Estate should regularly devolve to the next lawful *Heir,* whether Male or Female.

And my reason for this Proposal, is; because, considerable Estates, which probably would be squandered away among *Hounds, Horses, Hawks, Whores, Sharpers, Surgeons, Taylors, Pimps, Masquerades,* or *Architects,* if left to the Management of such Incurables; would, by this Means, become of some *real* Use both to the *Publick* and themselves. And perhaps this may be the only Method which can be found, to make such young *Spendthrifts* of any real Benefit to their Country.

And altho' the Estates of deceased Incurables might be permitted to descend to the next Heirs, the *Høspital* would probably sustain no great Disadvantage; because, it is very likely, that most of those *Heirs* would also gradually be admitted under some Denomination or other; and consequently their Estates would again devolve to the Use of the *Hospital*.

As to the wealthy *Misers*, &c. I would have their private Fortunes nicely examined and calculated; because, if they were *old Batchelors*, (as it would frequently happen) their whole Fortunes should then be appropriated to the Endowment; but, if married, I would leave two thirds of their Fortunes, for the Support of their Families; which Families would chearfully consent to give away the remaining third, if not more, to be freed from such peevish and disagreeable Governors.

So that, deducting from the two hundred thousand Incurables, the 40 thousand *Scriblers*, who, to be sure, would be found in very bad Circumstances; I believe, among the remaining hundred and sixty thousand *Fools*, *Knaves*, and *Coxcombs*, so many would be found of Large Estates and Easy Fortunes, as would at least produce two hundred thousand Pounds *per Annum*.

As a further Addition to our Endowment, I would have a TAX upon all *Inscriptions* on *Tombstones*, *Monuments*, and *Obelisks* erected to the Honour of the Dead, or on *Portico's* and *Trophies* to the Honour of the Living: Because these will naturally and properly come under the Article of *Lies*, *Pride*, *Vanity*, &c.

And, if all *Inscriptions* throughout this Kingdom, were impartially examined, in order to tax those which should appear demonstrably false or flattering, I am convinced, that not one fifth Part of the Number, would, after such a Scrutiny, escape exempted.

Many an *ambitious* turbulent *Spirit* would then be found, *belied* with the opposite Title of *Lover* of his *Country*; and many a *Middlesex Justice*, as improperly described, *sleeping in Hope of Salvation*.

Many an *Usurer*, discredited by the Appellations of *honest* and *frugal*; and many a *Lawyer*, with the Character of conscientious and *equitable*.

Many a British *Statesman* and *General*, decaying, with more Honour than they lived; and their *Dusts*, distinguished with a better Reputation, than when they were animated.

Many dull *Parsons*, improperly stiled *Eloquent*; and as many stupid *Physicians*, improbably stiled *Learned*.

Yet notwithstanding the Extensiveness of a *Tax* upon such *Monumental Impositions*, I will count only upon 20 thousand, at five Pounds *per Annum* each, which will amount to one hundred thousand Pounds annually.

To these Annuities, I would also request the *Parliament* of this Nation, to allow the Benefit of two LOTTERIES yearly; by which the Hospital would gain two hundred thousand Pounds clear. Nor can such a Request seem any way extra-ordinary, since it would be appropriated to the Benefit of *Fools* and *Knaves*, which is the sole Cause of granting one for this Present Year.

In the last Place, I would add the Estate of *Richard Norton* Esquire; and to do his Memory all possible Honour, I would have his *Statue* erected in the very *first* Apartment of the Hospital, or in any other which might seem more apt. And, on his Monument, I would permit a long Inscription, composed by his dearest Friends, which should remain *Tax-free* for ever.

From these several Articles therefore, would annually arise the following Sums.

	M. Th. H. *P. Ann.*
From the voluntary Contributions	3,500,000
From the Estates of the Incurables	200,000
By the Tax upon Tombstones, Monuments, *&c.* (that of *Richard Norton* Esq; always excepted)	100,000
By two annual Lotteries	200,000
By the Estate of *Richard Norton* Esq.	6,000
Total	4,006,000
And the necessary Sum for the Hospital being	3,650,000
There will remain annually over and above	356,000

Which Sum of 356,000 *l.* should be applied towards erect-ing the Building, and to answer accidental Expences, in such a manner, as should seem most proper to promote the De-sign of the *Hospital.* But the whole Management of it should be left to the Skill and Discretion of those, who are to be constituted Governors.

It may, indeed, prove a Work of some small Difficulty, to fix upon a commodious Place, large enough for a Build-ing of this nature. I should have thoughts of attempting to enclose all YORKSHIRE, if I were not apprehensive, that it would be crowded with so many incurable *Knaves* of its own Growth, that there would not be the least room left for the Reception of any *others*: By which Accident, our whole Project might be retarded for some Time.

Thus have I set this Matter in the plainest Light I could, that every one may judge of the Necessity, Usefulness, and Practicableness of this Scheme: And I shall only add a few scattered Hints, which, to me, seem not altogether un-profitable.

I think the PRIME-MINISTER for the Time being, ought largely to contribute to such a Foundation; because his high Station and Merits must of Necessity infect a great Number with *Envy, Hatred, Lying*, and such sort of Dis-tempers; and of Consequence furnish the Hospital annually with many *Incurables.*

I would desire, that the *Governors* appointed to direct this Hospital, should have (if such a thing were possible) some Appearance of *Religion*, and *Belief* in *God*; because, those who are to be admitted as incurable *Infidels, Atheists, Deists*, and *Freethinkers*, most of which Tribe are only so out of *Pride, Conceit*, and *Affectation*; might perhaps grow gradually into *Believers*, if they perceived it to be the *Custom* of the Place where they lived.

Altho' it be not customary for the Natives of *Ireland* to meet with any manner of Promotion in this Kingdom, I would, in this Respect, have that National Prejudice en-tirely laid aside; and request, that for the Reputation of both Kingdoms, a *large* Apartment in the *Hospital* may be fitted up, for *Irishmen* particularly, who either by *Knavery*, *Lewdness*, or *Fortune-Hunting* should appear qualified for Admittance: Because, their Numbers would certainly be very considerable.

I would further request, that a *Father*, who seems delighted at seeing his *Son* Metamorphosed into a *Fop*, or a *Coxcomb*, because he hath travelled from *London* to *Paris*; may be sent, along with the young Gentleman, to the *Hospital*, as an *old Fool*, absolutely incurable.

If a *Poet* hath luckily produced any thing, especially in the Dramatick Way, which is tolerably well received by the Publick, he should be sent immediately to the *Hospital*; because incurable *Vanity* is always the Consequence of a *little* Success. And, if his Compositions be ill received, let him be admitted as a *Scribler*.

And I hope, in regard to the great Pains I have taken, about this *Scheme*, that I shall be admitted upon the Foundation, as one of the *scribling Incurables*. But as an additional Favour, I intreat, that I may not be placed in an Apartment with a *Poet*, who hath employed his Genius for the *Stage*; because he will kill me with repeating his *own* Compositions; and I need not acquaint the World, that it is extremely painful to bear any Nonsense——, except *our own*.

My private Reason for solliciting so early to be admitted, is; because it is observed that *Schemers* and *Projectors* are generally reduced to Beggary; but, by my being provided for in the Hospital, either as an Incurable *Fool* or a *Scribler*; that discouraging Observation will for once be publickly disproved, and my Brethren in that way will be secure of a *publick* Reward for their Labours.

It gives me, I own, a great Degree of Happiness, to reflect, that altho' in this short Treatise, the Characters of many Thousands are contained, among the vast Variety of *Incurables*; yet, not any one Person is likely to be offended; because, it is natural to apply ridiculous Characters to all the World except our selves. And I dare be bold to say, that the most incurable *Fool*, *Knave*, *Scold*, *Coxcomb*, *Scribler*, or *Lier*, in this whole Nation, will sooner enumerate the Circle of their Acquaintance as addicted to those

Distempers, than once imagine *themselves* any way qualified for such an *Hospital*.

I hope indeed, that our *wise Legislature* will take this Project into their serious Consideration; and promote an Endowment, which will be of such eminent Service to Multitudes of his Majesty's unprofitable Subjects, and may in time be of use to *themselves* and their *Posterity*.

From my Garret, in *Moor-Fields*.
Aug. 10. 1733.

POLITE CONVERSATION

SELECTIONS

T

" SOME of my friends ", Swift wrote to his Irish publisher [to Faulkner, March 8, 1737/8], " wonder very much at your delay to publish that treatise of Polite Conversation &c., when you so often desired that I should hasten to correct the several copies you sent me, which, as ill as I have been, and am still, I dispatched as fast as I got them. . . . I hope you have observed all the corrections." Swift had given the original manuscript of the book to his penurious friend Mrs Barber, wife of a Dublin tailor, to be printed for her benefit, and editions were published simultaneously in London and Dublin in the early spring of 1737/8. According to Faulkner, the Dialogues were acted " at the theatre in Aungier street, Dublin ".

My decision to print only the Introduction and one of the three Dialogues was anticipated by an anonymous writer in the *Saint James's Chronicle* for March 12, 1767/8, who, in reference to Deane Swift's edition of his cousin's writings, says : " I should like to leave out *The Polite Conversation*, all except the Preface and six or eight pages of the Work. . . ."

Swift's object in writing this treatise—to ridicule cant words and expressions—is sufficiently explained in his Introduction. Many of the ideas it contains were present in his earlier *Hints towards an Essay in Conversation*, written in 1709. The subject— an admirable target for irony—had a peculiar fascination for Swift and he spent many years contemplating and projecting the book.

A COMPLETE COLLECT-
ion of Genteel and Ingenious
Conversation, according to
the Most Polite Mode and
Method now used at
Court, and in the
Best Companies
of England

AN INTRODUCTION TO THE
FOLLOWING TREATISE

As my Life hath been chiefly spent in consulting the Honour and Welfare of my Country for more than Forty Years past, not without answerable Success, if the World and my Friends have not flattered me; so, there is no Point wherein I have so much labour'd, as that of improving and polishing all Parts of Conversation between Persons of Quality, whether they meet by Accident or Invitation, at Meals, Tea, or Visits, Mornings, Noons, or Evenings.

I have passed perhaps more time than any other Man of my Age and Country in Visits and Assemblees, where the polite Persons of both Sexes distinguish themselves; and could not without much Grief observe how frequently both Gentlemen and Ladies are at a Loss for Questions, Answers, Replies and Rejoinders: However, my Concern was much abated, when I found that these Defects were not occasion'd by any Want of Materials, but because those Materials were not in every Hand: For Instance, One Lady can give an Answer better than ask a question: One Gentleman is happy at a Reply; another excels in a Rejoinder: One can revive a languishing Conversation by a sudden surprising Sentence; another is more dextrous in seconding; a Third can fill the Gap with laughing, or commending what hath been said: Thus fresh Hints may be started, and the Ball of Discourse kept up.

But, alas! this is too seldom the Case, even in the most select Companies: How often do we see at Court, at public Visiting-Days, at great Men's Levees, and other Places of general Meeting, that the Conversation falls and drops to nothing, like a Fire without Supply of Fuel; this is what we ought to lament; and against this dangerous Evil I take upon me to affirm, that I have in the following Papers provided an infallible Remedy.

It was in the Year 1695, and the Sixth of his late Majesty King *William* the Third, of ever glorious and immortal Memory, who rescued Three Kingdoms from Popery and Slavery; when, being about the Age of Six-and-thirty, my Judgment mature, of good Reputation in the World, and well acquainted with the best Families in Town, I determined to spend Five Mornings, to dine Four times, pass Three Afternoons, and Six Evenings every Week, in the Houses of the most polite Families, of which I would confine myself to Fifty; only changing as the Masters or Ladies died, or left the Town, or grew out of Vogue, or sunk in their Fortunes, (which to me was of the highest moment) or because disaffected to the Government; which Practice I have followed ever since to this very Day; except when I happened to be sick, or in the Spleen upon cloudy Weather; and except when I entertained Four of each Sex at my own Lodgings once a Month, by way of Retaliation.

I always kept a large Table-Book in my Pocket; and as soon as I left the Company, I immediately entered the choicest Expressions that passed during the Visit; which, returning Home, I transcribed in a fair Hand, but somewhat enlarged; and had made the greatest Part of my Collection in Twelve Years, but not digested into any Method; for this I found was a Work of infinite Labour, and what required the nicest Judgment, and consequently could not be brought to any Degree of Perfection in less than Sixteen Years more.

Herein I resolved to exceed the Advice of *Horace*, a *Roman* Poet, (which I have read in Mr. *Creech*'s admirable Translation) That an Author should keep his Works Nine Years in his Closet, before he ventured to publish them; and finding that I still received some additional Flowers of Wit and Language, although in a very small Number, I determined to defer the Publication, to pursue my Design, and exhaust, if possible, the whole Subject, that I might present a complete System to the World: For, I am convinced by long Experience, that the Critics will be as severe as their old Envy against me can make them: I foretel, they will object, that I have inserted many Answers and Replies which are neither witty, humorous, polite, or authentic; and have omitted others, that would have been highly useful, as well as entertaining: But let them come to Particulars, and I will boldly engage to confute their Malice.

For these last Six or Seven Years I have not been able to add above Nine valuable Sentences to inrich my Collection; from whence I conclude, that what remains will amount only to a Trifle: However, if, after the Publication of this Work, any Lady or Gentleman, when they have read it, shall find the least thing of Importance omitted, I desire they will please to supply my Defects, by communicating to me their Discoveries; and their Letters may be directed to SIMON WAGSTAFF, Esq; at his Lodgings next Door to the *Gloucester-Head* in *St. James's-street*, (they paying the Postage). In Return of which Favour, I shall make honourable Mention of their Names in a short Preface to the Second Edition.

In the mean time, I cannot but with some Pride, and much Pleasure, congratulate with my dear Country, which hath outdone all the Nations of *Europe* in advancing the whole Art of Conversation to the greatest Height it is capable of reaching; and therefore being intirely convinced that the Collection I now offer to the Public is full and complete, I may at the same time boldly affirm, that the whole Genius, Humour, Politeness and Eloquence of *England* are summed up in it: Nor is the Treasure small, wherein are to be found at least a Thousand shining Questions, Answers, Repartees,

Replies and Rejoinders, fitted to adorn every kind of Discourse that an Assemblee of *English* Ladies and Gentlemen, met together for their mutual Entertainment, can possibly want, especially when the several Flowers shall be set off and improved by the Speakers, with every Circumlocution, in proper Terms; and attended with Praise, Laughter, or Admiration.

There is a natural, involuntary Distortion of the Muscles, which is the anatomical Cause of Laughter: But there is another Cause of Laughter which Decency requires, and is the undoubted Mark of a good Taste, as well as of a polite obliging Behaviour; neither is this to be acquired without much Observation, long Practice, and a sound Judgment: I did therefore once intend, for the Ease of the Learner, to set down in all Parts of the following Dialogues certain Marks, Asterisks, or *Nota-bene's* (in *English*, *Markwell's*) after most Questions, and every Reply or Answer; directing exactly the Moment when One, Two, or All the Company are to laugh: But having duly considered, that the Expedient would too much enlarge the Bulk of the Volume, and consequently the Price; and likewise that something ought to be left for ingenious Readers to find out, I have determined to leave that whole Affair, although of great Importance, to their own Discretion.

The Readers must learn by all means to distinguish between Proverbs and those polite Speeches which beautify Conversation: For, as to the former, I utterly reject them out of all ingenious Discourse. I acknowledge indeed, that there may possibly be found in this Treatise a few Sayings, among so great a Number of smart Turns of Wit and Humour, as I have produced, which have a proverbial Air: However, I hope, it will be considered, that even these were not originally Proverbs, but the genuine Productions of superior Wits, to embellish and support Conversation; from whence, with great Impropriety, as well as Plagiarism (if you will forgive a hard Word) they have most injuriously been transferred into proverbial Maxims; and therefore in Justice ought to be resumed out of vulgar Hands, to adorn the Drawing-Rooms of Princes, both Male and Female, the

Levees of great Ministers, as well as the Toilet and Tea-table of the Ladies.

I can faithfully assure the Reader, that there is not one single witty Phrase in this whole Collection, which hath not received the Stamp and Approbation of at least one hundred Years, and how much longer, it is hard to determine; he may therefore be secure to find them all genuine, sterling, and authentic.

But before this elaborate Treatise can become of universal Use and Ornament to my native Country, Two Points, that will require Time and much Application, are absolutely necessary.

For, *First*, whatever Person would aspire to be completely witty, smart, humourous, and polite, must by hard Labour be able to retain in his Memory every single Sentence contained in this Work, so as never to be once at a Loss in applying the right Answers, Questions, Repartees, and the like, immediately, and without Study or Hesitation.

And, *Secondly*, after a Lady or Gentleman hath so well overcome this Difficulty, as to be never at a Loss upon any Emergency, the true Management of every Feature, and almost of every Limb, is equally necessary; without which an infinite Number of Absurdities will inevitably ensue: For Instance, there is hardly a polite Sentence in the following Dialogues which doth not absolutely require some peculiar graceful Motion in the Eyes, or Nose, or Mouth, or Forehead, or Chin, or suitable Toss of the Head, with certain Offices assigned to each Hand; and in Ladies, the whole Exercise of the Fan, fitted to the Energy of every Word they deliver; by no means omitting the various Turns and Cadence of the Voice, the Twistings, and Movements, and different Postures of the Body, the several Kinds and Gradations of Laughter, which the Ladies must daily practise by the Looking-Glass, and consult upon them with their Waiting-Maids.

My Readers will soon observe what a great Compass of real and useful Knowledge this Science includes; wherein, although Nature, assisted by a Genius, may be very instrumental, yet a strong Memory and constant Application, together with Exampleand Precept, will be highly necessary: For these Reasons I have often wished, that certain Male and Female Instructors, perfectly versed in this science, would set up Schools for the Instruction of young Ladies and Gentlemen therein.

I remember about thirty Years ago, there was a *Bohemian* Woman, of that Species commonly known by the name of *Gypsies*, who came over hither from *France*, and generally attended ISAAC the Dancing-Master when he was teaching his Art to Misses of Quality; and while the young Ladies were thus employed, the *Bohemian*, standing at some distance, but full in their Sight, acted before them all proper Airs, and turnings of the Head, and motions of the Hands, and twistings of the Body; whereof you may still observe the good Effects in several of our elder Ladies.

After the same manner, it were much to be desired, that some expert Gentlewomen gone to decay would set up publick Schools, wherein young Girls of Quality, or great Fortunes, might first be taught to repeat this following System of Conversation, which I have been at so much pains to compile; and then to adapt every Feature of their Countenances, every Turn of their Hands, every Screwing of their Bodies, every Exercise of their Fans, to the Humour of the Sentences they hear or deliver in Conversation. But above all to instruct them in every Species and Degree of Laughing in the proper seasons at their own Wit, or that of the Company. And, if the Sons of the Nobility and Gentry, instead of being sent to common Schools, or put into the Hands of Tutors at Home, to learn nothing but Words, were consigned to able Instructors in the same Art, I cannot find what Use there could be of Books, except in the hands of those who are to make Learning their Trade, which is below the Dignity of Persons born to Titles or Estates.

It would be another infinite Advantage, that, by cultivating this Science, we should wholly avoid the Vexations and Impertinence of Pedants, who affect to talk in a Language not to be understood; and whenever a polite Person offers accidentally to use any of their Jargon-Terms, have the Presumption to laugh at Us for pronouncing those Words in a genteeler Manner. Whereas, I do here affirm, that, whenever any fine Gentleman or Lady condescends to let a hard Word pass out of their Mouths, every syllable is smoothed and polished in the Passage; and it is a true Mark of Politeness, both in Writing and Reading, to vary the Orthography as well as the Sound; because We are infinitely better Judges of what will please a distinguishing ear than those, who call themselves *Scholars*, can possibly be; who, consequently, ought to correct their Books, and Manner of pronouncing, by the Authority of Our Example, from whose lips they proceed with infinitely more Beauty and Significancy.

But, in the mean time, until so great, so useful, and so necessary a Design can be put in execution, (which, considering the good Disposition of our Country at present, I shall not despair of living to see) let me recommend the following Treatise to be carried about as a Pocket-Companion, by all Gentlemen and Ladies, when they are going to visit, or dine, or drink Tea; or where they happen to pass the Evening without Cards, (as I have sometimes known it to be the Case upon Disappointments or Accidents unforeseen) desiring they would read their several Parts in their Chairs or Coaches, to prepare themselves for every kind of Conversation that can possibly happen.

Although I have in Justice to my Country, allowed the Genius of our People to excel that of any other Nation upon Earth, and have confirmed this Truth by an Argument not to be controlled, I mean, by producing so great a Number of witty Sentences in the ensuing Dialogues, all of undoubted Authority, as well as of our own Production; yet, I must confess at the same time, that we are wholly indebted for them to our Ancestors; at least, for as long as my memory reacheth, I do not recollect one new Phrase of Importance to have been added; which Defect in Us Moderns I take to have been occasioned by the Introduction of Cant-Words in the Reign of King *Charles* the Second. And those have so often varied, that hardly one of them, of above a Year's standing, is now intelligible; nor any where to be found, excepting a small Number strewed here and there in the Comedies and other fantastick Writings of that Age.

The Honourable Colonel JAMES GRAHAM, my old Friend and Companion, did likewise, towards the End of the same Reign, invent a Set of Words and Phrases, which continued almost to the Time of his Death. But, as those Terms of Art were adapted only to Courts and Politicians, and extended little further than among his particular Acquaintance (of whom I had the Honour to be one) they are now almost forgotten.

Nor did the late D. of *R——* and E. of *E——* succeed much better, although they proceeded no further than single Words; whereof, except *Bite*, *Bamboozle*, and one or two more, the whole Vocabulary is antiquated.

The same Fate hath already attended those other Town-Wits, who furnish us with a great Variety of new Terms, which are annually changed, and those of the last Season sunk in Oblivion. Of these I was once favoured with a compleat List by the Right Honourable the Lord and Lady *H——*, with which I made a considerable Figure one Summer in the Country; but returning up to Town in Winter, and venturing to produce them again, I was partly hooted, and partly not understood.

The only Invention of late Years, which hath any way contributed towards Politeness in Discourse, is that of abbreviating or reducing Words of many Syllables into one, by lopping off the rest. This Refinement, having begun about the Time of the *Revolution*, I had some Share in the Honour of promoting it, and I observe, to my great Satisfaction, that it makes daily Advancements, and I hope in Time will raise our Language to the utmost Perfection; although, I must confess, to avoid Obscurity, I have been very sparing of this Ornament in the following Dialogues.

But, as for Phrases, invented to cultivate Conversation, I defy all the Clubs or Coffee-houses in this town to invent a new one equal in Wit, Humour, Smartness, or Politeness, to the very worst of my Set; which clearly shews, either that we are much degenerated, or that the whole Stock of Materials hath been already employed. I would willingly hope, as I do confidently believe, the latter; because, having my self, for several Months, racked my Invention (if pos-

sible) to enrich this Treasury with some Additions of my
own (which, however, should have been printed in a different Character, that I might not be charged with imposing
upon the Publick) and having shewn them to some judicious
Friends, they dealt very sincerely with me; all unanimously
agreeing, that mine were infinitely below the true old Helps
to Discourse, drawn up in my present Collection, and
confirmed their Opinion with Reasons, by which I was
perfectly convinced, as well as ashamed, of my great Presumption.

But, I lately met a much stronger Argument to confirm
me in the same Sentiments: For, as the great Bishop
BURNET, of *Salisbury*, informs us in the Preface to his
admirable *History of his own Times*, that he intended to
employ himself in polishing it every Day of his Life, (and
indeed in its Kind it is almost equally polished with this
Work of mine:) So, it hath been my constant Business, for
some Years past, to examine, with the utmost Strictness,
whether I could possibly find the smallest Lapse in Style
or Propriety through my whole Collection, that, in Emulation with the Bishop, I might send it abroad as the most
finished Piece of the Age.

It happened one Day as I was dining in good Company
of both Sexes, and watching, according to my Custom, for
new Materials wherewith to fill my Pocket-Book, I succeeded well enough till after Dinner, when the Ladies retired to their Tea, and left us over a Bottle of Wine. But I
found we were not able to furnish any more Materials, that
were worth the Pains of transcribing: For, the Discourse
of the Company was all degenerated into smart Sayings of
their own Invention, and not of the true old Standard; so
that, in absolute Despair, I withdrew, and went to attend
the Ladies at their Tea. From whence I did then conclude,
and still continue to believe, either that Wine doth not inspire Politeness, or that our Sex is not able to support it
without the Company of Women, who never fail to lead
us into the right Way, and there to keep us.

It much encreaseth the Value of these Apophthegms, that
unto them we owe the Continuance of our Language, for

at least an hundred Years; neither is this to be wondered at; because indeed, besides the Smartness of the Wit, and Fineness of the Raillery, such is the Propriety and Energy of Expression in them all, that they never can be changed, but to Disadvantage, except in the Circumstance of using Abbreviations; which, however, I do not despair, in due Time, to see introduced, having already met them at some of the Choice Companies in town.

Although this Work be calculated for all Persons of Quality and Fortune of both Sexes; yet the Reader may perceive, that my particular View was to the OFFICERS of the ARMY, the GENTLEMEN of the INNS of COURTS, and of BOTH the UNIVERSITIES; to all COURTIERS, Male and Female, but principally to the MAIDS of HONOUR, of whom I have been personally acquainted with two-and-twenty Sets, all excelling in this noble Endowment; till for some Years past, I know not how, they came to degenerate into Selling of BARGAINS, and FREE-THINKING; not that I am against either of these Entertainments at proper Seasons, in compliance with Company, who may want a Taste for more exalted Discourse, whose Memories may be short, who are too young to be perfect in their Lessons. Or (although it be hard to conceive) who have no Inclination to read and learn my Instructions. And besides, there is a strong Temptation for Court-Ladies to fall into the two Amusements above-mentioned, that they may avoid the Censure of affecting Singularity, against the general Current and Fashion of all about them: But, however, no Man will pretend to affirm, that either BARGAINS or BLASPHEMY, which are the principal Ornaments of FREE-THINKING, are so good a Fund of polite Discourse, as what is to be met with in my Collection. For, as to BARGAINS, few of them seem to be excellent in their kind, and have not much Variety, because they all terminate in one single Point; and, to multiply them, would require more Invention than People have to spare. And, as to BLASPHEMY or FREE-THINKING, I have known some scrupulous Persons, of both Sexes, who, by a prejudiced Education, are afraid of Sprights. I must, however, except the MAIDS of HONOUR, who have been fully convinced, by an infamous Court-Chaplain, that there is no such Place as Hell.

I cannot, indeed, controvert the Lawfulness of FREE-THINKING, because it hath been universally allowed, that Thought is free. But, however, although it may afford a large Field of Matter; yet in my poor Opinion, it seems to contain very little of Wit or Humour; because it hath not been antient enough among us to furnish established authentick Expressions, I mean, such as must receive a Sanction from the polite World, before their Authority can be allowed; neither was the Art of BLASPHEMY or FREE-THINKING invented by the Court, or by Persons of great Quality, who, properly speaking, were Patrons, rather than Inventors of it; but first brought in by the Fanatick Faction, towards the end of their Power, and, after the Restoration, carried to *Whitehall* by the converted *Rumpers*, with very good Reasons; because they knew, that K. *Charles* the Second, who, from a wrong Education, occasioned by the Troubles of his Father, had Time enough to observe, that Fanatick Enthusiasm directly led to Atheism, which agreed with the dissolute Inclinations of his Youth; and, perhaps, these Principles were farther cultivated in him by the *French* Huguenots, who have been often charged with spreading them among us: However, I cannot see where the Necessity lies, of introducing new and foreign Topicks for Conversation, while we have so plentiful a Stock of our own Growth.

I have likewise, for some Reasons of equal Weight, been very sparing in DOUBLE ENTENDRES; because they often put Ladies upon affected Constraints, and affected Ignorance. In short, they break, or very much entangle, the Thread of Discourse; neither am I Master of any Rules, to settle the disconcerted Countenances of the Females in such a Juncture; I can, therefore, only allow *Inuendoes* of this Kind to be delivered in Whispers, and only to young Ladies under Twenty, who, being in Honour obliged to blush, it may produce a new Subject for Discourse.

Perhaps the Criticks may accuse me of a Defect in my following System of POLITE CONVERSATION; that there is one great Ornament of Discourse, whereof I have not produced a single Example; which, indeed, I purposely omitted for some Reasons that I shall immediately offer; and, if those Reasons will not satisfy the Male Part of my gentle Readers, the Defect may be supplied in some manner by an *Appendix* to the *Second Edition*; which *Appendix* shall be printed by it self, and sold for *Sixpence*, stitched, and with a Marble Cover, that my Readers may have no Occasion to complain of being defrauded.

The Defect I mean is, my not having inserted, into the Body of my Book, all the OATHS now most in Fashion for embellishing Discourse; especially since it could give no Offence to the *Clergy*, who are seldom or never admitted to these polite Assemblies. And it must be allowed, that Oaths, well chosen, are not only very useful Expletives to Matter, but great Ornaments of Style.

What I shall here offer in my own Defence upon this important Article, will, I hope, be some Extenuation of my Fault.

First, I reasoned with my self, that a just Collection of Oaths, repeated as often as the Fashion requires, must have enlarged this Volume, at least, to Double the Bulk; whereby it would not only double the Charge, but likewise make the Volume less commodious for Pocket-Carriage.

Secondly, I have been assured by some judicious Friends, that themselves have known certain Ladies to take Offence (whether seriously or no) at too great a Profusion of Cursing and Swearing, even when that Kind of Ornament was not improperly introduced; which, I confess, did startle me not a little; having never observed the like in the Compass of my own several Acquaintance, at least for twenty Years past. However, I was forced to submit to wiser Judgments than my own.

Thirdly, as this most useful Treatise is calculated for all future Times, I considered, in this Maturity of my Age, how great a Variety of Oaths I have heard since I began to study the World, and to know Men and Manners. And here I found it to be true what I have read in an antient Poet.

> *For, now-a-days, Men change their Oaths,*
> *As often as they change their Cloaths.*

In short, Oaths are the Children of Fashion, they are in some sense almost Annuals, like what I observed before of Cant-Words; and I my self can remember about forty different Sets. The old Stock-Oaths I am confident, do not mount to above forty five, or fifty at most; but the Way of mingling and compounding them is almost as various as that of the Alphabet.

Sir JOHN PERROT was the first Man of Quality whom I find upon Record to have sworn by *G*——*'s W*——*s.* He lived in the Reign of Q. *Elizabeth*, and was supposed to have been a natural Son of *Henry* the Eighth, who might also have probably been his Instructor. This Oath indeed still continues, and is a Stock-Oath to this Day; so do several others that have kept their natural Simplicity: But, infinitely the greater Number hath been so frequently changed and dislocated, that if the Inventors were now alive, they could hardly understand them.

Upon these Considerations I began to apprehend, that if I should insert all the Oaths as are now current, my Book would be out of Vogue with the first Change of Fashion, and grow useless as an old Dictionary: Whereas, the Case is quite otherways with my Collection of polite Discourse; which, as I before observed, hath descended by Tradition for at least an hundred Years, without any Change in the Phraseology. I, therefore, determined with my self to leave out the whole System of Swearing; because, both the male and female Oaths are all perfectly well known and distinguished; new ones are easily learnt, and with a moderate Share of Discretion may be properly applied on every fit Occasion. However, I must here, upon this Article of Swearing, most earnestly recommend to my male Readers, that they would please a little to study Variety. For, it is the Opinion of our most refined Swearers, that the same Oath or Curse, cannot, consistent with true Politeness, be repeated above nine Times in the same Company, by the same Person, and at one Sitting.

I am far from desiring, or expecting, that all the polite and ingenious Speeches, contained in this Work, should, in the general Conversation between Ladies and Gentlemen, come in so quick and so close as I have here delivered them. By no means: On the contrary, they ought to be husbanded better, and spread much thinner. Nor, do I make the least Question, but that, by a discreet thrifty Management, they may serve for the Entertainment of a whole Year, to any Person, who does not make too long or too frequent Visits in the same Family. The Flowers of Wit, Fancy, Wisdom, Humour, and Politeness, scattered in this Volume, amount to one thousand, seventy and four. Allowing then to every Gentleman and Lady thirty visiting Families, (not insisting upon Fractions) there will want but little of an hundred polite Questions, Answers, Replies, Rejoinders, Repartees, and Remarks, to be daily delivered fresh, in every Company, for twelve solar Months; and even this is a higher Pitch of Delicacy than the World insists on, or hath Reason to expect. But, I am altogether for exalting this Science to its utmost Perfection.

It may be objected, that the Publication of my Book may, in a long Course of Time, prostitute this noble Art to mean and vulgar People: But, I answer; That it is not so easy an Acquirement as a few ignorant Pretenders may imagine. A Footman can swear; but he cannot swear like a Lord. He can swear as often: But, can he swear with equal Delicacy, Propriety, and Judgment? No, certainly; unless he be a Lad of superior Parts, of good Memory, a diligent Observer; one who hath a skilful Ear, some Knowledge in Musick, and an exact Taste, which hardly fall to the Share of one in a thousand among that Fraternity, in as high Favour as they now stand with their Ladies; neither hath one Footman in six so fine a Genius as to relish and apply those exalted Sentences comprised in this Volume, which I offer to the World: It is true, I cannot see that the same ill Consequences would follow from the Waiting-Woman, who, if she hath been bred to read Romances, may have some small subaltern, or second-hand Politeness; and if she constantly attends the Tea, and be a good Listner, may, in some Years, make a tolerable Figure, which will serve, perhaps, to draw in the young Chaplain or the old Steward. But, alas! after all, how can she acquire those hundreds of

Graces and Motions, and Airs, the whole military Management of the Fan, the Contortions of every muscular Motion
in the Face, the Risings and Fallings, the Quickness and
Slowness of the Voice, with the several Turns and Cad-
ences; the proper Junctures of Smiling and Frowning, how
often and how loud to laugh, when to jibe and when to
flout, with all the other Branches of Doctrine and Discipline
above-recited?

I am, therefore, not under the least Apprehension that
this Art will be ever in Danger of falling into common
Hands, which requires so much Time, Study, Practice, and
Genius, before it arrives to Perfection; and, therefore, I
must repeat my Proposal for erecting Publick Schools, provided with the best and ablest Masters and Mistresses, at
the Charge of the Nation.

I have drawn this Work into the Form of a Dialogue,
after the Patterns of other famous Writers in History, Law,
Politicks, and most other Arts and Sciences, and I hope it
will have the same Success: For, who can contest it to be
of greater Consequence to the Happiness of these Kingdoms, than all human Knowledge put together. Dialogue
is held the best Method of inculcating any Part of Knowledge; and, as I am confident, that Publick Schools will
soon be founded for teaching Wit and Politeness, after my
Scheme, to young People of Quality and Fortune, I have
determined next Sessions to deliver a Petition to the *House
of Lords* for an Act of Parliament, to establish my Book, as
the Standard *Grammar* in all the principal Cities of the
Kingdom where this Art is to be taught, by able Masters,
who are to be approved and recommended by me; which
is no more than LILLY obtained only for teaching Words
in a Language wholly useless: Neither shall I be so far
wanting to my self, as not to desire a Patent granted of
course to all useful Projectors; I mean, that I may have
the sole Profit of giving a Licence to every School to read
my *Grammar* for fourteen Years.

The Reader cannot but observe what Pains I have been
at in polishing the Style of my Book to the greatest Exactness: Nor, have I been less diligent in refining the Ortho-

graphy, by spelling the Words in the very same Manner that they are pronounced by the Chief Patterns of Politeness, at Court, at Levees, at Assemblees, at Playhouses, at the prime Visiting-Places, by young Templers, and by Gentlemen-Commoners of both Universities, who have lived at least a Twelvemonth in Town, and kept the best Company. Of these Spellings the Publick will meet with many Examples in the following Book. For instance, *can't, han't, sha'nt, didn't, coodn't, woodn't, is n't, e'n't,* with many more; besides several Words which Scholars pretend are derived from *Greek* and *Latin,* but not pared into a polite Sound by Ladies, Officers of the Army, Courtiers and Templers, such as *Jommetry* for *Geometry, Verdi* for *Verdict, Lierd* for *Lord, Larnen* for *Learning*; together with some Abbreviations exquisitely refined; as, *Pozz* for *Positive; Mobb* for *Mobile; Phizz* for *Physiognomy; Rep* for *Reputation; Plenipo* for *Plenipotentiary; Incog* for *Incognito; Hypps,* or *Hippo,* for *Hypocondriacks; Bam* for *Bamboozle*; and *Bamboozle* for *God knows what*; whereby much Time is saved, and the high Road to Conversation cut short by many a Mile.

I have, as it will be apparent, laboured very much, and, I hope, with Felicity enough, to make every Character in the Dialogue agreeable with it self, to a degree, that, whenever any judicious Person shall read my Book aloud, for the Entertainment and Instruction of a select Company, he need not so much as name the particular Speakers; because all the Persons, throughout the several Subjects of Conversation, strictly observe a different Manner, peculiar to their Characters, which are of different kinds: But this I leave entirely to the prudent and impartial Reader's Discernment.

Perhaps the very Manner of introducing the several Points of Wit and Humour may not be less entertaining and instructing than the Matter it self. In the latter I can pretend to little Merit; because it entirely depends upon Memory and the Happiness of having kept polite Company. But, the Art of contriving, that those Speeches should be introduced naturally, as the most proper Sentiments to be delivered upon so great Variety of Subjects, I take to be a Talent somewhat uncommon, and a Labour that few people could hope to succeed in, unless they had a genius, particularly turned that way, added to a sincere disinterested Love of the Publick.

Although every curious Question, smart Answer, and witty Reply be little known to many People; yet, there is not one single Sentence in the whole Collection, for which I cannot bring most authentick Vouchers, whenever I shall be called; and, even for some Expressions, which to a few nice Ears may perhaps appear somewhat gross, I can produce the Stamp of Authority from Courts, Chocolate-houses, Theatres, Assemblees, Drawing-rooms, Levees, Card-meetings, Balls, and Masquerades, from Persons of both Sexes, and of the highest Titles next to Royal. However, to say the truth, I have been very sparing in my Quotations of such Sentiments that seem to be over free; because, when I began my Collection, such kind of Converse was almost in its Infancy, till it was taken into the Protection of my honoured Patronesses at Court, by whose Countenance and Sanction it hath become a choice Flower in the Nosegay of Wit and Politeness.

Some will perhaps object, that when I bring my Company to Dinner, I mention too great a Variety of Dishes, not always consistent with the Art of Cookery, or proper for the Season of the Year, and Part of the first Course mingled with the second, besides a Failure in Politeness, by introducing Black Pudden to a Lord's Table, and at a great Entertainment: But, if I had omitted the Black Pudden, I desire to know what would have become of that exquisite Reason given by Miss Notable for not eating it; the World perhaps might have lost it for ever, and I should have been justly answerable for having left it out of my Collection. I therefore cannot but hope, that such Hypercritical Readers will please to consider, my Business was to make so full and compleat a Body of refined Sayings, as compact as I could; only taking care to produce them in the most natural and probable Manner, in order to allure my Readers into the very Substance and Marrow of this most admirable and necessary Art.

I am heartily sorry, and was much disappointed to find, that so universal and polite an Entertainment as CARDS, hath hitherto contributed very little to the Enlargement of my Work; I have sate by many hundred Times with the utmost Vigilance, and my Table-Book ready, without being able in eight Hours to gather Matter for one single Phrase in my Book. But this, I think, may be easily accounted for by the Turbulence and Justling of Passions upon the various and surprising Turns, Incidents, Revolutions, and Events of good and evil Fortune, that arrive in the course of a long Evening at Play; the Mind being wholly taken up, and the Consequence of Non-attention so fatal.

Play is supported upon the two great Pillars of Deliberation and Action. The Terms of Art are few, prescribed by Law and Custom; no Time allowed for Digressions or Tryals of Wit. QUADRILLE in particular bears some Resemblance to a State of Nature, which, we are told, is a State of War, wherein every Woman is against every Woman: The Unions short, inconstant, and soon broke; the League made this Minute without knowing the Ally; and dissolved in the next. Thus, at the Game of QUADRILLE, female Brains are always employed in Stratagem, or their Hands in Action. Neither can I find, that our Art hath gained much by the happy Revival of MASQUERADING among us; the whole Dialogue in those Meetings being summed up in one sprightly (I confess, but) single Question, and as sprightly an Answer. DO YOU KNOW ME? YES, I DO. And, DO YOU KNOW ME? YES, I DO. For this Reason I did not think it proper to give my Readers the Trouble of introducing a Masquerade, meerly for the sake of a single Question, and a single Answer. Especially, when to perform this in a proper manner, I must have brought in a hundred Persons together, of both Sexes, dressed in fantastick Habits for one Minute, and dismiss them the next.

Neither is it reasonable to conceive, that our Science can be much improved by Masquerades; where the Wit of both Sexes is altogether taken up in continuing singular and humoursome Disguises; and their Thoughts entirely employed in bringing Intrigues and Assignations of Gallantry to an happy Conclusion.

The judicious Reader will readily discover, that I make Miss NOTABLE my Heroin, and Mr. THOMAS NEVEROUT my Hero. I have laboured both their Characters with my utmost Ability. It is into their Mouths that I have put the liveliest Questions, Answers, Repartees, and Rejoynders; because my Design was to propose them both as Patterns for all young Batchelors and single Ladies to copy after. By which I hope very soon to see polite Conversation flourish between both Sexes in a more consummate Degree of Perfection, than these Kingdoms have yet ever known.

I have drawn some Lines of Sir JOHN LINGER's Character, the *Derbyshire* Knight, on purpose to place it in Counterview or Contrast with that of the other Company; wherein I can assure the Reader, that I intended not the least Reflexion upon *Derbyshire*, the place of my Nativity. But, my Intention was only to shew the Misfortune of those Persons, who have the Disadvantage to be bred out of the Circle of Politeness; whereof I take the present Limits to extend no further than *London*, and ten Miles round; although others are pleased to compute it within the Bills of Mortality. If you compare the Discourses of my Gentlemen and Ladies with those of Sir JOHN, you will hardly conceive him to have been bred in the same Climate, or under the same Laws, Language, Religion, or Government: And, accordingly, I have introduced him speaking in his own rude Dialect, for no other Reason than to teach my Scholars how to avoid it.

The curious Reader will observe, that when Conversation appears in danger to flag, which, in some Places, I have artfully contrived, I took care to invent some sudden Question, or Turn of Wit, to revive it; such as these that follow. *What? I think here's a silent Meeting! Come, Madam, A Penny for your Thought*; with several other of the like sort. I have rejected all provincial or country Turns of Wit and Fancy, because I am acquainted with a very few; but, indeed, chiefly because I found them so very much inferior to those at Court, especially among the Gentlemen-Ushers, the Ladies of the Bed-Chamber, and the Maids of Honour; I must also add, the hither End of our noble Metropolis.

When this happy Art of polite Conversing shall be thoroughly improved, good Company will be no longer pestered with dull, dry, tedious Story-tellers, nor brangling Disputers: For, a right Scholar, of either Sex, in our Science, will perpetually interrupt them with some sudden surprising Piece of Wit, that shall engage all the Company in a loud Laugh; and, if after a Pause, the grave Companion resumes his Thread in the following Manner; *Well, but to go on with my Story*; new Interruptions come from the Left to the Right, till he is forced to give over.

I have made some few Essays toward *Selling of* BARGAINS, as well for instructing those, who delight in that Accomplishment, as in compliance with my Female Friends at Court. However, I have transgressed a little in this Point, by doing it in a manner somewhat more reserved than as it is now practiced at St *James's*. At the same time, I can hardly allow this Accomplishment to pass properly for a Branch of that perfect polite Conversation, which makes the constituent Subject of my Treatise; and, for which I have already given my Reasons. I have likewise, for further Caution, left a Blank in the critical Point of each *Bargain*, which the sagacious Reader may fill up in his own Mind.

As to my self, I am proud to own, that except some Smattering in the *French*, I am what the Pedants and Scholars call, a Man wholly illiterate, that is to say, unlearned. But, as to my own Language, I shall not readily yield to many Persons: I have read most of the Plays, and all the miscellany Poems that have been published for twenty Years past. I have read Mr. *Thomas Brown's* Works entire, and had the Honour to be his intimate Friend, who was universally allowed to be the greatest Genius of his Age.

. Upon what Foot I stand with the present chief reigning Wits, their Verses recommendatory, which they have commended me to prefix before my Book, will be more than a thousand Witnesses: I am, and have been, likewise, particularly acquainted with Mr. CHARLES GILDON, Mr. WARD, Mr. DENNIS, that admirable Critick and Poet, and several others. Each of these eminent Persons (I mean, those who are still alive) have done me the Honour to read this Production five Times over with the strictest Eye of friendly Severity, and proposed some, although very few, Amendments, which I gratefully accepted, and do here publickly return my Acknowledgment for so singular a Favour.

And here, I cannot conceal, without Ingratitude, the great Assistance I have received from those two illustrious Writers, Mr. OZEL, and Captain STEVENS, These, and some others, of distinguished Eminence, in whose Company I have passed so many agreeable Hours, as they have been the great Refiners of our Language; so, it hath been my chief Ambition to imitate them. Let the POPES, the GAYS, the ARBUTHNOTS, the YOUNGS, and the rest of that snarling Brood burst with Envy at the Praises we receive from the Court and Kingdom.

But to return from this Digression.

The Reader will find that the following Collection of polite Expressions will easily incorporate with all Subjects of genteel and fashionable Life. Those, which are proper for Morning-Tea, will be equally useful at the same Entertainment in the Afternoon, even in the same Company, only by shifting the several Questions, Answers, and Replies, into different Hands; and such as are adapted to Meals will indifferently serve for Dinners or Suppers, only distinguishing between Day-light and Candle-light. By this Method no diligent Person, of a tolerable Memory, can ever be at a loss.

It hath been my constant Opinion, that every Man, who is intrusted by Nature with any useful Talent of the Mind, is bound by all the Ties of Honour, and that Justice which we all owe our Country, to propose to himself some one illustrious Action, to be performed in his Life for the publick Emolument. And, I freely confess, that so grand, so important an Enterprize as I have undertaken, and executed to the best of my Power, well deserved a much abler Hand, as well as a liberal Encouragement from the Crown. However, I am bound so far to acquit my self, as to declare, that I have often and most earnestly intreated several of my above-named Friends, universally allowed to be of the first Rank in Wit and Politeness, that they would undertake a Work, so honourable to themselves, and so beneficial to the Kingdom; but so great was their Modesty, that they all thought fit to excuse themselves, and impose the Task on me; yet in so obliging a Manner, and attended with such Compliments on my poor Qualifications, that I dare not repeat. And, at last, their Intreaties, or rather their Commands, added to that inviolable Love I bear to the Land of my Nativity, prevailed upon me to engage in so bold an Attempt.

I may venture to affirm, without the least Violation of Modesty, that there is no Man, now alive, who hath, by many Degrees, so just Pretensions as my self, to the highest Encouragement from the CROWN, the PARLIAMENT, and the MINISTRY, towards bringing this Work to its due Perfection. I have been assured, that several great Heroes of antiquity were worshipped as Gods, upon the Merit of having civilized a fierce and barbarous People. It is manifest, I could have no other Intentions; and, I dare appeal to my very Enemies, if such a Treatise as mine had been published some Years ago, and with as much Success as I am confident this will meet, I mean, by turning the Thoughts of the whole Nobility and Gentry to the Study and Practice of polite Conversation; whether such mean stupid Writers, as the CRAFTSMAN and his Abettors, could have been able to corrupt the Principles of so many hundred thousand Subjects, as, to the Shame and Grief of every whiggish, loyal, and true Protestant Heart, it is too manifest, they have done. For, I desire the honest judicious Reader to make one Remark, that after having exhausted the Whole *In sickly payday* (if I may so call it) of Politeness and Refinement, and faithfully digested it in the following Dialogues, there cannot be found one Expression relating to Politicks; that the MINISTRY is never mentioned, nor the Word KING, above twice or thrice, and then only to the Honour of Majesty; so very cautious were our wiser Ancestors in

---

* This Word is spelt by *Latinists*, *Encyclopædia*; but the judicious Author wisely prefers the Polite Reading before the Pedantick.

forming Rules for Conversation, as never to give Offence to Crowned Heads, nor interfere with Party Disputes in the State. And indeed, although there seem to be a close Resemblance between the two Words *Politeness* and *Politicks*, yet no Ideas are more inconsistent in their Natures. However, to avoid all Appearance of Disaffection, I have taken care to enforce Loyalty by an invincible Argument, drawn from the very Fountain of this noble Science, in the following short Terms, that ought to be writ in Gold, MUST IS FOR THE KING; which uncontroulable Maxim I took particular Care of introducing in the first Page of my Book; thereby to instil early the best Protestant Loyal Notions into the Minds of my Readers. Neither is it meerly my own private Opinion, that Politeness is the firmest Foundation upon which Loyalty can be supported: For, thus happily sings the Divine Mr. *Tibbalds*, or *Theobalds*, in one of his Birth-Day Poems.

> *I am no Schollard; but I am polite:*
> *Therefore be sure I am no* Jacobite.

Hear likewise, to the same purpose, that great Master of the whole Poetick Choir, our most illustrious Laureat Mr. COLLY CIBBER.

> *Who in his Talk can't speak a polite Thing,*
> *Will never loyal be to* GEORGE *our King.*

I could produce many more shining Passages out of our principal Poets, of both Sexes, to confirm this momentous Truth. From whence, I think, it may be fairly concluded, that whoever can most contribute towards propagating the Science contained in the following Sheets, through the Kingdoms of *Great-Britain* and *Ireland*, may justly demand all the Favour, that the wisest Court, and most judicious Senate, are able to confer on the most deserving Subject. I leave the Application to my Readers.

This is the Work, which I have been so hardy to attempt, and without the least mercenary View. Neither do I doubt of succeeding to my full Wish, except among the TORIES and their Abettors; who being all *Jacobites*, and, consequently *Papists* in their Hearts, from a Want of true Taste, or by strong Affectation, may perhaps resolve not to read my Book; chusing rather to deny themselves the Pleasure and Honour of shining in polite Company among the principal Genius's of both Sexes throughout the Kingdom, than adorn their Minds with this noble Art; and probably apprehending (as, I confess nothing is more likely to happen) that a true Spirit of Loyalty to the Protestant Succession should steal in along with it.

If my favourable and gentle Readers could possibly conceive the perpetual Watchings, the numberless Toils, the frequent Risings in the Night, to set down several ingenious Sentences, that I suddenly or accidentally recollected; and which, without my utmost Vigilance, had been irrecoverably lost for ever: If they would consider with what incredible Diligence I daily and nightly attended at those Houses, where Persons of both Sexes, and of the most distinguished Merit, used to meet and display their Talents; with what Attention I listened to all their Discourses, the better to retain them in my Memory; and then, at proper Seasons, withdrew unobserved, to enter them in my Table-Book, while the Company little suspected what a noble Work I had then in Embryo: I say, if all these were known to the World, I think, it would be no great Presumption in me to expect, at a proper Juncture, the publick Thanks of both Houses of Parliament, for the Service and Honour I have done to the whole Nation by my single Pen.

Although I have never been once charged with the least Tincture of Vanity, the Reader will, I hope, give me leave to put an easy Question: What is become of all the King of *Sweden*'s Victories? Where are the Fruits of them at this Day? or, of what Benefit will they be to Posterity? were not many of his greatest Actions owing, at least in part, to Fortune? were not all of them owing to the Valour of his Troops, as much as to his own Conduct? could he have conquered the *Polish* King, or the *Czar* of *Muscovy*, with his single Arm? Far be it from me to envy or lessen the Fame he hath acquired; but, at the same time, I will venture to say, without Breach of Modesty, that I, who have alone with this Right-hand subdued Barbarism, Rudeness, and Rusticity, who have established and fixed for ever the whole System of all true Politeness and Refinement in Conversation, should think my self most inhumanely treated by my Country-men, and would accordingly resent it as the highest Indignity, to be put upon the level, in point of Fame, in After-ages, with CHARLES the Twelfth, late King of *Sweden*.

And yet, so incurable is the Love of Detraction, perhaps beyond what the charitable Reader will easily believe, that I have been assured by more than one credible Person, how some of my Enemies have industriously whispered about, that one ISAAC NEWTON, an Instrument-maker, formerly living near *Leicester-Fields*, and afterwards a Workman at the Mint in the *Tower*, might possibly pretend to vye with me for Fame in future times. The Man it seems was knighted for making Sun-Dials better than others of his Trade, and was thought to be a Conjurer, because he knew how to draw Lines and Circles upon a Slate, which no body could understand. But, adieu to all noble Attempts for endless Renown, if the Ghost of an obscure Mechanick shall be raised up to enter into competition with me, only for his Skill in making Pot-hooks and Hangers with a Pencil, which many thousand accomplished Gentlemen and Ladies can perform as well with a Pen and Ink upon a Piece of Paper, and, in a manner, as little intelligible as those of Sir ISAAC.

My most ingenious Friend already mentioned, Mr. COLLY CIBBER, who does too much Honour to the Laurel Crown he deservedly wears, (as he hath often done to many Imperial Diadems placed on his Head) was pleased to tell me, that, if my Treatise were formed into a Comedy, the Representation, performed to Advantage on our Theatre, might very much contribute to the Spreading of polite Conversation among all Persons of Distinction through the whole Kingdom.

I own, the Thought was ingenious, and my Friend's Intention good. But, I cannot agree to his Proposal: For, Mr. CIBBER himself allowed, that the Subjects handled in my Work, being so numerous and extensive, it would be absolutely impossible for one, two, or even six Comedies to contain them. From whence it will follow, that many admirable and essential Rules for polite Conversation must be omitted.

And here let me do justice to my Friend Mr. TIBBALDS, who plainly confessed before Mr. CIBBER himself, that such a Project, as it would be a great Diminution to my Honour, so it would intolerably mangle my Scheme, and thereby destroy the principal End at which I aimed, to form a compleat Body or System of this most useful Science in all its Parts. And therefore Mr. TIBBALDS, whose Judgment was never disputed, chose rather to fall in with my Proposal mentioned before, of erecting publick Schools and Seminaries all over the Kingdom, to instruct the young People of both Sexes in this Art, according to my Rules, and in the Method that I have laid down.

I shall conclude this long, but necessary Introduction, with a Request, or indeed rather, a just and reasonable Demand from all Lords, Ladies, and Gentlemen, that while they are entertaining and improving each other with those polite Questions, Answers, Repartees, Replies, and Rejoinders, which I have with infinite Labour, and close Application, during the Space of thirty-six Years, been collecting for their Service and Improvement, they shall, as an Instance of Gratitude, on every proper Occasion, quote my Name, after this or the like manner. *Madam, as our Master* WAGSTAFF *says*. *My Lord, as our Friend* WAGSTAFF *has it*. I do likewise expect, that all my Pupils shall drink my Health every Day at Dinner and Supper during my Life; and that they, or their Posterity, shall continue the same Ceremony to my *not inglorious Memory*, after my Decease, for ever.

DIALOGUE III

The Ladies at their Tea.

Lady Smart. Well, Ladies; now let us have a Cup of Discourse to ourselves.

Lady Answ[erall]. What do you think of your Friend, Sir *John Spendall*?

Lady Smart. Why, Madam, 'tis happy for him, that his Father was born before him.

Miss [*Notable*]. They say, he makes a very ill Husband to my Lady.

Lady Answ. But he must be allow'd to be the fondest Father in the World.

Lady Smart. Ay, Madam, that's true; for they say, the Devil is kind to his own.

Miss. I am told, my Lady manages him to Admiration.

Lady Smart. That I believe; for she's as cunning as a dead Pig; but not half so honest.

Lady Answ. They say, she's quite a Stranger to all his Gallantries.

Lady Smart. Not at all; but, you know, there's none so blind as they that won't see.

Miss. O Madam, I am told, she watches him, as a Cat would watch a Mouse.

Lady Answ. Well, if she ben't foully belied, she pays him in his own Coin.

Lady Smart. Madam, I fancy I know your Thoughts, as well as if I were within you.

Lady Answ. Madam, I was t'other Day in Company with Mrs. *Clatter*; I find she gives herself Airs of being acquainted with your Ladyship.

Miss. Oh, the hideous Creature! did you observe her Nails? they were long enough to scratch her Granum out of her Grave.

Lady Smart. Well, She and *Tom Gosling* were banging Compliments backwards and forwards; it look'd like Two Asses scrubbing one another.

Miss. Ay, claw me, and I'll claw thou: But, pray, Madam, who were the Company?

Lady Smart. Why, there was all the World, and his Wife; there was Mrs. *Clatter*, Lady *Singular*, the Countess of *Talkham*, (I should have named her first;) *Tom Gosling*, and some others, whom I have forgot.

Lady Answ. I think the Countess is very sickly.

Lady Smart. Yes, Madam; she'll never scratch a grey Head, I promise her.

Miss. And, pray, what was your Conversation?

Lady Smart. Why, Mrs. *Clatter* had all the Talk to herself, and was perpetually complaining of her Misfortunes.

Lady Answ. She brought her Husband Ten thousand Pounds; she has a Town-House and Country-House: Would the Woman have her A—— hung with Points?

Lady Smart. She would fain be at the Top of the House before the Stairs are built.

Miss. Well, Comparisons are odious; but she's as like her Husband, as if she were spit out of his Mouth; as like as one Egg is to another: Pray, how was she drest?

Lady Smart. Why, she was as fine as Fi'pence; but, truly, I thought, there was more Cost than Worship.

Lady Answ. I don't know her Husband: Pray, what is he?

Lady Smart. Why, he's a Concealer of the Law; you must know, he came to us as drunk as *David's* Sow.

Miss. What kind of Creature is he?

Lady Smart. You must know, the Man and his Wife are coupled like Rabbets, a fat and a lean; he's as fat as a Porpus, and she's one of *Pharaoh's* lean Kine: The Ladies and *Tom Gosling* were proposing a Party at Quadrille, but he refus'd to make one: Damn your Cards, said he, they are the Devil's Books.

Lady Answ. A dull unmannerly Brute! Well, God send him more Wit, and me more Money.

Miss. Lord! Madam, I would not keep such Company for the World.

Lady Smart. O Miss, 'tis nothing when you are used to it: Besides, you know, for Want of Company, welcome Trumpery.

Miss. Did your Ladyship play?

Lady Smart. Yes, and won; so I came off with Fidlers Fare, Meat, Drink, and Money.

Lady Answ. Ay; what says *Pluck*?

Miss. Well, my Elbow itches; I shall change Bed-fellows.

Lady Smart. And my Right Hand itches; I shall receive Money.

Lady Answ. And my Right Eye itches; I shall cry.

Lady Smart. Miss, I hear your Friend Mistress *Giddy*

has discarded *Dick Shuttle*: Pray, has she got another Lover?

Miss. I hear of none.

Lady Smart. Why, the Fellow's rich; and I think she was a Fool to throw out her dirty Water before she got clean.

Lady Answ. Miss, that's a very handsome Gown of yours, and finely made; very genteel.

Miss. I'm glad your Ladyship likes it.

Lady Answ. Your Lover will be in Raptures; it becomes you admirably.

Miss. Ay; I assure you I won't take it as I have done; if this won't fetch him, the Devil fetch him, say I.

Lady Smart. (*to Lady Answ.*) Pray, Madam, when did you see Sir *Peter Muckworm*?

Lady Answ. Not this Fortnight; I hear, he's laid up with the Gout.

Lady Smart. What does he do for it?

Lady Answ. Why, I hear he's weary of doctoring it, and now makes Use of nothing but Patience and Flannel.

Miss. Pray, how does He and my Lady agree?

Lady Answ. You know, he loves her as the Devil loves Holy Water.

Miss. They say, she plays deep with Sharpers, that cheat her of her Money.

Lady Answ. Upon my Word, they must rise early that would cheat her of her Money; Sharp's the Word with her; Diamonds cut Diamonds.

Miss. Well, but I was assur'd from a good Hand, that she lost at one Sitting to the Tune of a hundred Guineas; make Money of that.

Lady Smart. Well, but do you hear, that Mrs. *Plump* is brought to Bed at last?

Miss. And, pray, what has God sent her?

Lady Smart. Why, guess, if you can.

Miss. A Boy, I suppose.

Lady Smart. No, you are out; guess again.

Miss. A Girl then.

Lady Smart. You have hit it; I believe you are a Witch.

Miss. O Madam; the Gentlemen say, all fine Ladies are Witches; but I pretend to no such thing.

Lady Answ. Well, she had good Luck to draw *Tom Plump* into Wedlock; she ris' with her A—— upwards.

Miss. Fie, Madam! what do you mean?

Lady Smart. O Miss; 'tis nothing what we say among ourselves.

Miss. Ay, Madam; but they say, Hedges have Eyes, and Walls have Ears.

Lady Answ. Well Miss, I can't help it; you know, I am old Tell-Truth; I love to call a Spade a Spade.

Lady Smart. (*mistakes the Tea-tongs for the Spoon.*) What! I think my Wits are a Wool-gathering To-day.

Miss. Why, Madam, there was but a Right and a Wrong.

Lady Smart. Miss, I hear, that You and Lady *Coupler* are as great as Cup and Can.

Lady Answ. Ay, Miss; as great as the Devil and the Earl of *Kent.*

Lady Smart. Nay, I am told, you meet together with as much Love, as there is between the old Cow and the Hay-stack.

Miss. I own, I love her very well; but there's Difference betwixt staring and stark mad.

Lady Smart. They say, she begins to grow fat.

Miss. Fat! ay, fat as a Hen in the Forehead.

Lady Smart. Indeed, Lady *Answerall*, (pray, forgive me) I think, your Ladyship looks thinner than when I saw you last.

Miss. Indeed, Madam, I think not; but your Ladyship is one of *Job's* Comforters.

Lady Answ. Well, no matter how I look; I am bought and sold: but really, Miss, you are so very obliging, that I wish I were a handsome young Lord for your Sake.

Miss. O Madam, your Love's a Million.

Lady Smart. (*to Lady Answ.*) Madam, will your Ladyship let me wait on you to the Play To-morrow?

Lady Answ. Madam, it becomes me to wait on your Ladyship.

Miss. What, then, I'm turn'd out for a Wrangler.

(The Gentlemen come in to the Ladies to drink Tea.

Miss. Mr. *Neverout*, we wanted you sadly; you are always out of the Way when you should be hang'd.

Neverout. You wanted me! Pray, Miss, how do you look when you lye?

Miss. Better than you when you cry. Manners indeed! I find, you mend like sour Ale in Summer.

Neverout. I beg your Pardon, Miss; I only meant, when you lie alone.

Miss. That's well turn'd; one Turn more would have turn'd you down Stairs.

Neverout. Come, Miss; be kind for once, and order me a Dish of Coffee.

Miss. Pray, go yourself; let us wear out the oldest first: Besides, I can't go, for I have a Bone in my Leg.

Col[onel Atwit]. They say, a Woman need but look on her Apron-string to find an Excuse.

Neverout. Why, Miss, you are grown so peevish, a Dog would not live with you.

Miss. Mr. *Neverout*, I beg your Diversion; no Offence, I hope: but truly in a little time you intend to make the Colonel as bad as yourself; and that's as bad as bad can be.

Neverout. My Lord, don't you think Miss improves wonderfully of late? Why, Miss, if I spoil the Colonel, I hope you will use him as you do me; for, you know, love me, love my Dog.

Col. How's that, *Tom*? Say that again: Why, if I am a Dog, shake Hands, Brother.

(Here a great, loud, long Laugh.

Ld. Smart. But, pray, Gentlemen, why always so severe upon poor Miss? On my Conscience, Colonel and *Tom Neverout*, one of you two are both Knaves.

Col. My Lady *Answerall*, I intend to do myself the Honour of dining with your Ladyship To-morrow.

Lady Answ. Ay, Colonel; do if you can.

Miss. I'm sure you'll be glad to be welcome.

Col. Miss, I thank you; and, to reward You, I'll come and drink Tea with you in Morning.

U

Miss. Colonel, there's Two Words to that Bargain.

Col. (*to Lady Smart.*) Your Ladyship has a very fine Watch; well may you wear it.

Lady Smart. It is none of mine, Colonel.

Col. Pray, whose is it then?

Lady Smart. Why, 'tis my Lord's; for they say, a marry'd Woman has nothing of her own, but her Wedding-Ring and her Hair-Lace: But if Women had been the Law-Makers, it would have been better.

Col. This Watch seems to be quite new.

Lady Smart. No, Sir; it has been Twenty Years in my Lord's Family; but *Quare* put a new Case and Dial-Plate to it.

Neverout. Why, that's for all the World like the Man who swore he kept the same Knife forty Years, only he sometimes changed the Haft, and sometimes the Blade.

Ld. Smart. Well, *Tom*, to give the Devil his Due, thou art a right Woman's Man.

Col. Odd-so! I have broke the Hinge of my Snuff-box; I'm undone beside the Loss.

Miss. Alack-a-day, Colonel! I vow I had rather have found Forty Shillings.

Neverout. Why, Colonel; all that I can say to comfort you, is, that you must mend it with a new one.

(Miss *laughs.*

Col. What, Miss! you can't laugh, but you must shew your Teeth.

Miss. I'm sure you shew your Teeth when you can't bite: Well, thus it must be, if we sell Ale.

Neverout. Miss, you smell very sweet; I hope you don't carry Perfumes.

Miss. Perfumes! No, Sir; I'd have you to know, it is nothing but the Grain of my Skin.

Col. Tom, you have a good Nose to make a poor Man's Sow.

Ld. Sparkish. So, Ladies and Gentlemen, methinks you are very witty upon one another: Come, box it about; 'twill come to my Father at last.

Col. Why, my Lord, you see Miss has no Mercy; I wish

she were marry'd; but I doubt, the grey Mare would prove the better Horse.

Miss. Well, God forgive you for that Wish.

Ld. Sparkish. Never fear him, Miss.

Miss. What, my Lord, do you think I was born in a Wood, to be afraid of an Owl?

Ld. Smart. What have you to say to that, Colonel?

Neverout. O my Lord, my Friend the Colonel scorns to set his Wit against a Child.

Miss. Scornful Dogs will eat dirty Puddens.

Col. Well, Miss; they say, a Woman's Tongue is the last thing about her that dies; therefore let's kiss and Friends.

Miss. Hands off! that's Meat for your Master.

Ld. Sparkish. Faith, Colonel, you are for Ale and Cakes: But after all, Miss, you are too severe; you would not meddle with your Match.

Miss. All they can say goes in at one Ear, and out at t'other for me, I can assure you: Only I wish they would be quiet, and let me drink my Tea.

Neverout. What! I warrant you think all is lost, that goes beside your own Mouth.

Miss. Pray, Mr. *Neverout*, hold your Tongue for once, if it be possible; one would think, you were a Woman in Man's Cloaths, by your prating.

Neverout. No, Miss; it is not handsome to see one hold one's Tongue: Besides, I should slobber my Fingers.

Col. Miss, did you never hear, that Three Women and a Goose are enough to make a Market?

Miss. I'm sure, if Mr. *Neverout* or You were among them, it would make a Fair.

(Footman *comes in.*

Lady Smart. Here, take away the Tea-table, and bring up Candles.

Lady Answ. O Madam, no Candles yet, I beseech you; don't let us burn Day-Light.

Neverout. I dare swear, Miss, for her Part, will never burn Day-Light, if she can help it.

Miss. Lord, Mr. *Neverout*, one can't hear one's own Ears for you.

Lady Smart. Indeed, Madam, it is Blind-Man's Holiday; we shall soon be all of a Colour.

Neverout. Why, then, Miss, we may kiss where we like best.

Miss. Fogh! these Men talk of nothing but kissing.

(*She spits.*

Neverout. What, Miss, does it make your Mouth water?

Lady Smart. It is as good be in the Dark as without Light; therefore pray bring in Candles: They say, Women and Linen shew best by Candle-Light: Come, Gentlemen, are you for a Party at Quadrille?

Col. I'll make one with you three Ladies.

Lady Answ. I'll sit down, and be a Stander-by.

Lady Smart. (*to Lady Answ.*) Madam, does your Ladyship never play?

Col. Yes; I suppose her Ladyship plays sometimes for an Egg at *Easter.*

Neverout. Ay; and a Kiss at *Christmas.*

Lady Answ. Come, Mr. *Neverout*; hold your Tongue, and mind your Knitting.

Neverout. With all my Heart; kiss my Wife, and welcome.

> (*The* Colonel, *Mr.* Neverout, *Lady* Smart *and* Miss *go to Quadrille, and sit till Three in the Morning.*
> (*They rise from Cards.*)

Lady Smart. Well, Miss, you'll have a sad Husband, you have such good Luck at Cards.

Neverout. Indeed, Miss, you dealt me sad Cards; if you deal so ill by your Friends, what will you do with your Enemies?

Lady Answ. I'm sure 'tis time for honest Folks to be a-bed.

Miss. Indeed, my Eyes draws Straw.

(*She's almost asleep.*

Neverout. Why, Miss, if you fall asleep, somebody may get a Pair of Gloves.

Col. I'm going to the Land of *Nod.*

Neverout. Faith, I'm for *Bedfordshire.*

Lady Smart. I'm sure I shall sleep without rocking.

Neverout. Miss, I hope you'll dream of your Sweetheart.

Miss. Oh, no doubt of it: I believe I shan't be able to sleep for dreaming of him.

Col. (*to Miss.*) Madam, shall I have the Honour to escort you?

Miss. No, Colonel, I thank you; my Mamma has sent her Chair and Footmen. Well, my Lady *Smart*, I'll give you Revenge whenever you please.

(Footman *comes in.*

Footman. Madam, the Chairs are waiting.

(*They all take their Chairs, and go off.*

DIRECTIONS
TO
SERVANTS

SELECTION

" THE following Treatise ", according to the Preface [dated Nov. 8, 1745] prefixed by Faulkner to the Dublin edition of the year 1746, " was begun some years ago by the Author, who had not Leisure to finish and put it into proper Order, being engaged in many other Works of greater Use to his Country, as may be seen from most of his Writings. But, as the Author's Design was to expose the Villanies and Frauds of Servants to their Masters and Mistresses, we shall make no Apology for its Publication; but give it our Readers in the same manner as we find it in the Original."

Swift appears to have added to the work from time to time, until, his memory failing, he laid it aside for ever. Parts of the existing text are clearly only memoranda upon which Swift intended to enlarge. In a letter, written from Powerscourt in August 1731, he speaks of having retired to the country " for the public good, having two great works in hand ", one of them *Polite Conversation*, the other *Directions to Servants*. Several copies of the manuscript of this curious work seem to have existed. A fragment of one, with some corrections in Swift's hand, is in the Forster collection and has been used in the preparation of the text of the following extracts. The book, " very unfinished and incorrect " [Mrs Whiteway to Pope, May 16, 1740], was published posthumously, by Bowyer in London and Faulkner in Dublin, November 1745. An unfinished preface by Swift is printed by Scott in his life of the author.

DIRECTIONS
TO SERVANTS

Rules that concern
All Servants in
general

WHEN your Master or Lady call a Servant by
Name, if that Servant be not in the Way, none of
you are to answer, for then there will be no End
of your Drudgery: And Masters themselves allow, that if a
Servant comes when he is called, it is sufficient.

When you have done a Fault, be always pert and insolent,
and behave your self as if you were the injured Person; this
will immediately put your Master or Lady off their Mettle.

If you see your Master wronged by any of your Fellow-
servants, be sure to conceal it, for fear of being called a
Tell-tale: However, there is one Exception, in case of a
favourite Servant, who is justly hated by the whole Family;
you are therefore bound in Prudence to lay all the Faults
you can upon the Favourite.

The Cook, the Butler, the Groom, the Market-man, and
every other Servant who is concerned in the Expences of
the Family, should act as if his Master's whole Estate ought
to be applied to that Servant's particular Business. For
Instance, if the Cook computes his Master's Estate to be a
thousand Pounds a Year, he reasonably concludes that a
thousand Pounds a Year will afford Meat enough, and
therefore, he need not be sparing; the Butler makes the same
Judgment, so may the Groom and the Coachman, and thus
every Branch of Expence will be filled to your Master's
Honour.

When you are chid before Company, (which with Submission to our Masters and Ladies is an unmannerly Prac-

tice) it often happens that some Stranger will have the Good-nature to drop a Word in your Excuse; in such a Case, you will have a good Title to justify yourself, and may rightly conclude, that whenever he chides you afterwards on other Occasions, he may be in the wrong; in which Opinion you will be the more confirmed by stating the Case to your Fellow-servants in your own Way, who will certainly decide in your Favour: Therefore, as I have said before, whenever you are chidden, complain as if you were injured.

It often happens that Servants sent on Messages, are apt to stay out somewhat longer than the Message requires, perhaps, two, four, six, or eight Hours, or some such Trifle, for the Temptation to be sure was great, and Flesh and Blood cannot always resist: When you return, the Master storms, the Lady scolds; stripping, cudgelling, and turning off, is the Word: But here you ought to be provided with a Set of Excuses, enough to serve on all Occasions: For Instance, your Uncle came fourscore Miles to Town this Morning, on purpose to see you, and goes back by Break of Day To-morrow: A Brother-Servant that borrowed Money of you when he was out of Place, was running away to *Ireland*: You were taking Leave of an old Fellow-Servant, who was shipping for *Barbados*: Your Father sent a Cow to you to sell, and you could not find a Chapman till Nine at Night: You were taking Leave of a dear Cousin who is to be hanged next *Saturday*: You wrencht your Foot against a Stone, and were forced to stay three Hours in a Shop, before you could stir a Step: Some Nastiness was thrown on you out of a Garret Window, and you were ashamed to come Home before you were cleaned, and the Smell went off: You were pressed for the Sea-service, and carried before a Justice of Peace, who kept you three Hours before he examined you, and you got off with much a-do: A Bailiff by mistake seized you for a Debtor, and kept you the whole Evening in a Spunging-house: You were told your Master had gone to a Tavern, and came to some Mischance, and your grief was so great that you inquired for his Honour in a hundred Taverns between *Pall-mall* and *Temple-bar*.

Take all Tradesmens Parts against your Master, and when you are sent to buy any Thing, never offer to cheapen it, but generously pay the full Demand. This is highly to your Master's Honour; and may be some Shillings in your Pocket; and you are to consider, if your Master hath paid too much, he can better afford the Loss than a poor Tradesman.

Never submit to stir a Finger in any Business but that for which you were particularly hired. For Example, if the Groom be drunk or absent, and the Butler be ordered to shut the Stable Door, the Answer is ready, An please your Honour, I don't understand Horses: If a Corner of the Hanging wants a single Nail to fasten it, and the Footman be directed to tack it up, he may say, he doth not understand that Sort of Work, but his Honour may send for the Upholsterer.

Masters and Ladies are usually quarrelling with the Servants for not shutting the Doors after them: But neither Masters nor Ladies consider that those Doors must be open before they can be shut, and that the Labour is double to open and shut the Doors; therefore the best and shortest, and easiest Way is to do neither. But if you are so often teized to shut the Door, that you cannot easily forget it, then give the Door such a Clap as you go out, as will shake the whole Room, and make every Thing rattle in it, to put your Master and Lady in Mind that you observe their Directions.

If you find yourself to grow into Favour with your Master or Lady, take some Opportunity, in a very mild Way, to give them Warning, and when they ask the Reason, and seem loth to part with you, answer that you would rather live with them, than any Body else, but a poor Servant is not to be blamed if he strives to better himself; that Service is no Inheritance, that your Work is great, and your Wages very small: Upon which, if your Master hath any Generosity, he will add five or ten Shillings a Quarter rather than let you go: But, if you are baulked, and have no Mind to go off, get some Fellow-servant to tell your Master, that he had prevailed upon you to stay.

Whatever good Bits you can pilfer in the Day, save them to junket with your Fellow-servants at Night, and take in the Butler, provided he will give you Drink.

Write your own Name and your Sweet-heart's with the Smoak of a Candle on the Roof of the Kitchen, or the Servants Hall, to shew your Learning.

If you are a young sightly Fellow, whenever you whisper your Mistress at the Table, run your Nose full in her Cheek, or if your Breath be good, breathe full in her Face; this I have known to have had very good Consequences in some Families.

Never come till you have been called three or four Times; for none but Dogs will come at the first Whistle: And when the Master calls (*Who's there?*) no Servant is bound to come; for (*Who's there*) is no Body's Name.

When you have broken all your earthen Drinking Vessels below Stairs (which is usually done in a Week) the Copper Pot will do as well; it can boil Milk, heat Porridge, hold Small-Beer, or in Case of Necessity serve for a Jordan; therefore apply it indifferently to all these Uses; but never wash or scour it, for Fear of taking off the Tin.

Although you are allow'd Knives for the Servants Hall, at Meals, yet you ought to spare them, and make Use only of your Master's.

Let it be a constant Rule, that no Chair, Stool or Table in the Servants Hall, or the Kitchen, shall have above three Legs, which hath been the antient, and constant Practice in all the Families I ever knew, and is said to be founded upon two Reasons; first to shew that Servants are ever in a tottering Condition; secondly, it was thought a Point of Humility, that the Servants Chairs and Tables should have at least one Leg fewer than those of their Masters. I grant there hath been an Exception to this Rule, with regard to the Cook, who by old Custom was allowed an easy Chair to sleep in after Dinner; and yet I have seldom seen them with above three Legs. Now this epidemical Lameness of Servants Chairs is by Philosophers imputed to two Causes, which are observed to make the greatest Revolutions in States and Empires; I mean Love and War. A Stool, a

Chair or a Table is the first Weapon taken up in a general Romping or Skirmish; and after a Peace, the Chairs if they be not very strong, are apt to suffer in the Conduct of an Amour, the Cook being usually fat and heavy, and the Butler a little in Drink.

I could never endure to see Maid-Servants so ungenteel as to walk the Streets with their Pettycoats pinned up; it is a foolish Excuse to alledge, their Pettycoats will be dirty, when they have so easy a Remedy as to walk three or four times down a clean Pair of Stairs after they come home.

When you stop to tattle with some crony Servant in the same Street, leave your own Street-Door open, that you may get in without knocking, when you come back; otherwise your Mistress may know you are gone out, and you must be chidden.

I do most earnestly exhort you all to Unanimity and Concord. But mistake me not: You may quarrel with each other as much as you please, only bear in Mind that you have a common Enemy, which is your Master and Lady, and you have a common Cause to defend. Believe an old Practitioner; whoever out of Malice to a Fellow-Servant, carries a Tale to his Master, should be ruined by a general Confederacy against him.

The general Place of Rendezvous for all the Servants, both in Winter and Summer, is the Kitchen; there the grand Affairs of the Family ought to be consulted; whether they concern the Stable, the Dairy, the Pantry, the Laundry, the Cellar, the Nursery, the Dining-room, or my Lady's Chamber: There, as in your own proper Element, you can laugh, and squall, and romp, in full Security.

When any Servant comes home drunk, and cannot appear, you must all join in telling your Master, that he is gone to Bed very sick; upon which your Lady will be so good-natured, as to order some comfortable Thing for the poor Man, or Maid.

When your Master and Lady go abroad together, to Dinner, or to Visit for the Evening, you need leave only one Servant in the House, unless you have a Black-guard-boy to answer at the Door, and attend the Children, if there be any. Who is to stay at home is to be determined by short and long Cuts, and the Stayer at home may be comforted by a Visit from a Sweet-heart, without Danger of being caught together. These Opportunities must never be missed, because they come but sometimes; and you are always safe enough while there is a Servant in the House.

When your Master or Lady comes home, and wants a Servant, who happens to be abroad, your Answer must be, that he but just that Minute stept out, being sent for by a Cousin who was dying.

If your Master calls you by Name, and you happen to answer at the fourth Call, you need not hurry yourself; and if you be chidden for staying, you may lawfully say, you came no sooner, because you did not know what you were called for.

When you are chidden for a Fault, as you go out of the Room, and down Stairs, mutter loud enough to be plainly heard; this will make him believe you are innocent.

Whoever comes to visit your Master or Lady when they are abroad, never burthen your Memory with the Person's Name, for indeed you have too many other Things to remember. Besides, it is a Porter's Business, and your Master's Fault he doth not keep one, and who can remember Names; and you will certainly mistake them, and you can neither write nor read.

If it be possible, never tell a Lye to your Master or Lady, unless you have some Hopes that they cannot find it out in less than half an Hour. When a Servant is turned off, all his Faults must be told, although most of them were never known by his Master or Lady; and all Mischiefs done by others, charge to him. (Instance them.) And when they ask any of you, why you never acquainted them before? The Answer is, Sir, or Madam, really I was afraid it would make you angry; and besides perhaps you might think it was Malice in me. Where there are little Masters and Misses in a House, they are usually great Impediments to the Diversions of the Servants; the only Remedy is to bribe them with Goody Goodyes, that they may not tell Tales to Papa and Mamma.

I advise you of the Servants, whose Master lives in the Country, and who expect Vales, always to stand Rank and File when a Stranger is taking his Leave; so that he must of Necessity pass between you; and he must have more Confidence, or less Money than usual, if any of you let him escape, and according as he behaves himself, remember to treat him the next Time he comes.

If you are sent with ready Money to buy any Thing at a Shop, and happen at that Time to be out of Pocket, sink the Money and take up the Goods on your Master's Account. This is for the Honour of your Master and yourself; for he becomes a Man of Credit at your Recommendation.

When your Lady sends for you up to her Chamber, to give you any Orders, be sure to stand at the Door, and keep it open fidling with the Lock all the while she is talking to you, and keep the Button in your Hand for fear you should forget to shut the Door after you.

If your Master or Lady happen once in their Lives to accuse you wrongfully, you are a happy Servant, for you have nothing more to do, than for every Fault you commit while you are in their Service, to put them in Mind of that false Accusation, and protest yourself equally innocent in the present Case.

When you have a Mind to leave your Master, and are too bashful to break the Matter for fear of offending him, the best way is to grow rude and saucy of a sudden, and beyond your usual Behaviour, till he finds it necessary to turn you off, and when you are gone, to revenge yourself, give him and his Lady such a Character to all your Brother-servants, who are out of Place, that none will venture to offer their Service.

Some nice Ladies who are afraid of catching Cold, having observed that the Maids and Fellows below Stairs, often forget to shut the Door after them as they come in or go out into the back Yards, have contrived that a Pulley and a Rope with a large Piece of Lead at the End, should be so fixt as to make the Door shut of itself, and require a strong Hand to open it, which is an immense Toil to Servants, whose Business may force them to go in and out fifty Times in a Morning: But Ingenuity can do much, for prudent Servants have found out an effectual Remedy against this insupportable Grievance, by tying up the Pully in such a Manner, that the Weight of the Lead shall have no Effect; however, as to my own Part, I would rather chuse to keep the Door always open, by laying a heavy Stone at the Bottom of it.

The Servants Candlesticks are generally broken, for nothing can last for ever. But you may find out many Expedients: You may conveniently stick your Candle in a Bottle, or with a Lump of Butter against the Wainscot, in a Powder-horn, or in an old Shoe, or in a cleft Stick, or in the Barrel of a Pistol, or upon its own Grease on a Table, in a Coffee Cup or a Drinking Glass, a Horn Can, a Tea Pot, a Twisted Napkin, a Mustard Pot, an Inkhorn, a Marrowbone, a Piece of Dough, or you may cut a Hole in the Loaf, and stick it there.

When you invite the neighbouring Servants to junket with you at home in an Evening, teach them a peculiar way of tapping or scraping at the Kitchen Window, which you may hear, but not your Master or Lady, whom you must take Care not to disturb or frighten at such unseasonable Hours.

Lay all Faults upon a Lap-Dog or favourite Cat, a Monkey, a Parrot, a Child, or on the Servant who was last turned off: By this Rule you will excuse yourself, do no Hurt to any Body else, and save your Master or Lady from the Trouble and Vexation of chiding.

When you want proper Instruments for any Work you are about, use all Expedients you can invent, rather than leave your Work undone. For Instance, if the Poker be out of the Way or broken, stir up the Fire with the Tongs; if the Tongs be not at Hand, use the Muzzle of the Bellows, the wrong End of the Fire Shovel, the Handle of the Fire Brush, the End of a Mop, or your Master's Cane. If you want Paper to singe a Fowl, tear the first Book you see about the House. Wipe your Shoes, for want of a Clout, with the Bottom of a Curtain, or a Damask Napkin. Strip your

Livery Lace for Garters. If the Butler wants a Jordan, he may use the great Silver Cup.

There are several Ways of putting out Candles, and you ought to be instructed in them all: you may run the Candle End against the Wainscot, which puts the Snuff out immediately: You may lay it on the Floor, and tread the Snuff out with your Foot: You may hold it upside down until is choaked with its own Grease; or cram it into the Socket of the Candlestick: You may whirl it round in your Hand till it goes out: When you go to Bed, after you have made Water, you may dip the Candle End into the Chamber Pot: You may spit on your Finger and Thumb, and pinch the Snuff until it goes out: The Cook may run the Candle's Nose into the Meal Tub, or the Groom into a Vessel of Oats, or a Lock of Hay, or a Heap of Litter: The Housemaid may put out her Candle by running it against a Looking-glass, which nothing cleans so well as Candle Snuff: But the quickest and best of all Methods, is to blow it out with your Breath, which leaves the Candle clear and readier to be lighted.

There is nothing so pernicious in a Family as a Tell-Tale, against whom it must be the principal Business of you all to unite: Whatever Office he serves in, take all Opportunities to spoil the Business he is about, and to cross him in every Thing. For Instance, if the Butler be the Tell-Tale, break his Glasses whenever he leaves the Pantry Door open: or lock the Cat or the Mastiff in it, who will do as well: Mislay a Fork or a Spoon so as he may never find it. If it be the Cook, whenever she turns her Back, throw a Lump of Soot, or a Handful of Salt in the Pot, or smoaking Coals into the Dripping-Pan, or daub the roast Meat with the Back of the Chimney, or hide the Key of the Jack. If a Footman be suspected, let the Cook daub the Back of his new Livery; or when he is going up with a Dish of Soup, let her follow him softly with a Ladle-full, and dribble it all the Way up Stairs to the Dining-room, and then let the Housemaid make such a Noise, that her Lady may hear it: The Waiting-maid is very likely to be guilty of this Fault, in hopes to ingratiate herself. In this Case, the Laundress must be sure to tear her Smocks in the washing, and yet wash them but half; and, when she complains, tell all the House that she sweats so much, that her Flesh is so nasty, that she fouls a Smock more in one Hour than the Kitchen-maid doth in a Week.

DIRECTIONS TO THE BUTLER

In my Directions to Servants, I find from my long Observation, that you, Butler, are the principal Person concerned.

If any one desires a Glass of Bottled-Ale, first shake the Bottle, to see whether any thing be in it, then taste it, to see what Liquor it is, that you may not be mistaken; and lastly, wipe the Mouth of the Bottle with the Palm of your Hand, to shew your Cleanliness.

If an humble Companion, a Chaplain, a Tutor, or a dependent Cousin happen to be at Table, whom you find to be little regarded by the Master, and the Company, which nobody is readier to discover and observe than we Servants, it must be the Business of you and the Footman, to follow the Example of your Betters, by treating him many degrees worse than any of the rest, and you cannot please your Master better, or at least your Lady.

Take special Care that your Bottles be not musty before you fill them, in order to which, blow strongly into the Mouth of every Bottle, and then if you smell nothing but your own Breath, immediately fill it.

If you are sent down in haste to draw any Drink, and find it will not run, do not be at the Trouble of opening a Vent, but blow strongly into the Fosset, and you will find it immediately pour into your Mouth; or take out the Vent, but do not stay to put it in again, for fear your Master should want you.

If you are curious to taste some of your Master's choicest Ale, empty as many of the Bottles just below the Neck as will make the Quantity you want; but then take care to fill them up again with clean Water, that you may not lessen your Master's Liquor.

Because Butlers are apt to forget to bring up their Ale and Beer time enough, be sure you remember to have up yours two Hours before Dinner; and place them in the sunny Part of the Room, to let People see that you have not been negligent.

Clean your Plate, wipe your Knives, and rub the dirty Tables, with the Napkins and Table-cloths used that Day; for, it is but one washing, and besides it will save you wearing out the coarse Rubbers; and in Reward of such good Husbandry, my Judgment is, that you may lawfully make use of the finest Damask Napkins for Night-caps for yourself.

When you clean your Plate, leave the Whiting plainly to be seen in all the Chinks, for fear your Lady should not believe you had cleaned it.

Sconces are great Wasters of Candles, and you who are always to consider the Advantage of your Master, should do your utmost to discourage them: Therefore, your Business must be to press the Candle with both your Hands into the Socket, so as to make it lean in such a manner, that the Grease may drop all upon the Floor, if some Lady's Head-dress or Gentleman's Perriwig be not ready to intercept it: You may likewise stick the Candle so loose, that it will fall upon the Glass of the Sconce, and break it into Shatters; this will save your Master many a fair Penny in the Year, both in Candles, and to the Glass-man, and your self much Labour; for the Sconces spoiled cannot be used.

When you cut Bread for a Toast, do not stand idly watching it, but lay it on the Coals, and mind your other Business; then come back, and if you find it toasted quite through, scrape off the burned Side, and serve it up.

When you dress up your Side-board, set the best Glasses

as near the edge of the Table as you can; by which means they will cast a double Lustre, and make a much finer Figure; and the Consequence can be at most, but the breaking half a Dozen, which is a Trifle in your Master's Pocket.

Wash the Glasses with your own Water, to save your Master's Salt.

When any Salt is spilt on the Table, do not let it be lost, but when Dinner is done, fold up the Table-cloth with the Salt in it, then shake the Salt out into the Salt-celler to serve next Day: But the shortest and surest Way is, when you remove the Cloth, to wrap the Knives, Forks, Spoons, Salt-cellars, broken Bread, and Scraps of Meat all together in the Table-cloth, by which you will be sure to lose nothing, unless you think it better to shake them out of the Window amongst the Beggars, that they may with more Convenience eat the Scraps.

When a Message is sent to your Master, be kind to your Brother-servant who brings it; give him the best Liquor in your keeping, for your Master's Honour; and with the first Opportunity he will do the same to you.

When Company is expected at Dinner or in the Evenings, be sure to be abroad that nothing may be got which is under your Key, by which your Master will save his Liquor, and not wear out his Plate.

In bottling Wine, fill your Mouth full of Corks, together with a large Plug of Tobacco, which will give to the Wine the true Taste of the Weed, so delightful to all good Judges in drinking.

When you are to get Water on for Tea after Dinner (which in many Families is Part of your Office) to save Firing, and to make more Haste, pour it into the Tea-pot, from the Pot where Cabbage or Fish have been boyling, which will make it much wholsomer, by curing the acid and corroding Quality of the Tea.

Be saving of your Candles, and let those in the Sconces

of the Hall, the Stairs, and in the Lanthorn, burn down into the Sockets, until they go out of themselves, for which your Master and Lady will commend your Thriftiness, as soon as they shall smell the Snuff.

If a Gentleman leaves a Snuff-box or Pick-tooth-case on the Table after Dinner, and goeth away, look upon it as Part of your Vails, for so it is allowed by all Servants, and you do no Wrong to your Master or Lady.

That the Salt may lie smooth in the Salt-celler, press it down with your moist Palm.

When a Gentleman is going away after dining with your Master, be sure to stand full in View, and follow him to the Door, and as you have Opportunity look full in his Face, perhaps it may bring you a Shilling; but, if the Gentleman hath lain there a Night, get the Cook, the House-maid, the Stable-men, the Scullion, and the Gardiner, to accompany you, and to stand in his Way to the Hall in a Line on each Side him: If the Gentleman performs handsomely, it will do him Honour, and cost your Master nothing.

You need not wipe your Knife to cut Bread for the Table, because, in cutting a Slice or two it will wipe it self.

Put your Finger into every Bottle, to feel whether it be full, which is the surest Way, for feeling hath no fellow.

Always lock up a Cat in the Closet where you keep your *China* Plates, for fear the Mice may steal in and break them.

A good Butler always breaks off the Point of his Bottle-screw in two Days, by trying which is hardest, the Point of the Screw, or the Neck of the Bottle: In this Case, to supply the Want of a Screw, after the Stump hath torn the Cork in Pieces, make use of a Silver Fork, and when the Scraps of the Cork are almost drawn out, flirt the Mouth of the Bottle into the Cistern until you quite clear it.

If a Gentleman dines often with your Master, and gives you nothing when he goes away, you may use several Methods to shew him some Marks of your Displeasure, and quicken his Memory: If he calls for Bread or Drink, you may pretend not to hear, or send it to another who called after him: If he asks for Wine, let him stay a while, and then send him Small-beer; give him always foul Glasses; send him a Spoon when he wants a Knife; wink at the Footman to leave him without a Plate; By these, and the like Expedients, you may probably be a better Man by Half a Crown before he leaves the House, provided you watch an Opportunity of standing by when he is going.

The Profit of Glasses is so very inconsiderable, that it is hardly worth mentioning: It consists only in a small Present made by the Glassman, and about four Shillings in the Pound added to the Prices for your Trouble and Skill in chusing them. If your Master hath a large Stock of Glasses, and you or your Fellow-servants happen to break any of them without your Master's Knowledge, keep it a Secret till there are not enough left to serve the Table, then tell your Master that the Glasses are gone; this will be but one Vexation to him, which is much better than fretting once or twice a Week; and it is the Office of a good Servant to discompose his Master and his Lady as seldom as he can; and here the Cat and Dog will be of great Use to take the Blame from you. *Note*, That Bottles missing are supposed to be half stolen by Stragglers and other Servants, and the other half broken by Accident, and a general Washing.

Do all in the Dark to save your Master's Candles.

DIRECTIONS TO THE COOK

ALTHO' I am not ignorant that it hath been a long Time, since the Custom began among People of Quality to keep Men Cooks, and generally of the *French* Nation; yet because my Treatise is chiefly calculated for the general Run of Knights, 'Squires, and Gentlemen both in Town and Country, I shall therefore apply myself to you, Mrs. Cook, as a Woman: However, a great Part of what I intend may serve for either Sex; and your Part naturally follows the former, because the Butler and you are join'd in Interest;

your Vails are generally equal, and paid when others are disappointed: You can junket together at Nights upon your own Progue, when the rest of the House are abed; and have it in your Power to make every Fellow-servant your Friend; you can give a good Bit or a good Sup to the little Masters and Misses, and gain their Affections: A Quarrel between you is very dangerous to you both, and will probably end in one of you being turned off; in which fatal Case, perhaps, it will not be so easy in some Time to cotton with another. And now Mrs. Cook, I proceed to give you my Instructions, which I desire you will get some Fellow-servant in the Family to read to you constantly one Night in every Week when you are going to Bed, whether you serve in Town or Country, for my Lessons shall be fitted for both.

Never send up a Leg of a Fowl at Supper, while there is a Cat or a Dog in the House that can be accused of running away with it: But, if there happen to be neither, you must lay it upon the Rats, or a strange Greyhound.

It is ill Housewifry to foul your Kitchen Rubbers with wiping the Bottom of the Dishes you send up, since the Table-cloth will do as well, and is changed every Meal.

If you are employed in Marketing, buy your Meat as cheap as you can; but when you bring in your Accounts, be tender of your Master's Honour, and set down the highest Rate; which besides is but Justice, for no body can afford to sell at the same Rate that he buys, and I am confident that you may charge safely; swear that you gave no more than what the Butcher and Poulterer asked. If your Lady orders you to set up a Piece of Meat for Supper, you are not to understand that you must set it up all, therefore you may give half to yourself and the Butler.

Good Cooks cannot abide what they justly call fidling Work, where Abundance of Time is spent and little done: Such, for Instance, is the dressing small Birds, requiring a World of Cookery and Clutter, and a second or third Spit, which by the way is absolutely needless; for it will be a very ridiculous Thing indeed, if a Spit which is strong enough to turn a Surloyn of Beef, should not be able to turn a Lark; however, if your Lady be nice, and is afraid that a large Spit will tear them, place them handsomely in the Dripping-pan, where the Fat of roasted Mutton or Beef falling on the Birds, will serve to baste them, and so save both Time and Butter: for what Cook of any Spirit would lose her Time in picking Larks, Wheatears, and other small Birds; therefore if you cannot get the Maids, or the young Misses to assist you, e'en make short Work, and either singe or flay them; there is no great Loss in the Skins, and the Flesh is just the same.

The Kitchen Bellows being usually out of Order with stirring the Fire with the Muzzle to save the Tongs and Poker, borrow the Bellows out of your Lady's Bed-chamber, which being least used, are commonly the best in the House; and if you happen to damage or grease them, you have a Chance to have them left entirely for your own Use.

Always keep a large Fire in the Kitchen when there is a small Dinner, or the Family dines abroad, that the Neighbours seeing the Smoak, may commend your Master's Housekeeping: But, when much Company is invited, then be as sparing as possible of your Coals, because a great deal of the Meat being half raw will be saved, and serve next Day.

When you have Plenty of Fowl in the Larder, leave the Door open, in Pity to the poor Cat, if she be a good Mouser.

If you find it necessary to market in a wet Day, take out your Mistress's Riding-hood and Cloak to save your Cloaths.

To keep troublesome Servants out of the Kitchen, always leave the Winder sticking on the Jack to fall on their Heads.

If a Lump of Soot falls into the Soup, and you cannot conveniently get it out, stir it well in, and it will give the Soup a high *French* Taste.

Scrape the Bottoms of your Pots and Kettles with a Silver Spoon, for fear of giving them a Taste of Copper.

When you send up Butter for Sauce, be so thrifty as to let it be half Water; which is also much wholesomer.

Never make use of a Spoon in any thing that you can do with your Hands, for fear of wearing out your Master's Plate.

When you find that you cannot get Dinner ready at the Time appointed, put the Clock back, and then it may be ready to a Minute.

You are to look upon your Kitchen as your Dressing-room; but, you are not to wash your Hands till you have gone to the Necessary-house, and spitted your Meat, trussed your Fowl, picked your Sallad; nor indeed till after you have sent up your second Course; for your Hands will be ten times fouler with the many things you are forced to handle; but when your Work is over, one Washing will serve for all.

There is but one Part of your Dressing that I would admit while the Victuals are boiling, toasting, or stewing, I mean the combing your Head, which loseth no Time, because you can stand over your Cookery, and watch it with one Hand, while you are using your Comb in the other.

As soon as you have sent up the second Course, you have nothing to do in a great Family until Supper: Therefore scoure your Hands and Face, put on your Hood and Scarf, and take your Pleasure among your Cronies, till Nine or Ten at Night—But dine first.

Let there be always a strict Friendship between you and the Butler, for it is both your Interests to be united: The Butler often wants a comfortable Tit-bit, and you much oftener a cool Cup of good Liquor. However, be cautious of him, for he is sometimes an inconstant Lover, because he hath great Advantage to allure the Maids with a Glass of Sack or White Wine and Sugar.

When you roast a Breast of Veal, remember your Sweet-heart the Butler loves a Sweetbread; therefore set it aside till Evening: You can say, the Cat or the Dog has run away with it, or you found it tainted, or fly-blown; and besides, it looks as well at the Table without it as with it.

If your Dinner miscarries in almost every Dish, how could you help it? You were teized by the Footmen coming into the Kitchen; and, to prove it true, take Occasion to be angry, and throw a Ladle-full of Broth on one or two of their Liveries; besides, *Friday* and *Childermass-day* are two cross Days in the Week, and it is impossible to have good Luck on either of them; therefore on those two Days you have a lawful Excuse.

To save Time and Trouble, cut your Apples and Onions with the same Knife; and well-bred Gentry love the Taste of an Onion in everything they eat.

Lump three or four Pounds of Butter together with your Hands, then dash it against the Wall just over the Dresser, so as to have it ready to pull by Pieces as you have occasion for it.

When you send up a Mess of Broth, Water-gruel, or the like, to your Master in a Morning, do not forget with your Thumb and two Fingers to put Salt on the side of the Plate; for if you make use of a Spoon, or the End of a Knife, there may be Danger that the Salt would fall, and that would be a Sign of ill Luck. Only remember to lick your Thumb and Fingers clean, before you offer to touch the Salt.

DIRECTIONS TO THE FOOTMAN

Your Employment being of a mixt Nature, extends to a great Variety of Business, and you stand in a fair way of being the Favourite of your Master or Mistress, or of the young Masters and Misses; you are the fine Gentleman of the Family, with whom all the Maids are in Love. You are sometimes a Pattern of Dress to your Master, and sometimes he so is to you. You wait at Table in all Companies, and consequently have the Opportunity to see and know the World, and to understand Men and Manners; I confess your Vails are but few, unless you are sent with a Present, or attend the Tea in the Country; but you are called Mr. in the Neighbourhood, and sometimes pick up a Fortune, perhaps your Master's Daughter; and I have known many of your Tribe to have good Commands in the Army. In Town you have a seat reserved for you in the Play-House, where you have an Opportunity of becoming Wits and Criticks: You have no profest Enemy except the Rabble, and my Lady's Waiting-woman, who are sometimes apt to call you Skipkennel. I have a true Veneration for your Office, because I had once the Honour to be one of your Order, which I foolishly left by demeaning myself with accepting an Employment in the Custom-House.—But that you, my Brethren, may come to better Fortunes, I shall here deliver my Instructions, which have been the Fruits of much Thought and Observation, as well as of seven Years Experience.

In order to learn the Secrets of other Families, tell them those of your Master's; thus you will grow a Favourite both at home and abroad, and regarded as a Person of Importance.

Take off the largest Dishes, and set them on with one Hand, to shew the Ladies your Vigour and Strength of Back; but always do it between two Ladies, that if the Dish happens to slip, the Soup or Sauce may fall on their Cloaths and not daub the Floor: By this Practice two of our Brethren, my worthy Friends, got considerable Fortunes.

Learn all the new-fashion Words and Oaths, and Songs, and Scraps of Plays that your Memory can hold. Thus, you will become the Delight of nine Ladies in ten, and the Envy of ninety nine Beaux in a hundred.

When Dinner is done, carry down a great Heap of Plates to the Kitchen, and when you come to the Head of the Stairs, trundle them all before you: There is not a more agreeable Sight or Sound, especially if they be Silver, besides the Trouble they save you, and there they will lie ready near the Kitchen Door, for the Scullion to wash them.

If you are bringing up a Joint of Meat in a Dish, and it falls out of your Hand, before you get into the Dining Room, with the Meat on the Ground, and the Sauce spilled, take up the Meat gently, wipe it with the Lap of your Coat, then put it again into the Dish, and serve it up; and when your Lady misses the Sauce, tell her, it is to be sent up in a Plate by itself.

You are the best Judge of what Acquaintance your Lady ought to have, and therefore, if she sends you on a Message of Compliment or Business to a Family you do not like, deliver the Answer in such a Manner, as may breed a Quarrel between them, not to be reconciled : Or, if a Footman comes from the same Family on the like Errand, turn the Answer she orders you to deliver, in such a Manner, as the other Family may take it for an Affront.

Never clean your Shoes on the Scraper, but in the Entry, or at the Foot of the Stairs, by which you will have the Credit of being at home, almost a Minute sooner, and the Scraper will last the longer.

While Grace is saying after Meat, do you and your Brethren take the Chairs from behind the Company, so that when they go to sit again, they may fall backwards, which will make them all merry; but be you so discreet as to hold your Laughter till you get to the Kitchen, and then divert your Fellow-servants.

When you know your Master is most busy in Company, come in and pretend to fettle about the Room, and if he chides, say, you thought he rung the Bell. This will divert him from plodding on Business too much, or spending himself in Talk, or racking his Thoughts, all which are hurtful to his Constitution.

If you are ordered to break the Claw of a Crab or a Lobster, clap it between the Sides of the Dining Room

Door between the Hinges: Thus you can do it gradually without mashing the Meat, which is often the Fate of the Street-Door-Key, or the Pestle.

When you take a foul Plate from any of the Guests, and observe the foul Knife and Fork lying on the Plate, shew your Dexterity, take up the Plate, and throw off the Knife and Fork on the Table without shaking off the Bones or broken Meat that are left: Then the Guest, who hath more Time than you, will wipe the Fork and Knife already used.

It is much to be lamented, that Gentlemen of our Employment have but two Hands to carry Plates, Dishes, Bottles, and the like out of the Room at Meals; and the Misfortune is still the greater, because one of those Hands is required to open the Door, while you are encumbred with your Load: Therefore, I advise, that the Door may be always left at jar, so as to open it with your Foot, and then you may carry out Plates and Dishes from your Belly up to your Chin, besides a good Quantity of Things under your Arms, which will save you many a weary Step; but take Care that none of the Burthen falls till you are out of the Room, and, if possible, out of Hearing.

If you are sent to the Post-Office with a Letter in a cold rainy Night, step to the Alehouse, and take a Pot, until it is supposed you have done your Errand, but take the next fair Opportunity to put the Letter in carefully, as becomes an honest Servant.

If you are ordered to make Coffee for the Ladies after Dinner, and the Pot happens to boil over, while you are running up for a Spoon to stir it, or are thinking of something else, or struggling with the Chamber-maid for a Kiss, wipe the Sides of the Pot clean with a Dishclout, carry up your Coffee boldly, and when your Lady finds it too weak, and examines you whether it has not run over, deny the Fact absolutely, swear you put in more Coffee than ordinary, that you never stirred an Inch from it, that you strove to make it better than usual, because your Mistress had Ladies with her, that the Servants in the Kitchen will justify what you say: Upon this, you will find that the other

Ladies will pronounce your Coffee to be very good, and your Mistress will confess that her Mouth is out of Taste, and she will for the future suspect herself, and be more cautious in finding Fault. This I would have you do from a Principle of Conscience, for Coffee is very unwholesome; and out of Affection to your Lady, you ought to give it her as weak as possible: And upon this Argument, when you have a Mind to treat any of the Maids with a Dish of fresh Coffee, you may, and ought to substract a third Part of the Powder, on account of your Lady's Health and getting her Maids Good-will.

When you step but a few Doors off to tattle with a Wench, or take a running Pot of Ale, or to see a Brother Footman going to be hanged, leave the Street Door open, that you may not be forced to knock, and your Master discover you are gone out; for a Quarter of an Hour's Time can do his Service no Injury.

When you leave your Lady at Church on *Sundays,* you have two Hours safe to spend with your Companions at the Ale-House, or over a Beef Stake and a Pot of Beer at home with the Cook and the Maids; and indeed poor Servants have so few Opportunities to be happy, that they ought not to lose any.

Never wear Socks when you wait at Meals, on the Account of your own Health, as well as of them who set at Table; because as most Ladies like the Smell of young Mens Toes, so it is a sovereign Remedy against the Vapours.

In Winter time light the Dining-Room Fire but two Minutes before Dinner is served up, that your Master may see, how saving you are of his Coals.

When you are ordered to stir up the Fire, clean away the Ashes from betwixt the Bars with the Fire-Brush.

When you carry a Parcel of *China* Plates, if you chance to fall, as it is a frequent Misfortune, your Excuse must be, that a Dog ran across you in the Hall; that the Chamber-maid accidentally pushed the Door against you; that a Mop stood across the Entry, and tript you up; that your Sleeve stuck against the Key, or Button of the Lock.

When your Master and Lady are talking together in the Bed-chamber, and you have some Suspicion that you or your Fellow-servants are concerned in what they say, listen at the Door for the publick Good of all the Servants, and join all to take proper Measures for preventing any Innovations that may hurt the Community.

Be not proud in Prosperity: You have heard that Fortune turns on a Wheel; if you have a good Place, you are at the Top of the Wheel. Remember how often you have been stripped, and kick'd out of Doors, your Wages all taken up beforehand, and spent in translated red-heel'd Shoes, second-hand Toupees, and repair'd Lace Ruffles, besides a swinging Debt to the Ale-wife and the Brandy-shop. The neighbouring Tapster, who before would beckon you over to a savoury Bit of Ox-cheek in the Morning, give it you *gratis*, and only score you up for the Liquor, immediately after you were packt off in Disgrace, carried a Petition to your Master, to be paid out of your Wages, whereof not a Farthing was due, and then pursued you with Bailiffs into every blind Cellar. Remember how soon you grew shabby, thread-bare, and out-at heels, was forced to borrow an old Livery Coat, to make your Appearance while you were looking for a Place; and sneak to every House where you have an old Acquaintance to steal you a Scrap, to keep Life and Soul together; and upon the whole, were in the lowest Station of human Life, which, as the old Ballad says, is that of a Skipkennel turn'd out of Place: I say, remember all this now in your flourishing Condition. Pay your Contributions duly to your late Brothers the Cadets, who are left to the wide World: Take one of them as your Dependant, to send on your Lady's Messages when you have a Mind to go to the Ale-house; slip him out privately now and then a Slice of Bread, and a Bit of cold Meat, your Master can afford it; and if he be not yet put upon the Establishment for a Lodging, let him lie in the Stable, or the Coach-house, or under the Back-stairs, and recommend him to all the Gentlemen who frequent your House, as an excellent Servant.

The last Advice I give you, relates to your Behaviour when you are going to be hanged; which, either for robbing your Master, for House-breaking, or going upon the Highway, or in a drunken Quarrel, by killing the first Man you meet, may very probably be your Lot, and is owing to one of these three Qualities; either a Love of good Fellowship, a Generosity of Mind, or too much Vivacity of Spirits. Your good Behaviour on this Article, will concern your whole Community at your Tryal: Deny the Fact with all Solemnity of Imprecations: A hundred of your Brethren, if they can be admitted, will attend about the Bar, and be ready upon Demand to give you a good Character before the Court: Let nothing prevail on you to confess, but the Promise of a Pardon for discovering your Comrades: But, I suppose all this to be in vain, for if you escape now, your Fate will be the same another Day. Get a Speech to be written by the best Author of *Newgate*: Some of your kind Wenches will provide you with a *Holland* Shirt, and white Cap crowned with a crimson or black Ribbon: Take Leave chearfully of all your Friends in *Newgate*: Mount the Cart with Courage: Fall on your Knees: Lift up your Eyes: Hold a Book in your Hands although you cannot read a Word: Deny the Fact at the Gallows: Kiss and forgive the Hangman, and so farewell: You shall be buried in Pomp, at the Charge of the Fraternity: The Surgeon shall not touch a Limb of you; and your Fame shall continue until a Successor of equal Renown succeeds in your Place.

DIRECTIONS TO THE GROOM

You are the Servant upon whom the Care of your Master's Honour in all Journies entirely depends: Your Breast is the sole Repository of it. If he travels the Country, and lodgeth at Inns, every Dram of Brandy, every Pot of Ale extraordinary that you drink, raiseth his Character; and therefore his Reputation ought to be dear to you; and, I hope, you will not stint yourself in either. The Smith, the Sadler's Journeyman, the Cook at the Inn, the Ostler and the Boot-catcher, ought all by your Means to partake of your Master's Generosity: Thus, his Fame will reach from one County to another; and what is a Gallon of Ale, or a Pint of Brandy in his Worship's Pocket? And, although he should be in the Number of those who value their Credit less than their Purse, yet your Care of the former ought to be so much the greater. His Horse wanted two Removes; your Horse wanted Nails; his Allowance of Oats and Beans was greater than the Journey required; a third Part may be retrenched, and turned into Ale or Brandy; and thus his Honour may be preserved by your Discretion, and less Expence to him; or, if he travels with no other Servant, the Matter is easily made up in the Bill between you and the Tapster.

Consider your Master's Health, and rather than let him take long Journies, say the Cattle are weak, and fallen in their Flesh with hard riding; tell him of a very good Inn five Miles nearer than he intended to go; or leave one of his Horses Fore Shoes loose in the Morning; or contrive that the Saddle may pinch the Beast in his Withers; or keep him without Corn all Night and Morning, so that he may tire on the Road; or wedge a thin Plate of Iron between the Hoof and the Shoe, to make him halt; and all this in perfect Tenderness to your Master.

Hay and Oats, in the Management of a skilful Groom, will make excellent Ale as well as Brandy; but this I only hint.

In long Journies, ask your Master Leave to give Ale to the Horses; carry two Quarts full to the Stable, pour half a Pint into a Bowl, and if they will not drink it, you and the Ostler must do the best you can; perhaps they may be in a better Humour at the next Inn, for I would have you never fail to make the Experiment.

If your Horse drop a Fore-Shoe, be so careful to alight

x

and take it up: Then ride with all the Speed you can (the Shoe in your Hand that every Traveller may observe your Care) to the next Smith on the Road, make him put it on immediately, that your Master may not wait for you, and that the poor Horse may be as short a Time as possible without a Shoe.

You may now and then lend your Master's Pad to a Brother Servant, or your favourite Maid, for a short Jaunt, or hire him for a Day, because the Horse is spoiled for want of Exercise: And if your Master happens to want his Horse, or hath a mind to see the Stable, curse that Rogue the Helper who is gone out with the Key.

When you want to spend an Hour or two with your Companions at the Ale-house, and that you stand in need of a reasonable Excuse for your Stay, go out of the Stable Door, or the back Way, with an old Bridle, Girth, or Stirrup Leather in your Pocket, and on your Return come home by the Street Door with the same Bridle, Girth, or Stirrup Leather dangling in your Hand, as if you came from the Saddler's, where you were getting the same mended; if you are not missed all is well, but if you are met by your Master, you will have the Reputation of a careful Servant. This I have known practised with good Success.

DIRECTIONS TO THE CHAMBER-MAID

THE Nature of your Employment differs according to the Quality, the Pride, or the Wealth of the Lady you serve; and this Treatise is to be applied to all Sorts of Families; so, that I find myself under great Difficulty to adjust the Business for which you are hired. In a Family where there is a tolerable Estate, you differ from the House-Maid, and in that View I give my Directions. Your particular Province is your Lady's Chamber, where you make the Bed, and put Things in Order; and if you live in the Country, you take Care of Rooms where Ladies lie who come into the House, which brings in all the Vails that fall to your Share. Your usual Lover, as I take it, is the Coachman; but, if you are under Twenty, and tolerably handsome, perhaps a Footman may cast his Eyes on you.

Get your favourite Footman to help you in making your Lady's Bed; and, if you serve a young Couple, the Footman and you, as you are turning up the Bed-cloaths, will make the prettiest Observations in the World, which whispered about, will be very entertaining to the whole Family, and get among the Neighbourhood.

Do not carry down the necessary Vessels for the Fellows to see, but empty them out of the Window, for your Lady's Credit. It is highly improper for Men Servants to know that fine Ladies have Occasion for such Utensils; and do not scour the Chamber-pot, because the Smell is wholesome.

If you happen to break any *China* with the Top of the Wisk on the Mantle-tree or the Cabinet, gather up the Fragments, put them together as well as you can, and place them behind the rest, so that when your Lady comes to discover them, you may safely say they were broke long ago, before you came to the Service. This will save your Lady many an Hour's Vexation.

Oil the Tongs, Poker, and Fire-shovel up to the Top, not only to keep them from rusting, but likewise to prevent meddling People from wasting your Master's Coals with stirring the Fire.

When you are in haste, sweep the Dust into a Corner of the Room, but leave your Brush upon it, that it may not be seen, for, that would disgrace you.

In the Time when you leave the Windows open for Air, leave Books, or something else on the Window-seat, that they may get Air too.

Making Beds in hot Weather is a very laborious Work, and you will be apt to sweat; therefore, when you find the Drops running down from your Forehead, wipe them off with a Corner of the Sheet, that they may not be seen on the Bed.

When your Lady sends you to wash a *China* Cup, and it happen to fall, bring it up, and swear you did but just touch it with your Hand, when it broke into *three Halves*: And here I must inform you, as well as your fellow Servants, that you ought never to be without an Excuse; it doth no Harm to your Master, and it lessens your Fault: As in this Instance; I do not commend you for breaking the Cup; it is certain you did not break it on purpose, and the Thing is possible, that it might break in your Hand.

When you spread Bread and Butter for Tea, be sure that all the Holes in the Loaf be left full of Butter, to keep the Bread moist against Dinner; and let the Mark of your Thumb be seen only upon one End of every Slice, to shew your Cleanliness.

When you are ordered to open or lock any Door, Trunk or Cabinet, and miss the proper Key, or cannot distinguish it in the Bunch; try the first Key that you can thrust in, and turn it with all your Strength till you open the Lock, or break the Key; for your Lady will reckon you a Fool to come back and do nothing.

DIRECTIONS TO THE WAITING-MAID

Two Accidents have happened to lessen the Comforts and Profits of your Employment; First, that execrable Custom got among Ladies, of trucking their old Cloaths for *China*, or turning them to cover easy Chairs, or making them into Patch-work for Skreens, Stools, Cushions, and the like. The Second is, the Invention of small Chests and Trunks, with Lock and Key, wherein they keep the Tea and Sugar, without which it is impossible for a Waiting-maid to live: For, by this means you are forced to buy brown Sugar, and pour Water upon the Leaves, when they have lost all their Spirit and Taste: I cannot contrive any perfect Remedy against either of these two Evils. As to the former, I think there should be a general Confederacy of all the Servants in every Family, for the publick Good, to drive those *China* Hucksters from the Doors; and as to the latter, there is no other Method to relieve yourselves, but by a false Key, which is a Point both difficult and dangerous to compass; but, as to the Circumstance of Honesty in procuring one, I am under no Doubt, when your Mistress gives you so just a Provocation, by refusing you an ancient and legal Perquisite. The Mistress of the Tea-shop may now and then give you half an Ounce, but that will be only a Drop in the Bucket: Therefore, I fear you must be forced, like the rest of your Sisters, to run in Trust, and pay for it out of your Wages, as far as they will go, which you can easily make up other ways, if your Lady be handsome, or her Daughters have good Fortunes.

If you are in a great Family, and my Lady's Woman, my Lord may probably like you, although you are not half so handsome as his own Lady. In this Case, take Care to get as much out of him as you can; and never allow him the smallest Liberty, not the squeezing of your Hand, unless he puts a Guinea into it; so, by degrees, make him pay accordingly for every new Attempt, doubling upon him in proportion to the Concessions you allow, and always struggling, and threatning to cry out or tell your Lady, although you receive his Money: Five Guineas for handling your Breast is a cheap Pennyworth, although you seem to resist with all your Might; but never allow him the last Favour under a hundred Guineas, or a Settlement of twenty Pounds a Year for Life.

I must caution you particularly against my Lord's eldest Son: If you are dextrous enough, it is odds that you may draw him in to marry you, and make you a Lady: If he be a common Rake, (and he must be one or t'other) avoid him like *Satan*; for he stands less in awe of a Mother, than my Lord doth of a Wife; and, after ten thousand Promises, you will get nothing from him, but a big Belly or a Clap, and probably both together.

If you serve a Lady who is a little disposed to Gallantries, you will find it a Point of great Prudence how to manage: Three Things are necessary. First, how to please your Lady;

Secondly, how to prevent Suspicion in the Husband, or among the Family; and lastly, but principally, how to make it most for your own Advantage. To give you full Directions in this important Affair, would require a large Volume. All Assignations at home are dangerous, both to your Lady and yourself; and therefore contrive, as much as possible, to have them in a third Place; especially, if your Lady, as it is a hundred odds, entertains more Lovers than one, each of whom is often more jealous than a thousand Husbands; and, very unlucky Rencounters may often happen under the best Management. I need not warn you to employ your good Offices chiefly in favour of those, whom you find most liberal; yet, if your Lady should happen to cast an Eye upon a handsome Footman, you should be generous enough to bear with her Humour, which is no Singularity, but a very natural Appetite: It is still the safest of all home Intrigues, and was formerly the least suspected, until of late Years it hath grown more common. The great Danger is, lest this King of Gentry, dealing too often in bad Ware, may happen not to be sound; and then, your Lady and you are in a very bad Way, although not altogether desperate.

When you lock up a Silk Mantua, or laced Head in a Trunk or Chest, leave a Piece out, that when you open the Trunk again, you may know where to find it.

DIRECTIONS TO THE HOUSE-MAID

IF your Master and Lady go into the Country for a Week or more, never wash the Bed-chamber or Dining-room, until just the Hour before you expect them to return: Thus, the Room will be perfectly clean to receive them, and you will not be at the Trouble to wash them so soon again.

I am very much offended with those Ladies, who are so proud and lazy, that they will not be at the Pains of stepping into the Garden to pluck a Rose, but keep an odious Implement, sometimes in the Bed-chamber itself, or at least in a dark Closet adjoining, which they make Use of to ease their worst Necessities; and, you are the usual Carriers away of the Pan, which maketh not only the Chamber, but even their Cloaths offensive, to all who come near. Now, to cure them of this odious Practice, let me advise you, on whom this Office lies, to convey away this Utensil, that you will do it openly, down the great Stairs, and in the Presence of the Footmen; and, if any Body knocks, to open the Street-door, while you have the Vessel filled in your Hands: This, if any Thing can, will make your Lady take the Pains of evacuating her Person in the proper Place, rather than expose her Filthiness to all the Men Servants in the House.

Leave a Payl of dirty Water with the Mop in it, a Coal-box, a Bottle, a Broom, a Chamber-pot, and such other unsightly Things, either in a blind Entry, or upon the darkest Part of the Back-stairs, that they may not be seen; and, if People break their Shins by trampling on them, it is their own Fault.

Leave your Lady's Chamber-pot in her Bed-chamber Window, all Day to air.

Bring up none but large Coals to the Dining-room and your Lady's Chamber; they make the best Fires, and, if you find them too big, it is easy to break them on the Marble Hearth.

When you wash any of the Rooms towards the Street over Night, throw the foul Water out of the Street-door; but, be sure not to look before you, for fear those on whom the Water lights, might think you uncivil, and that you did it on purpose. If he who suffers, breaks the Windows in revenge, and your Lady chides you, and gives positive Orders that you should carry the Payl down, and empty it in the Sink, you have an easy Remedy. When you wash an upper Room, carry down the Payl so as to let the Water dribble on the Stairs all the way down to the Kitchen; by which, not only your Load will be lighter, but you will convince your Lady, that it is better to throw the Water out of the Windows, or down the Street-door Steps: Besides this latter Practice will be very diverting to you and the Family in a frosty Night, to see a hundred People falling on their Noses or Back-sides before your Door, when the Water is frozen.

DIRECTIONS TO THE DAIRY-MAID

FATIGUE of making Butter: Put scalding Water in your Churn, although in Summer, and churn close to the Kitchen Fire, and with Cream of a Week old. Keep Cream for your Sweet-heart.

DIRECTIONS TO THE CHILDREN'S-MAID

IF a Child be sick, give it whatever it wants to eat or drink, although particularly forbid by the Doctor: For what we long for in Sickness, will do us good; and throw the Physick out of the Window; the Child will love you the better; but bid it not tell. Do the same for your Lady, when she longs for any thing in Sickness, and engage it will do her good.

If your Mistress cometh to the Nursery, and offers to whip a Child, snatch it out of her Hands in a Rage, and tell her she is the cruellest Mother you ever saw: She will chide, but love you the better. Tell the Children Stories of Spirits, when they offer to cry, &c.

Be sure to wean the Children, &c.

DIRECTIONS FOR THE LAUNDRESS

IF you singe the Linen with the Iron, rub the Place with Flour, Chalk, or white Powder; and if nothing will do, wash it so long, till it be either not to be seen, or torn to Rags.

About tearing Linen in washing.

When your Linen is pinned on the Line, or on a Hedge, and it rains, whip it off, although you tear it, &c. But the Place for hanging them, is on young Fruit Trees, especially in Blossom; the Linen cannot be torn, and the Trees give them a fine Smell.

DIRECTIONS TO THE TUTORESS, OR GOVERNESS

SAY the Children have sore Eyes; Miss *Betty* won't take to her Book, *&c.*

Make the Misses read *French* and *English* Novels, and *French* Romances, and all the Comedies writ in King *Charles* II. and King *William's* Reigns, to soften their Nature, and make them tender-hearted, *&c.*

FINIS

JOURNAL
TO
STELLA

SELECTION

THE *Journal to Stella*—it was first referred to by this title by Nichols [*Advertisement*, Vol. XIV, *Works*. 4to. 1779]—was addressed to Esther Johnson, whom Swift had met as a girl in Temple's house in Surrey, and who, accompanied by a Miss Dingley, afterwards settled in Ireland at his suggestion. The *Journal* is a day by day record of Swift's life in London and it was dispatched in fortnightly packets to Ireland. The mystery of Swift's relations with Stella, as he called her, has never been cleared up, and this is not the place to discuss or summarise the numerous theories that have been advanced to account for their equivocal nature. Swift's early biographers—Deane Swift, Delany and Orrery—and later Sheridan, Scott and Craik, believed, on very imperfect evidence, that he went through a ceremony of marriage with her. What is certain is that they never lived together, and indeed it has been doubted if they ever met except in the presence of a third person [*v. note* p. 868].

The 65 letters, comprising the *Journal*, were printed for the first time in Vol. X, 1766, and Vol. XII, 1768, of the quarto edition of Swift's *Works*. Volume X contains letters 41-65; Volume XII letters 1-40. The text of the letters, especially of the first forty, was ruthlessly touched up by Hawksworth and Deane Swift. Nichols, in his Supplement to this edition [Vol. XIV, 1779] attempted to correct a portion of the *Journal* by reference to the original manuscripts of letters 1, 41-53 and 55-65, which are still preserved in the British Museum. It was not until almost a hundred years later [1875] that Forster in an appendix to his unfinished *Life* of Swift carried Nichols's work a stage further. The modernized text [Ed. F. Rylands], in Temple Scott's edition [Vol. II], is frequently inaccurate in its manuscript readings. The *Journal* was transcribed afresh by Mr J. K. Moorhead for "Everyman's Library"; this excellent edition, which preserves the spelling, &c., of the originals, whether printed or manuscript, is not only the best but also the most easily available.

The text of the following extracts is that of the first published edition for those letters of which the original MSS. have disappeared; and of the holographs in the British Museum for those of which the originals still exist. The relevant passages from these manuscripts have been freshly transcribed for this edition.

A note on " the little language " of the *Journal* will be found in the notes [p. 857].

JOURNAL

TO

STELLA

London. Sept. 23. 1710.

Here is such a stir and bustle with this little *MD* of ours; I must be writing every night; I can't go to-bed without a word to them; I can't put out my candle till I have bid them good night: O Lord, O Lord! Well, I dined the first time, to-day, with *Will Frankland* and his *Fortune*: she is not very handsome. Did I not say I would go out of town to-day; I hate lying abroad and clutter; I go to-morrow in *Frankland's* chariot, and come back at night. Lady *Berkeley* has invited me to *Berkeley-castle*, and lady *Betty Germain* to *Drayton* in *Northampton-shire*, and I'll go to neither. Let me alone, I must finish my pamphlet. I have sent a long letter to *Bickerstaff*: let the bishop of *Clogher* smoak it if he can. Well, I'll write to the bishop of *Killala*; but you might have told him how sudden and unexpected my journey was though. Deuce take lady S——; and if I know D——y, he is a rawboned-faced fellow, not handsome, nor visibly so young as you say: she sacrifices two thousand pounds a year, and keeps only six hundred. Well, you have had all my land journey in my second letter, and so much for that. So, you have got into *Presto's* lodgings; very fine, truly! We have had a fortnight of the most glorious weather on earth, and still continues: I hope you have made the best of it. *Ballygall* will be a pure good place for air, if Mrs. *Ashe* makes good her promise. *Stella* writes like an emperor: I am afraid it hurts your eyes; take care of that pray, pray, Mrs. *Stella*. Can't you do what you will with your own horse? Pray don't let that puppy *Parvisol* sell him. *Patrick* is drunk about three times a week, and I bear it, and he has got the better of me; but one of these days I will positively turn him off to the wide

world, when none of you are by to intercede for him.—
Stuff—how can I get her husband into the *Charter-house*?
get a . . . into the *Charter-house*.—Write constantly! Why,
sirrah, don't I write every day, and sometimes twice a day
to *MD*? Now I have answered all your letter, and the rest
must be as it can be: send me my bill. Tell Mrs. *Brent* what
I say of the *Charter-house*. I think this enough for one
night; and so farewel till this time to-morrow.

Sept. 29. [1710].

I wish *MD* a merry *Michaelmas*. I dined with Mr.
Addison, and *Jervas* the painter, at *Addison's* country place;
and then came home, and writ more to my lampoon. I
made a *Tatler* since I came: guess which it is, and whether
the bishop of *Clogher* smoaks it. I saw Mr. *Sterne* to-day:
he will do as you order, and I will give him chocolate for
Stella's health. He goes not these three weeks. I wish I
could send it some other way. So now to your letter, brave
boys. I don't like your way of saving shillings: nothing
vexes me but that it does not make *Stella* a coward in a
coach. I don't think any lady's advice about my ear signifies two-pence: however I will, in compliance to you, ask
Dr. *Cockburn*. *Radcliffe* I know not, and *Bernard* I never
see. *Walls* will certainly be stingier for seven years, upon
pretence of his robbery. So *Stella* puns again; why, 'tis well
enough; but I'll not second it, though I could make a dozen:
I never thought of a pun since I left *Ireland*.—Bishop of
Clogher's bill? Why, he paid it me; do you think I was such
a fool to go without it? As for the four shillings, I will give
you a bill on *Parvisol* for it on t'other side this paper; and
pray tear off the two letters I shall write to him and *Joe*, or
let *Dingley* transcribe and send them; though that to *Parvisol*, I believe, he must have my hand for. No, no, I'll eat
no grapes; I ate about six t'other day at sir *John Holland's*;
but would not give six-pence for a thousand, they are so bad
this year. Yes, faith, I hope in God *Presto* and *MD* will
be together this time twelvemonth: What then? Last year
I suppose I was at *Laracor*; but next I hope to eat my
Michaelmas goose at my two little gooses' lodgings. I drink

no *aile* (I suppose you mean *ale*) but yet good wine every day, of five and six shillings a bottle. O Lord, how much *Stella* writes: pray don't carry that too far, young women, but be temperate to hold out. To-morrow I go to Mr. *Harley*. Why; small hopes from the duke of *Ormond*: he loves me very well, I believe, and would, in my turn, give me something to make me easy; and I have good interest among his best friends. But I don't think of any thing further than the business I am upon: you see I writ to *Manley* before I had your letter; and I fear he will be out. Yes, Mrs. Owl, *Blighe's* corpse came to *Chester* when I was there, and I told you so in my letter, or forgot it. I lodge in *Bury-street*, where I removed a week ago. I have the first floor, a dining-room, and bedchamber, at eight shillings a week; plaguy deep, but I spend nothing for eating, never go to a tavern, and very seldom in a coach; yet after all it will be expensive. Why do you trouble yourself, Mistress *Stella*, about my *instrument*? I have the same the arch-bishop gave me; and it is as good now the bishops are away. The dean friendly; the dean be poxt: a great piece of friend-ship indeed, what you heard him tell the bishop of *Clogher*; I wonder he had the face to talk so: but he lent me money, and that's enough. Faith I would not send this these four days, only for writing to *Joe* and *Parvisol*. Tell the dean, that when the bishops send me any pacquets, they must not write to me at Mr. *Steele's*; but direct for Mr. *Steele*, at his office at the *Cockpit*; and let the inclosed be directed for me: that mistake cost me eighteen-pence t'other day.

[*From* LETTER IV.]

London. Oct. 4. 1710.

AFTER I had put out my candle last night, my landlady came into my room, with a servant of lord *Halifax*, to de-sire I would go dine with him at his house near *Hampton-court*; but I sent him word I had business of great import-ance that hindered me, &c. And, to-day, I was brought privately to Mr. *Harley*, who received me with the greatest respect and kindness imaginable: he has appointed me an hour on *Saturday* at four, afternoon, when I will open my business to him; which expression I would not use if I were a woman. I know you smoakt it; but I did not till I writ it. I dined to-day at Mr. *Delaval's*, the envoy for *Portugal*, with *Nic. Rowe* the poet, and other friends; and I gave my lampoon to be printed. I have more mischief in my heart; and I think it shall go round with them all, as this hits, and I can find hints. I am certain I answered your 2d letter, and yet I do not find it here. I suppose it was in my 4th: and why *N.* 2d, 3d; is it not enough to say, as I do, 1.2.3? &c. I am going to work at another *Tatler*: I'll be far enough but I say the same thing over two or three times, just as I do when I am talking to little *MD*; but what care I? they can read it as easily as I can write it: I think I have brought these lines pretty straight again. I fear it will be long before I finish two sides at this rate. Pray, dear *MD*, when I occasionally give you any little commission mixt with my letters, don't forget it, as that to *Morgan* and *Joe*, &c. for I write just as I can remember, otherwise I would put them all together. I was to visit Mr. *Sterne* to-day, and gave him your commission about handkerchiefs: that of chocolate I will do myself, and send it him when he goes, and you'll pay me *the giver's bread*, &c. To-night I will read a pamphlet, to amuse myself. God preserve your dear healths.

[*From* LETTER V.]

London. Oct. 13. 1710.

O LORD, here's but a trifle of my letter written yet; what shall *Presto* do for prittle prattle to entertain *MD*? The talk now grows fresher of the duke of *Ormond* for *Ireland*, though Mr. *Addison* says he hears it will be in commission, and lord *Gallaway* one. These letters of mine are a sort of journal, where matters open by degrees; and, as I tell true or false, you will find by the event whether my intelligence be good; but I don't care two-pence whether it be or no.— At night. To-day I was all about *St. Paul's* and up at the top like a fool, with sir *Andrew Fountain* and two more; and spent seven shillings for my dinner like a puppy: this is the second time he has served me so; but I'll never do it again, though all mankind should persuade me, unconsidering puppies! There's a young fellow here in town we are all fond of, and about a year or two come from the university, one *Harrison*, a little pretty fellow, with a great deal of wit, good sense, and good nature; has written some mighty pretty things; that in your 6th *Miscellanea*, about the *Sprig of an Orange*, is his: he has nothing to live on but being governor to one of the duke of *Queensbury's* sons for forty pounds a year. The fine fellows are always inviting him to the tavern, and make him pay his club. *Henley* is a great crony of his: they are often at the tavern at six or seven shillings reckoning, and always makes the poor lad pay his full share. A colonel and a lord were at him and me the same way to-night: I absolutely refused, and made *Harrison* lag behind, and persuaded him not to go to them. I tell you this, because I find all rich fellows have that humour of using all people without any consideration of their fortunes; but I'll see them rot before they shall serve me so. Lord *Halifax* is always teazing me to go down to his country house, which will cost me a guinea to his servants, and twelve shillings coach hire; and he shall be hanged first. Is not this a plaguy silly story? But I am vext at the heart; for I love the young fellow, and am resolved to stir up people to do something for him: he is a *Whig*, and I'll put him upon some of my cast *Whigs*; for I have done with them, and they have, I hope, done with this kingdom for our time. They were sure of the four members for *London* above all places, and they have lost three in the four. Sir *Richard Onslow*, we hear, has lost for *Surry*; and they are overthrown in most places. Lookee, gentlewomen, if I write long letters, I must write you news and stuff, unless I send you my verses; and some I dare not; and those on the *Shower in London* I have sent to the *Tatler*, and you may see them in *Ireland*. I fancy you'll smoak me in the *Tatler* I am going to write; for I believe I have told you the hint. I had a letter sent me to-night from sir *Matthew Dudley*, and found it on my table when I came in. Because it is extraordinary I will transcribe it from beginning to end. It is as follows (Is the devil in you? Oct. 13, 1710.) I would have answered every particular passage in it, only I wanted time. Here's enough for to-night, such as it is, &c.

Oct. 14. [1710].

Is that tobacco at the top of the paper, or what? I don't remember I slobbered. Lord, I dreamt of *Stella*, &c. so confusedly last night, and that we saw dean *Bolton* and *Sterne* go into a shop; and she bid me call them to her, and they proved to be two parsons I know not; and I walked without till she was shifting, and such stuff, mixt with much melancholy and uneasiness, and things not as they should be, and I know not how: and it is now an ugly gloomy morning.—At night. Mr. *Addison* and I dined with *Ned Southwell*, and walkt in the *Park*; and at the *Coffee-house* I found a letter from the bishop of *Clogher*, and a pacquet from *MD*. I opened the bishop's letter; but put up *MD's*, and visited a lady just come to town, and am now got into bed, and going to open your little letter: and God send I may find *MD* well, and happy, and merry, and that they love *Presto* as they do fires. Oh, I won't open it yet! yes I will! no I won't; I am going; I can't stay till I turn over: What shall I do? My fingers itch; and now I have it in my left hand; and now I'll open it this very moment.—I have just got it, and am cracking the seal, and can't imagine what's in it; I fear only some letter from a bishop, and it comes too late: I shall employ nobody's credit but my own. Well, I see though—Pshaw, 'tis from sir *Andrew Fountain*: What, another! I fancy this is from Mrs. *Barton*; she told me she would write to me; but she writes a better hand than this; I wish you would enquire; it must be at *Dawson's* office at the *Castle*. I fear this is from *Patty Rolt*, by the scrawl. Well, I'll read *MD*'s letter. Ah, no; it is from poor lady *Berkeley*, to invite me to *Berkeley-castle* this winter; and now it grieves my heart: she says she hopes my lord is in a fair way of recovery; poor lady. Well, now I go to *MD's* letter: faith, 'tis all right; I hoped it was wrong. Your letter, *N*.3. that I have now received, is dated *Sept*. 26, and *Manley's* letter, that I had five days ago, was dated *Oct*. 3.

that's a fortnight difference: I doubt it has lain in *Steele's* office, and he forgot. Well, there's an end of that: he is turned out of his place; and you must desire those who send me pacquets, to inclose them in a paper directed to Mr. *Addison*, at *St. James's Coffee-house*: not common letters, but pacquets: the bishop of *Clogher* may mention it to the archbishop when he sees him. As for your letter, it makes me mad: slidikins, I have been the best boy in *Christendom*, and you come with your two eggs a penny.— Well; but stay, I'll look over my book: adad, I think there was a *chasm* between my *N*.2. and *N*.3. Faith, I won't promise to write to you every week; but I'll write every night, and when it is full I will send it; that will be once in ten days, and that will be often enough: and if you begin to take up the way of writing to *Presto*, only because it is *Tuesday*, a *Monday* bedad, it will grow a task; but write when you have a mind.—No, no, no, no, no, no, no, no— Agad, agad, agad, agad, agad, agad; no, poor *Stellakins*. Slids, I would the horse were in your—chamber. Have not I ordered *Parvisol* to obey your directions about him? And han't I said in my former letters, that you may pickle him, and boil him, if you will? What do you trouble me about your horses for? Have I any thing to do with them?—Re-volutions a hindrance to me in my business; Revolutions— to me in my business? If it were not for the revolutions, I could do nothing at all; and now I have all hopes possible, though one is certain of nothing; but to-morrow I am to have an answer, and am promised an effectual one. I sup-pose I have said enough in this and a former letter how I stand with new people; ten times better than ever I did with the old; forty times more caressed. I am to dine to-morrow at Mr. *Harley's*; and if he continues as he has begun, no man has been ever better treated by another. What you say about *Stella's* mother, I have spoken enough to it already. I believe she is not in town; for I have not yet seen her. My lampoon is cried up to the skies; but nobody suspects me for it, except sir *Andrew Fountain*: at least they say noth-ing of it to me. Did not I tell you of a great man who re-ceived me very coldly? That's he; but say nothing; 'twas only a little revenge: I'll remember to bring it over. The bishop of *Clogher* has smoaked my *Tatler* about shortening of words, &c. But, God so! &c.

[*From* LETTER VI.]

London. Oct. 26. 1710.

I WAS to-day to see Mr. *Congreve*, who is almost blind with cataracts growing on his eyes; and his case is, that he must wait two or three years, until the cataracts are riper, and till he is quite blind, and then he must have them couched; and besides he is never rid of the gout, yet he looks young and fresh, and is as chearful as ever. He is younger by three years or more than I, and I am twenty years younger than he. He gave me a pain in the great toe, by mentioning the gout. I find such suspicions frequently, but they go off again. I had a second letter from Mr. *Morgan*; for which I thank you: I wish you were whipt for forgetting to send him that answer I desired you in one of my former, that I could do nothing for him of what he desired, having no credit at all, &c. Go, be far enough, you negligent baggages. I have had also a letter from *Parvisol*, with an account how my livings are set, and that they are fallen, since last year, sixty pounds. A comfortable piece of news. He tells me plainly, that he finds you have no mind to part with the horse, because you sent for him at the same time you sent him my letter; so that I know not what must be done. 'Tis a sad thing that *Stella* must have her own horse, whether *Parvisol* will or no. So now to answer your letter that I had three or four days ago. I am not now in bed, but am come home by eight; and it being warm, I write up. I never writ to the bishop of *Killala*, which, I suppose, was the reason he had not my letter. I have not time, there's the short of it.—As fond as the dean is of my letter, he has not written to me. I would only know whether dean *Bolton* paid him the twenty pounds; and for the rest, he may kiss——. And that you may ask him, because I am in pain about it, that dean *Bolton* is such a *whipster*. 'Tis the most obliging thing in the world in dean *Sterne* to be so kind to you. I believe he knows it will please me, and makes up, that way, his other usage. No, we have had none of your snow, but a little one morning; yet I think it was great snow for an hour or so, but no longer. I had heard of *Will Crowe's* death before, but not the foolish circumstance that hastened his end. No, I have taken care that captain *Pratt* shall not suffer by lord *Anglesea's* death. I'll try some contrivance to get a copy of my picture from *Jervas*. I'll make sir *Andrew Fountain* buy one as for himself, and I'll pay him again and take it, that is, provided I have money to spare when I leave this—Poor *John*! is he gone? and madam *Parvisol* has been in town? Humm. Why, *Tighe* and I, when he comes, shall not take any notice of each other; I would not do it much in this town, though we had not fallen out.—I was to-day at Mr. *Sterne's* lodging; he was not within, and Mr. *Leigh* is not come to town, but I will do *Dingley's* errand when I see him. What do I know whether china be dear or no? I once took a fancy of resolving to grow mad for it, but now 'tis off; I suppose I told you so in some former letter. And so you only want some salad dishes, and plates, and &c. Yes, yes, you shall. I suppose you have named as much as will cost five pounds. —Now to *Stella's* little postscript; and I am almost crazed that you vex yourself for not writing. Can't you dictate to *Dingley*, and not strain your dear little eyes? I am sure 'tis the grief of my soul to think you are out of order. Pray be quiet, and if you will write, shut your eyes, and write just a line, and no more, thus (How do you do, Mrs. *Stella*?) That was written with my eyes shut. Faith, I think it is better than when they are open: and then *Dingley* may stand by, and tell you when you go too high or too low.— My letters of business, with pacquets, if there be any more occasion for such, must be inclosed to Mr. *Addison*, at *St. James's Coffee-house*: but I hope to hear, as soon as I see Mr. *Harley*, that the main difficulties are over, and that the rest will be but form.—Make two or three nutgalls, make two or three —— galls, stop your receipt in your —— I have no need on't. Here's a clutter! Well, so much for your letter, which I will now put up in my letter-partition in my cabinet, as I always do every letter as soon as I answer it. Method is good in all things. Order governs the world. The Devil is the author of confusion. A general of an army, a minister of state; to descend lower, a gardener, a weaver, &c. That may make a fine observation, if you think it worth finishing; but I have not time. Is not this a terrible long piece for one evening? I dined to-day with *Patty Rolt* at my cousin *Leach's*, with a pox, in the city: he is a printer, and prints the *Postman*, oh ho, and is my cousin, God knows how, and he married Mrs. *Baby Aires* of *Leicester*; and my cousin *Thompson* was with us: and my cousin *Leach* offers to bring me acquainted with the author of the *Postman*; and says, he does not doubt but the gentleman will be glad of my acquaintance, and that he is a very ingenious man, and a great scholar, and has been beyond sea. But I was modest, and said, May be the gentleman was shy, and not fond of new acquaintance; and so put it off: and I wish you could hear me repeating all I have said of this in its proper tone, just as I am writing it. 'Tis all with the same cadence with oh hoo, or as when little girls say, I have got an apple, miss, and I won't give you some. 'Tis plaguy twelve-penny weather this last week, and has cost me ten shillings in coach and chair hire. If the fellow that has your money will pay it, let me beg you to buy *Bank Stock* with it, which is fallen nearly thirty *per cent*. and pays eight pounds *per cent*. and you have the principal when you please: it will certainly soon rise. I would to God lady *Giffard* would put in the four hundred pounds she owes you, and take the five *per cent*. common interest and give you the remainder. I will speak to your mother about it when I see her. I am resolved to buy three hundred pounds of it for myself, and take up what I have in *Ireland*; and I have a contrivance for it, that I hope will do, by making a friend of mine buy it as for himself, and I'll pay him when I can get in my money. I hope *Stratford* will do me that kindness. I'll ask him to-morrow or next day.

[*From* LETTER VII.]

London. Nov. 8. 1710.

HERE'S ado and a clutter! I must now answer *MD's* fifth; but first you must know I dined at the *Portugal* envoy's to-day, with *Addison, Vanburg*, admiral *Wager*, sir *Richard Temple, Methuen*, &c. I was weary of their company, and stole away at five, and came home like a good boy, and studied till ten, and had a fire; O ho! and now am in bed. I have no fire-place in my bed-chamber; but 'tis very warm weather when one's in bed. Your fine cap, madam *Dingley*, is too little, and too hot: I'll have that furr taken off; I wish it were far enough; and my old velvet cap is good for nothing. Is it velvet under the fur? I was feeling, but can't find: if it be, 'twill do without it, else I will face it; but then I must buy new velvet: but may be I may beg a piece. What shall I do? Well, now to rogue *MD's* letter. God be thanked for *Stella's* eyes mending; and God send it holds; but faith you writ too much at a time: better write less, or write it at ten times. Yes, faith, a long letter in a morning from a dear friend is a dear thing. I smoke a compliment, little mischievous girls, I do so. But who are those *Wiggs* that think I am turned *Tory*? Do you mean *Whigs*? Which *Wiggs* and *wat* do you mean? I know nothing of *Raymond*, and only had one letter from him a little after I came here. (Pray remember *Morgan*.) *Raymond* is indeed like to have much influence over me in *London*, and to share much of my conversation. I shall, no doubt, introduce him to *Harley*, and lord keeper, and the secretary of state. The *Tatler* upon *Milton's Spear* is not mine, madam. What a puzzle there was betwixt you and your judgment? In general you may be sometimes sure of things, as that about style, because it is what I have frequently spoken of; but guessing is mine— and I defy mankind, if I please. Why, I writ a pamphlet when I was last in *London*, that you and a thousand have seen, and never guest it to be mine. Could you have guest the *Shower in Town* to be mine? How chance you did not see that before your last letter went; but I suppose you in *Ireland* did not think it worth mentioning. Nor am I suspected for the lampoon; only *Harley* said he smoaked me, (have I told you so before?) and some others knew it. 'Tis called *The Rod of Sid Hamet*. And I have written several other things that I hear commended, and nobody suspects me for them; nor you shan't know till I see you again. What do you mean *That boards near me, that I dine with now and then*? I know no such person: I don't dine with boarders. What the pox! You know whom I have dined with every day since I left you, better than I do. What do you mean, sirrah? Slids, my ailment has been over these two months almost. Impudence, if you vex me, I'll give ten shillings a week for my lodging; for I am almost st——k out of this with the sink, and it helps me to verses in my *Shower*. Well, madam *Dingley*, what say you to the world to come? What *Ballad*? Why go look, it was not good for much: have patience till I come back: patience is a gay thing as, &c. I hear nothing of lord *Mountjoy's* coming for *Ireland*. When is *Stella's Birth-day*? in *March*? Lord bless me, my turn at *Christ-Church*; it is so natural to hear you write about that, I believe you have done it a hundred times; it is as fresh in my mind, the verger coming to you; and why to you? Would he have you preach for me? O pox on your spelling of *Latin*, *Jonsonibus atque*, that's the way. How did the dean get that name by the end? 'Twas you betrayed me: not I, faith; I'll not break his head. Your mother is still in the country, I suppose, for she promised to see me when she came to town. I writ to her four days ago, to desire her to break it to lady *Giffard*, to put some money for you in the *Bank*, which was then fallen to thirty *per cent*. Would to God mine had been here, I should have gained one hundred pounds, and got as good interest as in *Ireland*, and much securer. I would fain have borrowed three hundred pounds; but money is so scarce here, there is no borrowing, by this fall of stocks. 'Tis rising now, and I knew it would: it fell from one hundred and twenty-nine to ninety-six. I have not heard since from your mother. Do you think I would be so unkind not to see her, that you desire me in a style so melancholy? Mrs. *Raymond* you say is with child: I am sorry for it; and so is, I believe, her husband. Mr. *Harley* speaks all the kind things to me in the world; and, I believe, would serve me, if I were to stay here; but I reckon in time the duke of *Ormond* may give me some addition to *Laracor*. Why should the *Whigs* think I came to *England* to leave them? Sure my journey was no secret? I protest sincerely, I did all I could to hinder it, as the dean can tell you, although now I do not repent it. But who the Devil cares what they think? Am I under obligations in the least to any of them all? Rot 'em, for ungrateful dogs; I'll make them repent their usage before I leave this place. They say here the same thing of my leaving the *Whigs*; but they own they cannot blame me, considering the treatment I have had. I will take care of your spectacles, as I told you before, and of the bishop of *Killala's*; but I will not write to him, I han't time. What do you mean by my fourth, madam *Dinglibus*? Does not *Stella* say you have had my fifth, goody Blunder? You frighted me till I lookt back. Well, this is enough for one night. (Pray give my humble service to Mrs. *Stoyte* and her sister, *Kate* is it or *Sarah*? I have forgot her name, faith.) I think I'll e'en (and to Mrs. *Walls* and the archdeacon) send this to-morrow: no, faith, that will be in ten days from the last. I'll keep it till *Saturday*, though I write no more. But what if a letter from *MD* should come in the mean time? Why then I would only say, Madam, I have received your sixth letter; your most humble servant to command, *Presto*; and so conclude. Well, now I'll write and think a little, and so to bed, and dream of *MD*.

Nov. 11. [1710].

Morning by candlelight. You must know that I am in my night-gown every morning between six and seven, and *Patrick* is forced to ply me fifty times before I can get on my night-gown; and so now I'll take my leave of my own dear *MD* for this letter, and begin my next when I come home at night. God Almighty bless and protect dearest *MD*. Farewel, &c.

This letter's as long as a sermon, faith.

[*From* LETTER VIII.]

London. Nov. 11. 1710.

I DINED to-day, by invitation, with the secretary of state, Mr. *St. John*. Mr. *Harley* came in to us before dinner, and made me his excuses for not dining with us, because he was to receive people who came to propose advancing money to the government: there dined with us only Mr. *Lewis*, and Dr. *Freind* (that writ *Lord* Peterborow's *Actions in* Spain.) I staid with them till just now between ten and eleven, and was forced again to give my eighth to the bell-man, which I did with my own hands, rather than keep it till next post. The secretary used me with all the kindness in the world. *Prior* came in after dinner; and, upon an occasion, he (the secretary) said, the best thing he ever read is not your's, but Dr. *Swift's* on *Vanbrugh*; which I do not reckon so very good neither. But *Prior* was damped until I stuft him with two or three compliments. I am thinking what a veneration we used to have for sir *William Temple*, because he might have been secretary of state at fifty; and here is a young fellow, hardly thirty, in that employment. His father is a man of pleasure, that walks the *Mall*, and frequents *St. James's Coffee-house*, and the *Chocolate-houses*, and the young son is principal secretary of state. Is there not something very odd in that? He told me, among other things, that Mr. *Harley* complained he could keep nothing from me, I had the way so much of getting into him. I knew that was a refinement; and so I told him, and it was so: indeed it is hard to see these great men use me like one who was their betters, and the puppies with you in *Ireland* hardly regarding me: but there are some reasons for all this, which I will tell you when we meet. At coming home I saw a letter from your mother, in answer to one I sent her two days ago. It seems she is in town; but cannot come out in a morning, just as you said; and God knows when I shall be at leisure in an afternoon: for if I should send her a penny-post letter, and afterwards not be able to meet her, it would vex me; and, besides, the days are short, and why she cannot come early in a morning before she is wanted, I cannot imagine. I will desire her to let lady

Giffard know that she hears I am in town, and that she would go to see me to enquire after you. I wonder she will confine herself so much to that old *Beast's* humour. You know I cannot in honour see lady *Giffard*, and consequently not go into her house. This I think is enough for the first time.

[*From* LETTER IX.]

London. Nov. 26. 1710.

I HAVE got a cruel cold, and staid within all this day in my nightgown, and dined on six-pennyworth of victuals, and read and writ, and was denied to every body. Dr. *Raymond* called often, and I was denied; and at last, when I was weary, I let him come up, and asked him, without consequence, How *Patrick* denied me, and whether he had the art of it? So by this means he shall be used to have me denied to him; otherwise he would be a plaguy trouble and hindrance to me: he has sat with me two hours, and drank a pint of ale cost me five pence, and smoakt his pipe, and 'tis now past eleven that he is just gone. Well, my eighth is with you now, young women, and your seventh to me is somewhere in a post-boy's bag; and so go to your gang of deans, and *Stoytes*, and *Walls*, and lose your money; go, sauce-boxes, and so good night and be happy, dear rogues. Oh, but your box was sent to Dr. *Hawkshaw* by *Sterne*, and you will have it with *Hawkshaw*, and spectacles, &c. &c.

Nov. 30. [1710].

To-day I have been visiting, which I had long neglected; and I dined with Mrs. *Barton* alone; and sauntered at the *Coffee-house* till past eight, and have been busy till eleven, and now I'll answer your letter, sauce-box. Well, let me see now again. My wax-candle's almost out, but however I'll begin. Well then, don't be so tedious, Mr. *Presto*; what can you say to *MD's* letter? Make haste, have done with your preambles—Why, I say I am glad you are so often abroad; your mother thinks it is want of exercise hurts you, and so do I. (She called here to-night, but I was not within, that's by the bye.) Sure you don't deceive me, *Stella*, when you say you are in better health than you were these three weeks; for Dr. *Raymond* told me yesterday, that *Smyth* of the *Blind-Quay* had been telling Mr. *Leigh*, that he left you extreamly ill; and, in short, spoke so, that he almost put poor *Leigh* into tears, and would have made me run distracted; though your letter is dated the 11th instant, and I saw *Smyth* in the city above a fortnight ago, as I past by in a coach. Pray, pray, don't write, *Stella*, until you are mighty, mighty, mighty, mighty, mighty well in your eyes, and are sure it won't do you the least hurt. Or come, I'll tell you what; you, mistress *Stella*, shall write your share at five or six sittings, one sitting a day; and then comes *Dingley* all together, and then *Stella* a little crumb towards the end, to let us see she remembers *Presto*; and then conclude with something handsome and genteel, as your most humble-cumdumble, or, &c. O Lord! does *Patrick* write word of my not coming till *spring*? Insolent man! he know my secrets? No; as my lord *Mayer* said, No; if I thought my shirt knew, &c. Faith, I will come as soon as it is any way proper for me to come; but to say the truth, I am at present a little involved with the present ministry in some certain things (which I tell you as a secret) and soon as ever I can clear my hands, I will stay no longer: for I hope the *first-fruit* business will be soon over in all its forms. But, to say the truth, the present ministry have a difficult task, and want me, &c. Perhaps they may be just as grateful as others: but, according to the best judgment I have, they are pursuing the true interest of the publick; and therefore I am glad to contribute what is in my power. For God's sake, not a word of this to any alive.—Your chancellor? Why, madam, I can tell you he has been dead this fortnight. Faith, I could hardly forbear our little language about a nasty dead chancellor, as you may see by the blot. Ploughing? A pox plough them; they'll plough me to nothing. But have you got your money, both the ten pounds? How durst he pay you the second so soon? Pray, be good huswifes.—Aye, well, and *Joe*; why, I had a letter lately from *Joe*, desiring I would take some care of their poor town, who, he says, will lose their liberties. To which I desired Dr. *Raymond*

would return answer; That the town had behaved themselves so ill to me, so little regarded the advice I gave them,
and disagreed so much among themselves, that I was resolved never to have more to do with them; but that whatever personal kindness I could do to *Joe*, should be done.
Pray, when you happen to see *Joe*, tell him this, lest
Raymond should have blundered or forgotten.—Poor Mrs.
Wesley—Why these poligyes for being abroad? Why should
you be at home at all, until *Stella* is quite well?—So, here
is mistress *Stella* again with her two eggs, &c. My *Shower*
admired with You; why, the bishop of *Clogher* says, he
has seen something of mine of the same sort, better than
the *Shower*. I suppose he means *The Morning*; but it is not
half so good. I want your judgment of things, and not your
country's. How does *MD* like it? and do they taste it *all*?
&c. I am glad dean *Bolton* has paid the twenty pounds.
Why should not I chide the bishop of *Clogher* for writing
to the archbishop of *Cashel*, without sending the letter first
to me? It does not signify a ——; for he has no credit at
court. Stuff—they are all puppies. I'll break your head in
good earnest, young woman, for your nasty jest about Mrs.
Barton. Unlucky sluttikin, what a word is there? Faith, I
was thinking yesterday, when I was with her, whether she
could break them or no, and it quite spoiled my imagination. Mrs. *Walls*, does *Stella* win as she pretends? No
indeed, *doctor*; she loses always, and will play so *venter-
somely*, how can she win? See here now, an't you an impudent lying slut? Do, open *Domvile's* letter; what does it
signify, if you have a mind? Yes, faith, you write smartly
with your eyes shut; all was well but the *w*. See how I can
do it; *Madam Stella, your humble servant*. O, but one may
look whether one goes crooked or no, and so write on.
I'll tell you what you may do; you may write with your eyes
half shut, just as when one is going to sleep: I have done so
for two or three lines now; 'tis but just seeing enough to go
straight.—Now, madam *Dingley*, I think I bid you tell Mr.
Walls, that in case there be occasion, I will serve his friend
as far as I can; but I hope there will be none. Yet I believe
you will have a new *Parliament*; but I care not whether you

have or no a better. You are mistaken in all your conjectures about the *Tatlers*. I have given him one or two hints, and you have heard me talk about the *Shilling*. Faith, these answering letters are very long ones: you have taken up almost the room of a week in journals; and I'll tell you what, I saw fellows wearing crosses to-day, and I wondered what was the matter; but just this minute I recollect it is little *Presto's birth-day*; and I was resolved these three days to remember it when it came, but could not. Pray, drink my health to-day at dinner; do, you rogues. Do you like *Sid Hamet's Rod*? Do you understand it all? Well, now at last I have done with your letter, and so I'll lay me down to sleep, and about fair maids; and I hope merry maids all.

[*From* LETTER X.]

London. Dec. 13. 1710.

MORNING. I am to go traping with lady *Kerry* and Mrs. *Pratt* to see sights all this day: they engaged me yesterday morning at tea. You hear the havock making in the army: *Meredyth*, *Macartney*, and colonel *Honeywood*, are obliged to sell their commands at half value, and leave the army, for drinking Destruction to the present ministry, and dressing up a hat on a stick, and calling it *Harley*; then drinking a glass with one hand, and discharging a pistol with the other at the maukin, wishing it were *Harley* himself; and a hundred other such pretty tricks, as enflaming their soldiers, and foreign ministers, against the late changes at *Court*. *Cadogan* has had a little paring: his mother told me yesterday he had lost the place of envoy; but I hope they will go no further with him, for he was not at those mutinous meetings. Well, these saucy jades take up so much of my time, with writing to them in a morning; but faith I am glad to see you whenever I can: a little snap and away; and so hold your tongue, for I must rise: not a word for your life. How nowww? So, very well; stay till I come home, and then, perhaps, you may hear further from me. And where will you go to-day, for I can't be with you for these ladies? It is a rainy ugly day. I'd have you send for *Walls*, and go to the dean's; but don't play small games when you lose. You'll be ruined by *Manilio*, *Basto*, the *Queen*, and two small *Trumps* in red. I confess 'tis a good hand against the player: but then there are *Spadilio*, *Punto*, the *King*, strong *Trumps* against you, which, with one *Trump* more, are three tricks ten ace: for, suppose you play your *Manilio*—Oh, silly, how I prate and can't get away from this *MD* in a morning. Go, get you gone, dear naughty girls, and let me rise. There, *Patrick* lockt up my ink again the third time last night: the rogue gets the better of me; but I will rise in spite of you, sirrahs.—At night. Lady *Kerry*, Mrs. *Pratt*, Mrs. *Cadogan*, and I, in one coach; lady *Kerry's* son and his governor, and two gentlemen, in another; maids and misses, and little master (lord *Shelburn's* children) in a third, all hackneys, set out at ten o'clock this morning from lord *Shelburn's* house in *Piccadilly* to the *Tower*, and saw all the sights, lions &c. then to *Bedlam*; then dined at the *Chop-house* behind the *Exchange*; then to *Gresham College* (but the keeper was not at home) and concluded the night at the *Puppet-Shew*, whence we came home safe at eight, and I left them. The ladies were all in mobbs; how do you call it? undrest; and it was the rainiest day that ever dript; and I'm weary, and 'tis now past eleven.

[*From* LETTER XI.]

London. Dec. 24. 1710.

... LADY MOUNTJOY carried me home to dinner, where I staid not long after, and came home early, and now am got into bed, for you must always write to your *MD's* in bed, that's a maxim. Mr. *White* and Mr *Red*, Write to *MD* when abed; Mr. *Black* and Mr. *Brown*, Write to *MD* when you're down; Mr. *Oak* and Mr. *Willow*, Write to *MD* on your pillow.—What's this? faith I smell fire; what can it be; this house has a thousand s——ks in it. I think to leave it on *Thursday*, and lodge over the way. Faith I must rise, and look at my chimney, for the smell grows stronger, stay —I have been up, and in my room, and found all safe, only a mouse within the fender to warm himself, which I could not catch. I smelt nothing there, but now in my bed-chamber I smell it again; I believe I have singed the woolen curtain, and that's all, though I cannot smoak it. *Presto's* plaguy silly to-night, an't he? Yes, and so he be. Aye, but if I should wake and see fire. Well; I'll venture; so good night, &c.

[*From* LETTER XII.]

London. Jan. 14. 1710–11.

O FAITH, young women, I want a letter from *MD*; 'tis now nineteen days since I had the last: and where have I room to answer it, pray? I hope I shall send this away without any answer at all; for I'll hasten it, and away it goes on *Tuesday*, by which time this side will be full. I'll send it two days sooner on purpose out of spight, and the very next day after, you must know, your letter will come, and then 'tis too late, and I'll so laugh, never saw the like! 'Tis *Spring* with us already. I ate asparagus t'other day. Did you ever see such a frostless winter? Sir *Andrew Fountain* lies still extreamly ill; it costs him ten guineas a day to doctors, surgeons, and apothecaries, and has done so these three weeks. I dined to-day with Mr. *Ford*; he sometimes chuses to dine at home, and I am content to dine with him; and at night I called at the *Coffee-house*, where I had not been in a week, and talk'd coldly a while with Mr. *Addison*; all our friendship and dearness are off: we are civil acquaintance, talk words of course, of when we shall meet, and that's all. I have not been at any house with him these six weeks: t'other day we were to have dined together at the comptroller's; but I sent my excuses, being engaged to the secretary of state. Is not it odd? But I think he has used me ill, and I have used him too well, at least his friend *Steele*.

[*From* LETTER XIII.]

London. Jan. 16. 1710–11.

O FAITH, young women, I have sent my letter *N*.13, without one crumb of an answer to any of *MD's*, there's for you now; and yet *Presto* ben't angry faith, not a bit, only he will begin to be in pain next *Irish post*, except he sees *MD's* little hand-writing in the glass-frame at the bar of *St. James's Coffee-house*, where *Presto* would never go but for that purpose. *Presto's* at home, God help him, every night from six till bed-time, and has as little enjoyment or pleasure in life at present as any body in the world, although in full favour with all the ministry. As hope saved, nothing gives *Presto* any sort of dream of happiness but a letter now and then from his own dearest *MD*. I love the expectation of it, and when it does not come, I comfort myself, that I have it yet to be happy with. Yes faith, and when I write to *MD*, I am happy too; it is just as if methinks you were here and I prating to you, and telling you where I have been: Well, says you, *Presto*, come, where have you been to-day? come, let's hear now. And so then I answer; *Ford* and I were visiting Mr. *Lewis*, and Mr. *Prior*, and *Prior* has given me a fine *Plautus*, and then *Ford* would have had me dine at his lodgings, and so I would not; and so I dined with him at an eating-house; which I have not done five times since I came here; and so I came home after visiting Sir *Andrew Fountain's* mother and sister, and Sir *Andrew Fountain* is mending, though slowly.

[*From* LETTER XIV.]

London. Feb. 5. 1710–11.

MORNING. I am going this morning to see *Prior*, who dines with me at Mr. *Harley's*; so I can't stay fiddling and talking with dear little brats in a morning, and 'tis still terribly cold.—I wish my cold hand was in the warmest place about you, young women, I'd give ten guineas upon that account with all my heart, faith; oh, it starves my thigh; so I'll rise, and bid you good morrow, my ladies both, good morrow. Come stand away, let me rise: *Patrick*, take away the candle. Is there a good fire?—So—up a-dazy

[*From* LETTER XV.]

London. Feb. 18. 1710–11.

MY head has no fits, but a little disordered before dinner; yet I walk stoutly, and take pills, and hope to mend. Secretary *St. John* would needs have me dine with him to-day, and there I found three persons I never saw, two I had no acquaintance with, and one I did not care for: so I left them early and came home, it being no day to walk, but scurvy rain and wind. The secretary tells me he has put a cheat on me; for lord *Peterborow* sent him twelve dozen flasks of *Burgundy*, on condition that I should have my share; but he never was quiet till they were all gone, so I reckon he owes me thirty-six pound. Lord *Peterborow* is now got to *Vienna*, and I must write to him to-morrow. I begin now to be towards looking for a letter from some certain ladies of *Presto's* acquaintance, that live at *St. Mary's*, and are called in a certain language our little *MD*. No, stay, I don't expect one these six days, that will be just three weeks; an't I a reasonable creature? We are plagued here with an *October Club*, that is, a set of above a hundred parliament-men of the country, who drink *October* beer at home, and meet every evening at a tavern near the parliament, to consult affairs, and drive things on to extreams against the *Whigs*, to call the old ministry to account, and get off five or six heads. The ministry seem not to regard them, yet one of them in confidence told me, that there must be something thought on to settle things better. I'll tell you one great state secret; The queen, sensible how much she was governed by the late ministry, runs a little into t'other extream, and is jealous in that point, even of those who got her out of the others hands. The ministry is for gentler measures, and the other *Tories* for more violent. Lord *Rivers*, talking to me the other day, cursed the paper called The *Examiner*, for speaking civilly of the duke of *Marlborough*; this I happened to talk of to the secretary, who blamed the warmth of that lord and some others, and swore, that if their advice were followed, they would be blown up in twenty-four hours. And I have reason to think, that they will endeavour to prevail on the queen to put her affairs more in the hands

of a ministry than she does at present; and there are, I believe, two men thought on, one of them you have often met
the name of in my letters. But so much for politicks.

Feb. 21. [1710-11].

Morning. Faith I hope it will be fair for me to walk into
the city, for I take all occasions of walking.—I should be
plaguy busy at *Laracor* if I were there now, cutting down
willows, planting others, scouring my canal, and every kind
of thing. If *Raymond* goes over this summer, you must submit, and make them a visit, that we may have another eel
and trout fishing; and that *Stella* may ride by and see
Presto in his morning-gown in the garden, and so go up with
Joe to the *Hill of Bree*, and round by *Scurlock's Town*; O
Lord, how I remember names; faith it gives me short sighs:
therefore no more of that if you love me. Good morrow,
I'll go rise like a gentleman, my pills say I must.

[*From* LETTER XVI.]

London. March 7. 1710-11.

MORNING. Faith, a little would make me, I could find in my
heart, if it were not for one thing, I have a good mind, if I
had not something else to do, I would answer your dear
saucy letter. O Lord, I am going awry with writing in bed.
O faith, but I must answer it, or I shan't have room, for it
must go on *Saturday*; and don't think I'll fill the third side,
I an't come to that yet, young women. Well then, as for
your *Bernage*, I have said enough: I writ to him last week.
—Turn over that leaf. Now, what says *MD* to the world to
come? I tell you, madam *Stella*, my head is a great deal
better, and I hope will keep so. How came yours to be
fifteen days coming, and you had my fifteenth in seven?
Answer me that, rogues. Your being with goody *Walls* is
excuse enough: I find I was mistaken in the sex, 'tis a boy.
Yes, I understand your cypher, and *Stella* guesses right, as
she always does. He gave me al bfadnuk lboinlpl dfaonr
ufainfbtoy dpionufnad, which I sent him again by Mr.
Lewis, to whom I writ a very complaining letter that was

shewed him; and so the matter ended. He told me he had a quarrel with me; I said I had another with him, and we returned to our friendship, and I should think he loves me as well as a great minister can love a man in so short a time. Did not I do right? I am glad at heart you have got your palsey-water; pray God Almighty it may do my dearest little *Stella* good. I suppose Mrs. *Edgworth* set out last *Monday* se'nnight. Yes, I do read the *Examiners*, and they are written very finely, as you judge. I do not think they are too severe on the duke; they only tax him of avarice, and his avarice has ruined us. You may count upon all things in them to be true. The author has said, It is not *Prior*; but perhaps it may be *Atterbury*.—Now, madam *Dingley*, says she, 'tis fine weather, says she; yes, says she, and we have got to our new lodgings. I compute you ought to save eight pounds by being in the others five months; and you have no more done it than eight thousand. I am glad you are rid of that squinting, blinking *Frenchman*. I will give you a bill on *Parvisol* for five pound for the half year. And must I go on at four shillings a week, and neither eat nor drink for it? Who the D—— said *Atterbury* and your dean were alike? I never saw your chancellor, nor his chaplain. The latter has a good deal of learning, and is a well-wisher to be an author: your chancellor is an excellent man. As for *Patrick's* bird, he bought him for his tameness, and is grown the wildest I ever saw. His wings have been quilled thrice, and are now up again: he will be able to fly after us to Ireland, if he be willing.—Yes, Mrs. *Stella*, *Dingley* writes more like *Presto* than you; for all you superscribed the letter, as who should say, Why should not I write like our *Presto* as well as Dingley? You with your aukward SSs ; can't you write them thus, SS? No, but always SSS. Spiteful sluts, to affront *Presto's* writing; as that when you shut your eyes you write most like *Presto*. I know the time when I did not write to you half so plain as I do now; but I take pity on you both. I am very much concerned for Mrs. *Walls's* eyes. *Walls* says nothing of it to me in his letter dated after yours. You say, If she recovers she may lose her sight. I hope she is in no danger of her life. Yes, *Ford* is as sober as I please: I use him to walk with me as an easy companion, always ready for what I please, when I am weary of business and ministers. I don't go to a *Coffee-house* twice a month. I am very regular in going to sleep before eleven.——And so you say that *Stella's* a pretty girl; and so she be, and methinks I see her just now as handsome as the day's long. Do you know what? when I am writing in our language I make up my mouth just as if I was speaking it. I caught myself at it just now. And I suppose *Dingley* is so fair and so frêsh as a lass in *May*, and has her health, and no spleen.—In your account you sent do you reckon as usual from the 1st of *November* was twelvemonth? Poor *Stella*, won't *Dingley* leave her a little day-light to write to *Presto*? Well, well, we'll have day-light shortly, spight of her teeth; and zoo must cly Lele, and Hele, and Hele aden. Must loo mimitate *pdfr*, pay? Iss, and so la shall. And so leles fol ee rettle. Dood mollow.—At night. Mrs. *Barton* sent this morning to invite me to dinner; and there I dined, just in that genteel manner that *MD* used when they would treat some better sort of body than usual.

[*From* LETTER XVII.]

London. March 10. 1710–11.

PRETTY little *MD* must expect little from me till Mr. *Harley* is out of danger. We hope he is so now; but I am subject to fear for my friends. He has a head full of the whole business of the nation, was out of order when the villain stabbed him, and had a cruel contusion by the second blow. But all goes on well yet. Mr. *Ford* and I dined with Mr. *Lewis,* and we hope the best.

March 11. [1710–11].

This morning Mr. secretary and I met at *Court*, where he went to the queen, who is out of order and aguish: I doubt the worse for this accident to Mr. *Harley*. We went together to his house, and his wound looks well, and he is not feverish at all, and I think it is foolish in me to be so much in pain as I am. I had the penknife in my hand, which is broken within a quarter of an inch of the handle. I have a mind to write and publish an account of all the particularities of this fact: it will be very curious and I would do it when Mr. *Harley* is past danger.

March 12. [1710-11].

We have been in terrible pain to-day about Mr. *Harley*, who never slept last night, and has been very feverish. But this evening I called there, and young Mr. *Harley* (his only son) tells me he is now much better, and was then asleep. They let nobody see him, and that is perfectly right. The *parliament* cannot go on till he is well, and are forced to adjourn their money businesses, which none but he can help them in. Pray God preserve him.

March 13. [1710-11].

Mr. Harley is better to-day, slept well all night, and we are a little out of our fears. I send and call three or four times every day. I went into the city for a walk, and dined there with a private man; and coming home this evening broke my shin in the *Strand* over a tub of sand left just in the way. I got home dirty enough, and went straight to bed, where I have been cooking it with gold-beaters skin, and have been peevish enough with *Patrick*, who was near an hour bringing a rag from next door. It is my right shin, where never any humour fell when t'other used to swell; so I apprehend it less: however I shall not stir till 'tis well, which I reckon will be in a week. I am very careful in these sort of things; but I wish I had Mrs. *J[ohnson']s* water: she is out of town, and I must make a shift with allum. I will dine with Mrs. *Vanhomrigh* till I am well, who lives but five doors off; and that I may venture.

March 14. [1710-11].

My journals are like to be very diverting, now I cannot stir abroad, between accounts of Mr. *Harley's* mending, and of my broken shin. I just walkt to my neighbour *Vanhomrigh* at two, and came away at six, when little *Harrison* the *Tatler* came to me, and begged me to dictate a paper to him, which I was forced in charity to do. Mr. *Harley* still mends; and I hope in a day or two to trouble you no more with him, nor with my shin. Go to bed and sleep, sirrahs, that you may rise to-morrow and walk to *Donnybrook*, and lose your money with *Stoite* and the dean; do so, dear little rogues, and drink *Presto's* health. O, pray, don't you drink *Presto's* health sometimes with your deans, and your *Stoites*, and your *Walls*, and your *Manleys*, and your every body's, pray now? I drink *MD's* to myself a hundred thousand times.

March 15. [1710–11].

I was this morning at Mr. secretary *St. John's* for all my shin, and he has given me for young *Harrison*, the *Tatler*, the prettiest employment in *Europe*; secretary to my lord *Raby*, who is to be ambassador extraordinary at the *Hague*, where all the great affairs will be concerted; so we shall lose the *Tatlers* in a fortnight. I will send *Harrison* to-morrow morning to thank the secretary. Poor *Biddy Floyd* has got the small-pox. I called this morning to see lady *Betty Germain*; and when she told me so, I fairly took my leave. I have the luck of it; for about ten days ago I was to see lord *Carteret*; and my lady was entertaining me with telling of a young lady, a cousin, who was then ill in the house of the small-pox, and is since dead: it was near lady *Betty's*, and I fancy *Biddy* took the fright by it. I dined with Mr. secretary, and a physician came in just from *Guiscard*, who tells us he is dying of his wounds, and can hardly live till to-morrow. A poor wench that *Guiscard* kept, sent him a bottle of sack; but the keeper would not let him touch it, for fear it was poison. He had two quarts of old clotted blood come out of his side to-day, and is delirious. I am sorry he is dying; for they had found out a way to hang him. He certainly had an intention to murder the queen.

March 16. [1710–11].

I have made but little progress in this letter for so many days, thanks to *Guiscard* and Mr. *Harley*; and it would be endless to tell you all the particulars of that odious fact.

I do not yet hear that *Guiscard* is dead, but they say 'tis impossible he should recover. I walkt too much yesterday for a man with a broken shin; to-day I rested, and went no further than Mrs. *Vanhomrigh's*, where I dined; and lady *Betty Butler* coming in about six, I was forced in good manners to sit with her till nine; then I came home, and Mr. *Ford* came in to visit my shin, and sat with me till eleven: so I have been very idle and naughty. It vexes me to the pluck that I should lose walking this delicious day. Have you seen the *Spectator* yet, a paper that comes out every day ? 'Tis written by Mr. *Steele*, who seems to have gathered new life, and have a new fund of wit; it is in the same nature as his *Tatlers*, and they have all of them had something pretty. I believe *Addison* and he club. I never see them; and I plainly told Mr. *Harley* and Mr. *St. John*, ten days ago, before my lord keeper and lord *Rivers*, that I had been foolish enough to spend my credit with them in favour of *Addison* and *Steele*; but that I would engage and promise never to say one word in their behalf, having been used so ill for what I had already done.—So, now I am got into the way of prating again, there will be no quiet for me. When *Presto* begins to prate, Give him a rap upon the pate. —O Lord, how I blot; 'tis time to leave off, &c.

March 17. [1710–11].

Guiscard died this morning at two, and the coroner's inquest have found that he was killed by bruises received from a messenger, so to clear the cabinet counsellors from whom he received his wounds. I had a letter from *Raymond*, who cannot hear of your box; but I hope you have it before this comes to your hands. I dined to-day with Mr. *Lewis* of the secretary's office. Mr. *Harley* has abundance of extravasated blood comes from his breast out of his wound, and will not be well so soon as we expected. I had something to say, but cannot call it to mind (What was it ?).

March 18. [1710–11].

I was to-day at *Court* to look for the duke of *Argyle*, and give him the memorial about *Bernage*. The duke goes with the first fair wind: I could not find him, but I have given the memorial to another to give him; and, however, it shall be sent after him. *Bernage* has made a blunder in offering money to his colonel without my advice; however he is made captain-lieutenant, only he must recruit the company, which will cost him forty pounds, and that is cheaper than a hundred. I dined to-day with Mr. secretary *St. John*, and staid till seven, but would not drink his *Champaign* and *Burgundy*, for fear of the gout. My shin mends, but is not well. I hope it will by the time I send this letter, next *Saturday*.

March 19. [1710–11].

I went to-day into the city, but in a coach, and sossed up my leg on the seat; and as I came home I went to see poor *Charles Barnard's* books, which are to be sold by auction, and I itch to lay out nine or ten pounds for some fine editions of fine authors. But 'tis too far, and I shall let it slip, as I usually do all such opportunities. I dined in a *Coffeehouse* with *Stratford* upon chops, and some of his wine. Where did *MD* dine? Why, poor *MD* dined at home to-day, because of the archbishop, and they could not go abroad, and had a breast of mutton and a pint of wine. I hope Mrs. *Walls* mends; and pray give me an account what sort of godfather I made, and whether I behaved myself handsomely. The duke of *Argyle* is gone; and whether he has my memorial, I know not, till I see Dr. *Arbuthnott*, to whom I gave it. That hard name belongs to a *Scotch* doctor, an acquaintance of the duke's and me; *Stella* can't pronounce it. Oh, that we were at *Laracor* this fine day! the willows begin to peep, and the quicks to bud. My dream's out: I was a-dreamed last night that I eat ripe cherries.— And now they begin to catch the pikes, and will shortly the trouts (pox on these ministers), and I would fain know whether the floods were ever so high as to get over the holly bank or the river walk; if so, then all my pikes are gone; but I hope not. Why don't you ask *Parvisol* these things, sirrahs? And then my canal, and trouts, and whether the bottom be fine and clear? But hearkee, ought not

Parvisol to pay in my last year's rents and arrears out of his hands? I am thinking, if either of you have heads to take his accounts, it should be paid in to you; otherwise to Mr *Walls*. I will write an order on t'other side; and do as you will. Here's a world of business; but I must go sleep, I'm drowsy; and so good night, &c.

March 20. [1710–11].

This sore shin ruins me in coach hire; no less than two shillings to-day going and coming from the city, where I dined with one you never heard of, and passed an insipid day. I writ this post to *Bernage*, with the account I told you above. I hope he will like it; 'tis his own fault, or it would have been better. I reckon your next letter will be full of Mr. *Harley's* stabbing. He still mends, but abundance of extravasated blood has come out of the wound: he keeps his bed, and sees nobody. The speaker's eldest son is just dead of the small-pox, and the house is adjourned a week, to give him time to wipe off his tears. I think it very handsomely done; but I believe one reason is, that they want Mr. *Harley* so much. *Biddy Floyd* is like to do well: and so go to your dean's, and roast his oranges, and lose your money, do so, you saucy sluts. *Stella*, you lost three shillings and four pence t'other night at *Stoite's*, yes, you did, and *Presto* stood in a corner, and saw you all the while, and then stole away. I dream very often I am in *Ireland*, and that I have left my cloaths and things behind me, and have not taken leave of any body; and that the ministry expect me to-morrow, and such nonsense.

March 21. [1710–11].

I would not for a guinea have a letter from you till this goes; and go it shall on *Saturday*, faith. I dined with Mrs. *Vanhomrigh*, to save my shin, and then went on some business to the secretary, and he was not at home.

March 22. [1710–11].

Yesterday was a short day's journal: but what care I? what cares saucy *Presto*? *Darteneuf* invited me to dinner to-day. Don't you know *Darteneuf*? That's the man that knows every thing, and that every body knows; and that knows where a knot of rabble are going on a holiday, and when they were there last: and then I went to the *Coffee-house*. My shin mends, but is not quite healed: I ought to keep it up, but I don't; I e'en let it go as it comes. Pox take *Parvisol* and his watch. If I do not receive the ten pound bill I am to get towards it, I will neither receive watch nor chain; so let *Parvisol* know.

March 23. [1710–11].

I this day appointed the duke of *Ormond* to meet him at *Ned Southwell's*, about an affair of printing *Irish Prayer-Books*, &c. but the duke never came. There *Southwell* had letters that two pacquets are taken; so if *MD* writ then, the letters are gone; for they were pacquets coming here. Mr. *Harley* is not yet well, but his extravasated blood continues, and I doubt he will not be quite well in a good while: I find you have heard of the fact, by *Southwell's* letters from *Ireland*: What do you think of it? I dined with Sir *John Perci-val*, and saw his lady sitting in the bed, in the forms of a lying-in woman; and coming home my sore shin itched, and I forgot what it was, and rubbed off the s——b, and blood came; but I am now got into bed, and have put on allum curd, and it is almost well. Lord *Rivers* told me yesterday a piece of bad news, as a secret, that the Pretender is going to be married to the duke of *Savoy's* daughter. 'Tis very bad, if it be true. We were walking in the *Mall* with some *Scotch* lords, and he could not tell it until they were gone, and he bade me tell it to none but the secretary of state and *MD*. This goes to-morrow, and I have no room but to bid my dearest little *MÐ* good night.

March 24. [1710–11].

I will now seal up this letter, and send it; for I reckon to have none from you ('tis morning now) between this and night; and I will put it in the post with my own hands. I am going out in great haste; so farewel, &c.

[LETTER XVIII.]

London. March 26. 1711.

THIS was a most delicious day; and my shin being past danger, I walkt like lightning above two hours in the *Park*. We have generally one fair day, and then a great deal of rain for three or four days together. All things are at a stop in parliament for want of Mr. *Harley*; they cannot stir an inch without him in their most material affairs: and we fear by the caprice of *Radcliffe*, who will admit none but his own surgeon, he has not been well lookt after. I dined at an alehouse with Mr. *Lewis*, but had his wine. Don't you begin to see the flowers and blossoms of the field? How busy should I be now at *Laracor*? No news of your box? I hope you have it, and are this minute drinking the chocolate, and that the smell of the *Brazil* tobacco has not affected it. I would be glad to know whether you like it, because I would send you more by people that are now every day thinking of going to *Ireland*; therefore pray tell me, and tell me soon: and I will have the strong box.

April 1. [1711].

The duke of *Buckingham's* house fell down last night with an earth-quake, and is half swallowed up;—Won't you go and see it?—An *April* fool, an *April* fool, oh ho, young women. Well, don't be angry, I'll make you an *April* fool no more till the next time: we had no sport here, because it is *Sunday*, and *Easter-Sunday*. I dined with the secretary, who seemed terribly down and melancholy, which Mr. *Prior* and *Lewis* observed as well as I: perhaps something is gone wrong; perhaps there is nothing in it. God bless my own dearest *MD*, and all is well.

April 3. [1711].

I was this morning to see Mrs. *Barton*; I love her better than any body here, and see her seldomer. Why really now, so it often happens in the world, that where one loves a body best—pshah, pshah, you are so silly with your moral observations. Well, but she told me a very good story. An old gentlewoman died here two months ago, and left in her will, to have eight men and eight maids bearers, who should have two guineas apiece, ten guineas to the parson for a sermon, and two guineas to the clerk. But bearers, parson and clerk must be all true virgins; and not to be admitted till they took their oaths of virginity: so the poor woman lies still unburied, and so must do till the general resurrection.—I called at Mr. secretary's to see what the D—— ailed him on *Sunday*; I made him a very proper speech, told him, I observed he was much out of temper; that I did not expect he would tell me the cause, but would be glad to see he was in better; and one thing I warned him of, Never to appear cold to me, for I would not be treated like a school-boy; that I had felt too much of that in my life already (meaning from Sir *William Temple*) that I expected every great minister, who honoured me with his acquaintance, if he heard or saw any thing to my disadvantage, would let me know it in plain words, and not put me in pain to guess by the change or coldness of his countenance or behaviour; for it was what I would hardly bear from a crowned head, and I thought no subject's favour was worth it; and that I designed to let my lord keeper and Mr. *Harley* know the same thing, that they might use me accordingly. He took all right; said, I had reason, vowed nothing ailed him but sitting up whole nights at business, and one night at drinking; would have had me dine with him and Mrs. *Masham's* brother, to make up matters; but I would not. I don't know, but I would not. But indeed I was engaged with my old friend *Rollinson*, you never heard of him before.

April 4. [1711].

I sometimes look a line or two back, and see plaguy mistakes of the pen; how do you get over them? you are puzzled sometimes. Why, I think what I said to Mr. secretary was right. Don't you remember how I used to be in pain when Sir *William Temple* would look cold and out of humour for three or four days, and I used to suspect a hundred reasons. I have pluckt up my spirit since then, faith; he spoiled a fine gentleman. I dined with my neigh-

bour *Vanhomrigh*, and *MD*, poor *MD*, at home on a loin
of mutton and half a pint of wine, and the mutton was raw,
poor *Stella* could not eat, poor dear rogue, and *Dingley*
was so vext; but we'll dine at *Stoyte's* to-morrow. Mr.
Harley promised to see me in a day or two, so I called this
evening; but his son and others were abroad, and he asleep,
so I came away, and found out Mrs. *Vedeau*. She drew out
a letter from *Dingley*, and said she would get a friend to
receive the money. I told her I would employ Mr. *Tooke*
in it henceforward. Her husband bought a lieutenancy of
foot, and is gone to *Portugal*. He sold his share of the shop
to his brother, and put out the money to maintain her, all but
what bought the commission. She lodges within two doors
of her brother. She told me, It made her very melancholy
to change her manner of life thus, but trade was dead, *&c.*
She says, she will write to you soon. I design to engage
Ben. Tooke, and then receive the parchment from her.—I
gave Mr. *Dopping* a copy of *Prior's* verses on Mr. *Harley*, he
sent them yesterday to *Ireland*, so go look for them, for I
won't be at the trouble to transcribe them here. They will
be printed in a day or two. Give my hearty service to *Stoyte*
and *Catherine*; upon my word I love them dearly, and desire you will tell them so: pray desire goody *Stoyte* not to
let Mrs. *Walls* and Mrs. *Johnson* cheat her of her money at
ombre, but assure her from me, that she is a bungler. Dine
with her to-day, and tell her so, and drink my health, and
good voyage, and speedy return, and so you're a rogue.

April 5. [1711].

Morning. Now let us proceed to examine a saucy letter
from one Madam *MD*.—God Almighty bless poor dear
Stella, and send her a great many *Birth-days*, all happy and
healthy, and wealthy, and with me ever together, and never
asunder again, unless by chance. When I find you are
happy or merry there, it makes me so here, and I can hardly
imagine you absent when I am reading your letter, or
writing to you. No faith, you are just here upon this little
paper, and therefore I see and talk with you every evening

constantly, and sometimes in the morning, but not always
in the morning, because that is not so modest to young
ladies.—What, you would fain palm a letter on me more
than you sent; and I, like a fool, must look over all yours,
to see whether this was really *N*.12 or more. (*Patrick* has
this moment brought me letters from the bishop of *Clogher*
and *Parvisol*; my heart was at my mouth for fear of one
from *MD*; what a disgrace would it be to have two of yours
to answer together? But faith this shall go to night, for fear,
and then come when it will, I defy it.) No, you are not
naughty at all, write when you are disposed. And so the
dean told you the story of Mr. *Harley* from the archbishop;
I warrant it never spoiled your supper, or broke off your
game. Nor yet, have not you the box; I wish Mrs. *Edgworth* had the ——. But you have it now, I suppose; and
is the chocolate good, or has the tobacco spoiled it? *Leigh*
stays till *Sterne* has done his business, no longer; and when
that will be, God knows: I befriend him as much as I can,
but Mr. *Harley's* accident stops that as well as all things
else. You guess, Madam *Dingley*, that I shall stay a round
twelvemonth; as hope saved, I would come over, if I could,
this minute; but we will talk of that by and bye.—Your
affair of *Vedeau* I have told you of already; now to the next,
turn over the leaf. Mrs. *Dobbins* lies, I have no more provision here or in *Ireland* than I had. I am pleased that
Stella the conjurer approves what I did with Mr. *Harley*;
but your generosity makes me mad; I know you repine inwardly at *Presto's* absence; you think he has broken his
word of coming in three months, and that this is always
his trick; and now *Stella* says, she does not see possibly how
I can come away in haste, and that *MD* is satisfied, &c.
An't you a rogue to overpower me thus? I did not expect
to find such friends as I have done. They may indeed deceive me too. But there are important reasons (Pox on this
grease, this candle tallow!) why they should not. I have been
used barbarously by the late ministry; I am a little piqued
in honour to let people see I am not to be despised. The
assurances they give me, without any scruple or provocation, are such as are usually believed in the world; they may

come to nothing, but the first opportunity that offers, and is neglected, I shall depend no more, but come away. I could say a thousand things on this head, if I were with you. I am thinking why *Stella* should not go to the *Bath*, if she be told it will do her good; I will make *Parvisol* get up fifty pounds, and pay it you; and you may be good houswives, and live cheap there some months, and return in *Autumn*, or visit *London*, as you please: pray think of it. I writ to *Bernage*, directed to *Curry's*; I wish he had the letter. I will send the bohea tea, if I can. The bishop of *Kilmore*, I don't keep such company; an old dying fool whom I never was with in my life. So I am no godfather; all the better. Pray, *Stella*, explain these two words of yours to me, what you mean by *Villian*, and *Dainger*, and you Madam Dingley, what is *Christianing*?—Lay your letter *this way*, *this way*, and the devil a bit of difference between this way and t'other way. No; I'll shew you, lay them *this way*, *this way*, and not *that way*, *that way*.—You shall have your aprons; and I'll put all your commissions as they come, in a paper together, and don't think I'll forget *MD's* orders, because they are friends; I'll be as careful, as if they were strangers. I know not what to do about this *Clements*. *Walls* will not let me say any thing, as if Mr. *Pratt* was against him; and now the bishop of *Clogher* has written to me in his behalf. This thing does not rightly fall in my way, and that people never consider: I always give my good offices where they are proper, and that I am judge of; however, I will do what I can. But, if he has the name of a *Whig*, it will be hard, considering my lord *Anglesea* and *Hyde* are very much otherwise, and you know they have the employment of deputy treasurer. If the frolick should take you of going to the *Bath*, I here send you a note on *Parvisol*; if not, you may tear it, and there's an end. Farewel.

If you have an imagination that the *Bath* will do you good, I say again, I would have you go; if not, or it be inconvenient, burn this note. Or, if you would go, and not take so much money, take thirty pounds, and I will return you twenty from hence. Do as you please, sirrahs. I suppose it will not be too late for the first season; if it be, I would have you resolve however to go the second season, if the doctors say it will do you good, and you fancy so.

[*From* LETTER XIX.]

London. April 23. 1711.

So you expect an answer to your letter, do you so? Yes, yes, you shall have an answer, you shall, young women. I made a good pun on *Saturday* to my lord keeper. After dinner we had coarse *Doiley* napkins, fringed at each end, upon the table to drink with: my lord keeper spread one of them between him and Mr. *Prior*; I told him I was glad to see there was such a *Fringeship* between Mr. *Prior* and his lordship. *Prior* swore it was the worst he ever heard: I said I thought so too; but at the same time I thought it was most like one of *Stella's* that ever I heard. I dined to-day with lord *Montjoy*, and this evening saw the *Venetian* ambassador coming from his first publick audience. His coach was the most monstrous, huge, fine, rich, gilt thing that ever I saw. I loitered this evening, and came home late.

[*From* LETTER XXI.]

Chelsea. April 30. 1711.

MORN. I am here in a pretty pickle: it rains hard; and the cunning natives of *Chelsea* have outwitted me, and taken up all the three stage coaches. What shall I do? I must go to town: this is your fault. I can't walk: I'll borrow a coat. This is the blindside of my lodging out of town; I must expect such inconveniences as these. Faith I'll walk in the rain. Morrow.

May 2. [1711]

A fine day, but begins to grow a little warm; and that makes your little fat *Presto* sweat in the forehead. Pray, are not the fine buns sold here in our town; was it not *Rrrrrrrrrare Chelsea Buns*? I bought one to-day in my walk: it cost me a penny; it was stale, and I did not like it, as the man said, &c. Sir *Andrew Fountain* and I dined at Mrs. *Vanhomrigh's*; and had a flask of my *Florence*, which lies in their cellar; and so I came home gravely, and saw nobody of consequence to-day. I am very easy here, nobody plaguing me in a morning; and *Patrick* saves many a score lies. I sent over to Mrs. *Atterbury*, To know whether I might wait on her? but she is gone a visiting: we have exchanged some compliments, but I have not seen her yet. We have no news in our town.

May 4. [1711].

I dined to-day at lord *Shelburn's*, where lady *Kerry* made me a present of four *India* handkerchiefs, which I have a mind to keep for little *MD*, only that I had rather, &c. I have been a mighty handkerchief-monger, and have bought abundance of snuff ones since I have left off taking snuff. And I am resolved, when I come over, *MD* shall be acquainted with lady *Kerry*: we have struck up a mighty friendship; and she has much better sense than any other lady of your country. We are almost in love with one another: but she is most egregiously ugly; but perfectly well bred, and governable as I please. I am resolved, when I come, to keep no company but *MD*: you know I kept my resolution last time; and, except Mr. *Addison*, conversed with none but you and your club of deans and *Stoytes*. 'Tis three weeks, young women, since I had a letter from you; and yet, methinks, I would not have another for five pound till this is gone; and yet I send every day to the *Coffee-house*, and I would fain have a letter, and not have a letter; and I don't know what, nor I don't know how, and this goes on very slow; 'tis a week to-morrow since I began it. I am a poor country gentleman, and don't know how the world passes. Do you know that every syllable I write I hold my lips just for all the world as if I were talking in our own little language to *MD*. Faith, I am very silly; but I can't help it for my life. I got home early to-night. My solicitors, that used to ply me every morning, knew not where to find me; and I am so happy not to hear *Patrick*, *Patrick*, called a hundred times every morning. But I lookt backward, and find I have said this before. What care I? go to the dean, and roast the oranges.

[*From* LETTER XXII.]

Chelsea. May 14. 1711.

I WENT to town to-day by water. The hail quite discouraged me from walking, and there is no shade in the greatest part of the way: I took the first boat; and had a footman my companion; then I went again by water, and dined in the city with a printer, to whom I carried a pamphlet in manuscript, that Mr. secretary gave me. The printer sent it to the secretary for his approbation, and he desired me to look it over, which I did, and found it a very scurvy piece. The reason I tell you so, is because it was done by your parson *Slap, Scrap, Flap* (what d'ye call him) *Trap*, your chancellor's chaplain. 'Tis called *A Character* of the present set of *Whigs*, and is going to be printed, and no doubt the author will take care to produce it in *Ireland*. Dr. *Freind* was with me, and pulled out a two-penny pamphlet just published, called *The State of Wit*, giving a character of all the papers that have come out of late. The author seems to be a *Whig*, yet he speaks very highly of a paper called the *Examiner*, and says the supposed author of it is Dr. *Swift*. But above all things he praises the *Tatlers* and *Spectators*; and I believe *Steele* and *Addison* were privy to the printing of it. Thus is one treated by these impudent dogs. And that villain *Curl* has scraped up some trash, and calls it Dr. *Swift's* miscellanies, with the name at large: and I can get no satisfaction of him. Nay, Mr. *Harley* told me he had read it, and only laughed at me before lord keeper, and the rest. Since I came home I have been sitting with the prolocutor, dean *Atterbury*, who is my neighbour over the way; but generally keeps in town with his convocation. 'Tis late, &c.

May 15. [1711].

My walk to town to-day was after ten, and prodigiously hot: I dined with lord *Shelburn*, and have desired Mrs. *Pratt*, who lodges there, to carry over Mrs. *Walls's* tea; I hope she will do it, and they talk of going in a fortnight. My way is this; I leave my best gown and periwig at Mrs. *Vanhomrigh's*, then walk up the *Pall-mall*, through the *Park*, out at

Buckingham-house, and so to *Chelsea* a little beyond the *Church*: I set out about sun-set, and get here in something less than an hour; it is two good miles and just five thousand seven hundred and forty-eight steps; so there is four miles a day walking, without reckoning what I walk while I stay in town. When I pass the *Mall* in the evening it is prodigious to see the number of ladies walking there; and I always cry shame at the ladies of *Ireland*, who never walk at all, as if their legs were of no use, but to be *laid aside*. I have been now almost three weeks here, and I thank God, am much better in my head, if it does but continue. I tell you what, if I was with you, when we went to *Stoyte* at *Donnybrook*, we would only take a coach to the hither end of *Stephen's-Green*, and from thence go every step on foot, yes faith, every step; it would do: *DD* goes as well as *Presto*. Every body tells me I look better already; for faith I lookt sadly, that's certain. My breakfast is milk porridge: I don't love it, faith I hate it, but 'tis cheap and wholesome; and I hate to be obliged to either of those qualities for any thing.

May 23. [1711].

. . . O faith, I should be glad to be in the same kingdom with *MD*, however, although you were at *Wexford*. But I am kept here by a most capricious fate, which I would break through, if I could do it with decency or honour.— To return without some mark of distinction, would look extremely little; and I would likewise gladly be somewhat richer than I am. I will say no more, but beg you to be easy, 'till *Fortune* take her course, and to believe that *MD's* felicity is the great end I aim at in all my pursuits. And so let us talk no more on this subject, which makes me melancholy, and that I would fain divert. Believe me, no man breathing at present has less share of happiness in life than I: I do not say I am unhappy at all, but that every thing here is tasteless to me for want of being as I would be And so, a short sigh, and no more of this.

[*From* LETTER XXIII.]

Chelsea. May 24. 1711.

MORNING. Once in my life the number of my letters and of the day of the month is the same; that's lucky, boys; that's a sign that things will meet, and that we shall make a figure together. What, will you still have the impudence to say *London, England,* because I say *Dublin, Ireland*? Is there no difference between *London* and *Dublin,* saucy boxes? I have sealed up my letter, and am going to town. Morrow, sirrahs.

May 30. [1711].

I am so hot and lazy after my morning's walk, that I loitered at Mrs. *Vanhomrigh's,* where my best gown and periwig are, and out of mere listlessness dine there very often, so I did to-day, but I got little *MD's* letter, *N.*15. (you see, sirrahs, I remember to tell the number) from Mr. *Lewis,* and I read it in a closet they lend me at Mrs. *Van's,* and I find *Stella* is a saucy rogue and a great writer, and can write finely still when her hand's in, and her pen good. When I came here to-night, I had a mighty mind to go swim after I was cool, for my lodging is just by the river, and I went down with only my night-gown and slippers on at eleven, but came up again; however, one of these nights I will venture.

June 5. [1711].

I dined in the city to-day, and went from hence early to town, and visited the duke of *Ormond,* and Mr. secretary. They say, my lord treasurer has a dead warrant in his pocket, they mean, a list of those who are to be turned out of employment, and we every day now expect those changes. I past by the treasury to-day, and saw vast crowds waiting to give lord treasurer petitions as he passes by. He is now at the top of power and favour: he keeps no levees yet. I am cruel thirsty this hot weather.—I am just this minute going to swim. I take *Patrick* down with me to hold my nightgown, shirt and slippers, and borrow a napkin of my landlady for a cap—So farewel till I come up; but there's no danger, don't be frighted.—I have been swimming this half-hour and more; and when I was coming out I dived, to make my head and all through wet, like a cold bath; but as I dived, the napkin fell off and is lost, and I have that to pay for. O faith, the great stones were so sharp, I could hardly set my feet on them as I came out. It was pure and warm. I got to bed, and will now go sleep.

June 6. [1711].

Morning. This letter shall go to-morrow; so I will answer yours when I come home to-night. I feel no hurt from last night's swimming. I lie with nothing but the sheet over me, and my feet quite bare. I must rise and go to town before the tide is against me. Morrow, sirrahs; dear sirrahs, morrow.—At night. I never felt so hot a day as this since I was born. I dined with lady *Betty Germain*, and there was the young earl of *Berkeley* and his fine lady. I never saw her before, nor think her near so handsome as she passes for.—After dinner, Mr. *Bertue* would not let me put ice in my wine; but said my lord *Dorchester* got the bloody-flux with it, and that it was the worst thing in the world. Thus are we plagued, thus are we plagued; yet I have done it five or six times this summer, and was but the drier and the hotter for it. Nothing makes me so excessively peevish as hot weather. Lady *Berkeley* after dinner clapt my hat on another lady's head, and she in roguery put it upon the rails. I minded them not; but in two minutes they called me to the window, and lady *Carteret* shewed me my hat out of her window five doors off, where I was forced to walk to it, and pay her and old lady *Weymouth* a visit, with some more beldames. Then I went and drank coffee, and made one or two puns with lord *Pembroke*, and designed to go to lord treasurer; but it was too late, and beside I was half broiled, and broiled without butter; for I never sweat after dinner, if I drink any wine. Then I sat an hour with lady *Betty Butler* at tea, and every thing made me hotter and drier. Then I walkt home, and was here by ten, so miserably hot, that I was in as perfect a passion as ever I was in my life at the greatest affront or provocation. Then

I sat an hour, till I was quite dry and cool enough to go swim; which I did, but with so much vexation, that I think I have given it over: for I was every moment disturbed by boats, rot them; and that puppy *Patrick*, standing ashore, would let them come within a yard or two, and then call sneakingly to them. The only comfort I proposed here in hot weather is gone; for there is no jesting with those boats after 'tis dark: I had none last night. I dived to dip my head, and held my cap on with both my hands, for fear of losing it.——Pox take the boats! Amen. 'Tis near twelve, and so I'll answer your letter (it strikes twelve now) to-morrow morning.

[*From* LETTER XXIV.]

Chelsea. June 30. 1711.

MORNING. I am terrible sleepy always in a morning; I be-lieve it is my walk over-night that disposes me to sleep; faith 'tis now striking eight, and I am but just awake. *Patrick* comes early, and wakes me five or six times, but I have excuses, though I am three parts asleep. I tell him I sat up late, or slept ill in the night, and often it is a lie. I have now got little *MD's* letter before me, *N.*16, no more, nor no less, no mistake. *Dingley* says, "This letter won't be above six lines," and I was afraid it was true, though I saw it filled on both sides. The bishop of *Clogher* writ me word you were in the country, and that he heard you were well: I am glad at heart *MD* rides, and rides, and rides. Our hot weather ended in *May*, and all this month has been moder-ate: it was then so hot, I was not able to endure it; I was miserable every moment, and found myself disposed to be peevish and quarrelsome; I believe a very hot country would make me stark mad.——Yes, my head continues pretty tolerable, and I impute it all to walking. Does *Stella* eat fruit? I eat a little; but I always repent, and resolve against it. No, in very hot weather I always go to town by water; but I constantly walk back, for then the sun is down. And so Mrs. *Proby* goes with you to *Wexford*; she's admir-able company: you'll grow plaguy wise with those you fre-quent. Mrs. *Taylor*, and Mrs. *Proby*; take care of infection.

I believe my two hundred pounds will be paid; but that Sir *Alexander Cairnes* is a scrupulous puppy: I left the bill with Mr. *Stratford*, who is to have the money. Now, madam *Stella*, what say you? you ride every day; I know that already, sirrah; and if you rid every day for a twelvemonth, you would be still better and better. No, I hope *Parvisol* will not have the impudence to make you stay an hour for the money; if he does, I'll un-parvisol him; pray let me know. O Lord, how hasty we are, *Stella* can't stay writing and writing; she must write and go a cock-horse, pray now. Well; but the horses are not come to the door; the fellow can't find the bridle; your stirrup is broken; where did you put the whips, *Dingley*? *Marg'et*, where have you laid Mrs. *Johnson's* ribband to tie about her? reach me my mask: sup up this before you go. So, so, a gallop, a gallop: sit fast, sirrah, and don't ride hard upon the stones.——Well, now *Stella* is gone, tell me, *Dingley*, is she a good girl? and what news is that you are to tell me?—No, I believe the box is not lost: *Sterne* says, it is not.—No faith, you must go to *Wexford* without seeing your duke of *Ormond*, unless you stay on purpose; perhaps you may be so wise.—I tell you this is your sixteenth letter; will you never be satisfied? No, no, I'll walk late no more; I ought less to venture it than other people, and so I was told: but I'll return to lodge in town next *Thursday*. When you come from *Wexford* I would have you send a letter of attorney to Mr. *Benjamin Tooke*, bookseller in *London*, directed to me; and he shall manage your affair. I have your parchment safely lockt up in *London*.—O madam *Stella*, welcome home; was it pleasant riding? did your horse stumble? how often did the man light to settle your stirrup? ride nine miles? faith you have galloped indeed. Well, but where's the fine thing you promised me? I have been a good boy, ask *Dingley* else. I believe you did not meet the fine-thing-man: faith you are a cheat. So you'll see *Raymond* and his wife in town. Faith that riding to *Laracor* gives me short sighs, as well as you. All the days I have passed here, have been dirt to those: I have been gaining enemies by the scores, and friends by the couples, which is against the rules of wisdom; because they say, one enemy can do more hurt, than ten friends can do good. But I have had my revenge at least, if I get nothing else. And so let *Fate* govern.—Now I think your letter is answered; and mine will be shorter than ordinary, because it must go to-day. We have had a great deal of scattering rain for some days past, yet it hardly keeps down the dust. —We have plays acted in our town, and *Patrick* was at one of them, oh ho. He was damnably mauled one day when he was drunk; he was at cuffs with a brother footman, who dragged him along the floor upon his face, which lookt for a week after as if he had the leprosy; and I was glad enough to see it. I have been ten times sending him over to you; yet now he has new cloaths, and a laced hat, which the hatter brought by his orders, and he offered to pay for the lace out of his wages.—I am to dine to-day with *Dilly* at Sir *Andrew Fountain's,* who has bought a new house, and will be weary of it in half a year. I must rise and shave, and walk to town, unless I go with the dean in his chariot at twelve, which is too late: and I have not seen that lord *Peterborow* yet. The duke of *Shrewsbury* is almost well again, and will be abroad in a day or two: what care you? There it is now; you don't care for my friends. Farewel, my dearest lives, and delights, I love you better than ever, if possible, as hope saved, I do, and ever will. God Almighty bless you ever, and make us happy together; I pray for this twice every day; and I hope God will hear my poor hearty prayers.—Remember if I am used ill and ungratefully, as I have formerly been, 'tis what I am prepared for, and shall not wonder at it. Yet, I am now envied, and thought in high favour, and have every day numbers of considerable men teazing me to solicit for them. And the ministry all use me perfectly well, and all that know them, say they love me. Yet I can count upon nothing, nor will, but upon *MD's* love and kindness—They think me useful; they pretended they were afraid of none but me; and that they resolved to have me; they have often confessed this: yet all makes little impression on me.—Pox of these speculations! They give me the spleen; and that is a disease I was not born to. Let me alone, sirrahs, and be satisfied: I am, as long as *MD* and

Presto are well: Little wealth, And much health, And a life by stealth: that is all we want; and so farewel, dearest *MD*; *Stella*, *Dingley*, *Presto* all together, now and for ever all together. Farewel again and again.

[*From* LETTER XXV.]

London. July 9. 1711.

. . . I WAS at *Bateman's* the bookseller's, to see a fine old library he has bought; and my fingers itched, as yours would do at a china-shop; but I resisted, and found every thing too dear, and I have fooled away too much money that way already. So go and drink your waters, saucy rogue, and make your self well; and pray walk while you are there: I have a notion there is never a good walk in *Ireland*. Do you find all places without trees? Pray observe the inhabitants about *Wexford*; they are old *English*; see what they have particular in their manners, names and language: magpies have been always there, and no where else in *Ireland*, till of late years. They say the cocks and dogs go to sleep at noon, and so do the people. Write your travels, and bring home good eyes, and health.

[*From* LETTER XXVI.]

London. July 21. 22. 1711.

I DINED yesterday with lord treasurer, who would needs take me along with him to *Windsor*, although I refused him several times, having no linen, &c. I had just time to desire lord *Forbes* to call at my lodging, and order my man to send my things to-day to *Windsor* by his servant. I lay last night at the secretary's lodgings at *Windsor*, and borrowed one of his shirts to go to court in. The queen is very well. I dined with Mr. *Masham*; and not hearing any thing of my things, I got lord *Winchelsea* to bring me to town. Here I found that *Patrick* had broke open the closet to get my linen and night-gown, and sent them to *Windsor*, and there they are; and he not thinking I would return so soon, is gone upon his rambles: so here I am left destitute. and forced to borrow a night-gown of my landlady, and have not a rag to put on to-morrow: faith, it gives me the spleen.

July 24. [1711].

I dined to-day with a hedge friend in the city; and *Walls* overtook me in the street, and told me he was just getting on horseback for *Chester*. He has as much curiosity as a cow: he lodged with his horse in *Aldersgate-street*: he has bought his wife a silk gown, and himself a hat. And what are you doing? what is poor *MD* doing now? how do you pass your time at *Wexford*? how do the waters agree with you? Let *Presto* know soon; for *Presto* longs to know, and must know. Is not madam *Proby* curious company? I am afraid this rainy weather will spoil your waters. We have had a great deal of wet these three days. Tell me all the particulars of *Wexford*; the place, the company, the diversions, the victuals, the wants, the vexations. Poor *Dingley* never saw such a place in her life; sent all over the town for a little parsley to a boiled chicken, and it was not to be had: the butter is stark naught, except an old *English* woman's; and it is such a favour to get a pound from her now and then. I am glad you carried down your sheets with you, else you must have lain in sackcloth. O Lord!

July 27. [1711].

I dined to-day in the city, and saw poor *Patty Rolt*, and gave her a pistole to help her a little forward against she goes to board in the country. She has but eighteen pounds a year to live on, and is forced to seek out for cheap places. Sometimes they raise their price, and sometimes they starve her, and then she is forced to shift. *Patrick* the puppy put too much ink in my standish, and carrying too many things together, I spilled it on my paper and floor. The town is dull, and wet and empty: *Wexford* is worth two of it; I hope so at least, and that poor little *MD* finds it so. I reckon upon going to *Windsor* to-morrow with Mr. secretary, unless he changes his mind, or some other business prevents him. I shall stay there a week, I hope.

Windsor. July 31. [1711].

I have sent a noble haunch of venison this afternoon to Mrs. *Vanhomrigh*: I wish you had it, sirrahs: I dined gravely with my landlord the secretary. The queen was abroad to-day in order to hunt, but finding it disposed to rain, she kept in her coach: she hunts in a chaise with one horse, which she drives herself, and drives furiously, like *Jehu*, and is a mighty hunter, like *Nimrod*. *Dingley* has heard of *Nimrod*, but not *Stella*, for it is in the *Bible*. I was to-day at *Eton*, which is but just cross the bridge, to see my lord *Kerry's* son, who is at school there. Mr. secretary has given me a warrant for a buck; I can't send it to *MD*? It is a sad thing faith, considering how *Presto* loves *MD*, and how *MD* would love *Presto's* venison for *Presto's* sake. God bless the two dear *Wexford* girls.

August 4. 5. [1711].

I dined yesterday at *Buckleberry*, where we lay two nights, and set out this morning at eight, and were here at twelve, in four hours we went twenty-six miles. Mr. secretary was a perfect country gentleman at *Buckleberry*; he smoakt tobacco with one or two neighbours; he enquired after the wheat in such a field; he went to visit his hounds; and knew all their names; he and his lady saw me to my chamber just in the country fashion. His house is in the midst of near three thousand pounds a year he had by his lady, who is descended from *Jack* [of] *Newbury*, of whom books and ballads are written; and there is an old picture of him in the house. She is a great favourite of mine. I lost church to-day; but I dressed, and shaved, and went to *Court*, and would not dine with the secretary, but engaged myself to a private dinner with Mr. *Lewis*, and one friend more. We go to *London* to-morrow; for lord *Dartmouth*, the other secretary, is come, and they are here their weeks by turns.

August 8. [1711].

There was a drawing-room to-day at *Court*; but so few company, that the queen sent for us into her bed-chamber.

where we made our bows, and stood about twenty of us round the room, while she looked at us round with her fan in her mouth, and once a minute said about three words to some that were nearest her, and then she was told dinner was ready, and went out. I dined at the green-cloth, by Mr. *Scarborow's* invitation, who is in waiting. It is much the best table in *England*, and costs the queen a thousand pounds a month while she is at *Windsor* or *Hampton-Court*; and is the only mark of magnificence or hospitality I can see in the queen's family: it is designed to entertain foreign ministers, and people of quality, who come to see the queen, and have no place to dine at.

[*From* LETTER XXVII.]

London. August 15. 1711.

I DINED to-day with Mrs. *Van*, who goes to-night to her new lodgings. I went at six to see lord treasurer, but his company was gone, contrary to custom, and he was busy, and I was forced to stay some time before I could see him. We were together hardly an hour, and he went away, being in haste. He desired me to dine with him on *Friday*, because there would be a friend of his that I must see: my lord *Harley* told me when he was gone, that it was Mrs. *Masham* his father meant, who is come to town to lie-in, and whom I never saw, though her husband is one of our *Society*. God send her a good time; her death would be a terrible thing.— Do you know, that I have ventured all my credit with these great ministers, to clear some misunderstandings betwixt them; and if there be no breach, I ought to have the merit of it? 'Tis a plaguy ticklish piece of work, and a man hazards losing both sides. 'Tis a pity the world does not know my virtue.—I thought the clergy in convocation in *Ireland* would have given me thanks for being their solicitor, but I hear of no such thing. Pray talk occasionally on that subject, and let me know what you hear. Do you know the greatness of my spirit, that I value their thanks not a rush? but at my return shall freely let all people know, that it was my lord treasurer's action, wherein the duke of *Ormond* had no more share than a cat. And so they may go whistle, and I'll go sleep.

August 24. [1711].

I dined to-day with lord treasurer, who chid me for not dining with him yesterday; for it seems I did not understand his invitation: and their *Club* of the ministry dined together, and expected me. Lord *Radnor* and I were walking the *Mall* this evening; and Mr. secretary met us, and took a turn or two, and then stole away, and we both believed it was to pick up some wench; and to-morrow he will be at the cabinet with the queen: so goes the world. *Prior* has been out of town these two months, nobody knows where, and is lately returned. People confidently affirm he has been in *France*, and I half believe it. It is said, he was sent by the ministry, and for some overtures towards a Peace. The secretary pretends he knows nothing of it. I believe your parliament will be dissolved. I have been talking about the quarrel between your lords and commons with lord treasurer; and did, at the request of some people, desire that the queen's answer to the commons address might express a dislike of some principles, &c, but was answered dubiously. —And so now to your letter, fair ladies. I know drinking is bad; I mean writing is bad in drinking the waters; and was angry to see so much in *Stella's* hand. But why *Dingley* drinks them I cannot imagine; but truly she'll drink waters as well as *Stella*: why not? I hope you now find the benefit of them since you are returned: pray let me know particularly. I am glad you are forced upon exercise, which, I believe, is as good as the waters for the heart of them. 'Tis now past the middle of *August*; so by your reckoning you are in *Dublin*. It would vex me to the dogs that letters should miscarry between *Dublin* and *Wexford*, after scaping the salt seas. I will write no more [to] that nasty town in haste again, I warrant you. I have been four *Sundays* together at *Windsor*, of which a fortnight together; but I believe I shall not go to-morrow; for I will not, unless the secretary asks me. I know all about your news about the mayor: it makes no noise here at all, but the quarrel of your parliament does; it is so very extraordinary, and the language

of the commons so very pretty. The *Examiner* has been
down this month, and was very silly the five or six last
papers; but there is a pamphlet come out, in answer to a
letter to the seven lords who examined *Gregg*. The *Answer*
is by the real author of the *Examiner*, as I believe; for it
is very well written. We had *Trap's* poem on the duke of
Ormond printed here, and the printer sold just eleven of
them. 'Tis a dull piece, not half so good as *Stella's*; and she
is very modest to compare herself with such a poetaster.
I am heartily sorry for poor Mrs. *Parnel's* death; she seemed
to be an excellent good-natured young woman, and I believe
the poor lad is much afflicted: they appeared to live perfectly well together. *Dilly* is not tired at all with *England*,
but intends to continue here a good while: he is mighty
easy to be at distance from his two sisters-in-law. He finds
some sort of scrub acquaintance; goes now and then in disguise to a play; smoaks his pipe; reads now and then a little
trash, and what else the Lord knows. I see him now and
then; for he calls here, and the town being thin, I am less
pestered with company than usual. I have got rid of many
of my solicitors, by doing nothing for them: I have not
above eight or nine left, and I'll be as kind to them. Did
I tell you of a knight, who desired me to speak to lord
treasurer to give him two thousand pounds, or five hundred pounds a year, until he could get something better? I
honestly delivered my message to the treasurer, adding, The
knight was a puppy, whom I would not give a groat to save
from the gallows. *Cole, Reading's* father-in-law has been
two or three times at me to recommend his Lights to the
ministry; assuring me, that a word of mine would, &c. Did
not that dog use to speak ill of me, and profess to hate me?
He knows not where I lodge, for I told him I lived in the
country; and I have ordered *Patrick* to deny me constantly
to him.—Did the bishop of *London* die in *Wexford*? poor
gentleman! Did he drink the waters? Were you at his
burial? Was it a great funeral? So far from his friends?
But he was very old: we shall all follow. And yet it was a
pity, if God pleased. He was a good man; not very learned:
I believe he died but poor. Did he leave any charity lega-

cies? Who held up his pall? Was there a great sight of clergy? Do they design a tomb for him? Are you sure it was the bishop of *London*? because there is an elderly gentleman here that we give the same title to: or did you fancy all this in your water, as others do strange things in their wine? They say, these waters trouble the head, and make people imagine what never came to pass. Do you make no more of killing a bishop? Are these your whiggish tricks?—Yes, yes, I see you are in a fret. Oh faith, says you, saucy *Presto*, I'll break your head; what, can't one report what one hears, without being made a jest and a laughing-stock? Are these your *English* tricks, with a murrain? And *Sacheverell* will be the next bishop? He would be glad of an addition of two hundred pounds a year to what he has; and that is more than they will give him, for aught I see. He hates the new ministry mortally, and they hate him, and pretend to despise him too. They will not allow him to have been the occasion of the late change; at least some of them will not: but my lord keeper owned it to me t'other day. No, Mr. *Addison* does not go to *Ireland* this year: he pretended he would; but he is gone to *Bath* with Pastoral *Philips*, for his eyes.—So now I have run over your letter; and I think this shall go to-morrow, which will be just a fortnight from the last, and bring things to the old form again after your rambles to *Wexford*, and mine to *Windsor*. Are there not many literal faults in my letters? I never read them over, and I fancy there are. What do you do then? do you guess my meaning; or are you acquainted with my manner of mistaking? I lost my handkerchief in the *Mall* to-night with lord *Radnor*: but I made him walk with me to find it, and find it I did not. *Tisdall* (that lodges with me) and I have had no conversation, nor do we pull off our hats in the streets. There is a cousin of his (I suppose) a young parson, that lodges in the house too; a handsome genteel fellow. *Dick Tighe* and his wife lodged over-against us; and he has been seen, out of our upper windows, beating her two or three times: they are both gone to *Ireland*, but not together; and he solemnly vows never to live with her. Neighbours do not stick to say, that she has a tongue: in short, I am told, she is the most urging provoking devil that ever was born; and he a hot whiffling puppy, very apt to resent. I'll keep this bottom till to-morrow: I'm sleepy.

August 25. [1711].

I was with the secretary this morning, who was in a mighty hurry, and went to *Windsor* in a chariot with lord keeper; so I was not invited, and am forced to stay at home; but not at all against my will; for I could have gone, and would not. I dined in the city with one of my printers, for whom I got the *Gazette*, and am come home early; and have nothing to say to you more, but finish this letter, and not send it by the bell-man. Days grow short, and the weather grows bad, and the town is splenetick, and things are so oddly contrived, that I cannot be absent; otherwise I would go for a few days to *Oxford*, as I promised.—They say, 'tis certain that *Prior* has been in *France*; nobody doubts it: I had not time to ask the secretary, he was in such haste. Well, I will take my leave of dearest *MD* for a while; for I must begin my next letter to-night: consider that, young women; and pray be merry, and good girls, and love *Presto*. There is now but one business the ministry wants me for; and when that is done I will take my leave of them. I never got a penny from them, nor expect it. In my opinion, some things stand very ticklish; I dare say nothing at this distance. Farewell, dear sirrahs, dearest lives: there is peace and quiet with *MD*, and nowhere else. They have not leisure here to think of small things, which may ruin them; and I have been forward enough. Farewel again, dearest rogues; I am never happy, but when I write or think of *MD*. I have enough of *Courts* and ministries; and wish I were at *Laracor*: and if I could with honour come away this moment, I would. *Bernage* came to see me to-day; he is just landed from *Portugal*, and come to raise recruits: he looks very well, and seems pleased with his station and manner of life: he never saw *London* nor *England* before; he is ravished with *Kent*, which was his first prospect when he landed. Farewel again, &c, &c.

[*From* LETTER XXVIII.]

z

London. Sept. 1. 1711.

MORNING. I go to-day to *Windsor* with Mr. secretary; and lord treasurer has promised to bring me back. The weather has been fine for some time, and I believe we shall have a great deal of dust.—At night. *Windsor.* The secretary and I and brigadier *Sutton* dined to-day at *Parson's-Green*, at my lord *Peterborow's* house, who has left it and his gardens to the secretary during his absence. It is the finest garden I have ever seen about this town, and abundance of hot walls for grapes, where they are in great plenty, and ripening fast. I durst not eat any fruit, but one fig; but I brought a basket full to my friend *Lewis* here at *Windsor*. Does *Stella* never eat any? what, no apricocks at *Donnybrook*? nothing but claret and ombre? I envy people maunching and maunching peaches and grapes, and I not daring to eat a bit. My head is pretty well, only a sudden turn any time makes me giddy for a moment, and sometimes it feels very stufft; but if it grows no worse, I can bear it very well. I take all opportunities of walking; and we have a delicious park here just joining to the castle, and an avenue in the great park very wide and two miles long, set with a double row of elms on each side. Were you ever at *Windsor*? I was once a great while ago; but had quite forgotten it.

Sept. 8. [1711].

Morning. I go to *Windsor* with lord treasurer to-day, and will leave this behind me to be sent to the post. And now let us hear what says the first letter, *N.*19. You are still at *Wexford*, as you say, madam *Dingley*. I think no letter from me ever yet miscarried. And so *Inish-Corthy*, and the river *Slainy*; fine words those in a lady's mouth. Your hand like *Dingley's*, you scambling, scattering sluttekin? *Yes, mighty like indeed, is not it?* Pisshh, don't talk of writing or reading till your eyes are well, and long well; only I would have *Dingley* read sometimes to you, that you may not quite lose the desire of it. God be thanked that the ugly numming is gone. Pray use exercise when you go to town. What game is that ombra which Dr. *Elwood* and you play at? is it the

Spanish game ombre? Your card purse? you a card purse! you a fiddlestick. You have luck indeed; and luck in a bag. What a Devil is that eight shilling tea-kettle? copper or tin japanned? It is like your *Irish* politeness, raffling for tea-kettles. What a splutter you keep to convince me that *Walls* has no taste? My head continues pretty well. Why do you write, dear sirrah *Stella*, when you find your eyes so weak that you cannot see? what comfort is there in reading what you write, when one knows that? So *Dingley* can't write because of the clutter of new company come to *Wexford*? I suppose the noise of their hundred horses disturbs you; or, do you lie in one gallery, as in an hospital? What; you are afraid of losing in *Dublin* the acquaintance you have got in *Wexford*; and chiefly the bishop of *Rapho*, an old, doating, perverse coxcomb? Twenty at a time at breakfast. That is like five pounds at a time, when it was never but once. I doubt, madam *Dingley*, you are apt to lie in your Travels, though not so bad as *Stella*; she tells thumpers, as I shall prove in my next, if I find this receives encouragement.—So, Dr. *Elwood* says, There are a world of pretty things in my Works. A pox on his praises! an enemy here would say more. The duke of *Buckingham* would say as much, though he and I are terribly fallen out; and the great men are perpetually inflaming me against him: they bring me all he says of me, and, I believe, make it worse out of roguery.—No, 'tis not your pen is bewitched, madam *Stella*, but your old *scrawling*, *splay-foot* pot-hooks, s, ʃ, aye, that's it: there the s, ʃ, ʃ, there, there, that's exact. Farewel, &c.

Our fine weather is gone, and I doubt we shall have a rainy journey to-day. Faith, 'tis shaving day, and I have much to do.

When *Stella* says her pen was bewitched, it was only because there was a hair in it. You know the fellow they call God-help-it had the same thoughts of his wife, and for the same reason. I think this is very well observed, and I unfolded the letter to tell you it.

Cut off those two notes above; and see the nine pounds indorsed, and receive the other; and send me word how my accounts stand, that they may be adjusted by *Nov.* 1. Pray be very particular: but the twenty pounds I lend you is not to be included; so make no blunder. I won't wrong you; nor you shan't wrong me; that's the short. O Lord, how stout *Presto* is of late? But he loves *MD* more than his life a thousand times, for all his stoutness; tell him that; and that I'll swear it, as hope saved, ten millions of times, &c. &c.

I open my letter once more to tell *Stella*, that if she does not use exercise after her waters, it will lose all the effects of them: I should not live, if I did not take all opportunities of walking. Pray, pray do this to oblige poor *Presto*.]

[*From* LETTER XXIX.

Windsor. Oct. 3. 1711.

MR. MASHAM sent this morning to desire I would ride out with him, the weather growing again very fine: I was very busy, and sent my excuses; but desired he would provide me a dinner: I dined with him, his lady, and her sister, Mrs. *Hill*, who invites us to-morrow to dine with her, and we are to ride out in the morning. I sat with lady *Oglethorp* till eight this evening, then was going home to write; looked about for the woman that keeps the key of the house; she told me *Patrick* had it. I cooled my heels in the cloisters till nine, then went into the musick-meeting, where I had been often desired to go; but was weary in half an hour of their fine stuff, and stole out so privately that every body saw me; and cooled my heels in the cloisters again till after ten: then came in *Patrick*. I went up, shut the chamber-door, and gave him two or three swinging cuffs on the ear, and I have strained the thumb of my left hand with pulling him, which I did not feel until he was gone. He was plaguily afraid and humbled.

[*From* LETTER XXXI.]

London. Oct. 10. 1711.

IT cost me two shillings in coach-hire to dine in the city with a printer. I have sent, and caused to be sent, three pamphlets out in a fortnight. I will ply the rogues warm, and whenever any thing of theirs makes a noise, it shall have an answer. I have instructed an under-spur-leather to write so, that it is taken for mine. A rogue that writes a news-paper called *The Protestant Post-boy*, has reflected on me in one of his papers; but the secretary has taken him up, and he shall have a squeeze extraordinary. He says, that an ambitious *Tantivy*, missing of his towering hopes of preferment in *Ireland*, is come over to vent his spleen on the late ministry, &c. I'll *Tantivy* him with a vengeance. I sat the evening at home, and am very busy, and can hardly find time to write, unless it were to *MD*. I am in furious haste.

Oct. 11. [1711].

I dined to-day with lord treasurer. *Thursdays* are now his days when his choice company comes, but we are too much multiplied. *George Granville* sent his excuses upon being ill; I hear he apprehends the apoplexy, which would grieve me much. Lord treasurer calls *Prior* nothing but *Monsieur Baudrier*, which was the feigned name of the *Frenchman* that writ his journey to *Paris*. They pretend to suspect me, so I talk freely of it, and put them out of their play. Lord treasurer calls me now Dr. *Martin*, because *Martin* is a sort of a swallow, and so is a *Swift*. When he and I came last *Monday* from *Windsor*, we were reading all the signs on the road. He is a pure trifler; tell the bishop of *Clogher* so. I made him make two lines in verse for the *Bell and Dragon*, and they were rare bad ones. I suppose *Dilly* is with you by this time: what could his reason be of leaving *London*, and not owning it? 'Twas plaguy silly. I believe his natural inconstancy made him weary; I think he is the king of inconstancy. I stayed with lord treasurer till ten; we had five lords and three commoners. Go to ombre, sirrahs.

Oct. 20. [1711].

This day has gone all wrong, by sitting up so late last night. Lord treasurer is not yet well, and can't go to *Windsor*. I dined with Sir *Matthew Dudley*, and took occasion to hint to him that he would lose his employment, for which I am very sorry. Lord *Pembroke* and his family are all come to town. I was kept so long at a friend's this evening, that I cannot send this to-night. When I knocked at my lodgings, a fellow asked me where lodged Dr. *Swift*? I told him, I was the person: he gave me a letter he brought from the secretary's office, and I gave him a shilling: when I came up, I saw *Dingley's* hand: faith I was afraid, I do not know what. At last it was a formal letter from *Dingley* about her exchequer business. Well, I'll do it on *Monday*, and settle it with *Tooke*. And now, boys, for your letter, I mean the first, *N*.21. Let's see; come out, little letter.— I never had the letter from the bishop that *Raymond* mentions; but I have written to *Ned Southwel*, to desire the duke of *Ormond* to speak to his reverence that he may leave off his impertinence. What a pox can they think I am doing for the archbishop here? You have a pretty notion of me in *Ireland*, to make me an agent for the archbishop of *Dublin*.—Why; do you think I value your people's ingratitude about my part in serving them? I remit them their *First-Fruits* of Ingratitude, as freely as I got the other remitted to them. This lord treasurer defers writing his letter to them, or else they would be plaguily confounded by this time. For, he designs to give the merit of it wholly to the queen and me, and to let them know it was done before the duke of *Ormond* was lord lieutenant. You visit, you dine abroad, you see friends; you pilgarlick; you walk from *Finglass*, you a cat's foot. O Lord—Lady *Gore* hung her child by the waist; what is that *waist*, I don't understand the word; he must hang on till you explain or spell it.—I don't believe he was pretty, that's a liiii.—Pish; burn your *First-Fruits*; again at it. *Stella* has made twenty false spellings in her writing; I'll send them to you all back again on the other side of this letter, to mend them; I won't miss one. Why; I think there were seventeen bishops names to the letter lord *Oxford* received.—I will send you some pamphlets by *Leigh*; put me in mind of it on *Monday*, for I shall go then to the printer; yes, and the *Miscellany*. I am mightily obliged to *Walls*, but I don't deserve it by any

usage of him here, having seen him but twice, and once
en passant. Mrs. *Manley* forsworn ombre! What; and no
blazing star appear? no monsters born? no whale thrown
up? Have you not found out some evasion for her? She
had no such regard to oaths in her younger days. I got the
books for nothing, madam *Dingley*; but the wine I got not;
it was but a promise.—Yes, my head is pretty well in the
main, only now and then a little threatning or so.—You
talk of my reconciling some great folks. I tell you what.
The secretary told me last night, that he had found the
reason why the queen was cold to him for some months
past; that a friend had told it him yesterday; and it was,
that they suspected he was at the bottom with the duke of
Marlborough. Then he said, he had reflected upon all I had
spoken to him long ago; but he thought it had been only
my suspicion, and my zeal and kindness for him. I said I
had reason to take that very ill, to imagine I knew so little
of the world as to talk at a venture to a great minister;
that I had gone between him and lord treasurer often, and
told each of them what I had said to the other, and that I
had informed him so before; he said all that you may imagine to excuse himself, and approve my conduct. I told
him, I knew all along, that this proceeding of mine was the
surest way to send me back to my willows in *Ireland*, but
that I regarded it not, provided I could do the kingdom
service in keeping them well together. I minded him how
often I had told lord treasurer, lord keeper, and him together, that all things depended on their union, and that my
comfort was to see them love one another; and I had told
them all singly, that I had not said this by chance, &c. He
was in a rage to be thus suspected; swears he will be upon a
better foot, or none at all; and I do not see, how they can
well want him in this juncture. I hope to find a way of
settling this matter. I act an honest part; that will bring me
neither profit nor praise. *MD* must think the better of me
for it: nobody else shall ever know it. Here's politicks
enough for once; but madam *D.D.* gave me occasion for it.
I think I told you I have got into lodgings that don't smell
ill—O Lord! the spectacles: well, I'll do that on *Monday*

too; although it goes against me to be employed for folks that neither you nor I care a groat for. Is the eight pounds from *Hawkshaw* included in the thirty-nine pounds five shillings and two-pence? How do I know by this how my account stands? Can't you write five or six lines to cast it up? Mine is forty-four pounds *per annum*, and eight pounds from *Hawkshaw* makes fifty-two pounds. Pray set it right, and let me know; you had best.—And so now I have answered *N*.21, and 'tis late, and I will answer *N*.22 in my next: this cannot go to-night, but shall on *Tuesday*: and so go to your play, and lose your money, with your two eggs a penny; silly jade; you witty? very pretty.

Oct. 22. [1711].

I dined in the city to-day with Dr. *Freind*, at one of my printers; I enquired for *Leigh*, but could not find him: I have forgot what sort of apron you want. I must rout among your letters, a needle in a bottle of hay. I gave *Sterne* directions, but where to find him Lord knows. I have bespoken the spectacles; got a set of *Examiners*, and five pamphlets, which I have either written or contributed to, except the best, which is the *Vindication of the duke of Marlborough*; and is entirely of the author of the *Atalantis*. I have settled *Dingley's* affair with *Tooke*, who has undertaken it, and understands it. I have bespoken a *Miscellany*: what would you have me do more? It cost me a shilling coming home; it rains terribly, and did so in the morning. Lord treasurer has had an ill day, in much pain. He writes and does business in his chamber now he is ill: the man is bewitched; he desires to see me, and I'll maul him, but he will not value it a rush.——I am half weary of them all. I often burst out into these thoughts, and will certainly steal away as soon as I decently can. I have many friends, and many enemies; and the last are more constant in their nature. I have no shuddering at all to think of retiring to my old circumstances, if you can be easy; but I will always live in *Ireland* as I did the last time; I will not hunt for dinners there; nor converse with more than a very few.

Oct. 23. [1711].

... Here is a full and true account of *Stella*'s new spelling.

Plaguely,	— Plaguily.	A bout,	— About.
Dineing,	— Dining.	Intellegence,	— Intelligence.
Straingers,	— Strangers.	Aboundance,	— Abundance.
Chais,	— Chase.	Merrit,	— Merit.
Waist,	— Wast.	Secreet,	— Secret.
Houer,	— Hour.	Phamphlets,	— Pamphlets.
Immagin,	— Imagine.	Bussiness,	— Business.

Tell me truly, sirrah, how many of these are mistakes of the pen, and how many are you to answer for as real ill spelling? There are but fourteen; I said twenty by guess. You must not be angry, for I will have you spell right, let the world go how it will. Though after all, there is but a mistake of one letter in any of these words. I allow you henceforth but six false spellings in every letter you send me.

[*From* LETTER XXXII.]

London. Nov. 2. 1711.

IT has rained all day with a *continuendo*, and I went in a chair to dine with Mrs. *Van*; always there in a very rainy day. But I made a shift to come back afoot. I live a very retired life, pay very few visits, and keep but very little company; I read no news-papers. I am sorry I sent you the *Examiner*; for the printer is going to print them in a small volume; it seems the author is too proud to have them printed by subscription, though his friends offered, they say, to make it worth five hundred pounds to him. The *Spectators* are likewise printing in a larger and a smaller volume: so I believe they are going to leave them off, and indeed people grow weary of them, though they are often prettily written. We have had no news for me to send you now towards the end of my letter. The queen has the gout a little; I hoped the lord treasurer would have had it too; but *Radcliffe* told me yesterday it was the rheumatism in his knee and foot; however he mends, and I hope will be abroad in a short time. I am told they design giving away several employments before the parliament sits, which will be the thirteenth instant. I either do not like, or not understand this policy; and if lord treasurer does not mend soon, they must give them just before the sessions. But he is the greatest procrastinator in the world.

[*From* LETTER XXXIII.]

London. Nov. 9. 1711.

I DESIGNED a jaunt into the city to-day to be merry, but was disappointed; so one always is in this life; and I could not see lord *Dartmouth* to-day, with whom I had some business. Business and pleasure both disappointed. You can go to your dean, and for want of him, goody *Stoyte*, or *Walls*, or *Manley*, and meet every where with cards and claret. I dined privately with a friend on a herring and chicken, and half a flask of bad *Florence*. I begin to have fires now, when the mornings are cold; I have got some loose bricks at the back of my grate for good husbandry. Fine weather. *Patrick* tells me, my caps are wearing out; I know not how to get others. I want a necessary woman strangely; I am as helpless as an elephant.——I had three pacquets from the archbishop of *Dublin*, cost me four shillings, all about *Higgins*, printed stuff, and two long letters. His people forget to enclose them to *Lewis*; and they were only directed to Doctor *Swift*, without naming *London* or any thing else: I wonder how they reached me, unless the post-master directed them. I have read all the trash, and am weary.

Nov. 13. [1711].

I dined privately with a friend to-day in the neighbourhood. Last *Saturday* night I came home, and the drab had just washed my room, and my bed-chamber was all wet, and I was forced to go to bed in my own defence, and no fire: I was sick on *Sunday*, and now have got a swinging cold. I scolded like a dog at *Patrick*, although he was out with me: I detest washing of rooms: can't they wash them in a morning, and make a fire, and leave open the windows? I slept not a wink last night for hawking and spitting: and now every body has colds. Here's a clutter: I'll go to bed and sleep if I can.

[*From* LETTER XXXIV.]

London. Dec. 1. 1711.

PISH, sirrahs, put a date always at the bottom of the letter as well as the top, that I may know when you send it; your last is of *Nov.* 3d, yet I had others at the same time written a fortnight after. Whenever you would have any money, send me word three weeks before, and in that time you will certainly have an answer, with a bill on *Parvisol*: pray do this; for my head is full, and it will ease my memory. Why, I think I quoted you some of ——'s letter, so you may imagine how witty the rest was; for it was all of a bunch, as goodman *Peesley* says. Pray let us have no more *Bussiness*, but *Busyness*: the Deuse take me if I know how to spell it, your wrong spelling, madam *Stella*, has put me out: it does not look right; let me see, *Bussiness*, *Busyness*, *Business*, *Bisyness*, *Bisness*, *Bysness*; faith, I know not which is right, I think the second; I believe I never writ the word in my life before; yes, sure I must though; *Business*, *Busyness*, *Bisyness*.—I have perplexed myself, and can't do it. Prithee ask *Walls*. *Business*, I fancy that's right. Yes it is; I looked in my own pamphlet, and found it twice in ten lines, to convince you that I never writ it before. Oh, now I see it as plain as can be; so yours is only an *s* too much. The parliament will certainly meet on *Friday* next; the *Whigs* will have a great majority in the house of lords; no care is taken to prevent it; there is too much neglect; they are warned of it, and that signifies nothing: it was feared there would be some peevish address from the lords against a Peace. 'Tis said about the town, that several of the allies begin now to be content that a Peace should be treated. This is all the news I have. The queen is pretty well; and so now I bid poor dearest *MD* farewel till to-night, then I will talk with them again.

The fifteen images that I saw were not worth forty pounds, so I stretched a little when I said a thousand. The *Grub-street* account of that tumult is published. The *Devil* is not like lord treasurer; they were all in your odd antick masks, bought in common shops. I fear *Prior* will not be one of the plenipotentiaries.

I was looking over some of this letter, and find I make many mistakes of leaving out words; so 'tis impossible to find my meaning, unless you be conjurers. I will take more care for the future, and read over every day just what I have written that day; which will take up no time to speak of.]

[*From* LETTER XXXV.

London. Dec. 8. 1711.

I WAS early this morning with the secretary, and talkt over this matter. He hoped, that when it was reported this day in the house of lords, they would disagree with their committee, and so the matter would go off, only with a little loss of reputation to lord treasurer. I dined with Dr. *Cockburn*, and after a *Scotch* member came in, and told us that the clause was carried against the *Court* in the house of lords almost two to one; I went immediately to Mrs. *Masham*, and meeting Dr. *Arbuthnott* (the queen's favourite physician) we went together. She was just come from waiting at the queen's dinner, and going to her own. She had heard nothing of the thing being gone against us. It seems lord treasurer had been so negligent, that he was with the queen while the question was put in the house: I immediately told Mrs. *Masham*, that either she and lord treasurer had joined with the queen to betray us, or that they two were betrayed by the queen: she protested solemnly it was not the former, and I believed her; but she gave me some lights to suspect the queen is changed. For, yesterday when the queen was going from the house, where she sat to hear the debate, the duke of *Shrewsbury* lord chamberlain asked her, whether he or the great chamberlain *Lindsay* ought to lead her out; she answered short, Neither of you, and gave her hand to the duke of *Somerset*, who was louder than any in the house for the clause against Peace. She gave me one or two more instances of this sort, which convince me that the queen is false, or at least very much wavering. Mr.

Masham begged us to stay, because lord treasurer would call, and we were resolved to fall on him about his negligence in securing a majority. He came, and appeared in good humour as usual, but I thought his countenance was much cast down. I rallied him, and desired him to give me his staff, which he did; I told him, If he would secure it me a week, I would set all right: he asked, How? I said, I would immediately turn lord *Marlborough*, his two daughters, the duke and duchesss of *Somerset*, and lord *Cholmondely* out of all their employments; and I believe he had not a friend but was of my opinion. *Arbuthnott* asked, How he came not to secure a majority? He could answer nothing, but that he could not help it, if people would lie and forswear. A poor answer for a great minister. There fell from him a scripture expression, that *the hearts of kings are unsearchable*. I told him, It was what I feared, and was from him the worst news he could tell me. I begged him to know what we had to trust to; he stuck a little; but at last bid me not fear, for all would be well yet. We would fain have had him eat a bit where he was, but he would go home, it was past six: he made me go home with him. There we found his brother and Mr. secretary. He made his son take a list of all in the house of commons who had places, and yet voted against the *Court*, in such a manner as if they should lose their places: I doubt he is not able to compass it. Lord keeper came in an hour, and they were going upon business. So I left him, and returned to Mrs. *Masham*: but she had company with her, and I would not stay.—This is a long journal, and of a day that may produce great alterations, and hazard the ruin of *England*. The *Whigs* are all in triumph; they foretold how all this would be, but we thought it boasting. Nay, they said the parliament should be dissolved before *Christmas*, and perhaps it may: this is all your d——d duchess of *Somerset's* doings. I warned them of it nine months ago, and a hundred times since: the secretary always dreaded it. I told lord treasurer, I should have the advantage of him; for he would lose his head, and I should only be hanged, and so carry my body entire to the grave.

Dec. 9. [1711].

I was this morning with Mr. secretary; we are both of opinion that the queen is false. I told him what I heard, and he confirmed it by other circumstances. I then went to my friend *Lewis*, who had sent to see me. He talks of nothing but retiring to his estate in *Wales*. He gave me reasons to believe the whole matter is settled between the queen and the *Whigs*; he hears that lord *Somers* is to be treasurer, and believes, that sooner than turn out the duchess of *Somerset*, she will dissolve the parliament, and get a *Whiggish* one, which may be done by managing elections. Things are now in the crisis, and a day or two will determine. I have desired him to engage lord treasurer, that as soon as he finds the change is resolved on, he will send me abroad as queen's secretary somewhere or other, where I may remain till the new ministers recal me; and then I will be sick for five or six months till the storm has spent itself. I hope he will grant me this; for I should hardly trust myself to the mercy of my enemies while their anger is fresh. I dined to-day with the secretary, who affects mirth, and seems to hope all will yet be well. I took him aside after dinner, told him how I had served them, and had asked no reward, but thought I might ask security; and then desired the same thing of him, to send me abroad before a change. He embraced me, and swore he would take the same care of me as himself, &c. but bid me have courage, for that in two days my lord treasurer's wisdom would appear greater than ever; that he suffered all that had happened on purpose, and had taken measures to turn it to advantage. I said, God send it; but I do not believe a syllable; and as far as I can judge, the game is lost. I shall know more soon, and my letters will at least be a good history to shew you the steps of this change.

[*From* LETTER XXXVI.]

London. Dec. 25. 1711.

I WISH dearest *MD* a merry Christmas, and many a one; but mine is melancholy: I durst not go to church to-day, finding myself a little out of order, and it snowing prodigiously, and freezing. At noon I went to Mrs. *Van.* who had this week engaged me to dine there to-day: and there I received the news, that poor Mrs. *Long* died at *Lynn* in *Norfolk* on *Saturday* last, at four in the morning; she was sick but four hours. We suppose it was the asthma, which she was subject to as well as the dropsy, as she sent me word in her last letter, written about five weeks ago; but then said she was recovered. I never was more afflicted at any death. The poor creature had retired to *Lynn* two years ago, to live cheap, and pay her debts. In her last letter she told me she hoped to be easy by *Christmas*; and she kept her word, although she meant it otherwise. She had all sorts of amiable qualities, and no ill ones, but the indiscretion of too much neglecting her own affairs. She had two thousand pounds left her by an old grandmother, with which she intended to pay her debts, and live on an annuity she had of one hundred pounds a year, and *Newburg-house*, which would be about sixty pounds more. That odious grandmother living so long, forced her to retire; for the two thousand pounds was settled on her after the old woman's death, yet her brute of a brother, Sir *James Long*, would not advance it for her; else she might have paid her debts, and continued here, and lived still: I believe melancholy helped her on to her grave. I have ordered a paragraph to be put in the *Post-boy*, giving an account of her death, and making honourable mention of her; which is all I can do to serve her memory: but one reason was spite; for, her brother would fain have her death a secret, to save the charge of bringing her up here to bury her, or going into mourning. Pardon all this, for the sake of a poor creature I had so much friendship for.   [*From* LETTER XXXVII.]

London. Jan. 9. 1711–12.

I COULD not go sleep last night till past two, and was waked before three by a noise of people endeavouring to break open my window; for a while I would not stir, thinking it might be my imagination; but hearing the noise con-

tinued, I rise and went to the window, and then it ceased:
I went to bed again, and heard it repeated more violently;
then I rise, and called up the house, and got a candle: the
rogues had lifted up the sash a yard; there are great sheds
before my windows, although my lodgings be a story high;
and if they get upon the sheds, they are almost even with
my window. We observed their track, and panes of glass
fresh broken. The watchmen told us to-day, they saw them,
but could not catch them: they attacked others in the neighbourhood, about the same time, and actually robbed a
house in *Suffolk-Street*, which is the next street but one to
us. It is said, they are seamen discharged from service. I
went up to call my man, and found his bed empty; it seems
he often lies abroad. I challenged him this morning as one
of the robbers. He is a sad dog; and the minute I come to
Ireland I will discard him. I have this day got double iron
bars to every window in my dining-room and bed-chamber;
and I hide my purse in my thread stocking between the
bed's head and the wainscot. *Lewis* and I dined with an
old *Scotch* friend, who brought the duke of *Douglas*, and
three or four more *Scots* upon us.

[*From* LETTER XXXVIII.]

London. Feb. 8. 1711–12.

I DINED to-day in the city; this morning a scoundrel dog,
one of the queen's musick, a *German*, whom I had never
seen, got access to me in my chamber by *Patrick's* folly,
and gravely desired me to get an employment in the customs
for a friend of his, who would be very grateful; and likewise to forward a project of his own, for raising ten thousand pounds a year upon *Operas*: I used him civiller than he
deserved; but it vexed me to the pluck. He was told, I had
a mighty interest with lord treasurer, and one word of mine,
&c.——Well; I got home early on purpose to answer *MD's*
letter, *N*.26; for this goes to-morrow.——Well; I never saw
such a letter in all my life; so saucy, so journalish, so sanguine, so pretending, so every thing.——I satisfied all your
fears in my last; All is gone well, as you say; yet you are

an impudent slut to be so positive; you will swagger so upon your sagacity that we shall never have done. Pray don't mislay your reply; I would certainly print it, if I had it here: how long is it? I suppose, half a sheet: was the Answer written in *Ireland*? Yes, yes, you shall have a letter when you come from *Baligall*. I need not tell you again who's out and who's in: we can never get out the duchess of *Somerset*. —So, they say *Presto* writ the *Conduct*, &c. do they like it? I don't care whether they do or no; but the *Resolutions* printed t'other day in the Votes, are almost quotations from it; and would never have passed, if that book had not been written. I will not meddle with the *Spectator*, let him fair-sex it to the world's end. My disorder is over, but blood was not from the p—les.——Well, madam *Dingley*, the frost; why we had a great frost, but I forget how long ago; it lasted above a week or ten days: I believe about six weeks ago; but it did not break so soon with us I think as *December* 29; yet I think it was about that time, on second thoughts. *MD* can have no letter from *Presto*, says you, and yet four days before you own you had my thirty-seventh, unreasonable sluts! The bishop of *Gloucester* is not dead, and I am as likely to succeed the duke of *Marlborough* as him if he were; there's enough for that now. It is not unlikely that the duke of *Shrewsbury* will be your governour; at least I believe the duke of *Ormond* will not return.—Well, *Stella* again: why really three editions of the *Conduct*, &c, is very much for *Ireland*; it is a sign you have some honest among you.—Well; I will do Mr. *Manley* all the service I can: but he will ruin himself. What business had he to engage at all about the city? can't he wish his cause well, and be quiet, when he finds that stirring will do it no good, and himself a great deal of hurt? I cannot imagine who should open my letter; it must be done at your side.—If I hear of any thoughts of turning out Mr. *Manley*, I will endeavour to prevent it. I have already had all the gentlemen of *Ireland* here upon my back often, for defending him. So now I have answered your saucy letter. My humble service to goody *Stoyte* and *Catherine*; I will come soon for my dinner.

[*From* LETTER XL.]

[*Note : With the exception of the extract from Letter LIV, the remaining passages reproduce the text of the original manuscript.*]

London. March 12. 1711–12.

HERE is te d——— and all to do with these Mohocks, Grub-street Papers about them fly like Lightning; and a List Printed of near 80 put into severll Prisons, and all a Lye: and I begin almost to think there is no Truth or very little in te whole Story. He that chyd D'avenant was a drunken gentleman, none of that gang. My Man tells me, that one of te Lodgers heard in a Coffee-house publickly that one design of te Mohocks was upon me, if they could catch me. And tho I believe nothing of it, yet I forbear walking late, and they have put me to te Charge of some Shillings already. I dined to day with L^d.Treas^r. and two Gentlemen of te Highlands of Scotland, yet very polite men: I sate there till 9, and then went to L^d. Mashams, where L^d. Treas^r followd me, & we sate till 12, and I came home in a Chair for fear of te Mohocks, and I have given him warning of it too—little Harrison whom I sent to Holld is now actually made Qu[een']s Secty at te Hague, it will be in te Gazett to morrow, tis worth 12 hundred Pounds a Year. Here is a young Fellow has writt some Sea Eclogues, Poems of Mermen, resembling Pastorals of Shepherds, & they are very pretty, and te Thought is new. Mermen are he Mermaids: Tritons, Natives of te Sea; do y understand me. I think to recommend him to our Society to morrow. His Name is Diaper. P——— on him, I must do something for him, & get him out of te way. I hate to have any new Witts rise: but when they do rise I would encourage them. but they tred on our Heels, & thrust us off te Stage. Nite deelst Md.

[*From* LETTER XLIII.]

London. March 26. 1712.

I FORGOT to tell y that on Sunday last about 7 at night, it lightend above 50 times as I walkt te Mall wch I think is extdy at this time of te year. & te weather was very hot.

Had y any thing of this in Dublin? I intended to dine with
Ld Treas^r to day: but Ld Mansel & Mr Lewis made me
dine with them at Kit Musgrave's. Now y don't know who
Kit Musgrave is. I sate te Evening with Mrs Wesley who
goes to morrow morning to te Bath. She is much better
than she was. The News of te French desiring a Cessation
of Arms &c was but Town talk: We shall know in a few
days as I am told, whether there will be a Peace or no.
The d[uke] of Orm[on]d will go in a week for Flanders they
say: Our Mohawks go on still, & cut Peoples faces every
night; fais they shan't cut mine, I like it better as it is. The
Dogs will cost me at least a Crown a Week in Chairs. I believe te Souls of yr Houghers of Cattle have gott into them,
and now they don't distinguish between a Cow and a Christian. I forgot to wish y yesterday a happy new year, y
know te 25 of March is te first day of te year, and now
y must leave of Cards, and put out yr fire: I'll put out
mine the 1st of April, cold or not cold. I believe I shall
lose Credit with y by not coming over at te Beginning of
April: but I hoped te Session would be ended, and I must
stay till then, & yet I would fain be at te Beginning of my
willows growing. Percivall tells me that te Quicksetts upon
te flatt in te Garden do not grow so well as those famous
ones on te Ditch. They want Digging about them: The
Cherry trees by te River Side my Heart is sett upon.
Nite Md.

                                      March 29. [1712].

I am plagued with these Pains in my Shouldr: I believe
it is Rheumatick: I will do something for it to Night. Mr
Lewis & I dined with Mr Domvile to take our Leave of
him: I drunk 3 or 4 Glasses of Champagne by perfect teazing; thô it is bad for my Pain: but if it continue I will not
drink any wine without Water till I am well. The Weathr
is abominably cold and wet.—I am got into bed and have
put some old Flannel for want of new to my Shouldr, and
rubbd it with Hungary water.—Tis plaguy hard; I never
would drink any Wine if it were not for my Head, and
drinking has given me this Pain. I will try Abstemiousness

for a while. How does Md do now? how does dd and ppt? You must know I hate Pain, as te old woman sd—But I'll try to go seep; My Flesh sucks up Hungary Water rarely. My Man's an awkward Rascal, and makes me peevish. Do you know that tother day he was forcd to beg my Pardon that he could not shave my Head, his Hand shook so. He is drunk every day & I design to turn him off soon as ever I get to Ireld. I'll write no more now, but go to Sleep and see whether Sleep & Flannell will cure my Shouldr. Nite deelest Md.

March 30. [1712].

I was not able to go to Church or Court to day for my Shouldr; th Pain has left my Shouldr and crept to my neck and Collar bone. It makes me think of poor pooppt's blade-bone. Urge, urge, urge, dogs gnawing. I went in a Chair at 2 and dined with Mrs Van[homrigh], where I could be easy, & came back at 7. My Hungary water is gone, & to night I use Spirits of wine, wch my Landlady tells me is very good. It has raind terribly all day long; & is extreemly cold. I am very uneasy, and such cruell Twinges every moment. Nite deelest md.

March 31. April. 1. 2. 3. 4. 5. 6. 7. 8. [1712].

All these days I have been extreemly ill, tho I twice crawld out a week ago; but am now recovering, thô very weak. The violence of my Pain abated the night before last; I will just tell y how I was & then send away this Lettr wch ought to have gone Saturday last. Th Pain encreasd with mighty violence in my left Shouldr & Collar bone, & that side of my neck. On Thursday morning appeared great Red Spots in all those Places where my Pain was, and te Violence of te Pain was confined to my Neck behind a little on te left side; which was so violent that I not a minutes ease nor hardly a minutes sleep in 3 days & nights. te spots encreasd every day & bred little Pimples which are now grown white & full of corruption, [thô] small. te Red still continues too, and most prodigious hott & in-flamed. The disease is te Shingles. I eat nothing but Water gruell; I am very weak but out of all violent Pain.

The Doctrs say it would have ended in some violent Disease if it had not come out thus. I shall now recover fast. I have been in no danger of Life, but miserable Torture. I must not write too much.—So adieu deelest Md Md Md Fw Fw Me Me Me Lele I can say lele yet oo see—Fais I dont conceal a bitt. as hope savd.

I must purge and clyster after this; and my next Lettr will not be in te old order of Journall till I have done with Physick. An't oo surprised to see te Lettr want half a side.

[*From* LETTER XLIV.]

London. April 24. 1712.

I HAD yr 28th 2 or 3 days ago. I can hardly answer it now —Since my last I have been extremely ill. Tis this day just a Month since I felt a small pain on te tip of my left Shoulder, which grew worse & spread for 6 days; then broke all out by my collar, & left side of my neck in monstrous red Spotts, inflamed, & these grew to small Pimples. for 4 days I had no rest nor nights, for a Pain in my neck, then I grew a little bettr; afterwards where my Pains were a cruell Itching seised me beyond what ever I could imagine, & kept me awake severall Nights. I rubbed it vehemently but did not Scratch it. Then it grew into three or for great Sores like Blisters and run; at last I advised te Dr to use it like a Blister, so I did, with Melilot Plaisters, which still run, and I am now in pain enough; but am daily mending: I kept my Chambr a fortnight: then went out a day or 2; but then confined my self again. 2 days ago I went to a Neighbr to dine, but yesterday again kept at home: to day I will venture abroad a little; and hope to be well in a week or ten days: I never suffered so much in my life: I have taken my Breeches in above 2 Inches, so I am leaner, wch answers one Question in yr Letter. Th Weathr is mighty fine, I write in te morning, because I am better then. I will go and try to walk a little: I will give Dd's Certificate to Took to morrow

farewell md md md me me FW FW Me me—

[LETTER XLV.]

London. May 10. 1712.

I HAVE not yet ease or Humor enough to go on in my Journall Method, thô I have left my Chambr these 10 days. My Pain continues still in my Shouldr and Collar I keep Flannel on it, and rub it with Brandy; and take a nasty dyet Drink I still Itch terribly & have some few Pimples: I am weak and Sweat, & then the Flannell makes me mad with Itching: but I think my Pain lessens. A Journall while I was sick would have been a noble thing, made up of Pain and Physick, & Visits & Messages. The 2 last were almost as troublesom as te 2 first. One good Circumstance is that I am grown much leaner. I believe I told you, that I have taken in my Breeches 2 Inches. I had y^r N 29 last night. In answer to y^r good opinion of my disease, te D^{rs} sd they never saw any thing so odd of the kind; they were not properly Shingles, but Herpes miliaris, and 20 other hard names. I can never be sick like othr People, but always something out of te common way; and as for y^r notion of it coming without Pain, it neither came, nor stayd, nor went without Pain, & te most pain I ever bore in my Life — Madameris is retired in te Country with te Beast her Husband long ago—I thank te B[isho]p of Cl[ogher] for his Proxy; I will write to him soon. Here is Dilly's Wife in Town, but I have not seen her yet—No, Sinkerton [*Simpleton*] tis not a sign of Health, but a Sign that if it had not come out some terrible Fitt of Sickness would have followd. I was at our Society last Thursday, to receive a new Memb^r, te Chancellor of the Exchequer; but I drink nothing above wine & water—We shall have a Peace I hope soon, or at least entirely broke, but I believe te first. My Lettr to Ld Treas^r about te Engl[ish] Tongue is now printing; and I suffer my name to be put at te End of it, wch I nevr did before in my Life. The Appendix to th 3^d Part of John Bull was published yesterday: tis equall to te rest. I hope y read John Bull. It was a Scotch Gentleman a friend of mine that writ it; but they put it upon me. The Parlemt will hardly be up till June. We were like to be undone some days ago with a Tack, but we carryed it bravely, and the

Whigs came in to help us. Poor Ldy Masham I am afraid will lose her onely son, about a twelve Month old, with te King's Evil. I never would let Mrs Fenton see me in my Illness, tho she often came, but she has been once here since I recovered. Bernage has been twice to see me of late. His Regimt will be broke, and he onely upon half pay; so perhaps he thinks he will want me again. I am told here that the B[isho]p of Clogh[e]r & Family are coming over, but he says nothing of it himself.—I have been returning th Visits of those that sen Howdees in my Sickness, particularly te Dutchess of Hamilton, who came & satt with me 2 hours; I make Bargains with all people that I dine with, to let me Scrub my Back agst a Chair, & te Dutchess of Orm[on]d was forced to bear it tother day: Many of my Friends are gone to Kensington where te Qu[een] has been removed for some time—This is a long Lettr for a kick [*sick*] body; I will begin te next in te Journall way, thô my Journals will be sorry ones.—My left Hand is very weak & trembles; but my right side has not been toucht. This is a pitifull Letter for want of a better but Plagud with a Tetter my Fancy does fetter—Ah my poor willows & Quicksets— Well, but y must read John Bull. Do y understand it all? Did I tell y that young Parson Geree is going to be marryed, and asked my Advice—when it was too late to break off. He tells me Elwick has purchasd 40ll a year in Land adjoyning to his Living. Ppt does not say one word of her own little Health. I'm angry almost; but I won't tause see im a dood dallar in odle sings. Iss and so im dd too. G[o]d bless md & FW & Me, ay & Pdfr too. Farewell Md Md Md Fw Fw Fw Me Me

Lele. I can say lele it ung oomens iss I tan, well as oo.

[LETTER XLVI.]

London. May 31. 1712.

I CANNOT yet arrive to my Journall Letters, my Pains continuing still thô with less violence; but I don't love to write Journals while I am in pain, and above all not Journalls to Md; But however I am so much mended that I intend my next shall be in te old way; and yet I shall perhaps break my Resolution when I feel Pain. I believe I have lost Credit with you in relation to my coming over; but I protest, it is impossible to one who has any thing to do with this Ministry, to be certain, when he fixes any time. There is a Business which till it takes some Turn or other, I cannot leave this Place in Prudence or Hon^r. And I never wished so much as now, that I had staid in Ireld, but the Dye is cast and is now a spinning, and till it settles I can not tell whethr it be an Ace or a Sise. I am confident by what you know yr selves, that you will justify me in all this. The moment I am used ill, I will leave them, but know not how to do it while Things are in suspense. The Session will soon be over (I believe in a fortnight) and the Peace we hope will be made in a short time and then there will be no further Occasion for me, nor I have any thing to trust to but Court Gratitude; so that I expect to see my Willows a month after the Parlmt is up: but I will take Md in the way, and not go to Laracor like an unmannerly Spreenekick Ferrow. Have y seen my L^r to Ld Treas^r; there are 2 Answers come out to it already, thô tis no Politicks, but a harmlesss Proposall about te Improvemt of th Engl. Tongue. I believe if I writt an Essay upon a Straw some Fool would answer it. About ten days hence I expect a Lettr from Md N. 30. Y are now writing it near the end as I guess. I have not received Dd's money; but I will give y a Note for it on Parvisol, & bid a Paadon I have not done it before—I am just now thinking to go lodge at Kensington for te Air. Ldy Masham has teazd me to do it, but Business has hindred me, but now Ld Treas^r has removed thither. Fifteen of our Society dined togethr under a Canopy in an Arbour at Parsons Green last Thursday; I never saw any Thing so fine and Romantick. We got a great Victory last Wednesday in th H[ouse] of L[or]ds by a Majority I think of 28, and the Whigs had desired their Friends to bespeak Places to see Ld Treas^r carryed to the Tower. I mett y^r Higgins here yesterday; He roars at te Insolence of te Whigs in Ireld, talks much of his own sufferings and expences in asserting the Cause of the Church; and I find he would fain plead merit enough to desire that his Fortune should be mended. I believe he designs to make as much noise as he can in order to Prefermt. Pray let te Provost when he sees you give y ten English Shillings, and I will give as much here to te Man that deliverd me Rimers Books he knows te meaning: Tell him I will not trust him but that y can order it to be pd me here; And I will trust you till I see y; Have I told y that te Rogue Patrick has left me these two Months, to my great Satisfaction. I have got anothr, who seems to be much better, if he continues it. I am printing a threepenny Pamphlet, and shall print anothr in a fortnight; and then I have done, unless some new Occasion Starts. Is my Curate Warburton marryed to Mrs Melthrop in my Parish: So I heeear; Or is [it] a Lye. Has Raym[on]d got to his new House: Do y see Jo now and then. What luck have you at Ombre; How Stands it with te Dean? [*Words crossed out*.] My Service to Mrs Stoit and Catherine if she be come from Wales. I have not yet seen Dilly Ash's wife. I call'd once but she was not at home: I think she is under th Doctor's Hand; [*Words crossed out*] I believe the News of te D[uke] of Orm[on]d producing Letters in te Council of War, with orders not to fight, will surprise y in Ireld. Ld Treas^r sd in te House of L[or]ds that in a few days te Treaty of Peace should be layd before them; And our Court thought it wrong to hazard a Battle, and sacrifice many Lives in such a Juncture. If te Peace holds all will do well: otherwise, I know not how we shall weather it. And it was reckoned as a wrong Step in Politicks for Ld Treas^r to open himself so much. The Secrty would not go so far to satisfy the Whigs in the H[ouse] of Commons: but there all went swimmingly.—I'll say no more to oo to nite sollohs; becase I must send away te Lettr, not by th Bell, but early: and besides I have not much more to say at zis plesent liting. Does Md never reed at all now, pee? but oo walk plodigiousry I suppose, oo make nothing of walking to too to ay, to, Donibrook: I walk too as much as I can: because Sweating is good; but I'll walk more if I go to Kensington. I suppose I shall have no Apples this year neithr: for I dined tothr day with Ld Rivers who is sick, at his Country house: and he shewd me all his Cherryes blasted; Nite deelest sollahs: farewell deelest Rives; rove poopoopdfr, farewell deelest richar Md, Md, Md FW FW FW FW FW Me Me Lele, Me lele lele richar Md.

[LETTER XLVII.]

Kensington. June 17. 1712.

I HAVE been so tosticated about since my last that I could not go on in my Journall manner, thô my Shoulder is a great deal better: However I feel constant pain in it, but I think it diminishes, and I have cutt off some slices from my Flannel. I have lodged here near a fortnight, partly for the Air and Exercise; partly to be near the Court, where dinners are to be found. I generally get a lift in a Coach to Town, and in the evening I walk back. On Saturday I dined with te Dutchess of Orm[on]d at her Lodge near Sheen; and thought to get a Boat back as usuall; I walkt by te Bank to Cue [*Kew*]; but no Boat; then to Mortlack, but no boat: & it was 9 o clock; at last a little sculler calld, full of nasty People; I made him sett me down at Hammersmith; so walkt 2 miles to this Place, & got here by 11. Last night I had anothr such difficulty; I was in the City till past 10 at night; it raind hard; but no Coach to be had; It gave over a little and I walkt all te way here and gott home by 12. I love these shabby difficultyes when they are over; but I hate them because they rise from not having a thousd pd a year—I had yr N. 30 about 3 days ago, wch I will now Answer. And first, I did not relapse, but found I came out before I ought, and so and so, as I have told you in some of my last. The first coming abroad made People think I was quite recovered; & I had no more messages after-wards.—Well but John Bull is not writt by te Person y imagine, as hope—It is too good for anothr to own, had it been Grubstreet, I would have let People think as they please: and I think that's right, is not it now? So flap ee hand, & make wry mouth oo self sawci doxi: Now comes Dd: why sollah I did write in a fortnight; my 47th, and if it did not come in due time, can I help Wind and Weathr;

am I a Laplander, am I witch, can I work Miracles, can I make Easterly winds. Now I am agst Dr Smith: I drink little water with my wine; yet I believe he is right; Yet Dr Cockburn told me a little wine would not hurt me: But it is so hot and dry, and water is so dangerous. The worst thing here is my Evenings at Ld Mashams, where Ld Treasr comes, and we sitt till after 12, but it is convenient I should be among them for a while as much as possible; I need not tell oo why. But I hope that will be at an end in a Month or two one way or othr; and I am resolvd it shall. But I can't go to Tunbridge nor any where else out of te way in this Juncture. So Ppt designs for Templeoag (what a name is that) where abouts is that place; I hope not very far from Dublin.

Higgins is here roaring that all is wrong in Ired; & would have me gett him an Audience of Ld Treasr to tell him so. But I will have nothing to do in it: no not I fais. We have had no Thundr till last night; and till then we were dead for want of rain: but there fell a great deal. No field lookt green. I reckon te Qu[een] will go to Windsor in 3 or 4 weeks; and if te Secty takes a House there, I shall be sometimes with him. but how affecteedly ppt talks of my being here all Summer; wch I do not intend; nor to stay one minute longer in Engd than becomes te Circumstances I am in. I wish y would go soon into te Country, & take a good deal of it; & where better than Trim. Jo will be yr humble Servt: Parvisol yr slave, & Raym[on]d at yr Command, for he picques himself on good manners. I have seen Dilly's wife.—And I have seen once or twice old Bradly here. He is very well, very old, and very wise: I believe I must go see his wife when I have Leisure. I should be glad to see Goody Stoit, and her Husband; pray give them my humble Service, and to Katherine; and to Mrs Walls: I am not the least bit in love with Mrs Walls. I suppose te Cares of te Husband encrease with te fruitfullness of te wife. I am grad at halt to hear of Ppts good Health: pray let her finish it by drinking Waters. I hope dd had her Bill, & has her money. Remembr to write a due time before Me money is wanted; & be good galls, dood dallars I mean, & no crying dallars. I heard somebody coming up stairs, and forgot I was in te Country; & I was afraid of a Visiter; that's one Advantage of being here; that I am not teazd with Solliciters.—My Service to Dr Smith; Molt the Chymist is my Acquaintance. I sent te Questions to him about Sr W. Raleighs Cordial, and the Answer he returned is in these words *It is directly after Mr Boyle's Receit.* That Commission is performd; If he wants any of it, Molt shall use him fairly. I suppose Smith is one of y^r Physicians. So now oor Lettr is fully and impartially answerd, not as rascals answer me: I believe if I writt an Essay upon a Straw, I should have a Shoal of Answerers; but no mattr for that: Y see I can answr y without making any Reflections, as becomes men of Learning. Well, but now for te Peace: why, we expect it daily; but te French have te Staff in their own Hands, & we trust to their Honesty: I wish it were otherwise. Things are now in te way of being soon in te Extreams of well or ill. I hope and believe the first. Ld Wharton is gone out of Town in a Rage, and curses himself & friends for ruining themselves in defending Ld Marl[borough] and Godolphin, & taking Nottingham into their favor. He swears he will meddle no more during this Reign, a pretty Speech at 66, & te Qu[een] is 20 years youngr: & now in very good Health. For y must know her Health is fixt by a certain Reason, that she has done with Braces (I must use te Expression) and nothing ill has happened to her since; so she has a new Lease of her Life. Read te Lettr to a Whig Lord. Do y ever reed; why dont y say so; I mean does dd reed to ppt. Do y walk. I think ppt should walk to dd, as dd reeds to ppt. for ppt oo must know is a good walker; but not so good as pdfr. I intend to dine to day with Mr Lewis but it threatens rain, & I shall be too late to get a Lift; & I must write to te B[isho]p of Cl[ogher]. tis now 10 in te morning, & this is all writt at a heat. Farewell deelest lele deelest Md Md Md Md Md FW FW FW Me Me Lele Me lele me lele me lele lele lele me.

[LETTER XLVIII.]

Windsor. Sept. 15. 1712.

I NEVER was so long without writing to Md as now, since I left them, nor ever will again while I am able to write. I have expected from one week to anothr, that something would be done in my own Affairs, but nothing at all is nor I dont know when any thing will, or whethr ever at all, so slow are people at doing Favors.—I have been much out of order of late with te old giddyness in my Head. I took a vomit for it 2 days ago, and will take another about a day or two hence. I have eat mighty little Fruit, yet I impute my disorder to that little, and shall henceforth wholly forbear it. I am engaged in a long work, and have done all I can of it, and wait for some Papers from the Ministry for materialls for the rest, & they delay me as if it were a Favor I asked of them; so that I have been idle here this good while, and it happened in a right time, when I was too much out of order to study. One is kept constantly out of humor by a thousand unaccountable things in publick Proceedings and when I reason with some Friends we cannot conceive how Affairs can last as they are; God only knows; but it is a very melancholy subject for those who have any neer concern in it. I am again endeavoring as I was last year to keep People from breaking to pieces upon a hundred misunderstandings. One cannot withold them from drawing different ways while the enemy is watching to destroy both. See how my Stile is altered by living & thinking & talking among these People, instead of my Canal & river walk, and Willows. I lose all my money here among te Ladyes, so that I never play when I can help it, being sure to lose: I have lost 5¹¹ the five weeks I have been here, I hope Ppt is luckyer at Picquet with te Dean & Mrs Walls. The Dean never answerd my Letter thô. I have clearly forgot whether I sent a Bill for Me in any of my last Letters; I think I did: pray let me know, & always give me timely Notice. I wait here but to see what they will do for me; & whenever Prefermts are given from me, as hope savd I will come over.

Sept. 18. [1712].

I HAVE taken a vomit to day; and hope I shall be bettr. I have been very giddy since I writt what is before, yet not as I used to be, more frequent, but not so violent. Yesterday we were allarmd with te Queens being ill. She had an Aguish & feaverish Fitt and you never saw such Countenances as we all had; such dismal Melancholy. Her Physicians from Town were sent for; but towards night she grew better, to day she misst her Feet [*Fit*] and was up: We are not now in any Fear. It will be at worst but an Ague: and we hope even that will not return. Ld Treas^r would not come here from London because it would make a Noise, if he came before his usuall time, which is Saturday, & he goes away on Mondays. The Whigs have lost a great support in te E[arl] of Godolphin. Tis a good jest to hear te Ministers talk of him now with Humanity and Pity, because he is dead, and can do them no more hurt. Ldy Orkney, te late King's Mistress, who lives at a fine place 5 miles from hence calld Cliffden, and I are grown mighty Acquaintance. She is te wisest woman I ever saw, & Ld Treas^r made great use of her Advise in te late change of Affairs. I hear, Ld Marlbrow is growing ill of his Diabetis, whch if it be true, may soon carry him off; and then te Ministry will be something more at ease. Md has been a long time without writing to pdfr thô they have not the same Cause; tis seven weeks since y^r last came to my hands, wch was N. 32, that y may not be mistaken; I hope ppt has not wanted her health; y were then drinking waters. The Doctor tells me I must go into a Course of Steel, tho I have not te Spleen; for that they can never give me thô I have as much Provocation to it as any man alive. Bernage's Regimt is broke, but he is upon half pay: I have not seen him this long time; but I suppose he is overrun with Melancholy. My Ld Shrewsbury is certainly designed to be Governor of Ireld; and I believe te Dutchess will please te people there mightily. The Irish Whig Leaders promise great Things to themselves from His Governmt: but care shall be taken, if possible, to prevent them. Mrs Fenton has writ to me that she has been forced to leave L^{dy} G[iffard] and come to town for a Rheumatism; that L^{dy} does not love to be troubled with sick People. Mrs Fenton writes to me as one dying, & desires I would think of her Son: I have not answered her Lettr: She is retired to Mrs Povey's.—Is my Aunt alive yet; and do you ever see her. I suppose she has forgot te Loss of her Son. Is Raym[on]ds new house quite finished; and does he squander as he used to do? Has he yet spent all his Wive's Fortune? I hear there are 5 or 6 People putting strongly in for my Livings; God help them. But if ever te Court should give me any thing, I woud recommend Raym[on]d to te D[uke] of Orm[on]d, not for any particular Friendship to him, but because it would be proper for the Ministr of Trim to have Laracor. You may keep te gold studded snuffbox now, for my Brothr Hill. Govern^r of Dunkirk has sent me te finest that ever you saw; tis allowed at Court that none in Engld comes near it, thô it did not cost above 20^{ll}. And te Dutchess of Hamilton has made me Pockets for [it] like a womans, with a Belt and Buckle, for y know I wear no wastcoat in Summer: & there are severall divisions, and one on purpose for my box, oh ho,—We have had most delightfull weathr this whole week, but illness and vomiting have hindred me from sharing in a great Part of it. Ldy Masham made te Queen send to Kensington for some of her preserved Ginger for me, wch I take in te morning, and hope it will do me good. Mrs Brent sent me a Letter by a young Fellow a Printer, desiring I would recommend him here, which you may tell her, I have done: but I cannot promise what will come of it, for it is necessary they should be made free here before they can be employd: I remember I putt te Boy prentice to Brent. I hope Parvisol has sett my Tyths well this year: He has writt nothing to me about it; pray talk to him of it when y see him: & lett him give me an Account how Things are. I suppose te Corn is now off the Ground: I hope he has sold that great ugly Horse. Why don't you sell to him? He keeps me at Charges for Horses that I can never ride; yrs is lame, and will never be good for any thing. The Qu[een] will stay here about a month longer I suppose, but Ldy

Masham will go in ten days to lye in at Kensington, poor
Creature she fell down in te Court here t'other day. She
would needs walk a cross it, upon some displeasure with her
Chairmen; and was like to be spoild, so near her time.
but we hope all is over for a black eye and a sore side; tho
I shall not be at ease till she is brought to bed.—I find I can
fill up a Lettr some way or other without a Journall. If I
had not a Spirit naturally cheerfull, I should be very much
discontented at a thousand Things. Pray God preserve
Md's Health, and Pdfrs and that I may live far from te
Envy and Discontent that attends those who are thought
to have more Favour at Courts than they reelly possess.
Love pdfr., who loves md above all things. farewell deelest
ten thousand times deelest md md md FW FW Me Me Me
Me lele lele lele

lele——

[LETTER LII.]

London. Oct 30. 1712.

THE duchess of *Ormond* found me out to-day, and made me
dine with her. Lady *Masham* is still expecting. She has had
a cruel cold. I could not finish my letter last post for the
soul of me. Lord *Bolingbroke* has had my papers these
six weeks, and done nothing to them. Is *Tisdall* yet in the
world? I suppose writing controversies, to get a name with
posterity. The duke of *Ormond* will not be over these three
or four days. I design to make him join with me in settling
all right among our people. I have ordered the duchess to
let me have an hour with the duke at his first coming, to
give him a true state of persons and things. I believe the
duke of *Shrewsbury* will hardly be declared your governor
yet; at least, I think so now; but resolutions alter very often.
Duke *Hamilton* gave me a pound of snuff to-day, admirable
good. I wish *D.D.* had it; and *Ppt.* too, if she likes it. It
cost me a quarter of an hour of his politics, which I was
forced to hear. Lady *Orkney* is making me a writing-table
of her own contrivance, and a bed night-gown. She is perfectly kind, like a mother. I think the d—— was in it the

other day, that I should talk to her of an ugly squinting cousin of her's; and the poor lady herself, you know, squints like a dragon. The other day we had a long discourse with her about love; and she told us a saying of her sister *Fitzharding*, which I thought excellent, that *in men desire begets love*, and *in women love begets desire*. We have abundance of our old criers still hereabouts. I hear every morning your woman with the old sattin and taffata, &c. the fellow with old coats, s s suits or cloaks. Our weather is abominable of late. We have not two tolerable days in twenty. I lost money again at ombre, with lord *Orkney* and others; yet, after all, this year I have lost but three and twenty shillings; so that, considering card-money, I am no loser.

Our society hath not yet renewed their meetings. I hope we shall continue to do some good this winter; and lord treasurer promises the academy for reforming our language shall soon go forward. I must now go hunt those dry letters for materials. You will see something very notable I hope So much for that. God Almighty bless you.

[*From* LETTER LIV.]

London. Dec. 13. 1712.

MORN. I am so very seepy in te mornings, that my man wakens me above ten times, and now I can tell oo no News of this day (here is a restless dog crying Cabbages and Savoys plagues me every morning about this time, he is now at it: I wish his largest Cabbage was sticking in his Throat) I lodge over against te House in little Rider street where Dd lodged, don't oo lememble Maram.—To Night I must see te Abbè Gaultier, to get some particulars for my History: it was he who was first employd by France in te Overtures of Peace. & I have not had time this month to see him. He is but a Puppy too—Ldy Orkney has just sent to invite me to dinner. She has not given me te Bed nightgown; besides I am come very much off from writing in bed tho I am doing it this minute, but I stay till my fire is burnt up. My grate is very largely, 2 bushell of Coals a week, but I save it in lodgings. Ld Abercorn is come to

London, & will plague me, & I can do him no Service— D[uke of] Shrewsbury goes in a day or 2 for France, perhaps to day; We shall have a Peace very soon, te Dutch are almost entirely agreed, & if they stop we shall make it without them; that has been long resolved. One Squire Jones, a Scoundrel in my Parish has writt to me to desire I would engage Jo Beaum[on]t to give him his Interest for Parlm^t man for Trim: pray tell Jo this; & if he designed to vote for him already, then he may tell Jones that I received his Letter, & that I writt to Jo to do it: if Jo be engaged for any other, then he may do what he will; & Parvisol may say he spoke to Jo, but Jo's engaged &c. I receivd 3 pair of fine thread Stockins from Jo lately. Pray thank him when you see him, & that I say they are very fine & good (I never lookt at them yet, but that's no matter) This is a fine day, I am ruined with Coaches & Chairs this 12 penny weathr. I must see my Brother Orm[on]d at 11, & then te Dutchess of Hamilton, with whom I doubt I am in disgrace, not having seen her these ten days.—I send this to day, and must finish it now, & phaps some People may come & hindr me, for it is ten o Clock (but not shaving day) & I must be abroad at 11. Abbe Gautier sends me word I can't see him to night pots cake him. I don't value any thing but one letter he has, of Petcum's, shewing te Roguery of te Dutch. did not te Conduct of te Allyes make ye great Politicians, fais I believe y are not quite so ignorant as I thought you. I am glad to hear oo walked so much in te Country: does dd ever read to you ung ooman. O fais I shall find strange doings hen I tum ole [*home*].—Here is somebody coming that I must see that wants a little place, te son of Coz Rooks eldest daughter tht dyed many years ago. Hes here:—farewell deelest md md md me me me FW FW FW lele—

[From LETTER LVI.]

London.   Jan. 3. 1712 [–13].

L^D DUPPLIN & I went with L^d & L^{dy} Orkney this morning at ten to Wimbleton 6 miles off; to see Ld and Ldy Caermarthen. It is much te finest place about this Town;

did oo never see it. I was once there before about 5 years ago. You know Ldy Caermarthen is Ld Treas^{rs} Daughter, marryed about 3 weeks ago. I hope te young Fellow will be a good Husband.—I must send this away now. I came back just by night fall, cruell cold weathr. I have no smell yet, but my cold something better. [*words crossed out*] I forgett how [*words crossed out*] & pray give te Bill on tothr side to Mrs Brent as usuall. I believe I have not payd her this great while; [*words crossed out*] The six odd Shillings, tell Mrs Br[ent] are for her Newyears gift.

I am just now told that poor dear Lady Ashburnham, te Duke of Orm[on]d's daughter dyed yesterday at her Country House; th poor creature was with Child. She was my greatest Favorite and I am in excessive Concern for her Loss. I hardly knew a more valuable Person on all Accounts: y must have heard me talk of her. I am afraid to see te Duke and Dutchess: She was naturally very healthy; I am afraid she has been thrown away for want of care. Pray condole with me; tis extreemly moving, Her Lord's a Puppy, and I shall never think it worth my while to be troubled with him, now he has lost all that was valuable in his Possession. Yet I think he used her pretty well—I hate Life, when I think it exposed to such Accidents and to see so many thousand wretches burthening te Earth while such as her dye, makes me think God did never intend Life for a Blessing—Farewell.

[*From* LETTER LVII.]

London. Jan. 14. 1712-13.

To day I took te Circle of morning Visits I went to te Dutchess of Orm[on]d; & there was she & Ldy Betty, & Ld Ashburnham together: that was te first time te Mother & daughter saw each othr since Ldy Ashburnham's death, they were both in Tears, and I chid them for being together, & made Ldy Betty go to her own Chambr, then sate a while with te Dutchess, & went after Lady Betty, & all was well. there is something of Farce in all these Mournings let them be ever so serious. People will pretend to grieve more than they really do, & that takes off from their true Grief. I then went to Dutchess Hamilton, who never grieved but raged & stormed & railed. She is pretty quiet now, but has a diabolicall Temper. Ld Keeper & his son & their two Ladyes & I dined to day with Mr Cesar, Treasurer of te Navy at his House in te City where he keeps his Office— We happened to talk of Brutus, and I sd something in his Praise, when it struck me immediatly that I had made a Blunder in doing so, and therefore I recollected my self, and sd, Mr Cesar I beg y^r Pardon. So we laughed &c— [*words crossed out*].

[*From* LETTER LVIII.]

London. Feb. 12. 1712–13.

I HAVE reckond days wrong all this while for this is te 12, I don't know when I lost it. I dined to day with our Society, te greatest dinner I have ever seen; it was at Jack Hills te Governr of Dunkirk. I gave an Account of 60 Guineas I had collectd, & am to give them away to 2 Authors to morrow. and Ld Tr has promised us 100^ll to reward some others. I found a Letter on my Table last night to tell me that poor little Harrison te Queens Secrty that came lately from Utrecht with te Barrier Treaty was ill & desired to see me at Night but it was late & I could not go till to day. I have often mentioned him in my Letters. you may remembr [*words crossed out*] I went in te morning, & found him mighty ill, & got 30 Guinneas for him from Ld Bolinbroke; & an order for a 100^ll from te Treasury to be pd him to morrow. & I have got him removed to Knightsbridge for Air. He has a Feaver & Inflammation on his Lungs; but I hope will do well. Nite.

Feb. 13. [1712–13].

I was to see a poor Poet one Mr. Diaper, in a nasty Garret, very sick; I gave him 20 Guinneas from Ld Bolingbrok, & disposed the othr 60 to 2 other Authors, & desird a Friend to receive te 100^ll for poor Harrison; and will carry it him to morrow morning. I sent to see how he did, & he is extreamly ill, & I very much afflicted for him, for he is my own Creature, & in a very honorable Post, and very worthy of it. I dined in te City. I am in much concern for this poor Lad. His Mothr & Sister attend him, & he wants nothing. Nite poo dee MD.

Feb. 14. [1712–13].

I took Parnel this morning and we walkt to see poor Harrison, I had te 100ˡˡ in my Pocket. I told Parnel I was afraid to knock at te door; my mind misgave me. I knockt, & his man in Tears told me his Master was dead an hour before. Think what Grief this [is] to me; I went to his Mothr, & have been ordering things for his Funerall with as little Cost as possible, to morrow at ten at night. Ld Treasʳ was much concernd when I told him. I could not dine with Ld Tr nor any where, but got a bit of meat towards Evening. no loss ever grieved me so much. poor Creature.—Pray Gd Almighty bless poor MD.—adieu—

I send this away to night and am sorry it must go while I am in so much Grief.

[*From* LETTER LIX.]

London. Mar. 27. [1713].

PARNELS Poem is mightily esteemed, but Poetry sells ill, I am plagued with that [*two words crossed out*], poor Harrison's mother. Y would laugh to see how cautious I am of paying her te 100ˡˡ I received for her son from te Treasury: I have asked every Creature I know, whethr I may do it safely; yet durst not venture, till my Lᵈ Keeper assured me there was no danger. yet I have not payd her, but will in a day or two tho I have a great mind to stay till [Ppt] sends me [her] Opinion, because [Ppt] is a great Lawyer. I dined to day with a mixture of People at a Scotchmans, who made te Invitation to Mr Lewis & me, and has some design upon us wᶜʰ we know very well. I went afterwards to see a famous moving Picture, & I never saw any thing so pretty—Y see a sea ten miles wide, a town on tothr end, and ships sailing in te sea, & discharging their Canon. Y see a great Sky with moon & stars &c. I'm a fool. [*Words crossed out*].

[*From* LETTER LXII.]

CHARACTER

OF

STELLA

THREE
PRAYERS

The *Character of Stella*, which Swift began on the night of her death, was printed for the first time by Deane Swift in Vol. VIII, i, of the quarto edition, 1765.

Of the three prayers, written by Swift for Stella in her last illness, the first was originally printed in the same volume as her *Character*; the second and third in *Miscellanies*, Vol. XI, 1746, and also Vol. 8 of Faulkner's collected edition, 1746.

ON THE
DEATH OF MRS
JOHNSON

T HIS day, being Sunday, January 28th, 1727–8, about
eight o'clock at night a servant brought me a note,
with an account of the death of the truest, most virtuous, and valuable friend, that I or perhaps any other
person ever was blessed with. She expired about six in the
evening of this day; and, as soon as I am left alone, which
is about eleven at night, I resolve, for my own satisfaction,
to say something of her life and character.

She was born at Richmond in Surrey on the thirteenth
day of March, in the year 1681. Her father was a younger
brother of a good family in Nottinghamshire, her mother
of a lower degree; and indeed she had little to boast of her
birth. I knew her from six years old, and had some share
in her education, by directing what books she should read,
and perpetually instructing her in the principles of honour
and virtue; from which she never swerved in any one action
or moment of her life. She was sickly from her childhood
until about the age of fifteen: But then grew into perfect
health, and was looked upon as one of the most beautiful,
graceful, and agreeable young women in London, only a
little too fat. Her hair was blacker than a raven, and every
feature of her face in perfection. She lived generally in the
country, with a family, where she contracted an intimate
friendship with another lady of more advanced years. I
was then (to my mortification) settled in Ireland; and about
a year after, going to visit my friends in England, I found
she was a little uneasy upon the death of a person on whom
she had some dependance. Her fortune, at that time, was
in all not above fifteen hundred pounds, the interest of
which was but a scanty maintenance, in so dear a country,
for one of her spirit. Upon this consideration, and indeed

very much for my own satisfaction, who had few friends or acquaintance in Ireland, I prevailed with her and her dear friend and companion, the other lady,* to draw what money they had into Ireland, a great part of their fortune being in annuities upon funds. Money was then at ten *per cent.* in Ireland besides the advantage of turning it, and all necessaries of life at half the price. They complied with my advice, and soon after came over; but, I happening to continue some time longer in England, they were much discouraged to live in Dublin, where they were wholly strangers. She was at that time about nineteen years old, and her person was soon distinguished. But the adventure looked so like a frolic, the censure held, for some time as if there were a secret history in such a removal; which, however soon blew off by her excellent conduct. She came over with her friend on the [*blank*] in the year 170–; and they both lived together until this day, when death removed her from us. For some years past, she had been visited with continual ill-health: and several times, within these two years her life was despaired of. But, for this twelve-month past, she never had a day's health; and properly speaking, she hath been dying six months, but kept alive, almost against nature, by the generous kindness of two physicians, and the care of her friends. Thus far I writ the same night between eleven and twelve.

Never was any of her sex born with better gifts of the mind, or more improved them by reading and conversation. Yet her memory was not of the best, and was impaired in the latter years of her life. But I cannot call to mind that I ever once heard her make a wrong judgment of persons, books, or affairs. Her advice was always the best, and with the greatest freedom, mixed with the greatest decency. She had a gracefulness somewhat more than human in every motion, word, and action. Never was so happy a conjunction of civility, freedom, easiness and sincerity. There seemed to be a combination among all that knew her, to treat her with a dignity much beyond her rank: Yet people

---

* Mrs. Dingley.

of all sorts were never more easy than in her company. Mr. Addison, when he was in Ireland, being introduced to her, immediately found her out; and if he had not soon after left the kingdom, assured me he would have used all endeavours to cultivate her friendship. A rude or conceited coxcomb passed his time very ill, upon the least breach of respect; for in such a case she had no mercy, but was sure to expose him to the contempt of the standers by; yet in such a manner as he was ashamed to complain, and durst not resent. All of us, who had the happiness of her friendship, agreed unanimously, that, in an afternoon or evening's conversation, she never failed before we parted of delivering the best thing that was said in the company. Some of us have written down several of her sayings, or what the French call *Bon Mots*, wherein she excelled almost beyond belief. She never mistook the understanding of others; nor ever said a severe word, but where a much severer was deserved.

Her servants loved and almost adored her at the same time. She would, upon occasions, treat them with freedom, yet her demeanour was so awful, that they durst not fail in the least point of respect. She chid them seldom, but it was with severity, which had an effect upon them for a long time after.

January 29th, My head achs, and I can write no more.

January 30th, Tuesday.

This is the night of the funeral, which my sickness will not suffer me to attend. It is now nine at night, and I am removed into another apartment, that I may not see the light in the church, which is just over against the window of my bed-chamber.

With all the softness of temper that became a lady, she had the personal courage of a hero. She and her friend having removed their lodgings to a new house, which stood solitary, a parcel of rogues, armed, attempted the house, where there was only one boy: She was then about four and twenty: And, having been warned to apprehend some such attempt, she learned the management of a pistol; and the other women and servants being half-dead with fear, she stole softly to her dining-room window, put on a black hood, to prevent being seen, primed the pistol fresh, gently lifted up the sash; and, taking her aim with the utmost presence of mind, discharged the pistol loaden with the bullets, into the body of one villain, who stood the fairest mark. The fellow, mortally wounded, was carried off by the rest, and died the next morning, but his companions could not be found. The Duke of Ormond hath often drank her health to me upon that account, and had always an high esteem of her She was indeed under some apprehensions of going in a boat, after some danger she had narrowly escaped by water, but she was reasoned thoroughly out of it. She was never known to cry out, or discover any fear, in a coach or on horseback, or any uneasiness by those sudden accidents with which most of her sex, either by weakness or affectation, appear so much disordered.

She never had the least absence of mind in conversation, nor given to interruption, or appeared eager to put in her word by waiting impatiently until another had done. She spoke in a most agreeable voice, in the plainest words, never hesitating, except out of modesty before new faces, where she was somewhat reserved; nor, among her nearest friends, ever spoke much at a time. She was but little versed in the common topics of female chat; scandal, censure, and detraction, never came out of her mouth: Yet, among a few friends, in private conversation, she made little ceremony in discovering her contempt of a coxcomb, and describing all his follies to the life; but the follies of her own sex she was rather inclined to extenuate or to pity.

When she was once convinced by open facts of any breach of truth or honour, in a person of high station, especially in the church, she could not conceal her indignation, nor hear them named without shewing her displeasure in her countenance; particularly one or two of the latter sort, whom she had known and esteemed, but detested above all mankind, when it was manifest that they had sacrificed those two precious virtues to their ambition, and would much sooner have forgiven them the common immoralities of the laity.

Her frequent fits of sickness, in most parts of her life, had prevented her from making progress in reading which she would otherwise have done. She was well versed in the Greek and Roman story, and was not unskilled in that of France and England. She spoke French perfectly, but forgot much of it by neglect and sickness. She had read carefully all the best books of travels, which serve to open and enlarge the mind. She understood the Platonic and Epicurean philosophy, and judged very well of the defects of the latter. She made very judicious abstracts of the best books she had read. She understood the nature of government, and could point out all the errors of Hobbes, both in that and religion. She had a good insight into physic, and knew somewhat of anatomy; in both which she was instructed in her younger days by an eminent physician, who had her long under his care, and bore the highest esteem for her person and understanding. She had a true taste of wit and good sense, both in poetry and prose, and was a perfect good critic of style: Neither was it easy to find a more proper or impartial judge, whose advice an author might better rely on, if he intended to send a thing into the world, provided it was on a subject that came within the compass of her knowledge. Yet, perhaps, she was sometimes too severe, which is a safe and pardonable error. She preserved her wit, judgment, and vivacity to the last, but often used to complain of her memory.

Her fortune, with some accession, could not, as I have heard say, amount to much more than two thousand pounds, whereof a great part fell with her life, having been placed upon annuities in England, and one in Ireland. In a person so extraordinary, perhaps it may be pardonable to mention some particulars, although of little moment, further than to set forth her character. Some presents of goldpieces being often made to her while she was a girl, by her mother and other friends, on promise to keep them, she grew into such a spirit of thrift, that, in about three years, they amounted to above two hundred pounds. She used to shew them with boasting; but her mother, apprehending she would be cheated of them, prevailed, in some months, and with great importunities, to have them put out to interest:

When the girl lost the pleasure of seeing and counting her gold, which she never failed of doing many times in a day, and despaired of heaping up such another treasure, her humour took the quite contrary turn: She grew careless and squandering of every new acquisition, and so continued till about two and twenty; when, by advice of some friends, and the fright of paying large bills of tradesmen, who enticed her into their debt, she began to reflect upon her own folly, and was never at rest until she had discharged all her shop-bills, and refunded herself a considerable sum she had run out. After which, by the addition of a few years and a superior understanding, she became, and continued all her life a most prudent oeconomist; yet still with a strong bent to the liberal side, wherein she gratified herself by avoiding all expence in cloaths, (which she ever despised) beyond what was merely decent. And, although her frequent returns of sickness were very chargeable, except fees to physicians, of which she met with several so generous that she could force nothing on them, (and indeed she must otherwise have been undone;) yet she never was without a considerable sum of ready money. Insomuch that, upon her death, when her nearest friends thought her very bare, her executors found in her strong box about a hundred and fifty pounds in gold. She lamented the narrowness of her fortune in nothing so much, as that it did not enable her to entertain her friends so often, and in so hospitable a manner as she desired. Yet they were always welcome; and, while she was in health to direct, were treated with neatness and elegance: So that the revenues of her and her companion, passed for much more considerable than they really were. They lived always in lodgings, their domesticks consisting of two maids and one man. She kept an account of all the family-expences, from her arrival in Ireland to some months before her death; and she would often repine, when looking back upon the annals of her household bills, that every thing necessary for life was double the price, while interest of money was sunk almost to one half; so that the addition made to her fortune was indeed grown absolutely necessary.

(I since writ as I found time.)

But her charity to the poor was a duty not to be diminished, and therefore became a tax upon those tradesmen who furnish the fopperies of other ladies. She bought cloaths as seldom as possible, and those as plain and cheap as consisted with the situation she was in; and wore no lace for many years. Either her judgment or fortune was extraordinary, in the choice of those on whom she bestowed her charity; for it went further in doing good than double the sum from any other hand. And I have heard her say, she always met with gratitude from the poor: Which must be owing to her skill in distinguishing proper objects, as well as her gracious manner in relieving them.

But she had another quality that much delighted her, although it may be thought a kind of check upon her bounty; however it was a pleasure she could not resist: I mean that of making agreeable presents, wherein I never knew her equal, although it be an affair of as delicate a nature as most in the course of life. She used to define a present, That it was a gift to a friend of something he wanted or was fond of, and which could not be easily gotten for money. I am confident, during my acquaintance with her, she hath, in these and some other kinds of liberality, disposed of to the value of several hundred pounds. As to presents made to herself, she received them with great unwillingness, but especially from those to whom she had ever given any; being on all occasions the most disinterested mortal I ever knew or heard of.

From her own disposition, at least as much as from the frequent want of health, she seldom made any visits; but her own lodgings, from before twenty years old, were frequented by many persons of the graver sort, who all respected her highly, upon her good sense, good manners, and conversation. Among these were the late Primate Lindsay, Bishop Loyd, Bishop Ashe, Bishop Brown, Bishop Stearn, Bishop Pulleyn, with some others of later date; and indeed the greatest number of her acquaintance was among the clergy. Honour, truth, liberality, good nature, and modesty, were the virtues she chiefly possessed, and most valued in her acquaintance; and where she found them, would be ready to allow for some defects, nor valued them less, al-though they did not shine in learning or in wit; but would never give the least allowance for any failures in the former, even to those who made the greatest figure in either of the two latter. She had no use of any person's liberality, yet her detestation of covetous people made her uneasy if such a one was in her company; upon which occasion she would say many things very entertaining and humorous.

She never interrupted any persons who spoke; she laught at no mistakes they made, but helped them out with mod-esty; and if a good thing were spoken, but neglected, she would not let it fall, but set it in the best light to those who were present. She listened to all that was said, and had never the least distraction, or absence of thought.

It was not safe nor prudent, in her presence, to offend in the least word against modesty; for she then gave full em-ployment to her wit, her contempt, and resentment, under which even stupidity and brutality were forced to sink into confusion; and the guilty person, by her future avoiding him like a bear or a satyr, was never in a way to trans-gress a second time.

It happened one single coxcomb, of the pert kind, was in her company, among several other ladies; and, in his flip-pant way, began to deliver some double meanings: The rest flapt their fans, and used the other common expedients practised in such cases, of appearing not to mind or com-prehend was was said. Her behaviour was very different, and perhaps may be censured. She said thus to the man: " Sir, all these ladies and I understand your meaning very " well, having, in spite of our care, too often met with those " of your sex who wanted manners and good sense. But, " believe me, neither virtuous nor even vicious women love " such kind of conversation. However, I will leave you, " and report your behaviour: And, whatever visit I make, " I shall first enquire at the door whether you are in the " house, that I may be sure to avoid you." I know not whether a majority of ladies would approve of such a pro-ceeding; but I believe the practice of it would soon put an end to that corrupt conversation, the worst effect of dulness, ignorance, impudence, and vulgarity, and the highest affront to the modesty and understanding of the female sex.

By returning very few visits, she had not much company of her own sex, except those whom she most loved for their easiness, or esteemed for their good sense; and those, not insisting on ceremony, came often to her. But she rather chose men for her companions, the usual topics of ladies discourse being such as she had little knowledge of, and less relish. Yet no man was upon the rack to entertain her, for she easily descended to any thing that was innocent and diverting. News, politics, censure, family-management, or town-talk, she always diverted to something else; but these indeed seldom happened, for she chose her company better: And therefore many, who mistook her and themselves, having solicited her acquaintance, and finding themselves disappointed after a few visits, dropt off; and she was never known to enquire into the reason, or ask what was become of them.

She was never positive in arguing, and she usually treated those who were so, in a manner which well enough gratified that unhappy disposition; yet in such a sort as made it very contemptible, and at the same time did some hurt to the owners. Whether this proceeded from her easiness in general, or from her indifference to certain persons, or from her despair of mending them, or from the same practice which she much liked in Mr. Addison, I cannot determine; but when she saw any of the company very warm in a wrong opinion, she was more inclined to confirm them in it than oppose them. The excuse she commonly gave when her friends asked the reason, was, That it prevented noise, and saved time. Yet I have known her very angry with some whom she much esteemed for sometimes falling into that infirmity.

She loved Ireland much better than the generality of those who owe both their birth and riches to it; and, having brought over all the fortune she had in money, left the reversion of the best part of it, one thousand pounds, to Dr. Stephens's Hospital. She detested the tyranny and injustice of England, in their treatment of this kingdom. She had indeed reason to love a country, where she had the esteem and friendship of all who knew her, and the universal good-report of all who ever heard of her, without one exception, if I am told the truth by those who keep general conversation. Which character is the more extraordinary, in falling to a person of so much knowledge, wit, and vivacity, qualities that are used to create envy, and consequently censure; and must be rather imputed to her great modesty, gentle behaviour, and inoffensiveness, than to her superior virtues.

Although her knowledge, from books and company, was much more extensive than usually falls to the share of her sex; yet she was so far from making a parade of it, that her female visitants, on their first acquaintance, who expected to discover it, by what they call hard words and deep discourse, would be sometimes disappointed, and say, they found she was like other women. But wise men, through all her modesty, whatever they discoursed on, could easily observe that she understood them very well, by the judgment shewn in her observations as well as in her questions.

THREE PRAYERS
FOR STELLA

I

ALMIGHTY and most gracious Lord God, extend, we beseech thee, thy pity and compassion towards this thy languishing servant: Teach her to place her hope and confidence entirely in thee; give her a true sense of the emptyness and vanity of all earthly things; make her truly sensible of all the infirmities of her life past, and grant to her such a true sincere repentance as is not to be repented of. Preserve her, O Lord, in a sound mind and understanding, during this thy visitation; keep her from both the sad extremes of presumption and despair. If thou shalt please to restore her to her former health, give her grace to be ever mindful of that mercy, and to keep those good resolutions she now makes in her sickness, so that no length of time, nor prosperity, may entice her to forget them. Let no thought of her misfortunes distract her mind, and prevent the means towards her recovery, or disturb her in her preparations for a better life. We beseech thee also, O Lord, of thy infinite goodness to remember the good actions of this thy servant; that the naked she hath clothed, the hungry she hath fed, the sick and the fatherless whom she hath relieved, may be reckoned according to thy gracious promise, as if they had been done unto thee. Hearken, O Lord, to the prayers offered up by the friends of this thy servant in her behalf, and especially those now made by us unto thee. Give thy blessing to those endeavours used for her recovery; but take from her all violent desire, either of life or death, further them with resignation to thy holy will. And now, O Lord, we implore thy gracious favour towards us here met together; grant that the sense of this thy servant's weakness may add strength to our faith, that we, considering the infirmities of our nature, and the uncertainty of life, may by this example, be drawn to repentance before it shall please thee to visit us in the like manner. Accept these prayers, we beseech Thee, for the sake of thy dear Son Jesus Christ, our Lord; who, with Thee and the Holy Ghost, liveth and reigneth ever one God world without end. Amen.

II

Oct. 17. 1727.

MOST merciful Father, accept our humblest Prayers, in Behalf of this thy languishing Servant: Forgive the Sins, the Frailties and Infirmities of her Life past. Accept the good Deeds she hath done, in such a Manner, that, at whatever Time Thou shalt please to call her, she may be received into everlasting Habitations. Give her Grace to continue sincerely thankful to Thee for the many Favours Thou hast bestowed upon her, the Ability and Inclination and Practice to do Good, and those Virtues, which have procur'd the Esteem and Love of her Friends, and a most unspotted Name in the World. O God, thou dispensest thy Blessings and thy Punishments, as it becometh infinite Justice and Mercy; and since it was thy Pleasure to afflict her with a long, constant, weakly State of Health, make her truly sensible, that it was for very wise Ends, and was largely made up to her in other Blessings, more valuable and less common. Continue to her, O Lord, that Firmness and Constancy of Mind, wherewith thou hast most graciously endowed her, together with that Contempt of worldly Things and Vanities, that she hath shewn in the whole Conduct of her Life. O All-powerful Being, the least Motion of whose Will can create or destroy a World; pity us, the mournful Friends of thy distressed Servant, who sink under the Weight of her present Condition, and the Fear of losing the most valuable of our Friends: Restore her to us, O Lord, if it be thy gracious Will, or inspire us with Constancy and Resignation, to support ourselves under so heavy an Affliction. Restore her, O Lord, for the Sake of those Poor, who by losing her will be desolate, and those Sick, who will not only want her Bounty, but her Care and Tending; or else, in thy Mercy, raise up some other in her Place with equal Disposition and better Abilities. Lessen, O Lord, we beseech thee, her bodily Pains, or give her a double Strength of Mind to support them. And if thou wilt soon take her to thyself, turn our Thoughts rather upon that Felicity, which we hope she shall enjoy, than upon that unspeakable Loss we shall endure. Let her Memory be ever dear unto us; and the Example of her many Virtues, as far as human Infirmity will admit, our constant Imitation. Accept, O Lord, these Prayers poured from the very Bottom of our Hearts, in thy Mercy, and for the Merits of our Blessed Saviour. Amen.

III

Nov. 6. 1727.

O MERCIFUL Father, who never afflicted thy Children, but for their own Good, and with Justice, over which thy Mercy always prevaileth, either to turn them to Repentance, or to punish them in the present Life, in order to reward them in a better; take pity, we beseech thee, upon this thy poor afflicted Servant, languishing so long and so grievously under the Weight of thy Hand. Give her Strength, O Lord, to support her Weakness; and Patience to endure her Pains, without repining at thy Correction. Forgive every rash and inconsiderate Expression, which her Anguish may at any Time force from her Tongue, while her Heart continueth in an entire Submission to thy Will. Suppress in her, O Lord, all eager Desires of Life, and lessen her Fears of Death, by inspiring into her an humble, yet assured, Hope of thy Mercy. Give her a sincere Repentance for all her Transgressions and Omissions, and a firm Resolution to pass the Remainder of her Life in endeavouring to her utmost to observe all thy Precepts. We beseech thee likewise to compose her Thoughts; and preserve to her the Use of her Memory and Reason, during the Course of her Sickness. Give her a true Conception of the Vanity, Folly, and Insignificancy of all human Things; and strengthen her so as to beget in her a sincere Love of thee in the Midst of her Sufferings. Accept, and impute all her good Deeds, and forgive her all those Offences against thee, which she hath sincerely repented of, or through the Frailty of Memory hath forgot. And now, O Lord, we turn to thee in Behalf of ourselves, and the rest of her sorrowful Friends. Let not our Grief afflict her Mind, and thereby have an ill Effect on her present Distemper. Forgive the Sorrow and Weakness of those among us, who sink under the Grief and Terror of losing so dear and useful a Friend. Accept and pardon our most earnest Prayers and Wishes for her longer Continuance in this evil World, to do what thou art pleas'd to call thy Service, and is only her bounden Duty; that she may be still a Comfort to us, and to all others, who will want the Benefit of her Conversation, her Advice, her good Offices, or her Charity. And since thou hast promised, that, where two or three are gathered together in thy Name, thou wilt be in the Midst of them, to grant their Request; O Gracious Lord, grant to us who are here met in thy name, that those Requests, which in the utmost Sincerity and Earnestness of our Hearts we have now made in Behalf of this thy distressed Servant, and of ourselves, may effectually be answered; through the Merits of *Jesus Christ* our Lord. Amen.

POEMS

INTRODUCTION TO THE POEMS

"COUSIN Swift," observed Dryden, "you will never be a poet." Swift never forgave his kinsman for this taunt, and continued to write verses until the end of his life. Dryden, it is true, had only lived to read Swift's early pindaric odes. Swift's later verse might have caused him to reconsider his opinion. But whether anything Swift wrote in verse deserves the name of poetry is a question that cannot be answered here. The most indulgent critic will discover little trace in it either of fancy or imagination, little evidence, that is to say, of poetic sensibility. He will find, on the other hand, immense facility combined with technical ingenuity and correctness.

The small selection of his verse in the following pages is not representative of all that he wrote, though it does, I think, represent his best work. A wider selection would only have upset the balance I have tried to preserve between his writings in prose and verse. For this reason I have not included specimens of his juvenile odes, *vers d'occasion*, personal lampoons, poems relating to English and Irish politics, or those riddles and similar evaporations of wit, which occupied his leisure hours. Besides, I have omitted those coarse yet pungent verses, which express Swift's profound disgust for the natural functions of the body.

The first five pieces I have chosen reveal the light and almost playful side of Swift's nature before it was eclipsed by the sullenness and misanthropy of his later years. The *Verses written in an Ivory Table-Book* anticipate the uncompromising sarcasm and wry humour of such satires as *Betty the Grizette* and *The Furniture of a Woman's Mind*, written more than a quarter of a century after. *The Petition of Frances Harris*, composed early in 1701/2—a brilliant example of the clever doggerel Swift too seldom employed—recalls the happy domesticity of his life in Lord Berkeley's household at Dublin Castle. Frances Harris, the heroine of the tale, was a gentlewoman of Lady Berkeley's.

Swift's power of concentrated description is shown in the two accounts, one of an early morning in London, the other of a sudden shower of rain, in which he parodies (with an eye on his enemy Dryden) the heroic style by exalting mean subjects. As he grew older, Swift tended more and more to exercise his gift for naturalistic description on the squalid aspects of human life. The repellent nastiness of the Yahoos in *Gulliver's Travels* infects such pieces as *The Lady's Dressing Room* and *On a Beautiful Young Nymph going to Bed*.

In Sickness—written in October 1714—originated, according to Elrington Ball, " in the depression caused by learning of the complete eclipse of the Tory ministers ", when Swift, exiled from his friends in Ireland and suffering increasingly from the attacks of deafness and giddiness that were finally to drive him off his head, realized that all hope of political preferment had been swept away for ever. It might well be described as a rejected fragment of the more celebrated *Verses on the Death of Dr Swift*.

Two examples have been included of the poems which Swift addressed every year, with one exception [1725/6], to Stella Johnson on her birthday, March 13, from 1718/9 until the year preceding her death in January 1727/8.

Phillis, Or the Progress of Love—the date of composition given by Faulkner is probably too early—is a good specimen of Swift's use of his favourite octosyllables in narrative verse. The best of his early experiments in this kind is *Baucis and Philemon*, and the most polished example *Cadenus and Vanessa*, which is printed in full here.

On Poetry: A Rapsody, his most sustained satire in verse, and regarded by many critics as the greatest of his poems, was published in London by Swift's agent Matthew Pilkington on December 31, 1733. On account of its subversive political allusions, two of the persons concerned in its publication—Motte, Swift's London publisher, and the unfortunate Mrs Barber, who had brought the poem over from Dublin—were imprisoned for more than a year. It is believed that the miserable Pilkington informed against them.

The Day of Judgement, the most concentrated poem Swift ever wrote, was probably written at the same time as the verses on his own death, that is to say in 1731.

CADENUS AND VANESSA

Cadenus and Vanessa—Swift's longest poem—is an autobiographical fantasy. Its theme is the relations of Swift, in the character of Cadenus [an anagram of Decanus, i.e. Dean] with Esther Vanhomrigh [Vanessa], the daughter of a rich Dutch merchant, whom he had first met in London towards the end of the year 1707, and at whose mother's house he became a frequent and intimate visitor. Unknown to Stella Johnson, the affection which sprang up between the two ripened swiftly into love. Swift's biographers, in general, have attempted to save his face and his cloth by putting the responsibility for the passion on Vanessa. But even assuming, as they do without good reason, that Vanessa took the initiative, the letters that passed between them, particularly in the last four years of her life, show clearly enough to an unbiased reader that Swift did not wholly resent her advances and only grew cold and "terrible" when he realized he could not retreat.

Whether Vanessa finally suspected that she was being deceived, and, if so, whether she dragged an explanation out of Swift or Stella are questions that cannot be answered convincingly. It seems certain, however, that some rupture occurred before Vanessa's early death, on June 2, 1723, closed this tragic incident for ever. Some light is thrown on Stella's character and her attitude to the affair by her reply to one who observed that Vanessa must have been a remarkable woman to have inspired such a poem, that " it was well known the Dean could write finely upon a Broom-stick ".

On two occasions Swift stated that *Cadenus and Vanessa* was written at Windsor in the autumn of 1712, that is to say a year before he was entitled to call himself *Cadenus*. It may be that he was mistaken in the date, or wished to conceal the actual time of composition. The poem was revised in 1719 [*v.* Letter in French to Vanessa, May 12, 1719], and was published in London by three publishers, without Swift's consent, in 1726. There is some ground for believing that Vanessa gave instructions for its publication after her death. Swift's feelings are summed up in a remarkable passage from a letter addressed by him to Knightley Chetwode on April 19, 1726:

> " I am very indifferent what is done with it, for printing cannot make it more common than it is; and for my own part, I forget what is in it, but believe it to be only a cavalier business, and they who will not give allowances may choose, and if they intend it maliciously, they will be disappointed, for it was what I expected, long before I left Ireland.
>
> " Therefore what you advise me, about printing it myself, is impossible, for I never saw it since I writ it. Neither if I had, would I use shifts or arts, let people think of me as they please. Neither do I believe the gravest character is answerable for a private humorsome thing, which, by an accident inevitable, and the baseness of particular malice, is made public. I have borne a great deal more; and those who will like me less, upon seeing me capable of having writ such a trifle so many years ago, may think as they please, neither is it agreeable to me to be troubled with such accounts, when there is no remedy, and only gives me the ungrateful task of reflecting on the baseness of mankind which I knew sufficiently before."

There is no evidence to show which of the several printings of the poem is the first. Roberts's edition was published anonymously; Warner, who added to the title the words *A Law Case*, attributed it to " Dean Swift "; Blandford, who published at least seven editions or issues [" editions " 4 and 6, for example, are typographically identical] attributed it to " Dr. S——t". During the same year the poem was also printed in Dublin and Edinburgh. It was included in *The Last* [i.e. the *Third*] *Volume* of *Miscellanies*, 1727, and by Faulkner in 1735 in his collected edition of Swift's *Works*.

VERSES ON THE DEATH OF DR. SWIFT

The best example of Swift's mysterious methods of publishing his work is to be found in the history of the early editions of the poem he wrote in anticipation of his own death. Early in April 1733, a poem of 202 lines, dedicated to Pope, entitled *The Life and Genuine Character of Dean Swift*, was published in London and Dublin at the instance of the egregious and reverend Mr Matthew Pilkington. The Dedication, it was dated All Fools' Day, is significant. In a letter [To Gay. Dec. 1, 1731] written about eighteen months earlier, Swift mentions that he has been " several months writing near five hundred lines on a pleasant subject, only to tell what my friends and enemies will say on me after I am dead. I shall finish it soon, for I add two lines every week, and blot out four and alter eight. I have brought in you and my other friends as well as enemies and destructors." The poem was completed before February, 1731/2. Some eight years later, in 1739, Bathurst published in London three folio editions of a poem of 381 lines, including six blank lines, entitled *Verses on the Death of Dr Swift*. The MS. of this poem had been given by Swift to his friend Dr William King, an Oxford don, who, fearful of the consequences of printing the libels it contained on Queen Caroline and her first minister, Walpole, omitted Swift's notes and several passages and " assigned many judicious reasons (though some of them were merely temporary and prudential) " for the mutilation : but, adds Nichols, " they were so far from satisfying Dr Swift that a complete edition was immediately printed by Faulkner, with the Dean's express permission ". Accordingly, five impressions of the complete poem of 484 lines were published in Dublin by Faulkner in 1739. Several states of these impressions exist, containing a few corrections made while the sheets were in the press. These were afterwards incorporated by Faulkner in the version of the poem printed in Volume 8, 1746, of his collected edition. Even Faulkner, however, omitted words in the text and passages in the notes, which Swift had added after he had finished the poem. Fortunately these *lacunae* have been supplied in manuscript in three surviving copies. One of these—a copy of the first impression now in the Forster collection—contains six alternative lines, and is the basis of the present text. A second copy—the fifth impression—belongs to Mr Harold Williams. A third copy, hitherto unrecorded—a later state of the first impression, containing a few verbal corrections not in the Forster copy—has been collated for this edition. Purchased in Belfast in 1933 and generously lent to me by Mr Dudley Massey, this copy is now in Mr Williams's library. In none of these copies is there any indication of the source of these important MS. additions, but they are certainly authoritative.

Bathurst's edition, prepared by King with Pope's assistance, contains 65 lines which were not in Swift's original MS. but which appear with some variants in the earlier *Life and Character*. Scott printed these lines in the notes as rejections made by Swift, but Browning in his very unsatisfactory edition of the poems placed them in the text, thereby destroying the shape of the poem. It is almost certain that Swift was a party to the mysterious publication of the *Life and Character* and used it as an excuse for publishing the genuine poem while he was still alive. Lord Orrery, Faulkner and Mrs Letitia Pilkington never doubted his share in the conspiracy. Both poems were included by Faulkner in Vol. 8, 1746, of his collected edition, with an advertisement appended to the spurious poem, implying that Swift was the author.

The curious reader should consult an article by Mr H. Davis in *The Book Collector's Quarterly* [No. 11, March 1931], where the history of the poem is examined at length.

NOTE ON THE TEXT OF THE POEMS

THE majority of the poems that follow have been re-printed from the volumes in which they first appeared. The source of each piece and any later editions used in the preparation of the present recension are indicated in the Textual Notes. With two exceptions—*On the Day of Judgement* and *Verses on the Death of Dr Swift*—all these poems were collected by Faulkner in the second volume of his edition of Swift's *Works*, 1735. Faulkner's text, which there is good reason to believe Swift himself supervised, is still the most satisfactory for general purposes and is much to be preferred to the only modern edition of Swift's poems, prepared by W. E. Browning in 1910.* Faulkner's first edition of 1735 is unfortunately scarce. Smaller collections of Swift's verses had previously appeared in the volumes of *Miscellanies*, published in 1711, 1727 and 1732. *Cadenus and Vanessa* and *On Poetry: A Rapsody*, among others, were issued separately.

The Petition of Frances Harris was pirated by Hills in 1709 and published with *Baucis and Philemon*; and again in 1710 by the wicked Curll, in a slim volume containing *A Meditation on a Broomstick*. The first authorized printing was in the *Miscellanies* of the following year. The variants between these three editions are insignificant, but for the satisfaction of the curious reader I have given a collation of Curll's text.

Three poems — *Phillis, Or the Progress of Love* and the birthday poems for Stella—have been printed from a volume of Swift's poems, written in Stella Johnson's autograph, now in the Duke of Bedford's library at Woburn Abbey. This common-place book appears to have been in existence in the early 'twenties of the eighteenth century [cf. Swift's *To Stella, who Collected and Transcribed his Poems*, first printed in *Miscellanies the Third* [i.e. Fourth] *Volume* 1732]. After Stella's death Swift presented the volume to his friend Sir Arthur Acheson, the owner of Market Hill [Gosford Castle] in Ireland,

---

* Since the publication (1937) of Mr Harold Williams's definitive edition of the poems, this is no longer true. [ED.]

from one of whose descendants it passed into the possession of the Dukes of Bedford. From the textual point of view Stella's transcription is certainly as authoritative as if it had been made by Swift himself; but it is additionally valuable since it precedes in date the first printed version of the three poems in question [in *Miscellanies*, Vol. III, 1727, published shortly after Stella's death] by at least half a dozen years. A full collation of the manuscript and printed texts will be found in the notes.

A *Description of Morning* and *The Description of a City Shower* were originally given by Swift to Steele to fill out a number of *The Tatler*, which the latter was editing with Swift's encouragement. They were not printed in book form until 1711 in *Miscellanies in Prose and Verse*. The present text is based on the version given in *The Tatler* corrected by that of *Miscellanies* 1711.

On the Day of Judgement was not added to the canon of Swift's verse until 1775. [*Works*. Ed. Nichols. 4to. IX. ii.] According to Elrington Ball, Faulkner obtained Swift's holograph of the poem—probably after Swift's death—and gave it to his patron Lord Chesterfield, who sent a copy of it to Voltaire in a letter dated August 27, 1752. The covering letter with Chesterfield's comment on the poem in French is printed in the first edition of his *Letters to his Son* [pub. April 7, 1774] but the poem itself is missing. On April 12 of the same year, however, a copy of the poem appeared with the following note from an anonymous correspondent in the *Saint James's Chronicle*:—

> In return for the Pleasure which I often receive from the Perusal of your agreeable miscellaneous Paper, I send you an original poem of Dean Swift's, which he never published. ... You may be assured of the Authenticity of this little Poem, when I refer you to the Authority of Lord Chesterfield. ... His Lordship expressly says he had the Original, in the Dean's own Hand-writing; but there is no Copy of it in the Earl's Book. I am happy, however, in having it in my Power to send you a correct Copy for the entertainment of your Readers.
>
> I am, Sir, &c.
>
> KENSINGTON. *April* 7.   MERCUTIO.

The poem was printed again in *The Monthly Review* for July 1774 in the course of a criticism of Chesterfield's *Letters*, and reprinted, presumably from this source, in the fourth edition of the *Letters*, which was published on October 29. The whole subject has been ably discussed in an article by S. L. Gulich Jr. in *Pub. Mod. Lang. Ass. of America*, Vol. XLVIII, 3 Sept. 1933.

The complicated bibliography of *Verses on the Death of Dr. Swift* and of *Cadenus and Vanessa* has already been examined. The reader should consult the textual notes on the subject of the passages from *On Poetry: A Rapsody*, which were printed for the first time by Scott in 1824.

POEMS

Wrote in a Lady's *Ivory Table-Book*

Anno 1698

Peruse my Leaves thro' ev'ry Part,
　And think thou seest my owners Heart,
　　Scrawl'd o'er with Trifles thus, and quite
As hard, as sensless, and as light:
Expos'd to every Coxcomb's Eyes,
But hid with Caution from the Wise.
Here you may read (*Dear charming Saint*)
Beneath (*A new Receit for Paint*)
Here in Beau-spelling (*tru tel deth*)
There in her own (*far an el breth*)
Here (*lovely Nymph pronounce my doom*)
There (*A safe way to use Perfume*)
Here, a Page fill'd with Billet Doux;
On t'other side (*laid out for Shoes*)
(*Madam, I dye without your Grace*)
(*Item, for half a Yard of Lace*.)
Who that had Wit would place it here,
For every peeping Fop to Jear.
To think that your Brains Issue is
Expos'd to th'Excrement of his,
In power of Spittle and a Clout
When e're he please to blot it out;
And then to heighten the Disgrace
Clap his own Nonsense in the place.
Whoe're expects to hold his part
In such a Book and such a Heart,
If he be Wealthy and a Fool
Is in all Points the fittest Tool,
Of whom it may be justly said,
He's a Gold Pencil tipt with Lead.

To their Excellencies the Lords Justices of Ireland

THE HUMBLE PETITION OF
FRANCES HARRIS,

Who must Starve, and Die a Maid if it miscarries.

Anno 1700

Humbly Sheweth.

THAT I went to warm my self in Lady *Betty's* Chamber,
because I was cold,

And I had in a Purse, seven Pound, four Shillings and six
Pence, besides Farthings, in Money, and Gold;

So because I had been buying things for my *Lady* last Night,

I was resolved to tell my Money, to see if it was right:

Now you must know, because my Trunk has a very bad
Lock,

Therefore all the Money, I have, which, *God* knows, is a
very small Stock,

I keep in my Pocket ty'd about my Middle, next my
Smock.

So when I went to put up my Purse, as *God* would have it,
my Smock was unript,

And, instead of putting it into my Pocket, down it slipt:

Then the Bell rung, and I went down to put my *Lady* to
Bed,

And, *God* knows, I thought my Money was as safe as my
Maidenhead.

So when I came up again, I found my Pocket feel very light,

But when I search'd, and miss'd my Purse, *Lord !* I thought
I should have sunk outright:

Lord ! Madam, says *Mary*, how d'ye do? Indeed, says I,
never worse;

But pray, *Mary*, can you tell what I have done with my
Purse !

Lord help me, said *Mary*, I never stirr'd out of this Place !

Nay, said I, I had it in Lady *Betty's* Chamber, that's a
   plain Case.

So *Mary* got me to Bed, and cover'd me up warm;

However, she stole away my Garters, that I might do my
   self no Harm:

So I tumbl'd and toss'd all Night, as you may very well
   think,

But hardly ever set my Eyes together, or slept a Wink.

So I was a-dream'd, methought, that we went and search'd
   the Folks round,

And in a Corner of Mrs. *Dukes's* Box, ty'd in a Rag, the
   Money was found.

So next Morning we told *Whittle*, and he fell a Swearing;

Then my Dame *Wadgar* came, and she, you know, is thick
   of Hearing;

Dame, said I, as loud as I could bawl, do you know what
   a Loss I have had?

Nay, said she, my Lord **Collway's* Folks are all very sad,

For my Lord †*Dromedary* comes a *Tuesday* without fail;

Pugh! said I, but that's not the Business that I ail.

Says *Cary*, says he, I have been a Servant this Five and
   Twenty Years, come Spring,

And in all the Places I Liv'd, I never heard of such a
   Thing.

Yes, says the *Steward*, I remember when I was at my Lady
   Shrewsbury's,

Such a thing as this happen'd, just about the time of
   Goosberries.

So I went to the Party suspected, and I found her full of
   Grief;

(Now you must know, of all Things in the World, I hate
   a Thief.)

However, I was resolv'd to bring the Discourse slily about,

Mrs. *Dukes*, said I, here's an ugly Accident has happen'd
   out;

'Tis not that I value the Money three Skips of a Louse;

But the Thing I stand upon, is the Credit of the House;

---

* *Gallway*.   † *Drogheda*.

'Tis true, seven Pound, four Shillings, and six Pence, makes
   a great Hole in my Wages,
Besides, as they say, Service is no Inheritance in these
   Ages.
Now, Mrs. *Dukes*, you know, and every Body understands,
That tho' 'tis hard to judge, yet Money can't go without
   Hands.
The *Devil* take me, said she, (blessing her self,) if ever I
   saw't!
So she roar'd like a *Bedlam*, as tho' I had call'd her all to
   naught;
So you know, what could I say to her any more,
I e'en left her, and came away as wise as I was before.
Well: But then they would have had me gone to the Cun-
   ning Man;
No, said I, 'tis the same Thing, the *Chaplain* will be here
   anon.
So the *Chaplain* came in; now the Servants say, he is my
   Sweet-heart,
Because he's always in my Chamber, and I always take
   his Part;
So, as the *Devil* would have it, before I was aware, out I
   blunder'd,
Parson, said I, can you cast a *Nativity*, when a Body's
   plunder'd?
(Now you must know, he hates to be call'd *Parson*, like
   the *Devil*.)
Truly, says he, Mrs. *Nab*, it might become you to be more
   civil:
If your Money be gone, as a Learned *Divine* says, d'ye see,
You are no *Text* for my Handling, so take that from me:
I was never taken for a *Conjurer* before, I'd have you to
   know.
Lord, said I, don't be angry, I'm sure I never thought
   you so;
You know, I honour the Cloth, I design to be a *Parson*'s
   Wife,
I never took one in *Your Coat* for a *Conjurer* in all my
   Life.

With that, he twisted his Girdle at me like a Rope, as who
  should say,
Now you may go hang your self for me, and so went away.
Well; I thought I should have swoon'd; *Lord*, said I, what
  shall I do?
I have lost my *Money*, and shall lose my *True-Love* too.
Then my *Lord* call'd me; *Harry*, said my *Lord*, don't cry,
I'll give something towards thy Loss; and says my *Lady*,
  so will I.
Oh but, said I, what if after all my Chaplain won't *come to*?
For that, he said, (an't please your *Excellencies*) I must
  petition You.
The Premises tenderly consider'd, I desire your *Excellencies*
  Protection,
And that I may have a Share in next *Sunday's* Collection:
And over and above, that I may have your *Excellencies*
  Letter,
With an Order for the *Chaplain* aforesaid; or instead of
  Him, a Better:
And then your poor *Petitioner*, both Night and Day,
Or the *Chaplain*, (for 'tis his *Trade*) as in Duty bound, shall
  ever *Pray*.

A DESCRIPTION OF THE MORNING

April, 1709.

Now hardly here and there an Hackney-Coach
Appearing, show'd the Ruddy Morn's Approach.
Now *Betty* from her Master's Bed had flown,
And softly stole to discompose her own.
The Slipshod 'Prentice from his Master's Dore,
Had par'd the Street, and Sprinkled round the Floor.
Now *Moll* had whirl'd her Mop with dext'rous Airs,
Prepar'd to scrub the Entry and the Stairs.
The Youth with broomy Stumps began to trace
The Kennel Edge, where Wheels had worn the Place.
The Smallcoal-Man was heard with Cadence deep,
Till drown'd in shriller Notes of Chimney-sweep.
Duns at his Lordship's Gate began to meet;

And Brickdust *Moll* had scream'd through half a Street.
The Turn-key now his Flock returning sees,
Duly let out a' Nights to steal for Fees.
The watchful Bayliffs take their silent Stands;
And School-boys lag with Satchels in their Hands.

A DESCRIPTION OF A CITY SHOWER

October, 1710.

CAREFUL Observers may foretel the Hour
(By sure Prognosticks) when to dread a Show'r:
While Rain depends, the pensive Cat gives o'er
Her Frolicks, and pursues her Tail no more.
Returning Home at Night, you'll find the Sink
Strike your offended Sense with double Stink.
If you be wise, then go not far to dine,
You'll spend in Coach-hire more than save in Wine.
A coming Show'r your shooting Corns presage,
Old Aches throb, your hollow Tooth will rage.
Sauntring in Coffee-house is *Dulman* seen;
He damns the Climate, and complains of Spleen.

Mean while the South rising with dabbled Wings,
A Sable Cloud a-thawrt the Welkin flings,
That swill'd more Liquor than it could contain,
And like a Drunkard gives it up again.
Brisk *Susan* whips her Linen from the Rope,
While the first drizzling Show'r is born aslope.
Such is that Sprinkling which some careless Quean
Flirts on you from her Mop, but not so clean.
You fly, invoke the Gods; then turning, stop
To rail; she singing, still whirls on her Mop.
Not yet, the Dust had shun'd th'unequal Strife,
But aided by the Wind, fought still for Life;
And wafted with its Foe by violent Gust,
'Twas doubtful which was Rain, and which was Dust.
Ah! where must needy Poet seek for Aid,
When Dust and Rain at once his Coat invade;

His only Coat, where Dust confus'd with Rain,
Roughen the Nap, and leave a mingled Stain.

Now in contiguous Drops the Flood comes down,
Threat'ning with Deluge this *Devoted* Town.
To Shops in Crowds the daggled Females fly,
Pretend to cheapen Goods, but nothing buy.
The Templer spruce, while ev'ry Spout's a-broach,
Stays till 'tis fair, yet seems to call a Coach.
The tuck'd-up Sempstress walks with hasty Strides,
While Streams run down her oil'd Umbrella's Sides.
Here various Kinds by various Fortunes led,
Commence Acquaintance underneath a Shed.
Triumphant Tories, and desponding Whigs,
Forget their Fewds, and join to save their Wigs.
Box'd in a Chair the Beau impatient sits,
While Spouts run clatt'ring o'er the Roof by Fits;
And ever and anon with frightful Din
The Leather sounds, he trembles from within.
So when *Troy* Chair-men bore the Wooden Steed,
Pregnant with *Greeks*, impatient to be freed.
(Those Bully *Greeks*, who, as the Moderns do,
Instead of paying Chair-men, run them thro'.)
Laoco'n struck the Outside with his Spear,
And each imprison'd Hero quak'd for Fear.

Now from all Parts the swelling Kennels flow,
And bear their Trophies with them as they go:
Filth of all Hues and Odours seem to tell
What Street they sail'd from, by their Sight and Smell.
They, as each Torrent drives, with rapid Force
From *Smithfield* or St. *Pulchre's* shape their Course,
And in huge Confluent join at *Snow-Hill* Ridge,
Fall from the *Conduit* prone to *Holborn-Bridge*.
Sweepings from Butchers Stalls, Dung, Guts, and Blood,
Drown'd Puppies, stinking Sprats, all drench'd in Mud,
Dead Cats and Turnip-Tops come tumbling down the
Flood.

CORINNA

This Day, (the Year I dare not tell,)
　　Apollo play'd the Midwife's Part,
Into the World *Corinna* fell,
　　And he endow'd her with his Art.

But *Cupid* with a *Satyr* comes;
　　Both softly to the Cradle creep:
Both stroke her Hands, and rub her Gums,
　　While the poor Child lay fast asleep.

Then *Cupid* thus: This little Maid
　　Of Love shall always speak and write;
And I pronounce, (the *Satyr* said)
　　The World shall feel her scratch and bite.

Her Talent she display'd betimes;
　　For in twice twelve revolving Moons,
She seem'd to laugh and squawl in Rhimes,
　　And all her Gestures were Lampoons.

At six Years old, the subtle Jade
　　Stole to the Pantry-Door, and found
The Butler with my Lady's Maid;
　　And you may swear the Tale went round.

She made a Song, how little Miss
　　Was kiss'd and slobber'd by a Lad:
And how, when Master went to p——,
　　Miss came, and peep'd at all he had.

At twelve, a Wit and a Coquette;
　　Marries for Love, half Whore, half Wife;
Cuckolds, elopes, and runs in Debt;
　　Turns Auth'ress, and is *Curll's* for Life.

Her Common-Place-Book all gallant is,
　　Of Scandal now a *Cornucopia*;
She pours it out in an *Atlantis*,
　　Or *Memoirs* of the *New Utopia*.

IN SICKNESS

*Written soon after the Author's coming to live in Ireland,
upon the Queen's Death, October 1714.*

'Tis true,—then why should I repine,
To see my Life so fast decline?
But, why obscurely here alone?
Where I am neither lov'd nor known.
My State of Health none care to learn;
My Life is here no Soul's Concern.
And, those with whom I now converse,
Without a Tear will tend my Herse.
Remov'd from kind *Arbuthnot's* Aid,
Who knows his Art but not his Trade;
Preferring his Regard for me
Before his Credit or his Fee.
Some formal Visits, Looks, and Words,
What meer Humanity affords,
I meet perhaps from three or four,
From whom I once expected more;
Which those who tend the Sick for pay
Can act as decently as they.
But, no obliging, tender Friend
To help at my approaching End,
My Life is now a Burthen grown
To others, e'er it be my own.

Ye formal Weepers for the Sick,
In your last Offices be quick:
And spare my absent Friends the Grief
To hear, yet give me no Relief;
Expir'd To-day, entomb'd To-morrow,
When known, will save a double Sorrow.

PHILLIS: OR THE PROGRESS OF LOVE
Written. A.D. 1719.

DESPONDING *Phillis* was endu'd
With ev'ry Talent of a Prude,

She trembled when a Man drew near,
Salute her, and she turn'd her Ear;
If o'er against her you were plac't,
She durst not look above your Wast:
She'd rather take you to her Bed
Than let you see her dress her Head;
In Church you heard her thrô the Crowd
Repeat the *Absolution* loud;
In Church, secure behind her Fan
She durst behold that Monster, Man:
There practic'd how to place her Head,
And bit her Lips, to make them red:
Or on the Matt devoutly kneeling
Would lift her Eyes up to the Ceeling,
And heave her Bosom unaware
For neighb'ring Beaux to see it bare.

At length a lucky Lover came,
And found Admittance from the Dame.
Suppose all Partyes now agreed,
The Writings drawn, the Lawyer fee'd,
The Vicar and the Ring bespoke:
Guess, how could such a Match be broke?
See then what Mortals place their Bliss in!
Next Morn betimes the Bride was missing.
The Mother scream'd, the Father chid;
Where can this idle Wench be hid?
No News of Phil.   The Bridegroom came,
And thought his Bride had skulk't for shame,
Because her Father us'd to say,
The Girl had such a Bashfull way.

Now John the Butler must be sent,
To learn the Way that Phillis went.
The Groom was wisht to saddle Crop,
For John must neither light, nor stop;
But find her where so'er she fled,
And bring her back, alive or dead.
See here again the Dev'l to do;
For truly John was missing too:

The Horse and Pillion both were gone—
Phillis, it seems, was fled with John.
Old Madam who went up to find
What Papers Phil had left behind,
A Letter on the Toylet sees,
To my much honour'd Father. . . . These:
('Tis always done, Romances tell us,
When Daughters run away with Fellows)
Fill'd with the choicest common-places,
By others us'd in the like Cases;
That, long ago, a Fortune-teller
Exactly said what now befell her,
And in a glass had made her see
A serving-Man of low Degree:
It was her Fate; must be forgiven;
For Marriages are made in Heaven:
His Pardon begg'd; but to be plain,
She'd do't if 'twere to do again.
Thank God, 'twas neither Shame nor Sin,
For John was come of honest Kin:
Love never thinks of Rich and Poor,
She'd beg with John from Door to Door:
Forgive her, if it be a Crime,
She'll never do't another Time,
She ne'er before in all her Life
Once disobey'd him, Maid nor Wife.
One Argument she summ'd up all in,
The Thing was done, and past recalling:
And therefore hop'd she would recover
His Favor when his Passion's over.
She valued not what others thought her;
And was—His most Obedient Daughter.

Fair Maidens all attend the Muse
Who now the wandring Pair pursues:
Away they rode in homely sort
Their Journy long, their Money short;
The loving Couple well bemir'd,
The Horse and both the Riders tir'd:

Their Vittels bad, their Lodging worse;
Phil cry'd, and John began to curse;
Phil wisht, that She had strain'd a Limb
When first she ventur'd out with him.
John wisht, that he had broke a Leg
When first for her he quitted Peg.

But what Adventures more befell 'um
The Muse has now not time to tell 'um.
How Jonny wheadled, threatned, fawn'd,
Till Phillis all her Trinkets pawn'd:
How oft she broke her marriage Vows
In Kindness to maintain her Spouse;
Till Swains unwholsome spoyld the trade;
For now the Surgeon must be paid
To whom those Perquisites are gone
In Christian Justice due to John.
When food and Rayment now grew scarce
Fate put a Period to the Farce;
And with exact Poetick Justice;
For John is Landlord, Phillis Hostess;
They keep at *Staines*, the *Old Blue Boar*,
Are Cat and Dog, and Rogue and Whore.

STELLA'S BIRTH-DAY
Written. A.D. 1718.

STELLA this Day is thirty four,
(We wont dispute a Year or more)
However Stella, be not troubled,
Although thy Size and Years are doubled,
Since first I saw Thee at Sixteen
The brightest Virgin of the Green.
So little is thy Form declin'd
Made up so largly in thy Mind.
Oh, would it please the Gods, to Split
Thy Beauty, Size, and Years, and Wit,
No Age could furnish out a Pair
Of Nymphs so gracefull, Wise, and fair

With half the Lustre of your Eyes,
With half thy Wit, thy Years, and Size:
And then before it grew too late,
How should I beg of gentle Fate,
(That either Nymph might have her Swain,)
To split my Worship too in twain.

STELLA'S BIRTH-DAY

Written. A.D. 1720–21.

ALL Travellers at first incline
Where-e'er they see the fairest Sign,
And if they find the Chambers neat,
And like the Liquor and the Meat
Will call again and recommend
The Angel-Inn to ev'ry Friend:
And though the Painting grows decay'd
The House will never loose its Trade;
Nay, though the treach'rous Rascal Thomas
Hangs a new Angel two Doors from us
As fine as Dawbers Hands can make it
In hopes that Strangers may mistake it,
They think it both a Shame and Sin
To quit the true old Angel-Inn.

Now, this is Stella's Case in Fact,
An Angel's Face, a little crackt;
(Could Poets or could Painters fix
How Angels look at thirty six)
This drew us in at first to find
In such a Form an Angel's Mind:
And ev'ry Virtue now supplyes
The fainting Rays of Stella's Eyes:
See, at her Levee crowding Swains
Whom Stella freely entertains
With Breeding, Humor, Wit, and Sense,
And puts them to so small Expence:
Their Minds so plentifully fills,
And makes such reasonable Bills,

So little gets for what She gives,
We really wonder how She lives;
And, had her Stock been less, no doubt
She must have long ago run out.
Then who can think we'll quit the Place
When Doll hangs out a newer Face
Nail'd to her Window full in sight
All Christian People to invite;
Or stop and light at Cloe's Head,
With scraps and Leavings to be fed.

Then Cloe, still go on to prate
Of thirty six, and thirty eight;
Pursue thy Trade of Scandall-picking,
Thy Hints that Stella is no Chickin;
Your Innuendo's when you tell us
That Stella loves to talk with Fellows:
But let me warn thee to believe
A Truth for which thy Soul should grieve:
That should you live to see the Day
When Stella's Locks must all be grey,
When Age must print a furrow'd Trace
On every Feature of her Face;
Though you and all your Senceless Tribe
Could Art or Time or Nature bribe
To make you look like Beauty's Queen
And hold for ever at fifteen;
No Bloom of Youth can ever blind
The Cracks and Wrinckles of your Mind:
All Men of Sense will pass your Dore
And crowd to Stella's at fourscore.

CADENUS AND VANESSA

THE Shepherds and the Nymphs were seen
Pleading before the *Cyprian* Queen.
The Council for the Fair began,
Accusing that false Creature, Man.

The Brief with weighty Crimes was charg'd,
On which the Pleader much enlarg'd;
That *Cupid* now has lost his Art,
Or blunts the Point of ev'ry Dart;
His Altar now no longer smoaks,
His Mother's Aid no Youth invokes:
This tempts Free-thinkers to refine,
And bring in doubt their Pow'r divine.
Now Love is dwindled to Intrigue,
And Marriage grown a Money-League.
Which Crimes aforesaid (with her Leave)
Were (as he humbly did conceive)
Against our Sov'reign Lady's Peace;
Against the Statutes in that Case;
Against her Dignity and Crown:
Then pray'd an Answer, and sat down.

The Nymphs with Scorn beheld their Foes:
When the Defendant's Council rose,
And, what no Lawyer ever lack'd,
With Impudence own'd all the Fact.
But, what the gentlest Heart would vex,
Laid all the fault on t'other Sex;
That modern Love is no such Thing
As what those ancient Poets sing,
A Fire celestial, chaste, refin'd,
Conceiv'd and kindled in the Mind,
Which, having found an equal Flame,
Unites, and both become the same;
In different Breasts together burn,
Together both to Ashes turn.
But Women now feel no such Fire,
And only know the gross Desire,
Their Passions move in lower Spheres,
Where-e'er Caprice or Folly stears:
A Dog, a Parrot, or an Ape,
Or a worse Brute in human Shape,
Engross the Fancies of the Fair,
The few soft Moments they can spare,

From Visits to receive and pay,
From Scandal, Politicks and Play,
From Fans and Flounces and Brocades,
From Equipage and Park-parades,
From all the thousand female Toys,
From every Trifle that employs
The out or inside of their Heads,
Between their Toylets and their Beds.

In a dull Stream, which moving slow,
You hardly see the Current flow,
If a small Breeze obstructs the Course,
It whirls about for want of Force,
And in its narrow Circle gathers
Nothing but Chaff and Straws and Feathers.
The Current of a Female Mind
Stops thus, and turns with ev'ry Wind;
Thus whirling round, together draws
Fools, Fops, and Rakes, for Chaff and Straws.
Hence we conclude, no Women's Hearts
Are won by Virtue, Wit and Parts:
Nor are the Men of Sense to blame,
For Breasts incapable of Flame;
The fault must on the Nymphs be plac'd,
Grown so corrupted in their Taste.

The Pleader having spoke his best,
Had Witness ready to attest,
Who fairly could on Oath depose,
When Questions on the Fact arose,
That ev'ry Article was true;
Nor further those Deponents knew:
Therefore he humbly would insist,
The Bill might be with Costs dismist.

The Cause appear'd of so much Weight,
That *Venus*, from the Judgment Seat,
Desir'd them not to talk so loud,
Else she must interpose a Cloud:

For if the Heav'nly Folk should know
These Pleadings in the Courts below,
That Mortals here disdain to love,
She ne'er could shew her Face above:
For Gods, their Betters, are too wise
To value that which Men despise:
And then, said she, my Son and I
Must strole in Air 'twixt Earth and Sky;
Or else, shut out from Heaven and Earth,
Fly to the Sea, my Place of Birth;
There live with daggl'd *Mermaids* pent,
And keep on Fish perpetual *Lent*.

But since the Case appear'd so nice,
She thought it best to take Advice;
The Muses, by their King's Permission,
Tho' Foes to Love, attend their Session,
And on the Right Hand took their Places
In Order; on the Left, the Graces:
To whom she might her Doubts propose
In all Emergencies that rose.

The Muses oft were seen to frown;
The Graces half asham'd look'd down;
And 'twas observ'd there were but few ⎫
Of either Sex, among the Crew, ⎬
Whom she or her Assessors knew. ⎭
The Goddess soon began to see
Things were not ripe for a Decree,
And said she must consult her Books,
The *Lovers Fleta's, Bractons, Cokes.*

First to a dapper Clerk she beckon'd,
To turn to *Ovid,* Book the Second;
She then referr'd them to a Place
In *Virgil* (*vide Dido's* Case):
As for *Tibullus's* Reports,
They never pass'd for Law in Courts;
For *Cowley's* Briefs, and Pleas of *Waller*,
Still their Authority was smaller.

There was on both sides much to say:
She'd hear the Cause another Day,
And so she did, and then a Third,
She heard it—there she kept her Word.
But with Rejoinders and Replies,
Long Bills, and Answers, stuft with Lies,
Demurr, Imparlance, and Essoign,
The Parties ne'er cou'd Issue join:
For Sixteen Years the Cause was spun,
And then stood where it first begun.

Now, gentle *Clio*, sing or say,
What *Venus* meant by this Delay:
The Goddess much perplex'd in Mind,
To see her Empire thus declin'd,
When first this grand Debate arose,
Above her Wisdom to compose,
Conceiv'd a Project in her Head,
To work her Ends; which if it sped,
Wou'd shew the Merits of the Cause,
Far better than consulting Laws.

In a glad Hour *Lucina's* Aid
Produc'd on Earth a wond'rous Maid,
On whom the Queen of Love was bent
To try a new Experiment:
She threw her Law-books on the Shelf,
And thus debated with herself;
Since Men alledge they ne'er can find
Those Beauties in a female Mind,
Which raise a Flame that will endure
For ever, uncorrupt and pure,
If 'tis with Reason they complain,
This Infant shall restore my Reign;
I'll search where ev'ry Virtue dwells,
From Courts inclusive, down to Cells,
What Preachers talk, or Sages write,
These I will gather and unite,

And represent them to Mankind,
Collected in that Infant's Mind.

This said, she plucks in Heav'ns high Bow'rs
A Sprig of *Amaranthine* Flow'rs,
In Nectar thrice infuses Bays,
Three times refin'd in *Titan's* Rays:
She calls the Graces to her Aid,
And sprinkles thrice the new-born Maid,
From whence the tender Skin assumes
A Sweetness above all Perfumes;
From whence a Cleanliness remains,
Incapable of outward Stains;
From whence that Decency of Mind,
So lovely in the Female Kind,
Where not one careless Thought intrudes,
Less modest than the Speech of *Prudes*;
Where never Blush was call'd for aid,
That spurious Virtue in a Maid;
A Virtue but at second hand:
They blush because they understand.

The Graces next wou'd act their Part,
And shew'd but little of their Art;
Their Work was half already done,
The Child with native Beauty shone,
The outward Form no Help requir'd:
Each breathing on her thrice, inspir'd
That gentle, soft, engaging Air,
Which in old Times adorn'd the Fair;
And said, *Vanessa* be the Name
By which thou shalt be known to Fame:
Vanessa, by the Gods enroll'd:
Her Name on Earth—shall not be told.

But still the Work was not compleat,
When *Venus* thought on a Deceit:

Drawn by her Doves, away she flies,
And finds out *Pallas* in the Skies.
Dear *Pallas*, I have been this Morn
To see a lovely Infant born,
A Boy in yonder Isle below,
So like my own, without his Bow,
By Beauty cou'd your Heart be won,
You'd swear it is *Apollo's* Son;
But it shall ne'er be said, a Child
So hopeful has by me been spoil'd;
I have enough besides to spare,
And give him wholly to your Care.
Wisdom's above suspecting Wiles:
The Queen of Learning gravely smiles,
Down from *Olympus* comes with Joy,
Mistakes *Vanessa* for a Boy,
Then sows within her tender Mind
Seeds long unknown to Womankind,
For manly Bosoms chiefly fit,
The Seeds of Knowledge, Judgment, Wit;
Her Soul was suddenly endu'd
With Justice, Truth and Fortitude;
With Honour, which no Breath can stain,
Which Malice must attack in vain;
With open Heart and bounteous Hand:
But *Pallas* here was at a Stand;
She knew in our degenerate Days
Bare Virtue cou'dn't live on Praise,
That Meat must be with Money bought;
She therefore, upon second Thought,
Infus'd, yet as it were by Stealth,
Some small Regard for State and Wealth;
Of which, as she grew up, there stay'd,
A Tincture in the prudent Maid:
She manag'd her Estate with Care,
Yet lik'd three Footmen to her Chair.
But lest he shou'd neglect his Studies,
Like a young Heir, the thrifty Goddess,
For fear young Master shou'd be spoil'd,

Wou'd use him like a younger Child;
And, after long computing, found
'Twou'd come to just five thousand Pound.

The Queen of Love was pleas'd, and proud,
To see *Vanessa* thus endow'd;
She doubted not but such a Dame
Thro' ev'ry Breast wou'd dart a Flame,
That ev'ry rich and lordly Swain
With Pride wou'd drag about her Chain;
That Scholars wou'd forsake their Books
To study bright *Vanessa's* Looks:
As she advanc'd, that Womankind
Wou'd by her Model form their Mind,
And all their Conduct wou'd be try'd
By her, as an unerring Guide.
Offending Daughters oft wou'd hear
Vanessa's Praise rung in their Ear:
Miss *Betty*, when she does a Fault,
Lets fall her Knife, and spills her Salt,
Will thus be by her Mother chid,
'Tis what *Vanessa* never did.
Thus by the Nymphs and Swains ador'd,
My Pow'r shall be again restor'd,
And happy Lovers bless my Reign:
So *Venus* hop'd, but hop'd in vain.

For when in time the Martial Maid
Found out the Trick that *Venus* play'd,
She shakes her Helm, she knits her Brows,
And, fir'd with Indignation, vows,
To-morrow, ere the setting Sun,
She'd all undo, that she had done.

But Gods (we are by Poets taught)
Must stand to what themselves have wrought;
For in their old Records we find
A wholesome Law, thrice out of Mind,
Confirm'd long since by Fate's Decree,
That Gods, of whatsoe'er Degree,

Resume not what themselves have giv'n,
Or any Brother God in Heav'n:
Which keeps the Peace among the Gods,
Else they must always be at odds.
And *Pallas*, if she broke the Laws,
Must yield her Foe the Stronger Cause;
A Shame to one so much ador'd
For Wisdom, at *Jove's* Council-Board.
Besides, she fear'd the Queen of Love
Wou'd meet with better Friends above;
And tho' she must with Grief reflect,
To see a Mortal Virgin deckt
With Graces, hitherto unknown
To Female Breasts, except her own;
Yet she wou'd act as best became
A Goddess of unspotted Fame:
She knew, by Augury Divine,
Venus wou'd fail in her Design:
She study'd well the Point, and found
Her Foe's Conclusions were not sound
From Premisses erroneous brought,
And therefore the Deduction's nought,
And must have contrary Effects
To what her treach'rous Foe expects.
In proper Season *Pallas* meets
The Queen of Love, whom thus she greets,
(For Gods, we are by *Homer* told,
Can in Celestial Language scold)
Perfidious Goddess! but in vain
You form'd this Project in your Brain,
A Project for thy Talents fit,
With much Deceit, and little Wit;
Thou hast, as thou shalt quickly see,
Deceiv'd thy self, instead of me;
For how can Heav'nly Wisdom prove
An Instrument to earthly Love?
Know'st thou not yet that Men commence
Thy Votaries, for want of Sense?
Nor shall *Vanessa* be the Theme

To Marriage, thy abortive Scheme;
She'll prove the greatest of thy Foes:
And yet I scorn to interpose,
But using neither Skill, nor Force,
Leave all things to their Nat'ral Course.

The Goddess thus pronounc'd her Doom:
When, lo! *Vanessa* in her Bloom,
Advanc'd like *Atalanta's* Star,
But rarely seen, and seen from far;
In a new World with Caution stept,
Watch'd all the Company she kept,
Well knowing from the Books she read
What dangerous Paths young Virgins tread;
Wou'd seldom at the Park appear,
Nor saw the Play-house twice a Year;
Yet not incurious, was inclin'd
To have the Converse of Mankind.
First issu'd from Perfumers Shops
A Croud of fashionable Fops;
They ask'd her, how she lik'd the Play,
Then told the Tattle of the Day,
A Duel fought last Night at Two,
About a Lady——You know who;
Talk'd of a new *Italian*, come
Either from *Muscovy* or *Rome*;
Gave hints of who and who's together;
Then fell to talking of the Weather:
Last Night was so extremely fine,
The Ladies walk'd 'till after Nine.
Then in soft Voice and Speech absurd,
With Nonsense ev'ry second Word,
With Fustian from exploded Plays,
To celebrate her Beauty's Praise,
Run o'er their Cant of stupid Lies,
And tell the Murders of her Eyes.

With silent Scorn *Vanessa* sat,
Scarce list'ning to their idle Chat;

Further than sometimes by a Frown,
When they grew pert, to pull them down.
At last she spitefully was bent,
To try their Wisdom's full extent;
And said, she valu'd nothing less
Than Titles, Figure, Shape and Dress;
That Merit should be chiefly plac'd
In Judgment, Knowledge, Wit and Taste;
And these, she offer'd to dispute,
Alone distinguish'd Man from Brute:
With her, a wealthy Fool wou'd pass
At best but for a golden Ass;
That present Times have no pretence
To Virtue, in the Noblest Sense,
By *Greeks* and *Romans* understood,
To perish for our Country's Good.
She scan'd the antient Heroes round,
Explain'd for what they were renown'd;
Then spoke with Censure or Applause,
Of foreign Customs, Rites and Laws;
Thro' Nature and thro' Art she rang'd,
And gracefully her Subject chang'd:
In vain: her Hearers had no Share
In all she spoke, except to stare.
Their Judgment was upon the whole,
——That Lady is the dullest Soul——
Then tipt their Foreheads in a Jeer,
As who should say——she wants it here;
She may be handsome, young and rich,
But none will burn her for a Witch.

A Party next of glitt'ring Dames,
From round the Purlieus of St. *James*,
Came early out of pure Good-will,
To see the Girl in Deshabille.
Their Clamour, 'lighting from their Chairs,
Grew lowder, all the way up Stairs;
At Entrance loudest, where they found,
The Room with Volumes litter'd round;

Vanessa held *Montaigne*, and read,
Whilst Mrs. *Susan* comb'd her Head:
They call'd for Tea and Chocolate,
And fell into their usual Chat,
Discoursing with important Face,
On Ribbons, Fans, and Gloves and Lace;
Shew'd Patterns just from *India* brought,
And gravely ask'd her—what she thought,
Whether the Red or Green were best,
And what they cost: *Vanessa* guest,
As came into her fancy first,
Nam'd half the Rates, and lik'd the worst.
To Scandal next——What aukward Thing
Was that, last *Sunday* in the Ring?
——I'm sorry *Mopsa* breaks so fast;
I said——her face would never last.—
Corinna with that youthful Air,
Is thirty, and a Bit to spare.
Her Fondness for a certain Earl
Began, when I was but a Girl.
——*Phyllis*, who but a Month ago
Was marry'd to the *Tunbridge* Beau,
I saw coquetting t'other Night
In publick with that odious Knight.

They rally'd next *Vanessa's* Dress;
——That Gown was made for old Queen *Bess*.
——Dear Madam—Let me set your Head—
——Don't you intend to put on Red?
A Pettycoat without a Hoop!
—— Sure you are not asham'd to stoop;
With handsome Garters at your Knees,
No matter what a Fellow sees.
Fill'd with Disdain, with Rage inflam'd,
Both of her self and Sex asham'd,
The Nymph stood silent out of spight,
Nor wou'd vouchsafe to set them right.
Away the fair Detractors went,
And gave, by turns, their Censures vent.

——She's not so handsome, in my Eyes:
——For Wit—I wonder where it lies.
She's fair and clean, and that's the most,
But why proclaim her for a Toast?
A Baby Face, no Life, no Airs,
But what she learnt at Country Fairs;
Scarce knows what difference is between
Rich *Flanders* Lace, and Colberteen;
I'll undertake my little *Nancy*
In Flounces has a better Fancy;
With all her Wit, I wou'd not ask
Her Judgment, how to buy a Mask.
We beg'd her but to patch her Face,
She never hit one proper Place;
Which every Girl at five Years old
Can do, as soon as she is told.
I own that out-of-fashion Stuff
Becomes the Creature well enough.
The Girl might pass, if we cou'd get her
To know the World a little better.
To know the World! a modern Phrase,
For Visits, Ombre, Balls and Plays.

Thus, to the World's perpetual Shame,
The Queen of Beauty lost her Aim.
Too late with Grief she understood,
Pallas had done more Harm than Good;
For great Examples are but vain,
Where Ignorance begets Disdain.
Both Sexes, arm'd with Guilt and Spite,
Against *Vanessa's* Power unite;
To copy her, few Nymphs aspir'd,
Her Virtues fewer Swains admir'd:
So Stars beyond a certain height
Give Mortals neither Heat nor Light.

Yet some of either Sex, endow'd
With Gifts superior to the Crowd,
With Virtue, Knowledge, Taste and Wit,

She condescended to admit:
With pleasing Arts she could reduce
Men's Talents to their proper Use;
And with Address each Genius held
To that wherein it most excell'd;
Thus making others Wisdom known,
Cou'd please them, and improve her own.

A modest Youth said something new,
She placed it in the strongest View.
All humble Worth she strove to raise;
Wou'dn't be prais'd, yet lov'd to praise;
The Learned met with free Approach,
Although they came not in a Coach.
Some Clergy too she wou'd allow,
Nor quarrell'd at their aukward Bow;
But this was for *Cadenus*' sake,
A Gownman of a different Make,
Whom *Pallas*, once *Vanessa's* Tutor,
Had fix'd on for her Coadjutor.

But *Cupid*, full of Mischief, longs
To vindicate his Mother's Wrongs.
On *Pallas* all Attempts are vain;
One way he knows to give her Pain.
Vows on *Vanessa's* Heart to take
Due Vengeance, for her Patron's sake.
Those early Seeds by *Venus* sown,
In spight of *Pallas*, now were grown;
And *Cupid* hop'd they wou'd improve
By Time, and ripen into Love.
The Boy made use of all his Craft,
In vain discharging many a Shaft,
Pointed at Colonels, Lords and Beaux;
Cadenus warded off the Blows:
For placing still some Book betwixt,
The Darts were in the Cover fixt,
Or often blunted and recoil'd,
On *Plutarch's* Morals struck, were spoil'd.

The Queen of Wisdom cou'd foresee,
But not prevent, the Fates Decree;
And human Caution tries in vain
To break that Adamantine Chain.
Vanessa, tho' by *Pallas* taught,
By Love invulnerable thought,
Searching in Books for Wisdom's Aid,
Was in the very Search betray'd.

Cupid, tho' all his Darts were lost,
Yet still resolv'd to spare no Cost;
He cou'dn't answer to his Fame
The Triumphs of that stubborn Dame,
A Nymph so hard to be subdu'd,
Who neither was Coquette nor Prude;
I find, says he, she wants a Doctor,
Both to adore her and instruct her;
I'll give her what she most admires,
Among those venerable Sires;
Cadenus is a Subject fit,
Grown old in Politicks and Wit;
Caress'd by Ministers of State,
Of half Mankind the Dread and Hate.
Whate'er Vexations Love attend,
She need no Rivals apprehend.
Her Sex, with universal Voice,
Must laugh at her capricious Choice.
Cadenus many things had writ,
Vanessa much esteem'd his Wit,
And call'd for his Poetick Works;
Mean-time the Boy in secret lurks,
And while the Book was in her Hand,
The Urchin from his private Stand
Took Aim, and shot with all his Strength,
A Dart of such prodigious Length,
It pierc'd the feeble Volume thro'
And deep transfix'd her Bosom too.
Some Lines, more moving than the rest,
Stuck to the Point that pierc'd her Breast,

And born directly to her Heart,
With Pains unknown increas'd her Smart.

    Vanessa, not in Years a Score,
Doats on a Gown of forty-four;
Imaginary Charms can find,
In Eyes with reading almost blind;
Cadenus now no more appears
Declin'd in Health, advanc'd in Years,
She fancies Musick in his Tongue,
Nor further looks, but thinks him young.
What Mariner is not afraid,
To venture in a Ship decay'd?
What Planter will attempt to yoke,
A Sapling with a falling Oak?
As Years increase she brighter shines,
Cadenus with each Day declines,
And he must fall a Prey to Time,
While she is blooming in her Prime.

    Strange that a Nymph by *Pallas* nurs'd
In Love shou'd make Advances first.
Cadenus, common Forms apart,
In every Sense had kept his Heart,
Had sigh'd and languish'd, vow'd and writ,
For Pastime, or to shew his Wit;
But Time, and Books, and State Affairs,
Had spoil'd his fashionable Airs;
He now cou'd praise, esteem, approve,
But understood not what was Love;
This Conduct might have made him styl'd
A Father, and the Nymph his Child.
That innocent Delight he took
To see the Virgin mind her Book,
Was but the Master's secret Joy,
In School to hear the finest Boy.
Her Knowledge with her Fancy grew,
She hourly press'd for something new:

Ideas came into her Mind
So fast, his Lessons lagg'd behind.
She reason'd without pleading long,
Nor ever gave her Judgment wrong:
But now a sudden Change was wrought,
She minds no longer what he taught.
She wish'd her Tutor were her Lover;
Resolv'd she wou'd her Flame discover:
And when *Cadenus* wou'd expound
Some Notion, subtle and profound,
The Nymph wou'd gently press his Hand,
As if she seem'd to understand,
Or dext'rously dissembling Chance,
Wou'd sigh, and steal a secret Glance.

    Cadenus was amaz'd to find
Such Marks of a distracted Mind;
For tho' she seem'd to listen more
To all he spoke, than e'er before;
He found her Thoughts wou'd absent range,
Yet guess'd not whence cou'd spring the Change.
And first he modestly conjectures
His Pupil might be tir'd with Lectures;
Which help'd to mortify his Pride,
Yet gave him not the Heart to chide;
But in a mild dejected Strain,
At last he ventur'd to complain:
Said she shou'd be no longer teiz'd,
Might have her Freedom when she pleas'd;
Was now convinc'd he acted wrong,
To hide her from the World so long;
And in dull Studies to engage
One of her tender Sex and Age;
That ev'ry Nymph with Envy own'd,
How she might shine in the *Grand-Monde*,
And ev'ry Shepherd was undone
To see her cloister'd like a Nun!
This was a visionary Scheme,
He wak'd, and found it but a Dream;

A Project far above his Skill,
For Nature must be Nature still.
If he was bolder than became
A Scholar to a Courtly Dame,
She might excuse a Man of Letters;
Thus Tutors often treat their Betters.
And since his Talk offensive grew,
He came to take his last Adieu.

Vanessa, fill'd with just Disdain,
Wou'd still her Dignity maintain,
Instructed from her early Years
To scorn the Art of female Tears.

Had he employ'd his Head so long,
To teach her what was Right or Wrong,
Yet cou'd such Notions entertain,
That all his Lectures were in vain?
She own'd the wand'ring of her Thoughts,
But he must answer for her Faults;
She well remember'd to her Cost,
That all his Lessons were not lost.
Two Maxims she could still produce,
And sad Experience taught their Use:
That Virtue, pleas'd by being shewn,
Knows nothing which it dare not own:
Can make us without Fear disclose
Our inmost Secrets to our Foes:
That common Forms were not design'd
Directors to a noble Mind.
Now, said the Nymph, to let you see
My Actions with your Rules agree,
That I can vulgar Forms despise,
And have no Secrets to disguise,
I'll fully prove your Maxims true,
By owning here my Love to you.
I knew by what you said and writ,
How dang'rous Things were Men of Wit.
You caution'd me against their Charms,

But never gave me equal Arms:
Your Lessons found the weakest Part,
Aim'd at the Head, but reach'd the Heart.

Cadenus felt within him rise
Shame, Disappointment, Guilt, Surprize;
He knew not how to reconcile
Such Language, with her usual Style,
And yet her Words were so expresst,
He cou'd not hope she spoke in jest.
His Thoughts had wholly been confin'd
To form and cultivate her Mind;
He hardly knew, 'till he was told,
Whether the Nymph were Young or Old;
Had met her in a publick Place,
Without distinguishing her Face.
Much less shou'd his declining Age,
Vanessa's earliest Thoughts engage.
And if her Youth Indifference met,
His Person must Contempt beget:
Or grant her Passion be sincere,
How shall his Innocence be clear?
Appearances were all so strong,
The World must think him in the Wrong;
Wou'd say he made a treach'rous Use
Of Wit, to flatter and seduce:
The Town wou'd swear he had betray'd,
By magick Spells, the harmless Maid;
And ev'ry Beau wou'd have his Joke,
That Scholars were like other Folk;
That when Platonick Flights were over,
The Tutor turn'd a mortal Lover;
So tender of the Young and Fair,
It shew'd a true Paternal Care.
Five thousand Guineas in her Purse,
The Doctor might have fancy'd worse.

Hardly at length he Silence broke,
And faulter'd ev'ry Word he spoke;

Interpreting her Complaisance
Just as a Man *sans Consequence*:
She rally'd well, he always knew,
Her Manner now was something new;
And what she spoke was in an Air
As serious as a Tragick Player.
But those who aim at Ridicule,
Shou'd fix upon some certain Rule;
Which fairly hints they are in jest,
Else he must enter his Protest:
For let a Man be ne'er so wise,
He may be caught with sober Lies;
A Science which he never taught,
And, to be free, was dearly bought:
For take it in its proper Light,
'Tis just what Coxcombs call a Bite.

But not to dwell on things minute,
Vanessa finish'd the Dispute,
Brought weighty Arguments to prove
That Reason was her Guide in Love.
She thought he had himself describ'd,
His Doctrines when she first imbibed,
From his, transfus'd into her Breast,
With Pleasure not to be express'd.
What he had planted, now was grown,
His Virtues she might call her own;
As he approves, as he dislikes,
Love, or Contempt, her Fancy strikes.
Self-Love, in Nature rooted fast,
Attends us first, and leaves us last.
Why she loves him, admire not at her,
She loves herself, and that's the Matter.
How was her Tutor wont to praise
The Genius's of ancient Days!
Those Authors he so oft had nam'd
For Learning, Wit, and Wisdom, fam'd;
Was struck with Love, Esteem, and Awe,
For Persons whom he never saw.

Suppose *Cadenus* flourish'd then,
He must adore such Godlike Men.
If one short Volume cou'd comprise
All that was witty, learn'd and wise,
How wou'd it be esteem'd, and read,
Altho' the Writer long were dead?
If such an Author were alive,
How all wou'd for his Friendship strive;
And come in Crowds to see his Face:
And this she takes to be her Case.
Cadenus answers every End,
The Book, the Author, and the Friend.
The utmost her Desires will reach,
Is but to learn what he can teach;
This Converse is a System, fit
Alone to fill up all her Wit;
While ev'ry Passion of her Mind
In him is center'd and confin'd.

Love can with Speech inspire a Mute,
And taught *Vanessa* to dispute;
This Topick, never touch'd before,
Display'd her Eloquence the more:
Her Knowledge, with such Pains acquir'd,
By this new Passion grew inspir'd.
Thro' Love she made all Objects pass,
Which gave a Tincture o'er the Mass.
As Rivers, tho' they bend and twine,
Still to the Sea their Course incline;
Or as Philosophers, who find
Some fav'rite System to their Mind,
In ev'ry Point to make it fit,
Will force all Nature to submit.

Cadenus, who cou'd ne'er suspect
His Lessons wou'd have such Effect,
Or be so artfully apply'd,
Insensibly came on her Side;
It was an unforeseen Event,

Things took a Turn he never meant;
Who'er excells in what we prize,
Appears a Hero to our Eyes;
Each Girl when pleas'd with what is taught,
Will have the Teacher in her Thought.
When Miss delights in her Spinnet,
A Fidler may a Fortune get;
A Blockhead with melodious Voice
In Boarding-Schools can have his Choice;
And oft' the Dancing-Master's Art
Climbs from the Toe to touch the Heart.
In Learning let a Nymph delight,
The Pedant gets a Mistress by't.
Cadenus, to his Grief and Shame,
Cou'd scarce oppose *Vanessa's* Flame;
But tho' her Arguments were strong,
At least, cou'd hardly wish them wrong.
Howe'er it came, he cou'dn't tell,
But, sure, she never talk'd so well.
His Pride began to interpose,
Preferr'd before a Crowd of Beaux,
So bright a Nymph to come unsought,
Such Wonder by his Merit wrought;
'Tis Merit must with her prevail,
He never knew her Judgment fail.
She noted all she ever read,
And had a most discerning Head.

'Tis an old Maxim in the Schools,
That Vanity's the Food of Fools;
Yet now and then your Men of Wit
Will condescend to take a bit.

So when *Cadenus* cou'd not hide,
He chose to justify his Pride;
Const'ring the Passion she had shown,
Much to her Praise, more to his Own.
Nature in him had Merit plac'd,
In her a most judicious Taste.

Love, hitherto a transient Guest,
Ne'er held Possession of his Breast;
So long attending at the Gate,
Disdain'd to enter in so late.
Love, why do we one Passion call?
When 'tis a Compound of them all;
Where hot and cold, where sharp and sweet,
In all their Equipages meet;
Where Pleasures mixt with Pains appear,
Sorrow with Joy, and Hope with Fear:
Wherein his Dignity and Age
Forbid *Cadenus* to engage.
But Friendship in its greatest height,
A constant, rational Delight,
On Virtue's Basis fix'd to last,
When Love's Alurements long are past;
Which gently warms, but cannot burn,
He gladly offers in return:
His want of Passion will redeem,
With Gratitude, Respect, Esteem:
With that Devotion we bestow,
When Goddesses appear below.

While the *Cadenus* entertains
Vanessa in exalted Strains,
The Nymph in sober Words intreats
A Truce with all sublime Conceits.
For why such Raptures, Flights and Fancies,
To her, who durst not read Romances;
In lofty Style to make Replies,
Which he had taught her to despise.
But when her Tutor will affect
Devotion, Duty and Respect,
He fairly abdicates his Throne,
The Government is now her own:
He has a Forfeiture incurr'd,
She vows to take him at his Word,
And hopes he will not think it strange,
If both shou'd now their Stations change

The Nymph will have her turn, to be
The Tutor; and the Pupil, he:
Tho' she already can discern,
Her Scholar is not apt to learn;
Or wants Capacity to reach,
The Science she designs to teach:
Wherein his Genius was below
The Skill of ev'ry common Beau;
Who, tho' he cannot spell, is wise
Enough to read a Lady's Eyes;
And will each accidental Glance
Interpret for a kind Advance.
But what Success *Vanessa* met,
Is to the World a Secret yet:
Whether the Nymph, to please her Swain,
Talks in a high Romantick Strain;
Or whether he at last descends
To love with less Seraphick Ends;
Or, to compound the Business, whether
They temper Love and Books together;
Must never to Mankind be told,
Nor dare the conscious Muse unfold.

Mean-time the mournful Queen of Love
Led but a weary Life above.
She ventures now to leave the Skies,
Grown by *Vanessa's* Conduct wise;
For tho' by one perverse Event
Pallas had cross'd her first Intent,
Tho' her Design was not obtain'd,
Yet had she much Experience gain'd;
And, by the Project vainly try'd,
Cou'd better now the Cause decide.
She gave due Notice that both Parties,
Coram Regina prox' die Martis,
Should at their Peril without fail
Come and appear, to save their Bail.
All met, and Silence thrice proclaim'd,
One Lawyer to each Side was nam'd.

The Judge discover'd in her Face
Resentments for her late Disgrace;
And full of Anger, Shame and Grief,
Directed them to mind their Brief;
Nor spend their Time to shew their Reading,
She'd have a summary Proceeding.
She gather'd under ev'ry Head
The Sum of what each Lawyer said,
Gave her own Reasons last, and then
Decreed the Cause against the Men.

But in a weighty Cause like this,
To shew she did not judge amiss,
Which evil Tongues might else report,
She made a Speech in open Court;
Wherein she grievously complains,
How she was cheated by the Swains:
On whose Petition, humbly shewing
That Women were not worth the wooing,
And that unless the Sex would mend,
The Race of Lovers soon must end;
She was at Lord knows what Expence,
To form a Nymph of Wit and Sense;
A Model for her Sex design'd,
Who never cou'd one Lover find.
She saw her Favour was misplac'd,
The Fellows had a wretched Taste,
She needs must tell them to their Face,
They are a senseless stupid Race:
And were she to begin again,
She'd study to reform the Men;
Or add some Grains of Folly more
To Women, than they had before,
To put them on an equal Foot;
And this, or nothing else, wou'd do't.
This might their mutual Fancy strike,
Since every Being loves it's Like.
But now repenting what was done,
She left all Business to her Son,

She puts the World in his Possession,
And let him use it at Discretion.
The Cryer was order'd to dismiss
The Court, so made his last *O yes!*
The Goddess wou'd no longer wait;
But rising from her Chair of State,
Left all below at six and seven,
Harness'd her Doves, and flew to Heav'n

THE FURNITURE OF A WOMAN'S MIND

Written in the Year 1727.

A SET of Phrases learn't by Rote;
A Passion for a Scarlet-Coat;
When at a Play to laugh, or cry,
Yet cannot tell the Reason why:
Never to hold her Tongue a Minute;
While all she prates has nothing in it.
Whole Hours can with a Coxcomb sit,
And take his Nonsense all for Wit:
Her Learning mounts to read a Song,
But, half the Words pronouncing wrong;
Has ev'ry Repartee in Store,
She spoke ten Thousand Times before.
Can ready Compliments supply
On all Occasions, cut and dry.
Such Hatred to a Parson's Gown,
The Sight will put her in a Swown.
For Conversation well endu'd;
She calls it witty to be rude;
And, placing Raillery in Railing,
Will tell aloud your greatest Failing;
Nor makes a Scruple to expose
Your bandy Leg, or crooked Nose.
Can, at her Morning Tea, run o'er
The Scandal of the Day before.
Improving hourly in her Skill,
To cheat and wrangle at Quadrille.

In chusing Lace a Critick nice,
Knows to a Groat the lowest Price;
Can in her Female Clubs dispute
What Lining best the Silk will suit;
What Colours each Complexion match:
And where with Art to place a Patch.

If chance a Mouse creeps in her Sight,
Can finely counterfeit a Fright;
So, sweetly screams if it comes near her,
She ravishes all Hearts to hear her.
Can dext'rously her Husband teize,
By taking Fits whene'er she please:
By frequent Practice learns the Trick
At proper Seasons to be sick;
Thinks nothing gives one Airs so pretty;
At once creating Love and Pity.
If *Molly* happens to be careless,
And but neglects to warm her Hair-Lace,
She gets a Cold as sure as Death;
And vows she scarce can fetch her Breath.
Admires how modest Women can
Be so *robustious* like a Man.

In Party, furious to her Power;
A bitter Whig, or Tory sow'r;
Her Arguments directly tend
Against the Side she would defend:
Will prove her self a Tory plain,
From Principles the Whigs maintain;
And, to defend the Whiggish Cause,
Her Topicks from the Tories draws.

O yes! If any Man can find
More virtues in a Woman's Mind,
Let them be sent to Mrs. **Harding*;
She'll pay the Charges to a Farthing:

---

* *A Printer.*

Take Notice, she has my Commission
To add them in the next Edition;
They may out-sell a better Thing;
So, Holla Boys; God save the King.

BETTY THE GRIZETTE

Written in the Year 1730.

QUEEN of Wit and Beauty, *Betty*,
Never may the Muse forget ye:
How thy Face charms ev'ry Shepherd,
Spotted over like a Le'pard!
And, thy freckled Neck display'd,
Envy breeds in ev'ry Maid.
Like a fly blown Cake of Tallow,
Or, on Parchment, Ink turn'd yellow:
Or, a tawny speckled Pippin,
Shrivel'd with a Winter's keeping.

And, thy Beauty thus dispatcht;
Let me praise thy Wit unmatcht.

Sets of Phrases, cut and dry,
Evermore thy Tongue supply.
And, thy Memory is loaded
With old Scraps from Plays exploded.
Stock't with Repartees and Jokes,
Suited to all Christian Fokes:
Shreds of Wit, and senseless Rhimes,
Blunder'd out a Thousand Times.
Nor, wilt thou of Gifts be sparing,
Which can ne'er be worse for wearing.
Picking Wit among Collegions,
In the Play-House upper Regions;
Where, in Eighteen-penny Gall'ry,
Irish Nymphs learn *Irish* Raillery:
But, thy Merit is thy Failing,
And, thy Raillery is Railing.

Thus, with Talents well endu'd
To be scurrilous, and rude;
When you pertly raise your Snout,
Fleer, and gibe, and laugh, and flout;
This, among *Hibernian* Asses,
For sheer Wit, and Humour passes!
Thus, indulgent *Chloe* bit,
Swears you have a World of Wit.

ON POETRY: A RAPSODY

ALL Human Race wou'd fain be *Wits*,
And Millions miss, for one that hits.
Young's universal Passion, *Pride*,
Was never known to spread so wide.
Say *Britain*, cou'd you ever boast,——
Three *Poets* in an Age at most?
Our chilling Climate hardly bears
A *Sprig* of Bays in Fifty Years:
While ev'ry Fool his Claim alledges,
As if it grew in common Hedges.
What Reason can there be assign'd
For this Perverseness in the Mind?
Brutes find out where their Talents lie:
A *Bear* will not attempt to fly:
A founder'd *Horse* will oft debate,
Before he tries a five-barr'd Gate:
A *Dog* by Instinct turns aside,
Who sees the Ditch too deep and wide.
But *Man* we find the only Creature,
Who, led by *Folly*, fights with *Nature*;
Who, when *she* loudly cries, *Forbear*,
With Obstinacy fixes there;
And, where his *Genius* least inclines,
Absurdly bends his whole Designs.

Not *Empire* to the Rising-Sun,
By Valour, Conduct, Fortune won;

Nor highest *Wisdom* in Debates
For framing Laws to govern States;
Nor Skill in Sciences profound,
So large to grasp the Circle round;
Such heavenly Influence require,
As how to strike the *Muses Lyre*.

Not Beggar's Brat, on Bulk begot;
Nor Bastard of a Pedlar *Scot*;
Nor Boy brought up to cleaning Shoes,
The Spawn of *Bridewell*, or the Stews;
Nor Infants dropt, the spurious Pledges
Of *Gipsies* littering under Hedges,
Are so disqualified by Fate
To rise in *Church*, or *Law*, or *State*,
As he, whom *Phebus* in his Ire
Hath *blasted* with poetick Fire.

What hope of Custom in the *Fair*,
While not a Soul demands your Ware?
Where you have nothing to produce
For private Life, or publick Use?
Court, *City*, *Country* want you not;
You cannot bribe, betray, or plot.
For Poets, Law makes no Provision:
The Wealthy have you in Derision.
Of State-Affairs you cannot smatter,
Are awkward when you try to flatter.
Your Portion, taking *Britain* round,
*Was just one annual Hundred Pound.
Now not so much as in Remainder
Since *Cibber* brought in an Attainder;
For ever fixt by Right Divine,
(A Monarch's Right) on *Grubstreet* Line.
Poor starv'ling Bard, how small thy Gains!
How unproportion'd to thy Pains!

---

* Paid to the Poet Laureat, which place was given to one *Cibber*,
a Player.

And here a *Simile* comes Pat in:
Tho' *Chickens* take a Month to fatten,
The Guests in less than half an Hour
Will more than half a Score devour.
So, after toiling twenty Days,
To earn a Stock of Pence and Praise,
Thy Labours, grown the Critick's Prey,
Are swallow'd o'er a Dish of Tea;
Gone, to be never heard of more,
Gone, where the *Chickens* went before.

How shall a new Attempter learn
Of diff'rent Spirits to discern,
And how distinguish, which is which,
The Poet's Vein, or scribling Itch?
Then hear an old experienc'd Sinner
Instructing thus a young Beginner.

Consult yourself, and if you find
A powerful Impulse urge your Mind,
Impartial judge within your Breast
What Subject you can manage best;
Whether your Genius most inclines
To Satire, Praise, or hum'rous Lines;
To Elegies in mournful Tone,
Or Prologue sent from Hand unknown.
Then rising with *Aurora's* Light,
The Muse invok'd, sit down to write;
Blot out, correct, insert, refine,
Enlarge, diminish, interline;
Be mindful, when Invention fails,
To scratch your Head, and bite your Nails.

Your Poem finish'd, next your Care
Is needful, to transcribe it fair.
In modern Wit all printed Trash, is
Set off with num'rous *Breaks*— and *Dashes*—

To Statesman wou'd you give a Wipe,
You print it in *Italick Type*.

When Letters are in vulgar Shapes,
'Tis ten to one the Wit escapes;
But when in *Capitals* exprest,
The dullest Reader smoaks the Jest:
Or else perhaps he may invent
A better than the Poet meant,
As learned Commentators view
In *Homer* more than *Homer* knew.

Your Poem in its modish Dress,
Correctly fitted for the Press,
Convey by Penny-Post to *Lintot*,
But let no Friend alive look into't.
If *Lintot* thinks 'twill quit the Cost,
You need not fear your Labour lost:
And, how agreeably surpriz'd
Are you to see it advertiz'd!
The Hawker shews you one in Print,
As fresh as Farthings from the Mint:
The Product of your Toil and Sweating;
A Bastard of your own begetting.

Be sure at *Will's* the following Day,
Lie Snug, and hear what Criticks say.
And if you find the general Vogue
Pronounces you a stupid Rogue;
Damns all your Thoughts as low and little,
Sit still, and swallow down your Spittle.
Be silent as a Politician,
For talking may beget Suspicion:
Or praise the Judgment of the Town,
And help yourself to run it down.
Give up your fond paternal Pride,
Nor argue on the weaker Side;
For Poems read without a Name
We justly praise, or justly blame:
And Criticks have no partial Views,
Except they know whom they abuse.

And since you ne'er provok'd their Spight,
Depend upon't their Judgment's right:
But if you blab, you are undone;
Consider what a Risk you run.
You lose your Credit all at once;
The Town will mark you for a Dunce:
The vilest Doggrel *Grubstreet* sends,
Will pass for yours with Foes and Friends.
And you must bear the whole Disgrace,
'Till some fresh Blockhead takes your Place.

Your Secret kept, your Poem sunk,
And sent in Quires to line a Trunk;
If still you be dispos'd to rhime,
Go try your Hand a second Time.
Again you fail, yet Safe's the Word,
Take Courage, and attempt a Third.
But first with Care imploy your Thoughts,
Where Criticks mark'd your former Faults.
The trivial Turns, the borrow'd Wit,
The *Similes* that nothing fit;
The *Cant* which ev'ry Fool repeats,
Town-Jests, and Coffee-house Conceits;
Descriptions tedious, flat and dry,
And introduc'd the Lord knows why;
Or where we find your Fury set
Against the harmless Alphabet;
On A's and B's your Malice vent,
While Readers wonder whom you meant.
A publick, or a private *Robber*;
A *Statesman*, or a South-Sea *Jobber*.
A *Prelate* who no God believes;
A [Parliament], or a Den of Thieves.
A Pick-purse at the Bar, or Bench;
A Duchess, or a Suburb-Wench.
Or oft when Epithets you link,
In gaping Lines to fill a Chink;
Like stepping Stones to save a Stride,
In Streets where Kennels are too wide:

Or like a Heel-piece to support
A Cripple with one Foot too short:
Or like a Bridge that joins a Marish
To Moorlands of a diff'rent Parish.
So have I seen ill-coupled Hounds,
Drag diff'rent Ways in miry Grounds.
So Geographers in *Afric*-Maps
With Savage-Pictures fill their Gaps;
And o'er unhabitable Downs
Place Elephants for want of Towns.

But tho' you miss your third Essay,
You need not throw your Pen away.
Lay now aside all Thoughts of Fame,
To spring more profitable Game.
From Party-Merit seek Support;
The vilest Verse thrives best at Court.
A Pamphlet in Sir *Rob's* Defence
Will never fail to bring in Pence;
Nor be concern'd about the Sale,
He pays his Workmen on the Nail.

A Prince the Moment he is crown'd,
Inherits ev'ry Virtue round,
As Emblems of the sov'reign Pow'r,
Like other Bawbles of the Tow'r.
Is gen'rous, valiant, just and wise,
And so continues 'till he dies.
His humble *Senate* this professes,
In all their *Speeches, Votes, Addresses*.
But once you fix him in a Tomb,
His Virtues fade, his Vices bloom;
And each Perfection wrong imputed
Is fully at his Death confuted.
The Loads of Poems in his Praise,
Ascending make one Funeral-Blaze.
As soon as you can hear his Knell,
This God on Earth turns *Devil* in Hell.

And, lo, his Ministers of State,
Transform'd to Imps, his Levee wait:
Where, in this Scene of endless Woe,
They ply their former Arts below:
And as they sail in *Charòn's* Boat,
Contrive to bribe the Judge's Vote.
To *Cerberus* they give a Sop,
His triple-barking Mouth to stop:
Or in the Iv'ry Gate of Dreams,
Project [Excise] and [*South-Sea* Schemes]:
Or hire their Party-Pamphleteers,
To set *Elysium* by the Ears.

Then *Poet*, if you mean to thrive,
Employ your Muse on Kings alive;
With Prudence gath'ring up a Cluster
Of all the Virtues you can muster:
Which form'd into a Garland sweet,
Lay humbly at your Monarch's Feet;
Who, as the Odours reach his Throne,
Will smile, and think 'em all his own:
For *Law* and *Gospel* both determine
All Virtues lodge in royal Ermine.
(I mean the Oracles of Both,
Who shall depose it upon Oath.)
Your Garland in the following Reign,
Change but their Names, will do again.

But if you think this Trade too base,
(Which seldom is the Dunce's Case)
Put on the Critick's Brow, and sit
At *Wills* the puny Judge of Wit.
A Nod, a Shrug, a scornful Smile,
With Caution us'd, may serve a-while.
Proceed no further in your Part,
Before you learn the Terms of Art:
(For you may easy be too far gone,
In all our Modern Criticks Jargon.)
Then talk with more authentick Face,

Of *Unities, in Time and Place.*
Get Scraps of *Horace* from your Friends,
And have them at your Fingers Ends.
Learn *Aristotle's* Rules by Rote,
And at all Hazards boldly quote:
Judicious *Rymer* oft review:
Wise *Dennis*, and profound *Bossu.*
Read all the *Prefaces* of *Dryden*,
For these our Criticks much confide in,
(Tho' meerly writ at first for filling
To raise the Volume's Price, a Shilling.)

A forward Critick often dupes us
With sham Quotations *Peri Hupsous*:
And if we have not read *Longinus*,
Will magisterially out-shine us.
Then, lest with *Greek* he over-run ye,
Procure the Book for Love or Money,
Translated from *Boileau's* Translation,†
And quote *Quotation* on *Quotation.*

At *Wills* you hear a Poem read,
Where *Battus* from the Table-head,
Reclining on his Elbow-chair,
Gives Judgment with decisive Air.
To whom the Tribe of circling Wits,
As to an Oracle submits.
He gives Directions to the Town,
To cry it up, or run it down.
(Like *Courtiers*, when they send a Note,
Instructing *Members* how to Vote.)
He sets the Stamp of Bad and Good,
Tho' not a Word be understood.
Your Lesson learnt, you'll be secure
To get the Name of *Connoisseur.*
And when your Merits once are known,
Procure Disciples of your own.

---

* A famous Treatise of *Longinus*   † By Mr. *Welsted.*

Our Poets (you can never want 'em,
Spread thro' *Augusta Trinobantum*)
Computing by their Pecks of Coals,
Amount to just Nine thousand Souls.
These o'er their proper Districts govern,
Of Wit and Humour, Judges sov'reign.
In ev'ry Street a City-bard
Rules, like an Alderman his Ward.
His indisputed Rights extend
Thro' all the Lane, from End to End.
The Neighbours round admire his *Shrewdness*,
For Songs of *Loyalty* and *Lewdness*.
Out-done by none in Rhyming well,
Altho' he never learnt to spell.

Two bordering Wits contend for Glory;
And one is *Whig*, and one is *Tory*.
And this, for Epicks claims the Bays,
And that, for Elegiack Lays.
Some famed for Numbers soft and smooth,
By Lovers spoke in *Punch's* Booth.
And some as justly Fame extols
For lofty Lines in *Smithfield* Drols.
Bavius in *Wapping* gains Renown,
And *Mævius* reigns o'er *Kentish-Town*:
Tigellius plac'd in *Phoebus*' Car,
From *Ludgate* shines to *Temple-bar*.
Harmonius *Cibber* entertains
The Court with annual Birth-day Strains;
Whence *Gay* was banish'd in Disgrace,
Where *Pope* will never show his Face;
Where *Y[oung]* must torture his Invention,
To flatter *Knaves*, or lose his *Pension*.

But these are not a thousandth Part
Of Jobbers in the Poets Art,
Attending each his proper Station,
And all in due Subordination;

Thro' ev'ry Alley to be found,
In Garrets high, or under Ground:
And when they join their *Pericranies*,
Out skips a *Book of Miscellanies*.
Hobbes clearly proves that ev'ry Creature
Lives in a State of War by Nature.
The Greater for the Smaller watch,
But meddle seldom with their Match.
A Whale of moderate Size will draw
A Shole of Herrings down his Maw.
A Fox with Geese his Belly crams;
A Wolf destroys a thousand Lambs.
But search among the rhiming Race,
The Brave are worried by the Base.
If, on *Parnassus'* Top you sit,
You rarely bite, are always bit:
Each Poet of inferior Size
On you shall rail and criticize;
And strive to tear you Limb from Limb,
While others do as much for him.

The Vermin only teaze and pinch
Their Foes superior by an Inch.
So, Nat'ralists observe, a Flea
Hath smaller Fleas that on him prey,
And these have smaller Fleas to bite 'em,
And so proceed *ad infinitum*:
Thus ev'ry Poet in his Kind,
Is bit by him that comes behind;
Who, tho' too little to be seen,
Can teaze, and gall, and give the Spleen;
Call Dunces, Fools, and Sons of Whores,
Lay *Grubstreet* at each others Doors:
Extol the *Greek* and *Roman* Masters,
And curse our modern Poetasters.
Complain, as many an ancient Bard did,
How Genius is no more rewarded;
How wrong a Taste prevails among us;
How much our Ancestors out-sung us;

Can personate an awkward Scorn
For those who are not Poets born:
And all their Brother Dunces lash,
Who crowd the Press with hourly Trash.

O, *Grubstreet*! how do I bemoan thee,
Whose graceless Children scorn to own thee!
Their filial Piety forgot,
Deny their Country like a Scot:
Tho' by their Idiom and Grimace
They soon betray their native Place:
Yet *thou* hast greater Cause to be
Asham'd of them, than they of thee.
Degenerate from their ancient Brood,
Since first the Court allow'd them Food.

Remains a Difficulty still,
To purchase Fame by writing ill:
From *Flecknoe* down to *Howard's* Time,
How few have reach'd the *low Sublime*?
For when our high-born *Howard* dy'd,
Blackmore alone his Place supply'd:
And least a Chasm should intervene,
When Death had finish'd *Blackmore's* Reign,
The *leaden Crown* devolv'd to thee,
Great *Poet of the *Hollow-Tree*.
But, oh, how unsecure thy Throne!
A thousand Bards thy Right disown:
They plot to turn in factious Zeal,
Duncenia to a Common-weal;
And with rebellious Arms pretend
An equal Priv'lege to *descend*.

In Bulk there are not more Degrees,
From *Elephants* to *Mites* in Cheese,
Than what a curious Eye may trace
In Creatures of the rhiming Race.

---

* Lord *G[rimston]*.

From bad to worse, and worse they fall,
But, who can reach the Worst of all?
For, tho' in Nature Depth and Height
Are equally held infinite,
In Poetry the Height we know;
'Tis only infinite below.
For Instance: When you rashly *think,
No Rhymer can like *Welsted* sink.
His Merits ballanc'd you shall find,
The Laureat leaves him far behind.
Concannen, more aspiring Bard,
Climbs downwards, deeper, by a Yard:
Smart JEMMY MOOR with Vigor drops,
The Rest pursue as thick as Hops:
With Heads to Points the Gulph they enter,
Linkt perpendicular to the Centre:
And as their Heels elated rise,
Their Heads attempt the nether Skies.

O, what Indignity and Shame
To prostitute the Muse's Name,
By flatt'ring Kings whom Heaven design'd
The Plagues and Scourges of Mankind.
Bred up in Ignorance and Sloth,
And ev'ry Vice that nurses both.

Fair *Britain* in thy Monarch blest,
Whose Virtues bear the strictest Test;
Whom never *Faction* cou'd bespatter,
Nor *Minister*, nor *Poet* flatter.
What Justice in rewarding Merit?
What Magnanimity of Spirit?
What Lineaments divine we trace
Thro' all the Features of his Face;
Tho' Peace with Olive bind his Hands,
Confest the conqu'ring Hero stands.
Hydaspes, *Indus*, and the *Ganges*,
Dread from his Hand impending Changes.

---

* *Vide* The Treatise on the *Profound*, and Mr. *Pope's Dunciad*.

From him the *Tartar*, and *Chinese*,
Short by the Knees intreat for Peace.
The *Consort* of his Throne and Bed,
A perfect Goddess born and bred.
Appointed sov'reign Judge to sit
On Learning, Eloquence and Wit.
Our eldest Hope, divine *Iülus*,
(Late, very late, O, may he rule us.)
What early Manhood has he shown,
Before his downy Beard was grown!
Then think, what Wonders will be done
By going on as he begun;
An Heir for *Britain* to secure
As long as Sun and Moon endure.

The Remnant of the royal Blood,
Comes pouring on me like a Flood.
Bright Goddesses, in Number five;
Duke *William*, sweetest Prince alive.

Now sing the *Minister* of *State*,
Who shines alone, without a Mate.
Observe with what majestick Port
This *Atlas* stands to prop the Court:
Intent the Publick Debts to pay,
Like prudent **Fabius* by *Delay*.
Thou great Vicegerent of the King,
Thy Praises ev'ry Muse shall sing.
In all Affairs thou sole Director,
Of Wit and Learning chief Protector;
Tho' small the Time thou hast to spare,
The Church is thy peculiar Care.
Of pious Prelates what a Stock
You chuse to rule the Sable-flock.
You raise the Honour of the Peerage,
Proud to attend you at the Steerage.
You dignify the noble Race,
Content yourself with humbler Place.

---

* *Unus Homo nobis* Cunctando *restituit rem.*

Now Learning, Valour, Virtue, Sense,
To Titles give the sole Pretence.
St. George beheld thee with Delight,
Vouchsafe to be an azure Knight,
When on thy Breast and Sides *Herculean*,
He fixt the *Star* and *String Cerulean*.

Say, Poet, in what other Nation,
Shone ever such a Constellation.
Attend ye *Popes*, and *Youngs*, and *Gays*,
And tune your Harps, and strow your Bays.
Your Panegyricks here provide,
You cannot err on Flatt'ry's Side.
Above the Stars exalt your Stile,
You still are low ten thousand Mile.
On *Lewis* all his Bards bestow'd,
Of Incense many a thousand Load;
But *Europe* mortify'd his Pride,
And swore the fawning Rascals ly'd:
Yet what the World refus'd to *Lewis*,
Apply'd to *George* exactly true is:
Exactly true! Invidious Poet!
'Tis fifty thousand Times below it.

Translate me now some Lines, if you can,
From *Virgil*, *Martial*, *Ovid*, *Lucan*;
They could all Pow'r in Heaven divide,
And do no Wrong to either Side:
They'll teach you how to split a Hair,
*Give *George* and *Jove* an equal Share.
Yet, why should we be lac'd so straight;
I'll give my Monarch Butter-weight.
And Reason good; for many a Year
Jove never intermeddl'd here:
Nor, tho' his Priests be duly paid,
Did ever we *desire* his Aid:
We now can better do without him,
Since *Woolston* gave us Arms to rout him.

Cætera desiderantur

---

* *Divisum Imperium cum* Jove Cæsar *habet*

ON THE DAY OF JUDGEMENT

WITH a Whirl of Thought oppress'd,
I sink from Reverie to Rest.
An horrid Vision seiz'd my Head,
I saw the Graves give up their Dead.
Jove, arm'd with Terrors, burst the Skies,
And Thunder roars, and Light'ning flies!
Amaz'd, confus'd, its Fate unknown,
The World stands trembling at his Throne.
While each pale Sinner hangs his Head,
Jove, nodding, shook the Heav'ns, and said,
"Offending race of Human Kind,
By Nature, Reason, Learning, blind;
You who thro' Frailty stepp'd aside,
And you who never fell—*thro' Pride*;
You who in different Sects have shamm'd,
And come to see each other damn'd;
(So some Folks told you, but they knew
No more of Jove's Designs than you)
The World's mad Business now is o'er,
And I resent these Pranks no more,
I to such Blockheads set my Wit!
I damn such Fools!—Go, go, you're bit."

VERSES
ON
THE
DEATH
OF
DR SWIFT

VERSES ON THE DEATH OF
D^R S[WIFT], D.S.P.D.

Occasioned by reading a Maxim in *Rochefoulcault.*

*Dans l'adversité de nos meilleurs amis nous trouvons
quelque chose, qui ne nous deplaist pas.*

*In the Adversity of our best Friends, we find something
that doth not displease us.*

Written by Himself, *November* 1731.

THE PUBLISHER'S ADVERTISEMENT.

The following Poem was printed and published in London,
*with great Success. We are informed by the supposed
Author's Friends, that many Lines and Notes are omitted in
the* English *Edition; therefore we hope, that such Persons
who have seen the Original Manuscript, will help us to procure those Omissions, and correct any Things that may be
amiss, and the Favour shall be gratefully acknowledged.*

As *Rochefoucault* his Maxims drew
From Nature, I believe 'em true:
They argue no corrupted Mind
In him; the Fault is in Mankind.

This Maxim more than all the rest
Is thought too base for human Breast;
" In all Distresses of our Friends
" We first consult our private Ends,
" While Nature kindly bent to ease us,
" Points out some Circumstance to please us."

If this perhaps your Patience move
Let Reason and Experience prove.

We all behold with envious Eyes,
Our *Equal* rais'd above our *Size*;

Who wou'd not at a crowded Show,
Stand high himself, keep others low?
I love my Friend as well as you,
But would not have him stop my View;
Then let him have the higher Post;
I ask but for an Inch at most.

If in a Battle you should find,
One, whom you love of all Mankind,
Had some heroick Action done,
A Champion kill'd, or Trophy won;
Rather than thus be over-topt,
Would you not wish his Lawrels cropt?

Dear honest *Ned* is in the Gout,
Lies rackt with Pain, and you without:
How patiently you hear him groan!
How glad the Case is not your own!

What Poet would not grieve to see,
His Brethren write as well as he?
But rather than they should excel,
He'd wish his Rivals all in Hell.

Her End when Emulation misses,
She turns to Envy, Stings and Hisses:
The strongest Friendship yields to Pride,
Unless the Odds be on our Side.

Vain human Kind! Fantastick Race!
Thy various Follies, who can trace?
Self-love, Ambition, Envy, Pride,
Their Empire in our Hearts divide:
Give others Riches, Power, and Station,
'Tis all on me an Usurpation.
I have no Title to aspire;
Yet, when you sink, I seem the higher.
In POPE, I cannot read a Line,
But with a Sigh, I wish it mine:

When he can in one Couplet fix
More Sense than I can do in Six:
It gives me such a jealous Fit,
I cry, Pox take him, and his Wit.

Why must I be outdone by GAY,
In my own hum'rous biting Way?

ARBUTHNOT is no more my Friend,
Who dares to Irony pretend;
Which I was born to introduce,
Refin'd it first, and shew'd its Use.

ST. JOHN, as well as PULTNEY knows,
That I had some Repute for Prose;
And till they drove me out of Date,
Could maul a Minister of State:
If they have mortify'd my Pride,
And made me throw my Pen aside;
If with such Talents Heav'n hath blest 'em
Have I not Reason to detest 'em?

To all my Foes, dear Fortune, send
Thy Gifts, but never to my Friend:
I tamely can endure the first,
But, this with Envy makes me burst.

Thus much may serve by way of Proem,
Proceed we therefore to our Poem.

The Time is not remote, when I
Must by the Course of Nature dye:
When I foresee my special Friends,
Will try to find their private Ends:
Tho' it is hardly understood,
Which way my Death can do them good;
Yet, thus methinks, I hear 'em speak;
See, how the Dean begins to break:

Poor Gentleman, he droops apace,
You plainly find it in his Face:
That old Vertigo in his Head,
Will never leave him, till he's dead:
Besides, his Memory decays,
He recollects not what he says;
He cannot call his Friends to Mind;
Forgets the Place where last he din'd:
Plyes you with Stories o'er and o'er,
He told them fifty Times before.
How does he fancy we can sit,
To hear his out-of-fashion'd Wit?
But he takes up with younger Fokes,
Who for his Wine will bear his Jokes:
Faith, he must make his Stories shorter,
Or change his Comrades once a Quarter:
In half the Time, he talks them round;
There must another Sett be found.

For Poetry, he's past his Prime,
He takes an Hour to find a Rhime:
His Fire is out, his Wit decay'd,
His Fancy sunk, his Muse a Jade.
I'd have him throw away his Pen;
But there's no talking to some Men.

And, then their Tenderness appears,
By adding largely to my Years:
" He's older than he would be reckon'd,
" And well remembers *Charles* the Second.

" He hardly drinks a Pint of Wine;
" And that, I doubt, is no good Sign.
" His Stomach too begins to fail:
" Last Year we thought him strong and hale;
" But now, he's quite another Thing;
" I wish he may hold out till Spring."

Then hug themselves, and reason thus;
" It is not yet so bad with us."

In such a Case they talk in Tropes,
And, by their Fears express their Hopes:
Some great Misfortune to portend,
No Enemy can match a Friend;
With all the Kindness they profess,
The Merit of a lucky Guess,
(When daily Howd'y's come of Course,
And Servants answer; *Worse and Worse*)
Wou'd please 'em better than to tell,
That, GOD be prais'd, the Dean is well.
Then he who prophecy'd the best,
Approves his Foresight to the rest:
" You know, I always fear'd the worst,
" And often told you so at first:"
He'd rather chuse, that I should dye,
Than his Prediction prove a Lye.
Not one foretels I shall recover;
But, all agree, to give me over.

Yet shou'd some Neighbour feel a Pain,
Just in the Parts, where I complain;
How many a Message would he send?
What hearty Prayers that I should mend?
Enquire what Regimen I kept;
What gave me Ease, and how I slept?
And more lament, when I was dead,
Than all the Sniv'llers round my Bed.

My good Companions, never fear,
For though you may mistake a Year;
Though your Prognosticks run too fast,
They must be verify'd at last.

" Behold the fatal Day arrive!
" How is the Dean? He's just alive.
" Now the departing Prayer is read:
" He hardly breathes. The Dean is dead.
" Before the Passing-Bell begun,
" The News thro' half the Town has run.

" O, may we all for Death prepare!
" What has he left? And who's his Heir?
" I know no more than what the News is,
" 'Tis all bequeath'd to publick Uses.
" To publick Use! A perfect Whim!
" What had the Publick done for him!
" Meer Envy, Avarice, and Pride!
" He gave it all:——But first he dy'd.
" And had the Dean, in all the Nation,
" No worthy Friend, no poor Relation?
" So ready to do Strangers good,
" Forgetting his own Flesh and Blood?"

Now Grub-street Wits are all employ'd;
With Elegies, the Town is cloy'd:
Some Paragraph in ev'ry Paper,
*To *curse* the *Dean*, or *bless* the *Drapier*.

The Doctors tender of their Fame,
Wisely on me lay all the Blame:
" We must confess his Case was nice;
" But he would never take Advice:
" Had he been rul'd, for ought appears,
" He might have liv'd these Twenty Years:
" For when we open'd him we found,
" That all his vital Parts were sound."

From *Dublin* soon to *London* spread,
†'Tis told at Court, the Dean is dead.

‡ Kind Lady *Suffolk* in the Spleen,
Runs laughing up to tell the [Queen,]

---

* *The Author supposes, that the Scriblers of the prevailing Party,
which he always opposed, will libel him after his Death; but that others,
who remember the Service he had done to* Ireland, *under the Name of*
M. B. Drapier, *by utterly defeating the destructive Project of* Wood's
Half-pence, *in five Letters to the People of* Ireland, *at that Time read
universally, and convincing every Reader, will remember him with
Gratitude.*
† *The Dean supposeth himself to dye in* Ireland.
‡ *Mrs* Howard, *afterwards Countess of* Suffolk, *then of the Bed-
chamber to the Queen, professed much Favour for the Dean. The
Queen then Princess, sent a dozen times to the Dean* (then in London)

The [Queen] so Gracious, Mild, and Good,
Cries, " Is he gone? 'Tis time he shou'd.
" He's dead you say; [Why, let him] rot;
*" I'm glad [the medals were] forgot.
" I promis'd [him, I own, but] when?
" I only [was a Princess] then;
" But now as Consort of [a King]
" You know 'tis quite a different Thing."

† Now, *Chartres* at Sir *R[obert]'s* Levee,
Tells, with a Sneer, the Tidings heavy:
" Why, is he dead without his Shoes?
‡ (Cries *B[ob]*) " I'm sorry for the News;
" Oh, were the Wretch but living still,
§ " And, in his Place my good Friend *Will*;

---

with her Command to attend her; which at last he did, by Advice of all his Friends. She often sent for him afterwards, and always treated him very Graciously. He taxed her with a Present worth Ten Pounds, which she promised before he should return to Ireland, *but on his taking Leave, the Medals were not ready.*

* *The Medals were to be sent to the* Dean *in four Months, but* [*She forgot, or thought them too dear. The Dean being in Ireland sent Mrs Howard a piece of plad made in that Kingdom, which the Queen seeing took it from her and wore it herself, and sent to the Dean for as much as would clothe herself and Children—desiring he would send the charge of it. He did the former: it cost 35l. but he said he would have nothing except the medals: he went next summer to England and was treated as usual, and she being then Queen, Ye Dean was promised a settlement in England but return'd as he went, and instead of receiving of her intended favours or ye medals hath been ever since under her Majesty's displeasure.*]

† *Chartres is a most infamous, vile Scoundrel, grown from a Foot-Boy, or worse, to a prodigious Fortune both in* England *and* Scotland: *He had a Way of insinuating himself into all Ministers under every Change, either as Pimp, Flatterer, or Informer. He was Tryed at Seventy for a Rape, and came off by sacrificing a great Part of his Fortune (he is since dead, but this Poem still preserves the Scene and Time it was writ in.)*

‡ *Sir* Robert Walpole, *Chief Minister of State, treated the Dean in* 1726, *with great Distinction, invited him to Dinner at* Chelsea, *with the Dean's Friends chosen on Purpose; appointed an Hour to talk with him of* Ireland, *to which* Kingdom *and* People *the Dean found him no great Friend; for he defended* Wood's *Project of Half-pence, &c. The Dean would see him no more; and upon his next Year's return to* England, *Sir* Robert *on an accidental Meeting, only made a civil Compliment, and never invited him again.*

§ *Mr.* William Pultney, *from being Mr.* [Walpole]'s *intimate Friend, detesting his Administration, became his mortal Enemy, and joyned with my* Lord Bolingbroke *to expose him in an excellent Paper, called the* Craftsman, *which is still continued.*

" Or, had a Mitre on his Head
* " Provided *Bolingbroke* were dead."
† Now, *Curl* his Shop from Rubbish drains;
Three genuine Tomes of *Swift's* Remains.
And then, to make them pass the glibber,
‡ Revis'd by *Tibbalds*, *Moore*, and *Cibber*.
He'll treat me as he does my Betters.
§ Publish my Will, my Life, my Letters.
Revive the Libels born to dye;
Which POPE must bear, as well as I.

Here shift the Scene, to represent
How those I love, my Death lament.
Poor POPE will grieve a Month; and GAY
A Week; and ARBUTHNOTT a Day.

ST. JOHN himself will scarce forbear,
To bite his Pen, and drop a Tear.
The rest will give a Shrug, and cry,
I'm sorry; but we all must dye.
Indifference Clad in Wisdom's Guise,
All Fortitude of Mind supplies:

---

* Henry St. John, *Lord Viscount* Bolingbroke, *Secretary of State to* Queen Anne of blessed Memory. *He is reckoned the most Universal Genius in* Europe; [Walpole] *dreading his Abilities, treated him most injuriously, working with* [King George] *who forgot his Promise of restoring the said Lord, upon the restless Importunity of* [Sir Robert Walpole].

† Curl, *hath been the most infamous Bookseller of any Age or Country: His Character in Part may be found in Mr.* POPE's *Dunciad. He published three Volumes all charged on the Dean, who never writ three Pages of them: He hath used many of the Dean's Friends in almost as vile a Manner.*

‡ *Three stupid Verse Writers in* London, *the last to the Shame of the Court, and the highest Disgrace to Wit and Learning, was made Laureat.* Moore, *commonly called* Jemmy Moore, *Son of* Arthur Moore, *whose Father was Jaylor of* Monaghan *in* Ireland. *See the Character of* Jemmy Moore, *and* Tibbalds, Theobald *in the Dunciad.*

§ Curl *is notoriously infamous for publishing the Lives, Letters, and last Wills and Testaments of the Nobility and Ministers of State, as well as of all the Rogues, who are hanged at* Tyburn. *He hath been in Custody of the House of Lords for publishing or forging the Letters of many Peers; which made the Lords enter a Resolution in their Journal Book, that no Life or Writings of any Lord should be published without the Consent of the next Heir at Law, or Licence from their House.*

For how can stony Bowels melt,
In those who never Pity felt;
When *We* are lash'd, *They* kiss the Rod;
Resigning to the Will of God.

The Fools, my Juniors by a Year,
Are tortur'd with Suspence and Fear.
Who wisely thought my Age a Screen,
When death approach'd, to stand between:
The Screen remov'd, their Hearts are trembling,
They mourn for me without dissembling.

My female Friends, whose tender Hearts,
Have better learn'd to Act their Parts,
Receive the News in *doleful Dumps*,
" The Dean is Dead, (*and what is Trumps?*)
" Then Lord have Mercy on his Soul.
" (Ladies I'll venture for the *Vole*.)
" Six Dean's they say must bear the Pall.
" (I wish I knew what *King* to call.)
" Madam, your Husband will attend
" The Funeral of so good a Friend.
" No Madam, 'tis a shocking Sight,
" And he's engag'd To-morrow Night!
" My Lady *Club* wou'd take it ill,
" If he shou'd fail her at *Quadrill*.
" He lov'd the Dean. (*I led a Heart*.)
" But dearest Friends, they say, must part.
" His Time was come, he ran his Race;
" We hope he's in a better Place."

Why do we grieve that Friends should dye?
No Loss more easy to supply.
One Year is past; a different Scene;
No further mention of the Dean;
Who now, alas, no more is mist,
Than, if he never did exist.
Where's now this Fav'rite of *Apollo*?
Departed; *and his Works must follow*:

Must undergo the common Fate;
His Kind of Wit is out of Date.
Some Country Squire to *Lintot goes,
Enquires for SWIFT in Verse and Prose:
Says *Lintot*, " I have heard the Name:
" He dy'd a Year ago." The same.
He searches all his Shop in vain;
" Sir you may find them in †*Duck-lane*:
" I sent them with a Load of Books,
" Last *Monday*, to the Pastry-cooks.
" To fancy they cou'd live a Year!
" I find you're but a Stranger here.
" The Dean was famous in his Time;
" And had a Kind of Knack at Rhyme:
" His way of Writing now is past;
" The Town hath got a better Taste:
" I keep no antiquated Stuff;
" But, spick and span I have enough.
" Pray, do but give me leave to shew 'em,
" Here's *Colley Cibber's* Birth-day Poem.
" This Ode you never yet have seen,
" By [*Stephen Duck*], upon the Queen.
" Then, here's a Letter finely penn'd
" Against the *Craftsman* and his Friend;
" It clearly shews that all Reflection
" On Ministers, is Disaffection.
‡ " Next, here's Sir *R*[*obert*]'s Vindication,
§ " And Mr. *Henly's* last Oration:
" The Hawkers have not got 'em yet,
" Your Honour please to buy a Set?

---

* Bernard Lintot, *a Bookseller in* London, *Vide Mr.* Pope's *Dunciad.*
    † *A Place where old Books are sold in* London.
    ‡ [Walpole] *hath a Set of Party Scriblers, who do nothing else but write in his Defence.*
    § Henly *is a Clergyman who wanting both Merit and Luck to get Preferment, or even to keep his Curacy in the Established Church, formed a new Conventicle, which he calls an Oratory. There, at set Times, he delivereth strange Speeches compiled by himself and his Associates, who share the Profit with him: Every Hearer pays a Shilling each Day for Admittance. He is an absolute Dunce, but generally reputed crazy.*

*" Here's *Wolston's* Tracts, the twelfth Edition;
" 'Tis read by ev'ry Politician:
" The Country Members, when in Town,
" To all their Boroughs send them down:
" You never met a Thing so smart;
" The Courtiers have them all by Heart:
" Those Maids of Honour (who can read)
" Are taught to use them for their Creed.
" The rev'rend Author's good Intention,
" Hath been rewarded with a Pension:
" He doth an Honour to his Gown,
" By bravely running *Priest-craft* down:
" He shews, as sure as GOD's in *Gloc'ster*,
"That [*Jesus*] was a Grand Impostor:
" That all his Miracles were Cheats,
" Perform'd as Juglers do their Feats:
" The Church had never such a Writer:
" A Shame, he hath not got a Mitre!"

Suppose me dead; and then suppose
A Club assembled at the *Rose*;
Where from Discourse of this and that,
I grow the Subject of their Chat:
And, while they toss my Name about,
With Favour some, and some without;
One quite indiff'rent in the Cause,
My Character impartial draws.

" The Dean, if we believe Report,
" Was never ill receiv'd at Court.
" As for his Works in Verse and Prose,
" I own my self no Judge of those:
" Nor, can I tell what Criticks thought 'em;
" But, this I know, all People bought 'em;

---

* Wolston *was a Clergyman, but for want of Bread, hath in several Treatises, in the most blasphemous Manner, attempted to turn* Our Saviour *and his Miracles into Ridicule. He is much caressed by many great Courtiers, and by all the Infidels, and his Books read generally by the Court Ladies.*

" As with a moral View design'd
" To cure the Vices of Mankind:
" His Vein, ironically grave,
" Expos'd the Fool, and lash'd the Knave:
" To steal a Hint was never known,
" But what he writ, was all his own.

    " He never thought an Honour done him
" Because a Duke was proud to own him:
" Would rather slip aside, and chuse
" To talk with Wits in dirty Shoes:
" Despis'd the Fools with Stars and Garters,
" So often seen caressing *Chartres:
" He never courted Men in Station,
" *Nor Persons had in Admiration*;
" Of no Man's Greatness was afraid,
" Because he sought for no Man's Aid.
" Though trusted long in great Affairs,
" He gave himself no haughty Airs:
" Without regarding private Ends,
" Spent all his Credit for his Friends:
" And, only chose the Wise and Good;
" No Flatt'rers; no Allies in Blood;
" But succour'd Virtue in Distress,
" And seldom fail'd of good Success;
" As Numbers in their Hearts must own,
" Who, but for him, had been unknown.

    " With Princes Kept a due Decorum,
" But never stood in Awe before 'em:
" He follow'd *David's* Lesson just,
" *In Princes never put thy Trust.*
" And, would you make him truly sower;
" Provoke him with *a Slave in Power*:
" The [Irish] S[enate], if you nam'd,
" With what Impatience he declaim'd!
" Fair LIBERTY was all his Cry;
" For her he stood prepar'd to die;

---

* *See the Notes before on* Chartres.

" For her he boldly stood alone;
" For her he oft expos'd his own.
*" Two Kingdoms, just as Faction led,
" Had set a Price upon his Head;
" But, not a Traytor cou'd be found,
" To sell him for Six Hundred Pound.

  " Had he but spar'd his Tongue and Pen,
" He might have rose like other Men:
" But, Power was never in his Thought;
" And, Wealth he valu'd not a Groat:
" Ingratitude he often found,
" And pity'd those who meant the Wound:
" But, kept the Tenor of his Mind,
" To merit well of human Kind:
" Nor made a Sacrifice of those
" Who still were true, to please his Foes.
†" He labour'd many a fruitless Hour
" To reconcile his Friends in Power;
" Saw Mischief by a Faction brewing,
" While they pursu'd each others Ruin.
" But, finding vain was all his Care,
" He left the Court in meer Despair.

  " And, oh! how short are human Schemes!
" Here ended all our golden Dreams.
" What St. John's Skill in State Affairs,
" What Ormond's *Valour*, Oxford's Cares,
" To save their sinking Country lent,
" Was all destroy'd by one Event.

---

  * *In the Year* 1713, *the late Queen was prevailed with by an Address of the House of Lords in* England, *to publish a Proclamation, promising Three Hundred Pounds to whatever Person would discover the Author of a Pamphlet called,* The Publick Spirit of the Whiggs; *and in* Ireland, *in the Year* 1724, *my Lord* Carteret *at his first coming into the Government, was prevailed on to issue a Proclamation for promising the like reward of Three Hundred Pounds, to any Person who could discover the Author of a Pamphlet called,* The Drapier's Fourth Letter, &c. *writ against that destructive Project of coining Half-pence for* Ireland; *but in neither Kingdoms was the Dean discovered.*

  † *Queen* Anne's *Ministry fell to Variance from the first Year after their Ministry began:* Harcourt *the Chancellor, and Lord*

*" Too soon that precious Life was ended,
" On which alone, our Weal depended.

†" When up a dangerous faction starts,
" With Wrath and Vengeance in their Hearts;
" *By solemn League and Cov'nant bound,*
" To ruin, slaughter, and confound;
" To turn Religion to a Fable,
" And make the Government a *Babel*:
" Pervert the Law, disgrace the Gown,
" Corrupt the [Senate], rob the [Crown];
" To sacrifice old [England's] Glory,
" And make her infamous in Story.
" When such a Tempest shook the Land,
" How could unguarded Virtue stand?

" With Horror, Grief, Despair the Dean
" Beheld the dire destructive Scene:
" His Friends in Exile, or the Tower,
‡" Himself within the Frown of Power;
" Pursu'd by base envenom'd Pens,
§" Far to the Land of [Slaves] and Fens;

Bolingbroke *the Secretary, were discontented with the Treasurer* Oxford, *for his too much Mildness to the Whig Party; this Quarrel grew higher every Day till the Queen's Death: The Dean, who was the only Person that endeavoured to reconcile them, found it impossible; and thereupon retired to the Country about ten Weeks before that fatal Event: Upon which he returned to his Deanry in* Dublin, *where for many Years he was worryed by the new People in Power, and had Hundreds of Libels writ against him in* England.

* *In the Height of the Quarrel between the Ministers, the Queen died.*

† *Upon Queen* ANNE'S *Death the Whig Faction was restored to Power, which they exercised with the utmost Rage and Revenge; impeached and banished the Chief Leaders of the Church Party, and stripped all their Adherents of what Employments they had, [after which* England *was never known to make so mean a figure in Europe: The greatest preferments in the Church in both Kingdoms were given to the most ignorant men. Fanaticks were publickly caressed;* Ireland *utterly ruined and enslaved; only great Ministers heaping up Millions; and so affairs continue to this* 3d. *of* May 1732, *and are likely to remain so.*]

‡ *Upon the Queen's Death, the Dean returned to live in* Dublin, *at his Deanry-House: Numberless Libels were writ against him in* England, *as a Jacobite; he was insulted in the Street, and at Nights he was forced to be attended by his Servants armed.*

§ *The Land of* [Slaves] *and Fens, is* Ireland.

" A servile Race in Folly nurs'd,
" Who truckle most, when treated worst.

" By Innocence and Resolution,
" He bore continual Persecution;
" While Numbers to Preferment rose;
" Whose Merits were, to be his Foes.
" When, *ev'n his own familiar Friends*
" Intent upon their private Ends;
" Like Renegadoes now he feels,
" *Against him lifting up their Heels.*

" The Dean did by his Pen defeat
*" An infamous destructive Cheat.
" Taught Fools their Int'rest how to know;
" And gave them Arms to ward the Blow.
" Envy hath own'd it was his doing,
" To save that helpless Land from Ruin;
" While they who at the Steerage stood,
" And reapt the Profit, sought his Blood.

" To save them from their evil Fate,
" In him was held a Crime of State.
†" A wicked Monster on the Bench,
" Whose Fury Blood could never quench;
" As vile and profligate a Villain,
" As modern ‡*Scroggs*, or old *Tressilian*;

---

* *One* Wood, *a Hardware-man from* England, *had a Patent for coining Copper Half-pence in* Ireland, *to the Sum of* 108,000 l. *which in the Consequence, must leave that Kingdom without Gold or Silver* (*See* Drapier's *Letters.*)

† *One* W[hitshed] *was then Chief Justice: He had some Years before prosecuted a Printer for a Pamphlet writ by the Dean, to per-swade the People of* Ireland *to wear their own Manufactures.* Whit-shed *sent the Jury down eleven Times, and kept them nine Hours, until they were forced to bring in a special Virdict. He sat as Judge afterwards on the Tryal of the Printer of the* Drapier's *Fourth Letter: but the Jury, against all he could say or swear, threw out the Bill: All the Kingdom took the* Drapier's *Part, except the Courtiers, or those who expected Places. The* Drapier *was celebrated in many Poems and Pamphlets: His Sign was set up in most Streets of* Dublin (*where many of them still continue*) *and in several Country Towns.*

‡ Scroggs *was Chief Justice under King* Charles *the Second: His Judgment always varied in State Tryals, according to Directions from*

" Who long all Justice had discarded,
" *Nor fear'd he GOD, nor Man regarded;*
" Vow'd on the Dean his Rage to vent,
" And make him of his Zeal repent;
" But Heav'n his Innocence defends,
" The grateful People stand his Friends:
" Not Strains of Law, nor Judges Frown,
" Nor Topicks brought to please the [Crown],
" Nor Witness hir'd, nor Jury pick'd,
" Prevail to bring him in convict.

    *" In Exile with a steady Heart,
" He spent his Life's declining Part;
" Where, Folly, Pride, and Faction sway,
†" Remote from ST. JOHN, POPE, and GAY.
‡" His Friendship there to few confin'd,
" Were always of the midling Kind:
" No Fools of Rank, a mungril Breed,
" Who fain would pass for [Lords] indeed;
§" Where Titles give no Right or Power,
" And [Peerage] is a wither'd Flower,
" He would have held it a Disgrace,
" If such a Wretch had known his Face.
" On Rural Squires, that Kingdoms Bane,
" He vented oft his Wrath in vain:
‖ " [Biennial] Squires, to Market brought;

Court. Tressilian *was a wicked Judge, hanged above three Hundred Years ago.*

* *In* Ireland, *which he had Reason to call a Place of Exile; to which Country nothing could have driven him, but the Queen's Death, who had determined to fix him in* England, *in Spight of the Dutchess of* Somerset, &c.

† Henry St. John, *Lord Viscount* Bolingbroke, *mentioned before.*

‡ *In* Ireland *the Dean was not acquainted with one single Lord Spiritual or Temporal. He only conversed with private Gentlemen of the Clergy or Laity, and but a small Number of either.*

§ *The Peers of* Ireland *lost their Jurisdiction by one single Act,* [*and tamely submitted to the infamous mark of slavery without the least resentment or remonstrance.*]

‖ *The* [*Parliament, as they call it, in* Ireland *meet but once in two years, and after having given five times more than they can afford return home to reimburse themselves by all country jobs and oppressions of which some few only are mentioned.*]

" Who sell their Souls and [Votes] for Naught;
" The [Nation stripp'd] go joyful back,
" To [rob] the Church, their Tenants rack,
* " Go Snacks with [Rogues and Rapparees]
" And, keep the Peace, to pick up Fees:
" In every Jobb to have a Share,
† " A Jayl or [Barrack] to repair;
" And turn the [Tax] for publick Roads
" Commodious to their own Abodes.

    " Perhaps I may allow, the Dean
" Had too much Satyr in his Vein;
" And seem'd determin'd not to starve it,
" Because no Age could more deserve it.
" Yet, Malice never was his Aim;
" He lash'd the Vice, but spar'd the Name.
" No Individual could resent,
" Where Thousands equally were meant.
" His Satyr points at no Defect,
" But what all Mortals may correct:
" For he abhorr'd that senseless Tribe,
" Who call it Humour when they jibe:
" He spar'd a Hump, or crooked Nose,
" Whose Owners set not up for Beaux.
" True genuine Dullness mov'd his Pity,
" Unless it offer'd to be witty.
" Those, who their Ignorance confess'd,
" He ne'er offended with a Jest;
" But laugh'd to hear an Idiot quote,
" A Verse from *Horace*, learn'd by Rote.

    " He knew an hundred pleasant Stories,
" With all the Turns of *Whigs* and *Tories*:
" Was chearful to his dying Day,
" And Friends would let him have his Way.

---

  * [*The Highwaymen in* Ireland, *are, since the late wars there, usually called* Rapparees, *which was a name given to those* Irish *soldiers who in small parties used at that time to plunder* Protestants.]

  † [*The army in* Ireland *are lodged in Barracks, the building and repairing whereof and other charges have cost a prodigious sum to that unhappy Kingdom.*]

" He gave the little Wealth he had,
" To build a House for Fools and Mad:
" And shew'd by one satyric Touch,
" No Nation wanted it so much:
*" That Kingdom he hath left his Debtor,
" I wish it soon may have a Better."

---

* *Meaning* Ireland, *where he now lives, and probably may dye.*

THE EPITAPH ON SWIFT'S TOMB
IN SAINT PATRICK'S CATHEDRAL
DUBLIN

WRITTEN BY HIMSELF.

HIC DEPOSITVM EST CORPVS

JONATHAN SWIFT, *S.T.P.

HVIVS ECCLESIAE CATHEDRALIS

DECANI,

VBI SAEVA INDIGNATIO

VLTERIVS COR LACERARE NEQUIT.

ABI, VIATOR,

ET IMITARE, SI POTERIS,

STRENVVM PRO VIRILI LIBER-

TATIS VINDICEM.

OBIIT ANNO MDCCXLV

MENSIS OCTOBRIS DIE 19

AETATIS ANNO LXXVIII

---

* The Monument in St. Patrick's Cathedral reads S.T.D. (*i.e.* Sacræ Theologiæ Doctor) for the more usual S.T.P[rofessor] of the printed texts of Swift's Will, in which the epitaph was first published. The version given here is taken from *Works, Vol. VIII. 4to 1765.* [ED.]

TEXTUAL
NOTES

NOTE: In the following notes, '*f.b.*' after a line reference indicates that the number of the line has been counted from the bottom of the page.

TEXTUAL NOTES

PROSE

GULLIVER'S TRAVELS

Text from: VOLUME III. / Of the Author's / WORKS. / containing, / TRAVELS / into several / Remote Nations of the WORLD. / In Four Parts, . . . / By *LEMUEL GULLIVER*, first a Surgeon,/ and then a Captain of several Ships. / . . . / In this Impression several Errors in the *London* and *Dublin* / Editions are corrected. / *DUBLIN*: / Printed by and for GEORGE FAULKNER, Printer / and Bookseller, in *Essex-Street*, opposite to the / Bridge. MDCCXXXV. /
Copy: Editor.
Collated with: First Edition 2 vols.: 1726. Ford's annotated and interleaved large-paper copy of Edn. 1 in the Forster Collection, South Kensington. [*v*. P. 2].

In the following list of variants, corrections and emendations the first edition of the Travels, printed by Motte in October 1726, is referred to as *M.*; the text of Volume III of Faulkner's *Works, 1735*, reprinted in this volume, as *F.*; Ford's " paper " of errata, sent to Motte in a letter [Jan. 3. 1726/7], as *P.*; and Ford's corrections, written in the interleaved, large-paper copy of Motte's first edition, as *C.*

The following Advertisement *appears in F. after the general title*:— Mr *Sympson's* Letter to Captain *Gulliver*, prefixed to this Volume, will make a long Advertisement unnecessary. Those Interpolations complained of by the Captain, were made by a Person since deceased, on whose Judgment the Publisher relyed to make any Alterations that might be thought necessary. But, this Person, not rightly comprehending the Scheme of the Author, nor able to imitate his plain simple Style, thought fit among many other Alterations and Insertions, to compliment the Memory of her late Majesty, by saying, *That she governed without a ·Chief Minister*. We are assured, that the Copy sent to the Bookseller in *London*, was a Transcript of the Original, which Original being in the Possession of a very worthy Gentleman in *London*, and a most intimate Friend of the Authors; after he had bought the Book in Sheets, and compared it with the Originals, bound it up with blank Leaves, and made those Corrections, which the Reader will find in our Edition. For, the same Gentleman did us the Favour to let us transcribe his Corrections.
The " very worthy Gentleman " is, of course, Ford; the interleaved copy mentioned, the volume, now at South Kensington, referred to in these notes as C.
PAGE 5. " A Letter from Capt. Gulliver to his Cousin Sympson ", *printed almost certainly at Swift's instigation, appeared for the first time in F.* [1735].
P. 10, LINE 4 *f.b.* " The Publisher to the Reader." I shall be. *M. This preface is followed in F. by a list of Contents, which has been omitted here.*

Part I. A Voyage to Lilliput

Chap. 1.

P. 16, l. 5. my Eyes. *C.* mine
Eyes. *F. The correction*—my *for*
mine—*also occurs in the following places:*—

P. 19, l. 17.	P. 105, l. 4 *f.b.*
P. 31, l. 15.	P. 134, l. 13.
P. 32, l. 6 *f.b.*	P. 139, l. 8.
P. 47, l. 19.	P. 145, *last line.*
P. 69, l. 17.	P. 146, l. 18.
P. 72, l. 20.	P. 192, l. 3 *f.b.*
P. 84, l. 9.	P. 236, l. 13 *f.b.*
P. 104, l. 2.	P. 277, l. 9 *f.b.*

Ford [C.] *omitted to make this
correction in three other passages:*
P. 15, *last line.* P. 17, l. 5 *f.b.*
P. 141, l. 4 *f.b.*
These I have emended accordingly.
　P. 17, ll. 10-11. Noise . . .
greater. Noise I heard, I knew
their Numbers encreased. *M.*
　l. 13. like People. like that of
People. *M.*
　l. 13 *f.b.* who was. that was. *M.*
　l. 11 *f.b.* who held. that held.
M.
　P. 18, l. 17. *M. omits:* as fast.
　l. 16 *f.b.* hardly held. did not
hold. *M.*
　P. 19, l. 3. those. these. *M.*
　l. 8. on my. upon my. *M.*
　P. 20, l. 17. sleeping Potion.
sleepy Potion. *M.*
　P. 21, l. 3. buildeth. builds. *M.*
　P. 22, l. 1. the Day. that Day.
M.
　l. 15. common Uses. *P.* common Use. *F.*
　l. 25. on the other. on t'other.
M.

Chap. II.

P. 24, l. 19. although. though.
M.
*This variant also occurs in the
following passages:*—
P. 42, l. 14.　　　P. 62, l. 1.
P. 87, l. 17.
P. 91, Chap. II, ll. 8 and 12.
P. 93, *last line.* P. 105, l. 2 *f.b.*
P. 136, Chap. VIII, l. 2
P. 138, l. 3 *f.b.* P. 149, l. 13.
P. 150, l. 2 *f.b.*
P 202, l. 7 *f.b.* P. 224, l. 17 *f.b.*
P. 226, l. 5 *f.b.* P. 280, l. 14 *f.b.*

　l. 22. until. till. *M.*
*This variant also occurs in the
following passages:*—
P. 24, l. 11 *f.b.* P. 30, l. 15.
P. 47, l. 9.　　　P. 48, l. 12.
P. 57, ll. 8 *f.b.* and 2 *f.b.*
P. 69 *last line.* P. 247, l. 8.
P. 263, l. 20.　　P. 281, l. 3.
　l. 25. beyond. without. *M.*
　l. 26. Chains. Chain. *M.*
　l. 29. these vehicles. those
vehicles. *M.*
　P. 27, l. 4. was as much. was
looked upon to be as much.
M.
　l. 3 *f.b.* be exercised. be frequently exercised. *M.*
　P. 28, l. 7. apprehend, was.
apprehend it, was. *M.*
　l. 9. of his Council. *P. F.* of
Council. *M.*
　l. 9 *f.b.* Necessaries of. Necessaries that were of. *M.*
　P. 30, l. 11. was at the end of
that. was fastened to that. *M.*
　P. 31, l. 10. directed me to.
directed me, although in very
gentle terms, to. *M.*
　l. 9 *f.b.* escape. scape. *M.*
　l. 8 *f.b.* that all . . . provide
against. against which all . . .
provide. *M.*
　P. 32, l. 10. He asked. and
asked. *M.*

Chap. III.

　P. 34, ll. 15-14 *f.b.* Blue . . .
Red . . . Green. *B. F.* Purple . . .
Yellow . . . White. *M.*
*These variants recur in the same
paragraph:*—P. 35, ll. 3-4.
　P. 36, l. 20 *f.b.* Kinds of. kind
of. *M.*
　P. 38, l. 6 *f.b.* at our. to our.
M.
　P. 39, l. 12. require. requires.
M.
　l. 4 *f.b.*-P. 40, ll. 12, 6 *f.b.*
Motte's 3rd edition, [1726] *reads
correctly:*—1728. *Ford, followed
by Faulkner, omits to make the
correction and retains the reading
of M.*—1724.

Chap. IV.

P. 41, l. 13 *f.b.* who might. that
might. *M.*

P. 43, l. **13.** *Reldresal. Keld-resal. M.*

l. 18. as of the. as the. *M.*

l. 26. we appear. we may appear. *M.*

Chap. V.

P. 46, l. 8 *f.b.* walked to. walked towards. *M.*

l. 7 *f.b.* where. lying. and, lying. *M.*

P. 47 l. 9 arrived at. *P.* arrived to. *F.*

l. 17 *f.b.* escaped. scaped. *M.*

l. 9 *f.b.* boldest Part. *P.F.* bold Part. *M.*

P. 48, l. 2 *f.b.* remain sole. remain the sole. *M.*

P. 49, l. 14. Junta. Junto. *M.*

l. 4 *f.b.* interrupt. trouble. *M. The phrase* trouble the Reader *occurs earlier in the paragraph.*

P. 52, l. 14. assured, that the. assured, the. *M.*

Chap. VI.

P. 53, l. 4 *f.b.* make. maketh. *M.*

P. 54, l. 5. doth. does. *M. The same variant occurs on :—*

P. 54, l. 4 *f.b.* P. 118, l. 2 *f.b.*

l. 12. Honesty hath. Honesty has. *M.*

P. 55, l. 13 *f.b.* to multiply. and multiply. *M.*

l. 6 *f.b.* acteth. acts. *M.*

P. 56, l. 11. they have. he hath. *M.*

l. 24. nor intended. or intended. *M.*

P. 57, l. 19. not to last above. to last but. *M.*

l. 21. standeth. stands. *M.*

l. 9 *f.b.* seven. Eleven. *M.*

l. 8 *f.b.* Exercises until. Nurseries till. *M.*

P. 58, l. 5. Parts. Part. *M.*

l. 13. their Maxim. the Maxim. *M.*

ll. 24-25. seven . . . eleven. nine . . . thirteen. *M.*

P. 59, l. 4 *f.b.* not have been able. not be able. *M.*

P. 60, l. 2 *f.b.* that I had. that in short I had. *M.*

P. 61, l. 6 *f.b.* let them. let 'em. *M.*

P. 62, l. 1. although I had. though I had then. *M.*

l. 5. *England*; yet. *England*, although. *M.*

l. 7. made the Treasurer. made Flimnap the Treasurer. *M.*

l. 9. For although. and although. *M.*

Chap. VII.

P. 64, l. 11. *M. reads* his Majesty's dear Imperial Consort.

P. 65, l. 10 *f.b. M. omits* and Sheets.

P. 68, l. 8 *f.b.* Yet, as to. And as to. *M.*

P. 69, l. 6 *f.b.* I carryed. I brought. *M.*

Chap. VIII.

P. 74, l. 16 *f.b.* and as I. and I. *M.*

P. 75, l. 2. I had left. *P.* I left. *F.*

l. 21. Blefuscu. *P.F.* Lilliput. *M.*

Part II. A Voyage to Brobdingnag

Chap. I.

P. 79, l. 2. two Months. *The necessary correction to* two Months *was made by Motte in his 4th edition* [1727]. *F. & M. read* ten months.

P. 81, l. 11 *f.b.* but run. but ran. *M.*

P. 82, l. 6. utmost. uppermost. *M.*

l. 11 *f.b.* However. *P.F. M. omits.*

P. 86, l. 16. two Gallons. three Gallons. *M.*

l. 9 *f.b.* the Fall. my Fall. *M.*

P. 87, l. 4. Master understand. Master to understand. *M.*

Chap. II.

P. 91, l. 19 *f.b.* towardly. forward. *P.* toward. *M.*

P. 92, l. 16. Fields. *C.* Field. *F.*

P. 93, l. 16. conceive it to be *M.* conceive to be. *F.*

l. 21. as soon as it. *M.* as soon it. *F.*

P. 96, l. 8. by Leading-strings. by a Leading-string. *M.*

Chap. III.

P. 97, l. 9. to bring. to carry. *M.*
P. 98, l. 8 *f.b.* Majesty perhaps would. *P.*
Majesty would. *F.*
P. 99, l. 9. Hand. Hands. *M.*
l. 13. Splacknuck. Splacnuck. *M.*
l. 16 *f.b.* Dominions; and had. *P.* Dominions; had. *F.*
P. 100, l. 18. One of them. One of these Virtuosi. *M.*
P. 103, l. 13 *f.b.* those Creatures. these Creatures. *M.*
P. 104, l. 20 *f.b.* so insolent. *M. omits* so.
l. 16 *f.b.* smart Word. small Word. *M.*
P. 105, l. 9. Extremitys. *C.* Extremity. *F.*
l. 18. mounted the stool that she.
upon the stool she. *M.*
P. 106, l. 7 *f.b.* Insects. *C.F.* Creatures. *M.*

Chap. IV.

P. 108, l. 18 *f.b.* Houses. Houses, and about six hundred thousand Inhabitants. *M.*
P. 109, l. 6. *European C.F. English. M.*

Chap. V.

P. 114, 17 *f.b.* hop back. turn back. *M.*
P. 115, l. 9 *f.b.* Motions. emotions. *M.*
P. 116, l. 17. at one Blow. at a blow. *M.*
l. 22. at least an. at least half an. *M.*
P. 117, l. 14. my Diversion. my own Diversion. *M.*
l. 15. agreeably. well. *M.*
P. 118, l. 5 *f.b.* seized. caught hold of. *M.*
l. 4 *f.b.* Silk. Cloth. *M.*
P. 119, l. 10 *f.b.* five Hundred. three Hundred *M.*
P. 120, l. 11 *f.b.* Courage *P.F.* Honour. *M.*

Chap. VI.

P. 121. Chap. [VI]. *misprinted* Chap. III. *F.*
P. 123, l. 16 *f.b.* End. ends. *M.*
P. 124, l. 7. Mind, that he. Mind he. *M.*
l. 15 *f.b.* the Praises. *P.* the Praise. *F.*
l. 2 *f.b.* born to.
Faulkner in his editions of 1759 *and* 1752 *reads:*—both to.
P. 125, l. 13. and wisest. and his wisest. *M.*
P. 126, l. 4. what Questions. several Questions. *P.* all Questions. *M.*
The reading of M. is to be preferred to that of F. or P.
l. 15 *f.b.* constantly. always. *M.*
l. 5 *f.b.* Landlords. Landlord. *M.*
P. 128, l. 6. we found. we should find. *M.*
l. 8 *f.b.* as Cordials. for Cordials. *M.*
P. 129, l. 19 *f.b.* are the proper Ingredients. *C.F.* may be sometimes the only Ingredients. *M.*
l. 12 *f.b.* Perfection. Virtue. *M.*
l. 10 *f.b.* are ennobled. *P.F.* were ennobled. *M.*
l. 9 *f.b.*. are advanced. *P.F.* were advanced *M.*

Chap. VII.

P. 130, l. 3 *f.b.* that mighty Monarch. *C.* that Monarch. *F.*
P. 131, l. 8 *f.b.* Pavement. Pavements. *M.*
last line. two hundred. an hundred. *M.*
P. 132, l. 3 *f.b.* by not having. they not having. *M.*
P. 133, l. 13 *f.b.* only of. only in. *M.*
P. 134, l. 16 *f.b.* the latter. the rest. *M.*
l. 5 *f.b.* from the Inclemencies *P.* front Inclemencies. *F.*
P. 135, l. 3. Man. *F.* Men. *P.*
P. 136, l. 2. Ninety Foot. an hundred Foot. *M.*
l. 14. to which the whole . . . is Subject. *C.F.* to which so many other Governments are subject. *M.*

l. 19. more than once. once or more. *M.*

Chap. VIII.

P. 136, l. 5 *f.b.* it were. it was. *M.*

P. 137, l. 16 *f.b.* wide. I had. wide. And, I had. *M.*

l. 11 *f.b.* set not directly over. not directly over. *M.* Just over. *C.*

P. 138, l. 16 *f.b.* the Box. my Box. *M.*

P. 139, l. 7 *f.b.* Misfortune. Misfortunes. *M.*

P. 140, l. 9. my self from being. myself some Hours longer than by being. *M.*

l. 15 *f.b.* I were. I was. *M.*

P. 143, l. 11. ordered his Men. ordered them. *M.*

P. 144, l. 19. kept the Key. had the Key. *M.*

l. 21. his Presence. *P.F.* his own Presence. *M.*

P. 146, l. 13. for me. *P.F. M. omits.*

Part III. A Voyage to Laputa, *etc.*

Chap. I.

P. 150, l. 11. We stayed. *M. omits:* We.

l. 16. several Months. some Months. *M.*

l. 18 *f.b.* to traffick, while. to traffic for two Months, while. *M.*

l. 2 *f.b.* he were. he was. *M.*

Chap. II.

P. 155, l. 7 *f.b.* or attend. nor attend. *M.*

last line. two or more. two or three more. *M.*

P. 157, l. 8. his Order. the Kings Order. *M.*

P. 159, l. 7 *f.b.* else. *M. omits.*

P. 161, l. 5 *f.b.* Sprites. *P.F.* Spirits. *M.*

P. 162, l. 8. wrapped. rapt. *M.*

last line. Womankind. *P.F.* Womenkind. *M.*

Chap. III.

P. 164, l. 11. to do so in. to do in. *M.*

P. 166, ll. 18-20 For . . . Clearness. *F. This passage is not in M. P. varies slightly from F., viz.:—*. . . more than those of an hundred Yards among us, and at the same time shew the Stars . . .

l. 20. This Advantage. For this Advantage. *M.*

l. 21. their Discoveries. *P.F.* the Discoveries. *M.*

P. 167, l. 15. Dearth. *P.F.* Death. *M.*

P. 168, l. 13. *After the words* fall to the Ground *in C. there is added in Ford's hand the following passage, first printed in G. A. Aitken's edition, 1896, as an appendix to the text :—*About three Years before my Arrival among them, while the King was in his Progress over his Dominions there happened an extraordinary Accident which had like to have put a Period to the Fate of that Monarchy, at least as it is now instituted. Lindalino the second City in the Kingdom was the first his Majesty visited in his Progress. Three Days after his Departure, the Inhabitants who had often complained of great Oppressions, shut the Town Gates, seized on the Governor, and with incredible Speed and Labour erected four large Towers, one at every Corner of the City (which is an exact Square) equal in Heighth to a strong pointed Rock that stands directly in the Center of the City. Upon the Top of each Tower, as well as upon the Rock, they fixed a great Loadstone, and in case their Design should fail, they had provided a vast Quantity of the most combustible Fewel, hoping to burst therewith the adamantine Bottom of the Island, if the Loadstone Project should miscarry.

It was eight Months before the King had perfect Notice that the Lindalinians were in Rebellion. He then commanded that the Island should be wafted over the City. The People were unanimous, and had laid in Store of Provisions, and a great River runs through the middle of the Town. The King hovered over them several Days to deprive them of the Sun and Rain. He ordered many Packthreads to be let down, yet not a Person offered to send up a Petition, but instead thereof, very bold Demands, the Redress of all their Grievances, great Immunitys, the Choice of their own Governor, and other the like Exorbitances. Upon which his Majesty commanded all the Inhabitants of the Island to cast great Stones from the lower Gallery into the Town; but the Citizens had provided against this Mischief by conveying their Persons and Effects into the four Towers, and other strong Buildings, and Vaults under Ground.

The King being now determined to reduce this proud People, ordered that the Island should descend gently within fourty Yards of the Top of the Towers and Rock. This was accordingly done; but the Officers employed in that Work found the Descent much speedier than usual, and by turning the Loadstone could not without great Difficulty keep it in a firm position, but found the Island inclining to fall. They sent the King immediate Intelligence of this astonishing Event and begged his Majesty's Permission to raise the Island higher; the King consented, a general Council was called, and the Officers of the Loadstone ordered to attend. One of the oldest and expertest among them obtained leave to try an Experiment. He took a strong Line of an Hundred Yards, and the Island being raised over the Town above the attracting Power they had felt, He fastened a Piece of Adamant to the End of his Line, which had in it a Mixture of Iron mineral, of the same Nature with that whereof the Bottom or lower Surface of the Island is composed, and from the lower Gallery let it down slowly towards the Top of the Towers. The Adamant was not descended four Yards, before the Officer felt it drawn so strongly downwards, that he could hardly pull it back. He then threw down several Pieces of Adamant, and observed that they were all violently attracted by the Top of the Tower. The same Experiment was made on the other three Towers, and on the Rock with the same Effect.

This Incident broke entirely the King's Measures and (to dwell no longer on other Circumstances) he was forced to give the Town their own Conditions.

I was assured by a great Minister, that if the Island had descended so near the Town, as not to be able to raise it self, the Citizens were determined to fix it for ever, to kill the King and all his Servants, and entirely change the Government.

Chap. IV.

P. 170, l. 5. Abode there. *P.F.* Abode here. *M*.

P. 172, l. 12. Dress or Looks. *C*. Dress and Looks. *F*.

P. 173, l. 10. into such. in such. *M*

Chap. V.

P. 175, *last line*. more, that he. more, he. *M*.

P. 177, l. 8. Masts. Maste. *M*.

l. 15 *f.b.* would be. should be. *M*.

P. 178, l. 15. recovers. recover. *M*.

P. 179, l. 21. Books in. *P.F.* both in. *M*.

l. 10 *f.b.* Papers. *C*. Paper. *F*.

P. 180, l. 6 *f.b.* as the. *P.F.* or the. *M*.

P. 181, l. 7. emptyed. employed. *M*.

l. 9. is in Books. *P.F.* is in the Book. *M*.

l. 9 *f.b.* The other, was. The other Project, was. *C*.

P. 182, l. 6. Forefathers. Ancestors. *M*.

l. 17. Sacks. *P.F.* Saddles. *M*.

l. 9 *f.b.* And thus, Embassa-dors. *P.F.* And the Embassa-dors. *M.*

Chap. VI.

P. 183, *Chap. Head.* PROPOSETH. PROPOSES. *M.*

P. 184, l. 14 *f.b.* Methods. *P.F.* method. *M.*

l. 4 *f.b.* and might. and would. *M.*

P. 185, l. 17 *f.b.* dispose them. dispose of them. *M.*

l. 3 *f.b.* they came. *C.F.* they come. *M.*

P. 186, l. 19. Person. Persons. *M.* Person's. *P.*

P. 187, l. 6. to take. *P.F. M. omits :* to.

l. 15 *f.b.* to P. 188, l. 7 *f.b.* I told him ... Anagrammatik Method. *M. reads as follows :*—I told him, that should I happen to live in a Kingdom where Plots and Con-spiracies were either in Vogue from the turbulency of the meaner People, or could be turned to the use and service of the higher Rank of them, I first would take care to cherish and encourage the breed of Discov-erers, Witnesses, Informers, Ac-cusers, Prosecutors, Evidences, Swearers, together with their several subservient and subaltern Instruments; and when I had got a competent Number of them of all sorts and Capacities, I would put them under the Colour and Conduct of some dextrous Per-sons in sufficient power both to protect and reward them. Men thus qualified and thus empow-ered might make a most excellent use and advantage of Plots, they might raise their own Characters and pass for most profound Poli-ticians, they might restore new Vigor to a crazy Administration, they might stifle or divert general Discontents; fill their Pockets with Forfeitures, and advance or sink the Opinion of Publick Credit, as either might answer their private Advantage. This might be done by first agreeing and settling among themselves what suspected Persons should

be accused of a Plot. Then effec-tual care is taken to secure all their Letters and Papers, and put the Criminal in safe and secure Custody. These Papers might be delivered to a Sett of Artists of Dexterity sufficient to find out the mysterious Meanings of Words, Syllables, and Letters. They should be allowed to put what Interpretation they pleased upon them, giving them a Sense not only which has no relation at all to them, but even what is quite contrary to their true In-tent and real Meaning; thus for Instance, they may, if they so fancy, interpret a *Sieve* to signify a *Court Lady*, a *lame Dog* an *In-vader*, the *Plague* a *standing Army*, a *Buzzard* a *great States-man*, the *Gout* a *High Priest*, a *Chamber-pot* a *Committee of Grandees*, a *Broom* a *Revolution*, a *Mouse-trap* an *Imployment*, a *Bottomless-pit* a *Treasury*, a *Sink* a *Court*, a *Cap and Bells* a *Favorite*, a *broken Reed* a *Court of Justice*, an *empty Tun* a *Gen-eral*, a *running Sore* an Administra-tion.

But should this Method fail, re-course might be had to others more effectual, by Learned Men called *Acrosticks* and *Anagrams*. First, might be found Men of Skill and Penetration who can discern that all initial Letters have political Meanings. Thus *N* shall signify a Plot, *B* a Regi-ment of Horse, *L* a Fleet at Sea. Or secondly, by transposing the Letters of the Alphabet in any suspected Paper, who can dis-cover the deepest Designs of a disconnected Party. So for ex-ample, if I should say in a Letter to a Friend, *Our Brother* Tom *has just got the Piles*, a Man of Skill in this Art would discover how the same Letters which compose that Sentence, may be analysed into the following Words; *Resist, —a Plot is brought Home—The Tour*. And this is the Anagram-matick Method.

This passage was crossed out by Ford in his copy [C] *and in its place was substituted another which Faulkner subsequently printed, with the following slight variations from Ford's MS. :—*

P. 187, l. 14 *f.b.* long sojourned, the Bulk. *F.* [Faulkner, 1735.] sojourned, some time in my travels, the Bulk. *C.* [Ford's Copy.]

l. 13 *f.b.* consisted wholly. *F.* consisted in a manner, wholly. *C.*

ll. 10, 9 *f.b.* all . . . Deputies. *F.* all under Colours, and Conduct of Ministers of State and their Deputies. *C.*

P. 188, l. 1. and other Papers. *F.* and Papers. *C.*

l. 2. Owners. *F.* Criminals. *C.*

l. 5. decypher. *F.* discover. *C.*

l. 6. an Invader; the Plague. *F.* an Invader; a Codshead a ——; the Plague. *C.*

l. 7. a Minister. *F.* a prime Minister. *C.*

l. 11. a C——t. *F.* the Court. *C.*

l. 13 *f.b.* they can lay open. *F.* they can discover. *C.*

l. 11 *f.b.* hath just. *F.* has just. *C.*

l. 11 *f.b.* a Man . . . this Art. *F.* a skillful Decypherer. *C.*

l. 10 *f.b.* how the same. *F.* that the same. *C.*

Chap. VII.

P. 189. Chap. V[II]. *misprinted* Chap. V. *F.M.*

l. 1. is a part. *P.F.* was a part. *M.*

P. 192, l. 3. into the Room. *P.F.* in the room. *M.*

l. 13. a modern Representative. *C.F.* an Assembly of somewhat a latter Age. *M.*

l. 12 *f.b.* Ancestor. *P.F.* Ancestors. *M.*

Chap. VIII.

P. 194, l. 12. who pretend. who pretended. *C. This may not be Ford's correction, the handwriting differing at this point in C.*

P. 195, l. 14. Fidlers, Players. *M.* omits.

l. 14 *f.b.* Factions. *P.F.* Faction. *M.*

P. 196, l. 3. true Causes. secret Causes. *M.*

P. 197, l. 12. Among others. Among the rest. *M.*

l. 18 *f.b.* the War. this War. *M.*

l. 15 *f.b.* a Boy. a Youth. *M.*

l. 14 *f.b.* of a Libertina. of *Libertina. M.*

l. 12 *f.b.* Vessel. Vessels. *M.*

Chap. IX.

P. 199, l. 5. 1708. 1711. *M.* 1709. *P.*

l. 6. River of *Clumegnig.* River *Clumegnig. M.*

l. 11. the Passage. *P.F.* a Passage. *M.*

l. 16 *f.b.* a *Hollander.* an *Hollander. M.*

l. 2 *f.b.* invited. *Faulkner's editions of* 1759 *and* 1772 *read:—* visited.

last line. reported I. reported that I. *M.*

P. 200, l. 1. they had never. *P.F.* they never. *M.*

l. 7. that came. who came. *M.*

l. 14. Service. At. Service, and at. *M.*

l. 17 *f.b.* upon. on. *M.*

l. 15 *f.b* it so clean. it swept so clean. *M.*

P. 201, l. 9 *f.b. Dwuldum . . . mirplush, Dwuldom . . . mirpush. M.*

Chap. X.

P. 205, l. 8. Fashions of Dress. *P.* Fashions, Dress. *F.*

l. 18. choise. choice. *P.* Choice. *M.*

P. 206, l. 11 *f.b.* both those. *P.F.* both these. *M.*

l. 2 *f.b.* oldest. *P.F.* eldest. *M.*

P. 207, l. 12 *f.b.* Age, they were. *P.F.* Age, were. *M.*

P. 208, l. 16. comes to. *P.F.* come to. *M.*

l. 7 *f.b.* continue. *P.F.* continuing. *M.*

l. 6 *f.b.* they forget. *P.F.* they forgot. *M.*

P. 209, l. 12. the youngest. *This should read* the oldest.

l. 13. brought to me. *P.F.* brought me. *M.*

l. 19 *f.b.* despised. *P.F.* deprived *M.*

l. 19 *f.b.* Sorts of. sort of. *M.*

l. 3 *f.b.* there were. there was. *M.*

Chap. XI.

P. 211, l. 4. the Language. that Language. *M.*

l. 15 *f.b.* Part. Point. *M.*

P. 212, l. 5 *f.b.* to convey. *P.F.* to conver. *M.*

P. 213, l. 15. performed. *P.F.* petformed. *M.*

l. 11 *f.b.* safe at. *P.F.* safe to. *M.* safely at. *C.*

l. 6 *f.b.* [2]0th of *April* [Ed.]. *This seems to be the most plausible emendation of the error in all the early editions:* 10th of April.

l. 3 *f.b.* whither. where. *M.*

Part IV. A Voyage to the Country of the Houyhnhnms

Chap. I.

P. 215, l. 11. 7th . . . 1710. Second Day of *August*, 1710. *M.*

last line. at this Time. *M. places these words after* Family *in the next line.*

P. 216 l. 17. then unbound. then they unbound. *M.*

l. 12 *f.b.* kept close. kept a close. *M.*

P. 217, l. 6. discovered. could discover. *M.*

l. 8. and bade. and so bad. *M.*

P. 218, l. 3. on sharp. in sharp. *M.*

l. 3. hooked. and hooked. *P.*

l. 6. Heads, and only. Faces, nor any thing more than. *M.*

P. reads Heads, but none on their Faces, and only. . .

l. 12. or one. nor one. *M.*

l. 8 *f.b.* into the. in the. *M.*

l. 5 *f.b.* the Tree. *M.* a Tree. *F.*

P. 219, l. 16. Left. right. *M.*

P. 221, l. 10. it were. it was. *M.*

l. 7 *f.b.* before him. *P.F.* before them. *M.*

Chap. II.

P. 222, *Chap. Head.* THAT COUNTRY. THIS COUNTRY. *M.*

l. 14. The last. They. *M.*

P . 223, l. 4. I heard. I observed. *M.*

l. 12. as the. like the. *M.*

l. 13. my Eyes. *M.* mine Eyes. *F.*

l. 3 *f.b.* which. whom. *M.*

P. 224, l. 7. a Yard. the Yard. *M.*

l. 17 *f.b.* although. tho'. *M.*

P. 226, l. 19 *f.b.* he was. that he was. *M.*

P. 227, l. 2. It is. 'Tis. *M.*

l. 12 *f.b.* fare. fared. *P.*

Chap. III.

P. 230, l. 9. all which. all these. *M.*

P. 231, l. 11 *f.b.* in the Whiteness. in the Softness, and Whiteness. *M.*

P. 232, l. 2. of my having. *P.F.* of having. *M.*

l. 15 *f.b.* those Means. these means. *M.*

Chap. IV.

P. 234, ll. 15, 16. and . . . practised. *M. omits.*

l. 16 *f.b.* where. *P.F.* when. *M.*

last line. and drawing. or drawing. *M.*

P. 235, l. 1. treated. *P.F.* treasted. *some copies of M.*

l. 2. but then. and then. *M.*

l. 9. feed. fed. *M.*

l. 18. weakest. *P.* meanest. *F.*

l. 20. rouling. rolling. *P.*

l. 14 *f.b.* the common. common. *M.*

l. 3 *f.b.* to express. to represent. *M.*

P. 236, l. 9. Offices. *P.F.* Office. *M.*

l. 10 *f.b.* one of. *P.F. M. omits.*

P. 237, l. 6. the Matter. that matter. *C.*

l. 17 *f.b.* Trade it is. *P.* Trade is. *F.*

l. 14 *f.b.* a *Queen. P.* Queen. *F.*

P. 238, l. 4. deserting to the. *M.* deserting the. *F.*

l. 9. pleased . . . me.

pleased to interrupt me several times. *M.*

l. 13 *f.b.* making. making of. *M.*

last line. especially. but especially. *M.*

Chap. **V.**

P. 239, l. 3. Points, which. *P.F.* Points of which. *M.*

l. 3 *f.b.* five times. thrice. *M.*

P. 240, l. 11 *f.b.* into a War. into War. *M.*

l. 10 *f.b.* when one. where one. *C.*

l. 9 *f.b.* compact. compleat. M.

P. 241, l. 2. sufficient. frequent. *M.*

l. 6. these Reasons. *P.F.* those Reasons. *M.*

l. 11. There is. *C.F.* There are. *M.*

l. 11. a Kind. *P.F.* another Kind. *M.*

l. 11. beggarly. *C.F. M. omits.*

ll. 15, 16. in many . . . *Europe.* in Germany and other *Northern* Parts of *Europe. C.*

l. 18 *f.b.* For your Mouths. *M. begins a new paragraph.*

l. 8 *f.b.* Bayonets, Battles, Sieges. *C.*

Bayonets, Sieges. *F.*

P. 242, l. 20. his Hoof. *P.F.* my Hoof. *M.*

l. 9 *f.b.* said. informed him. *M.*

l. 4 *f.b. to* P. 244, l. 11. what I meant by *Law* . . . fail of directing accordingly. *C.F. M. reads as follows:*—what I meant by *Law*, and what sort of Dispensers thereof it could be by whose Practices the Property of any Person could be lost, instead of being preserved. He added, he saw not what great Occasion there could be for this thing called *Law*, since all the Intentions and Purposes of it may be fully answered by following the Dictates of *Nature* and *Reason*, which are sufficient Guides for a Reasonable Animal, as we pretended to be, in shewing us what we ought to do, and what to avoid.

I assured his Honour, that *Law* was a Science wherein I had not much conversed, having little more Knowledge of it than what I had obtained by employing Advocates, in vain, upon some Injustices that had been done me, and by conversing with some others who by the same Method had first lost their Substance and then left their own Country under the Mortification of such Disappointments, however I would give him all the Satisfaction I was able.

I said that those who made profession of this Science were exceedingly multiplied, being almost equal to the Caterpillars in Number; that they were of diverse Degrees, Distinctions, and Denominations. The Numerousness of those that dedicated themselves to this Profession were such that the fair and justifiable Advantage and Income of the Profession was not sufficient for the decent and handsome Maintenance of Multitudes of those who followed it. Hence it came to pass that it was found needful to supply that by Artifice and Cunning, which could not be procured by just and honest Methods: The better to bring which about, very many Men among us were bred up from their Youth in the Art of proving by Words multiplied for the Purpose that *White* is *Black* and *Black* is *White*, according as they are paid. The Greatness of these Mens Assurance and the Boldness of their Pretensions gained upon the Opinion of the Vulgar, whom in a Manner they made Slaves of, and got into their Hands much the largest Share of the Practice of their Profession. These Practitioners were by Men of Discernment called *Pettifoggers*, (that is, *Confounders*, or rather, *Destroyers of Right*,) as it was my ill Hap as well as the Misfortune of my suffering Acquaintance to be engaged only with this Species of the Profession. I desired his Honour to understand the Description I had to give, and the Ruin I had complained of to relate to these Sectaries only, and how and by what means the Misfortunes we met with were brought upon us by the Management of these Men, might be more easily conceived by explaining to him their Method of Proceeding, which could not be better done than by giving him an Example.

My Neighbour, said I, I will suppose, has a mind to my *Cow*, he hires one of these Advocates to prove that he ought to have my *Cow* from me. I must then hire another of them to defend my Right, it being against all Rules of *Law* that any Man should be allowed to speak for himself. Now in this case, I who am the Right Owner lie under two great Disadvantages. First, my Advocate, being as I said before practised almost from his Cradle in defending Falshood, is quite out of his Element when he would argue for the Right, which as an Office unnatural he attempts with great Awkwardness, if not with an Ill-will. The Second Disadvantage is that my Advocate must proceed with great Caution; for, since the Maintenance of so many depend on the keeping up of Business, should he proceed too summarily, if he does not incur the Displeasure of his Superiors, he is sure to gain the Ill-will and Hatred of his Brethren, as being by them esteemed one that would lessen the Practice of the Law. This being the Case, I have but two Methods to preserve my *Cow*. The first is, to gain over my Adversary's Advocate with a double Fee; from the Manner and Design of whose Education before mentioned it is easy to expect he will be induced to drop his Client and let the Ballance fall on my Side. The Second Way is for my Advocate not to insist on the Justice of my Cause, by allowing the *Cow* to belong to my Adversary; and this if it be dexterously and skilfully done will go a great Way towards ob-

taining a favourable Verdict, it having been found, from a careful Observation of Issues and Events, that the wrong Side, under the Management of such Practitioners, has the fairer Chance for Success, and this more especially if it happens, as it did in mine and my Friend's Case, and may have done since, that the Person appointed to decide all Controversies of Property as well as for the Tryal of Criminals, who should be taken out of the most knowing and wise of his Profession, is by the Recommendation of a great Favourite, or Court Mistress chosen out of the Sect before mentioned, and so, having been under a strong Bias all his life against Equity and fair dealing, lies as it were under a fatal Necessity of favouring, shifting, double dealing and Oppression, and besides through Age, Infirmity and Distempers grown lazy, unactive and inattentive, and thereby almost incapacitated from doing any thing becoming the Nature of his Imployment, and the Duty of his Office. In such Cases, the Decisions and Determinations of Men so bred, and so qualified, may with Reason be expected on the wrong side of the Cause, since those who can take Harangue and Noise, (if pursued with Warmth, and drawn out into a Length,) for Reasoning, are not much to be wondered at, if they infer the weight of the Argument from the heaviness of the Pleading.

It is a Maxim among these Men, That whatever has been done before may legally be done again: And therefore they take special Care to record all the Decisions formerly made, even those which have through Ignorance or Corruption contradicted the Rules of common Justice and the general Reason of Mankind. These, under the Name of *Precedents*, they produce as Authorities, and thereby endeavour to justify the most iniquitous Opinions; and they are so lucky in this Practice, that it rarely fails of Decrees answerable to their Intent and Expectation.

The following variants from Ford's MS. occur in Faulkner's text:—

P. 243, l. 18. true Owner. *F.* [Faulkner, 1735.] right Owner. *C.* [Ford's Copy.]

l. 18 *f.b.* great . . . if not with. *F. C. omits.*

l. 14 *f.b.* one who. *F.* one that. *C.*

last line. lie under. *F.* are under. *C.*

P. 244. l. 1. some . . . refused. *F.* several of them to refuse. *C.*

l. 11. of directing accordingly. *F.* of decreeing. *C.*

l. 19. she were. she was. *M.*

l. 12 *f.b.* have wholly confounded. have gone near to confound. *M.*

l. 11 *f.b.* it will. it may. *M.*

l. 9 *f.b.* belong. belongs. *M.*

l. 6 *f.b.* commendable: The Judge . . . Law. *F.C. M. reads:* —commendable: For if those in power, who know well how to choose Instruments fit for their Purpose, take care to recommend and promote out of this Clan a proper Person, his Method of Education and Practice makes it easy for him, when his Patrons Disposition is understood, without Difficulty or Study either to condemn or acquit the Criminal, and at the same time strictly preserve all due Forms of Law.

P. 245, l. 1. Lawyers. Advocates. *M.*

l. 4. I assured his Honour . . . Profession. *F.C. M. reads:* — I assured his Honour that the Business and Study of their own Calling and Profession so took up all their Thoughts and engrossed all their Time, that they minded nothing else, and that therefore, in all points out of their own Trade, many of them were of so great Ignorance and Stupidity, that it was hard to pick out of any Profession a

Generation of Men more despicable in common Conversation, or who were so much looked upon as avowed Enemies to all Knowledge and Learning, being equally disposed to pervert the general reason of Mankind in every other Subject of Discourse, as in that of their own Calling.

l. 5. were usually the most. *C. omits* usually.

Chap. VI.

P. 245, *Chap. Head. M. reads:* —A CONTINUATION OF THE STATE OF ENGLAND, SO WELL GOVERNED BY A QUEEN AS TO NEED NO FIRST MINISTER. THE CHARACTER OF SUCH AN ONE IN SOME EUROPEAN COURTS *C. follows F. but omits* UNDER QUEEN ANNE *and* IN THE COURTS OF EUROPE.

l. 19 *f.b.* by engaging. and engage. *M.*

P. 247, l. 14. or. *P.F.* and. *M.*

l. 13 *f.b.* worketh. works. *M.*

l. 11 *f.b.* thought. thought it. *M.*

l. 9 *f.b.* operated contrary. operated the one contrary. *M.*

P. 248. l. 6. to each. to them. *M.*

l. 18. Bones, Birds, Beasts. *C.* Bones, Beasts. *F.*

l. 20. detestable, that they. detestable, they. *M.*

l. 12 *f.b. Clyster. Glyster. M.*

l. 9 *f.b.* Posterior. *P.F. M. omits.*

P. 249, ll. 19, 18 *f.b.* I told him . . . Creature wholly exempt. *C.F. M. reads:*—I told him, that our She Governor or Queen having no Ambition to gratify, no Inclination to satisfy of extending her Power to the Injury of her Neighbours, or the Prejudice of her own Subjects, was therefore so far from needing a corrupt Ministry to carry on or cover any sinister Designs, that She not only directs her own Actions to the Good of her People, conducts them by the Direction, and restrains them within the Limitation of the Laws of her own Country; but submits the

Behaviour and Acts of those She intrusts with the Administration of Her Affairs to the Examination of Her great Council, and subjects them to the Penalties of the Law; and therefore never puts any such Confidence in any of her Subjects as to entrust them with the whole and entire Administration of her Affairs: But I added, that in some former Reigns here, and in many other Courts of *Europe* now, where Princes grew indolent and careless of their own Affairs through a constant Love and Pursuit of Pleasure, they made use of such an Administrator, as I had mentioned, under the Title of *first* or *chief Minister of State*, the Description of which, as far as it may be collected not only from their Actions, but from the Letters, Memoirs, and Writings published by themselves, the Truth of which has not yet been disputed, may be allowed to be as follows: That he is a Person wholly exempt. . . .

The following variant between F. and C. should be noted:—

P. 249, l. 19 *f.b. State*, whom. *F.* [Faulkner, 1735.] *State*, who was the Person. *C.* [Ford's Copy.]

l. 16 *f.b.* makes use. made use. *C.*

P. 250, l. 8. an Expedient called. *C.F. M. omits.*

l. 10. secure. secured. *M.*

l. 11. retire. retired. *M.*

l. 15 *f.b.* Day, my. Day in Discourse my. *M.*

P. 251, l. 13 *f.b.* Wife take. Wife takes. *M.*

l. 12 *f.b. to end.* her Neighbours . . . Appeal. *F.C. M. reads:—* her Neighbours or Acquaintance, in order to improve and continue the Breed. That a weak diseased Body, a meager Countenance, and sallow Complexion, are no uncommon Marks of a *Great Man*; and a healthy robust Appearance is so far disgraceful in a Man of Quality, that the World is apt to conclude his real Father to have been one of the Inferiors of the Family, especially when it is seen that the Imperfections of his Mind run parallel with those of his Body, and are little else than a Composition of Spleen, Dulness, Ignorance, Caprice, Sensuality, and Pride. [*M. omits last 3 lines of F.C.*]

The following variants between F. and C. should be noted:—

p. 251, l. 2 *f.b.* enacted. *F.* [Faulkner, 1735.] made. *C.* [Ford's Copy.]

l. 2 *f.b.* these Nobles have. *F.* these have. *C.*

last line. likewise. *F. C. omits.*

Chap. VII.

P. 252, l. 8. my eyes. *M.* mine eyes. *F.*

l. 8. enlarged. *P.F.* enlightened. *M.*

P. 255, l. 9. out, and. out, then. *M.*

l. 2 *f.b.* some. some kind of. *M.*

P. 256, l. 5. never. *C.P.F.* seldom. *M.*

l. 9. undistinguished. undistinguishing. *M.*

l. 10. corrupted. the corrupted. *M.*

l. 19. something. somewhat. *M.*

l. 20. fought for. sought for. *M.*

l. 21. It. and it. *M.*

l. 21. produced. produced in them. *P.*

l. 16 *f.b.* and roul. and reel. *C. M. omits.*

l. 15 *f.b.* Mud. Dirt. *M.*

l. 4 *f.b.* known . . . taken. *P.F.* taken myself. *M.*

l. 3 *f.b.* here. *M. omits.*

P. 257, l. 14 *f.b.* hath. has. *M.*

l. 4 *f.b.* the Females. *P.F.* Females. *M.*

P. 258, l. 8. the last Article. *P.F.* the Article. *M.*

l. 20. fat, and wanted. fat, wanted. *M.*

l. 21. nor did. *P.F.* nor could. *M.*

l. 15 *f.b.* plainly discover. *C.F.* discover. *M.*

Chap. VIII.

P. 259, l. 9 *f.b.* Honour. Favour. *M.*

P. 261, l. 6. search. *P.F.* scratch. *M.*

P. 262, l. 5. already. *M. omits.*

P. 263, l. 7. proceedeth. proceeds. *M.*

l. 17. again; or. again. Or. *C.* again, or. *M.*

l. 19. bestows on him. bestow on him. *M.* bestow him. *C.*

l. 20. a second Time. again. *M.*

l. 21. be pregnant. is pregnant. *M.*

last line. in a reasonable. of a Rational. *M.*

P. 264, l. 7. deserveth. deserves. *M.*

l. 11. as many. as long. *M.*

l. 13. the Grass. their Grass. *M.*

l. 17 *f.b.* their Children. our Children. *M.*

l. 13 *f.b.* hard stony. *P.F.* hard and stony. *M.*

l. 11 *f.b.* River. *C.F.* Rivet. *M.*

l. 10 *f.b.* certain Districts. a certain District. *M.*

l. 10 *f.b.* shew their. *M.* shew the. *F.*

l. 4 *f.b.* Brutes are. *P.F.* Brutes were. *M.*

P. 265, l. 1. continueth. continues. *M.*

l. 11. Family in the District shall. *C.* Family shall. *F.*

Chap. IX.

P. 265, l. 11 *f.b.* that ever. which ever. *C.*

l. 11 *f.b.* in their. in that. *M.*

P. 266, l. 4. in their. in that. *M.*

l. 8. and Froth. *P.F.* or Froth. *M.*

l. 13. Older. old Ones. *M.* elder. *P.*

P. 268, l. 9. Memories. Memorys. *P.* Memory. *M.*

P. 269, l. 10. certain. *P.F.* several. *M.*

l. 15 *f.b. Lhnuwnh. Shnuwnh. M.*

l. 8 *f.b.* rest: She died. rest, and died. *M.*

P. 270, l. 10 *f.b.* cuts. *P.F.* cut. *M.*

Chap. X.

P. 271, *Chap. Head.* HATH NOTICE. HAS NOTICE. *M.*

l. 2. to be made. *P.F. M. omits.*

l. 11 *f.b.* I likewise made. *C.F.* I made. *M.* I also made. *P.*

l. 2 *f.b.* feel. find. *M.*

P. 272, l. 9. Spleneticks, *C.F.* Splenaticks, *P.* splenetick tedious Talkers. *M.*

l. 19. upon the Merit of. for the sake of. *M.*

l. 6 *f.b.* (as . . . said). *M. omits.*

P. 273, l. 3. their Minds. the Thoughts. *M.* their Thoughts. *P.*

l. 4. the Discourse. *P.F.* their Discourse. *M.*

l. 5. on Order. or Order. *C.*

l. 18. *Yahoos. M. adds:*—in all Countries.

P. 274, l. 1. Friends, my. *P.F.* Friends, and my. *M.*

l. 3. perhaps. only. *M.C.*

l. 4. more. *C.F. M. omits.*

l. 9. Fountain. a Fountain. *M.*

l. 20. when. and when. *M.*

l. 7 *f.b.* or a. nor a. *M.*

P. 276, l. 7. of an unnatural. *P.F.* of unnatural. *M.*

P. 278, l. 3. Detractors. For my Detractors. *M.*

Chap. XI.

P. 278, l. 10 *f.b.* probably. *M. omits.*

P. 279, l. 11 *f.b.* climbing. climbing up. *M.*

P. 281, l. 5 *f.b.* or a Yahoo. as a Yahoo. *M.*

P. 282, l. 3. Ship, to inform. Ship, inform. *M.*

P. 283, l. 2. five. three. *M.*

l. 8. of his. in his. *M.*

l. 16. and he. and then he. *M.*

l. 19. of my Veracity. *M. adds:* —of my Veracity, and the rather because he confessed, he met with a *Dutch* Skipper, who pretended to have landed with Five others of his Crew upon a certain Island or Continent *South* of *New-Holland,* where they went for fresh Water, and observed a Horse driving before him several Animals exactly resembling those I described under the Name of *Yahoos*, with some other Particulars, which the Captain said he had forgot; because he then concluded them all to be Lies. But he added . . .

l. 10 *f.b.* against. to. *M.*

P. 284, l. 8 *f.b.* a Point. a Matter. *M.*

P. 285, l. 8. this last. the last. *M.*

l. 13. *Redriff. Rotherhith. M.*

l. 15 *f.b.* had become. *P.F.* became. *M.*

Chap. XII.

P. 286, *Chap. Head.* CONCLUDETH. CONCLUDES. *M.*

l. 12 *f.b.* as of Truth. as Truth. *M.*

P. 287, l. 19. Temptation. *P.F.* temptations. *M.*

l. 2 *f.b.* ever I was. I was ever. *M.*

P. 288, l. 19. not the least with. *C. F.* not with. *M.*

l. 10 *f.b.* Tribes. Tribe. *C.*

P. 289, l. 15 *f.b.* in modern. *P.F.* in some modern. *M.*

l. 12 *f.b.* Discoveries. Discoverys. *P.* Discovery. *M.*

l. 4 *f.b.* the King. their King. *M.*

P. 290, l. 15 *f.b.* any Desire. *P.* a Desire. *F.*

l. 11 *f.b.* may concern. more concerns. *P.*

l. 7 *f.b.* to be believed. *M. adds:* —to be believed; unless a Dispute may arise about the two *Yahoos*, said to have been seen many Ages ago on a Mountain in *Houyhnhnmland*, from whence the Opinion is, that the Race of those Brutes hath descended; and these, for any thing I know, may have been *English*, which indeed I was apt to suspect from the Lineaments of their Posterity's Countenances, although very much defaced. But, how far that will go to make out a Title, I leave to the Learned in Colony-Law.

But as to the Formality . . . *last line.* the *only.* the only. *M.*

P. 291, l. 17. asked her. ask her. *C.* ask'd her. *M.*

P. 292, *last line.* appear. come. *M.*

A TALE OF A TUB

Text from *Fifth Edition*: A / TALE / OF A / TUB. / Written for the Universal Im- / provement of Mankind. / *Diu multumque desideratum.* / . . . The Fifth Edition: With the Au- / thor's Apology and Explanatory Notes. / By *W. W.. tt .. n,* B.D. and others. / London: Printed for *John Nutt,* near / *Stationers-Hall.* MDCCX.
Copy: Editor.
Collated with: First Edition: 1704. Edn. 2: 1704. Edn. 3: 1704. Edn. 4: 1705.

To . . . Lord Summers.

P. 295, l. 1. *The* large Dedication [*not printed here*] *is addressed to* Prince Posterity.

The Preface.

P. 299, l. 8 *f.b.* Number of Wits, *i.e.* The number of livings in England. *Note in the Pate MS.* [*v. Works.* Ed. Nichols. 1808.]

P. 301, l. 23. Postures. Posture. *edns. 1-4.*

P. 306, l. 5 *f.b.* Rapins. *edns. 4, 5.* Rapine. *edns. 1-3.*

Concerning Criticks.

P. 309, l. 2. padling in. padling in it. *edn. 4.*

l. 3 *f.b.* as Hercules. *edns. 1-4. edn. 5 omits:* as.

P. 310, l. 16. Augea's. Augeas's. *edns. 1-3.*

l. 21. true. *True. edns. 1-2.*

P. 314, l. 6. of *True.* of the *True. edns. 1-4.*

P. 315, l. 19. to these. *edns. 1-4.* to those. *edn. 5.*

In the Modern Kind.

P. 318, *note* 1. been ever any. *edn. 1711.* been any. *edns. 1-5..*
P. 319, l. 11 *f.b.* Sendivogius. *edn. 4.* Sendivogus. *edns. 1-3, 5.*

Of Digressions.

P. 322, l. 2 *f.b.* an *Iliad. edns. 1,* 2. a *Iliad. edns. 3-5.*
P. 325, l. 11 *f.b.* the *Pudenda.* the *Genitals. edns. 1-4.*
P. 327, l. 2. happily. haply. *edn. 1.*
l. 24. he pleases. he please. *edns. 1-2.*

Of Madness.

P. 328, l. 9 *f.b.* differs. *edns. 1-4.* differ. *edn. 5.*
last line. Expectations. Expectation. *edns. 1-3.*
P. 329, l. 2 *f.b.* — *Teterrima. Cunnus Teterrima. edns. 1-4.*
P. 330, l. 13. of [the] Human. of Human. *edns. 1-5.*
P. 331, l. 12 *f.b.* and there. and thence. *edn. 1.*
P. 333, l. 8. unhappily. *edns. 1-3.* happily. *edns. 4-5.*

P. 336, l. 11 *f.b.* Vapours, Vapor. *edns. 1-3.* Vapour. *edn. 4.*
P. 337. l. 6. Season. Seasons. *edns. 1-4.*
l. 9. whence. thence. *edns. 1-4.*
ll. 26-28. *These Names were printed in full in edn. 1720, with the following note:*—These were at the time topping Members of the House of Commons.
last line. State, For the principal Management of affairs Ecclesiasticall. *edn. 1720.* State, * * * Civil. *edns. 1-5.*
P. 338, l. 13 *f.b.* Window. *Edns. 1-4 omit.*

To the Readers.

P. 340, *Title.* THE AUTHORS COMPLIMENT &c. . . . *from edn. 1720. In edns. 1-5, this section is headed:*—A TALE OF A TUB.
P. 341, l. 1. Acknowledgement. Acknowledgements. *edns. 1-4.*
P. 342, l. 13. Part of. Part in. *edns. 1-4.*
P. 345, *note* 1, l. 7. *are really. were really. edn. 1711.*

THE CONDUCT OF THE ALLIES

Text from *First Edition*: THE / CONDUCT / OF THE / ALLIES, / AND OF THE / Late Ministry, / IN / Beginning and Carrying on / THE / Present War. / . . . *LONDON*, / Printed for *John Morphew*, near *Statio-* / *ners-Hall.* 1712. [1711.]
Copy: Editor.
Collated with: Edn. 7: 1711.

P. 349, l. 7. Man. Person. *edn. 7.*
P. 353, l. 6 *f.b.* enriched our selves. enriched our Allies. *edns. 2 & 6.*
enriched our Selves. *edns. 3-7.*
P. 354, l. 6 *f.b. a Nation. the Nation. edn. 7.*
P. 355, l. 7. War, to have. War, and to have. [*Temple Scott's edn. 1911.*]
P. 356, l. 22. to continue. to go on with. *edn. 7.*
P. 357, l. 13. *General.* G——l. *edn. 7.*

l. 16. working out some. working some. *edn. 7.*
P. 358, l. 8 *f.b.* And if it . . . new paragraph. *edn. 7.*
l. 2 *f.b.* Duke of *Marlbrough.* D—— of M——h's. *edn. 7.*
P. 360, l. 6. were bound. are bound. *edn. 7.*
ll. 12, 14. Queen. Qu—n. *edn. 7.*
P. 361, l. 3 *et seq.* Guarantee, how much . . . require it.
Guarantee; however our Posterity may hereafter, by the Tyranny and Oppression of any succeeding Princes, be reduced to the fatal Necessity of break-

ing in upon the excellent and happy Settlement now in force. *edn.* 7.

l. 11 *f.b.* Manufacturers. Manufactures. *edn.* 7.

P. 362, l. 13 *f.b.* side the. side of the. *edn.* 7.

l. 13 *f.b.* he then had. he had then. *edn.* 7.

P. 363, l. 7. King *Charles.* K—g C——s. *edn.* 7.

l. 11 *f.b.* at our Court. to our Court. *edn.* 7.

l. 7 *f.b.* same Cause. same grievous Cause. *edn.* 7.

P. 364, l. 10. time. *edn.* 7 omits.

l. 13. particular. particulars. *edn.* 7.

l. 18. Earl of G—y. *edn.* 7. E. of G—. *edn.* 1.

P. 365, l. 18. *Godolphin.* G——n. *edn.* 7.

P. 367, l. 4. a certain *Great Man.* my Lord G——n. *edn.* 7.

l. 7. serve him no. serve no. *edn.* 7.

l. 16. Her Majesty's. her M——y's. *edn.* 7.

last line. Princes. *Powers. edn.* 7.

P. 368, l. 3. unmeasurable. *edn.* 7. unanswerable. *edn.* 1.

P. 369, l. 6 *f.b.* That it was indeed. That indeed it was. *edn.* 7.

l. 2 *f.b.* General . . . Ministry. G——l . . . M——y. *edn.* 7.

P. 370, l. 4. Opportunity that fell, which. Opportunity, which. *edn.* 7.

l. 7. the Queen. the Q——. *edn.* 7.

l. 9. *wexed. waxed. edn.* 7.

l. 11. immediate Alarm. immediately the Alarm. *edn.* 7.

l. 12 *f.b.* in Her Story. in Story. *edn.* 7.

P. 371, l. 3. *to live . . . in a large house.* to dwell in a corner of the House-top, than with a brawling Woman in a wide House. *edn.* 7.

l. 8. the Queen. the Qu—n. *edn.* 7.

l. 14. became. become. *edn.* 7.

l. 16. *General.* G——l. *edn.* 7.

P. 376, l. 20. strong Delusion. *strong Delusion. edn.* 7.

P. 378, l. 1. *lay heavy. lay the heavy. edn.* 7.

P. 379, l. 1. For an absolute . . . Countries. *Edn.* 7. *edn.* 1 omits.

P. 380, l. 16. desire. would desire. *edn.* 7.

AN ARGUMENT, &c.

Text from *earliest version in*: MISCELLANIES / IN / PROSE / AND / VERSE / LONDON : / Printed for John Morphew, near *Stationer's Hall*, MDCCXI. / [*It would seem that Benjamin Tooke, not Morphew, was the publisher.*]

Copy: R. Jennings. [The 2nd edn. 1713, of which there are two issues, is textually almost identical with edn. 1.]

Collated with : Miscellanies in Prose and Verse. The First Volume: 1727 [*M.*]. Faulkner, Vol. I : 1735 [*F.*].

P. 383, l. 5. several. severe. *F.*

l. 6. the *Union. F.* the ——. *1711.*

l. 14. seem so. appear so. *F.*

l. 19. Nay though. Nay, although. *F.*

P. 384, l. 14. abolishing of. abolishing. *F.*

l. 11 *f.b.* betwixt. between. F.

l. 9 *f.b.* Real. *real. F.*

l. 4 *f.b.* all the Wit. *all* the Wit.

l. 4 *f.b.* half the. *half* the. *F.*

P. 385, l. 4. of a Cure. of Cure. *F.*

l. 10. Nominal. *nominal. F.*

l. 12. with all our. with our. *F.*

l. 19. System. *F.* Systems. *1711.*

l. 8 *f.b.* real Hopes. great Hopes. *F.*

last line. obsolete. *obsolete. F.*

last line. broke for. broke only for. *F.*

P. 386, l. 23. we know. I know. *F.*

l. 7 *f.b.* shook off. shaken off. *F.*

l. 3 *f.b.* pleases. pleaseth. *F.*

last line. if it serves. if it serve. *F.*

P. 387, l. 4. and to be confirmed. and confirmed. *F.*

last line. Productions. *F.* Production. *1711.*

P. 388, l. 16. Play-houses. Theatres. *F.*

P. 389, l. 5. mutual. grievous. *F.*

l. 6. and are apt to. and dispose men to. *F.*

l. 6 *f.b.* no other. *F.* no others. *1711.*

ll. 5, 4 *f.b. F. notes:—*Italian Singers then in Vogue.

P. 390, l. 3. and would serve. *F.* and serve. *1711.*

l. 5. Religion. And therefore. Religion. Therefore. *F.*

l. 9. 'Tis. It is. *F.*

l. 21. Taste. *F.* Test. *1711.*

l. 11 *f.b.* 'Tis. It is. *F.*

last line. though. although. *F.*

P. 391, l. 2. some Years. several Years. *F.*

l. 3. deep Thinkers. Deep-Thinkers. *F.*

l. 5. are said. *F.* were said. *1711.*

l. 8 *f.b.* 'tis. it is. *F.*

P. 392, l. 2. t'other. the other. *F.*

l. 10. nor it's. or it's. *F.*

l. 17. Forms and. *F. omits.*

l. 24. into a Flame. in a Flame. *F.*

l. 9 *f.b.* which may. that may. *F.*

P. 393, l. 3. in not coming in. in refusing to enter. *F.*

l. 12. choqued. choaked. *M.*

l. 13. that happen. who happen. *F.*

l. 23. how would. how could. *M.F.*

l. 3 *f.b.* Art or Nature. *F.* Art of Nature. *1711. M.*

P. 394, l. 21. they may. this may. *F.*

l. 10 *f.b.* has been. hath been. *F.*

P. 395, l. 13. it still be. it shall still be. *F.*

l. 6 *f.b.* Sorites. *Sorites. F.*

P. 396, l. 16. For they are. Because, the Turks are. *F.*

A LETTER TO A YOUNG GENTLEMAN

Text from *First Edition*: A / LETTER / TO A / Young Gentleman, / Lately enter'd into / HOLY ORDERS. / By a Person of Quality / *It is certainly known, that the following Treatise was / writ in* Ireland *by the Reverend Dr.* SWIFT, *Dean / of St.* Patrick's *in that Kingdom.* / *LONDON:* / Printed for J. Roberts at the *Oxford Arms* in / *Warwick-Lane.* MDCCXXI. Price 6d. /

Copy: British Museum.

Collated with : Miscellanies. Vol. I: 1727 [*M.*]. Faulkner, Vol. I: 1735 [*F.*].

P. 399. *Heading. M. reads:—*Dublin, January 9.

l. 1. it was. it were. *F.*

l. 3. Dispositions. Disposition. *M.*

ll. 10, 24. 'till. until. *F.*

P. 400, l. 2. 'tis. it is. *F.*

P. 401, l. 4. makes the. make the. *F.*

l. 22. which they. which the Preacher. *F.*

l. 9 *f.b.* or to reject. or reject. *F.*

P. 402, l. 9. I observe. I have observed. *M. F.*

l. 11. of all those. of those. *F.*

P. 403, l. 9. a Gentlemans . . . have. some Gentlemen's Families may have. *F.*

P. 404, l. 4. in the Style. in a Style. *M.*

l. 16 *f.b.* is too. be too. *F.*

P. 405, l. 5. though. although. *F.*

l. 18. accused. *M.F.* accursed. *1721.*

l. 20. the Oratory. the Orators. *M.F.*

l. 12 *f.b.* moving the Passions. moving Passions. *F.*

P. 406, l. 7. as any Man. as every Man. *F.*

l. 10. if you are. if you be. *F.*

l. 18. or seems. *F.* nor seems. *1721.*

P. 407, l. 1. this first. the former. *F.*

l. 9. Argument. Arguments. *M.F.*

l. 5 *f.b.* Compromise. Compremise. *M.F.*

P. 408, l. 2. Forms. Form. *M.*

l. 3. Morning, took. Morning, he took. *F.*

l. 12. so directly. *M.F.* too directly. *1721.*

l. 3 *f.b.* Sermon. *F.* Sermons. *1721. M.*

P. 409, l. 11 *f.b.* justly be. be justly. *F.*

P. 410, l. 8. because I. because, as I. *F.*

l. 9. bestowing on us. *M.F.* bestowing us. *1721.*

l. 19. has over. hath over. *F.*

l. 9 *f.b.* or Learning. and Learning. *M.F.*

P. 411, l. 24. than turn. than to turn. *M.F.*

l. 26. tho'. though *M.* although. *F.*

P. 412, l. 14 *f.b.* wisest. wise. *M.F.*

ll. 7, 6 *f.b.* Plowman . . . born. Plowman knows well enough, although he never heard of *Aristotle* or *Plato. F.*

l. 4 *f.b.* would trust their. would rather trust to their. *F.*

P. 413, l. 7. does to. do to. *M. F.*

l. 19. has been. hath been. *F.*

l. 7 *f.b.* those kinds. *F.* those kind. *1721. M.*

last line. Orthodoxy. *M. F.* Orthodox. *1721.*

P. 414, l. 1. seems to be. *M. F.* seem to be. *1721.*

l. 5. Occasion; upon. Occasion, is upon. *M.F.*

l. 21. by People. by the People. *M.*

l. 24. *No paragraph in F.*

l. 9 *f.b.* an hundred. a hundred. *M. F.*

l. 3 *f.b.* Among. Amongst. *M.F.* *The catch-word in M. reads:—* Among.

P. 415, l. 14. at least forty. above Forty. *F.*

l. 14. latter Sort now. *F. omits* Sort.

P. 416, l. 6. among a People. among People. *F.*

l. 9. interpreted. *M.F.* interrupted. *1721.*

l. 18. Administration. Add. *M.F.* Admiration. And. *1721.*

P. 417, l. 6. Though. Although. *F.*

l. 19. whoever knows. whoever knoweth. *F.*

l. 12 *f.b.* that the Clergy. that many of the Clergy. *F. F. notes:* —*N.B.*—This Discourse was written Fourteen Years ago; since which Time, the Case is extremely altered by Deaths and Successions.

l. 7 *f.b.* Man: And. Man: For. *F.*

l. 5 *f.b.* is not. be not. *F.*

P. 418, l. 5. in Life. in the World. *F.*

Signature. M. and F. omit the initials: A.B.

TO A YOUNG POET

Text from *First Edition*: A / LETTER / OF / ADVICE / TO A / Young Poet; / TOGETHER / With a PROPOSAL for the Encouragement / of POETRY in this Kingdom. / . . . DUBLIN : / Printed by J. HYDE, in *Dames-street*, 1721. /

Copy: Forster Collection.

Collated with : 1st English Edition : 1721 [*E.*].

P. 421, l. 2. and for that Reason. and have therefore been. *E.*

P. 424, l. 21. to a man. all to a man. *E.*

P. 425, l. 2 *f.b.* it necessary. it is necessary. *E.*

P. 426, l. 10. perceive 'twas. *E.* perceive was. *1721.*

P. 427, l. 12 *f.b.* Turn, and. *E.* Turn, which. *1721.*

P. 428, l. 11 *f.b.* and Summaries. *E. omits :* and.

P. 430, l. 1. is Body. is a Body. *E.*

P. 431, l. 20. an Improvement. and Improvement. *E.*

P. 432, l. 5 *f.b.* because that upon. because upon. *E.*

l. 4 *f.b.* Heroicks. Heroes. *E.*

P. 433, l. 19. to call. to all. *E.*

l. 11 *f.b.* affect. effect. *1721.*

l. 8 *f.b.* is as poor. *E.* is poor. *1721.*

P. 434, l. 22. score of Reputations. score Reputations. *E.*

l. 11 *f.b.* travail. travel. *E.*

P. 435, l. 8. *Char-woman.* Chairwoman. *E.*

l. 13 *f.b.* in the great. in great. *E.*

P. 437, l. 13. pestilent. pestilential. *E.*

l. 18. and the *Common.* and *Common. E.*

P. 439, l. 6. Countenance it; and were. *E.* Countenance it. [*1721 ends a paragraph.*]

l. 8. manner. *E.* [*E. opens a new paragraph with :*—I have heard.] manner. I have heard. *1721.*

P. 441, l. 8. take my leave. *E.* make my leave. *1721.*

TO A VERY YOUNG LADY

Text from *earliest version in*: MISCELLANIES / [IN / *PROSE* and *VERSE.* /] [THE / FIRST VOLUME] THE SECOND VOLUME [THE LAST VOLUME] / LONDON : / Printed for Benjamin Motte, at the *Middle- / Temple Gate* in *Fleet-Street.* M.DCC. XXVII / .

Copy : Editor.

Collated with : Faulkner, Vol. I : 1735 [*F.*].

P. 445. *Title.* a Very Young. a Young. *F. F. adds :*—Written in the Year 1723.

P. 446, l. 14. Witness. Witnesses. *F.*

l. 16. exceeding. extremely. *F.*

l. 19. has too. hath too. *F.*

l. 23. has a. hath a. *F.*

l. 7 *f.b.* the Servants. their Servants. *F.*

l. 6 *f.b.* happens. happen. *F.*

l. 4 *f.b.* has been. hath been. *F.*

P. 447, l. 6. were apt. are apt. *F.*

l. 12. a little hard. somewhat hard. *F.*

l. 5 *f.b.* will not. may not. *F.*

P. 449, l. 20. is not. be not. *F.*

l. 10 *f.b.* has no. hath no. *F.*

P. 450, l. 21. uncapable. incapable. *F.*

l. 7 *f.b.* Dresses. Petticoats. *F.*

last line. has more. hath more. *F.*

P. 451, l. 5. as all. which all. *F.*

l. 13. though. although. *F.*

l. 21. remote. *F.* remoter. *1727.*

P. 453, l. 1. which seems to be. which is. *F.*

l. 8. a hundred. an hundred. *F.*

l. 12. worth. worthy. *F.*

l. 21. Liberties. *F.* liberty. *1727.*

l. 12 *f.b.* happens. happen. *F.*

P. 454, l. 3. is generally. be generally. *F.*

l. 4. to be a mark. for a mark. *F.*

l. 5. he wants. the Person you have chosen wants. *F.*

A MEDITATION UPON A BROOM-STICK

Text from *First Edition*: A / Meditation / upon a / Broom-Stick, / and / *Somewhat Beside*; / of / The Same Author's. / . . . London : / Printed for *E. Curll,* at the *Dial* and *Bible* against / St. *Dunstan's*

Church in *Fleetstreet;* and sold by / *J. Harding*, at the *Post-Office* in St. *Martins-Lane.* / 1710. / (Price 6*d.*)

Copy : Elkin Mathews.

Collated with : Miscellanies : 1711 [1711]. Miscellanies. Vol. II : 1727 [*M*.]. Faulkner, Vol. I : 1735 [*F*.].

P. 457. *Title. 1711 adds :* Written *August*, 1704. *F. adds :*—According to the Style and Manner of the Honourable Robert Boyle's Meditations. Written in the Year 1703. *M. follows F., but omits the last sentence.*

ll. 6, 9, 12. 'tis. It is. *F.*

l. 13. its last. the last. *M.F.*

l. 14. Fires. a Fire. *1711 M.F.*

l. 15. **Surely Man.** Surely

Mortal Man. *1711 M.F.*

l. 20. unto Art. to Art. *1711 M.F.*

l. 21. *Peruque.* Perriwig. *1711 M.F.*

P. 458. l. 1. you'll. you will. *1711*

l. 4. a-Cock-Horse and Rational. mounted on his Rational. *1711 M.F.*

l. 14. he's. he is. *1711*

THOUGHTS ON VARIOUS SUBJECTS

[numbers supplied by Editor]

Nos. 1-20. Text from *earliest version in* : Miscellanies in PROSE and VERSE. 1711.

Copy : R. Jennings.

Collated with : Miscellanies. Vol. I : 1727 [*M*.]. Faulkner, Vol. I : 1735 [*F*.].

P. 458. *Title. Supplied by Editor.* Nos. 1-20 *are headed in Misc. 1711 :*—Various Thoughts, Moral and Diverting. Written October the 1. 1706.

l. 9 *f.b.* enough Religion. Religion enough. *F.*

l. 6 *f.b.* &c. and the like. *F.*

P. 459, l. 9. seems to allude. may allude. *F.*

l. 17. this Sign. this infallible Sign. *F.*

P. 460, l. 2. of the Censure of the World. of a censorious World. *F.*

l. 10. &c. and the like. *F.*

l. 13. ignorant of. Miscellanies. *edn. 2, 1713. F.* ignorant. *1711.*

l. 2 *f.b.* who Dirts. who fouls. *F.*

Nos. 21-38. Text from *earliest version in :* Miscellanies in Prose and Verse. The First Volume : *1727.*

Copy : Editor.

Collated with : Faulkner, Vol. I : 1735. [*F*.].

P. 462, l. 1. has once. hath once. *F.*

l. 3. do to a Whore. do a Whore. *F.*

P. 463, l. 9. Sorts of. Kinds of. *F.*

l. 10. are an. *F.* is an. *1727.*

l. 17. as easy a one. *F.* as easy one. *1727.*

Nos. 39-47. Text from *earliest version in* : Faulkner, Vol. VIII : 1746. Copy : R. Jennings.

Nos. 48-49. Text from *earliest version in :* Works. Ed. Hawksworth. Vol. VIII. 4to : 1765. Copy : R. Jennings.

THOUGHTS ON RELIGION

Text from *earliest version in* : Works. Ed. Hawksworth. Vol. VIII. i. 4to : 1765. Copy : R. Jennings.

RESOLUTIONS, &c.

Text from *Swift's autograph MS.* in the Forster Collection.

P. 467. *Title. Supplied from Works.* Vol. VIII. 4to: 1765. p. 240, *where these* Resolutions *were first printed. The MS. heading, retained here, though omitted in* Works, 1765, *is simply:—* When I come to be old 1699.

l. 16 *f.b.* or let . . . hardly. *this*

sentence is deleted in the MS., though not by Swift.

l. 9 *f.b.* over. *This word is inserted above the line in the MS.*

l. 3 *f.b.* desire. *Swift originally wrote* conjure [not covet *as a recent editor supposes*], *but deleted it and substituted* desire.

THE DRAPIER'S FIRST LETTER

Text from *First Edition*: A / LETTER / TO THE / *Shop-Keepers, Tradesmen, Farmers,* / and *Common-People* of IRELAND, / Concerning the / Brass Half-Pence / Coined by / **Mr. Woods**, [*sic*] with / A DESIGN to have them Pass in this / KINGDOM. / . . . / (Very Proper to be kept in every FAMILY.) / By M. B. Drapier. / *Dublin*: Printed by *J. Harding* in Moles- / worth's Court. / [1724.]

[Reprinted in: FRAUD DETECTED: / OR, THE / *Hibernian* Patriot. / CONTAINING, / All the *Drapier's* Letters to the People of *Ireland,* / on *Wood's* Coinage, &c. / . . . With a PREFACE, explaining / the Usefulness of the Whole. / *Dublin*: Re-printed and Sold by *George Faulkner* / in *Pembroke-Court, Castle-street*, 1725. (Copy: Maggs Brothers.)]

Copies: British Museum and Pickering & Chatto [*Mac*]. Owing to the unexpected demand for this cheap, ill-printed pamphlet, fresh issues had to be printed off after the original type had been distributed; in consequence it will be found that copies of the first edition are distinguished by numerous variants, chiefly in spelling and punctuation. A folio edition, 2 leaves double columns, is recorded. Collated with: *Fraud Detected:* 1725 [*H.*]. Faulkner, Vol. IV: 1735 [*F.*].

P. 473. *Title.* Common People. Country People. *F.*

l. 7 *f.b.* three Years. four Years. *H.F.*

l. 6 *f.b. F. notes:* — Vide . . . A Proposal for the Use of Irish Manufactures.

l. 4 *f.b. any Man.* Person whatsoever. *F.*

P. 474, l. 4. and *Loss of Money.* and to be fined and imprisoned. *F.*

l. 20. Wood. *H.* Woods. *The first edition adds an* s *to* Wood *throughout. On the last two pages of the copy* [*Mac.*], *of the first edition, lent by Pickering & Chatto, the name is correctly spelled.*

l. 22. FOURSCORE . . .

108000 l. *F. passim.* [*Actually the sum should be £100,800, the value of 360 tons of copper as stated in the patent.*]

l. 12 *f.b.* lose above. lose much above. *F.*

l. 9 *f.b.* would not. would hardly. *F.*

P. 475. l. 20. could tell. would tell. *F.*

P. 476, l. 2. these. those. *H.F.*

l. 11. by help. by the help. *Mac.*

l. 14. shall Receive. will Receive. *Mac.*

l. 16. will be. shall be. *Mac.*

l. 7 *f.b. Bere. F. notes:*—A sort of Barley in Ireland.

P. 477, l. 1. are between. is between. *F.*

l. 4. *Pound. Pounds.* H.F.
l. 5. Two Hundred Pound. Two-Hundred Pounds. *Mac.*
l. 9. Horse. Horses. *H.F.*
l. 15. loaden. loaded. *H.F.*
l. 18. CONOLLY. *F.* C——Y. *1724.*
l. 20. *Forty Horses. Fifty Horses.* H.F.
l. 6. *f.b.* till. until. *F.*
P. 478, l. 23. *Cottiers. Cottagers. F.*
l. 11 *f.b.* hoard up or. hoard up to. *H.F.*
P. 479, l. 4. does not. doth not. *F.*
l. 19. Thousand. Thousandth. *F.*
l. 24. thus much. this much. *H.F.*
l. 8 *f.b.* . *Articles Charters. F.*
l. 6 *f.b.* Change, Impair . . . Money. Change *or* impair *the* Money. *F.*
P. 480, l. 2. Law. Laws. *H.F. Mac.*
l. 2. the several. and several. *H.* several. *F.*
l. 13. *into prison. to prison. H.*
l. 7 *f.b.* is most evident. is more evident. *H.* is evident. *F.*

l. 6 *f.b.* Henry the 4th. Chap. 4. [*This should be* 4. Henry IV. cap. 10.]
l. 6 *f.b.* by which. whereby. *F.*
P. 481, l. 1. Word. Words. *F.*
l. 3. *are meant. is meant. F.*
l. 8. *Vessel. Vessels. F.*
l. 8. *nor any. or any.* H.F.
l. 14. *Metal*, and that these. *Metal.* And these. *F.*
l. 15. farther. further. *H.F.*
l. 10 *f.b.* such power. such legal power. *F.*
P. 482, l. 3. are not obliged. are oblig'd. *H.* are not oblig'd. *F.*
l. 4. no not the. not only the. *H.F.*
l. 5. or of any. but of any. *F.*
l. 6. only for. meerly for. *F.*
l. 8. I will suppose. I suppose. *F.*
l. 10. you obliged. we oblig'd. *H.F.*
l. 17. so ill. such ill. *F.*
l. 22. poor Sort. poorer Sort. *F.*
l. 2 *f.b.* an half-penny. a half-penny. *F.*
P. 483, l. 7. *a King. the King. F.*
l. 6 *f.b.* made it their. *F.* made their. *1724. H.*
l. 3 *f.b.* all Persons. that all Families. *F.*

THE DRAPIER'S FOURTH LETTER

Text from *First Edition*: A / LETTER / TO THE / WHOLE People / OF / IRELAND. / *By* M. B. *Drapier* / AUTHOR of the LETTER to the / *SHOP-KEEPERS, &c.* / DUBLIN: / Printed by *John Harding* in *Moles-* / *worth's Court* in *Fishamble Street.* / [1724.] Copy: University Library, Cambridge.
Collated with: 2nd issue: [1724], *Fraud Detected:* 1725 [*H.*]. Faulkner, Vol. IV: 1735 [*F.*].

P. 484. *After the title F. adds :*— This was the Letter against which the Lord Lieutenant (*Carteret*) and Council, issued a Proclamation, offering three Hundred Pounds to discover the Author; and for which, *Harding* the Printer was tried before one *Whitshed*, then Chief Justice: But the noble Jury would not find the Bill; nor would any Person discover the Author.
l. 4. conceived. conceive. *H.* conceived. *F.*
l. 10. proceeds. proceed. *F.*
l. 6. *f.b.* probably. certainly. *F.*

l. 6 *f.b.* no good Design. a bad Design. *F.*
last line. Number. Numbers. *H.F.*
P. 485. *last line.* and these. and those. *F.*
P. 486, l. 2 *f.b.* has Power. hath Power. *F.*
P. 489, l. 5. Project is. Project are. *F.*
l. 5. the last. their last. *F.*
l. 7 *f.b. Keeper. Keepers. H. Keeper. F.*
l. 7 *f.b. Records* of. *Records* in. *F.*
l. 3 *f.b.* Favourite. *F. notes:*—

Mr Hopkins, Secretary to the Duke of Grafton.

P. 490, l. 1. 8000 1. 9000 1. *F.*

l. 3. Jest. *F.* Test. *1724.*

P. 491. l. 5. hath been given. was lately given. *F.*

l. 7. Noble. *F. omits.*

l. 18. were in. are in. *H.F.*

l. 24. under Pain. under the Pain. *F.*

l. 27. *Closeting.* It would. *Closeting ;* it might. *F.*

l. 29. though. although. *F.*

P. 492. l. 8 *f.b. Irish Man,* upon. *Irishman,* at least, upon. *F.*

l. 8 *f.b. this Article.* this one *Article. F.*

P. 493, l. 10 *f.b.* without finding. finding, *1st issue. Corrected in errata, 2nd issue.*

l. 8 *f.b.* does upon. doth upon. *F.*

P. 494, l. 4. am so far. am far, *1st issue. Corrected in errata, 2nd issue.*

l. 13. 'Tis. It is. *F.*

l. 3 *f.b. Same Person. F. notes :* —Mr. Walpole, now Sir Robert.

P. 495, l. 4. it lay in. to lay it in. *H.* to leave it in. *F.*

P. 496, l. 8. I would. I should. *F.*

l. 12. merely for. even for, *1st issue. Corrected in errata, 2nd issue.*

l. 7 *f.b.* intended. intend. *F.*

P. 497. l. 13. *or Silver.* and *Silver. F.*

P. 498, l. 10. to his own Place. *to his own Place. F.*

l. 12. probably. *F. omits.*

l. 24. without one. without any. *F.*

l. 28. and his *Hirelings.* and *Hirelings, 1st issue. Corrected in errata, 2nd issue.*

l. 2 *f.b.* P. 499, ll. 4, 8, 4 *f.b.* P. 500, l. 21. Mr. W——. Mr. *Walpole. F.*

P. 499, ll. 7, 8. He orders . . . Paper, that. In another printed Paper of his contriving, it is roundly expressed, that. *F.*

l. 9. *this brass. his brass. F.*

P. 500, l. 9. this Kingdom. the Kingdom. *F.*

l. 30. Remote. . . . *F. notes :*— Procul à Jove, procul à fulmine.

A CHARACTER OF THE EARL OF WHARTON

Text from *First Edition*: A Short / Character / of / His Ex. T. E. of W. / L. L. of I. . . . / With / An Account of some smaller Facts, du- / ring His Government, which will not / be put into the Articles of Impeach- / ment. / London : / Printed for *William Coryton*, Bookseller, at the / *Black-Swan* on *Ludgate-hill,* 1711. / Price 4^d. /

Copy : London Library.

P. 503, l. 16. that Kingdom. *Later texts, printed after Swift's death, read :*—Ireland.

A SHORT VIEW OF THE STATE OF IRELAND

Text from *First Edition*: A / SHORT VIEW / of the / STATE / of / IRELAND. / Dublin : / Printed by *S. Harding,* next Door to / the *Crown* in *Copper-Alley,* 1727–8. /

Copy : Pickering & Chatto.

Collated with : Faulkner, Vol. IV : 1735 [*F.*]. Miscellanies. Volume the Fifth : 1735 [*M.*].

P. 504. *F. and M. add after title :*—Written in the Year 1727.

ll. 11, 12. cordially . . . obligingly. *cordially . . . obligingly. M.F.*

P. 505, l. 3. the Liberty. the Priviledge. *M.F.*

l. 15. Prince. *M.F.* Princes. *1727–8.*

l. 16. Administrator. *M.F.* Administrators. *1727–8.*

P. 506, l. 8 *f.b.* Nature . . . is. Nature hath bestowed so liberally on this Kingdom is. *M.F.*

l. 5 *f.b.* this Kingdom. *Ireland.*
M.F.

P. 507, l. 5. Privilege. *M.F.*
1727–8 omits.

l. 15. L— C— J— W—'s. Lord
Chief Justice *Whitshed's. M.F.*

l. 16. LIBERTAS . . . SOLUM. Liberty and my native Country.
note : *M.F.*

l. 18. was Perjuring himself.
was —— himself. *M.*

l. 22. decide. *M.F.* divide.
1727–8.

P. 508, l. 22. in great quantity.
M.F. omit.

l. 10 *f.b.* Improvement. *M.F.*
Improvements. 1727-8.

l. 9 *f.b.* half of the. half the.
M.F.

last line. C——*rs. Commis-*
soiners. M.F.

P. 509, l. 14. these. those.
M.F.

P. 510, l. 9. although they. although themselves. *M.F.*

l. 14 *f.b.* that shall. who shall.
M.F.

l. 6 *f.b.* those. *M.F.* these.
1727–8.

A MODEST PROPOSAL

Text from *First Edition* : A Modest / Proposal / For preventing
the / Children / of / Poor People / From being a / Burthen to their
Parents, / or the / Country, / and / For making them Beneficial to
the / Publick. / Dublin: / Printed by *S. Harding*, opposite the *Hand*
and / *Pen* near Fishamble-Street, on the *Blind Key.* / MDCCXXIX. ɪ
Copy: Forster Collection.
Collated with: Third Edition 1730 [*B.*]. Miscellanies. The Third
Volume [*actually the Fourth*] : 1732 [*M.*]. Faulkner, Vol. IV : 1735 [*F.*].

P. 512. *F. adds after title :—*
Written in the Year 1729.

P. 513, l. 3. of other. of our.
M. errata.

l. 22. this Kingdom. *Ireland.*
F.

ll. 29, 32. an hundred. one
hundred. *B.*

l. 10 *f.b.* I again . . . *new para-*
graph. B.

P. 514, l. 1. till. until. *F.*

l. 15. or the Kingdom. or
Kingdom. *M.*

l. 24. or a *Ragoust.* or *Ra-*
goust. F.

l. 4 *f.b.* in the. *M.F.* of the.
1729.

P. 515, l. 6. Pound. Pounds.
M.F.

l. 13. a grave Author. Rabe-
lais. *Note. F.*

l. 8 *f.b.* neat. net. *F.*

l. 5 *f.b.* flay. flea. *M.*

P. 516, l. 12 *f.b.* however so
well. how well soever. *M.F.*

P. 517, l. 5. at the. at a. *M.*

l. 14. about the. upon that.
M.F.

l. 22. are happily. are in a fair
Way of being soon. *F.*

l. 4 *f.b.* an Episcopal. an idolatrous, Episcopal. *F.*

P. 518, l. 8 *f.b. to the Market.*
to Market. *B.*

l. 4 *f.b.* as it is. as is. *M.*

P. 519, l. 4. which are. and are.
F.

l. 5. Yearling. Yearly. *M.F.*

l. 12. *Weddings.* at *Weddings.*
M. F.

l. 19. be thereby. thereby be. *B.*

l. 20. and it was. *F.* and was.
1729. and 'twas. *B.*

l. 21. I desire . . . *new para-*
graph. B.

P. 520, l. 6. *and earnestly.* in
earnest. *B.*

l. 8. some Glimpse. a Glimpse.
F.

l. 25. But before . . . *new para-*
graph. B.

l. 11 *f.b.* an hundred. one
hundred. *B.* a hundred. *M.F.*

l. 10 *f.b.* And *Secondly* . . . *new*
paragraph. B.

l. 6 *f.b.* Million. Millions. *M.F.*

l. 3 *f.b.* I desire those . . . *new*
paragraph. B.

P. 521, l. 8. of Weather. of the
Weather. *M.F.*

AN EXAMINATION OF CERTAIN ABUSES

Text from *First Edition*: An / Examination / of certain / *Abuses, Corruptions*, / and / Enormities / in the / City of *Dublin*. / *Dublin* ⋅ Printed in the Year 1732. /
Copy: British Museum.
Collated with: Faulkner, Vol. IV: 1735 [*F.*].

P. 522, l. 9. these. those. *F.*
l. 13. their most profound. their profound. *F.*
l. 7 *f.b.* touch at. touch the. *F.*
P. 523, ll. 8, 22. till. until. *F.*
l. 9. these. those. *F.*
P. 524, l. 15. *Sweet-hearts.* A Sort of Sugar-Cakes in the Shape of Hearts. *Note. F.*
l. 13 *f.b. Toupees.* A new Name for a modern Periwig, and for its Owner; now in Fashion. Dec. 1, 1733. *Note. F.*
P. 526, l. 21. and *Tory.* and a *Tory. F.*
P. 527, l. 8 *f.b.* a *Cock.* a *Cock*, in the same Posture. *F.*
l. 6 *f.b.* speaking, either fit. speaking, fit. *F.*
P. 528, l. 4. Guest. Guests. *F.*
l. 6. is a. being a. *F.*
l. 7. For the Birds, as they. For, as they. *F.*
l. 8. Sign, are. Sign, they are. *F.*
P. 529, l. 8. the *Protestant.* the *true* Protestant. *F.*
l. 16. those Signs. the Signs. *F.*
l. 18. the most. *F. omits.*
l. 24. those. these. *F.*
P. 530, l. 1. till. until. *F.*
l. 13. to that. to the. *F.*
P. 531, l. 1. our most able. our able. *F.*
l. 14 *f.b.* great Offence. much Offence. *F.*

l. 8 *f.b. worst of Times.* A Cant-Word used by Whigs for the four last Years of Queen Anne's Reign, during the Earl of Oxford's Ministry; whose Character here is an exact Reverse in every Particular. *Note. F.*
l. 2 *f.b.* Gold Plate. *F. omits* Gold.
P. 532, l. 12 *f.b.* after they. until they. *F.*
l. 10 *f.b.* the fine Cries. the Cries. *F.*
P. 533, l. 4. the wicked. this wicked. *F.*
l. 6. and is in. *F.* and in. *1732.*
ll. 14, 15. after . . . aspired. they have so long aimed at. *F.*
l. 17. And the. Whereby. *F.*
P. 534, l. 8. Voice . . . upon. Voice, as to have the Honour of being mentioned upon. *F.*
l. 21. have often since. have since. *F.*
last line. P——*n.* Peyton. *F. F. adds in note :*—A famous Whig Justice in those Times.
P. 536, l. 5. that Party. the Party. *F.*
P. 537, l. 3 *to end.* Having already . . . my superiors. *This final paragraph was printed for the first time in Scott's edition 1808, from which it is here transcribed.*

A SERIOUS AND USEFUL SCHEME

Text from *First Edition*: A / Serious and Useful / Scheme, / To make an / Hospital for Incurables, / of / Universal Benefit to all His Majesty's / Subjects. / Occasioned by a Report, that the Estate of / Richard Norton Esq; was / to be appointed by Parliament / for such an Endowment. / . . . . / By a Celebrated Author in *Ireland*. / . . . . / London: / Printed for J. Roberts, at the *Oxford Arms* in / *Warwick-Lane*. MDCCXXXIII. / Price 6d. /
Copy: University Library, Cambridge.
Collated with: First Dublin Edition. " Printed by George Faulkner . . . 1733." [Swift's initials do not appear on the title-page of this edition.]
Note: The few variant readings in the first London edition and the first Dublin edition of the same year have no textual significance.

But two points should be noticed. (i) On P. 553, l. 3 *f.b.*, both editions give the total incorrectly as £4,600,000: this has been silently corrected in the present text. (ii) P. 556, last line, the Dublin edition is dated *Aug. 20, 1733*.

POLITE CONVERSATION

Text from *First Edition*: A Complete / Collection / Of Genteel and Ingenious / Conversation, / According to the Most / Polite Mode and Method / now used / At Court, and in the Best / Companies of England. / In Three Dialogues. / By Simon Wagstaff, Esq; / *LONDON:* / Printed for B. Motte, and C. Bathurst, at / the *Middle Temple-Gate* in *Fleet-street*. / M.DCC.XXXVIII. /
Copy: Editor.

DIRECTIONS TO SERVANTS

Text from *First Edition*: Directions / to / Servants / In General; / And in particular to / The Butler, Cook, / Footman. . . . / By the Reverend Dr. Swift, D.S.P.D. / . . . . London: / Printed for R. Dodsley, in *Pall-Mall*, and / M. Cooper, in *Pater-Noster-Row*, / MDCCXLV. / (Price One Shilling and Six-Pence.)
Copy: Birrell & Garnett.
Collated with: MS. fragment, corrected by Swift in the Forster Collection. [The readings of this MS. are indicated in the notes as *MS*. Swift's own manuscript corrections as *MS. Swift*.] Faulkner, Vol. VIII: 1746 [*F.*].

P. 596, l. 1. The Preface. *From Vol. viii. Faulkner's edition, 1746.*

RULES . . . IN GENERAL

P. 597, l. 5. comes. cometh. *F.*

l. 13. you are therefore. *F.* who therefore are. *1745.*

l. 19. computes. computeth. *F. alters the termination throughout.*

l. 22. sparing. saving. *MS.*

P. 598, l. 6. more confirmed. *MS. Swift*. better confirmed. *1745.*

l. 24. find. *MS. Swift*. get. *1745.*

P. 599, l. 3. highly to. highly for. *MS.*

l. 21. and shortest. the Shortest. *MS.*

l. 24. as you go out. at going out. *MS.*

l. 10 *f.b.* give . . . Warning. *underlined by Swift in MS.*

P. 600, ll. 18, 19. Porridge . . . Jordan. Porridge, And or in case . . . Jordan, or hold Small-Beer. *MS.*

l. 10 *f.b* a Point. a Part. *F.*

l. 2 *f.b.* observed. observable. *MS.*

P. 601, ll. 11-15. When you . . . chidden. *Note by Swift:*—Better if put in another place.

l. 15. must be. will be. *MS.* you may be. *F.*

l. 22. should be. *MS. Swift*. shall be. *1745.*

l. 3 *f.b.* to Visit. *MS. Swift*. on a Visit. *1745.*

P. 602, l. 5. and you . . . safe. & is safe. *MS.*

l. 9. he but just. he is just. *MS.*

l. 10. was dying. is dying. *MS.*

l. 12 *f.b.* less than. *MS. omits*.

l. 12 *f.b.* When a Servant . . . *new paragraph. MS.*

l. 5 *f.b.* Where there are . . . *new paragraph. MS.*

P. 603, l. 1. Master lives. Masters live. *MS.*

l. 8. are sent. be sent. *MS.*

l. 9. Pocket. *MS. adds:* which is very usual.

l. 13 *f.b.* the best. your best. *MS.*

P. 604, l. 5. shall have. will have. *MS.*

l. 10. find out. find. *MS.*

l. 12. Wainscot, in. Wainscot, or in. *MS.*

l. 17. Dough, or. Dough, a bundle of shavings or. *F.*

l. 17. the Loaf. a loaf. *MS.*

l. 20. peculiar. particular. *MS.*

l. 25. upon a Lap-Dog or. on a Lap-Dog, a. *F.*

l. 26. Parrot, a Child. Parrot, a Magpye, a Child. *F.*

l. 6 *f.b.* Tongs be. Tongs are. *MS.*

last line. a Curtain. the Curtain. *MS.*

P. 605, l. 1. Jordan, he. Jordan, in case of need he. *MS.*

l. 6. Floor. *MS. Swift.* Ground. *1745.*

l. 13. until. till. *MS.*

l. 26. Pantry Door. *MS.* omits Door.

RULES . . . IN PARTICULAR

To the Butler.

P. 606, l. 7. Person. party. *MS.*

l. 18. Footman. Footmen. *MS.*

ll. 20, 21. and you . . . Lady. *MS.* omits.

l. 8 *f.b.* If you . . . Drink. When you are drawing Ale. *MS.*

ll. 5-3 *f.b.* or take . . . want you. *MS.* omits.

l. 2 *f.b.* choicest Ale. *MS. Swift.* choice Bottles. *1745.*

last line. of the Bottles. *MS. Swift.* of them. *1745.*

last line. Neck. necks. *MS.*

P. 607, l. 11. it will save you. you save. *MS.*

l. 6 *f.b.* spoiled cannot. spoiled they cannot. *MS.*

P. 608, l. 10 *f.b.* give to the. give the. *F.*

l. 5 *f.b.* Tea-pot. Tea-kettle. *MS. F.*

P. 609, l. 1. of the Hall. *MS.* omits : of the.

l. 2. until. till. *MS.*

l. 4. they shall smell. they smell. *MS.*

l. 5. leaves a. leaves his. *MS.*

l. 12. in View. in his view. *MS.*

l. 11 *f.b.* of his. of the. *MS.*

l. 5 *f.b.* Cistern until. Cistern three or four times, till. *MS.*

P. 610, l. 16. till. until. *F.*

l. 25. Dark to. dark, (as clean Glasses &c.) to. *MS.*

To the Cook.

P. 610, l. 5 *f.b.* 'Squires. Esquires. *F.*

l. 4 *f.b.* myself. *F. omits.*

P. 611, l. 3. Progue. Progg. *F.*

l. 5. or a good. or good. *MS.*

l. 15. for both. to both. *MS.*

l. 9 *f.b.* If your . . . *new paragraph. MS.*

l. 5 *f.b.* they justly. they very justly. *MS.*

P. 612, ll. 7-12. Butter : for . . . the same. Butter ; And least the Pen Feathers should offend the Gentry, I advise you to flay all small Birds instead of pulling them. *MS.*

l. 13. with stirring. by stirring. *F.*

l. 12 *f.b.* serve next. serve for next. *MS.*

l. 2 *f.b.* well in, and. well, and. *F.*

P. 613, l. 13. and spitted. *MS.* omits : and.

l. 14. till. until. *F.*

l. 15. up your. up the. *MS.*

l. 16. fouler. fouled. *MS.*

l. 19. There is . . . *no paragraph. MS.*

l. 20. toasting. roasting. *MS. F.*

l. 23. in the. with the. *MS.*

P. 614, l. 4. at the. on the. *MS.*

l. 4. without it. without the Sweet-bread. *MS.* '

l. 10 *f.b.* would be. *MS. Swift.* will be. *1745.*

To the Footman. *The arrangement of the text in the MS. varies from that of the 1st edition.*

P. 615, l. 12. Skipkennel. Skipkennels. *MS.*

l. 14 *f.b.* the largest Dishes . . . them on with. a heavy Dish of Soupe from the Table with. *MS.*

l. 13 *f.b.* to shew . . . Strength of Back. to shew your Strength. *MS.*

l. 12 *f.b.* the Dish. it. *MS.*

l. 11 *f.b.* slip, the Soup or Sauce. spill, the Liquor. *MS.*

ll. 10, 9 *f.b.* By this . . . Fortunes. *MS. omits.*

P. 616, l. 12 *f.b.* to sit. *F.* to it.
1745.

P. 617, l. 20. till. until. *F.*

P. 618, l. 11 *f.b.* set. sit. *F.*
l. 4 *f.b.* betwixt. between. *F.*
l. 3 *f.b.* if you. if they. *MS.F.*

P. 619, l. 1. a Mop. *MS.F. a*
Map. *1745.*

P. 620, l. 3. I give. I shall give.
MS.

l. 11. Community at your
Tryal. *MS. Swift.* Community.
1745.

l. 17. escape. scape. *MS.*

l. 23. Eyes. *MS. Swift.* Hands.
1745.

To the Chamber-Maid.

P. 623, ll. 4-8. Bed ; and . . .

Neighbourhood. Bed. *F.*
F. omits the rest of the paragraph.

To the Waiting-Maid.

P. 625, l. 8 *f.b.* Rake (and . . .
t'other) avoid. Rake, or a Fool,
(and . . . t'other) but, if the
former, avoid. *F.*
l. 7 *f.b.* less in. in less. *F.*

To the Children's-Maid.

P. 628, l. 11. for your. to your.
MS.

l. 13. cometh. comes. *MS.*

To the Laundress.

P. 628, l. 7 *f.b.* Rags. *F. adds:*
—Always wash your own Linen
first.

THE JOURNAL TO STELLA

Text of extracts from Letters IV-XL from *earliest version in*:
Works. Ed. Deane Swift. Vol. XII. 4to : 1768.

Text of extract from Letter LIV from *earliest version*: Works.
Ed. Hawkesworth. Vol. X. 4to : 1766.

Copies : R. Jennings.

Text of extracts from Letters XLIII-LXII from : Swift's holograph
MS. in the British Museum. Add. MS. 4804. First printed, very
imperfectly, in Works. Ed. Hawkesworth. Vol. X. 4to : 1766.

The so-called " little language ", in which Swift disguised his more
playful and affectionate addresses to Stella and Dingley, was either
suppressed or " edited " beyond recognition in the early printed
copies. Deane Swift took it for granted that " the strange spelling
. . . could be no entertainment to the reader " and omitted it with
the exception of the code letters by which Swift designated himself
and his two correspondents; and even these he " improved ". " In
these letters ", he remarked, " *pdfr* stands for Dr Swift ; *Ppt* for
Stella ; *D* for Dingley ; *DD* generally for Dingley, but sometimes for
Stella and Dingley ; and *MD* generally stands for both these ladies ;
yet sometimes only for Stella. But to avoid perplexing the reader,
it was thought more advisable to use the word *Presto* for Swift ; instead of *Ppt.*, Stella is used for Mrs Johnson, and so for *D.* Dingley ;
but as *MD* stands for both Stella and Dingley, it was thought more
convenient to let it remain a cypher in the original state." A comparison between the printed and MS. versions of the Journal reveals
the extent of this tiresome meddling. It is generally assumed
that *pdfr* signifies " poor dear foolish rogue "; *ppt* " poppet " or
" poor pretty thing "; *D. DD. MD.* " Dingley ", " Dear Dingley ",
" My Dear or Dears " respectively. *F.W.* remains a mystery.
" Lele, lele . . ." which usually appears at the end of the letters has
been taken to mean " there, there . . .", and the letters *l* and *r*, and
g and *d* are occasionally interchanged. For the rest, the reader, if
he wishes, may exercise his own ingenuity. It is scarcely incumbent
upon an editor to explain, even if he could, such very intimate and
peculiar nonsense.

P. 655, l. 3 *f.b.* al bfadnuk &c. *i.e.* a bank-bill for fifty pound. *The cypher is solved by reading only every alternate letter.*

P. 657, l. 15. *Deane Swift* [Works]. Vol. XII. 1768.] *annotates this passage as follows:*—Here is just one specimen given of his way of writing to *Stella* in these journals. The reader, I hope, will excuse my omitting it in all other places where it occurs. The meaning of this pretty language is: " And you must cry, There, and Here, and Here again. Must you imitate *Presto*, pray? Yes, and so you shall. And so there's for your letter. Good morrow.

Neither the transcription nor the interpretation of these lines can be called correct.

P. 704, l. 4 *f.b.* [thô] *the MS. is torn at this place.*

P. 708, l. 19. Spreenekick Ferrow. *i.e.* Splenetick Fellow.

P. 719, ll. 6, 7. *The obliterated words appear to be:*—Nite [?] sollahs ; I'll take my reeve. [I forgett how] Md Accounts are ; pray let me know always timely before Md wants.

l, 9. *According to Mr. Moorhead* [*Journal to Stella.* Everyman edn.], *the obliterated passage should read:* Go play Cards & be melly dee sollahs, & rove pdfr who roves Md bettle zan his Rife. Farewell deelest Md Md Md Md Md . . . Me Me Me Fw Fw Fw Me Me lele Lele Lele Lele.

P. 720, l. 11. *The following phrase is crossed out:*—Nite my own deelest richar logues MD.

P. 721, l. 12 *f.b. The two words obliterated are:* Nasty Bawd.

P. 722, *last line. Read:* Nite dee Md.

ON THE DEATH OF MRS JOHNSON

Text from *earliest version in*: Works Vol. VIII. pt. i. 4to : 1765.
Copy : R. Jennings.

THREE PRAYERS

Text of the first Prayer from *earliest version in*: Works. Vol. VIII pt. i. 4to : 1765.
Copy : R. Jennings.

Text of the second and third Prayers from *earliest version in*: Miscellanies &c. The Eleventh Volume. London. Printed for C. Hitch, C. Davis, R. Dodsley, and M. Cooper. MDCCXLVI.
Copy : British Museum.

POEMS

IN A LADY'S IVORY TABLE-BOOK

Text from *earliest version in*: Miscellanies : 1711.
Collated with : Miscellanies. The Last Volume [*actually the Third*]: 1727 [*M.*]. Faulkner, Vol. II : 1735 [*F.*].

P. 749, *Title.* Wrote in. Wrote on. *M.F.*
Anno 1698. *M. omits.* Written in the Year 1706. *F.*

ll. 19, 20. To think . . . of his. *M.F. omit this couplet.*
l. 6 *f.b.* hold. *M.F.* holds. *1711.* last line. Golden *M.*

TO THEIR EXCELLENCIES, &c.

Text from *first authorized version in*: Miscellanies: 1711.
Collated with: Curll's Edition: 1710 [*C.*]. Miscellanies. Vol. III:
1727 [*M.*]. Faulkner, Vol. II: 1735 [*F.*].

P. 750. *Title*. Lords . . . Ireland. *C. omits.*
Anno 1700. Written in the Year 1701. *F.*
l. 4. Pound, four. Pound, and four. *C.*
l. 5. besides Farthings. (besides Farthings). *F.*
l. 10. which . . . Stock. (which . . . Stock). *F.*
l. 12. my Pocket. a Pocket. *C.*
l. 14. went to. *C. omits.*
l. 17. down to. down Stairs to. *C.*
l. 19. And. When. *C.*
l. 21. feel. *C. omits.*
l. 5 *f.b.* says I. said I. *F.*
P. 751, l. 9. a-dream'd. dream'd. *C.*
l. 13. *Whittle*. Earl of Berkeley's Valet. *note F.*
l. 14. my Dame. Mrs. *C.*
l. 14. *Wadgar*. The old deaf House-Keeper. *note F.*
l. 15. of Hearing. o' Hearing. *C.*
note 2. Drogheda. F. adds:—
who with the Primate were to succeed the two Earls.
l. 20. that I. *C. omits* that.

l. 21. *Cary*. Clerk of the Kitchen. *note F.*
l. 25. I remember. *C. omits.*
l. 9 *f.b.* and I found. and found. *C.*
l. 7 *f.b.* must. *C. omits this word and the brackets.*
l. 4 *f.b.* Mrs. *Dukes*. A Servant, one of the Footmen's Wives. *note F.*
l. 4 *f.b.* an ugly accident. *C. M.F.* an Accident. *1711.*
l. 2 *f.b.* three Skips . . . An usual Saying of hers. *note F.*
P. 752, l. 1. Pound, four. Pound, and four. *C.*
l. 6. yet. ——. *C.*
l. 8. *C. omits brackets.*
l. 8. ever I. *C.M.F.* I ever. *1711.*
l. 10. all. *C. omits.*
ll. 26, 27. *C. omits brackets.*
l. 9 *f.b.* so. *C. omits.*
l. 6 *f.b.* I'm. I am. *M.F.*
P. 753, l. 1. at me. *C. omits.*
l. 6. and shall. and I shall. *F.*
l. 7. Then my. So, my. *F.*
l. 7. *Harry*. Harris. *C.*
l. 21. *C. omits brackets.*
l. 22. ever. *C. omits.*

A DESCRIPTION OF THE MORNING

Text from *earliest version in*: The Tatler. Number 9. From Thursday April 28 to Saturday April 30, 1709.
Copy: H. Williams.
Collated with: Miscellanies: 1711 [1711]. Miscellanies. Vol. III: 1727 [*M.*]. Faulkner, Vol. II: 1735 [*F.*].

P. 753. *Title*. April 1709. *M. omits.* Written about the Year 1712. *F.*
l. 13 *f.b.* an. a. *F.*

l. 8 *f.b.* Street. Dirt. *1711. M.F.*
l. 5 *f.b.* The Youth. To find old Nails. *note F.*

A CITY SHOWER

Text from *earliest version in*: The Tatler. No. 238. From Saturday October 14 to Tuesday October 17, 1710.
Copy: H. Williams.

Collated with : Miscellanies : 1711. Miscellanies. Vol. III : 1727 [*M.*]. Faulkner, Vol. II : 1735 [*F.*].

P. 754. *Title*. October, 1710. *M. omits*. Written in the Year 1712. *F. In Imitation of* Virgil's Georg. *M.*

ll. 10, 13. you'll. you. *F.*

l. 6 *f.b.* Not yet. Nor yet. *F.*

l. 3 *f.b. F. notes :*—" 'Twas doubtful which was Sea, and which was Sky." Garth. Disp[ensary].

P. 755, ll. 1, 2. *F. reads :*—
Sole Coat, where Dust cemented by the Rain,
Erects the Nap, and leaves a cloudy Stain.

l. 13. Triumphant Tories. This was the first Year of the Earl of Oxford's Ministry. *note F.*

l. 10 *f.b.* Filth. Filths. *M.F.*

l. 9 *f.b.* Street . . . their. Streets . . . the. *F.*

final triplet. F. notes :—These three last lines were intended against that licentious Manner of modern Poets, in making Three Rhimes together, which they called *Triplets* ; and the last of the three, was two or sometimes more Syllables longer, called an *Alexandrian*. These *Triplets* and *Alexandrians* were brought in by DRYDEN, and other Poets in the Reign of CHARLES II. They were the mere Effect of Haste, Idleness, and want of Money ; and have been wholly avoided by the best Poets, since these Verses were written.

CORINNA

Text from *earliest version in :* .Miscellanies. The Last Volume [*i.e.* Vol. III] : 1727.
Collated with : Faulkner, Vol. II : 1735 [*F.*].

P. 756. *Title*. Written in the Year 1712. *F.*

l. 8 *f.b. F. reads :*—At twelve a Poet, and Coquette.

IN SICKNESS

Text from *earliest version in* : Faulkner, Vol. II : 1735.
Collated with : Miscellanies. Vol. V : 1735 [*M.*].

P. 757, l. 10. his Trade. the Trade. *M.*

PHILLIS : OR THE PROGRESS OF LOVE

Text from : Woburn Abbey MS. in Stella's autograph. [*v. note,* p. 746].
Collated with : Miscellanies. Vol. III : 1727 [*M.*]. Faulkner, Vol. II : 1735 [*F.*].
No italics in MS. Supplied from *M.* 1727.

P. 757. Title. Written . . . 1719. *M. omits*. Written in the Year 1716. *F.*

P. 758, l. 18. from the. to the. *M.F.*

l. 7 *f.b.* Way. Road. *M.F.*

l. 5 *f.b.* nor stop. or stop. *M.*

l. 2 *f.b. new paragraph. M.F.*

P. 759, l. 3. *new paragraph. M.F.*

l. 16. are made. were made. *M.F.*

l. 10 *f.b.* would recover. should recover. *M.F.*

P. 760, ll. 7, 8. 'um. 'em. *M.F.*

l. 8. has now not. hath now no. *M.F.*

l. 21. *Staines,* the *Old Blue Boar. M.F.* Stains the old blue Boar. *Woburn MS.*

STELLA'S BIRTH-DAY 1718

Text from: Woburn Abbey MS. in Stella's autograph. [*v. note*, p. 746].
Collated with: Miscellanies. Vol. III : 1727 [*M.*]. Faulkner, Vol. II : 1735 [*F.*].
Italics supplied from *M.* 1727.

P. 760. *Title*. Written A.D. 1718. 1718. *M.* Written in the Year 1718. *F.*
l. 11 *f.b.* won't. shan't. *M.F.*

l. 7 *f.b.* of the. on the. *M.F.*
l. 3 *f.b. new paragraph M.F.*
P. 761, l. 2. thy . . . thy. your . . . your. *M.F.*

STELLA'S BIRTH-DAY 1720-21

Text from: Woburn Abbey MS. in Stella's autograph. [*v. note*, p. 746].
Collated with: Miscellanies. Vol. III : 1727 [*M.*]. Faulkner, Vol. II : 1735 [*F.*].
Italics supplied from *M.* 1727.

P. 761. Title. Written A.D. 1720–21. 1720. *M.* Written in the Year 1720. *F.*
l. 13. And. What. *M.F.*
l. 15. Rascal. Tapster. *M.F.*
l. 19. They think. We think. *M.F.*
l. 3 *f.b.* to so. but to. *M.*
l. 2 *f.b.* Minds. Mind. *M.*
P. 762, l. 5. *new paragraph.* *M.F.*

ll. 7, 8. *This couplet omitted in M.F.*
l. 13. thy Trade. your Trade. *M.F.*
l. 14. Thy Hints. Your Hints. *M.F.*
l. 17. But let . . . thee. And let . . . you. *M.F.*
l. 18. thy Soul. your Soul. *M.F.*

CADENUS AND VANESSA

Text from: CADENUS / AND / VANESSA. / A / POEM. / *LON-DON*, / Printed: And Sold by *J. Roberts* at the *Oxford-* / *Arms* in *Warwick-Lane*, 1726. Price 6*d.* / [*This edition is referred to in the following notes as : 1726.*]
Copy : Pickering & Chatto.
Collated with : Edn. 7 (pub. H. Blandford) : 1726 [*7*]. Miscellanies. Vol. III : 1727 [*M.*]. Faulkner, Vol. II : 1735 [*F.*].

P. 762. *Title*. *F. adds:—* Written at *Windsor, Anno* 1713. *M. omits* at *Windsor.*
P. 763, l. 1. *new paragraph. M.*
l. 3. has lost. had lost. *7.*
l. 14. Statutes. Statute. *F.*
l. 3 *f.b.* a worse. some worse. *M.F.*
P. 764, l. 9 *f.b.* Questions. *7. M.F.* Question. *1726.*
P. 765, l. 1. Folk. Folks. *7.*
l. 8. Earth. Land. *F.*
l. 15. *new paragraph. 7.*

l. 17. took their. took the. *7. M.F.*
l. 20. In all. On all. *7.M.F.*
l. 21. *no paragraph. 7.M.*
l. 8 *f.b. no paragraph. M.*
P. 766, l. 11. *Clio,* sing or say. *M.F. Clio,* say. *1726.*
l. 10 *f.b. new paragraph. 7. M.F.*
P. 767, l. 3. in. from. *7.*
l. 7. She calls. Then calls. *7. M.F.*
l. 15. not one. not a. *7.*

l. 16. Prudes. 7.*M.F.* Druids. *1726.*

l. 17. for aid. in aid. *M.F.*

P. 768, l. 13. *new paragraph.* 7.*M.F.*

l. 4 *f.b.* lik'd. 7.*M.F.* lock'd. *1726.*

P. 769, l. 2. computing. 7. *M.F.* confuting. *1726.*

l. 10. That. 7.*M.F.* What. *1726.*

l. 19. her Salt. the Salt. 7. *M.F.*

ll. 32-3. *M.F. omit this couplet.*

l. 4 *f.b. M.F. read:*—But in the Poets we may find.

l. 3 *f.b.* thrice . . . Mind. Time out of Mind. 7.*M.F.*

l. 2 *f.b. M.F. read:*—Had been confirm'd by Fate's Decree.

P. 770, l. 4. Else. Or. *M.F.*

l. 14. Breasts. Breast. 7.

l. 25. *new paragraph.* 7.*M.F.*

l. 7 *f.b.* as thou. 7.*M.F.* as you. *1726.*

P. 771, l. 1. Marriage. manage. 7.*M.F.*

l. 17. To have. To know. 7. *M.F.*

l. 18. *new paragraph.* 7.*M.F.*

l. 24. Talk'd of a. Mention'd a. *M.F.*

l. 3 *f.b.* Murders. 7.*M.F.* Murder. *1726.*

last couplet. sat . . . Chat. sate . . . Prate. 7.

P. 772, l. 6. Figure. *M.F.* Figures. 1726. 7.

l. 9. these. 7.*M.F.* those. *1726.*

ll. 11-12. *M.F. omit this couplet.*

l. 14. Noblest. Noble. 7.

l. 17. scan'd. nam'd. 7.*M.F.*

l. 20. Rites. 7.*M.F.* Rights. *1726.*

l. 12 *f.b.* Foreheads. 7.*M.F.* Forehead. *1726.*

l. 12 *f.b.* a Jeer. 7.*M.F.* the Jeer. *1726.*

l. 7 *f.b.* Purlieus. 7.*M.F.* Parlours. *1726.*

l. 2 *f.b.* loudest. 7.*M.F.* louder. *1726.*

P. 773, l. 2. Whilst. While. 7.

l. 13. *new paragraph.* 7.

l. 9 *f.b.* you are. *M.F.* you're. 7. *1726.*

l. 6 *f.b. new paragraph.* 7. *M.F.*

l. 2 *f.b. new paragraph.* 7.

P. 774, l. 11 *f.b.* but vain. in vain. 7.

P. 775, l. 8. *no paragraph.* 7. *M.F.*

l. 18. Whom. 7. *M. F.* Who. *1726.*

l. 6 *f.b.* Pointed at. Pointed with. 7.

P. 776, l. 4. that. the. 7.

l. 15. says he. said he. 7.*F.*

l. 22. and Hate. or Hate. 7.

l. 12 *f.b. new paragraph.* 7. *M.F.*

P. 777, l. 2. her Smart. the Smart. 7.*F.*

l. 4. Doats on. Dreams of. *M.F.*

l. 18. is blooming. continues. *M.F.*

ll. 19-20. *M.F. omit this couplet.*

l. 8 *f.b.* This. His. 7.*M.F.*

l. 4 *f.b.* the Master's. a Master's. 7.

l. 3 *f.b.* School. Schools. 7.

P. 778, l. 3. pleading. plodding. 7.*M.F.*

l. 5. *new paragraph.* 7.

ll. 7-14. *M.F. omit these lines.*

l. 10. and profound. or profound. 7.

l. 15. *no paragraph.* *M.F.*

P. 779, l. 3. he was. he were. *F.*

l. 13. Head. Time. 7.*M.F.*

l. 14. or Wrong. and Wrong. 7.*F.*

l. 22. their Use. her Use. *M.*

l. 23. by being. with being. 7.

l. 24. dare. dares. 7.

l. 9 *f.b.* to let. I'll let. *M.*

ll. 5-4 *f.b. M.F. omit this couplet.*

l. 4 *f.b.* to you. for you. 7.

P. 780, l. 5. Guilt. Grief. 7.

l. 16. shou'd. could. *M.F.*

ll. 28-9. Joke . . . Folk. Jolks . . . Folks. 7.*M.F.*

l. 8 *f.b.* Flights were. Heights were. 7. Flights are. *F.*

l. 7 *f.b.* turn'd. turns. *F.*

P. 781, l. 2. as a . . . like a . . . 7.

l. 2. Consequence. 7.*M.F* Complaisance. *1726.*

l. 3. rally'd. railly'd. *M. F.*
l. 10. enter. alter. *F.*
l. 20. in Love. *7.M.F.* to Love. *1726.*
ll. 23-4. *M.F. omit this couplet.*
l. 23. From his. From him. *7.*
l. 25. now was. *7.M.F.* how was: *1726.*
l. 26. might. may. *7.*
l. 8 *f.b.* loves. likes. *M.F.*
ll. 4-3 *f.b.* *M.F. enclose this couplet in brackets.*
P. 782, l. 11. answers. answer'd. *F.*
l. 15. This. His. *7.M.F.*
l. 13 *f.b.* Thro' Love. Thro' this. *M.F.*
l. 9 *f.b.* who. that. *7.*
l. 5 *f.b.* ne'er. *7.M.F.* her. *1726.*
P. 783, l. 3. to our. in our. *7.*
l. 12. a Nymph. the Nymph. *7.*
l. 13. a Mistress. the Mistress.
l. 14. *new paragraph. 7.*
l. 16. But tho'. And tho'. *F.* But thought. *7.*
l. 18. cou'dn't. could not. *7. M.F.*
l. 23. Wonder. Wonders. *7.*
l. 9 *f.b.* Vanity's. Flattery's. *F.*
l. 6 *f.b. no paragraph. 7.F.*

l. 4 *f.b.* Const'ring. Construing. *7.*
P. 785, l. 13. *new paragraph. M.F.*
l. 18. To love. To like. *M.* To act. *F.*
l. 22. Nor dare. Nor dares. *7.* Nor shall. *M.F.*
l. 6 *f.b. new paragraph. M.F.*
l. 5 *f.b.* note. *7.F.:* Before the Queen on *Tuesday* next.
l. 2 *f.b. new paragraph. 7.*
P. 786, l. 5. their Time. the Time. *7.*
l. 5. Reading. *7.M.F.* Breeding. *1726.*
l. 11. Cause. Case. *M.F.*
ll. 17-20. humbly . . . end. (humbly . . . end). *M.F.*
l. 11 *f.b.* They are. They were. *M.F.*
l. 11 *f.b.* senseless stupid. stupid senseless. *7.M.F.*
l. 2 *f.b. new paragraph. M.F.*
P. 787, l. 3. *new paragraph. M.F.*
l. 4. The Court . . . *yes! M. 1726 reads :*—The Court, with his last *O yes! 7. reads :*—The Court; who made his last *O yes! F. reads :*—The Court : who made his last *O yes!*

THE FURNITURE OF A WOMAN'S MIND

Text from *earliest version in* : Faulkner, Vol. II : 1735.
Collated with: Miscellanies. Vol. V : 1735.

BETTY THE GRIZETTE

Text from *earliest version in*: Faulkner, Vol. II : 1735.
Collated with: Miscellanies. Vol. V : 1735.

ON POETRY

Text from *First English Edition* : On / Poetry : / A / Rapsody. / Printed at Dublin, and Re-printed at *London* : / And sold by J. Huggonson, next to *Kent*'s Coffee- / House, near *Serjeant*'s-Inn, in *Chancery-Lane*; and / at the Booksellers and Pamphlet-shops, 1733./ (Price One Shilling.) [*Spencer Jackson does not record the Dublin edition of which this presumably is a reprint. I have been unable to discover whether such an edition exists.*]
Copy: H. Macdonald.

Collated with: Faulkner. Vol. II.: 1735 [*F.*]. Miscellanies. Vol. V: 1735 [*M.*]. Works. Ed. Scott. 2nd edn.: 1824. [*v. infra.*]

P. 790, l. 19. there. their. *1733. corrected in errata.*
l. 7 *f.b.* fights with. combats. *F.*
P. 791, ll. 1, 3, 8, 9, 11. Nor. Not. *F.*
l. 2 *f.b. new paragraph.* *F.*
P. 792, l. 1. *no paragraph.* *F.*
l. 2. Month. week. *F.*
l. 24. *Italics.* *F.*
P. 793, l. 4. the Jest. a Jest. *F.*
l. 7. learned. learn'd *1733. corrected in errata.*
l. 11. *Lintot.* A Bookseller in London. *note.* *F.*
l. 21. *Will*'s. The Poet's Coffee-House. *note.* *F.*
P. 795, after l. 16. *The four following lines were printed for the first time by Scott in the second edition of his* Swift [*1824*]. *No indication of source is given. They were incorporated in the text by* W. E. Browning *in his edition of* Swift's *poems* [*2 vols. 1910*]. *It seems probable that they belong to an earlier draft of the poem and were rejected by Swift for reasons of discretion before publication.*

And may you ever have the luck
To rhyme almost as ill as Duck ;
And, though you never learn'd
to scan verse
Come out with some lampoon
on D'Anvers.

l. 17. *Rob*'s. *Bob*'s. *F.*
After l. 20. *Scott* [*Works 1824*] *adds the following lines.* [*v. supra.*]:—
Display the blessings of the nation,
And praise the whole administration.
Extol the bench of b[isho]ps round,
Who at them rail, bid —— confound.
To b[isho]p-haters answer thus:
(The only logic used by us)
What though they don't believe in [Christ]
Deny them Protestants—thou lyest.

l. 5 *f.b.* Is fully at. *F.* Is Folly, at. *1733.*
l. 3 *f.b.* Funeral. Fun'ral. *F.*
After l. 3 *f.b. Scott adds.* [*v. supra.*]:—
His panegyrics then are ceased,
He grows a tyrant, dunce, or beast.
P. 796, l. 3. this Scene. the Scenes. *F.*
l. 10. Project E——e and S—— Schemes. *F.*
l. 12 *f.b.* do again. serve again. *F.*
l. 3 *f.b.* may easy. can never. *F.*
P. 797, l. 13. Peri Hupsous. Peri Hupesous. *1733, corrected in errata. not corrected in F. and M.*
l. 12 *f.b.* To whom. To him. *F.*
P. 798, l. 2. *Augusta . . .* The antient Name of London. *note.* *F.*
l. 6 *f.b.* Y——. Y——g. *F.*
P. 799, l. 5. *new paragraph.* *F.*
l. 7. Smaller. *F.* Smallest. *1733.*
l. 19. strive. try. *F.*
l. 21. *no paragraph.* *F.*
l. 24. smaller Fleas. smaller yet. *F.*
P. 800, *note.* Lord G——. Lord Grimston, lately deceased. *note.* *F.*
P. 801, l. 10. The Laurcat. *F.* That Feilding. 1733. *F. notes:*—
In the London Edition, instead of Laureat, was maliciously inserted Mr. Fielding, for whose ingenious Writings the supposed Author hath manifested a great Esteem.
l. 21. flatt'ring Kings. *Scott*. 1824. flatt'ring ——. *1733. M.F.*
l. 22. Plagues. Plague. *F.*
after l. 24. *Scott adds the following paragraphs.* [*v. supra.*]:—
Perhaps you say, Augustus shines,
Immortal made in Virgil's lines,
And Horace brought the tuneful quire,

To sing his virtues on the lyre;
Without reproach for flattery, true,
Because their praises were his due.
For in those ages k[ing]s, we find,
Were animals of human kind.
But now, go search all E[u]r[o]pe round
Among the *savage monsters* [found]
With vice polluting every th[ro]ne,
(I mean all th[rone]s except our own ;)
In vain you make the strictest view
To find a [king] in all the crew,
With whom a footman out of place
Would not conceive a high disgrace,
A burning shame, a crying sin,
To take his morning's cup of gin.
Thus all are destined to obey
Some beast of burthen or of prey.
'Tis sung, Prometheus, forming man,
Through all the brutal species ran,
Each proper quality to find
Adapted to a human mind;
A mingled mass of good and bad,
The best and worst that could be had;

Then from a clay of mixture base
He shaped a [king] to rule the race,
Endow'd with gifts from every brute
That best the * * nature suit.
Thus think on [king]s : the name denotes
Hogs, asses, wolves, baboons, and goats.
To represent in figure just,
Sloth, folly, rapine, mischief, lust ;
Oh ! were they all but Neb-cad-nezers,
What herds of [king]s would turn to grazers !

l. 10 *f.b.* cou'd. can. *F.*
l. 5 *f.b.* Thro' all his Figure, Mien and Face. *F.*
l. 2 *f.b.* *Hydaspes* . . .—Super et Garamant[a]s, et Indos, Proferet imperium—Jam nunc et Caspia, regna Responsis horrent Divum—[*Virg. Aen.* vi.] note F.
last line. Hand. Arm. *F.*
P. 802, l. 2. Short . . . Knees. F. *notes*: Genibus minor. Hor.
P. 803, l. 20. to *George. Scott 1824.* to——. *1733. F.M.*
l. 28. give *George. Scott 1824.* give ——. *1733. F.M*
l. 5 *f.b.* my Monarch. *Scott 1824.* my ——. *1733. F.M.*
l. 3 *f.b.* *Jove* never. *F.* —— never. *1733.*
note. Jove. Jovi. *note F.*

ON THE DAY OF JUDGEMENT

Text from *earliest version in*: The Saint James's Chronicle. April 12. 1774.
Copy : British Museum.
Collated with : Works. Ed. Nichols. Vol. IX. ii. 4to. 1775.
Note : The following variants in Nichols' text, with some unimportant typographical changes, will also be found in a version of the poem printed in the *Monthly Review* for July 1774. No earlier authority is known for these readings, which Nichols followed when he added the poem to the Swift canon.

P. 804. Title. *1775 omits:* On.
l. 4. sink. sunk. *1775.*
l. 7. burst. bursts. *1775.*
l. 11. hangs. hung. *1775.*
l. 17. have shamm'd. were shamm'd. *1775.*
l. 19. Folks. folk. *1775.*
last line. you're bit. you're *bit. 1775.*

VERSES ON THE DEATH OF Dr. SWIFT

Text from *First complete and authorised edition*: VERSES / on the / DEATH / of / Dr. S——, D.S.P.D. / occasioned / By reading a Maxim in *Rochefoulcault*. / *Dans l'adversité de nos meilleurs amis nous trouvons quelque chose, qui ne nous deplaist pas.* / In the Adversity of our best Friends, we find something that doth not displease us. / Written by Himself, *November* 1731. / *LONDON* Printed : / *DUBLIN* : Reprinted by George Faulkner, / M,DCC,XXXIX. [*In the following notes this edition is referred to as* : *D*.]

Copy : P. J. Dobell.

Collated with : Bathurst's London edns., 1. 2. 3. 1739. [*B. 1, 2, 3*.]. Faulkner, Vol. VIII 1746. [*1746*.] Copy of *D*., with contemporary MS. additions, in the Forster Collection [*Forst*.]. A similar copy to the foregoing, now belonging to Harold Williams, Esq., and lent by Messrs. Pickering & Chatto [*P*.].

Note : The readings attributed to *Forst*. in the following notes are inserted in that copy in MS. The MS. insertions in *P*. are almost identical with those in *Forst*., but the text of P. agrees with the printed text of *1746* in a few places independently of *Forst*. Since the fifth and last issue of *D*. [1739] contains these variants, it must be inferred that corresponding sheets from this issue were, for some reason, substituted for the appropriate first edition sheets in *P*.

P. 807. Advertisement. *1746 reads :* The following Poem was printed and published in London, with great Success. Many Lines and Notes were omitted in the English Edition [*i.e. Bathurst's*] ; which we have here inscribed, to make this Work as compleat as possible.

P. 808, l. 2. keep. *1746*. keeps. *D*. *B. 1, 2, 3* omit this and the preceding line.

l. 4. *B. 1, 2, 3 read :*—But why shou'd he obstruct my view.

l. 6. *B. 1, 2, 3 read :*—Suppose it but an inch at most.

l. 17. grieve. mourn. *B. 1, 2, 3*.

l. 18. Brethren. Brother. *B. 1, 2, 3*.

P. 809, l. 5. *B. 1, 2, 3 read :*—I grieve to be outdone by GAY.

l. 4 *f.b.* Tho' it is. And tho' 'tis. *B. 1, 2, 3*.

P. 811, l. 12. his Foresight. his Judgment. *B. 1, 2*. the Judgement. *B. 3*.

P. 812, l. 5. *B. 1, 2, 3 read :*—To publick Uses ! there's a Whim !

notes. l. 1. supposes. imagines. *P. 1746*.

notes. l. 2 *et seq*. that, others who. that others will remember . . . Gratitude. remember him with Gratitude, who consider . . . every Reader. *P. 1746*.

notes. l. 8. Ireland. Ireland, where he was born. *1746*.

notes. l. 10. Favour. Friendship. *P. 1746*.

last line; P. 813, l. 1. Queen. *Forst. P.* ——. *B. 1, 2, 3*. *D*.

P. 813, ll. 3-8. *B. 1, 2, 3 print six lines of asterisks.*

l. 3. say : Why, let him rot. *Forst. P.* say : —— rot. *D*. say then let him rot. *1746*.

notes. l. 1. Command. Commands. *1746*.

l. 4. the medals were. *Forst. P.* ——. *D*. the M——ls were. *1746*.

l. 5. him, I own, but. *Forst. P. reads :* I promis'd them, I own, but. ——. *D. Forst. gives the following alternative :*—
I promised him, but that's the most
I cannot send them to his ghost.

l. 6. only was a Princess then. *Forst*. only was the Princess then. *P*. only —— then. *D*. only was the —— then. *1746*.

l. 7. Consort of a King. *Forst*. Consort of ——. *D*. Consort of the King. *P*.

l. 9. Sir *Robert's*. *Forst*. P. Sir
R——'s. D.

notes. ll. 7-16. She forgot . . .
displeasure. *Forst*. P. *not in* D.

*The following variants in this
note occur in* P. :—l. 8 : Indian
plad. (*v. P. 508. l. 17 et seq.*)
*The material of course was of
Irish manufacture, the whole
point of the gift being to encourage trade in Irish wool.*) l. 9. took
from her. l. 12. nothing but. l.
15. instead of favour or medals.
l. 11. is he dead. if he died. *B.
1, 2, 3.*

l. 12. *Bob*. *Forst*. *1746*. *P.
B*——. *D.*

notes. l. 8 *f.b.* Half-pence, &c.
The. Half-pence, &c. for which
the. *1746*.

notes. l. 6 *f.b.* only. *1746
omits*.

notes. l. 5 *f.b.* and . . . again.
but, the Dean never made him
another Visit. *1746*.

notes. l. 4 *f.b.* Mr. Walpole's.
Forst. P. Mr. ——'s. D. Sir
R——t's. *1746*.

notes. l. 3 *f.b.* became his
mortal enemy. opposed his
measures. *P. 1746*.

notes. l. 2 *f.b.* to expose him. to
represent his conduct. *P. 1746*.

P. 814, *notes*. l. 3. Walpole.
Forst. P. ——. D. W——e.
1746.

notes. l. 4. King George.
Forst. P. ——. D. K——George
I. *1746*.

notes. l. 5. Sir Robert Walpole.
Forst. Walpole. P. ——. D.
the said W——. *1746*.

P. 815, l. 14. and what. pray
what. *B. 1, 2, 3.*

l. 23. wou'd take. will take.
B. 3.

l. 25. led. lead. *P.*

l. 5 *f.b.* further. farther. *B.
2, 3.*

P. 816, l. 7. searches. search-
eth. *1746*.

l. 11. to fancy. *the catchword
in* D. *reads* :—I keep. In *P.* it is
printed correctly.

l. 22. By Stephen Duck. *Forst*.
P. By ——. *D.*

l. 27. Sir *Robert's*. *Forst*. P.
1746. Sir R——'s. D.

notes. l. 4. Walpole hath.
Forst. —— hath. D. Walpole
hires. P. hath *is struck out in* P.
W——le hath. *1746*.

P. 817, ll. 1-18. *B. 1, 2, 3*
omit.

l. 14. That Jesus. *Forst*. That
——. D. That J—s. *P.*

ll. 23-26. *B. 1, 2, 3* omit.

l. 5 *f.b.* *After this line B. 1, 2, 3
add the following couplet* :—

Altho' ironically grave,
He sham'd the Fool, and lash'd
   the Knave.

P. 818, l. 2. *B. 1, 2, 3 read* :—
To *please*, and to *reform* Mankind.

ll. 3-4. *B. 1, 2, 3 omit but cf.
note, on P. 817.* l. 5 *f.b.*

l. 8. Duke. Peer. *B. 1, 2, 3.*

l. 11. Despis'd the Fools. And
scorn the Tools. *B. 1, 2, 3.*

ll. 13-26. *B. 1, 2, 3 omit*.

l. 10 *f.b.* *B. 1, 2, 3 read* :—He
kept with Princes due Decoram.

l. 9 *f.b.* But. Yet. *B. 1, 2, 3.*

after l. 9 *f.b.* *Forst*. adds :—
And to her Majesty, God bless
   her,
Would speak as free as to her
   Dresser;
She thought it his peculiar whim
Nor took it ill as come from him.

l. 7 *f.b.* thy Trust. his Trust.
B. 1, 2, 3.

l. 4 *f.b.* to P. 822, l. 14. *B. 1, 2,
3* omit.

l. 4 *f.b.* The Irish Senate.
Forst. P. The —— S——. D.
The I—— S——. *1746*.

P. 819. *notes*. l. 3. *whatever
Person would*. *1746 omits*.

P. 820, *notes*. ll. 13-19. they
had after . . . remain so. *Forst*. P.
they had, Etc. D. *1746*.

*The following variants in this
note occur in* P. :—l. 18. until
this present 3rd of May. l. 18.
and are likely to go on in the
same manner.

l. 9. Law. Laws. *1746*.

l. 10. the Senate, rob the
Crown. *Forst*. P. the ——, rob
the ——. *D. 1746*.

l. 11. old England's Glory.
Forst. P. old —— Glory. *D.
1746*.

l. 20, *and notes last line.* of
Slaves and. *Forst. P. P. omits*
Slaves *in note 2.* of —— and.
D. of Sl——s and. *1746.*

P. 821, *notes.* l. 5. One Whit-
sed was. *Forst. P.* One W——
was. *D. 1746.*

P. 822, l. 8. the Crown. *Forst.*
P. the ——. *D.* the C——.
1746.

l. 15. there to. still to. *B. 1,*
2, 3.

l. 18. for Lords indeed. *Forst.*
P. for —— indeed. *D. 1746.*

l. 20. And Peerage. *Forst. P.*
And ——. *D.* And P——.
1746.

l. 21. held it. deem'd it. *B. 1,*
2, 3.

l. 23 to P. 823, l. 9. *B. 1, 2, 3*
om t.

l. 25. Biennial Squires. *Forst.*
P. —— Squires. *D. 1746.*

notes. l. 8. one single Lord.
many Lords. *1746.*

notes. ll. 12-13. and tamely
. . . remonstrance. *Forst. P.*
D. 1746 omit.

The following variant in this
note occurs in P. :—l. 12. this
infamous.

notes. ll. 14-17. Parliament

. . . mentioned. *Forst. P. D.*
1746 omit.

The following variants in this
note occur in P. :—l. 15. after giving. l. 17. are here mentioned.

P. 823, l. 1. and Votes for.
Forst. P. and —— for. *D. 1746.*

l. 2. The Nation stripp'd go.
Forst. P. The —— go. *D. 1746.*

l. 3. To rob the Church. *Forst.*
P. To —— the Church. *D.*
1746.

l. 4. Rogues and Rapparees.
Forst. Thieves and Rapparees.
P. Go Snacks with ——. *D.*
1746.

l. 7. or Barrack to. *Forst. P.*
or —— to. *D. 1746.*

l. 8. the Tax for. *Forst.* the
Ways for. *P.* the —— for. *D.*
the T——e for. *1746.*

notes * and †. *Forst. P.*
D. 1746 omit.

The following variants in these
notes occur in P. :—l. 3. the Protestants. l. 4. is lodged.

ll. 14-33. *B. 1, 2, 3 omit.*

P. 824, l. 3. And shew'd. to
shew. *B. 1, 2, 3.*

last couplet. B. 1, 2, 3 omit.

note. he . . . dye. he lived, was
born, and dyed. *1746.*

ADDITIONAL NOTES

P. 470. The reader is referred
to "The Drapier's Letters." Ed.
Herbert Davis. 1935, published
since the first appearance of this
edition. Professor Davis's volume contains a full account of
Wood's Coinage as well as a
history, bibliography and complete text of the letters.

P. 632. An examination of the
whole question will be found in
Maxwell Gold's "Swift's Marriage to Stella," 1937.

P. 851. *Note to* P. 484.
Faulkner's note originally read :
" before that infamous Wretch
Whitshed." This was cancelled in
almost all copies and replaced
by : " before one *Whitshed.*"